WITHDRAWN

My Struggle for Freedom

"MY STRUGGLE FOR FREEDOM"

ଽୠଔୠଔ

MEMOIRS

Hans Küng
Translated by John Bowden

William B. Eerdmans Publishing Company
Grand Rapids, Michigan / Cambridge, U.K.

Novalis
Saint Paul University, Ottawa

Originally published in German as *Erkämpfte Freiheit. Erinnerungen*
© 2002 Piper Verlag GmbH, Munich

English translation © 2003 John Bowden

English edition published 2003

in the United States of America by
Wm. B. Eerdmans Publishing Company
255 Jefferson Ave. S.E., Grand Rapids, Michigan 49503 /
P.O. Box 163, Cambridge CB3 9PU U.K.
www.eerdmans.com

in Canada by
Novalis, Saint Paul University
223 Main Street, Ottawa, Ontario, Canada K1S 1C4
Business office: 49 Front Street East, 2nd Floor
Toronto, Ontario, Canada M5E 1B3
www.novalis.ca
Toll-free: 1-800-387-7164

and in the United Kingdom by
Continuum, London

Printed in the United States of America

07 06 05 04 03   7 6 5 4 3 2 1

Library of Congress Cataloging-in-Publication Data

Eerdmans ISBN 0-8028-2659-8

National Library of Canada Cataloguing in Publication Data

A catalogue record for this book is available
from the National Library of Canada.
Novalis ISBN 2-89507-411-9

To the towns of Sursee and Tübingen,
in heartfelt gratitude to each of them for making me
an honorary citizen

Contents

⳨⳥⳨⳥⳨⳥

List of Illustrations

Appearing between pages 78 and 79

1. My parents' house Zur Krone (1651) with the town hall and the parish church of St George
2. My corner room with the statue of Mary by the sculptor Tüfel
3. Emma and Hans Küng-Gut
4. Two years old
5. Four years old
6. The Küng houses by the Sempachersee with a view of the Alps between the Rigi and the Pilatus
7. Eleven years old
8. Pastor Franz Xaver Kaufmann
9. The Küng family in Sursee, Shrove Tuesday 1948
10. Pontificium Collegium Germanicum et Hungaricum, Rome
11. A study, Collegium Germanicum 1948
12. Pius XII Pacelli: Proclamation of the Marian Dogma 1950, with Bishop von Streng (Basle)
13. *'Studium per totum diem'*
14. My fellow Germanicum student Otto Wüst, later Bishop of Basle
15. Cardinal Pizzardo presents silver medals for the licentiate in philosophy, 1951 (the Jesuit General Janssens is on the right)
16. Papal audience with Pius XII: 400th anniversary of the Collegium Germanicum, 1952
17. The summer villa of San Pastore in the Roman campagna
18. Spiritual Wilhelm Klein SJ
19. Rector Franz von Tattenbach SJ

Appearing between pages 174 and 175

20. The Küng family at my ordination to the priesthood, Rome 1954
21. First mass in the grottos of St Peter's, 1954
22. 1960: Professor at Tübingen at the age of 32
23. Hans Urs von Balthasar, Basle
24. Otto Karrer, Lucerne

Acknowledgements for Illustrations

Foto-Jung, Sursee: nos 1, 62

Gesellschaft für Schweizerische Kunstgeschichte, Berne: no. 2

Manfred Grohe, Tübingen: nos 22, 25, 28, 29, 32, 55, 61

Matthias Grünewald Verlag, Mainz: no. 41

Bernhard Moosbrugger, Zürich: nos 30, 31, 34, 35, 36, 37, 38, 39, 42, 43, 44, 45, 46, 47, 48, 49, 50, 53, 54

Seerestaurant Bellevue, Sursee: no. 6

University Archive, Tübingen: nos 40 (signature p. 35/1, no. 711), 51 (signature 35/1, no. 622)

The caricature (no. 64) is by David Levine (New York), the original being the private property of Hans Küng

Illustrations not otherwise mentioned are the private property of Hans Küng

Why I am Telling the Story of My Life

EVERYTHING could have been very different. But I am grateful that things turned out as they did, and not otherwise. I am grateful to the many very different people who have been my companions over seven sometimes stormy decades, supporting and strengthening me. And at the same time I am grateful to that hidden sustaining Power which in retrospect I think that I can recognize in my life, even in the bitter times. So gratitude is the basic mood in which I am giving this account of my life.

However, throughout my life there is also a thread of militancy, which is not to be confused with quarrelsomeness. I have been involved in many controversies, most of which I have neither sought nor avoided, but none of them have been about incidental matters which I could easily have ignored; they have been about a great cause in which I believe. The struggle for this cause has been worthwhile, and in these memoirs I hope that it will come through as clearly as the person who seeks to serve it. It is the cause of the true form of the Catholic Church, the ecumenical world, indeed of Christianity generally, and I want to tell its story. I remarked in jest to those who urged me years ago to write my autobiography that it would be my 'last polemic'. But will it really be my last book? Whether it is or not, at all events I have postponed plans for further books because it has become clear to me that an account of my life should appear now, and not later. There are personal reasons for this decision: how long will I be able to go on writing? And there are also political decisions: isn't a shift now taking place towards a new period of the world and the church? After a long life and much experience I have no doubt that it is, so my memoirs, which often involve other people who are still alive, should not seem presumptuous.

Of course I am aware that any history, including the history of my life, is interpreted history. But as autobiography it is history that I have interpreted myself, and so it has an authenticity of its own. I certainly do not share the view of Oscar Wilde that while everyone has his disciples, it is usually the Judas who writes the biography – after all, the author can also be the beloved disciple John. But while I am still alive I would like as far as I can to prevent the formation of legends, whether malicious or well-meaning. And at the same time I want to counter harmonizing historians who in the most recent histories of the church, theology or councils (Vatican II!) conceal unwelcome developments and trivialize conflicts. An autobiography with first-hand information can contribute towards avoiding hypotheses, conjectures and false interpretations – even if there is less need in my difficult professional sphere to be afraid of biographical charlatans and jackals than there is in politics and show business.

Structuralists, above all those of French provenance, have for some time now wanted to see only structures and processes in history; they have even thought that they could proclaim the 'death of the subject'. Certainly the self referred to here has taken form in response to the social and intellectual climate. But even the 'new historiography' (*'nouvelle histoire'*), finally correcting itself, has had to give up its contempt for the event, the history of facts, narrative history and biography. I have made this point elsewhere with reference to figures of world history like King David and Martin Luther. Throughout history there is an effective dialectic of structures and persons, institutions and mentalities.

Such narration must always be concerned with the historical truth, which does not allow any confusion between reality and invention, fact and fiction. However, I was tempted when in the 1980s the Australian writer Morris West, author of global bestsellers like *The Shoes of the Fisherman*, paid a special visit to Tübingen in an attempt to convince me that I could not defend myself on my increasingly difficult way. He very much wanted to do this for me in a 'true novel'. But I had no interest in existing in a novel in which truth and poetic licence need constant sifting, and could not allow Morris West to inspect a documentation which was far too large for him to cope with. I am also the opposite of Umberto Eco, who as a 'philosopher of obfuscation' gives the hero of his novel *Baudolino* a bit of episcopal advice: 'If you want to become a man of letters, you must also lie and invent tales, otherwise your History would become monotonous.' Life itself probably writes the most interesting stories, because they are true. My history will observe chronology throughout, but it will by no means simply relate facts one after another in a chronicle; rather, I shall be interweaving chronicle with a thematic treatment, so that it becomes evident how everything hangs together with everything else.

As an involved witness to our time and as a Christian, I attempt to combine intensity of experience with clarity of analysis in order to understand the past better in the light of the present. Like any biographer, I have to select, interpret and evaluate the facts. But despite all the passion, which I cannot and will not put aside, I want to achieve the greatest possible objectivity – towards my opponents as well. It is more important to me to describe political and contemporary events that I have experienced myself than the most private of matters. But I shall not omit personal experiences of life and crises. If something like a central theme seems to have been worked into my first four decades, it is that of freedom: the struggle for freedom in nation and church, theology and personal life, my struggle for freedom.

Since I am well aware how easily memory can deceive, I have taken the trouble to check what could be checked in the sources; after that I gave the individual chapters to several contemporary witnesses to read and correct. I have been particularly fortunate in having two extraordinarily competent colleagues and friends going back over decades who have read the manuscript several times and have given me invaluable advice and suggestions on both style and content: Dr Walter Jens, professor of rhetoric and writer, and Professor Dr Karl-Josef Kuschel, specialist in theology and literature. The manuscript has also been read intensively and checked by Dr Günther Gebhardt, Dr Thomas Riplinger, Marianne Saur, Stephan Schlensog, Bettina Schmidt and Dr Wolfgang Seibel, SJ. Several members of my family, friends and acquaintances have read parts of the manuscript. Anette Stuber-Rousselle was responsible for producing the countless versions of the manuscript, supported where necessary by my trusty secretaries Inge Baumann and Eleonore Henn. As in all my most recent books the layout and format have once again been in the hands of Stephan Schlensog.

I would like to express my thanks to all of them. They stand for the countless unnamed men and women who have supported me through my long life and to whom I dedicate these memoirs.

One last thing: intensive reflection on the past helps untiring thought about the future. Throughout these memoirs my gaze continues to be directed, *Deo bene volente*, not backwards, but forwards, full of curiosity about what may come. I hope that the second (and last) volume of my autobiography will be able to relate more of that.

HANS KÜNG
Tübingen,
1 August 2002

I

ဒေါ်ကြီးဒေါ်ကြီး

Roots of Freedom

*'Indeed it is impracticable to assume
that we must abandon our primordial ties
in order to become global citizens'*

UN Manifesto for the Dialogue among Civilizations 2001

Homeland?

IN its manifesto *Crossing the Divide*, addressed to the UN General Assembly, the 'Group of Eminent Persons' convened by the UN Secretary-General Kofi Annan to which I belong, which also includes Richard von Weizsäcker, Jacques Delors, Nadime Gordimer, Prince Hassan of Jordan, Amartya Sen and a dozen other personalities, has stated:

> It is ill advised to consider primordial ties as necessarily detrimental to the cosmopolitan spirit. We know that our strong feelings, lofty aspirations and recurring dreams are often attached to a particular group, expressed through a mother tongue, associated with a specific place and targeted to people of the same age and faith. We also notice that gender and class feature prominently in our self-definition. We are deeply rooted in our primordial ties, and they give meaning to our daily existence. They cannot be arbitrarily whisked away any more than one could consciously choose to be a totally different person.

Back to the roots, then? That is not an easy undertaking. Each individual has a whole web of roots: historical, natural, cultural, spiritual – land, history, nature, family, community, church. So back to the roots it is. Nowadays my relationship with my homeland, Switzerland, is more critical than that of the Catholic conservatives and more conservative than that of the left-wing intellectual critics. And I do not write at such length about my Swiss roots in this chapter out of a sheer delight in telling stories. What I want to do is to answer the question I am sometimes asked, how the Swiss boy (though by no means uncosmopolitan) became a world citizen (though by no means alienated from Switzerland).

4

Freedom threatened

Not only personal and private events but also political events can stir and shake a child. My childhood falls in the time of Adolf Hitler's seizure of power and the threat to our national and personal freedom. This more than anything else shapes my early years.

Politics is a constant presence in our family in the little Swiss town of Sursee. Later I hear that after 1933, in many German families, parents have to be careful of making political remarks in the presence of their children. At our family table, as at countless others in Switzerland, there is constantly open, free and often passionate discussion of all that takes place in local, cantonal, national and international politics during those increasingly dramatic years in our country. We all feel that we are 'politicians', and because of direct democracy, those of male gender have manifold possibilities of engaging in politics.

Neither my father ('Papa') nor my mother ('Mutti') are great readers of books, but that makes them all the more avid readers of newspapers and magazines. And just as grace is said together at midday and evening meals, so too regularly at midday and in the evening we listen to the news from the German-Swiss radio station of Beromünster. Its transmission towers are about five kilometres from my home town in the canton of Lucerne, so to speak in the heart of Switzerland.

During the war, as the voice of a free country, Radio Beromünster always broadcasts statements from both the German and the Allied sides, with a calm and objective commentary on Fridays in the 'World Chronicle' given by the historian J. R. von Salis. For us he is an intellectual authority and a figure with whom we identify. Many Germans also listen secretly to 'Beromünster', but like the BBC it is soon banned in Germany. And it is particular shocking political events in my early years that make me listen, read and act in a new way – 'political' if you like.

Shocking dates I: 25 July 1934

On this day a radio bulletin is broadcast which is the first to be engraved deeply on my memory: the murder of the Austrian Chancellor and Foreign Minister Engelbert Dollfuss – the victim of a National Socialist coup. I am six years old. I gather from the terrified reaction of my parents that something extremely threatening must have happened. Of course I don't know that this Christian Socialist politician not only banned the National Socialist and the Communist parties but even excluded the Social Democrats, in order to establish an authoritarian Catholic *Ständesstaat*, dominated by the upper classes, though this was essentially different from the totalitarian Nazi state.

The one thing I sense is the shock. In the country bordering on ours, in time of peace, an anti-Nazi head of government has been murdered by Nazis. This is also a storm warning for Switzerland! From then on the 'Third Reich' seems to me to be a threat to freedom. And I look with extreme mistrust even at harmless photographs which my aunt has brought with her of two laughing German soldiers on the frontier in Basle. People at our family table ask anxiously what will happen next, to Germany, to Austria, to Switzerland?

Almost five decades later I am invited by Bruno Kreisky, the Social Democrat Chancellor of Austria, to give a lecture in the Hofburg in Vienna. Before the lecture I ask him to show me the place in his office in the Ballhausplatz where Dollfuss collapsed, fatally wounded. It is still appropriately marked and decorated with flowers.

Shocking dates II: 12 March 1938

The day when I begin to read the daily paper. The German army has invaded Austria! It's the week before my tenth birthday. We Swiss are deeply disturbed: our neighbour and friend offers no resistance. It does not defend its freedom. It even welcomes the German soldiers with boisterous jubilation, and the Austrian army joins in. As early as 14 March, Adolf Hitler (who was born in Austria) can celebrate the 'Liberation Festival' quite personally with hundreds of thousands of people in the Heldenplatz in Vienna, after a triumphal procession.

It is clear to us in a flash that our country could very well be Hitler's next victim. However, people in my family and all around me are convinced that Hitler would encounter bitter resistance from us in Switzerland – regardless of the sacrifices! Hitler's Austrian spokesman Arthur Seyss-Inquart, forced on the Austrians as Minister of the Interior, who asked Hitler for military help and now signs the capitulation to 'Greater Germany', seems to us to be the prototype of the traitor. Indeed he is the predecessor of Vidkun Quisling, who the very next year proposed that Hitler should occupy Norway and whose name is synonymous with being a Nazi collaborator.

Dollfuss's successor as Austrian Chancellor, the shrewd and liberal Kurt von Schuschnigg, is a very different matter at that time. Under massive pressure from Hitler he had concluded a discriminatory agreement at Berchtesgaden on the Obersalzberg, but immediately attempts to subvert it by a plebiscite on the independence of Austria. Hitler takes this as a pretext for occupying Austria. Immediately after the invasion he has Schuschnigg arrested and put in a concentration camp. After the end of the war I will see and listen to this brave Schuschnigg in the hall of my grammar school in Lucerne with respect and interest: a great speech which makes me buy his long apologia with the sad title *Requiem in Rot-Weiss-Rot* (Requiem in Red, White and Red). By contrast, a few years later I will listen with understandable scepticism and mistrust to an after-dinner speech at the Collegium Germanicum et Hungaricum in Rome by the affable Theodor Innitzer, Cardinal of Vienna, who even sent a covering letter with a hand-written 'Heil Hitler' to accompany the Austrian episcopate's declaration of capitulation on 18 March 1938.

Times have become so dramatic by March 1938 that every day I turn eagerly to the newspaper, the 'Catholic conservative central organ' with the patriotic name *Vaterland* (it is published in Lucerne). However, I do so also because of its serialized love story (my first), which turns on the battle of Sempach in 1386; I devour the episodes as zealously as the reports of world political events. These cast increasing gloom on the political horizon of Europe, not least because of the incomprehensible inactivity and empty protest notes of those Western powers with which we in Switzerland openly sympathize. The British premier Neville Chamberlain with his umbrella, the exponent of an appeasement policy, is a figure of fun for us. Thus a few months later the 'bringing home' of Austria is followed by the 'annexation' of the Sudetenland enforced by Hitler and the expulsion of the Czechs. Then, despite – or better, because of – the appeasement conference of the four great powers of Germany, Great Britain, France and Italy in Munich (September 1938), in March 1939 comes the 'crushing' of Czechoslovakia threatened by Hitler: the surprise invasion of Prague by German troops and the establishment of the German protectorate of Bohemia and Moravia. And a few days later there is the violent annexation of the Memel region in Lithuania. Great Britain, the power supposed to be protecting it, doesn't even send a protest note.

We Swiss ask ourselves: who would stand by us if our country came next? People are already hawking round the German verse, 'And Switzerland, the porcupine, on the way back it will be mine.' Or perhaps even on the way out – to Paris?

Shocking dates III: 1 September 1939

The outbreak of the Second World War and general mobilization. I become an *active* patriot. Of course, at the age of eleven I am not among the 400,000 soldiers who are called up, among them the Protestant theologian Karl Barth. Barth has been expelled from Germany and teaches in Basle. Within three days those who have been mobilized and provided with uniform, rifles and ammunition (traditionally kept at home) also inundate Sursee – as an official centre with a large armoury the mustering point for the Nineteenth Lucerne Regiment of the Eighth Division.

In my leisure time I am already involved in the patriotic Catholic youth movement (the Jungwacht), whose 'law' also includes 'love your country'. After an examination I am soon promoted to 'auxiliary leader'. Some years later I become the youngest local soldier, likewise armed with a rifle, firmly resolved to defend the freedom of our country and my home town against any attack. Later, for two winters I go on voluntary courses for radio operators, so that fortunately I won't be conscripted into the infantry, which I don't like because of the drill, but into the troops which supply the air force and the anti-aircraft units. Because of my permanent leave abroad I don't have to do military service after the Second World War.

The 'Blitzkrieg' by the German army against Poland, completed in four weeks, and the cession of East Poland to the Soviet Union, and then the rapid occupation of Norway and Denmark, suggest that Hitler will now turn against France. As the power responsible for protecting Poland, along with Great Britain, France had declared war on Germany, but without venturing to come to its relief with an offensive on the Western front, which has largely been stripped of German troops. The question which oppresses us all is: in order to by-pass the heavily fortified Maginot Line, will the German attack be into the unprotected hinterland through Belgium and Holland or through Switzerland? In 1939 the Swiss Army is still badly prepared to resist invasion by a highly-equipped German army. Most troops are simply ordered to the frontiers, to make it clear that we will not accept a march through any more than in the First World War.

At the time, the First World War had led to a tense situation over provisions. Now we are better prepared: food dumps have been arranged in good time, and each family has its emergency stocks (among other things, ours includes a big sack of sugar in the attic). All at once the shadow organization for a war economy is brought to life: a comprehensive system of rationing extending from milk and coffee to clothes and shoes, along with price control and a conversion of the rural economy into increased areas of arable land and a greater yield. I too have to join the 'Land Army' in the holidays – happily with my farmer relatives.

In 1940, at the age of twelve, I write the longest school essay of my life, 32 pages. My teacher is clearly annoyed that I keep picking up four-page sets of paper from his desk: but in no way will he give me more than one at a time. The topic which fascinates me is: 'How the Second World War Broke Out'. I describe very precisely what happened between Berlin, Paris, London and Rome in those dramatic days. I give not only the names of the heads of governments, but also the names of various ambassadors and generals. 'Where does your boy get all that from?' our neighbour asks my mother on the day of the examination, after she has taken a look at my exercise book, which is on display. My mother goes on to tell me this, not without adding, as so often, 'But don't be proud!' The times are serious enough, and our cities, which used to be brightly lit, but are now totally blacked-out at the demand of the Germans, remind us every evening that although so far we are not bothered by the war, we too are nevertheless involved in it.

Conform or resist?

The basic problem with which I was to be confronted so often later in life is presented to me by national politics as it were in the cradle: conform and go along with events, or stand firm and resist? In the 1930s and 1940s there is a conflict over freedom and slavery both within politics and outside it, and this stirs me deeply, as it does everyone else in our country. For me, freedom is not something that I discover later in my life; nor does 'the search' for freedom shape my life as it shapes that of others; rather, it is important for me to maintain and preserve freedom. And so in this sense, time and again there is a new 'struggle for freedom'.

In all the years of National Socialist rule in Europe I never get to know a single Swiss Nazi, and I am seventeen years old when the war ends. On the contrary, all my acquaintances, everyone I know, are resolutely anti-Nazi. Even before the war, in Lucerne, in a villa by the Vierwaldstätter See, young officers founded a semi-private information centre under Captain Hans Hausammann ('H Bureau'), with the best channels of news, extending as far as the highest circles in Berlin. At the beginning of the war it is incorporated into the Army news organization – to combat the strong German underground organization made up of agents, spies, propagandists, collaborators and fellow-travellers. During the war years, throughout Switzerland 283 Swiss, 142 Germans and 40 other foreigners are condemned to death or to long periods in prison for espionage. As well as two foreigners, fifteen Swiss are summarily shot, two of them from Lucerne at the foot of the Pilatus. The two houses of the Federal Assembly refuse to pardon them – deservedly, according to public opinion.

However, in Switzerland there are various 'fronts' (against Bolshevism, Judaism, freemasonry, profiteering, died-in-the-wool conservatism) which are directly dependent on Hitler's Germany or want to replace democracy with the Führer principle within a Swiss national framework. There are also organizations of the around 130,000 expatriate Germans who are taxed from Germany; National Socialist party meetings can take place openly. None of the indigenous groups has an effective political following among my fellow-countrymen. But against the background of the terrifying military power of Germany and aggressive German diplomacy they form a threat which can hardly be underestimated. And it is by no means clear in advance what the right strategy is: firmer resolve or more tolerance and conciliation – that is the question.

Heroes of freedom

During the war, without any Führer cult, my heroes (and the heroes of the majority of our people) are the two historic figures of the democratic resistance to Nazism, who long stood in the shadow of history. First, Winston Churchill: he was ostracized in his own Tory party for a whole decade because of his criticism of Chamberlain's appeasement policy. But on 10 May 1940, at the beginning of the German western campaign, under public pressure he is appointed Prime

Minister and Minister of Defence and is now the symbol of the British will to stand firm. We also hear his message in Switzerland: 'I have nothing to offer but blood, sweat and tears.'

And then Charles de Gaulle: initially, as an officer he too for many years called in vain for rearmament and the concentration of the French tanks into coherent units with a deliberate plan. The capitulation of France forced him to flee to England, where he founded a national committee of Free French to continue the resistance. In his London radio broadcast of 18 June 1940, which we too pick up, he calls for a continuation of the war: 'This war has not been decided by the battle over France. This war is a world war!'

The symbol of resistance among us in Switzerland is not the federal government, reacting by yielding all too often to German intimidation, public and concealed. Rather, it is the man who two days before the attack on Poland at a solemn session of the two chambers of Parliament is appointed supreme commander of the army for the duration of the national emergency, the only man with the right to bear the title General. Henri Guisan is a somewhat quiet, restrained, 65-year-old landowner from a family in the liberal Waadtland, commandant of the First Army Corps, a militia soldier and a statesman all in one. Granted, left-wing critics have accused him of making positive statements about Mussolini and of tendencies towards authoritarianism; among us, by comparison with Hitler, Mussolini generally came off considerably better – he was laughed at rather than feared. But as supreme commander Guisan – and this unites him with Churchill and de Gaulle (whom historians also criticize in some respects) – is a convinced democrat, as remote from Hitlerism as from Stalinism. Guisan's will to resist and his growing resolution arise from a deep moral conviction, and his humanity quickly wins the hearts of the German Swiss as well.

I am highly delighted when I have an opportunity to observe this congenial and unassuming man only a few paces away in Sursee. One of his remarks is: 'When a man stands upright before me and looks me in the eye, I see behind him his home, his family, his worries.' Along with the general antipathy to Nazi Germany, the sovereign, humane General Guisan, a French speaker, sees to it that there is no new division in the land between the Francophile Romands and the Germanophile German Swiss, as happened under the German-speaking general Ulrich Wille in the First World War.

Our foreign minister, Marcel Pilet-Golaz, who in 1940 is also President, is a different matter. I catch sight of him among the other six federal councillors in Lucerne at the great procession for the Swiss shooting competition in 1939, immediately before the outbreak of the Second World War, and am allowed to clap. Pilet-Golaz, who is also a French-speaking Swiss, is certainly not a Nazi nor even a Nazi sympathizer. But he is in favour of assimilation to all-powerful National Socialist Germany. A pun of my father's has made me antipathetic to this conformist politician with his quite un-Swiss white or grey spats: '*Man sollte den Pilet go lah* – They should drop Pilet'. In fact, when the Nazi star begins to wane, he has to resign. Our man in the Federal Council is Guisan's friend Rudolf Minger, a natural, highly intelligent Berne farmer. Countless jokes are told about him, but in the government he is the competent exponent of the will for freedom and energetic resistance. In the procession he is applauded with special sympathy.

Conformist and unyielding

The military threat is greatest in the summer of 1940: the German Blitzkrieg – now, however, thrusting not through Switzerland, which is ready to fight, but through the Netherlands and Belgium, which capitulate rapidly – also compels France to capitulate after a few weeks. Recently discovered documents will confirm after the war that Hitler thinks of liquidating Switzerland immediately after the French campaign in operation 'Tannenbaum'. Almost overnight, apart from our tiny land, Europe from the North Cape to Sicily and Crete has become Nazi and Fascist; France has collapsed ('Vichy'). The Balkans, Yugoslavia and Greece are occupied. Italy and Spain are loyal allies of Germany.

Now in Switzerland we see ourselves totally surrounded and susceptible to blackmail: an island of freedom, certainly, but a people without coal, iron, steel and oil; on the instructions of Reich Marshal Goering, on 2 July 1940 Switzerland is threatened with the suspension of coal deliveries. A policy of direct confrontation with the all-powerful, dangerous and deceitful enemy is hardly advisable. But how far can one go in the fragile equilibrium between refusal and co-operation? Excessive sycophancy can also be a step too far.

The Federal Council is of the opinion that despite all the Swiss will to resist, only concessions will help in this desperate situation: over transit to Italy, deliveries from the machine and clock industry, financial clearing and transmission of the credits of the French government to Germany. In this context the national bank and the big banks are all too ready to collaborate with the National Socialist regime, but this is kept secret from the people. We read little about foreign trade or refugee policy in the Swiss press: our small country is to be a staging post for refugees (around 300,000); we hear later that more than 20,000 refugees have been refused or expelled; now and then there are protests against the harsh exclusionary policy of the Federal Council, and that has consequences. But not a single Swiss bishop criticizes the official refugee policy . . .

Most people think that the economic co-operation necessary for survival is unavoidable, but that there must be no political collaboration. This will be confirmed in 2002 by the Independent Commission of Swiss experts on Switzerland in the Second World War under Professor Jean-François Bergier (of whom I, too, have a high opinion), in a multi-volume report: no trains with deported Jews or 'slave' transports run through Switzerland. But the rumour goes the rounds that weapons could also be found in the sealed German trains; the lack of control will later be branded a violation of the law of neutrality.

11

General Guisan, above all, is convinced that, conversely, Germany remains dependent on Switzerland. Resistance makes sense at the centre of the Alps, controlling the transport routes. A system of destruction which is constructed rapidly would ensure that the Alpine roads and tunnels, especially the Gotthard and the Simplon, can be made impassable. Without the knowledge of the Federal Council, the General negotiates with the French army command, which according to the other side is a violation of the law of neutrality – the occasion for an intrigue of senior officers against him.

There is no question that in 1940 encircled Switzerland is by no means 'a single people of brothers'. Along with Pilet-Golaz, the conformists in the Federal Council, the army leadership and business are convinced of a final German victory; Switzerland should shape relations with Nazi Germany positively to its own advantage. Hence demobilization and a friendly co-existence with Hitler's 'New Europe' are called for. However, the unyielding – and with the leading media of German Switzerland (*NZZ, Tages-Anzeiger, Vaterland*) banned in Germany, that is the vast majority, which includes all my relatives and acquaintances – are convinced that a final German victory is by no means certain; that neutrality in foreign policy cannot be neutrality of mind towards a regime of violent rulers with a state party, the Gestapo, terror and concentration camps; that a peaceful co-existence with Hitler's new totalitarian Europe would only lead to total subjection and loss of freedom. So there must be no demobilization, but militant resistance to any attack from outside and within the country to the Nazi ideology and any agitation.

Being free as our fathers were

Precisely in this confused hour of the utmost danger General Henri Guisan now demonstrates an unconditional determination to resist at home and abroad. On 12 July 1940 he presents the secret plan for an 'Alpine redoubt' to the Federal Council and gets it approved. Frontier troops will be used only as an organization for sounding the alarm. There will be a few troops in the Mittelland, to hold up the enemy, supported by the local defence forces in every town and village. The hard core of the army will be in the 'redoubt' – the Alpine fortress which is almost inaccessible to tanks and planes (as will soon become evident in the mountains of Yugoslavia) – with the heavily fortified ring of rocks of St Maurice in the West, Sargans in the East and Gotthard in the south.

As early as 25 July 1940 the General summons all senior officers from battalion commanders upwards to report to the Rütli. To call this 'rash' from a later perspective is to overlook the towering significance of this action. Here on the famous meadow in the mountains above the Urnersee, where saga has it that the original Swiss canons of Uri, Schwyz and Nidwalden swore a covenant (clearly documented in the federal letter of 1291 for the 'beginning of August'), he gathers together the leadership of the army in the name of traditional freedom, independence, democracy. Without naming the opponents, Guisan calls for resolute resistance to any outside attack and to doubt, defeatism and submission in our own land. Only a few weeks after his election he had given all soldiers clear orders that retreat or capitulation were ruled out; rather, the fight had to go on to the last bullet, and those who no longer had ammunition had to continue to fight with bayonet and knife.

The next day the mustering at the Rütli is widely publicized in word and image. With it Guisan makes himself 'the figure who unites a whole generation', as the Zurich historian Jakob Tanner was later to remark: 'he gathers together in a critical moment the fears and hopes of the population'. The general is then immediately understood in the country, too. 'We will be a single people of brothers, and will not separate in any need or danger.' This Rütli oath, in the words of Friedrich Schiller, is no longer an empty phrase. Indeed: 'We will be free as our fathers were; better death than a life in slavery.' Here it is not just a question of life but of survival, in freedom and dignity!

These historical experiences of Switzerland shape me. How could it be otherwise? I experience the fellowship of a nation in distress with quite definite freedoms and spiritual values. And I will feel that I belong to this Switzerland! If it is to survive in Europe, which has now become Fascist, it cannot orientate itself on the outside, where the dictators Hitler, Mussolini, Franco, Salazar and Stalin rule, but must take its bearings from within. From a later perspective it is easy to talk about putting down the shutters and curling up into a ball, distancing oneself from all that is foreign, un-Swiss, defeatist. 'The enemy is listening' is in fact on one of the posters which warn us everywhere. But can anyone now grudge us reflection on ourselves in our distinctive Swiss way, cultivating the traditional values, strengthening the original Swiss democratic consciousness and profiling our spiritual character?

Political freedom — without leader and led

This is expressed both programmatically and tangibly at the Swiss National Exhibition by the Zurichsee in 1939, immediately before the outbreak of war. For many of the 10,000,000 visitors the Landi is 'the abiding exhibition experience' of their lives (as the Zurich historian Peter Stadler was to put it 50 years later). For me personally this is particularly true, since I almost ruined it for myself. During the preceding weeks, as a result of some rivalries, there has been a big row between classes in my school at Sursee, so that in the breaks we now play dodgeball in two teams instead of all together. One player from the other party has the audacity to kick our ball, my ball (and I am the only one to have a leather ball), in a high arc right over the playground, and then runs away in fear. Up and away, I catch him by the wire fence, where in fury I hold the scoundrel in an armlock.

13

They claim that I almost strangled him, which I dispute. Anyway, it's a great scandal. There is an investigation at school; the teacher visits my parents. They too condemn my misdeed and pronounce the punishment: 'You can't go to the Landi!' Just a few days before the trip the punishment is changed: instead, I am not allowed to go with my father to the celebration of the battle of Sempach.

Thank God for this change, for in fact, as I write in my second-longest school essay (26 pages), for me too the Landi is an unforgettable experience. It looks so impressive from the outside, from the Landidörfli, the little village, and the cable car over the Zurichsee, the Schifflibach running through the great exhibition, the highly modern industrial display, to the Höhenweg with the thousand community coats of arms. It doesn't strike us that there is no mention of particular problem areas in Switzerland, like poverty or alcoholism. Because of the emotional mood, other problems stand in the foreground: in 1939 moral armament to defend the country in spirit and by force of arms is the demand of the hour. There is a more than life-size statue of a free and well-built Swiss man putting on his uniform with a defiant gesture. And hundreds of Swiss in fact have to do this – in the middle of the exhibition, because of the outbreak of the Second World War.

So it makes good political sense in 1941 for our schools all to travel to the Rütli a year after the Rütli mustering for the 650th anniversary of the Confederacy. I am thirteen years old. The schools of Sursee also go from Lucerne in a big paddle steamer across the lake of the 'four forest states' (Uri, Schwyz, Unterwalden and Lucerne), between the Upper Nose (Rigi) and the Lower Nose (Bürgenstock), to the Rütli meadow under the Seelisberg. I have now started grammar school, and am given the task of pronouncing those decisive sentences from Schiller's Rütli oath, solemnly but at the same time in a matter-of-fact way, and all the pupils repeat them in solemn dedication: 'We will be a single people of brothers, and will not separate in any need or danger. We will be free as our fathers were; better death than a life in slavery.'

Anyone from Germany who thinks that this solemnity is exaggerated should remember that in that same year, in a strictly confidential instruction, Hitler had banned performances of Schiller's *William Tell* in German theatres and schools, though in the first years of Nazi rule he had prized it highly as a drama of nation and Führer. Now he was afraid of the ever-present possibility of a Tell shot. And whereas Rossini's *William Tell* never became popular in Switzerland, for a long time Schiller's drama had been a national epic. As early as 1859 the rock obelisk in Lake Lucerne, which towers more than 25 metres above the water, had been engraved in golden letters with the words: 'To the singer of Tell, Friedrich Schiller. The original cantons.' Although the Swabian Schiller never visited Switzerland, he grasped much of Swiss nature better than some German and sometimes even Swiss intellectuals.

For all our defects, our ideal is and remains political freedom without leaders and led, without master and servants. Three decades later I will bring to Tübingen my grandfather's Tell desk, an heirloom, decorated with a beautiful intarsia figure: not the image of a saint, nor just a 'conversation piece', but a depiction of the will for freedom and self-determination against all foreign rule expressed in the Tell saga (which probably has a historical nucleus). Tell is something like an archetype in the collective unconscious of the Swiss. He does not express the arrogant challenge and the militancy of the legendary Danish bowman Toko (allegedly Tell's model), who flaunts the skill of archery, but rather the right of the original Swiss to resist, which is rooted deep in mediaeval thought. How often I will appeal to that later: no respect for Gessler hats – empty symbols of authority – whether secular or spiritual!

Living by a history of freedom

Switzerland is a free, multicultural community which preserves the identity of the different groups of peoples, languages, cultures and confessions. We are patriots but not nationalists. We celebrate our 1 August – the anniversary of the legendary events of 1291 – without national pomp and splendour, without march-pasts and parades. But on this evening I will always love hearing the sound of the bells round our lake and looking at the fires high on the mountains – and also some fireworks and red Chinese lanterns with the white cross – at a good simple meal accompanied with a glass of St Saphorin or Dôle.

Even the great Swiss writer Max Frisch, so often critical of his country, concedes that 'the confederacy is a household, and as such is admirable'. But why isn't what Frisch rejects also admirable: a confederate 'project, through commitment to a future'? Isn't this a model for Europe? On his state visit to Switzerland on 29 June 2001, the place that the Czech freedom-fighter and state president Václav Havel wants to visit above all is the Rütli. Why? Myths, above all myths of freedom for self-determination, are not to be preserved artificially but to be made fruitful in their potency, through critical illumination.

Perhaps it is now possible to understand better my quite realistic pride in a history of freedom which has shaped me deeply – despite all the failure, not least in this period of Nazism and despite all the recurrent pressures and defeats? I don't come from that tradition of Swiss big banks and big businesses which has been so censured abroad for its excessive compliance with the Nazi regime in matters of currency and arms, and has put us all in a moral twilight. I will later be able to identify with the report by the Geneva historian Jean-François Bergier which I have already mentioned, but not with the tendentious, indeed frivolous, publications of the Geneva sociologist Jean Ziegler, which, especially with their grotesque caricatures – as if economic relations prolonged the war and the Swiss banks built their success on what the Nazi victims left behind – are avidly read in Germany. Indeed I am always proud of being a Swiss. And I cannot understand why, even in the year 2003, as a German one may not be proud of being a German, despite the catastrophic collapse of civilization in German history. Being proud of history does not mean being a proud German. We already learn that at school from our national poet Gottfried Keller: 'Respect the fatherland of every human being, but love your own!'

Yes, I come from a tradition with a sense of civic freedom and will never deny it. Our national 'project' and my Swiss nature have an almost instinctive antipathy to all dictatorship in state, church and society, to all state totalitarianism and ecclesiastical integralism; they are also resistant to the worship of church leaders and the idolization of institutions, whether party or church. And there is commitment, if need be against right or left wing, to democracy, federalism, tolerance and the freedom and dignity of the individual and smaller communities. Hence there is a sense of responsibility – realistic, down-to-earth and public-spirited.

For me, from my youth, public spirit has been symbolically bound up with the little town of Sempach, directly on our lake: for all Swiss this is the place of the second battle for freedom in a long war against the Habsburgs. It was there on 9 July 1386 that the army of peasants and citizens from central Switzerland inflicted a devastating defeat on the proud army of the knights of Count Leopold of Austria. Initially, though, the Swiss, armed with short halberds and spiked maces, made no progress against the knights in armour, who had formed a front with their long spears – until, as the saga has it (the Zurich chronicle of 1476 is the first to mention the heroic act of an individual), Arnold Winkelried from Stans in the Nidwald resolved to seize a bundle of lances and 'to make a passage-way for his men'. Here is a man who fearlessly and without restraint sacrificed himself for the common cause.

In his Laudatio when I am awarded the Theodor Heuss Prize in 1998 (Heuss was the first President of the Federal Republic of Germany), Carl Friedrich von Weizsäcker, a physicist and philosopher with much experience of Switzerland, will declare in my justification (or perhaps to excuse me): 'Those who seek to overcome harsh oppositions will also come into conflict with their advocates. If I may, Herr Küng, I would like to say that your role in the debate has sometimes reminded me of your Swiss fellow-countryman Winkelried, who in 1386 in the battle of Sempach seized the spears of a line of knights confronting him and thrust them into his chest. That made a gap in the front and the Swiss won.' My reply was: 'You are right, dear Carl Friedrich von Weizsäcker, to refer in your Laudatio to Winkelried and the battle of Sempach in 1386; I live by the Sempachersee, almost opposite the battlefield. They say of Winkelried in Switzerland "One for all", but also "all for one" – and I've also experienced that.'

But enough of historical considerations; I am not rooted only in history. In any case, for me historical reminiscences and experiences of nature overlap. Both shape me, and the latter will time and again be a source of strength and joy for me of which city dwellers have little inkling. Nature, in which I grew up and which I seek time and again, belongs at the roots of my existence.

Living with nature: lake and mountains

Some say that human beings are not free. Some say that they are governed by their environment, almost pre-formed by its influences. Conversely, others say that human beings are genetically pre-programmed, shaped and driven on by inherited programmes. I know that I am both conditioned by the environment and pre-programmed by heredity. And at the same time I know that I am not totally conditioned by either of these. Within the limits of what is innate and what is conditioned by the environment I am free, and therefore not simply predictable. I am not an animal and I am not a robot. But it is worth reflecting a little on both these factors: first on the environment which forms me and my will, but which I too form.

So it is in the little town of Sursee on the Sempachersee, which was called Sursee before the battle and from which our little river, the Sure, takes its course into the Surental, that I am born on 19 March 1928, under the sign of Pisces. Don't worry, I don't believe in the constellations imagined by human beings, the individual stars of which often lie billions of light-years apart. But even later, in Tübingen, I will rarely go to bed without having first looked at the stars or at least the clouds.

Beyond doubt I am a 'fish', since all my life I have been fond of swimming, but I am not a mountaineer. Certainly in my young years I climb many mountains in Central Switzerland, in Graubünden and especially round Zermatt: by the long approach from Randa I go many, many hours on foot, say to the Gornergrat, the Schwarzsee and the Hörnlihütte at the foot of the Matterhorn and back again, dead tired. But there is something which will later serve me as an excuse for not embarking on further mountain adventures: I have climbed the highest mountain that stands completely on Swiss soil, with the imposing name 'Dom', directly opposite the Matterhorn and even a couple of dozen metres higher, 4545 metres above sea level.

For me at the age of seventeen, having shot up and in Sursee being the tallest in the class, but (as a doctor will discover only decades later) suffering from low blood pressure and tending to tire more quickly than others, this is a challenge. The ascent, which takes many hours, starting early around 4 a.m. from the Domhütte at around 3000 metres, demands my last ounce of strength, especially on the final 200 metres, sinking deep into the snow of the summit at every step. This becomes an almost fatal adventure for Otto Wüst, the third member, with the guide, of our team of three, who is later to be my bishop: he suddenly falls on a rock wall below me, hanging by the rope over a crevasse several hundred metres deep, trying to stop by seizing the bare rock with both hands; fortunately we had secured our rope. But then, around midday, we've done it. Finally up. A fabulously beautiful view of the other mountains of the Valais above 4000 metres and dozens of smaller peaks. But the winds are icy and we can only picnic below the summit in the lee of the wind. Then very soon it's back down the mountain, no less effort, over an ice field which goes on and on and on for ever. Everyone takes it in turns to go first, laboriously cutting step after step in the ice with the axe. A slip would be fatal.

In the end all turns out well. With a feeling of pride and at the same time totally exhausted, I fall asleep. But nothing will persuade me to repeat such an adventure. Ski lifts and cable cars, which as at the Klein-Matterhorn go up to around 4000 metres, will give me the same glorious view in my later years; and then descents on skis, which in the white landscape and winter air, given reasonably good condition and technique, provide an incomparably greater pleasure. I will continue to enjoy this sport even in my eighth decade – not least because with it for a few hours at least I can 'air' my brain and forget all scholarship, often defying the cold, wind, snow and storm, but preferably of course in winter sunshine above the cloud layer which covers the Mittelland.

I can ski only for a few weeks in the year, but depending on the circumstances I can swim all the year round. Our lake, barely 20 kilometres in front of the great wall of the Alps, was formed in prehistoric times, after the tongue of the ice-age Reuss glacier withdrew and made a great hollow in front of the hill of the murrain. If as schoolchildren we swim straight across the lake as far as Gamma Island (named after my biology teacher who was President of the Swiss Naturalist Society) – this is regarded as a record achievement – we mustn't think too much about the depth of the lake, which on average is 45 metres but at its deepest is almost 90 metres. Only in 1806 was the lake lowered by two metres. Over the course of the time this dried out the Zellmoos, where according to the saga an early mediaeval church was submerged in the sea; in 1941 it was in fact rediscovered, during the building of a fisherman's house, with foundation walls from the Carolingian period. Soon I will build my own little house by the lake, only a few hundred metres away; for its foundations in the chalk floor of the lake a whole series of eight-metre piles are required. It will be a pile-dwelling in modern times – with the marvellous ever-changing view into the world of the mountains, when they are not hidden by clouds or mist!

Our lake between the gentle green hills of the Lucerne Mittelland is always a couple of degrees warmer than the nearby Vierwaldstätter See, fed directly from the glacier water, but because of the excessive use of fertilizer it is also more threatened with algae (happily it has proved possible to stop this with firm environmental measures). We learn to swim at an early age, self-taught among others of the same age. It impresses me deeply that one day I have the experience that 'the water's supporting me'. I come home radiant: 'I can swim.' For me this experience remains an illustration of the venture of faith, which cannot first be proved theoretically by a course on 'dry land' but simply has to be attempted: a quite rational venture, though the rationality only emerges in the act.

Happily my father buys a beautiful solid mahogany rowing boat for the whole family (of course my brothers and sisters and I would have preferred a motor boat). When I grow older I go out in it countless times alone on the lake, or moor somewhere and read and write there. It is on the lake that I shall be writing a good deal of my book on the Council (1960).

Nature mysticism?

Swimming all by myself far out on the lake, right at the beginning, especially under a cloudy sky, I feel a little uneasy at the thought of the tremendous depth of the lake. I am not a nature mystic who finds 'God in the forest' or on the lake. And for me 'Sursee' is not a place of metaphysical experience to be praised lyrically – as the little Odenwald town of Amorbach was for the philosopher Theodor W. Adorno or the 'Feldweg' was for Martin Heidegger – something that could even replace the experience of God for me. But I can very well find that on 'my' lake I completely and utterly forget myself. One cannot have this experience anywhere as one can have it here: the self is taken up into a great all-embracing whole, yet does not become a drop of water but remains itself. Countless ideas, notions, inspirations have come to me on the lake as I forget myself. And also prayers of gratitude: 'You hold me behind and before and you have laid your hand on me' (Ps. 139.5).

And so in this lake I shall swim over all the decades and at every season, and often at the same time meditate and reflect. I like it best in the early morning sunlight with flat, calm water, but also under a grey sky, often in rain and storm, when the lake, ruffled a garish green with white foam, seems to have been stirred up in anger. Indeed, once in a research semester I will swim in my lake right through a whole winter, even between Christmas and New Year. Quickly through the snow and into the water as soon as possible, otherwise the calf muscles hurt too much! And after a couple of dozen strokes back to the bank and over the snow, which now burns almost like fire, into the house under the hot shower. As I often sit at my desk from early to late at all hours of the day with little sleep, I need such variation and sometimes even physical challenge.

But as time goes on, it is not so much the challenge that is in the foreground as the constant need to keep fit and to contemplate, indeed wonder at, nature. My little house with a terrace on two sides will make that possible; on the left the massive mountain block of the Rigi and on the right the Pilatus, which rises sheer from the Mittelland with the Titlis, the Stanserhorn and the Bürgenstock in between. In clear weather I can see the whole chain of the Alps from the Glarner Alps to the Berne Alps with the Eiger, the Mönch and the Jungfrau. The lake glitters silver in the morning light, in the twilight only glowing from the opposite shore. Its colours and moods always point towards heaven. And it is at its most mysterious in the full moon, in winter often quite clear and white, with the Alps in the background. In summer in the distance are the warning lights on the peaks and on the other shore the reflection of the chain of village lights. Often I will be on my terrace until well past midnight, looking, reading and writing; above me is the Milky Way, which can be seen better than in the cities. My house is orientated exactly north–south, and I can see the North Star through the skylight of my little bedroom.

Later I will find compensation from the lake for the fact that as a child I am not allowed to have pets: there are plenty of animals round the house. And sometimes also under the house: foxes and badgers, so strong that they take on the three hunting dogs sent against them. In our peaceful bird sanctuary, with the head-quarters of the Swiss Society for the Protection of Birds on the other shore of the lake, there is no lack of birds, from pied wagtails in the garden to a great heron patrolling to and fro; he often proudly enthrones himself on the bow of our fisherman's boat. There are great flocks of gulls and starlings, and swallows display their acrobatic flying skills, swooping low to announce a storm. This then rushes over our lake, but usually does damage only nearer the Alps.

Sometimes when I get into the water a peaceful pair of swans go by in all their majesty with immaculate white feathers, but this doesn't just remind me of Saint-Saëns' *Carnival of the Animals*. For later one spring it's a sunny day, and the ice-blue water calls. On my bit of land a pair of swans have made a nest of grass and twigs in the belt of reeds and are hatching their young. Utter calm prevails as I swim out into the cold lake. Only when I want to swim back do I see the mother swan deftly gliding in the utmost haste through the reeds to the nest, while the father swan comes flying from the far distant peninsula with outstretched neck and legs sticking out behind, flapping his giant wings, to land upright in front of me with a threatening attitude. Moving to and fro amazingly quickly, paddling with both feet, he angrily attempts to prevent my return: his beak, as long as his head, points straight at my eyes; his wings, ready to beat, are ruffled up to drive me from the neighbourhood of the nest. Fortunately my old and experienced housekeeper, Charlotte Renemann from Oldenburg, disturbed that I have been out so long, runs to the nest with bread. She lures the swan away from me so that I can swim quickly to land. I don't seek a repetition of the event.

I like the peaceful great crested grebes much better; they live silently within view, in the same peaceful long-term marriage as the swans. Certainly they can't fly as well as the swans or the friendly mallards with their beautiful feathers, who often waddle cheerfully on land by the half-dozen. But grebes swim and dive fabulously. Time and again I attempt to compete with them in swimming or to separate them from each other, but I always lose. At the crucial moment they submerge, and it's impossible to work out where they will emerge again. It's utterly entrancing when they swim past with their chicks in the knapsack of their thick feathers.

The grebes are the most constant inhabitants of our part of the lake, where they find their food by diving for little fish that swim on the surface. There are big fish: bream, sea trout, a few carp and also pike, deeper down. 'A carp pool also needs a pike,' the wise Lucerne theologian Otto Karrer, a specialist in mysticism, will say to explain the particular function of his young colleague in the area of scholastic theology. However, I didn't come into the world right on the edge of the lake, but in the middle of our little town, in the shadow of the town hall and the parish church.

Three generations

Back to the roots. My family? I've reflected for a long time whether I should offer an extensive family history here – it's less important than the story of the church, theology and the Council that I shall be telling later. But anyone who picks up the memoirs of an author wants not only to have a few pieces of information about his youth but also to know: Who is this person? Where does he come from? How has he become who he is? So now something about my family.

I am born in an impressive house built of stone which bears the date 1651, but is already attested at the beginning of the fifteenth century. It can easily be recognized on my copperplate engraving of Sursee by the famous Basle engraver Merian. Today it is a favourite subject for all the photographers because of its two decorations. First there is the powerful wrought-iron shield with the Sursee coat of arms, an arm formed of acanthus and naturalistic flowers ending in a gryphon's head wearing a laurel wreath with a gilded crown hovering round it – a sign that this was originally the tavern Zur Krone. Then immediately alongside it, at the corner of the house, under a baldachin on a console, there is the almost life-size statue of Mary with a child in front of a mandorla of flames, her garment folded in a vivid way: a work by the widely-known Sursee sculptor Hans Wilhelm Tüfel. It is a reminder that it proved possible to stop the great fire by which our town was visited more than others in 1650 at this precise point, at the transition from the upper town to the lower town, according to legend by the intercession of Mary. It is in this beautiful corner room with a view on two sides, protected by the Madonna, that I live all those years, until our father buys a piece of land for me and my sisters by the lake, divided into three, and at the beginning of the 1960s I can build my 'Seehüsli' on it.

For a hundred years, now in the third generation, shoes are sold under the name 'Küng' in our house on the town hall square, in a good location, at the centre of a large catchment area. The name Küng is unusual in Germany, but comes from the Middle High German 'Künec' and the Old High German 'Kuni(n)g'. When I was at grammar school I read in a multi-volume Swiss-German dictionary (given the Greek title *Idiotikon* in the nineteenth century) how 'König', 'king', 'koning' (Dutch), 'konung' (Swedish) presumably derive from the word 'kühn' (bold). Be this as it may, I never felt this to be an obligation.

I have never got involved in genealogical research. But because one of the most important architects of Berne cathedral was called 'Küng' (Erhart), one of my uncles amused himself by taking over his coat of arms, conjecturing that the Küngs had come to Sursee from the region of Berne via Entlebuch. But all this is quite unimportant, given the historically indisputable fact that my grandfather Johann Küng began with literally nothing – except a solid education. As a 24-year-old master shoemaker from the region of Lucerne, having previously been an apprentice in the region of Berne and West Switzerland, in the first years he went round Sursee as a journeyman calling on customers and for a daily wage of three 'Fränkli' repaired all the shoes of the family and servants at farmhouses.

As early as 1901 he established a little cobbler's shop in the inn Zur Krone. Often it was late in the evening before he had repaired the shoes handed in there by the customers during the day. But from the beginning he also kept a little shoe shop, selling wooden or leather shoes to the farmers. With the new workshop in the Krone he extended this business, rented further rooms, and in 1916, in the middle of the First World War, to the amazement of our town bought the whole of the Krone. Much later he had another big building erected with storerooms, two dwellings and two marvellous big terraces. We have lunch on one of them in the summer and I also spend much of my youth there, hence probably my hunger for sun, light and warmth and my predilection for working in the open air. As Ingeborg Bachmann put it, 'There is nothing better under the sun than to be under the sun.'

My grandfather? I revere him; a powerful man who easily gets angry and at the same time is modest and affable, who soon gained many friends among the up-and-coming businessmen. He meets with three of them regularly every Sunday noon to play jass, the popular Swiss card game. Our neighbour from across the road, Siegmund Heimann, from the only Jewish family in our town, who has a drapery and clothes shop, is always there. When his second son, the 17-year-old Werner, drowns, walking on the lake in snowshoes to save a friend, everyone mourns. The friendly relations with this family over three generations make our relationship to Judaism seem quite unproblematical. No one in our family knows anything of the effects of a 'Jew stamp' for refugees from Nazi Germany and certain financial transactions of our big banks, and it is only towards the end of the war that we hear of the extent of the Nazi annihilation of the Jews. The Holocaust was implemented in the utmost secrecy, and when isolated bits of information came over the frontier into the free world, this far surpassed anything anyone could imagine. For us too the absolutely unimaginable will become horrific reality only with pictures from the liberated concentration camps.

The grandfather and godfather ('Götti') attentively observes the progress of his grandson and favourite, who now goes to kindergarten. When the grandson is able to write his first and second names with chalk on the parquet floor (only the 's' was the wrong way round), his grandfather gives him a five-franc coin with the head of William Tell on it. Grandfather's gifts at Christmas and other festivals are often bigger than those of my parents: skis, a mouth organ and the big Herder encyclopedia, and from the Basle fair a carousel with six seats which, when erected on our terrace and turned quickly, makes all the school friends who are allowed to come to visit us go pale. Sometimes it also has worse effects –

enormous fun. But I also remember the day when grandfather's piano is transported down from the upper floor. His three sons and his daughter have all had piano lessons, but no one wants to play. So why have a piano? He immediately sells it. My mother buys another one later, but for me it is now too late to learn to play the piano properly – which is perhaps a very good thing, in view of other intensive activity.

Grandfather's tragedy is a car accident in 1934 on the way back from a pilgrimage to Einsiedeln, a few kilometres before Sursee, in which his car turns over as the result of an engine fault. My grandmother is dead. The one who gave me sweets so often lies there peacefully, with a red mark on her forehead but no other visible wound. She is the first dead person of whom I have a vivid memory, at the age of six. To make the loneliness more tolerable for my grandfather, who doesn't want to marry again and is looked after by a faithful but somewhat cranky housekeeper, I am allowed to sleep in my own bed in his big bedroom, and chat with him a bit in the living room before going to bed. I regularly smuggle a book into the bedroom and can go on reading illicitly until he comes too. So I gobble up *Robinson Crusoe* and *Uncle Tom's Cabin,* and as well as many travel books and adventures almost all the books of Karl May and soon also historical novels like *Ben Hur* and *Quo Vadis*, and of course also detective stories, Edgar Wallace for preference. When my grandfather dies at the age of 76 he has made it possible for each of his sons to carry on a lucrative shoe business: in Sursee, Zofingen and Aarau. Happily the often-quoted saying 'the first generation builds it up, the second pulls it down and the third squanders it' doesn't seem to have been true in our family.

How much depends on genes?

My father? Johann Küng's oldest son Hans, my father, also needs courage to begin with. He has taken over the now already considerable shoe business in the difficult year 1936, in the midst of the great recession following the world economic crisis. Businesses are doing badly – what an effort it was to survive in these years! And even worse is to come when the Second World War breaks out in 1939. Leather and shoes become scarce and expensive, and sales are strictly controlled – how difficult it is to get the necessary supplies of the right quality! And how often I have to help, sticking all those hundreds of 'ration coupons' on big sheets!

My mother? My father's marriage to my mother, Emma Gut, a self-confident farmer's daughter from a tough, rising family from nearby Kaltbach, was great good fortune for all of us. She made him court her a long time and only married him at the age of 27 (it was not until late in her life that in connection with the papal encyclical on the pill, which she too rejected, she confessed to me that she didn't want to have too many children too early, as her mother did). She had grown up among numerous energetic brothers and sisters, all of whom were to achieve something in life. The Gut family was freethinking and liberal, and two of their number were community presidents in the neighbourhood. But the grandfather on mother's side had 'converted' – a sensation throughout the area: he had resolutely gone over to the Catholic conservative party. For when in 1918 he became seriously ill during a dangerous wave of influenza and his whole family had got into serious financial difficulties, his liberal relations had left him and his thirteen children in the lurch; only the Catholic conservative relations helped his wife. Big and gaunt, with a beard, and the first to ride through the village on a bicycle, he remained the undisputed and not always comfortable patriarch in the Gut family.

After the marriage my mother took it for granted that she should involve herself in our business with all her energy. So during the day she was a businesswoman, but also a housewife with finally two sons, after me Georg, and five daughters – Marlis, Rita, Margrit, Hildegard and Irene. However, she was always supported by a cook and sometimes also by a nursemaid, who was usually very popular with us children. The bigger and more complex the business, which had been taken on in difficult times – it is now far and wide the largest – the more important for the whole concern becomes her sure aesthetic feeling for each of the seasonal six-monthly orders which decide the success or failure of a shoe business. She is a wise, indeed skilful woman, who was not allowed more than a primary school education and the girls' school in Lucerne, and who acquired her distinctive education through indefatigable reading and courses of further education. In this way she remains spiritually alert and open to new things.

Both father and mother have a cheerful disposition, and a natural stature and dignity. Our father, now back at the piano from time to time, plays games with us like Lotto, for which he awards prizes; in due course he teaches us to drink wine in moderation on Sunday. He is involved in the town music and loves festivals more than anything. Quickly angered, he is also quickly reconciled again. I continue to remember my mother as a youthful woman with a good sense of humour, fond of jokes and also arguments. She is a strong woman, who doesn't create problems but solves them, and everyone can count on her good will. Both parents keep open house, and their hospitality is praised decades later. On Sunday grandfather often comes to breakfast from Kaltbach in his carriage and pair after early mass. And after the main service there is always the aperitif offered by my father, when all the many uncles and aunts fill our home and discuss God and the world, often at considerable volume, over a glass of Fendant and biscuits. My father follows politics closely, but avoids political office.

Cheerfulness, energy, concern, kindness, but also earnestness, are the principal characteristics of my mother. There were some dramatic personal incidents in her life: one was certainly the death of her son Rudolf in 1936, the year they took on the business, after a long bout of pneumonia, when he was only a year old. And then, even more, the death of her second son Georg when he was 23. This brother was the wilder of the two of us and ready for any joke, trick and argument. After joining the bank and continuing his training at the Morgan Bank in Paris, he was meant to be the owner of the business in the third generation, but this boy who so enjoyed life died an early death in 1955 after suffering for a long time from a brain tumour. We shall have to talk about this later.

People so often ask: how much is due to the genes and how much to upbringing? As the firstborn who saw the light of the world two years after my parents' marriage, I always think of Küng-Gut as a happy synergy. 'Küng' alone would probably have been all too light-footed and hedonistic; 'Gut' alone would have been rather too earnest and energetic. According to the popular theory I would define my temperament as choleric-sanguine, sometimes with a touch of melancholy, but without any phlegm. At any rate, I shall attribute the somewhat unusual capacity for physical and psychological effort and persistence which I needed later in every possible situation and crisis not to my own efforts but to the legacy I have been given. 'If one has been indisputably mother's favourite,' writes Sigmund Freud (I know this only from my sisters), 'then one retains for life that feeling of conquest, that confidence of success which quite often brings real success in its wake.' Beyond doubt my feelings and emotions towards my mother and father will remain fundamental to me all my life. But there is no trace of an Oedipus complex.

Of course, as in any family, there are also tensions and disputes among us, disputes between the parents, with the parents, and even more between the brothers and sisters, especially between my brother and me. My mother occasionally gets on our nerves with her religious demands. My father can react in a very impatient and unjust way. And I am extremely sensitive in my reactions to unfair treatment, whether from parents or teachers. For a long time my slogan is, '*Fiat justitia, pereat mundus!* – Let justice be done, even if the world should perish!' I will retain this unexpressed sense of justice, but later think up better slogans. But there are no fundamental conflicts with my parents – no letters to my father à la Kafka or Hesse.

A cheerful nature and seriousness about life, the mercantile sense of the entrepreneur and the vitality of a farmer, intelligence given by nature and a pragmatic sense of reality, all in a modesty which has been learned, an inner humility, and a friendliness which is taken for granted: perhaps this mixture isn't a bad basis for a natural sovereignty, growing up in a family which is well-to-do but not rich, clever but not academic, which enjoys respect but isn't an élite. 'What do you want to be?' the elderly shoemaker Enrico Erbini, who comes from Italy, asks the child who likes to keep watching him because he tells such interesting stories. 'Probably a shoemaker, too,' replies the child. Erbini laughs gently, 'You'll never be a shoemaker.' The child doesn't know what to make of this enigmatic prophecy.

Civic honour and honorary citizen

Back to the roots: our community. Every day in our house on the town hall square I hear the bells of the church opposite. They don't disturb me; rather, I'm glad when on the festivals the seventh bell, the 'big' bell, also rings. Every day I look at the great dial of the church clock and hardly need my own watch, which was given to me at my confirmation. And I'm very fond of the beautiful sundial on the town hall opposite us with the fresco of the great reaper and the hour glass, which recall the transitoriness of all things. However, Buddenbrookian decadence and a desire for death would be the last things to move me.

Our town hall, a building detached on all sides, the most extensive and most important official mediaeval building in the Lucerne district, bears witness to the civic pride of our town. It is almost incredible that between 1539 and 1546 — during these seven years the amount of goods transported over the Gotthard was a record — a town of perhaps 800 souls could afford such a town hall and market, still impressive today. It was built by the Lucerne master builder and stonemason Jakob Zumsteg, who has been eternalized as the hero of the novel *Der Rathausbaumeister* (The Town Hall Architect) by the native Sursee author Otto Helmut Lienert. When the town hall is renovated at the beginning of the 1970s and sponsors are being sought, I insist on bearing the cost of renovating the sundial.

I have close connections with the town hall. I go there very frequently for my grandfather to have documents authenticated by town clerk Randegger or to pay small change, and sometimes my own small savings, in at the cantonal bank on the first floor. Now and then I go up the spiral staircase of the tower as far as the great council room on the second floor. One day I look at its heavy coffered oak roof, constructed by the same sculptor Tüfel who carved our Madonna, gilded with sunlight. Overwhelmed, I think that sometime, somewhere, somehow, I too would like to have an oak ceiling to my room; later in the lake house the sun may not be shining on a coffered roof, but it does shine on my roof truss, and gild it in a similar way when the light falls on it.

However, it is not so much around the town hall, but rather in the alleyways which drop down to the Sure, that we discuss and gossip, play ball, fight and shout. The enclosed structure of alleyways and the fortifications of our town, some of which remain, provide the romantic framework for all kinds of noisy games, not just with balls and bicycles, but often quite rough fights between two sides or districts. Here fights are usually over the scarf pinned to our belts and sometimes they involve blows; however, no one is seriously injured, and never without our being reconciled again. In 'capture the flag' which we play in the breaks at St George's school, the important thing is to capture the enemy camp. Because of my size and physical strength I usually start by being able to make an attack on a camp with nine opponents, since on my approach the first three give way, the second three do not offer any serious resistance, and only the last three really have to be overcome.

The class reunion of St George, Sursee 1928 will allude to this and much more when at its jubilee meeting on 24 October 1998 it solemnly resolves to bestow 'honorary citizenship for life' on 'Professor Hans Küng, who by virtue of the year and place of his birth was necessarily made a founder member' (at this particular time he was in Kyoto for matters relating to the global ethic). The document is sealed with the signatures of all present, with the humorous yet serious explanation: 'in gratitude for his services to the reputation of our class association and the militant activity which he learned in the primary school class association, and to commemorate his civil courage'.

Looking at these years of my youth, it is understandable why the award of the honorary citizenship of my home town will be something quite special for me. The presentation of this document to me by the town president of Sursee in the great council chamber on my seventieth birthday, on the unanimous vote of the assembled community (I am the first and only person to receive such an honour), is unforgettable. The banquet – accompanied by Mozart's music for wind instruments based on *The Marriage of Figaro* – will not take place just in a circle of 'dignitaries'. It will be a joy for me to see family and relations, friends and schoolmates, neighbours and assistants again. And on that same occasion my sister Rita and my brother-in-law Bruno Frei, who to the great relief of the family were ready to take over the business, will show me our parents' big house, now in the third generation, restored in marvellous Tuscan red along with Madonna and crown. This will considerably increase my joy and that of our town at the banquet.

Time and again over all the years, to my great satisfaction I will hear from my former playmates and school friends, 'You really haven't changed'. Or that I've changed – yet remained the same.

From a closed Catholic world

Back to the roots: the church? The Catholicism of my grandparents and parents and also of my own early years has remained fundamentally mediaeval and baroque. With all its customs and usages this is a varied and colourful church life: by no means just superfluous and damaging ballast from its previous history, but also quite valuable religious substance. It isn't gloomy; rather, it delights the senses, like our parish church, dedicated to the patron saint of our town, St George. I cannot see why in the time after the Council this particular mythical fighter against incarnate evil will be removed from the church's calendar simply because the bold officer from Cappadocia or at least his dragon aren't historical, so that the powerful motif of killing the dragon is left to Richard Wagner and his Siegfried.

Our parish church admirably symbolizes something that I shall analyse in depth only many decades later: how in the religious sphere, in complete contrast to the scientific sphere, a quite specific 'constellation of beliefs, values and techniques', a 'paradigm', here the mediaeval one, can persist – of course with appropriate adaptations. The first predecessor of our parish church, built at the highest point and in the oldest part of the town, comes from the early Middle Ages, perhaps the seventh century. Today's church is one of the few examples of sacred Renaissance architecture in Switzerland; however, it was made baroque at the time of the triumphalism of the Counter-Reformation and now in my own youth has been renovated and extended for pastoral reasons – to the annoyance of some purist art experts. Round-arched arcades on Tuscan pillars carry the high walls of the central nave, the vault of which is decorated with pictures of the four evangelists and delicate, elegant rococo stucco work. All in all it's a cheerful church which gives delight, particularly in the evening when it is fully lit.

To serve at the mass here isn't so much a duty as an honour and a joy for me and many of my friends (girls aren't allowed to serve). Of course I can't know that our attractive little red and white robes possibly had their origin in the Collegium Germanicum in Rome. At all events the artistically embroidered heavy brocade vestments of our priest, especially as worn at festivals, would have also made a good show in baroque Rome. So too would the many valuable chalices and the two monstrances, which I can inspect closely so often in the sacristy: the slender and delicate late-Gothic tower monstrance from the beginning of the Reformation period (1523) and above all the baroque monstrance, set with great precious stones, made by Hans Peter Staffelbach, who is famous all around as the main witness to the goldsmith's art which flourished in Sursee above all from the seventeenth to the nineteenth century.

It's exciting for me when during the week now and again I am allowed to replace the sacristan. I then use the quiet time during holy mass to climb the high church tower very quickly and look from the open lantern ('*Känzeli*') under the beautifully curved cupola, down on our house, the whole city, indeed the broad landscape stretching as far as the mountains. Often when on travels all over the world I am asked what I would most like to see in this or that city, I reply 'the highest point' – to get a view, a panorama, and some insight.

That is the mediaeval aspect of our Catholicism: the whole of Christian life in our little town is quite naturally dominated by the church, which is in league with the Catholic conservative people's party. The church is already present acoustically with every stroke of the bell, announcing the time and important events: the sound of the angelus in the early morning, at noon and in the evening; the special sounds before the great festivals; and the passing bell which announces a death or a burial, to which careful attention is always paid. Visually the church is no less dominant, clearly towering over all the buildings, including our town hall; one goes 'up' a monumental flight of stairs to our church. Indeed the church still also continues to dominate life in spiritual terms: our local school, though in the hands of laity, is inconceivable without the presence of the clergy. The school inspector, the rector of the preparatory school, teachers of religion, Latin and Greek – all are clergy, supported by the fathers of the Capuchin monastery founded at the beginning of the seventeenth century, which also appoints the 'town preacher' (once a month).

The worship is still unrivalled, with its baroque colour, its golden vessels and its unsurpassable solemnity; the processions, hymns and powerful organ music. At festivals there is even an orchestral mass by Mozart or Haydn and a motet by Bruckner. The great festivals of the church's year are a community event forming a welcome interruption to everyday life, which flows placidly on. But there is also no question that the obligatory worship on Sundays and feast days makes possible a social control that gently inserts everyone into the collective. This is almost inevitable in that time of limited mobility. The hour of instruction in the church catechism on Thursday and the unpopular half-hour of Christian doctrine on Sunday, both for young people, are to be seen in this framework. In the medi-aeval manner, church and society aren't yet separated.

Here collective joy is often mixed with collective fear. This is expressed in some forms of pious superstition, in the pious works of the many blessings, processions, pilgrimages and above all the confessional, associated with arbitrary laws (against mixed marriages), casuistic precepts (sobriety before receiving communion), and many abstruse ideas of heaven, hell and purgatory. All children are brought to confession before they may receive communion towards the end of their first year at school, so that they can confess even their smallest 'sins' to the priest: 'I have stolen,' I say in one of my first confessions, and am deeply terrified when the priest asks, 'What and how much?' My halting answer: 'A couple of blackcurrants, by the garden fence, on the way back from the baths.' I never returned to this inquisitive confessor, who happened to be the parish priest.

This parish priest, Dr Robert Kopp, is the head of the Catholic establishment in Sursee (at that time we saw the Reformed community and its minister as being only peripheral). He is an honourable, condescending but friendly and musical prelate who always offers us boys his hand only from above, with his fingertips. In his last years he is allowed to bear the Roman title of apostolic protonotary (we mock him by calling him the 'apostolic protomotor'); of course this title has nothing to do with the apostles but with the mitre, the bishop's hat, which he now wears at the liturgy at high festivals – to the delight of the whole com-munity, which may now own to something like a quasi-bishop. That for us is 'the church': built up in stages like a pyramid. At the very bottom are the priests and religious; then the bishops, archbishops and cardinals; and right at the top, remote yet near, is the 'Holy Father', who stands above all criticism. They, the clergy, the hierarchy, *are* the church. We, the laity, *belong to* the church.

A picture will remain with me of this 'reverend father', Dr Kopp, going through the town with the senior curate, Eduard Pfister. Both are in black cassocks and broad-brimmed hats; they are greeted and return the greetings in a friendly way. What a different age – what a Catholic world shut off from the outside world! I would never have become a clergyman on this model. So why was I ordained?

One man was different

In a conversation at the beginning of the 1960s between the then two youngest professors at the University of Tübingen, the sociologist Ralf Dahrendorf will frankly tell me that he assumes that someone like me has become a theologian with a view to one day becoming prelate, bishop or cardinal; in other words for the sake of office, prestige, power. I dispute this, but don't know whether I have convinced my conversation partner. He was probably already planning his own career in politics (he rose to become an EU commissioner). I can't tell him the long story that I am telling here to explain why I chose the 'clerical' profession with no thought of career.

One person is different from the 'reverend fathers' of Sursee. He isn't a representative of the Catholic conservative establishment, which in fierce electoral battles is able to maintain its dominance over liberals and future socialists by preventing industrialization. Franz Xaver Kaufmann came to Sursee in 1937 as a 29-year-old auxiliary priest and youth chaplain and then in 1954, as is customary in Switzerland, was democratically elected by the congregation to be the sixty-fifth parish priest of Sursee. He will follow my life, initially very closely and then more from a distance, until he dies in 1986 as a hospital chaplain, at the age of 78. What I relate here doesn't apply exclusively to me; many of my generation have a similar experience. Without this man and his understanding nature some of us wouldn't have coped with the problems of puberty and adolescence so easily, and more than a dozen I know wouldn't have considered priestly ordination. He didn't invite, challenge, even press a single one. Rather, what happened just happened. That raises the question of the reasons for his influence.

What lies behind all the pastoral activities of this man, who isn't an activist? What lies behind the demonstrations, processions and renovations of a pastor who isn't a political demonstrator, a keen liturgist or a thwarted church builder? What, people ask later, perhaps even more than during his lifetime, is the secret of this unique pastor whom many of us simply call chaplain? He is neither president nor prelate, yet at the same time is more than either of these. For everyone, literally for everyone in Sursee, he is simply 'the priest', and we never feel that he is the kind of parish priest who gives himself airs.

If we want to feel our way towards the mystery of this man, with his actions and passions, his strengths and weaknesses, then we may begin quite confidently from outside, from the most external feature of all. 'Clothes make people,' perhaps, but certainly 'the black cassock and the Roman collar do not make the pastor'. Franz Xaver Kaufmann is convinced of this, and to the end likes to wear ordinary clothes. Only those who compare him with those other 'reverend fathers of the Herrenrain' can judge what it means to us young people that our young chaplain, more revered and loved than respected, also takes part in shirt and trousers in the treasure hunts and other games in the woods round about, and afterwards skilfully joins in cooking on the camp fire.

Once half-a-dozen of us even tackle six passes in four days on bicycles (Oberalp-Lukman-Gotthard-Furka-Grimsel-Brünig), spending the night in Disentis and Gletsch in a cold tent and in Airolo in the waiting room. What a difference from the bourgeois comfort that we are all accustomed to at home! In this way another lifestyle is made possible for us, shaped by the youth movement, which in Switzerland fortunately the Nazis can't commandeer.

He's a phenomenon – this youth chaplain who organizes holiday camps in the mountains lasting several weeks. Some people in Sursee will count these as the best experiences of their youth. He shapes the whole life of a crowd of some-times 100 boys from early in the morning until late in the evening, with demanding tours of the mountains, cooking and entertainment evenings. He puts on Punch and Judy shows, tells chilling stories of ghosts and robbers, and at the same time as a Samaritan can administer first aid for all our scratches and wounds. He truly practises the care of souls, and in many respects also the care of bodies; he isn't just a man of holidays and trips, but a 'man for all seasons'. And all through the year he keeps his ground floor open until well into the night on Sundays and weekdays: it's a 'club' where young people can meet; the thought of finding other places of entertainment simply doesn't occur to them. He inspires gripping forest Christmases in December and lavish carnival night processions in February, and even acts as a theatre director. He's never at a loss for ideas for financing his numerous enterprises by collecting paper and building cribs, and at the same time zealously runs the box office in person, annoying us by a policy of being sparing with information that would do credit to a big Swiss bank. However, in this way he ensures that the money which has been collected with great effort isn't given away again all too effortlessly. Truly he is a chaplain who at the same time is also an actuary and a cashier; as priest, too, in an old-fashioned way he deals with everything in a one-man business with no secretariat or card index, certainly economically and more cheaply than it will ever be again in the Sursee church.

So once again, what is the secret of this priest whose extraordinary dedication isn't exhausted in busy activities? He isn't a man of spiritual routine or a func-tionary but a pastor through and through; he isn't fond of visiting, yet is active in face-to-face encounters, in the youth group and in the school. He is also extremely discreet at the confessional, by the sickbed, in pastoral conversation. He isn't a doctrinaire defender of old bastions but the modest forerunner of a pastoral approach which is open to the world. He takes the tormenting problems of young people seriously and not least understands the sexual needs of those growing up. With winning humanity he finds the right tone and the right word for both individuals and groups, the younger and the older, in a variety of situations, happy or not so happy. He embodies authority without hidden authoritarianism, and in a quite Pauline way isn't the lord of our faith but the servant of our joy. He can pass on his unassuming piety credibly in conversations and addresses, in the service of God and his fellow men and women; and in everything he enjoys the confidence of all, small or great, strong or weak. And in all his secular activity he remains a true man of the spirit.

Truly he is a pastor for each and everyone, not for a circle of the pious and super-pious, but also for the less pious; not only for the 'conservatives' but also for the 'liberals'; not only for the strictly orthodox but also for the more worldly; not only for adult church people but for the ever-new generation of those who are growing up. And in all this he is not so much one who believes in miracles as one who performs many inconspicuous little miracles in the hearts of many people. Perhaps these miracles can be seen only in those who in his time take up the priestly vocation – and they are more numerous than any before or any afterwards – because by his way of life he can convey to them a compelling picture of this vocation, this calling. Here he is by no means always comfortable. He has his weaknesses; he can sulk and grumble, be annoyed and flare up in the stress of pastoral care. There are also tensions and disputes when we become more independent and want to implement our own ideas. But they never last long.

Our priest won't find church recognition 'from above', being more an inspiration than an organizer, more a dallier than an agitator, more a spiritual go-between than a wily politician. He is one of the 'quiet ones' among the clergy and feels lonely at clergy meetings where others love speaking; though beloved by the people below, he hardly makes himself popular with the hierarchy. He will never become canon or dean, episcopal commissioner or papal monsignor, although all who get to know him more closely value his shrewd and well-considered judgement in ecclesiastical and political matters. He has never sought places of honour, but will suffer a lack of church recognition and the isolation of his last dozen years under a parish priest with a traditionally Roman orientation, who keeps the hospital chaplain away from the pulpit and the community.

So to ask the question one last time: what is the secret of this obviously charismatic youth leader, confessor, preacher, pastor – the sort of man one would want to find more often among our clergy? As I shall understand better later on, the secret of this utterly human and sometimes all-too-human pastor of souls is that in him the spirit is at work of that spirit of the man who 2000 years ago attached no importance to clerical dress and clerical gestures. He took everyone as they were in their weakness and fragility, and treated them with utter seriousness as the people they were, the creatures whom God wanted to be like this. He didn't simply want to make people someone else, didn't condemn them, but gave them a new chance. He never interrogated anyone in inquisitorial fashion about their beliefs and condemned them, but was able to look into their hearts. He avoided all exaggerated piety, didn't build up any position of sacral power, but went before them in the service of humanity.

One could go on like this, but it must already have become clear that it is simply the spirit of this Jesus of which the youth chaplain, parish priest and finally hospital chaplain can speak and preach about to the end of his days in such an uncomplicated, direct and attractive way. Indeed at his funeral I shall say this quite plainly: it is the spirit of Jesus that is at work inconspicuously and gently in this clergyman; the liberating features of Jesus are the secret behind all the human charm and the all-too-human limitations of this priest. And it is the depth of this Jesus-like character that calls me as a young man along the way of the 'clergy' and will remain my model.

The next question I am often asked is when I decided on a priestly calling.

An early decision

This question usually has a note of unbelieving astonishment about it. How could someone like me – in particular – have wanted to become a Catholic priest? Some people were already amazed at this at the time. However, this vocation isn't like a job that one accepts, above all to earn a living, and which one gives up again when it ceases to be enjoyable. This vocation is a real calling, in which one hears something like an inner voice, not normally directly from heaven, but in one's own heart. It's a choice of life which turns one's whole existence upside down and embraces it; in it the financial reward (which in any case is not very splendid) is the most incidental of matters.

That's how I understand my decision: a choice of life, but one which is in fact something like a 'choice of estate'. Whereas with the end of the First World War the nobility largely lost the symbols and privileges of its estate, the 'clerical estate' largely continued to preserve them. And the 'reverend fathers' in Sursee and elsewhere still seem clearly distinct from the rest of the population – with particular rights (in Switzerland, for example, exemption from military service) and especially obligations, above all the obligation of celibacy.

For me this calling takes place very early and in an amazingly simple way, probably when I'm around eleven. My parents have nothing to do with this choice. They don't talk about it with me and I don't talk about it with them. Nor do I talk about it directly with my youth chaplain, though the choice would have been quite impossible without his example. In conversation with an older friend, Hans Zurkirchen, at that time the admired leader of our group, I ask what profession he has chosen: 'I want to become a priest like our chaplain' is his reply. And then suddenly it flashes through my head and heart like lightning: that would be a great calling for you too! And I say yes. In this way I have made my first fundamental decision in life. It will ask much of me, but I shall never waver in it. I have decided for the ordained ministry.

For me this is the 'call of God' – not of course in a supernatural and miraculous way directly from above, but in the real situation as it imposes itself, communicated through the voice of my friend. It is a calling which expresses itself in the inner compulsion, the inner recognition that one is capable of it; in being driven to this specific ministry. Neither a prelate nor a bishop has the least to do with this, though it is clear from the start that the church authorities also have the right to examine a candidate who thinks himself suitable. I subsequently reveal this choice of profession to my mother and my chaplain – in few words. Both are delighted, but don't exert any pressure. At all events it will be another twelve years before my definitive decision: who knows how everything will turn out?

Later, as an academic assistant for a year in distant Münster in Westphalia I spend my lonely Sunday afternoons playing the best game of my life, listening to classical music while calculating and drawing quite precisely on graph paper the outlines of my future little lake house. My architect friend Josef Suter then translates these detailed plans into a design which is interesting in quite a different way. At that time I think that being an architect could also have been a good profession. Or a historian, because of my immense interest in history, above all world history. Or when my leadership qualities find recognition in the youth movement and I am quickly made a successful group, team and district leader, some leadership post in politics or business?

But all these are pure flights of fancy and not options that I consider seriously. Untroubled by questions of money and power, I feel called to something else, which seems to me personally to be a far higher vocation, but of course also a more difficult one. For this decision for the ordained ministry is coupled with the extremely serious decision to be celibate. And at this time celibacy is regarded as a human but in fact irreversible church law which one simply has to take into account for the sake of the great calling in life: no priestly vocation without celibacy. No one in the Catholic Church at that time told us that according to Jesus and also Paul, celibacy had to be a calling freely chosen (a 'charisma': only 'those who can should do it'), which cannot be made a universally binding law on those in office (almost without exception, the apostles and the first bishops were married). The distinction between law and charisma will first dawn on us all at the time of the Council.

So isn't celibacy a problem at that time? It isn't as simple as that. I was no stranger to falling in love, even at grammar school, and more than once. I know very well the incomparable feeling of happiness that Friedrich Schiller has described with his 'blushing he follows her footsteps and is made happy by her greeting'. And like some people, I also cherish the hope, bewitched, that perhaps there may be some possibility of combining the priesthood with a woman, this woman. After a couple of weeks I ask the advice of my chaplain, who also knows and values the pretty girl. But what else can he say to me than 'Decide for yourself'? And so I decide – for distance, though I get on the same train to Lucerne every day, hold back my tears at such cruelty for me, and kiss her good-bye – the only time.

But I have the inestimable good fortune to grow up not only in the company of boys in the Jungwacht but also in the company of girls, in an uninhibited relationship to the 'other' sex. There are my five sisters – all younger than me, all pretty, intelligent and vivacious. I am proud of my sisters: Marlis, Rita, Margrit, Hildegard and Irene are very close to my heart, each in her own way. Later I will play my part in seeing that we also take account of the three who have not yet come of age in dividing up the site by the lake, so that in the summer we shall have months together in our three lake houses, and I shall also experience the growing up of the next generation. When many years later the great conflict with Rome develops, all my sisters will boldly make a public stand for me in a way which moves me.

Cock of the walk? No, my brother Georg is still there. And there are my many cousins: I am allowed to go with one of them, Liselotte, to Paris for two weeks before the school-leaving examination. And then there are the holiday children from Germany and France whom my mother particularly likes to welcome into the family in the distressed post-war years. Her argument is that we are privileged and should do something for the others, just as she also regularly sends us with some groceries to poor families in the Surengasse and elsewhere. Later we put up exchange students who at an early stage give us international contacts with Holland, France and Italy. Indeed the atmosphere is often noisy and wild in our big house, and for parents and visiting relations it is right that on festivals we should rampage in the office premises and storerooms instead of on the upper floors.

Farewell to ghetto Catholicism

After getting through the six classes of elementary school without too great an effort – except in discipline and calligraphy – in Sursee I enter the first class of grammar school. This is preceded in the summer with a 'preliminary course' with the emphasis on Latin, ten hours a week. I find the teachers, now 'professors', considerably more interesting than my former teachers, especially our class teacher Dr Paul Cuoni, who allows us to write as we want provided that it is orderly and looks good. So initially I write sloping backwards, disposed as I am to oppose many things, but in an orderly and beautiful way, so that for the first time in calligraphy my mark is 6 = very good.

However, then the rector of our preparatory school (this covers the first four classes) confronts us with a new regulation that in future the 'preliminary course' will be dropped and therefore the bottom class, which in any case we do not rate very highly, will be combined with ours. General indignation: in fact that will put us back a year! Resistance is organized. There is an unprecedented conference of the rebels with the class teacher. Our proposal is that if any of us passes a test we should be allowed to go up into the next class. A reasonable proposal, but rejected by the rector. What now?

In the end I am the only one who decides to leave the school. My parents don't object, but suggest: 'You can go to a Catholic boarding school, like all children from Catholic families, a college run by Benedictines or Capuchins. Appenzell would be the best; your father also studied there.' But I'm firmly opposed to this: 'I certainly won't enter such "castes"!' Supported by my chaplain I finally get my way: I am allowed to go to the grammar school of the canton in Lucerne, where two of our Jungwacht leaders are already studying; in the Catholic milieu it has a reputation for being 'liberal' and freethinking.

So every day for six years, from 1942 to 1948, I travel by train, a journey of three-quarters of an hour, to the capital of our canton. In fact for me this means giving up the ghetto of Catholic education which was also built up in Switzerland in the nineteenth and first third of the twentieth century in a defensive reaction involving Catholic schools and colleges – to ward off the 'liberal' spirit of the time and to disseminate Catholic thought in state and society. After my decision to be ordained, this is my second serious decision, a farewell to intellectual, termino-logical, religious ghetto Catholicism and a move to an openly humanistic culture.

However, in the transition I make perhaps the only serious mistake in my grammar school education. On the advice of my older friends I skip the second class. Such a 'skip' is regarded as a sign of special gifts. But only when I have passed the entrance examinations, after about three weeks, may I move into the third class. So I am now backward in practically all subjects and have got left behind particularly in algebra and Greek, two new and initially very difficult subjects. It isn't easy to catch up all this mostly by teaching myself (only in French do I have private lessons) and to ask a fellow-student only every now and then. And it takes a long time for me to work my way back from the bottom of the class to the top. The positive element isn't so much the year that I have gained as the many friends, boys and soon also girls, whom I have made in this particular year.

Whereas during the war years my contemporaries in Germany get only a fragmentary classical grammar-school education, I will be confronted with the whole gamut of the humanistic ideal of education – by outstanding teachers of the classical languages like Josef Vital Kopp, who even writes and publishes novels under the titles 'Socrates Dreams' and 'The Fair Damaris': he particularly enthuses us about the ideal of the Greek *kalokagathia*, the 'good and the beautiful', the humane, the truly humane. This is humanity through the development of both physical and intellectual forces. There is no question that in this grammar school I am stimulated to strive for as universal an education as possible, which is not to be dismissed as an old-fashioned classical education. If only we had more of it!

The best two years at grammar school are the last two, called 'lyceum'. There are new teachers, and there are girls. The fact that we are now joined by girls from the girls grammar school, which had previously been separate, has a very positive influence on the atmosphere. We live in times where crushes are normal, girl friends are permitted, but sex is unusual. Relations between the sexes are uninhibited. We have a good time, and I think back with pleasure to all the school trips, some lasting several days, which are so full of experiences. Of course there is mutual respect, trust, honesty, loyalty. Friendships for life come out of this, and at least once a year our 'club' (André Zund, Dora Meyer, Madeleine von Wolff, René Buri and Trudy Blume) will meet – usually by our lake, with trips together to the Valais, Alsace or to Greece.

Apart from physics and chemistry, our teachers are masters of their subject, usually dispensing with textbooks and inviting us to take notes. We are well prepared for university. We are enthused by the introduction to the history of German literature by Heinrich Bühlmann, who originally gained a doctorate in law, and is now a mixture of Goethe and Jeremias Gotthelf: at any time we can enjoy the way in which without any notes he can describe the various eras and tendencies and the representative figures of prose, drama and poetry.

No less exciting is Adolf Hüppi's teaching in history and the history of art. He gives us some idea of the drama of historical developments and makes us see the wider connections. By means of slides which we have to sketch, he introduces us to the history of art, first to modern art, Egyptian and Greek art; he thinks that we can easily pick up the art of the Middle Ages and the Renaissance for ourselves. That is where my preference for classical modernity comes from, and in later days I shall even dare to guide my fellow students in Rome through an exhibition by Henri Matisse in the Palazzo Barberini. Our preoccupation with contemporary sacred art is also intensive, especially church architecture, which in Switzerland is experiencing a unique heyday after the war. The stimulating, but also rather remote, teaching of philosophy by Joseph Rüttimann – my first dealings above all with Greek philosophy, but also 'Tao te ching' – is a good preparation for my later study of philosophy. My only bad memories are of the teaching of French by the capricious tyrant 'Joly', which has nothing to do with practical conversation. He is particularly unfriendly towards one of our two Jewish fellow-pupils, who are universally popular. When this 'Joly' later asks me as a rising professor to organize lectures on Paul Claudel for him in Germany, I remain friendly but do nothing.

In a break, my history teacher Hüppi once asks me what I want to study. With my fellow pupils I always smile meaningfully and give the symbolic and ambiguous answer 'civil engineering'. I give him a straight answer: 'Theology'. 'Good, good,' he remarks, 'but remain open, remain open.' 'Certainly,' I reply, and ask myself what I am to remain open to.

Switzerland and Europe

Summer 1947: I go for the first time to Germany, before the currency reform. Because of the world war that it has sparked off and lost, the whole country is at the absolute nadir. But I want to get to know it. I report with around a dozen Lucerne grammar-school children to take part in a holiday camp for German young people from the Ruhr basin in the Weser hills near Warburg. There we are to make a contribution to the 'democratization' of German youth.

The strongest impression made on me by the whole journey in Germany, which is largely destroyed – only the beautiful towns in the Rhine gorge were intact – is the city of Cologne. Our train goes in a great circle round the city to the station: apart from the cathedral, which amazingly has been preserved intact and now seems even bigger, there is virtually nothing but destroyed houses! 'Where do the people live here?' we ask ourselves in dismay before we are driven eastwards from Cologne station on an English military transport.

So I live there in tents for two or three weeks like everyone else. Like everyone else I'm hungry, with the one difference that I've taken enough Nescafé and saccharine to have with cold coffee, mixed in Ovaltine mugs, which drives away the hunger that remarkable dishes like pink semolina and a few potatoes can only take the edge off. Once when two of us have an excursion to the little town of Warburg, we can't get anything at all to eat in a restaurant although we have money. But coming as I do from the youth movement, I'm very pleased to play with the German young people, to discuss openly in the evening, now without any Nazi ideology, to sing with accompaniment, and once even go to a violin concert by an artist in the nearby monastery of Hardehausen. No one shows any longing for Hitler and his regime, and there seems to be little need for efforts at democratization. We can eat our fill again only at Frankfurt station on the way back, where as Swiss we have the right to drink orange juice and eat doughnuts with the Americans, until we are almost sick.

Yes, what will become of Germany, what will become of Europe? We can't ignore this question even on our Swiss 'Isle of the Blessed'. The first speech arguing for a united Europe has been given a year before at Zurich University, on 19 September 1946, by Winston Churchill. Why shouldn't our land, spared the war, the home of the League of Nations and the Red Cross, be the first country to take up this idea? But like England, which (including Churchill) believes above all in the commonwealth of English-speaking peoples, so too our Switzerland, which now arrogantly believes primarily in itself, chooses 'splendid isolation'. Above all in German-speaking Switzerland, particularly among those who don't know any Germans, for a long time there continues to be virulent resentment against 'the Germans', though we did not have to suffer any German occupation, like the Dutch and the Belgians.

So people fail to notice that what was in principle right for our country during the war has now in fact become wrong – why? In my speech at the ceremony celebrating the 700th anniversary of the Confederacy in 1991, likewise in Zurich, just next to the university at the Federal Institute of Technology, one day I will spell it out clearly: because the whole situation of the world and Europe has changed – and this also has consequences for Switzerland. For – as far as the external situation is concerned – Switzerland is no longer the 'Alpine fortress' threatened by hostile military powers. Rather, it is a land which threateningly cuts itself off in the midst of what is in principle a peaceful Europe, co-operating more and more politically and constantly growing stronger economically. But – as far as the internal situation is concerned – soon Switzerland is no longer the much-envied 'model democracy', no longer the land without scandals. Rather, it is the average normal democracy with weaknesses and failures, whose image abroad in the post-war period gets worse rather than better, above all because of the concessions to Nazi Germany that I have mentioned, the rejection of many Jews, and the ambiguous activities of its banks and businesses during the war. Only after 1995, under the pressure of the criticism of Switzerland (and then of course also other countries) for its failure during and after the war – partly rightly and partly wrongly – will there be a general searching of consciences.

On 19 March 1948 I celebrate my twentieth birthday in Sursee. Only now am I a full citizen, with the right to take part in all elections and referenda at a communal, cantonal and national level. I remain convinced that more direct democracy (through referenda and popular initiatives), a judicial system with integrity (in which the guilty cannot buy their freedom 'legally'), a federalism with an applied principle of subsidiarity (not state supervision), and a high degree of independence for communities and cantons, could also serve as a model for the European Union which is taking shape, in which people are increasingly passed over. Switzerland isn't 'the land of unlimited possibilities', but it is certainly the land of 'limited impossibilities', as the Zurich professor of literature Adolf Muschg wittily put it. And that's already a good deal.

However, I will hardly be able to take part in the political life of my country in the next seven years, since from now on I shall almost always be abroad. But precisely because of this I will realize earlier than some others in the circle of my relations and acquaintances that Switzerland, too, is again caught up in a major political paradigm change, as in 1798 (the abolition of the *ancien régime*) and 1848 (the federal state), and that a good Swiss patriot should also be a good European. If there is to be 'neutrality' (exaggerated at the time of the Cold War), then it should no longer be passive and even parasitical, but active and show solidarity.

And now as I look through this chapter about my Swiss roots for the last time on 3 March 2002 I see with no little satisfaction that my fellow-countrymen are finally voting in a referendum (in direct democracy everything takes rather longer) about entry into the United Nations. Twelve cantons for, eleven against, and my own canton Lucerne tips the scales, with the extremely narrow majority of only 4563 votes. Will my appearances on television also perhaps have convinced some of those who are sceptical about the UN? At any rate previously I have received thanks from the Bundeshaus in Berne for my resolute plea for entry into the United Nations Organization.

Decision for Rome

We celebrate our Matura (leaving school) at the beginning of July 1948 on the Bürgenstock, in a fine big hotel, all night. In the grey dawn we march down to Stansstad, to catch the early boat to Lucerne where, as we expect, in the first-class

39

station buffet we can greet our German teacher Bühlmann, who goes there every morning.

But my fellow pupils, the boys and especially the girls, are utterly perplexed when I take this occasion to tell them quite openly what 'civil engineer' really means: a Catholic theologian – and in Rome at that! I had already made this decision, my third fateful decision, around three years earlier, curiously in the Lucerne opera house. I no longer remember whether it was at Nicolai's *Merry Wives of Windsor,* Donizetti's *Daughter of the Regiment,* Verdi's *Rigoletto* or Beethoven's *Fidelio.* Anyway, I'm sitting there with my friend Otto Wüst and chaplain Kaufmann in the middle of the dress circle. In the interval the chaplain draws our attention to Professor Schenker, who is sitting in the stalls on the left. He tells us that Schenker is a moral theologian in the faculty here and has studied in Rome: at the Pontificium Collegium Germanicum, seven years in the red cassock, all the lectures in Latin and at the end two doctorates, in philosophy and theology. 'That could also be something for you,' he suggests.

At home I read the article on the Collegium Germanicum in the big Herder encyclopedia to get some information and am impressed by its history and importance. Soon afterwards Otto Wüst and I go to Professor Alois Schenker and interrogate him thoroughly about life in this college and the lectures at the Pontificia Universitas Gregoriana. We are impressed by the knowledgeable yet relaxed way in which as an insider he talks to us about some things in Rome. At any rate he promises to recommend our acceptance if the question arises. At the time of the Council, as chief editor of the *Schweizerische Kirchenzeitung*, the arch-conservative Germanicum alumnus Schenker proves to be my sternest opponent in matters of church reform.

My decision for Rome is now firm. And I'm well aware that I've chosen the more difficult way. But after all, I have enjoyed a free life in Sursee and done respectably at grammar school. Can it do me any harm to submit to strict discipline for a few years, to expose myself to the famous and well-tried Jesuit education? If I study at the centre of Catholic Christianity, so to speak under the eyes of the pope, and gain a profound knowledge of classical Roman theology in Latin? If in this way I get doctorates in philosophy and theology and have an excellent preparation for my pastoral activity? I don't aspire to high church office, far less to a professorial chair. I want to be a youth chaplain, and later if possible a parish priest, and a doctorate seems to me to be appropriate for that.

So I don't hesitate very long. Like Otto Wüst, I write to the Rector of the Collegium Germanicum and give him my reasons for wanting to study there. He is somewhat amazed that two students are writing directly and not through the bishop. It had never occurred to us to ask the bishop. As free Swiss citizens we think that we can decide for ourselves where we want to study. Happily the answer from Rome is a positive one. Otto Wüst, a year before me, and then I, are accepted.

After leaving school I get to know another European country. I go by myself for some weeks to England, to London and Cornwall, to learn English, which I had postponed in favour of French, Latin and Greek. I make my first acquaintance with the fascinating metropolis of London and its famous sights, and also with two classic films of 1948 which I remember all my life: Sir Laurence Olivier's magnificently staged and acted *Hamlet*, and David Lean's film of Charles Dickens' *Oliver Twist*, the first social novel, whose attack on social abuses gave rise to social reforms. I also make the acquaintance of two Swiss girls with whom I get on very well and go on several expeditions with them. A good twenty years later I see one of them again after a lecture in Riverside Church in New York. I keep looking at her, but in no way associate the cosmetically made-up face that is now before me with her former naturally pretty face. The nice Swiss girl has become an elegant New York lady. And what has happened to me in the meanwhile? Have I changed as much?

I return from England to Switzerland and know that the time has come to say goodbye to my former world. Goodbye to my parents and family, goodbye to my friends, male and female, goodbye to my town, the lake, the mountains, my lovely little land. For seven long years. I say goodbye with happy eyes and deep melancholy in my heart. October 1948 – an autumnal mood. The satirical weekly *Der Nebelspalter* which I buy in Lucerne doesn't cheer me up. Two people whom I don't know, Eduard Ackermann and Josef Fischer, get into the compartment. They, especially the latter, are to become my two faithful contemporaries in all the years in Rome. A new part of life begins with this long railway journey to the 'eternal city'.

II
ଔଔଔଔ

Education for Freedom?

'There is no determinism,
man is free,
indeed man is freedom.'

Jean-Paul Sartre

A Babylonian exile in Rome freely chosen?

'ALL roads lead to Rome': that was true when all the great roads of the empire were still measured from the golden milestone zero in the Forum Romanum. Today it is true only for people like me, so to speak 'dyed-in-the-wool Catholics', who want to be educated at the centre of Catholic Christianity in order to find their way back into the world from there.

'They take these young men out of their world, put them in a red cassock for seven years, and then let them loose on people again . . .' remarks the Federal Chancellor Konrad Adenauer to Monsignor Bruno Wüstenberg of the Papal Secretariat of State, after a visit to the Collegium Germanicum. The diplomatic answer of the Vatican diplomat is: 'There are two sides to that, Chancellor.' And Adenauer – one needs to hear his Rhineland accent – retorts: 'No, now you're not acting very wisely, Monsignor.' Moreover Adenauer had to leave the 'first lady', his daughter Libet, in the reception room of the college, since on principle only persons of the male sex are welcome at lunch in the refectory.

So is it a Babylonian exile in Rome? I never feel that these seven years in Rome are like that. I live them to the full and use them as intensively as possible. At the age of 20 I arrive as a free citizen, and at the age of 27 I will leave again as the same free person, and yet as someone completely different. 'So now you want to do your doctorate in Paris?' Pius XII's social expert, Professor Gustav Gundlach, will remark in a very sceptical tone of voice, as I say goodbye. 'You don't seem to like that, Fr Gundlach,' I will reply, 'but over these seven years I've learned all there is to be learned in Rome and I've always got top marks.' Then comes Gundlach's happily unambiguous answer: 'In that case I'm not worried about you, you can confidently go to Paris.'

So in the early days of October 1948 – for me the most attractive month in Rome – our Swiss trio arrives in Rome, lit by an autumnal sun which is no longer hot, greeted by the reddish brown of the many tiled roofs and the buildings, old and new, so different from the grey of the north. From the super-modern Termini station, which is not yet finished, we go over the Piazza Esedra (with one of the most beautiful fountains in Rome) to the modern district of airlines and banks. In the middle of that is Via San Nicolò da Tolentino 13, my future residence, with big letters chiselled into the Travertine gateway: 'Collegium Germanicum et Hungaricum'.

Time and again I am overwhelmed by the view from the giant roof terrace on the ninth floor, the 'highest point' of the college, at the feet of the Eternal City, which *ab urbe condita*, since its legendary founding by Romulus and Remus, has preserved all its centuries in it. The great historical panorama hardly changes over the years. On the left is our neighbour, the Palazzo Barberini, the masterpiece of baroque palace architecture built by Bernini. More in the foreground is the Quirinal palace, the former summer residence of the popes, then the seat of the Italian king and now the seat of the state president; alongside it runs one possible 'way to school', to our Pontificia Universitas Gregoriana. Alongside the tower of the Capitol, colossal in its white nineteenth-century wedding-cake style, is the Italian Counter-Vatican, the national monument to Vittorio Emanuele II in the Piazza Venezia, the scene of Mussolini's mass demonstrations. And against the background of the Janiculum hill with the statue of Garibaldi, the hero of Italian freedom, are a whole series of domes. The Jesuit Al Gesù church is important for us. It is the first baroque church in the world, and there our college forms the liturgical guard of honour on the vigils of the high festivals. Sant' Ignazio, where many of us will be ordained, and San Andrea della Valle, where we sing at Christmas, are also important. In between is the flat dome of the Pantheon, the circular building dedicated to all the gods, formerly in the Field of Mars, and now in the midst of the countless alleyways and passages of the mediaeval capital, through which we usually take the second 'way to school' at the Gregorian, past the splendid Fontana di Trevi. And then, on the right of the Janiculum, St Peter's and the Vatican are enthroned in the background.

It is truly a glorious view, which I now have before me every day. On the other side of the terrace to the right there is a view over the great Pincio Park with the Villa Borghese, to which the wide Via Vittorio Veneto leads up, soon known to all the world through Fellini's film *La Dolce Vita*. And then on the extreme right and somewhat below us is the American embassy. In my first years in Rome, more than once it has to be protected against Communist demonstrators by substantial numbers of Roman police. These are uncertain times.

Democracy or Communism?

In the three years following the Second World War the world-political situation has completely changed: not only is the 'thousand-year empire' of Nazism in rubble and ashes, but Mussolini's fascist Imperium Romanum has likewise collapsed. But the anti-Hitler coalition between the Western powers and the Soviet Union has also fallen apart: there is the Cold War with the Berlin blockade and later the Korean War. The other European countries are also involved.

Since 1946, on the basis of a referendum (contrary to the unexpressed wish of Pius XII), Italy has been a republic. The biggest Communist party in Europe under Palmiro Togliatti is fighting against the Christian Democrat government of Alcide de Gasperi, an honest Democrat, who during the war worked as a librarian in the Vatican but was never received by the pope then, nor has been yet. In April 1948 there is a tremendous electoral battle, attested by the countless posters which are still up on our arrival in Rome in October. It is won by Democrazia Cristiana, but with only 48.5 per cent of the vote, so that they always depend on splinter parties to form a government. The average duration of Italian governments since 1945 has been ten months.

The situation remains fluid in view of the threat from Stalinist Communism. It is the time of the show trial of the Hungarian Cardinal Mindszenty, whose Roman titular church, Santo Stefano Rotondo, Rome's biggest circular church, on Monte Celio, is in the possession of the Collegium Germanicum et Hungaricum. Archbishop Stepinac of Zagreb, our fellow Germanicum alumnus, had been condemned to sixteen years of forced labour under Tito in 1946. He is freed in 1951, interned in his homeland, and prevented from exercising his office. In 1953 he is elevated to cardinal. However, no one in college wants to talk about his silence over the crimes of the Croat Ustashas in collaboration with Hitler's troops any more than they do about Pius XII's silence over the Croat massacres in Serbia and the Vatican sympathies for Hitler's Panzer divisions, which as God's strong arm would be thought to be fulfilling Fatima's prophecy of the conversion of Russia.

In Italy, Mario Scelba, the Minister of the Interior, has organized the police forces into 'nuclei celeri', police in fast, manoeuvrable jeeps, who also counter threatening Communist mass demonstrations. Normally we get to know about Italian politics only by reading the Roman *Messagero* every day and (after a delay) the *Frankfurter Allgemeine Zeitung* and the Lucerne *Vaterland*. Later, however, from my solitary place of study on the sixth floor one day I discover on the balcony immediately opposite none other than Mario Scelba, now Prime Minister, and then the unmistakably sharp profile of Alcide de Gasperi. No one will believe me. A fellow-student from Trent, Piergiorgio Piechele, son of a senator, bets. And loses. The President of the Consiglio dei Ministri thanks us on his visiting card, our evidence, for our Easter bouquet of flowers, which my friend Josef Fischer and I have handed over for the promoter of the new Europe to the two carabinieri who stopped us at the lift on the ground floor of the house.

Some time after that session of the Senate, out of curiosity the two of us also attend a big Communist electoral rally in the Piazza Dodici Apostoli, wearing our red cassocks. Rows and rows of heads turn in amazement at these two *'frati rossi'* slowly moving forward on the edge of the crowd: the Vice-General Secretary of the Partito Communista Italiano, Piettro Secchia, is standing against the *'governo-clerico-fascista'*, the 'clerical fascist government'. In so doing he is involuntarily confirming the strategy of Pope Pacelli, that there is only the alternative of Roman Catholicism or Communist atheism. More and more people are turning to the political left, whereas the Vatican is increasingly identifying its interests with those of the conservative right.

Only fear of having our photograph on the front page of the Communist *Unità* makes us start back, unhindered, after spending a long time listening. Not very long beforehand, in fact, a professor from the Gregorian, Fr Tondi, has gone over to the Communist party, and still continues to be a member of the Society of Jesus. It is a tremendous scandal which occupies the Roman papers for days. I firmly decide that I will make a thorough study of the Communist ideology.

Putting off the old man – putting on the new

Our rooms in the Germanicum are simple, but big enough and with running water. They contain an iron bedstead and bright wooden furniture: desk, wardrobe, bookshelves and prayer desk, and later also a little typewriter table. There is no bedside rug on the linoleum of my first room on the fifth floor, occupied by the 'first-years'. I can do without, I think, ready to put up with any shortcomings in my new situation.

In the next two or three days there now follows what, in keeping with a saying of Paul, one can call the putting off of the old man and the putting on of the new. To begin with this can be understood quite externally, but very much with an inner meaning. We take off our civilian clothes – we shall see them again only some years later for our return home. We also hand over our underwear – in future fresh underwear will be brought to our rooms on Saturdays. We leave our money with the Fr Minister – except for pocket money, which we can replenish every now and then, for bus journeys and the like. We are measured and fitted for the red cassock, which has already been prepared, with its black zingulum (girdle), hat and biretta. In addition, for the house we have an attractive red 'domestica', and for going out an armless Roman cloak, called 'scholastica', which is also red, all reaching modestly down to the ground.

It was the cardinal protectors who had decided for red, their colour, at the founding of the college; this was sensational even for the colourful Roman world of the sixteenth century, and sometimes provoked exclamations and mockery from Romans. When the first German students asked for something to be done about this, they were given a good Roman answer by the cardinals, *'Pazienza!'* People in Rome quickly got used to the red of the Germanicum students, who are now more tenderly called *'gamberi cotti'*, 'boiled prawns', or *'cardinaletti'*, 'little cardinals', and are featured on some coloured pictures and postcards.

45

I think that as long as the other clergy go through the street in their sad black cassocks ('I keep thinking of Nietzsche's wicked saying, 'they have beaten their corpses black') it is right for us to show ourselves in our cheerful, happy red. 'You are the last to wear the red cassock,' we are told by Pater Graf Franz von Tattenbach, later the Rector of the college, 'so do so with dignity.' The days not only of the nobility but also of the clerical estate seem to him to be numbered. An amazing prospect.

The Roman cadre school

The most important Catholic Reformation historian, Professor Joseph Lortz of the Germanicum, with whom I have close contact in 1952 in connection with the 400th anniversary of the Germanicum, has shown in his epoch-making work *Die Reformation in Deutschland* (two vols, 1948) how at the height of the Lutheran Reformation the end of the Catholic Church under Roman domination seemed only a matter of time. It is true that when Luther died in 1546 the one Catholic Church of the West no longer existed, but the Roman system had failed to collapse. There was a change in Rome under Paul III (1534–49). Three factors led to reform within Catholicism: the nomination of important reform cardinals (1535), permission for the novel 'Society of Jesus' (1540), and the opening of the reform Council of Trent (1545).

One of the leaders of the Roman reform party, Cardinal Giovanni Morone, had the idea of a Collegium Germanicum as early as Luther's time. As papal legate at the Reichstags of Speyer and Augsburg Morone is only too well aware of the complete ruination of the Catholic Church in Germany: the failure of theology, the decadence of the clergy, and the lack of new vocations. He convinces the only man who can help here, the Basque knight and former officer Iñigo or Ignatius of Loyola, founder of the strictly organized and élite order of the Jesuits. The reform of Catholicism in Germany seems to him, too, to be an urgent task. Morone's idea is that this shall take place through a cadre educated in Rome: through secular clergy (not Jesuits!), who are to prove themselves in their home dioceses as pastors, priests, professors or bishops, with a high spiritual motivation and the best possible academic training.

Pope Julius III establishes the Collegium Germanicum as a papal foundation in 1552. In 1580 the Collegium Hungaricum, which was founded twelve years previously, is integrated into the Collegium Germanicum for financial reasons. Since then it has been called the Pontificium Collegium Germanicum et Hungaricum and is in fact open to students from all over the Roman Empire of the German Nation under the Habsburg crown, from the Netherlands to the Balkans, from Scandinavia to the South Tyrol.

This college is no 'prison of nations', a title sometimes given to the Habsburg empire. But there is no doubt that the spirituality and discipline of our college, like that of the Jesuit order, are stamped by the unconditional character, the radicalism and the orientation on praxis of its founder Ignatius of Loyola. As is well known, he dispensed with the choral prayer of the traditional orders in favour of active commitment, and also got the popes to agree to this. If historically the spirituality of the Benedictines with their concern for liturgy and culture ('pray and work') is the basis for the cultivation of northern Europe in the sixth century, and the spirituality of the Dominicans is the foundation for the crusades, cathedrals and theological Summas in the twelfth century, the spirituality of the Jesuits is the foundation for humanism and the missionary conquest of the world in the sixteenth century.

The way in which the Collegium Germanicum is ordered became significant for church politics since it serves as the basis for the 1563 decree on studies by the reform Council of Trent, whose president at the time is the self-same Cardinal Morone. This decree makes it obligatory to establish such seminaries in all the dioceses of the Catholic Church. Thus in contrast to the Protestant Christianity of Northern and Western Europe (and later of North America), such seminaries give rise not least to a Mediterranean Catholicism with an Italian-Spanish stamp, which also makes its way into Central and South America.

1928 – 1948 – 1968

We newcomers, too, are involved on 10 and 11 October 1948, the days of ordination to the priesthood and first masses. Because of the war there are only eight deacons, whose ordination to the priesthood we attend in Al Gesù, the Jesuit church. Every new priest can celebrate his first mass the next day in a church of his choice, and this is usually attended by relatives from home and friends from nearby. The mass is celebrated for us in the college church by the Hungarian Ludwig Kada, later a papal diplomat and nuncio, with whom I have ties of friendship over all the years since his first mass, despite the very different ways that we have taken.

Also because of the war, to begin with we are only seven 'new-reds', *neo-rubri*, who now appear for the first time in our cassocks, completely transformed, and are accepted into the community. Of course this is in the expectation that we will also fit in with the new form of life inwardly. Soon there will be eighteen of us, a complete year again for the first time; after six years, sixteen will be ordained priest.

We were almost all born in 1928, and are the same age as the anti-aircraft auxiliaries in Germany, the first year not to be decimated in the war. What good fortune to be able to enter professional life at the precise age of twenty, immediately after the currency reform which took place in June 1948 and which ushered in the German economic miracle; many important leading businessmen are of the same age. In the new Federal Republic of Germany a period is beginning in which the new generation sees the meaning of life above all in tireless work: there is a tremendous commitment first to rebuilding and safe-guarding life and then to a rising standard of living. This is a society of work and achievement, which unfortunately largely suppresses the problems of guilt and atonement in relation to the unprecedented German crimes against humanity and then has to justify itself to the demands of the generation of 1968.

Between the solemn service and the ceremonial lunch which follows we newcomers are solemnly greeted and embraced in the Gregorius Saal of the college. This also marks our complete incorporation into the order of the college. The lunch is a real *pranzone*. In the Germanicum every day we eat in fine Italian style: after soup comes pasta (or rice) and then a meat course, with dessert or fruit. At ceremonial meals there is also an antipasto or a second meat course with a big dessert and *vino secondo*, sweet Italian wine.

We drink wine every day, one carafe per four students at lunch and dinner, which is always enough. It's a simple country wine from the college estates. I take time to get a taste for it, being accustomed to Swiss white wines and French red wines. In the long hot summer wine has always been drunk Roman-style with water, as is still also prescribed for the Catholic celebration of the mass (for deep mystical reasons).

A life of regulations

In an extremely personal way Ignatius had composed a constitution which was both brief and precise: it was meant to be a harmonious combination of piety and study, aimed at shaping priests trained both spiritually and academically by a regulated day. However, as happens with laws, this brief college rule, completely orientated on isolation from the world, has been made more and more precise, and is now more than 40 pages long. Two basic rules above all are inculcated:

Studium per totum diem: study for the whole day. So it is not the times of study but the times of recreation that are prescribed: around half an hour after lunch and dinner, below in the courtyard, in the Gregorius Saal, or, especially in the eve-ning, on the ninth-floor terrace. This takes places in spontaneously formed groups of between three and five students, in which one or two walk backwards, to make it possible to maintain a face-to-face conversation. It is perhaps 70 metres to the end of the terrace, where those who have been walking forwards now walk backwards. One quickly gets used to this strange form of alternating promenade.

Silentium religiosum: strict silence after evening recreation at 9 p.m. until after breakfast at 8 a.m. This isn't burdensome for me, since it provides the necessary quiet for religious exercises (with pious exaggeration, the prefect of our philoso-phy group, Josef Stimpfle, later Bishop of Augsburg, calls this being 'alone with the most holy Trinity'). And there is reading during lunch and dinner – except on Sundays and festivals and on visits of bishops and old members of the college.

The reading is given from the lectern in the refectory; any shortcomings are immediately corrected loudly by the reading prefect up in the refectory (*'altius'*, 'louder!', or *'repetas, domine'*, 'repeat it'). There is a different student each week, reciting *in tono recto*, with a monotonous singing tone on the same note. The main readings in the evening are from Ludwig Freiherr von Pastor's *History of the Popes*; they've now got to the Barberini pope Urban VIII, where problems over some royal wedding or the trial of Galileo can be spun out over several dinners. Alessandro Manzoni's classic Italian novel *I promessi sposi* is also read aloud in the same monotone. In later years attempts are made to provide rather more exciting reading: C. W. Ceram's *Gods, Graves and Scholars*, or the army doctor Peter Bamm's *The Invisible Flag*, Thor Heyerdahl's *Kon-Tiki*, or *I Believed* by the ex-Communist Douglas Hyde. Or there are vividly written biographies of the pastor Augustine, the great mystic Teresa of Avila or the brave Munich Jesuit Rupert Mayer. The Latin account of the pilgrimage of Etheria from Constantinople to the Holy Land around 400 is rather boring (it is read during Lent).

Of course the devotional exercises are central. Usually announced with the loud ringing of a bell in all the corridors, they structure our whole day. The wake-up call for each individual, *'Deo gratias et Mariae'*, resounds as early as 5.30 a.m. − a normal time for me. At 6 there is brief, silent morning prayer in the chapel. After that everyone spends half an hour meditating in his room. Then there is a joint eucharist, usually a German pray-and-sing mass or the Latin choral mass. At noon before lunch there is the angelus prayer in the chapel and also a short *adoratio* afterwards. Finally there are devotions before dinner, often with the Litany of All Saints (no one can pray this aloud as fast as the Hungarians), and afterwards there is again *adoratio* in the chapel. The *silentium religiosum* begins at 9, after the recreation and notices from the prefect. Half an hour for self-examination, spiritual reading and preparation of morning meditation. Finally there is silent night prayer in the chapel and then complete rest for the night. And by now one needs it. But − what room is there for interpersonal relations?

No particular friendships

To begin with, quite specific rules of behaviour are strange to us. The formal second-person plural rule above all: 'You (*Sie*), Mr Fischer, can you please . . .' However, it was known and tacitly tolerated that when Swiss are talking together in their language, which is in any case incomprehensible, they use the forbidden second person singular, *Du*, with first names. Then there is the *regula liminis*, the 'threshold rule': no conversations in the room, even with the door closed, but on the threshold, softly and with due brevity. And finally the *regula tactus,* the prohibition against touching: one never proffers a hand, and exchanges the liturgical peace (*amplex*) only on specific festal occasions.

Obviously fear of homosexual relations underlies these rules, but during my seven years in the same house I can observe virtually none of these. We are in fact warned emphatically against 'particular friendships'. Of course there are always some fellow-students whom one finds more congenial than others and with whom one gets on particularly well. There were deep friendships, but these did not necessarily have an erotic, or even a sexual character. In gratitude for years of friendship I would mention here – alongside my contemporaries and fellow countrymen – Peter Lengsfeld, Otto Riedel, Wolfgang Seibel and Donato Vanzetta.

In any case the fears of homosexuality seem to me to be much exaggerated, as especially do further precautionary measures against 'particular friendships' and 'attachment to things' generally: every year a different room and the removal of all books and possessions. Every month there has to be a different group of four for the walk to the university, although when it is busy, two at most can walk together straight across the Piazza Barberini. Every month there is also a different order of seating in the refectory, pinned to the blackboard. I am annoyed when once again, probably on purpose, I am put with a less congenial contemporary; then I often prefer the reading at table to the laborious conversation. But all these commands and prohibitions have not prevented very stable friendships arising for life in these seven years (and probably were not intended to), so that even those who go extremely different ways within the church time and again still feel close ties with one another. After their college days, old alumni of the Germanicum address one another with the familiar second-person-singular *Du* and first name, whether they are cardinals or chaplains.

The 'defensive measures' against the female sex are even more thorough, indeed comprehensive. Women are not tolerated either at the Germanicum or at the university. We are marked out and at the same time segregated by our red cassocks. 'Impossible,' exclaims Rector Vorspel to me when I enter his room at his summons. I had been speaking at the college gate, immediately under the rector's room, with two smartly dressed girls. 'Im-poss-ible,' he exclaims even louder when I tell him I had been saying goodbye to my dear sisters Marlis and Rita, who in any case had only been allowed as far as the gloomy visitors' room. In fact any contact with women, apart from visits from relatives and friends from the north, is impossible.

I cannot recall ever having ventured into one of the numerous Roman espresso bars, far less restaurants, in the very first years. We are well looked after: in the late morning and the middle of the afternoon there is always coffee for a *'merenda'* in front of our refectory. But there are no relationships with Italian families. So in all the seven years, while I learn Italian, I do not get to know a single Italian woman or a single Italian family. '*La forza del destino* – the power of fate?' Only at our summer villa San Pastore is there the family of the caretaker Angelino and his wife Bice, whom we always greet in a friendly way. With the best will in the world I can't be as enthusiastic about their daughter as a fellow-student from the diocese of Trent, who then later marries – a German woman. No *'matrimonio segreto'*.

Those who can't endure this isolation in a clerical milieu have no alternative but to leave. Only two of our year do so. The rest of us had our reasons for keeping to our original decision for the priesthood, though even in papal Rome each had to seek his own way. Not least in our relationship with the pope.

'Our' pope: Pius XII

The new apostolic visitor for Germany, Alois Muench, Bishop of Fargo, USA, tells us in his after-dinner talk on the day of the ordination of priests in 1948 that dark shadows lie over the world. However, he goes on, never has the rock of Peter stood so unshaken as it does today. This is shown by the great devotion and recognition which the Holy Father receives on all sides. We listen with excitement to the pope's congratulatory telegram for our new priests, signed on his behalf by Giovanni Battista Montini, the most important man in the Secretariat of State.

For our spiritual training, submission to the pope is of capital importance. I have been in Rome only a few days when we go with the new priests and their families to the papal summer residence of Castel Gandolfo, to be received personally there by Pius XII, on 13 October 1948. There is no doubt that it is a great experience. Even Protestants and Social Democrats are enthusiastic about this pope. A tall slim figure, a spiritual face, eloquent hands. With his perfect gestures, his knowledge of languages and his rhetoric, Pius XII appears generally as *the* model pope.

Moreover, for those of us who speak German he is 'the pope of the Germans': markedly a Germanophile before, during and after the Nazi period. Since his time in Germany he has been looked after by a capable German nun of around the same age, his extremely influential confidante 'Madre' Pasqualina Lehnert, and surrounded by German co-workers or staff, mostly Jesuits, who are our professors at the Gregorian. At this time as yet no public criticism is expressed of Pacelli's highly diplomatic 'Jewish policy', nor has his dictatorial 'domestic policy' become notorious. He appears as the *'Pastor angelicus'* – as the saying about him, the 106th pope, has it in the 'prophecy' of the Irish bishop Malachi. There are to be 111 popes in all before the end of the world; soon we will wonder at the 111 medallions with the portraits of the popes (at that time five of them still empty), along with the sayings about them, in the basilica of San Paolo Fuori le Mura. However, by then we have come to know that this 'prophecy' is a forgery from 1590. Nevertheless, many people believe it.

What is also important for us is that Eugenio Pacelli is unmistakably a supporter of our college. Hardly had the former nuncio in Munich and Berlin, who was able to conclude the concordats with Bavaria and Prussia, been nominated Cardinal Secretary of State by Pius XI when he paid an official visit to the Collegium Germanicum. That was on 12 January 1933. It is not known in the college that at this time the same Pacelli urges his friend the chairman of the

Catholic Centre Party, Prelate Ludwig Kaas, an old alumnus of the Germanicum, to enter into a coalition with Hitler. On 30 January 1933 Hitler is nominated Chancellor, and he concludes the 'Reich concordat' with Pacelli as early as 20 July of the same year. This is an inestimable gain in prestige for the German dictator.

What Pacelli states at that time in the Germanicum as Cardinal Secretary of State is illuminating. He says that the experiences of his mission beyond the Alps have shown him 'the providential significance' of the college in a convincing and tangible form. Study in Rome has three advantages: 'Rome makes one open to the world! Without letting one's sense of homeland wither, the Eternal City gives an understanding of fellow men of other countries and zones, respect for their character, union with them through the miraculous bond of unity of the same love of Christ, and thus also that brotherly disposition from which the true reconciliation of the nations and longed-for peace sprang. Rome gives a love of the church and Christ's representative! It is not as if the rest of the clergy of the homeland lacked this love. But personal experience supports the firmness of love even more strongly and gives it the precious overtone of personal familiarity. Rome, education in this house, is an extremely valuable seedbed for your later priestly activity. I believe that we can best describe the spirit of your home with two terms: self-discipline and the supernatural.' Pacelli concludes: 'If priesthood is grace, then the way to the priesthood at the tomb of the man of the rock under the pope's hand raised in blessing is twofold grace and twofold responsibility.' That, in a nutshell, was the whole Catholic ideology of Rome. And the Germanicum students applauded enthusiastically.

However, Josef Stimpfle, who later becomes Bishop of Augsburg, tells me that when on 2 March 1939 white smoke rises from the Sistine Chapel on the Piazza San Pietro, those at the Germanicum by no means expected that the same Pacelli could be elected pope. The Cardinal Secretaries of State have always been regarded as politically too exposed and therefore unsuitable for the papacy. But when the 'Habemus Papam' involves the name 'Eugenium Pacelli', the students of the Germanicum rejoice more than all the rest. As early as 1939 they know what we know even more in 1948: in development, orientation and sympathy this pope is in a quite special way 'our pope'. Self-discipline and the supernatural! Pacelli's closing words will occupy us later.

And in fact never were so many old alumni of the Germanicum nominated bishop as under Pius XII: from Luxembourg to Brixen, including Speyer, Freiburg, Eichstätt, Munich, Limburg, Würzburg. The new Bishop of Würzburg, Julius Döpfner, with whom I later have something of a battle when he is Cardinal of Munich and President of the German Episcopal Conference, visits us in our first year in college as Germany's youngest bishop. It is a unique event in the history of the college; there are still five alumni here who wore the red cassock with him and were there in St Peter's Square in 1939. But whereas Döpfner advanced from chaplain to vice-regent of the priests' seminary and finally bishop, the others, including the Josef Stimpfle I have already mentioned, first had to complete their studies here because they were called up for military service.

Back to Castel Gandolfo, 13 October 1948: so I see Pius XII for the first time 'in the flesh', as he wishes our new priests much success in their apostolate and us *neo-rubri* courage and perseverance in our studies. Isn't it elevating to meet the Summus Pontifex at such close quarters and to feel his sympathy? Given the apostolic blessing, we return in a cheerful mood to Rome, where life now begins in earnest after all the celebrations. Only two days later, on 15 October, we go for the first time to our university, the Pontificia Universitas Gregoriana, where the new academic year is solemnly inaugurated by the Rector. In the year 2001 it will celebrate its 450th anniversary and count twenty-one saints, ten popes and more than a third of the present cardinals among its former students.

Philosophical substructure first

I have three years of studying philosophy at this university before me, followed by four years study of theology – both no longer concluded, as before the reform of studies at the Gregorian, with a doctorate, but with two licentiates, which can then possibly be followed by a doctorate. This clear separation between philosophy and theology corresponds to the distinction between the two capacities for knowledge (natural reason – supernatural faith) and two levels of knowledge (the natural truth of reason – the supernatural truth of revelation) carried through by Thomas Aquinas. So there are two storeys all the way through, philosophy and theology, clearly distinct but in no way contradictory; rather, the lower one, philosophy, is clearly orientated on the upper, higher one. Philosophy is *ancilla theologiae*, 'handmaid of theology'.

Ignatius himself based the Society of Jesus, his Collegium Romanum (later the Pontificia Universitas Gregoriana) and our college (founded a year afterwards) on the teaching of that Thomas Aquinas who during his lifetime in the thirteenth century in Paris was notorious as an innovator, was condemned, and only became established in the church in Spain and France in the fifteenth/sixteenth centuries. But our neo-Thomist professors constantly work within a logical–rational structure of proof to a much greater degree than Thomas himself did. That means that everything possible is moulded into syllogisms: the conclusion is derived from two proven or evident premises in accordance with quite definite rules. Indeed the syllogism forms the core even in Aristotle's logic or theory of thought. And it is precisely in this formal logic of Aristotle that we shall now first be trained, in order to think 'correctly' and to be able to unmask false conclusions and any illogicalities. It is certainly an extremely dry discipline, all presented in Latin, and difficult to impress on the memory. But we are told that precisely such training will in future give us the quick-witted clarity to come out victorious in all debates. Will it really?

I love philosophy. To begin with I find work at the university utterly liberating; at last I am no longer required simply to be a 'listener' every day. Because I have been taught Latin and philosophy at grammar school I am better prepared for these lectures than most of my German fellow-students, who enter these weeks utterly unprovided-for by their education in Germany. So I also need be less anxious about our first public examination, the notorious '*actus publicus*', which takes place as early as the beginning of December.

We first-years now all sit there nicely – chairs on the splendid coloured carpet – in the Gregorius Saal, looking at the assembled community. One after another we have to come up and to engage with the professor of logic, Francesco Morandini, and the professor of psychology, Georges Delannoye, speaking and answering in Latin, of course to the satisfaction of all those who already have this pain behind them. They all scrutinize us curiously and with a touch of *Schadenfreude* as we struggle with definitions, conclusions and false conclusions. But in each case, after around seven minutes the Rector ends the torture with an '*optime*', '*bene*' or '*satis*'. Thus at any rate right from the beginning we see ourselves urged on to an intensive sport of thinking and learning.

Logic is in fact only a preparation for metaphysics or the theory of being generally, to which we are introduced by the Rector of the Gregorian, Fr Paolo Dezza, in perfect Latin and with great clarity; later he is to be my colleague as a *peritus* at the Second Vatican Council. In the course of the three years there now follow at the 'natural' level epistemology, psychology, cosmology and ethics, which are less satisfying, and finally the strictly rational doctrine of God from the Frenchman René Arnou, whom I value no less highly.

Certainly the Roman Thomism that we meet there doesn't simply set out to expound the Summas of Thomas Aquinas. It doesn't regard them as a timeless oracle for all the questions of philosophy or theology. Nor are we brought up in a hatred of everything modern, as was customary at the climax of the antimodernism campaign, as Yves Congar will later tell me happened in his case. On the contrary, we are invited – above all in the history of philosophy taught by the great expert Alois Naber and in special courses on contemporary questions by Arnou – to grapple with modern and contemporary thought. Thus with Naber I take a special course on Hegelian philosophy and later also write for this man who understands all the modern tendencies my philosophical licentiate thesis on the existentialist humanism of Jean-Paul Sartre. But only part of our training takes place at the Gregorian; the part which is in some respects more important takes place in the Collegium Germanicum.

Who says here when time is up?

The lectures take place in the morning, the seminars in the afternoon, and in college we have the unpopular repetitions, in which what has been learned is chewed through once again in German in accordance with the Latin theses. At precisely this point it becomes clear to us that this scholastic philosophizing, disputing and distinguishing can easily degenerate into playing with concepts in a way that is remote from reality. Our repetitor in philosophy is a knowledgeable, intelligent and industrious Jesuit scholastic only a little older than we are, Brother Peter Gumpel. He has no sense of humour and easily gets bogged down. He is the cause of my first conflict, because regularly he overzealously goes beyond the time in repetitions, to the dissatisfaction of all. Now right at the beginning I was nominated *bidellus scholae*, the school beadle, the only office to be bestowed in the first year. In later years everyone is given an office, in keeping with the self-administration of the college, starting from the prefects and beadles of the philosophy and theology groups.

One of the modest tasks of the school beadle, right at the bottom of the college hierarchy, is to give a sign when time is up. I do this with a friendly gesture of the hand, but the Frater Repetitor tends to overlook this. I repeat the sign again. Visibly annoyed, Brother Gumpel finally remarks, 'Here I'm the one who says when time is up.' Whereupon I retort, 'No, Frater Repetitor, here *I* say when time is up.' He can hardly believe his ears and explodes. All my contemporaries, most of whom have been brought up in blind obedience, are utterly horrified at my blunt speaking. 'If you go on like that, Herr Küng,' Josef Kötter from Münster goes on to tell me, 'I guarantee that you'll leave this college before the year is out and your feet won't touch the ground.'

We shall see. I have no intention of giving in, but turn to my 'superior', the tutor of our first year, Otto Wüst, and we then both go to the ever-understanding senior tutor, Hermann-Josef Weisbender (later canon and apostolic protonotary in Dresden). I complain about Gumpel and claim that I had only been doing my duty. The senior tutor agrees and presents the case to the Rector, Fr Brust. His decision is that Herr Küng has acted rightly. So students, too, may speak openly in this college. However, there is to be another much more serious conflict with Brother Gumpel, who after a year will be replaced by Fr Emmerich Coreth from Vienna and then the German Fr Walter Kern (both universally popular, skilful and capable of discussion), but will return in later years in the post of theology repetitor.

Three years of philosophy: I will not have to work as hard for any other examination in all my years of study as I do for the licentiate in philosophy in summer 1951. A whole 100 theses have to be prepared, on epistemology, metaphysics, cosmology, psychology, natural theology and ethics. Most of them run to between one and several dozen pages. And to put all this into Latin! Truly it isn't a simple matter: in each thesis first comes the question (*status quaestionis*), then the definition of the terms used, then the opponents of the thesis, in the main part the arguments for, and finally the answers to objections. In the examination at the Gregorian there is no skating round the matter, as tends to happen when the vernacular is used in German universities. Either one knows it or one doesn't. '*Nescio*,' quite a few mutter, 'I don't know.'

However, in these years of philosophy I learn one thing thoroughly for life, something that I never want to be without: intellectual self-discipline. I've always loved ordered thinking. But now I learn terminological precision, transparent structure, coherent argument, the art of distinction, in short a Latin clarity of thought. And much more.

An early 'third way'

Alongside philosophy there is also much that is informative and attractive for us philosophers in the Germanicum. For example, there are the lectures by the Rector of the Pontifical Biblical Institute, who is also the pope's confessor, Augustinus Bea. Bea was able to convince the pope of the need for a progressive encyclical on the Bible (*Divino afflante spiritu*, 1941) – welcomed by the Catholic exegetes as a real liberation – and a new translation of the psalms; he is also available to us as a confessor and gently introduces us to the Old Testament prophets. There is also the fiery New Testament scholar Karl Prümm, author of *Das Christentum als Neuheitserlebnis* (Christianity as an Experience of Newness), who time and again interprets the letters of the apostle Paul to us in a lively way. In addition there are quite different lectures by visitors from all over the world.

At an early stage I get used to studying the Gregorian textbooks as soon as possible at the beginning of the new academic year and underlining them intensively, to see what is important in them. This leaves me more time for broadening my general education. In the splendid Villa Maraini, donated by the Swiss Confederacy as a cultural institute, which is close by, there is a modern library in which I enthusiastically occupy myself with modern art, but also with the psychology of C. G. Jung and much else.

Early on, social philosophy becomes a new focal point for me, combined with the social teaching of the church, which we discuss in the sociological circle or 'Social Circle' (founded as early as 1904) – under the moderation of the social scientist Gustav Gundlach, who impresses us with his knowledge, perspicacity, wit and aggressiveness. He is a pupil of the great national economist Werner Sombart and the pope's social expert. He is the one who makes me aware for the first time that there is a 'third way' between individualism and collectivism, capitalism and socialism, which regulates 'solidarism' through the principle of personality, solidarity and subsidiarity.

This is a conception which was given an academic foundation decades before any 'communitarianism' (and before Tony Blair, who will come to Tübingen for the first time in the year 2000 for the first Global Ethic Lecture), by Heinrich Pesch SJ, Oswald von Nell-Breuning SJ and Gustav Gundlach SJ. It will become important for the social market economy of Ludwig Erhard and finally also for my later works on the problems of a global ethic and the global economy. On the basis of thoroughly worked-out reports there is a presentation and serious critique of a variety of topics: in 1949/50 the idea of the state over changing times, from Aristotle and Thomas to Frantz and Jellinek; in 1951/52 the various socialisms of Proudhon, Bernstein, Lassalle and Natorp; in 1952/53 the 'professional order'; and in 1953/54 democracy.

For the series in the second year I write a time-consuming paper on the revolutionary syndicalism of the French social philosopher Georges Sorel; for the third year a paper on the interdependence of the three functionaries of any social order, family, property and state, and the effect of their hypertrophic and hypotrophic false developments. Finally, for the democracy series I engage in theological speculation on the ontic relationship between state and church in a way which attempts to combine christology, anthropology and sociology. I can no longer identify with this today.

But at the same time, in view of the strong Communism in Italy and France, I am interested in Soviet Marxism. So I personally organize a study group on Soviet philosophy, above all that of Lenin and Stalin. As a moderator I get the Rector of the Pontificium Collegium Russicum, Fr Gustav Wetter, who has written a book on Soviet philosophy, based on original Russian sources. In this group I write a paper on Marx's and Stalin's view of history compared with the Christian view. I do not need to study all this again in 1968. The theses of the young Marx and the Communist Manifesto of 1949 provide me at least theoretically with many insights, but I feel only abhorrence for Stalin's Communist system (he didn't die until 1953).

Distinguished visits

Readers shouldn't imagine everyday life at the Germanicum as being excessively monastic – as if all the time there we lived only for scholarship and piety. Totally isolated from the world? Not at any rate from the Catholic world. Who gets to know the heads of the Society of Jesus so soon? Since the re-establishment of the Collegium Germanicum after the Napoleonic wars the Jesuit General has been the one who bears the rights and duties of the cardinal protectors. 'His Paternity' General J. B. Janssens, a Fleming of great simplicity and matter-of-factness, tells us in his after-dinner talk that the Collegium Germanicum is *'una opera di prima importanza'* for the Society of Jesus. He is accompanied by the 'German' assistant Fr van Gestel, a Dutchman (responsible for all German-language, Dutch and Scandinavian provinces), delegate for our college, and the Slavonic assistant Fr Prešeren, an old alumnus of the Germanicum (responsible for all Hungarian and Slavonic provinces).

And who gets to know all the German cardinals, archbishops and bishops so soon? When they visit Rome they like to stay at the Germanicum or to accept an invitation for a meal. They either give a talk after dinner or speak to us in the Gregorius Saal. We also meet the Curia cardinals, who are heavyweights in every respect: Tisserant (Dean of the Sacred College), Micara (papal legate at the consecration of Cologne cathedral), Piazza, Aloisi Masella, Valeri and some others. Of course the visits of statesmen are great events: those of the German Chancellor Adenauer and the Austrian Chancellor Figl, but also those of Prime Minister Arnold (North Rhine-Westphalia) and Ehard (Bavaria), and the young federal minister Franz-Josef Strauss. It doesn't strike us that Social Democrats hardly ever find their way to our college, because they aren't in fact in the government.

A poet like Werner Bergengruen receives just as much attention as some professors from the north (Cullmann, Heer, Lortz, Schmaus . . .). He is the author of a fine 'Book of Roman Reminiscences'; he reads us his Roman poems and extracts from his novella 'The Sultan's Rose'. While I was still at school in Lucerne he signed his book 'The Great Tyrant and the Judgement' for me, my first book autographed by the author. The famous Paul Claudel, the dramatist of 'The Silk Shoe', comes to the city as a pilgrim in the holy year, and after his lecture I am able to shake hands with him in gratitude.

And music? Not much worth listening to! We can't have a radio or a gramophone in our rooms. There is just one radio in the whole college and a small collection of records – both in a tiny room where I often attempt to listen to some music, particularly at dinner time. But now and again we are allowed to go to the Accademia di Santa Cecilia, where over the years I attend splendid concerts conducted by Bohm, Jochum, Karajan, Knappertsbuch, Krips, Scherchen, de Sabata and others. I am even more impressed by Edwin Fischer than by Wilhelm Backhaus or Artur Rubinstein: he plays and conducts Beethoven's piano concertos 1, 3 and 4 like a second Beethoven.

In the college itself the music is usually orientated on the liturgy, where the all-too-numerous rehearsals for Gregorian chant are not among my favourite hours. In any case I sing bass and do not like the relatively high, floating, 'angelic' nature of Gregorian chant, influenced by the French Benedictine monastery of Solesmes, which lacks all masculinity. I prefer to sing in a Russian liturgy, where the basso profundo has the main role. Our guests – especially the many former alumni – are always welcomed in the refectory with a powerful polyphonic chorus *Salve in Domino*, which is never practised and handed down only in the singing, and on high feast days with the old *Laudes* of Hincmar of Reims and a piece by our orchestra. On such extraordinary occasions there is just a brief reading at table from the *Martyrologium romanum* for the day. Then the Rector calls *'Deo gratias'*, we reply *'Deo gratias'*, and cheerful conversation is allowed.

A longing for higher office?

Will all the hierarchical 'pomp and circumstance' perhaps lure me along the way to episcopal office or to papal diplomacy? Certainly not. For of course we young men always inspect our distinguished visitors with a by no means uncritical eye.

Thus we tell a joke about a theologically ignorant Curia cardinal who in a library surveys the dozens of volumes of the church fathers edited by Migne and comments, *'ha scritto molto, questo Migne'*; 'he's written a lot, this Migne'. And on seeing the *Patrologia graeca,* the Greek church fathers: 'Oh, he wrote in Greek, too.' *Se non è vero, è ben trovato.* If it isn't true, it's still a good story.

Of course I'm glad when in my first year at our summer villa Rector Brust, who takes good care of the sick, brings into my sickroom the Cardinal Bishop of Palestrina, Benedetto Aloisi Masella; with a few words and a nasal 'Bravo, bravo' he inspires me with courage. He will become the favourite papal candidate (*'papabile'*) of the conservatives; the Armenian Agagianian, who resides in Rome opposite our college, will become the favourite of the (relatively) progressive. But it will be the patriarch of Venice, Angelo Roncalli, and neither of these two, who succeeds Pius XII as pope in 1958.

All this, though, means that at a very early stage I get used to those who wear purple and violet and am not too impressed by them. In no way do I long to end my career in Rome, as meanwhile two well-known German professors of theology, neither members of the Germanicum, who alienated themselves at an early stage from the indigenous clergy, have attempted to do and – fortunately? – achieved. I don't long for a post in Rome but for home.

Far from my homeland, I also experience some hours of sorrow and home-sickness, regularly on Christmas Eve. Like everyone else I spend the long time between supper and midnight mass in my room. Then homesickness becomes really painful and I long for an end to this self-chosen seven-year exile. I am glad to go to midnight mass at St Peter's or Santa Maria Maggiore, where in the festive lighting under the ceiling gilded with the first gold from America we join in the service in front of the wonderful mosaic of the Coronation of Mary from the end of the thirteenth century.

Holidays in the Roman countryside

Of course there are yet other sides to college life. There are the regular enter-tainment evenings. We certainly don't need the 'Now let's enjoy ourselves' from Rector Vorspel, who immediately leaves the room again without the slightest smile and returns to self-discipline. Then in the three months of summer holidays – we aren't allowed to go home at all during the first three years – we lead a freer life at our summer villa San Pastore, in the middle of enormous olive groves around 30 kilometres from Rome on the road to Palestrina, in the heart of the Roman campagna: there is enough room for sports and – which I like best – an attractive elliptical swimming pool. Here I can even gain a life-saving quali-fication for swimmers which is recognized in Germany.

Then there is the theatre – a means of teaching and entertaining people which has had much encouragement from the Jesuits since the baroque period. For us first-years at any rate it's a tremendous pleasure to be taken completely out of ourselves (*'ecstasis'*) and slip into an entirely different role. I suggest to our year a play by the Swiss nationalist writer F. H. Achermann, *Die Kammerzofe Robespierres* ('Robespierre's Chambermaid'); I see myself in the role of Robespierre. It's a tremendous success, not least because we play only three of the five acts. At the end of the third act, Robespierre in the Conciergerie aims his pistols at the prison governor, who allows the two members of the Swiss guard (one of them his 'dumb' chambermaid) to escape: 'I acquit you of your sins – in the name of freedom, equality and brotherhood.' A shot. End. Curtain. Exhaustion and clapping. The audience thinks it really 'existentialist'.

Every week there is a day excursion, but after my experiences in the Swiss mountains, walking through the countryside in red cassocks and climbing every possible bare hill seems to me to be a waste of time. But the nocturnal pilgrimage to the Mentorella or the excursion to ancient Tusculum in the Alban hills, where Cicero, Lucullus, Brutus and Caesar had their villas at a height of around 600 metres, are exceptions. And we make the most of the innovation of a four-day excursion in groups of three or four, though within a clearly restricted area. So we can't go, say, to Naples, which is dangerously buzzing with life, but only as far as boring Gaeta. Our group of three cuts short our stay there – in favour of a secret trip from Pozzuoli on a boat carrying vegetables to the island of Ischia, where we spend two wonderful days *'in piena libertà'*.

Finally there are the regular summer courses, like the introduction to the church fathers by the patristic scholar Hugo Rahner, brother of the famous dogmatic theologian Karl Rahner, who never shows himself in Rome during my whole time because he is unpopular there. And there is the elocution course by the former opera singer and author of a 500-page book on 'Vocal Expression in the Service of the Church' (1946), Professor Fritz Schweinsberg of Walberberg, which is the occasion of many controversies. We are to speak, sing and preach not from the head, almost in a falsetto tone, but from the diaphragm, using our whole body as a sounding board. Schweinsberg finds agreement among most – but not masters of ceremonies and choral directors – with his polemic against the eunuch-like excessively high tessitura of choral singing and against the *tonus rectus* in the refectory. After vigorous discussions this is abolished.

My favourite place in San Pastore, too, is the 'highest point': the little roof terrace on the tower of our villa, which has more than 100 rooms. There in zealous study for my own pleasure, all by myself, especially in the morning and evening hours, I enjoy the sun and often also a breeze. There is the view over our olive groves and the whole campagna, the nearest village far away over the ravine. In the intense twilight the sun is often amazingly big, and the dome of St Peter's is very tiny on the horizon.

Very near to the pope

1950 is a special, a 'holy', year in Rome! For the first time a tremendous number of German pilgrims can come to Rome. There is a great need for pilgrim guides – why shouldn't they be students of the Germanicum? This is the argument of Don Carlo Bayer, himself a former alumnus, head of the German pilgrim committee. The Rector agrees. And soon we're particularly popular among pilgrims, because in our flowing red cassocks we're easily visible everywhere. We aren't ordinary tourist guides, but young theologians who try to communicate to people not only external dates and facts but also the inner spirit of the traditional places of Christianity. As well as having a welcome way of spending the day, at the end we receive a respectable sum of pocket money from our pilgrim groups. I deposit the money with the Fr Minister, in order to accumulate some capital for the return journey home after three years, for which at an early stage I plan a big detour via Vienna.

For most pilgrims, the high point of their journey to Rome is the papal audience, now usually in St Peter's because of the great crowds. My groups always prove quite surprised when they suddenly see their pilgrim guide standing before them by the papal throne in front of Bernini's great Confessio. I no longer know who first took me there through the rear entrances into the basilica, so that as the spokesman of the German-speakers I could lead the 'Our Father' and strike up 'Great God, we praise thee'. At any rate, in this way, directly under Michelangelo's dome, I see how the whole basilica is suddenly radiant with light and how the Summus Pontifex is carried into St Peter's on the sedia gestatoria, how he descends, how he greets the guest of honour, how he allows his hands to be kissed by enthusiasts. And also how he then comes to the Confessio and alongside me has his hands disinfected by his physician. Understandable and human. Our microphone is now put in front of his throne. From there he gives his official greeting and an address. It all concludes with the solemn apostolic blessing. Of course I delightedly write home how close I have been to the 'Holy Father'.

Another Germanicum student doesn't have the same good fortune. We take mostly groups of women and girls round Rome; there are more of them. I still enjoy looking at the attractive photographs which were sent to me at the time. Of course those 'reds' who don't have a place by the Confessio, as I do, also remain in the midst of their groups even in St Peter's. But the Holy Father doesn't like this. And just as his predecessor Pius X had the college telephoned because from his window he saw a 'red' all by himself in St Peter's Square, so from his throne one day Pius XII gestures a Germanicum student away from his group of girls. Evidently here the pope sees the 'self-discipline' of the candidate for priestly office in danger. Indeed he pauses in his address until the poor student, now blushing deeply, has taken up a position right in front, away from his group.

But this doesn't satisfy the Pastor Angelicus. He promptly informs our Rector through his private secretary, Fr Robert Leiber, that His Holiness does not want students of the Germanicum to guide groups of women or girls. We're perplexed. There's a great discussion. But the pope's 'wish' is obeyed. In the second half of the year we are able to guide only a few pilgrims. I find this quite incomprehensible, and ask our master of exercises, Fr Johannes Hirschmann from St Georgen, Frankfurt, a well-known moral theologian, about it. He opens my eyes for the future with the disarming explanation that even popes are not immune from sexual complexes. So 'self-discipline' can also mean a lack of inner freedom.

The college authorities are also anxious that the strict college discipline could suffer under the guiding of pilgrims. Be this as it may, one evening the prefect of the philosophy group, Josef Stimpfle, tells us in great earnestness in the evening notices before the *silentium religiosum* – in keeping with the self-administration of the college these are always given out by the 'senior' student – that today he has seen a fellow student in the city 'just like this, just like this'. And with a stern face he strokes his hands over his cassock from top to bottom, as if this fellow student had gone naked through the streets of Rome. But the 'just like this' – it became proverbial among us – simply referred to the fact that in the baking heat of Rome the brother had gone through the city without the scholastica, which reaches down to the feet, and only in his cassock. Something that doesn't strike anyone outside can seriously shake order within the church. Just like this.

After the Holy Year, all pilgrim leaders are given a bronze medal of merit on a green ribbon, which is presented by Cardinal Frings of Cologne. As well as Cardinal Valerio Valeri, the newly created Cardinal of Munich, Joseph Wendel of the Germanicum also attends the ceremony. For a whole week we experience at very close quarters what courtly ceremonies are due when the pope installs one of his 'sons' (cardinals are utterly 'creatures' of the pope, whereas bishops are to be respected as his 'brothers'): the presentation of the *bigliettos* of nomination, '*visite di calore*' by the cardinals and the diplomatic corps, a formal banquet, a holy stir, all in our college. Then comes the semi-public consistory in the Vatican, followed by the public consistory, and finally the taking possession of the Roman titular church of Santa Maria Nuova. SCV on the limousines is an abbreviation for 'Stato e Città del Vaticano'; it is translated by the mocking Romans as '*Se Cristo vedesse* – If Christ could have seen this.' What has all this to do with Jesus Christ? But fortunately hierarchical exercises are not the only kind.

Spiritual exercises

My expectations of spiritual training aren't disappointed, and I truly don't want to miss this – particularly in view of the rather scanty spiritual training that is usually given today to theological students, especially Protestants. I emphasize: this is spiritual and not simply ascetic training, of the kind that I had sometimes already practised at grammar school in Lucerne during Lent, with fasts of up to twelve hours. Such asceticism for the sake of asceticism isn't usually recommended to us in Rome. But otherwise there is a maximum of spiritual training, both extensive and intensive, which is assumed to be an optimum. Looking back, I can give a very good account of it through my Spiritual Journal (and the newsletter of the Germanicum).

To put it in purely quantitative terms: in the seven years, there are well over 2500 morning meditations and approximately the same number of half-hours in the evening for self-examination, spiritual reading and preparation for morning contemplation. In addition, at the end of the San Pastore holidays there are eight full days of Ignatian exercises, always in strict silence. As early as in the last three days of 1948 we first-years engage in the first exercises, which after a general confession call us very resolutely to the discipleship of Jesus (prayer of Ignatius). Likewise, there are exercises over several days before the 'tonsure', when a circular bunch of hair is cut off at the time of our legal admission to the clerical state, though we quickly let it grow again (the tonsure was abolished in 1973). There are also exercises lasting several days before the four 'lower ordinations'. Then there are even more exercises before the three higher ordinations: before the subdiaconate, where we promise to be celibate and pray the breviary regularly, before the diaconate, and (coinciding with the major exercises) before ordination to the priesthood.

Every day there are also daily meditations: mass together, morning and evening prayer together, *adoratio* before and after lunch and dinner – first still in the crypt, then soon in the new dark college church built of rough-hewn brown tuff. It has a red marble floor, with a big mosaic in the apse. We are expected to pray the rosary every day, and even before the subdiaconate the lesser 'hours' ('breviary'); after ordination to the priesthood we are to pray the great prayer of about an hour, spread over the day.

On the vigils before particular feasts a large part of the college takes part in the cardinal's benedictions in the Jesuit church Al Gesù. At this ceremony the Curia cardinals like to be led to the altar by several dozen students in white albs carrying big long candles. We gape attentively at the particular *'eminentissimus Dominus'*, patient or impatient in the sacristy before entering the church. No one says more to us than *'grazie'*. In Gesù we also sing the Holy Week masses. Finally, the papal masses at the opening of the holy year, at canonizations or beatifications or on other occasions, are liturgical highpoints; happily we often get very good seats – and the Easter blessing 'Urbi et orbi' is memorable.

But all this of course is only the quantitative, external side, which one can sometimes feel a burden. In time I get used to rising an hour before the others to perform meditation and other duties of prayer very early and to take part in the quiet 'early masses' for Jesuit brothers and the Italian staff instead of the community mass. To this day I have retained an antipathy to excessively long and pompous liturgies, for which in fact Ignatius of Loyola also had little time.

Abiding insights

However, what is decisive is all that we get inwardly and is to shape us for life. I owe much to the Spiritual Exercises (not spiritual theories) of Ignatius for my reflection on the foundations of a Christian life. Of course one has to abstract some Ignatian contemplations from a context in the history of spirituality which we can no longer accept, like the 'two banners' or camps: those of Satan and his hell and of the king Christ and his kingdom. On the other hand, they are not about 'emptying' the spirit, which I am to practise later in aniconic Buddhist meditation. They involve the utmost concentration on God, on scenes and words from the life of Jesus, a quite practical orientation on discipleship of him. Decisive basic insights from these exercises are still important to me today. They are high ideals, but they must be earthed and put in quite concrete situations.

What to live for? *Ad maiorem Dei gloriam*, 'to the greater glory of God': time and again I keep writing AMDG in my diary over the beginning of the year. This is to remind me of the meaning of human life: not living simply for myself but for my creator and perfecter, origin and goal: God alone as the absolute, everything else on earth relative. To live to God's glory and not simply for myself; not to be obsessed with myself but to go my way conscious of my own creatureliness, fragility and sinfulness.

What to decide for? *Fiat voluntas tua*, 'Thy will be done': to attempt to recognize in concrete situations of decision what is the quite personal will and wish of God for me and to apply the rules for 'discerning the spirits' to this end. Here is laid down something that will later be decisive for me: the last norm for me, my conscience, is not a law or an authority of the state or the church. It is the will of God, though in complex situations this can be discovered only through a critical searching of the conscience and a balanced weighing up of the alternatives. Even now it is important for me to check myself out on difficult questions whether in a particular decision about a person or a cause I am gaining something quite personal for myself or whether I really am concerned with 'the cause'.

How to deal with the goods of this world? *Tantum quantum*: I may freely use 'as much' money and possessions, calling and honour, as help me on my way to God. Nothing created, not even the human body and sexuality, is bad, even 'demonic'. All is good, but nothing must be absolutized. That means freedom, relaxation, active indifference.

What to strive for? *Magis*, 'ever more': always orientate myself more perfectly, stimulated by meditation, on the life, suffering and death of Jesus, following his example and being like him. The central commandment is love of neighbour born of love of God. Love of neighbour is the criterion of love of God. 'Perfection' is to be achieved biblically, not by going into the cloister but by going into the world, practising an active religion open to the world which finds God not only in the church but in all things. Will I be able to hold on to these ideals and want them for my life? But what does reality look like?

A threatening lack of freedom

In retrospect I will be able to note that in all the seven years in Rome I took virtually none of my spiritual training lightly. On the contrary, time and again there are new monthly resolutions like 'I will live and study in the presence of God,' 'I will always be cheerful,' 'I will be helpful and loving,' 'I will fight every stirring of my pride.' And in self-examination every evening I tabulate in precise spiritual bookkeeping whether I have fulfilled a rule or failed; for a long period I go to confession every day. Every day in prayer I also think of all my loved ones far away, concentrating on my parents or brother and sisters, my former friends, this or that fellow-student or acquaintance. This may be sublimated home-sickness, but it's truly more than just that.

There is no question that such a regulated life can lead to tension, fearfulness, indeed a lack of freedom. Just imagine. Always be cheerful? Never turn down a request? Do something good for someone every day? And counter all distractions in prayer and all 'unclean thoughts'? How is that to be possible? And eat less of something every meal, as the first master of exercises, Fr Vorspel, recommended? This leads to constant casuistic considerations: is one to hold back on the pasta, the main course or the dessert? Only in time will doubts arise for me: is the fulfilment of the will of God – in the spirit of Jesus! – identical with total faithfulness to the rules, painful self-control and complete submission?

Now serious reflection on the will of God can also prompt quite critical reflections on the direction of freedom. For example, on going to lectures, attendance at which is strictly compulsory. I write in my Spiritual Journal: 'If fruitful, write down the lecture! If useless, don't conform but work through the material right at the beginning of the year!' So just skip the lectures? It is precisely on this point that I am later to get entangled in a difficult conflict with the former master of exercises, Fr Fritz Vorspel. After the painful death from cancer on 1 November of Fr Karl Brust, whom I find congenial, he is summoned back from Germany as Rector of our college as early as December. This is a problematical decision for the Jesuit curia in view of the otherwise clear separation of *forum externum* (external sphere) and *internum* (sphere of conscience).

But I owe it to the same strict master of exercises, Fr Vorspel, that I have *not* become a Jesuit (in contrast, say, to Wolfgang Seibel, Anton Rauscher, Franz-Josef Steinmetz, Vladimir Kos). As students of a papal foundation, intrinsically our allegiance isn't to the Jesuit order but to our home dioceses, and in accordance with the will of the pope this allegiance is even sworn formally in a 'juramentum' during the first year.

However, we know that we can be dispensed from this oath relatively easily, by the pope through the Jesuit General. So, I reflect in the first year's exercises, should the *magis* and the striving for perfection lead me to become a Jesuit? I ask this in a personal conversation with the master of exercises. 'Not at all,' says Fr Vorspel in an amazingly unequivocal way, 'you don't need to become a Jesuit;

you can also strive for "perfection" as a secular priest.' An impressive answer from a Jesuit. That settles the question for me once for all. On 11 April 1949 I, too, with the others on my course, take the jurament not to become a Jesuit but to put myself at the service of my home diocese of Basle. Now I am greeted by the 'old inhabitants' as a full member and from now on am no longer under the supervision of a senior tutor and two tutors.

A first rebellion

I owe the fact that I am now finding my way in all the difficult personal questions facing me not to the Rector but to that old alumnus who returns to the college with us in October 1948 and here, approaching 60, takes on the extremely important office of spiritual director, known as the Spiritual. Fr Wilhelm Klein, severely wounded in the head as a divisional chaplain in 1918, is a highly intelligent, widely travelled former professor of philosophy with much experience. He is a great expert on Hegel, was rector and provincial of the North German province in Cologne during the Nazi period, visitor of the Society of Jesus in Japan and China, and much else. Just as the Rector is responsible for the *forum externum,* so the Spiritual is responsible for the *forum internum.* One can also speak to him about quite personal matters under the seal of silence, without fear of the consequences. When at a very early stage I think that something in the college rules isn't very good, he suggests that I should propose a change. 'Can one really change something in this college?' I ask in amazement. 'Men can change all human rules,' was his answer.

For me the problematical side of the little book of Exercises is the eighteen rules on *Sentire cum ecclesia*: a 'feeling with the church', which according to Ignatius in Rule 13 should go so far as believing 'that the white that I see is black if the hierarchical church so defines it'. Wilhelm Klein explains to me that the title does not mean *'sentire cum ecclesia'* (= with the hierarchy), but *'sentire in ecclesia'* (= in the church community). And what did Ignatius himself do, he observes pragmatically, when the fanatical and conservative pope Paul IV Caraffa wanted to suppress the Society of Jesus? He didn't give in, but sought out a number of cardinals and fought for his work, until the pope died four years after his election. So resistance can be allowed.

I truly didn't make my way into the opposition lightly. Evidence of this is that in these early years, after a meditation on the dispute between Peter and Paul in Antioch in the second chapter of the apostle Paul's letter to the Galatians I write in my Spiritual Journal: 'Lord, make me always stand by the pope in *all* things' (18 September 1949) – with a prayer for Pius XII and Fr Rector. And in fact apart from the initial conflict with the repetitor Gumpel, in the first three years of philosophy I get through college without serious conflicts – apart from one in the third year. Having held the harmless office of assistant editor of the newsletter for old alumni, for the third year I am appointed beadle of the philosophers, number two after the prefect. I am scrupulous about the small duties of this post of trust and moreover admire my prefect, Stimpfle, who unlike me is always gracious and friendly. He never gets angry, never speaks critically about fellow-students, and truly is far more perfect than I am. Unfortunately I am no lamb. In the first years I have faithfully 'reported' to him, the prefect, my own small offences against the rule, as is desired by the rule, in the evening after the *adoratio* before chapel: 'I've talked too long with a fellow-brother', or, 'I've talked with a theologian' (*separatio* from whom had to be observed by the philosophers) or . . . And Stimpfle has always given a gracious smile as an 'absolution'.

So in my first three years in Rome I am extraordinarily loyal to the rule. I decided on that once for all, at the beginning, and am constantly strengthened in it by the exercises. Therefore every day in all minor matters I make efforts to guard against distractions in prayer, unnecessary conversations, mockery of fellow-brothers,' muttering about the choir rehearsals and other things. It is no exaggeration to say that in my third year I have become something like a model student, whom Rector Vorspel presents as an example to two Swiss first-years: 'You should be like Küng!', they say that they have been told.

Yet, when I think back on this: what could have become of me if I had continued simply to observe the rule in 'holy obedience' and toed the prescribed line in college and university, apart from exceptions which were readily forgiven? Had he really wanted it, this model student could certainly have had a rapid Roman career (in Rome or at home in Switzerland).

But now one day this same prefect of philosophy, Stimpfle, requires the beadle of philosophy, Küng, to check on his fellow-students in their rooms at meditation next morning – by opening doors unannounced and inspecting them. The beadle: 'I won't do that: I won't check on my fellow-students at prayer.' The prefect: 'But you must.' The beadle: 'I still won't.' The prefect: 'It's always been done.' The beadle: 'I don't care, I still won't do it.' The prefect: 'Then I must report this to the Rector.' The beadle: 'You do that.' The prefect does so, and pronounces the Rector's verdict next day: 'If Herr Küng doesn't want to do it, he needn't do it.' Fr Vorspel was also like that.

Unlimited freedom?

All in all I am extremely content with my first three years in Rome. Also with my licentiate work, which gets top marks. Whereas at that time some of us had been attracted by Martin Heidegger's *Being and Time*, I was more fascinated by Jean-Paul Sartre, the main representative of French existentialism, and his radical positions. The German existentialist philosopher, originally a theological student, veils the question of God in the question of being – and avoids censure from the church. But the French existentialist, alienated from religious ties at an early stage, takes up the question of God directly and confesses a humanistic atheism – and in 1948 all his works are put on the index of forbidden books by the Holy Office.

Sartre's theoretical philosophical writings – his *magnum opus* is *Being and Nothingness* (*L'être et le néant*) – like his plays and novels, all grapple with an existential problem: human freedom. This is a topic in which for me the emphasis now shifts from civic freedom to the concept of personal and existential freedom. Doesn't the philosophy of the Gregorian, like Sartre, also confront the denial of freedom in materialism and mechanistic science? Doesn't it, too, emphasize the *liberum arbitrium*, human free will? Certainly, but there is little talk at the Gregorian of a possible suppression of human freedom in a particular understanding of God. However, precisely this is Jean-Paul Sartre's concern: human beings, often demoted to being objects by science and life, and often also humiliated by religion, are to be given back their *'dignité'*. And human dignity lies in human freedom: that is the atheist Sartre's central thesis. Freedom constitutes the being or the existence of man. Freedom does not depend on success but is even heightened by real obstacles.

'I *am* my freedom. Hardly did you create me when I ceased to obey you', cries Orestes, the man, in Sartre's play *The Flies* (*Les mouches*), to Jupiter, God. 'There is no determinism, man is free, indeed man is freedom', we read in Sartre's programmatic writing *Existentialism is a Humanism*. So this is a challenging confrontation – with the outcome that human beings, atheistically dependent on themselves, have to endure the lack of foundation and the absurdity of their existence.

I express a desire that we should put on *The Flies* in college. This provokes a discussion. Plays and films are not on the Index – even the Roman heresy hunt has remained behind the times; one may hear and look at what one may not read. But Sartre's *The Flies* in a papal Roman college? The Rector thinks that is too bold an undertaking. Which I understand.

Of course my objection to Sartre is that human existence may not be defined exclusively as freedom. Does existence freely developed, as Sartre's thesis on freedom has it, really presuppose any human essence or nature? No, this existence of mine isn't really undetermined. My freedom isn't completely unlimited. So my responsibility isn't total either. I don't freely invent and create all values, morality and the meaning of life. Sartre's alternative in *Being and Nothingness*, 'Man is either wholly and always free, or he is not', does not convince me. From my youth I have experienced things quite differently: we are free and yet not free. We are genetically pre-programmed and are conditioned by the environment and yet – within these specific limits – are free.

But Sartre is right over against any philosophical, physiological, psychological or sociological determinism. Within the specific limits of the human, which finally he too must acknowledge in the form of an unalterable human condition (*'conditio humaine'*), Orestes is right: 'I am a man, Jupiter, and every man must invent his way.' In the face of all false self-certainty and bourgeois satiety, it seems

68

to me that Sartre is right: the man who is not what he is has given himself up. And he will be what he has sketched himself as being. In other words, he must realize himself. His freedom is fulfilled only in the realization. Self-realization: 'Man is what he makes of himself.'

And it is also correct when Sartre sees individual actions as the expression of a more original choice: 'I can belong to a party, write a book, want to marry: all this is only the manifestation of a more original choice.' There is an 'original choice' (*'choix originel'*, *'choix fondamental'*): choice of myself in the world and thus at the same time discovery of the world.

I had made this choice and have no inkling of it: soon I myself will have sufficient opportunity to struggle for this freedom in life instead of depicting it on the stage: struggle in the sphere of college and church, but also in the solitude of my subjective existence – confronted with God. It is in fact a free basic choice in the face of man and the world, a free standpoint over against reality. But my fundamental decision will look different from that of Sartre. Questions had remained open.

An unshakable rational foundation?

Finally, after six semesters, I complete my philosophical licentiate according to plan, so that at the great inauguration ceremony at the beginning of the coming semester the Chancellor of the university and Prefect of the Vatican Congregation of Studies, Cardinal Giuseppe Pizzardo, presents me with a silver medal bearing a portrait of Pius XII on a blue ribbon. The photograph of me kneeling, according to protocol, to accept the honour from the cardinal, shows me in retrospect that after three years of Rome I was close to fitting into the Roman system. How great a value is attached to such Vatican honours by others will be shown me later by an intruder into my Tübingen house, who takes away only the bronze medal and this silver one.

Infinitely more important than these honours: in the first three years I have acquired a thorough knowledge of the classical *'philosophia perennis'*, grappling with the moderns, above all Kant, Hegel, Sartre and the Marxists in West and East. So I can be convinced that in this way, laboriously enough, I have worked out for myself a sure, indeed unshakable, rational foundation. Thus in June 1951, relaxed before we go on holiday, I walk up the Via Vittorio Veneto from the college to the Pincio with my friend Josef Fischer and jokingly speak to him of this conviction: 'Now in the next four years we've only to build on this foundation and get a serious theology for ourselves. Then we'll be academically prepared in the best way possible for our pastoral work.' However, neither of us thinks in any way of an academic career. Like children we now look forward to the first journey home after three long, long years.

So in cheerful mood, with the academic degree of a licentiate in philosophy, we travel north in civilian clothing. In the express to Florence we can at last again carry on 'normal' conversations as 'normal' people with our 'normal' fellow men and women. In the evening we boldly have ourselves driven in a carriage to the Boboli Gardens, the great city park of Florence. There Carl Maria von Weber's romantic fairy opera *Oberon* is being performed in the open air under a starry sky. What music, what a night! The next day on to Bologna, then after stops in Ferrara and Padua to Venice and finally to Trieste, where we are given a warm welcome by the family of Viljem Zerjal, the Germanicum student from Slovenia. After the Second World War Trieste, which was originally an Austrian free state, has become the great bone of contention between Tito's Yugoslavia and Italy, where there are nationalist demonstrations over Trieste.

From Trieste we have a train journey up to the Semmering pass, which goes on and on, on wooden seats without armrests. There we have difficulty in convincing Russian passport control that as Swiss citizens we do not need a 'stamp', 'stamp', 'stamp' – until the 1955 treaty, Austria was still divided into zones of occupation. Utterly shaken up, we finally arrive in Vienna: at the Burg Theatre we see Schiller's *Robbers*, at the State Opera Verdi's *Trovatore,* and in the Theater an der Wien Franz von Suppé's *Boccacio*. Finally, after stays in Linz, Salzburg and Innsbruck, which we likewise use to the full, we travel via Zürich to Sursee.

When I go up to the town hall through the lower gate, my town seems very much smaller than I had remembered. But I'm happy to be back with my parents and family and to have my old corner room on the town hall square. After three years everything is still as it was: 'still the old streets, the old alleys' and – in contrast to the beautiful song by Friedrich Silcher of Tübingen – also 'still the old friends'? Yes, they too are still there. I enjoy the weeks at home, make only a small trip to explore Europe, to Alsace, Mulhouse, Strasbourg and Colmar: and see Grünewald's unique Isenheim altar for the first time.

The days fly past. All too soon it is time to say goodbye. Again there is homesickness in my heart. What will the second period in Rome bring? After three years of philosophy, four years of theology. Will they pass as peacefully and generally as harmoniously as the first three?

III

Breakthrough to Freedom of Conscience

'The Catholics are the subjects of the pope
and the prisoners of an ecclesiastical clerical system
in which consciences are enslaved,
and the relations of the soul with God seem derived and controlled.'

Yves Congar OP (1937)

Entrenched fronts

BACK in Rome: on 13 October 1951 Pius XII formally ends the solemnities of the Holy Year 1950 with a radio broadcast to a million pilgrims in the Portuguese pilgrimage centre of Fatima. Cardinal legate Tedeschini reports to the public that in the previous year in Rome the pope – wonder of wonders – has observed the phenomena in the heavens which since 1917 have been called the solar miracle of Fatima. Even those among us at the Germanicum who intensively venerate Mary have no such experiences at this time.

I too am slowly beginning to take a critical view of the way in which Pius XII exercises office. His early encyclical *Divino afflante Spiritu* of 1941, essentially inspired by the Rector of the Biblical Institute, Augustine Bea, represented a true liberation for biblical scholarship: modern methods allowed; archaeology, palaeontology, study of the Semitic languages and the literature of antiquity desired; the different literary forms of the texts to be noted. But I was already alienated by the instruction *Ecclesia catholica* of the inquisitorial authority, the Sanctum Officium, dated 20 December 1949, against the ecumenical movement. This underlines the refusal of the Catholic Church to take part in the World Council of Churches, founded the previous year in Amsterdam.

However, at that time there is much that I don't know or understand. For example, that as early as 1926 the Jesuit Pierre Teilhard de Chardin had lost his chair at the Institut Catholique and since then has been persecuted by the Roman Inquisition; that he is not allowed to see a single of his theological works printed during his lifetime; indeed that in the course of the purge following the 1951 encyclical *Humani generis* he is banished somewhere into the backwoods of New York State, where on Easter Day 1955 just one person will follow his coffin to the grave. As a visiting professor in New York in 1968, one day I will travel 160 kilometres along the Hudson to his burial place and will be distressed that the tomb of the great palaeontologist and theologian is not marked in any way, so that I have difficulty finding it. '*Damnatio memoria* – obliterated from memory' – an old Roman custom!

There is no doubt that in 1950 in the Vatican the last reactionary phase of Pius XII's pontificate has begun; it brings to theology the peace of the graveyard and is a catastrophe for the worker-priests in France. And little seems to be moving in the great-power politics between East and West either. The Cold War has hardened into a war of entrenched positions, which at best allows vicarious wars, as in Korea. In Moscow, Stalin's rule has likewise entered the final phase. President Truman will soon be replaced by General Eisenhower. He pursues a 'policy of strength' towards the Soviet Union, the exponent of which is his foreign minister John Foster Dulles, uncle of the Jesuit theologian and convert to Catholicism Avery Dulles, who is even to become a cardinal under John Paul II.

In the Federal Republic of Germany, integration with the West follows the rebuilding. In 1951 the Western powers end the state of war with Germany. On 10 April, despite the pope's objection, the law on worker participation in the supervisory boards of West German mines and the steel industry is passed. On 10 September the Federal Republic concludes a treaty of reparation with the state of Israel, whereas for ideological reasons the Vatican still refuses diplomatic recognition to the Jewish state. The Vatican is increasingly playing the role of the world's political rearguard. The decree of the Holy Office of 1 July 1949 on Communism still applies: anyone who joins the Communist party, promotes it, publishes Communist books or journals, reads them or writes in them, is *ipso facto* excommunicated. But in 'The Little World of Don Camillo' – we too in San Pastore are shown the delightful film starring Fernandel – this is not taken too seriously. The laws are made in Rome and observed (only) in Germany.

A public disputation

I have the best memories of the first year of theology, which begins in the middle of October 1951. It literally warms my heart when after three years of philosophy I once again hear the name 'Jesus Christ' mentioned as a matter of course in the lectures. I am suddenly reminded of why I had really come to Rome.

To begin with, the lectures by the jovial Dutchman Sebastian Tromp on fundamental theology, which have a completely logical and transparent structure, enthuse me, as they do most of us: about the possibility of a revelation, about the fact of the revelation in Christ (miracle, prophecies, resurrection) and about the appropriateness of the revelation. Tromp is generally regarded as the real author of Pius XII's 1943 encyclical *Mystici corporis*, on the church as the mystical body of Christ. We laugh at Tromp's frequent witticisms. He sometimes slips the Italian term 'sciocchezze' (dumb talk) into his lectures in perfect Latin when he comes to talk of critical modern authors like Reimarus or David Friedrich Strauss.

Only later will it dawn on me that he never really takes his opponents seriously, but treats them as a priori enemies of the true faith who are on the wrong track, and whom he can easily deal with by his arguments. He also argues that some things are a matter of course, in accordance with the 'Principium Helveticum' that he has invented, according to which 'in Switzerland all rivers flow downwards'. That is the eternal order of things. 'What is "thinking historically"?' he remarks to a German professor of theology. 'My students don't even know that there is such a thing as history.' To that degree this fundamental theology is completely at the service of an anti-modern apologetic which fears nothing so much as a historical-critical investigation of the Bible and of the history of the church and dogma.

One particular honour makes me only half happy because of the 'terrible amount of work' involved in it: in the very first year of theology – on 29 April 1952, in honour of St Thomas Aquinas – I am to expound and defend Tromp's ten theses *De revelatione* before the professors and students of the theological faculty in a scholastic *disputatio publica* in the circular Auditorium Maximum of the Gregorian. Am I to do this in my own words or keep precisely to his wording? I ask my professor in a preliminary discussion. After all, I had also studied German theologians like Karl Adam, Michael Schmaus and Matthias Joseph Scheeben. Tromp remarks somewhat bad-temperedly, 'If you can do it better yourself, then do it.' Whereupon of course I keep faithfully to Tromp's text.

The disputation is to be purely rational and completely unemotional. But both in my explanation of the thesis and in my reply to the objections of my two opponents – an Italian Jesuit and a Mexican – I sometimes laugh mischievously. This, as my friend Robert Trisco from Chicago says later, makes the audience more attentive. He says that they had the impression that in the end I wasn't taking it all completely seriously. That is true in respect of the scholastic form, which with its rigid syllogisms seems to me to be out of date. But I make distinctions according to all the rules of the art and refute the objections. The defender of the theses proves the victor – as planned. Fr Tromp is very contented and afterwards drinks a glass of sherry with me, a very rare privilege for a student of the Gregorian. He thinks that it has once again proved that this kind of scholastic disputation has not yet had its day.

How can I have any inkling that only a few years later the same Tromp will be the influential secretary of the theological commission of an ecumenical council and that his particular understanding of revelation will become the subject of vigorous debates in which with the best will in the world I can now no longer defend him? There won't be another sherry with Tromp, who now develops into the reactionary exponent of a fossilized Roman theology.

The 'ordinary' magisterium – for every day

The doctrine of the church (ecclesiology) is summed up so precisely by the Spaniard Timotheus Zapelena, the author of a two-volume textbook, attacked by Tromp on secondary issues, that I write it out exactly in Latin. As always, I use small script with my own abbreviations, all very systematically, filling two ring binders which I still have today. *'Tempus currit velociter'*, 'Time is running away from us,' Zapelena often remarks, looking at his watch. At any rate I learn the theses of Roman ecclesiology which I am later to criticize sharply with infinitely more thoroughness than those German theologians who subsequently think that they have to accuse me of 'exaggerations' of Roman teaching – a charge which the Roman authorities never made. Zapelena presents the church in an utterly Roman way: as the kingdom of God beginning on earth, instituted by Christ himself as a church which from the very beginning was hierarchical and monarchical, and in no way democratic or charismatic.

I write 45 pages in my ring binder on the primacy of the pope. It is very much easier to imprint these indelibly on my memory than the corresponding 190 printed pages of Zapelena's textbook with its countless quotations. The one, holy, catholic and apostolic church is realized only in the Roman Catholic Church, the only true and legitimate church! Not only is the pope infallible when he speaks *ex cathedra* and thus exercises his 'extraordinary teaching office' (*magisterium extraordinarium*). So too is the episcopal college when it teaches that a particular doctrine of faith or morals is to be held definitively (*magisterium ordinarium*, the teaching office exercised every day): this is demonstrated to us broadly and at length, and no one in Rome disputes it.

In the later controversies over this *magisterium ordinarium* which is to guarantee the infallibility of the Roman teaching on contraception, the impossibility of the ordination of women and much else, I will often be surprised at the contortions that even alumni of the Germanicum, who have sat with me in the same lecture room, will see themselves compelled to make because of this Roman teaching which is uncomfortable for them. Cardinal Ratzinger, who was not at the Germanicum, will accept it completely in Rome. The declaration of the Congregation of Faith of 11 December 1995 succinctly states that the alleged divine prohibition of the ordination of women is 'infallible teaching' on the basis of this *magisterium ordinarium*. Nothing new. Roman. But is it Christian?

What I find most fascinating, however, are the lectures on moral theology, given in a sovereign and clear fashion by the German Franz Hürth. He keeps interrupting his traditional Roman teaching on the virtues and the various commandments with exciting case studies from real life. Often he gives no solution: we are to form our own views. But, *'Cauti sitis!'*, 'Be careful!' he keeps repeating. Hürth's lectures carry particular weight: everyone knows that he is the papal moral expert and thus an eminent 'Holy Ghost Writer' of the 'ordinary', everyday papal magisterium. He exercises this role, for example, over the pope's address to the Italian midwives association. In it Pius XII puts forward the doctrine that the direct killing of a foetus is always immoral; consequently the life of the mother or even the life of mother and child are to be sacrificed rather than performing an abortion. This is a speech which causes much indignation all over the world.

However, the selfsame Fr Hürth can justify abortions shortly afterwards – in the case of the white nuns in the Congo raped by black soldiers (which is allegedly quite different). Hürth attempts in his lecture with a tortured argument to demonstrate the correctness of what now even the pope declares to be permissible. For me this is the only blatant case of 'Jesuitism', that refined ambiguous moral casuistry, which I come across at the Gregorian. The American moral theologian Fr Healy, who lectures to us on sexual morality with a sense of humour, teaches us rather less ceremoniously, but just as traditionally. When in his lectures with a clearly American accent 'Stella, puella pulcherrima, etsi pessima – Stella, a girl who is very beautiful but extremely corrupt', appears, we already know that now we are dealing with a case in which a bad 'Sigismundus' is usually entangled. Everything is orientated on the confessional. 'Cauti sitis!'

Critical questions

What is congenial about the Gregorian is that anyone who summons up the courage can visit a professor in his room at any time. They all live on the third floor, and truly their accommodation is no better than that of us students. It's Spartan: just one room, which serves at the same time as study, bedroom and reception room. This is asking rather a lot of them, particularly in the Roman summer heat. Fr Gundlach thinks that they have the Jesuit General Vladimir Ledochowski, a Pole but an alumnus of the Germanicum, to thank for this.

So one day I too go to Fr Franz Hürth. Always sitting very upright, he gives information in a way which is both pontifical and friendly, but doesn't make the slightest concessions in personal conversation. All my questions turn on the 'ordinary' (everyday) magisterium of the pope, exercised by Pius XII through a growing flood of encyclicals, addresses and other documents (which are not in themselves infallible). A complicated 'reordering' (instead of simple abolition) of the fast before receiving communion ('ieiunium eucharisticum') is also inspired by Hürth, and he gives a special lecture on its interpretation.

Under the influence of Gundlach, in his message to the Katholikentag in Bochum in 1949 the pope had spoken out sharply against the plan for worker participation on the boards of businesses in Germany, against which Gundlach gave us three lectures at the Germanicum. Is it binding on Catholics? Hürth drummed into us in his lectures that one had in any case at least to offer an 'obedient silence' ('silentium obsequiosum', 'assensus externus') to the ordinary magisterium, as courtesy alone required, and also an 'inner assent' ('assensus *internus'*). So – as I was gradually becoming familiar with Rome – I had my questions about this.

First, on the matter of worker participation, must a German Catholic professor of social sciences present the teaching of the pope, which he regards as wrong, or his own, for which he has good reasons? Hürth's reply: first he must objectively present the papal teaching, and then, without polemic, his objections, and in the end refrain from a final verdict (I think: so he needs by no means keep silent).

Secondly, may I give 'inner consent' to a teaching that I regard as an error? Hürth's answer: inner consent may be given only to a truth. However, unlike many German professors, one shouldn't react to the statements of papal teaching in a critical-negative way, but with good will (I think: so one need by no means consent inwardly in every case).

Thirdly, couldn't the pope's experts exploit their position by writing their own doctrinal views into papal documents? Hürth's answer: 'To my knowledge the Summus Pontifex does not put his name to anything that he has not studied closely beforehand. Of course he is then free to follow a particular doctrinal view' (I think: if the pope is not convincingly offered an alternative view, he has no other choice).

So slowly and *'caute'*, in my study and in conversation with professors and fellow students, I work out a differentiated critical view of controversial problems, not least the papal magisterium. In college such questions are constantly discussed openly. Even when we are climbing the Tusculan hill at Frascati on an expedition we discuss papal infallibility vigorously. Johannes Demmeler, with Otto Wüst our tutor in the first year (he later becomes director of the Study Seminary in Kempten), puts forward a view which some Catholics still defend today: theoretically the pope may be infallible only when he speaks *ex cathedra*, but in fact he is always infallible.

I can see my doubts confirmed very well in personal conversations with younger professors like the moral theologian Josef Fuchs, an alumnus of the Germanicum, for example in respect of the notorious axiom *'In sexto mandato non datur parvitas materiae'*. In the sixth commandment (in remarkable opposition to the eighth, on truthfulness) every sin committed with full insight and full free will is a *peccatum grave*, a deadly sin, because sexual impulses always affect the whole. So is any 'unclean', 'shameful', 'unchaste' thought intrinsically a grave sin? That seems to me to be illogical and above all inhuman. As it does to Fr Fuchs. But I was soon to discover what the papal magisterium knew 'infallibly'.

The 'extraordinary magisterium': the Marian dogma of 1950

On 1 November 1950 I see my professors Bea, Hürth, Tromp and other members of the Sanctum Officium immediately in front of me in St Peter's Square. They are sitting with the French Foreign Minister Robert Schuman –

one of the first Europeans – in the places of honour at a great event of the 'extraordinary' papal magisterium: the definition of a new dogma – on Mary. 'The immaculate Mother of God and perpetual virgin Mary was', Pius XII solemnly declares as binding on all Catholics, 'taken up after the completion of her earthly career, body and soul, into heavenly glory' (the pope deliberately leaves open the question whether she died).

An infallible *ex cathedra* statement by the supreme teacher and pastor of the Catholic Church with the special support of the Holy Spirit: for the first time since the definition of papal infallibility by Vatican I in 1870! And this now against all the objections of Protestants, Orthodox and not least Catholics, who find no proof whatsoever in the Bible of this 'truth of faith revealed by God'. My own diocesan bishop, Franziskus von Streng, Bishop of Basle, plays a prominent role there as a papal throne assistant with a candle. Why? Because our diocese was allowed to pay for the sinfully expensive new bronze door for the Holy Year. However, not even the name of our bishop was engraved on the tremendous door, but that of prelate Ludwig Kaas, former President of the German Centre and the pope's friend, and now director of the Vatican Fabbrica di San Pietro. This too is old Roman tradition: letting others pay for one's own laurels. But what does Kaas get out of it? Barely two years later he has to 'pass on' from the world that was so dear to him.

Do we then have no problems at all with this infallible dogma? German theological students from Bonn who are guests in our refectory ask us this. After all, a long article had appeared by the leading German patrologist Berthold Altaner, demonstrating with much evidence that this dogma has no historical basis in the first centuries, but goes back to the legend of a fifth-century apocryphal writing which is addicted to miracles. We Germanicum students – under the influence of men like Tromp and Hürth – will have nothing of these objections. We think that the German theological students have been kept by their 'rationalistic' professors from the knowledge widespread in the Gregorian, that such a dogma 'developed' only slowly, as it were 'organically', in the course of the history of dogma, but is already suggested, 'implicitly' contained, in biblical statements like 'Mary full of grace'.

In my time in Sursee, too, in the Jungwacht we also practised a quite natural veneration of Mary, above all May devotions and forest Christmases – without any problems. But in Rome the veneration of Mary is now deliberately being exploited strategically by Pius XII, as it had already been exploited by Pius IX, not least with the help of the great Italian popular preacher Fr Riccardo Lombardi SJ. At the triumphal conclusion of his 'Crusade for a Better World' there was a giant procession in the city of Rome on 8 December 1949 – of course always with the Communists in view – involving hundreds of thousands, in which we Germanicum students were allowed proudly to take turns with other seminarians in carrying the image of the Virgin from Santa Maria Maggiore to St Peter's. The closing ceremony of the Crusade then took place at night in Santa Maria

Maggiore with a powerful sermon of Fr Lombardi broadcast in Rome's parish churches. Significantly for this piety it ended: *'Evviva Gesù! Evviva la Madonna! Evviva l'Italia!'*

However, for us such veneration of Mary is associated with an increasingly critical attitude to new appearances of Mary like those in the 1940s and 1950s in Heroldsbach in Bavaria. Our fellow Germanicum student, Arthur Michael Landgraf, Bishop of Bamberg and a scholar of early scholasticism, will soon give us detailed reports on them. According to his sober criteria, the appearances of Fatima, too, would certainly never have been recognized by the church.

Now on this radiant 1 November of the Holy Year 1950 I am enthusiastically present at the definition of the dogma. In silence I, too, make that devotion of complete dedication to Mary and through Mary to Jesus which was propagated by Grignion de Montfort, missionary to the French people and the founder of an order (he died in 1716, and was canonized by Pius XII in 1947). It has been recommended to me by Fr Klein, our Spiritual, who is otherwise so critical; he venerates Mary ardently and by 'spiritual exegesis' even tries to find Mary (as 'created grace') in the letters of Paul. With developing knowledge of critical exegesis I shall increasingly distance myself from this.

Dogmatics Roman-style

I now diligently make a thorough study of all the treatises of dogmatics on which one day I am later to lecture myself: thesis upon thesis, from the doctrine of God and the Trinity, through the doctrines of creation, grace and the sacraments, to the doctrine of the 'last things'. The doctrines and the textbooks which contain them have an almost unassailed authority. This theology has to be learned by heart, not investigated critically. Thomas Aquinas himself had first put a negation of the thesis at the beginning of each thesis: *'Videtur quod non* – it does not appear that . . .' But the Thomists see here only objections which Thomas answers.

I also have personal contact with the more interesting professors. I don't go to hear old Fr Filograssi, who has provided the 'foundation' of Marian dogma from the tradition on the basis of 'organic' development. But I learn much from the Spaniard Juan Alfaro, with whom I can have very constructive discussions about the pre-existence of Christ and the 'supernatural'; he constantly encourages me to make my own way. Also from the Frenchman Henri Vignon, who proves open to my questions about nature and grace. And finally from the Italian Maurizio Flick, with whom I talk at length about the problems of a 'supernatural order'; I then ask him to supervise my work for the theological licentiate. I learn less from the Canadian Bernard Lonergan, well known in America; he leans towards philosophy and bores us with his dry traditional lectures on christology. In vain he tries to convince me in personal conversation that Thomas Aquinas anticipated Einstein's theory of relativity.

My parents' house Zur Krone (1651) with the town hall and the parish church of St George

My corner room with the statue of Mary by the sculptor Tüfel

Emma and Hans Küng-Gut

The Küng houses by the Sempachersee with a view of the Alps between the Rigi and the Pilatus
View from Hotel Bellevue, Sursee

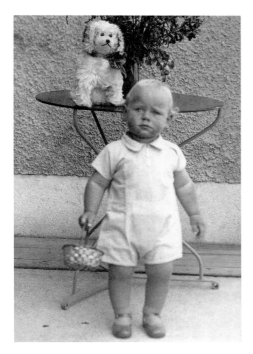

Two years old

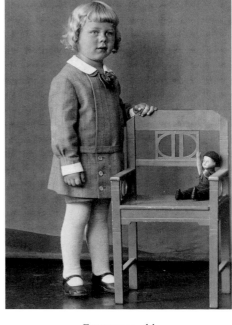

Four years old

Eleven years old

Pastor Franz Xaver Kaufmann

The Küng family in Sursee, Shrove Tuesday 1948

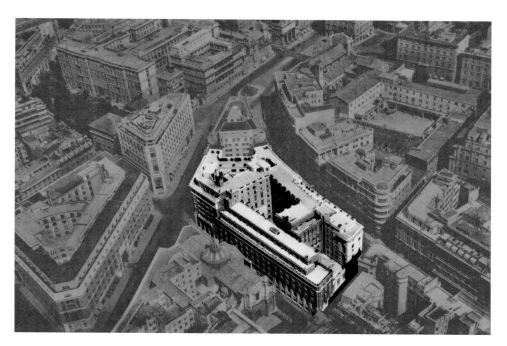

Pontificium Collegium Germanicum et Hungaricum, Rome

A study, Collegium Germanicum 1948

Pius XII Pacelli: Proclamation of the Marian Dogma 1950, with Bishop von Streng (Basle)

'Studium per totum diem'

My fellow Germanicum student Otto Wüst,
later Bishop of Basle

Cardinal Pizzardo presents silver medals for the licentiate in philosophy, 1951
(the Jesuit General Janssens is on the right)

Papal audience with Pius XII: 400th anniversary of the Collegium Germanicum, 1952

The summer villa of San Pastore in the Roman campagna

Spiritual Wilhelm Klein SJ

Rector Franz von Tattenbach SJ

At the Angelicum, the Dominican college, Josef Fischer and I once sit quite alone in red cassocks hearing a lecture by the famous Thomist Réginald Garrigou-Lagrange. We note that this man is even more conservative. This declared opponent of French *'nouvelle théologie'* and above all of his fellow Dominicans Chenu and Congar, this *consultor* of the Holy Office, simply comments on the *Summa* of Thomas! By comparison the theses of the Gregorian seem even modern to us. On another occasion there is a very lively discussion with a younger Dominican, Jérôme Hamer, a specialist on Thomas and Barth, and later my opponent as Secretary of the Sanctum Officium. But I like fencing with foils, even *à la française*.

During those years a certain Karol Wojtyla from Krakow is also preparing for his doctorate in theology at the Angelicum. He has been rejected at the Gregorian, the top place in Rome, because he hasn't completed his studies in Poland satisfactorily. So he has to content himself with the Roman Dominican university (a hotbed of traditional theology in contrast to the first-class French Dominican college, Le Saulchoir). It is reported that he secretly went to a series of lectures at the Gregorian, presumably by the Yugoslavian Fr Truhlar, whom we found rather boring. Rejection from the Gregorian must have been quite a blow for the ambitious Wojtyla. That he then as pope, in contrast to all his predecessors, turns to Opus Dei instead of the Jesuits is regarded in Rome as late revenge for his student days. Whether or not this is true, to the present day it is more important for the church that while this Polish student learned some philosophy, he evidently has a very thin theological foundation – not to mention a lack of knowledge of modern exegesis, the history of dogmas and the church. At that time – at the Gregorian or the Angelicum – did he spy out a certain Swiss Germanicum student in the red cassock?

Some Gregorian professors, however, like an American lecturing on the doctrine of the sacraments, simply read out their textbooks. These offer all the definitions, elements of the concept, arguments and explanations, with compelling logic, as in geometry (*'more geometrico'*, as Spinoza put it). The question arises: why then go to their lectures? Precisely at this point I am now – and I am already in my fifth year in Rome and 25 years old – hurled into my first serious crisis of authority.

A crisis of obedience

With the beginning of 1952, slowly dark clouds gather over the college for me. Fr Friedrich Vorspel, at first warmly welcomed as Rector, who had announced and carried out reforms (looking after one's own money, four-day excursions, reforms over possessions), did not succeed in the long run in winning the hearts of many by his manner, which, while jovial, was nevertheless stiff. Certainly this pastor and youth chaplain from the Ruhr, who was fond of recommending cold showers and Kneipp methods for every possible difficulty, encountered increasing opposition.

On New Year's Day 1952 the Rector – he had forbidden us to have a New Year's Eve celebration (after the solemn blessing and devotion with a cardinal in Al Gesù) – thought that in the service right at the beginning of the year he had to preach about obedience. He sharply admonished us to observe particular rules, and preached against world-shaking bad habits like closing lift doors loudly, whistling in the corridors and running up and down stairs (his saying, 'He whistles, and such a person wants to become a priest', had already been bandied around in San Pastore). And all this with a text from St Paul (in Galatians 4.4f.): 'He (Christ) was under the law', though the Rector, and I find this particularly scandalous, simply omitted the focal point of Paul's statement, 'that he might redeem from the law those who stand under the law'.

Redemption, liberation from the law is not foreseen here. On the contrary, only five days later the visitation of the college on behalf of the Jesuit General by his strict delegate, the Dutchman Fr Petrus van Gestel, begins: he is a big man with a slight stoop, and one of his eyelids constantly quivers. He is very much respected by us as a former inmate of Dachau concentration camp. However, he is an authoritarian personality, with a concealed resentment of the Germans, and because the Flemish General is rather weak, he is the real commander of the Compania. He now comes from the Jesuit curia in Borgo to the Vatican to spend whole weeks with us so that he can talk with each of the 100 students in detail about their views and about the college. *'Il Collegio Germanico – una opera di prima importanza.'*

Granted, I've already experienced such a visitation in my first year in Rome, but this was carried out by the gentle Fr Augustinus Bea, Rector of the Pontifical Biblical Institute; we called it *'visitatio beatifica'* because it had no bad consequences. At that time in a long friendly conversation I even defended the Rector, Fr Karl Brust, against the constant, often exaggerated criticism and satire of those 'providential students of the Germanicum' who came to the college directly from the German campaign in Italy and after their wild lives as soldiers understandably found the order of our Roman seminary difficult.

But now I cannot defend Rector Vorspel to Fr van Gestel against a criticism which I share. On the contrary, in conversation with the Pater Visitator I make very concrete proposals for a reform of the repetitions, for home leave and other matters. Fr Vorspel sees our college as an élite institution which is to train only students who are fully capable in spirit and body. When my Sursee friend Otto Wüst, who has already been ill more than once, has to go to Switzerland for a one-year cure, it takes a real campaign by his friends in the college to persuade the Rector and also the Bishop of Basle that he should be allowed to return to college; the then prefect of theology, Alois Wagner (later suffragan bishop of Linz and finally Curia archbishop), was of decisive help here.

I now speak very clearly with Fr van Gestel about the authoritarian method of education and the legalism in our college. Two pages of college rules had been enough for Ignatius Loyola, I remark (the college archivist, Josef Fischer, had informed me of this); the present Rector, Fr Vorspel, needs 24. The Fr Delegate, this most powerful man in college, begins to make notes. But then he puts down his pencil and simply listens in silence to all the criticisms that I present. After this conversation I go straight to Josef Fischer: 'If they don't throw me out now, they deserve every respect.' They don't throw me out, and so do deserve every respect.

The Holy Experiment

A third crisis factor, likewise in January 1952, plays a part in Fr Vorspel's stricter approach and Fr van Gestel's visitation: it had been decided to perform in college the Austrian Fritz Hochwälder's play *The Holy Experiment*, about the downfall of the Indian Jesuit state in Paraguay – a success all over the world. This now gives our discussion on obedience in the church an almost historic dimension. After all, Hochwälder is concerned to give a dramatic presentation of the conflict of obedience among the Jesuits, who at the command of the Spanish king and the pope are to sacrifice their enclave of social justice for the Indians to the new white Spanish masters of the land.

I am assigned the role of the Spanish visitor Don Pedro de Miura, who carries out the royal command in the spirit of reasons of state. Georg Zur (later a Vatican diplomat, nuncio, and president of the papal academy of diplomats) plays the role of Querini, the disguised legate of the General of the order, who has to preserve the interests of the Society of Jesus, which are threatened by Spain. And Johannes Singer (later professor and bishop's chaplain in Linz) is the Jesuit provincial Fernandez, shattered by the conflict of conscience between saving the Indian state and obedience to the Jesuit General and the pope. The provincial dies, the leaders of the revolt against the visitor are shot, the fathers deported. Curtain – and all the questions are left open.

The problem of obedience is hotly discussed in the college for weeks. Finally the first performance takes place in the new banqueting hall on Sunday, 20 January 1952, before the community and many guests of honour. Despite the footlights I see Fr Delegate van Gestel and the Slavonic assistant Prešeren in the front row exchanging agitated remarks even before the performance. But the applause is loud.

The next day I meet Fr van Gestel by chance on the stairway. He immediately addresses me in his Dutch accent, which I can imitate at any time: 'So, you're the one who played the Spanish visitor last night.' 'Yes,' I reply, 'you don't seem to have liked it, Fr Delegate. But I kept strictly to the text.' Thereupon he retorts, 'Certainly, but it's the tone, the tone . . . that makes it . . .' In fact I had taken trouble to express clearly in language and gesture the whole cynicism of this

Spanish-Roman enterprise ('Because you are right, you must be annihilated'), which brought the Jesuits in Paraguay to grief over the alternative of opposition or obedience. The representatives of Spain and Rome were less concerned with some hundreds of thousands of human lives than with their own eternal principles and claims to power.

It is announced that His Paternity, the Jesuit General, will also attend our performance. But – Fr Janssens doesn't come, and we think that we know why. It's an uncomfortable play, all too provocative (probably in van Gestel's judgement), particularly for Rome and the General of the order. However, that doesn't prevent our theatrical troupe from again celebrating until well past midnight with an illegal feast and much wine backstage after the second performance, which is equally enthusiastically applauded. The popular Jesuit brother, Wilhelm Dankl, the chief cook, always understands us.

The reaction of Fr van Gestel – not to our play but to the experiences of his visit – doesn't fail to materialize: he draws extremely unpleasant conclusions from it, not so much for our life in Rome, where some improvements in the timetable are introduced, as for life at our summer villa. The freer life there is strictly curtailed: even in the brutal Roman heat, instead of open-neck shirts we now wear the Roman collar; times for using the swimming pool are restricted; and there is strict 'separation' of philosophers and theologians. Further measures are introduced along the lines of a 'planned economy', which immediately earns van Gestel the nickname 'Malik', after the Soviet ambassador to the UN, Jakob Malik, who is notorious for saying no.

There is a general stir. Some of us are so furious that in the *silentium religiosum* we meet in the olive grove outside college territory proper to give free rein to our indignation and to resolve to stop observing any rules for a while. So there is passive resistance and active counter-propaganda. Van Gestel's measures seem to me to be completely irrational. Even our Spiritual can't explain them to me. Only Fr Gundlach, interrogated on a visit by our small group of the faithful from the social circle in the park of the villa, enlightens us: it all is 'Sulpicianism in the education of priests' (from the religious order at St Sulpice in Paris). He puts it roughly like this: 'We now have our high spiritual principles which do not change with the changing morals of the world; the worldly may run around naked, but we wear our cassocks and our Roman collars.' *Voilà, c'est ça.*

Freedom of conscience

The problem of going to lectures has now been worrying me for a long time; a rather ridiculous issue for present-day students. But my dilemma is easy to understand. I was honestly concerned the whole time to observe the college rule. And that strictly prescribes going to lectures (except when it snows in Rome, which happens perhaps once every seven years). On the other hand, certain lectures are deadly boring for some of us, and can usually be read in a textbook. So should I waste the time I urgently need for other studies for the sake of the 'law'?

The issue is now no longer our political freedom, as it was in my young years, but my existential freedom. Finally I ask my Spiritual. His answer is fundamental: the demand for obedience never, really never, makes the decision of my conscience superfluous. And this can't be taken in the abstract, but only in a particular situation. I have to decide for myself. It's a decision in myself, which is my *conscience,* though that conscience becomes transparent to another authority. I am reminded of Sartre; however, this freedom is not against God, but before God, before God's 'face'.

So I am to seek the will of God, seriously weighing up the pros and cons. The Spiritual tells me that the will of God is not a priori identical with the will of the superior. If the will of God were identical with the will of the Rector, then to be consistent this would also have to be the case with all other 'superiors', from the pope down to the last beadle or policeman. However, blind obedience leads to absurdities; indeed it is an absurdity. Were everyone to obey like this, the whole world would become one Prussian army, with the obvious consequences. After all, there was only the one incarnation of God, in Jesus Christ, and already at the age of twelve he had by no means shown blind obedience to his parents.

All very well, but what if after calm consideration the reasons against going to lectures are stronger? Then I needn't go to them. But I mustn't expect the Rector, who is probably more aware of the trouble caused by the absences than the waste of time, to be of the same opinion. If I were caught, I would be punished, and I would then have to endure bravely. What is the conclusion? The searching of my conscience, which includes not only my *bonum proprium* but also the *bonum commune* and the *bonum professoris,* leads to the choice of freedom: go to lectures only if they are worthwhile. However, unfortunately this is becoming less and less the case.

Now I am rash enough openly to announce my view to the new theology prefect, the friendly Slovene Janez Zdešar, with whom I am fond of having discussions: he lives on the sixth floor near the sociological library with Anton Rauscher and me. I haven't considered, as I did previously even when our fellow-student from Basle (later provost of the cathedral) Anton Cadotsch, so reasonable in character, was prefect of theology, how much an office, however lowly a one, changes a person. The person promoted now suddenly sees all problems officially 'from above'. As does Zdešar. He says that I should observe the rules. The will of God? Offer unconditional obedience to God alone? What does such freedom mean? What specifically do I want to obey? My reply is: 'My conscience!' That's clear. Freedom in action. But what I don't reckon with is that the theology prefect Zdešar, good-natured but only obedient, thinks that he has to report my free decision to Fr Rector Vorspel.

The Rector has in any case been following the increasingly critical development of his former 'model student' with misgivings. Certainly he expresses his admiration to me openly when in his course on homiletics I am able to give a trial sermon on the transfiguration of Jesus from the retrospect of 1 Peter, internalized in a wholly spiritual way: 'What a variety of capacities your God has given you!' This is a reason for gratitude and compliance. But on 8 November 1952 he instructs me to stop staying away from dinner, although this is allowed by the college rule: I am bored by Pastor's history of the papacy and above all I can use dinner time (and sometimes also recreation) for my studies. Furthermore the Rector doesn't allow me to accept an invitation from the Swiss military attaché to lunch: as chairman of the Helvetia Romana (more an academic Swiss club than the usual student association) I have invited him to give a lecture on the strategic situation of Switzerland. However, the Rector's prohibition doesn't prevent us from cheerfully celebrating with Frascati, as always, in the canteen of the Swiss Guard, where the Germanicum student's code of conduct doesn't apply.

Soon the Rector wants to persuade me to take over the leadership of the social circle, but I don't want to accept – because this is a 'choice from above'. Thereupon Anton Rauscher, who is a year older, is elected, as always in a secret ballot, by the around 50 members (I become his successor the next year). Is this why the Rector denies me the several days of recreation at San Pastore which was promised me after the Tromp disputation? He has no conversation with me, but simply has this passed on to me indirectly by the theology repetitor. Is something brewing here?

A silent duel

This Rector doesn't seek open discussion. Instead, he now writes me a letter, something that is quite unusual within the house. On 28 January 1953 it is stuck to my door: two pages of accusations, apart from that of skipping lectures all unjustified or ridiculous (I am said often to look discontented and gloomy during the reading in the refectory). And it all culminates in the verdict on the former 'model pupil' that my relationship with God is not in order! I am indignant. And I am to take this letter back with my signature on it.

I go straight to the Spiritual. He thinks that Fr Rector sometimes has attacks of conscientiousness: I shouldn't take the letter so seriously and should sign it. But may I ignore the fact that such a verdict signed personally by me could at any time be the irrefutable basis for a *'consilium abeundi'* ('advice to leave')? After a discussion with my friend Josef Fischer, I decide to resist and go straight to the Rector.

'I knew that Herr Küng wouldn't be able to wait!' is his welcome. I retort no less sharply: 'If I hadn't come immediately, Fr Rector, you would have said, I knew that Herr Küng would think he might wait.' So begins an endless unpleasant discussion of individual points and of his monstrous arrogance in thinking that he could pass judgement on my relationship with God. But the Rector won't budge from his demand for a signature. 'Good,' he finally says, 'good,' and taps his right middle finger on his left sleeve, 'good.' That's a well-known sign for us to leave.

But I remain sitting, with the slightly lowered gaze that I shall later practise in Buddhist meditation. I maintain a persistent silence, firmly resolved not to leave the Rector's room until he withdraws his demand for my signature to his letter. But he is equally silent. It's a wordless duel of a kind that I've never experienced either before or afterwards. It seems to me to go on for an eternity. I know only one thing: the one who now speaks first has lost. So I hang on. And *he* speaks first. The result is that I needn't sign the letter. I will recall this scene more than twenty years later when the Kultusminister of Baden-Württemberg wants to force me to travel to the ministry in Stuttgart immediately after the church's permission for me to teach has been withdrawn, before I have clarified and safeguarded my position in the university and faculty of Tübingen. I learned that early in Rome: to resist.

But I never harbour grudges. Later I have a conversation about *The Holy Experiment* and about the Jesuits in Switzerland with Fr van Gestel at a reception for our college in October 1953 in the summer villa of the Jesuit General ('Villa Cavaletti') on a splendid site near Frascati; I also have another long discussion the next year. However, Fr Vorspel is unexpectedly taken seriously ill and one day is transported by plane to Germany without being able to say goodbye. Presumably I am one of the few to send him a warm letter of thanks in hospital. He recovers to some degree after many months, but has long had a successor. When a few years later, before the Council, as a young professor I give a lecture in the big new Auditorium Maximum of Hamburg University, the old man will send two fathers to give me his greetings and express his appreciation. I reciprocate this with great warmth. I don't want any enmities.

A crisis of theology

In autumn 1953, Franz Graf von Tattenbach, the last scion of an old Bavarian family, follows Fritz Vorspel as my third Rector. At first glance he seems a nice man, who attaches no importance to his title; he is natural, likeable, open to the world, shrewd. I like him from the beginning and don't have the slightest inkling that with him I shall have to go through the most severe conflicts of my seven years in Rome.

Moreover in the first months Fr von Tattenbach has virtually no difficulties with the 'community', as our college fellowship is called. He had first come to our college as the second Spiritual, and he gives far less penetrating moralizing Sunday exhortations than his predecessor. Moreover his introductions to the practice of confession and liturgical actions – our year will very soon be going forward to the 'higher orders' – are sensitive down to words and gestures, and free from moral casuistry and liturgical bombast.

We are pleased to see that very soon the new Fr Rector gets himself a German Mercedes instead of the Italian Fiat which has hitherto been customary. Only on the entertainment evening do we mock this with the song *'Mercedes nostra in coelis est'* (instead of *'Merces nostra* – our reward is in heaven', as in the scriptural saying). Because since childhood I have always felt sick in buses – at an early stage a subject of mockery at an entertainment evening – I am occasionally allowed to go to San Pastore with him in his Mercedes. Indeed, as the last of my three Rectors Fr von Tattenbach would in fact have been the best – if only it hadn't been for theology. Unfortunately that isn't Tattenbach's strength, although he maintained a friendship to the bitter end with the well-known Jesuit theologian Alfred Delp – who as a member of the anti-Nazi Kreisau circle was condemned to death by a popular court shortly before the end of the war and executed in Berlin.

Meanwhile the discussions on questions of discipline within the college have shifted in an explosive way to problems of theology. Whereas our senior years – represented, say, by Helmut Riedlinger and Johannes Singer, later professors of dogmatics at Freiburg and Linz respectively – content themselves with a more external and superficial criticism of the practices at the Gregorian and the neo-scholastic theses, in the middle years the criticism concentrates on their basic approach: the sharp division between philosophy and theology, the 'natural' truth of reason and the 'supernatural' truth of faith, nature and grace. We are against 'thinking in storeys', which makes God's grace appear to be a merely beautiful but really unnecessary superstructure to human nature. So there are passionate discussions both in the repetitions and in the recreations.

We are in fact truly not the only ones to criticize this neoscholastic way of thinking in storeys. That happened above all through the schools of *'nouvelle théologie'*, the French theologians Henri de Lubac and Henri Bouillard, whom Pius XII criticized in his encyclical *Humani generis* of 1950 and at the same time removed from their professorial chairs. They and others were alleged not to preserve the completely unmerited character of grace and to 'corrupt' the 'unmerited' supernatural order. They were said to accept that a 'desire' (*'desiderium'*) for the blissful vision of God was implanted in human nature; a purely natural order (*'natura pura'*) without grace was quite impossible.

However, more influential for us in the Germanicum are the first articles by the German Jesuit theologian Karl Rahner. Skilled in dialectic and more difficult for Rome to put a finger on, he wants to attribute only a 'supernatural existential' to human nature (my copy of the first volume of Rahner's *Theological Investigations* containing the article on 'Nature and Grace' bear's Otto Wüst's dedication 'On your ordination and first mass'). The imaginative description and interpretation of the theology of the most significant Protestant theologian of the twentieth century, Karl Barth, by the Swiss ex-Jesuit Hans Urs von Balthasar, who treats the whole problem of nature and grace in a very differentiated way, becomes even more important for me. However, my own personal stimulus, theological adviser and mentor continues to be Wilhelm Klein, whom I can visit at any time.

A ban on meetings

A dozen like-minded students now form a theological study group to examine these problems. This 'dogmatic circle' certainly doesn't 'toe the line', but questions the theses of neoscholasticism. However, it's anything but 'heretical'; it doesn't speculate wildly. It examines neglected statements of the church's teaching, especially the Councils of Carthage (fourth/fifth century) and Orange (Arausicanum II in the sixth century) which were under the influence of Augustine's theology of grace, and the Council of Trent against the Reformers (in the sixteenth century).

I spend several weeks working almost to the point of exhaustion on a new interpretation of the decree of the Council of Trent on the justification of the sinner. The result is 30 close-written sheets of typing paper on the history, method and content of the decree on justification. They are all focused on a unitary 'supernatural' overall view of reality (with a christological structure). A purely natural order is accepted only as a mere hypothesis (with Rahner against de Lubac). But we cannot be content with a 'supernatural existential' (Rahner) or a 'natural longing for the vision of God' (de Lubac). My essay is discussed paragraph by paragraph in four sessions of the dogmatic circle and largely accepted.

The discussions in our circle take place throughout the winter semester of 1953/54, without a moderator – we would hardly have been able to find one – but at a high level. In a few years a number of the members of our circle become university professors or occupy other important positions: Bernhard Casper (philosopher of religion in Freiburg), Josef Fischer (grammar school teacher and educational adviser in Lucerne), Peter Hünermann (dogmatic theologian in Münster and Tübingen), Peter Lengsfeld (ecumenist in Münster), Oswald Loretz (Old Testament scholar in Münster), Wolfgang Seibel (chief editor of *Stimmen der Zeit* in Munich).

So we meet, but not at all in secret: no one who is interested is turned away. Nevertheless we are regarded as an élitist group and provoke curiosity, jealousy and heresy-hunting. But since we really have nothing to hide, we decide in the coming summer semester of 1954 to meet openly in college, to avert false suspicions. And we draw a considerable audience. Even Fr Rector von Tattenbach is present at the first session.

Presumably all would have gone off peacefully had not an old acquaintance emerged; he has meanwhile finished his theological education and is no longer a brother but an ordained father. Our former repetitor in philosophy and now in theology, Peter Gumpel SJ, reappears. It now emerges more clearly that Gumpel, who, coming from a half-Jewish family, has lost almost all his relatives in the

Holocaust, is a convert to the Catholic faith. Whereas his pointed index finger, his slightly exaggerated logic and his lack of sensitivity to new questions did little damage in philosophy, they now prove to be a 'danger to the community' in theology, where he is overbearingly concerned for Roman Catholic orthodoxy.

There is an explosion. Certainly not out of personal ambition but out of concern for the faith of the church, Gumpel falls upon poor Herbert Biesel (later a student chaplain in Düsseldorf), who in all good faith is giving a paper on nature and grace which he has possibly not thought through to the end. Gumpel argues and acts like a born little inquisitor. After all, he is one of those of whom Spiritual Klein remarks that they see the whole edifice of dogma collapsing if someone shakes a single stone in it. At any rate, the discussion is vigorous, and the arguments go to and fro, up and down. This is one of the very few times in my seven years in Rome when the sounding of the bell which otherwise rings out at 12.45 p.m. to the second is postponed, and lunch begins almost half an hour late in an oppressed mood.

'What will the consequences be?' we ask ourselves. We hope for support from Rector Tattenbach, who listens a lot to our Spiritual Klein; we know that in principle he is on our side. But we are mistaken. He listens to the repetitor Gumpel, since, as everyone knows, Gumpel is the protégé and spy of the powerful delegate Fr van Gestel, who regards the Rector as his agent. The surprising decision taken by the Rector is to ban the theological study circle. It is made clear to us that we students of around 25 years old, with licentiates in philosophy and many semesters of theology behind us, are forbidden to gather to discuss specialist questions in our own house. This is a scandal which is vigorously discussed. However, Hans Urs von Balthasar later tells me in Basle that we were lucky: had we been Jesuit students we would have been dispersed all over Europe as dangerous 'dissenters' and thus made harmless.

That, then, is my first personal experience of the Inquisition – without the Sanctum Officium on the other side of the Tiber having had to be involved. Those of us involved are infuriated and hurt. Now everyone continues to work more for himself, although personal contacts cannot be forbidden. Of course Fr von Tattenbach is made aware that by his ban on meetings he has deeply shattered his previously good relations, in particular with the most enlightened.

Some weeks later he summons me: we can continue our theological circle. Really? Yes, on condition that we take the theses of the Gregorian as the basis for our discussions. I reject this politely, but firmly. After all, what we want to discuss is the utterly questionable foundation of these theses in the Bible and tradition. All the neoscholastic definitions and explications, argumenta and responsa, seem largely prefabricated, without any ultimate foundation. But the Rector will not or may not concede this. So the ban remains. No further 'dogmatic circle' until my departure. No freedom in theology. I concentrate on my personal work but remain in conversation with my closest like-minded friends. Usually resistance doesn't dampen my energies but heightens them, if I am convinced of my cause. I involve myself even more vigorously in theology, which is at first practised in a very academic way.

Salvation for non-Christians?

I now work passionately for weeks on a question connected with the 'justification of the sinner', the Catholic extra-dogma: '*extra ecclesiam nulla salus* – outside the church no salvation'. Is the Roman Catholic Church really the 'only true' church, the 'church which alone brings salvation'? This is a question that I had already discovered at grammar school in Lucerne and taken with me into my Roman years. At the Gregorian the seminar of Fr Domenico Grasso on the salvation of non-Christians ('*infideles*', 'unbelievers') offers much that is interesting from the history of theology, but no solution which convinces me.

So I now venture my first completely independent theological essay, consisting of sixteen packed pages of typing paper with the title 'On Faith: An Essay'. I have kept it to the present day. It begins with the words: 'Since the beginnings of Christianity the salvation of unbelievers has been a crux of theology. The universal will of God for salvation – the absolute necessity of faith: both are truths of revelation which cannot be discussed. Yet the combination of them in the mystery of the Gentiles is more of a contradiction than a mystery ... Today there is relative clarity about the universal will of God for salvation – after many heresies of church history. But the necessity of faith? What kind of faith is necessary? What is faith? ... This short essay – it cannot be more – will simply investigate this mystery of faith to some degree in the hope that it will also shed some light on the salvation of unbelievers, which is so obscure for us.'

To make my question more precise: what minimum of 'faith' is necessary and sufficient for a 'pagan' in Central Africa or 'Christian Europe' to attain salvation? My answer, developed broadly and at length in terms of exegesis, the history of dogma and systematic theology, is as follows:

If according to Paul's letter to the Romans the Gentiles can know God's invisible being and eternal power from the works of creation if they want to (Rom 1);

if Jews and Christians should not take pride in their special revelation, since the Gentiles can fulfil this demand of the law written in their heart in accordance with conscience, and it is not 'the hearers but the doers of the law' who 'will be justified' by God (Rom 2);

if also according to the speeches of Paul in the later Acts of the Apostles God bears witness to the Gentiles in his own acts of kindness (Acts 14), indeed if the Gentiles are to seek the unknown God who is near to them, in whom they live, move and have their being and whose family they are (Acts 17);

and if all these testimonies of scripture are also confirmed by documents of church teaching and by Thomas Aquinas:

then indeed there must be something like a very primitive 'lowest level of faith' which in principle is accessible to every human being, even to non-Christians – and this 'before' any explicit faith in God, indeed in Christ, a trusting reason (*'ratio fidelis'*) or faith endowed with reason (*'fides rationabilis'*): in order to distinguish it from explicit belief in God and Christ I shall later give this the name 'faith', that is, primal or fundamental trust which is by no means irrational.

But those who read this extremely demanding theological concoction (begun on 21 March 1954 and finished on 1 May) will have no inkling that behind it is a spiritual experience which I must report here. The catalyst is a pastoral conversation with a non-Christian in Berlin in which I struggle for an answer and don't find one. In summer 1953 – one of the reforms introduced in the meantime by Fr Vorspel – after the second year of theology we are allowed a second home leave for a 'vacation diaconate'.

What a delight when on 28 June 1953, after a long overnight journey, I can greet my parents and my brother and sisters at Sursee station at 8 a.m., well and cheerful. There is a family walk, and a conversation with my brother Georg until 3 the next morning, a reunion with Chaplain Kaufmann, old friends and many acquaintances. But as early as 9 July I set out on a journey of exploration across Europe, lasting several weeks, which combines cultural, scholarly and pastoral interests and will finally take me to Berlin. First of all I go back to Paris (harmonious conversations with Anton Cadotsch on pastoral problems, then with various professors on the possibility of a doctorate in theology, which will be reported in a separate chapter). Then on to Brussels (JOC: Christian workers' and women's movement) and with stops in Bruges, Ghent and Antwerp to Amsterdam, where I make more than one lasting friendship. From my base in Amsterdam I go to other Dutch cities, where I get my bearings in the extremely active Dutch Catholicism, from parish and youth work to radio and ecumenical work, and make the acquaintance of a series of interesting theologians and church officials. Finally via Nijmegen to Essen (I visit Fr Vorspel in hospital, go down a coal mine and on my back make a laborious traverse of a coal seam), and from Essen via Hanover by air to Berlin.

There from 7 to 28 August I am engaged in the planned Berlin vacation diaconate in the very lively parish of St Lawrence in Moabit. I help the congenial pastor Johannes Kurka, his chaplain and his parish secretary in every possible way: at worship, with work on the card indexes, with difficult religious education (put at the edge of the timetable), with slide lectures and house visits. There are often difficult situations: mixed marriages, the marriage of divorced persons, the baptism of infants.

Among others I meet there a young artist who involves me in a long, deep conversation about the meaning of life. It has never before become so clear to me that my apparently unshakable philosophical basis ultimately does not hold: that evidently it is impossible to demonstrate the meaning of life and my freedom rationally. If I am to be honest with myself, that puts in question the whole rational substructure of my faith, which I assumed to be certain. Had I where possible largely suppressed my fundamental questions, or at least 'put them on ice'?

The significance of my freedom?

In fact I had never ruled out an ultimate doubt, though initially I didn't take it very seriously. Indeed on a purely intellectual level everything seemed crystal-clear. But at the existential level there remained an uncertainty which emerged again during the first semester of theology and showed me that ultimately everything was not as clear, provable and quantifiable as was assumed in the theology that was taught us. These are also the questions of that artist in Berlin-Moabit:

What is the meaning of my life? Is it evident that my life has a meaning? Why am I as I am? Why should I accept myself as I am, with my strengths and weaknesses? Accept myself solely on the basis of rational arguments? That is highly questionable.

And what is the meaning of my freedom? Why isn't it simply orientated on the good? What drives me? Why is guilt possible? And doesn't the possibility of failure, mistakes, guilt rebound on the one who willed human beings to be like this, so that I myself am excused? So can my freedom be asserted only on the basis of rational insight? That is more than questionable.

Here is Sartre's question about freedom, which is an unavoidable necessity and excludes a God, but precisely in so doing shows the lack of foundation and the absurdity of human existence. As early as 11 September 1949 I had written in my Spiritual Journal (after a meditation on Galatians 1.4): 'I simply cannot understand why God has given human beings the will to evil. How much could have been simpler and more beautiful.' Is this a naïve thought?

The allegedly evident principles of being in Greek-Thomistic metaphysics don't help me further in the face of such questions and oppression. Nor, however, does the modern approach of René Descartes, which I have studied intently, with his allegedly self-evident starting point in human subjectivity. No, his 'Cogito' makes the question more acute. 'I think, therefore I am?' Is my self really accessible? Am I not a being equipped with mind *and* will, disposition *and* a structure of drives, head *and* heart, conscious *and* unconscious? Am I not a self which in many respects is highly contradictory, as Descartes' counterpart Blaise Pascal makes clear?

And may not someone want in his heart to be rather better, a very little bit more intelligent, gifted, rich, handsome? Presumably there are more people than one thinks who say, 'I don't want to be as I am.' Many neuroses have their foundation here. It's often easier to accept the world than oneself as one is or as one has been made to be by others. 'But the simple thing is always the most difficult', I read in C. G. Jung's writings on philosophy and religion: 'In reality,

91

being simple is the supreme art, and thus accepting oneself is the embodiment of the moral problem and the core of a whole world-view.'

A few years later, I will find an apt description of what I then feel in a book by Romano Guardini, a Catholic theologian who teaches in Tübingen a good decade before me, likewise outside the faculty of Catholic theology, under the title 'The Acceptance of Oneself': 'The task can become very difficult. There is the rebellion against having to be oneself. Why should I? Have I desired to be? ... I keep coming up against the self-same limits. I keep making the same mistake, experiencing the same failure ... All this can lead to an infinite monotony, a fearful satiety.'

But in the face of this ambivalent reality, how can I arrive at a basic positive attitude to the world and myself without succumbing to irrationality? That is my essential question. In what way can I arrive at a deliberate constructive decision and attitude (basic choice, 'choix originel') which now embraces, colours, shapes the whole experience, conduct, action of my person, given that this highly ambivalent reality of the world and myself doesn't provide compelling evidence that it is meaningful? In the face of such threatening absurdity how can I gain a firm standpoint, as it were an Archimedean point from which I can fundamentally determine, move, understand, change my reality?

I have the choice

Evidently this fundamental question is about a free and thus a responsible standpoint. Here, simply to resort to the many ways in which I am determined, which are certainly a given, seems to me to be a demoralizing get-out which relieves me of all moral obligation and responsibility. After all, I have so often experienced that I am neither totally pre-programmed by my heredity or my unconscious nor totally conditioned by my environment. No, I am neither an animal nor a robot. I am free at the limits of my innate character and of my determination by the environment: freedom is understood as self-determination and responsibility for myself. Though I cannot 'prove' this freedom of choice and decision, I can experience it immediately at any moment, whenever I want. At any time I can also be different!

A fundamental alternative opens up for me:

I can more or less deliberately say no to a meaning in my life and my freedom, to reality generally. That is the nihilistic alternative, active or passive, philosophical or pragmatic ('It's all the same,' to avoid more trivial words), which time and again finds enough that is negative to assert that life is absurd and empty, lacks value and meaning, indeed to assert the nothingness of reality generally.

However, I can also more or less deliberately say yes, even if only in an apparently passive readiness for surrender: yes to the foundation and meaning of my life and my freedom despite all meaninglessness, to reality generally despite all nothingness. Beyond doubt this is a venture in the face of the manifest risk of disillusionment and the failure that is time and again possible in this burdensome life which is full of suffering.

But why should I say yes? I well recall how I perplexed my very first director of exercises, Fr Vorspel, with this question. He refers me to God. But the question of my own standpoint, the meaning of my life, my freedom, reality generally, seems to me to be more fundamental and therefore more urgent than the question of God, which logically should be considered at a secondary stage. He tells me reproachfully that in the last resort my question is rebellion against God. But how can I accept God if I cannot yet even accept myself? He tells me that I must 'believe'. But I was brought up to think that 'believing' holds only at the 'upper level' of the real, Christian truths of revelation. After all, faith has nothing to seek on the 'lower', natural level of reason. There only knowledge, insight, evidence is to prevail.

Now it becomes evident to me in my last years in Rome that Protestant theology too, as I slowly get to know it at that time by reading the works of Karl Barth, which are so impressive, is also in confusion in this respect. In this basic question does one a priori rely on God's Word? Simply read the Bible? But what about those who do not read the Bible because of their origin, education, attitude? Is it perhaps impossible for all these non-Christians to find any fixed standpoint in their lives, to attain any trust in life? Is belief in the Christian God really a presupposition for any yes to reality and any ethic which builds on it? These are questions on which Protestant theology, too, has hardly reflected sufficiently to the present day.

During that conversation in Berlin-Moabit, in which with all my philosophical education and a theological education that has already lasted for two years, I prove incapable of giving my conversation partner a convincing answer, and even excursions into aesthetics are of little use, I resolve after my return from the north to seek out in Rome my spiritual director, Wilhelm Klein.

Venturing fundamental trust

Of course I'm again given the answer to which I've long been allergic. I had firmly planned to attack it, in order finally to force a resolution of the conflict: 'One must just believe!' Believe? Always only belief? But suddenly – in the middle of this conversation – an insight seeps through to me. I don't like speaking of an 'illumination'. It was a spiritual experience. At any rate this intuitive insight doesn't come simply from my conversation partner. Nor, though, does it come through my own conceptual efforts. It comes suddenly from deep inside me. Or from outside, from above?

'Believe?' The solution certainly isn't offered by faith in the Catholic sense of the intellectual acceptance of supernatural truths of faith and dogmas. Nor, however, is it faith in the Protestant sense of the justifying acceptance of God's grace in Christ. My knowledge perhaps has something to do with that, but it is simpler, more elementary, more fundamental. It's initially a matter of the conscious foundation of human existence, not just Christian existence. It's a matter of that very question which arises for both Christians and non-Christians even before any reading of the Bible. How can I attain a firm standpoint? How can I accept my own self with all its shadow sides? How can I accept my own freedom, which is also open to evil? How can I affirm a meaning in my life of suffering despite all meaninglessness? How can I say yes to the reality of the world and human beings despite their enigmatic nature and contradictoriness?

What suddenly dawns on me is that an elementary choice is being asked of me, a venture of trust! This is the challenge: dare to say Yes! Instead of an abysmal mistrust, venture a fundamental trust in this ambivalent reality! Instead of fundamental mistrust, venture fundamental trust: in yourself, in others, in the world, in life, in questionable reality generally. And meaning shines out, makes things clear, becomes light!

Can you sense how this strange experience filled me with unbounded joy? It is lived-out, realized freedom; to say yes, to venture basic fundamental trust, to risk trust in life. So I can in fact adopt a particular basic attitude; I can go on with my head held high. No, my freedom of conscience isn't given once for all, but has constantly to be developed in my career.

Such fundamental trust and such a fundamental conviction doesn't have the slightest thing to do with blissful trust, an uncritical optimism. The reality of the world and my self hasn't changed, but only my fundamental attitude to it. It has by no means become a whole world; it remains stamped with contradictoriness and threatened by chaos and absurdity. Nor has my self in any way lost its shadows. It remains unfathomable, fallible, threatened by guilt, mortal. My freedom is still capable of everything, as is that of my fellow men and women. Thus along with all the trust in life at the same time shrewdness is required of me: a balance between justified restraint and trust, in individual cases also scepticism, indeed mistrust. Indeed even the possibility of a fundamental mistrust about reality is not ruled out once and for all.

But I now know that this my fundamental trust is by no means irrational: it can be examined, and that remains important for me. Granted – like the basic experiences of love or hope – it cannot be proved in advance by an argument, nor can it be proved after the event. Fundamental trust cannot be demonstrated as a premise before my decision, nor can it only be demonstrated as a consequence after my decision. No, it can be experienced as quite meaningful, indeed rational, only when I am actually making my decision. This reminds me of my lake: that the water will support my body, as it supports other bodies, cannot be demonstrated by a swimming course on dry land, however skilful; it can be experienced only when I am swimming. Without venturing to entrust myself to the reality of the water I will never experience how it bears me, me too, here and now.

I will announce my very first series of lectures in Tübingen (only six years later, I note with astonishment), as is usual in fundamental theology, under the title 'revelation'. However, in a way which some find enigmatic I shall begin with 'the question of human existence'. I have experienced that the answer lies in fundamental trust. Without this fundamental trust, any Christian faith is left hanging in the air. Without confidence in life there is no true life. Wouldn't it have been good to discuss this spiritual experience and its consequences in a theological circle? But under the 'rule' of Pius XII this isn't welcome.

A crisis of the church

As early as August 1950, after my second year of philosophy, I take the encyclical *Humani generis* as it is presented to us by professors in Rome and also by commentators subservient to Rome in Germany and France: as an allegedly necessary correction of highly dangerous views about the essence of 'supernature' as grace, the value of dogmatic formulations, the possibility of proving the existence of God, evolution and original sin, Christian philosophy and the doctrine of Thomas Aquinas (Thomism). At that time the Catholic press passes over as far as possible the fact that the important heads of the school of theologians in Lyons, their Spiritus Rector Henri de Lubac, and also other Jesuits like Henri Bouillard, Jean Rondet and Gaston Fessard have all been dismissed (apart from the wily Jean Daniélou, who will eventually manage to become a cardinal).

It will dawn on me later how shamefully the best theologians of France have been silenced when I send Henri de Lubac a manuscript in which I write about the 'discussion' on his 'supernatural'. He gives me a blunt answer: *'Il n'y avait pas de discussion.'* Was there really 'no discussion'? In fact there was only the suppression of any discussion by Rome, with the dismissal of those involved and a ban on publishing and speaking. But – all Jesuit professors submit silently in obedience. Where is the protest, where is there still freedom?

On 12 March 1952 I am still deeply impressed when taking part in the ceremony of the papal coronation of Pius XII in the Sistine chapel – through the good offices of the chaplain of the Swiss Guard, Monsignor Paul Krieg, also an alumnus of the Germanicum, who is always well disposed to me. What a sacral spectacle: all the Curia cardinals and diplomats from every country in formal dress, a high mass in the presence of His Holiness – in front of Michelangelo's Last Judgement, which forms a shattering contrast. This is then relativized for me personally by a lecture given by the French existentialist Gabriel Marcel in the afternoon, in the city, on 'Philosophie et théâtre', in which he rejects the theatre of ideas (J. P. Sartre!) in principle, but hardly in a convincing way.

The 400th anniversary of the college in autumn 1952 already casts long shadows forward. There is also to be a papal audience in Castel Gandolfo in the framework of a week of celebrations. News seeps through that our Rector Fr

Vorspel had been asked to draft a speech and that he is now in the process of writing his rigorous ideas about college discipline and obedience into the papal speech. There is great indignation among us 'reformers'. We complain to Fr Klein. He intervenes with his friend, the papal private secretary Fr Robert Leiber, so that now a 'moderate' address is expected. In favour of Fr Vorspel is his desire in principle to maintain the self-administration of the college. By contrast, Fr van Gestel wants to appoint Jesuits in place of the Germanicum prefects to tighten up discipline. Fr Vorspel wants to prevent that, and in the draft of the pope's address he writes a passage about self-administration which is retained in the version delivered by the pope: 'College discipline, which puts no small demands on you,' says Pius XII, 'is by an old and praiseworthy tradition of your house lightened to the degree that you yourselves play a part in its administration. Self-education is half the effort, and the trust which is put in you is upheld.' In this way Gestel's plans are thwarted from the top – but at the same time Vorspel's fate as Rector is sealed: he will soon be replaced when he falls sick.

Four hundred years of the Germanicum: many bishops and others who are alumni of the Germanicum have announced their intention of attending. I prefer talking with the Mainz church historian Joseph Lortz to talking with the Lucerne moral theologian Schenker. Lortz is the author of two famous volumes on 'The Reformation in Germany'. I also accompany him to Termini station in Rome and he gives me a copy of his 'History of the Church from the Perspective of the History of Ideas' in gratitude. He also tells us that the educational system at the Germanicum produces two kinds of people: the smooth and those with rough edges. Indeed the great Berlin pastor Carl Sonnenschein; August Pieper, the leading mind in the Catholic Volksverein; and Lorenz Werthmann, the founder of the German Caritas association, were all students at the Germanicum.

I am shocked when I see from close up Pius XII entering the audience chamber on 9 October 1952, marked by an almost terminal illness. His face is a greenish yellow. For the first time the pope, who hitherto has learned all his speeches by heart in his garden, reads his speech word for word from notes. In it he defends the nomination of so many alumni of the Germanicum as bishops. Later he talks with many of us. But for me a clear demystification of the pope and his declarations has already begun. Then we are guests at the summer villa of the American College in Castel Gandolfo, and I have the opportunity to have a long conversation about all this with my friend from Chicago, Robert Trisco. The next day I receive the third and fourth lower orders on the occasion of the ordination of my fellow students as priests; not only the German-speaking bishops and Vatican ambassadors, but also Lord Mayor Rebecchini of Rome and Signora Francesca de Gasperi can be seen at the reception which follows.

Reform of the church – from above or from below?

The next year, on 18 May 1953, as editorial assistant for the 'newsletter' of the Germanicum (a position which I share with Peter Lengsfeld and Georg Zur), I have an interview with the great popular preacher Fr Riccardo Lombardi SJ. After the Second World War he had carried on extremely popular 'radio crusades' in a variety of Italian cities – as a result of which he is called *'il microfono di Dio'* – and then had brought into being *'il Movimento per un Mondo Migliore'*, 'the movement for a better world'. On 3 May Lombardi had spoken to us in college (as, at another time, had the popular preacher Fr Johannes Leppich SJ, who was active in Germany) about his new conception of a reform of the church from below. We have listened to some of his sermons, which call clergy and people to a Christian and social *'rinnovamento'*. This is the first movement of church renewal in which I personally am involved; initially it enthuses me, despite its clearly Marian, papal and national overtones.

There are two issues, Lombardi tells us: 'creating a movement of the conscience and personal zeal' and 'systematically examining all our positions and mobilizing all our forces'. With the support of the pope, which has been given him in a major address to the faithful of Rome on 10 February 1952, first the city of Rome and then the church and the world are to be renewed on a broad front. Rather later (on 12 October 1952), Pius XII has required of all the dioceses of Italy what is to take place for the diocese of Rome under the leadership of the cardinal vicar Clemente Micara. It seems to us that Fr Lombardi has the full backing of the pope. Towards midnight that same evening I transcribe the interview with Lombardi, which we publish in a prominent place in the newsletter of November 1953.

What is unusual is that Lombardi recognizes the deep crisis of the church behind the Roman façade, presented brilliantly by Pius XII and his manifestations of pomp and power. But what we do not know (it will be made known only after Lombardi's death in 1979 by the 'Vaticanista' Giancarlo Zizola, on the basis of Lombardi's private notes) is that Lombardi initially attempted the direct reform of the church from above – but failed. As early as 1948, on the day after the great electoral victory of Democrazia Cristiana over the Communists which was won with his help (5 May 1948), at a private audience Lombardi had implored Pius XII in almost apocalyptic tones to prescribe a comprehensive plan of reforms both of the Vatican authorities and of the bishops, the clergy and the orders, and finally the laity for the church in its crisis.

In fact the pope commissioned Lombardi to work out a comprehensive 'project for the renewal of the church'. Agreed with the Jesuit General and other advisers, as early as August 1948 a 60-page document of very concrete proposals for reform, culminating in a council, was transmitted to the pope. However, leading Curia cardinals understandably had little time for a limitation on their time in office, de-Italianizing of the central administration and measures against careerism and bureaucracy. They also had little time for ecumenism, the reform of seminaries, a reorganization of the Italian dioceses and much more. And what about the sole ruler Pius XII? He hesitated. Was he, too, in the end perhaps a prisoner of the Curia?

Five years later, now, as Fr Lombardi speaks in our college about the reform of the church 'from below', his relations to those 'above' have already cooled off considerably – especially since this Jesuit with a sense of mission has been too insistent in demanding that the pope should dismiss that very cardinal vicar Clemente Micara who in his view is the main obstacle to a renewal of the diocese of Rome. In fact Micara, the pope's representative incarnate for his very own diocese, is a rather inefficient, good-natured and lazy *bon viveur*, for example, after a relatively simple dinner in our college (in the middle of the day there had been a ceremonial lunch), as he went out he said in an insolent and loud voice, '*E adesso, Monsignore, dove andiamo mangiare?* – And now, where shall we eat?' But is the pope simply to dismiss this 'curial heavyweight'? No, the Jesuit father is at a disadvantage sitting there, and it is little use for him to end every sermon with '*Viva Maria, Viva il Papa*'. Even the German Jesuits around Pius (as I note from Gundlach's reaction) have their reservations about the enthusiastic-apocalyptic mass preacher and his proposals for reform.

Regardless of the reform of the church, in any case in 1953 the Vatican has other concerns: the problem child is no longer Italy, where the rule of Demo-crazia Cristiana seems to be solidly established. France, with its equally large Communist party, strong trade unions and countless strikes, is turning into the real hotspot for the Catholic Church.

The worker-priests – a test case

The bishops of France had been alarmed by the sociological investigation by Abbés Godin and Daniel, *France, pays de mission?*: in France almost all the labour force has been lost; only 2 per cent are still religiously active. It is above all the Cardinal Archbishop of Paris, Emmanuel Suhard, who now reacts decisively to this finding, although he, too, like the majority of the French bishops, is com-promised by his collaboration with the authoritarian Pétain regime and initially is very conservative. At a very early stage I read the precise analysis in his pastoral letter *Essor ou declin de l'Eglise?* ('Rise or Fall of the Church?'), which is known far beyond France. In March 1953 the secretary of the Semaines Sociales de France, Professor Folliet from Lyons, discusses the French workers movement and the social-Catholic movement with us at the Germanicum.

The sociology of religion – established by Gabriel le Bras at the Sorbonne – is suspect to the Vatican, since in contrast to the prevalent triumphalism it paints a realistic picture of the sometimes desolate situation of the church at the grass roots. Of course there are also suspicions of a 'return to the sources', since in this way a different theology and a less legalistic picture of the church from that prevalent in neoscholasticism is developed from scripture and the church fathers. Of course there are also suspicions of any 'ecumenism' which claims to find what is true and good, and even the church, in the other Christian churches. Given all these circumstances, there is also particular suspicion of the worker-priests.

Thus I keenly follow the experiment of the 'Mission de Paris', later 'Mission de France', started after the war under Suhard's protectorate, which seeks to regain the workers through priests as workers (*'prêtres ouvriers'*). Experiments that had already been made during the war among the French forced labourers in German armament factories are now to be tried out in France: sending priests as workers into the factories to work there as pastors among the workers. This is an almost impossible task, given the long-standing alienation of the now mostly socialist and Communist working class from the bourgeois, 'capitalist' church since the revolutions of 1789 and 1848. Will the worker-priests avoid making the justified demands of the working class their own? Will they even join trade unions, which are often also Communist? Of the seven million wage-earners in France in 1953, more than one million earn less than $30 a month. Because of their better education, individual worker-priests will be elected to works committees or even become trade union secretaries. I ardently read Gilbert Cesbron's novel *Les saints vont en enfer* ('The Saints Go to Hell'), which is based on personal experiences.

And now in fact the worker-priests indeed go to 'hell'. Not, however, into the hell of totalitarian Communism but into the hell of the totalitarian Roman Inquisition. This may no longer be able to burn deviants physically, but it can burn them psychologically. It is that Cardinal Pizzardo, Secretary of the Vatican Congregation of Seminaries, to whom I owe my silver medal for a licentiate in theology, who under the direction of the Sanctum Officium and in collaboration with Nuncio Marella of Paris rolls out the broad Roman repression in August/September 1953. From now on no French seminarians are allowed to work in factories during vacations. All worker-priests are recalled from the factories to the religious houses of the orders and dioceses. The seminary of the Mission de France is closed. The professors are sent home. And of course all this is at the personal wish of the Holy Father ...

There are 90 worker-priests (in any case, no more had been tolerated by Rome). Do these represent such a tremendous danger for the church, among almost 50,000 secular priests and members of orders? The world press follows events attentively, and the issue is discussed passionately everywhere, as it is in our college. For the first time I am firmly convinced that Pius XII is wrong. The end of the worker-priests is a tragedy! And the end of the worker-priests is also the end of the theology which supports them.

Purging theologians: Yves Congar

A second purge (and deliberate intimidation of those not directly involved) now begins, no longer of the Jesuits, who after the encyclical *Humani generis* (1950) have withdrawn from the Mission de France in time with burnt fingers, but of the Dominicans. Just as in authoritarian or totalitarian systems of government, leading members are removed from their posts without any legal proceedings and with no possibility of defence. No one, let alone any pope, talks of human rights. Because the orders have preserved a remnant of their autonomy from Roman centralism on the basis of their constitution, deriving from the Middle Ages, they are to be compelled with every possible means to submit politically to the will of the power cartel ruling in Rome.

Not only the pope but also the Sanctum Officium likes to keep in the background in such actions. In February 1954 the Dominican General, the Spaniard Emanuel Suárez, is instructed to remove from office the three provincials of Paris, Lyons and Toulouse, Frs Avril, Belaud and Nicolas. Tragically, on 29 June Suárez is killed in a car crash between Perpignan and the Spanish frontier, having taken part in the feast of St Peter and St Paul in Rome and driven back right through the night. The élite of the order is paralysed. For four more famous Dominican theologians, whom I get to know later, are banished from Paris: Boisselot (Director of Éditions du Cerf), Féret (Professor of Catechetics), Chenu (the great stimulus, expert in Thomas and historian of theology, the critical author of a theology of work and the main support of the worker-priests), and above all Yves Congar. In February 1954 Congar is thrown out of the house of Le Saulchoir near Paris which is his home and banished to Jerusalem; then he is shifted to Cambridge and has a complete ban imposed on public speaking and publications. The only thing that doesn't happen to him is to be sent to a mental hospital (as in the Soviet Union): for anyone who is against the system ('church' or 'party') can only be mad.

To my surprise, in the winter of 1954/55 I meet Yves Congar, this most important ecumenist and ecclesiologist of our church, but now an *'auteur suspect'* to be avoided, in Rome, where he is staying between his exiles in Jerusalem and Cambridge. I later hear that he had been urgently called by the Sanctum Officium to Rome but without ever being interviewed. That is how they torture people. In Rome he may neither preach nor give lectures, nor even receive students in the parlour. As a member of a small international ecumenical circle, led in succession to Fr Boyer by Herman Schmidt SJ, the outstanding Dutch liturgical scholar whose lectures I zealously attend, I spend a good two hours with him. The host is the Unitas centre on the Piazza Navona, which is run by the marvellously committed Dutch ladies of the lay order of the Grail.

Congar, who was born in Sedan in the Ardennes in 1904, had experienced the First World War as a child and the Second as a soldier. And although between 1940 and 1945 he was a German prisoner of war in harsh conditions, he has more than overcome his understandable resentment against the Germans. He is a Dominican with all his heart: not a mystic and a contemplative but deeply committed to preaching (OP: *Ordo praedicatorum*: Order of Preachers), proclamation and theology. He found the days of silence in the exercises boring. Under the influence of his teacher Chenu, nine years older, at an early stage he became passionately interested in history and a historical approach to everything and also put the theology of Thomas Aquinas in its historical context. But he has made an intensive study of German theology, Luther, Möhler, Barth and above all historical works, so he is both a dogmatic theologian and a historian. As early as 1937, under the influence of Chenu and on the basis of his encounter with Protestants, with his 'Conférences' in Sacré Coeur of Montmartre, he writes a pioneering work under the title *Chrétiens désunis* ('Disunited Christians', from which the motto for this chapter is taken). Its subtitle is 'principles of a Catholic ecumenism'. But nowhere can I now get hold of his even bolder 1950 book on 'True and False Reform in the Church' – as early as 1952 the Holy Office bans any new edition or translation. Even Congar can't get me a copy.

We students can hardly imagine what is happening to the Dominican who is sitting in a calm and friendly way with us in our circle, vilified and condemned to public inactivity. Here he speaks of his understanding of the church, which is orientated on the future: it builds on the laity and has an ecumenical orientation. Only in 2000 – six years after his elevation to the cardinalate and five years after his death! – will his shattering *Journal d'un théologien 1946-1956* be published: this covers Congar's darkest decade in his struggle against the 'Roman hydra' (*l'hydre romaine*'). Because of his cruel experiences with the unholy Roman Inquisition – he always puts the term 'Holy Office' in quotation marks – he has long seen through this sick religious system and its symptoms more deeply than we critical Roman students: the Roman methods which claim to be serving God by suppressing the freedom of the gospel. Congar wrote as early as 1937 about this 'ecclesiastical clerical system in which consciences are enslaved, and the relations of the soul with God seem derived and controlled': 'a religion through authentication (*'procuration'*) in favour of the clergy, a church empire whose autocrat is the pope'.

But Congar hasn't given up hope. For he is convinced that this church must reform if it is not to collapse. There must be discussion with those who have left it, not a fight against them: *'débattre plutôt que combattre!'* And he wrote the much-quoted sentence about the worker-priests: '*On peut condamner une solution si elle est fausse, on ne peut condamner un problème* – One can condemn a solution if it is false; one cannot condemn a problem' (*Témoignage Chrétien*, 1953).

Congar never wanted to leave the order, the ministry, or the church, far less provoke a schism. But he deeply abhors the system, which he compares with that of Stalin (and the 'Holy Office' with the Gestapo), because with denunciation and secrecy it creates an atmosphere of suspicion and rumours in the church and is ultimately based on fear, fear not only of Communism but of any change to the *status quo*. Congar struggles seriously with the question whether he isn't making himself an accomplice if he gives unconditional obedience to the General of his order, in whom he always sees the successor of the founder of his order, St Dominic. This is a General who, while defending him against the Holy Office, is still doing so only within a system, without ever rejecting the lies inherent in this system. 'Today I am afraid that the absoluteness and simplicity of obedience is drawing me into a complicity with this abhorrent system of secret denunciations which is the essential condition of the "Holy Office", the centre and culmination of all the rest. For in fact if the Fr General has taken sanctions against Chenu, Féret, Boisselot and me without reason – I mean without any other reason than the dissatisfaction of the "Holy Office" and its scribes of the papal court – he is working for the suspicions and the lies which falsely burden us.' Congar's conclusion is: 'It is the system and the lies inherent in it which one must utterly reject' (*Journal*, 23 March 1954).

Would I myself have made other decisions about my career had Congar told me what at that time he was entrusting only to his *Journal*? The danger of such unconditional obedience, even contrary to one's own conscience, had already become painfully clear to me previously, and I have formed my own opinion about this. Faith is not submission to a human authority, but unconditional trust in God himself.

Submissive in the spirit of obedience

De Lubac and the Jesuits have outwardly submitted to church authority – and are silent. The church is *'quand-même notre Mère* – nevertheless our mother', de Lubac will say to me by way of rebuke during the Council, under the dome of St Peter's after I have given my first critical lecture on 'Truthfulness in the Church'. Yves Congar and the Dominicans have also submitted outwardly to the authority of the church – and are silent. To this degree it is incorrect in the year 2000 to praise Yves Congar's quite private *Journal* of the years 1946–56 as 'La révolte d'un théologien'. In the 1950s it can triumphantly be proclaimed in Rome that all French priests and theologians had 'submitted' in the spirit of obedience: *'Humiliter se subiecerunt* – they have humbly submitted' is the traditional formula. All? Apart from 40 (out of 90) worker-priests, who refuse to give up factory work and submit! Nothing more has been heard of them. *Damnatio memoriae*. Their names are forgotten. Will someone perhaps write their story one day?

In the midst of the controversies over the worker-priests, on 5 November 1953 the three French cardinals Feltin (Suhard's successor in Paris), Gerlier (Lyons) and Liénart (Lille) fly to Rome to intervene personally with Pius XII. With no success. Three years later in Paris at a small dinner to which I am invited by the open Monsignor Lalande, head of 'Pax Christi' and former secretary of Cardinal Suhard, I have the opportunity to ask Cardinal Pierre Gerlier about this conversation. The Primate of Gaul thinks that the pope could not be convinced. At the end he apparently said, '*Ma conscience de pape m'oblige d'agir ainsi* – my conscience as pope obliges me to act like this.' And now, turning towards me, Cardinal Gerlier says: '*Et alors, qu'est-ce que vous voulez faire* – what would you have done, *cher Monsieur l'Abbé?*' I shrug my shoulders and am later annoyed with myself that the answer did not occur to me: '*Démissionez, Eminence.*' 'Or even better, '*Résistez!* – Resist.' But '*Résistez*' was the slogan of the French Huguenots against Cardinal Richelieu, and in the face of such an episcopal conscience ('*conscience d'évêque*') and the threatened resignation of the three leaders of the '*Église de France*', would the conscience of this particular pope really have changed?

Even now I don't know. At that point the position of Pius XII, who was as self-confident as he was self-righteous, was still unassailed. Of course people already knew that neither the Italian attack on Albania on Good Friday 1939 nor the outbreak of the Second World War with the German attack on Poland in September 1939, nor the Holocaust, which was already known to the pope in 1942, could lead Papa Pacelli, the 'representative', to issue a public condemnation. After all, Hochhuth's 'tragedy' wouldn't appear until 1963.

The failure of any prophetic protest by totalitarian powers in the face of all the crimes against humanity on the one hand and the authoritarian action by the same pope against the innovators in his own theology and church on the other have fundamentally the same roots: there is an unmistakable affinity between the pope's authoritarian, i.e. anti-Protestant, anti-liberal, anti-socialist, anti-modern, understanding of the church and an authoritarian, i.e. Fascist, understanding of the state. Hence also Pacelli's concordats with Hitler's Germany, Salazar's Portugal and Franco's Spain. Significantly Pius XII once again allowed the nationalistic-fascistoid Action Française (for which democracy is the absolute evil and the monarchy the absolute means of salvation), banned in 1926 by Pius XI, to be revived just a few weeks after his election. But he drops the encyclical against Nazism and antisemitism which his predecessor had already prepared – Gustav Gundlach was one of the three who drafted it. Marshal Pétain's Catholic supporters were recruited from the hard core of Action Française in 1940, while the Catholics in the Resistance (de Gaulle, Bidault, Schuman, Abbé Pierre) often had to appeal to the primacy of their conscience against the hierarchy.

The bad thing about this authoritarian, quasi-fascist understanding of the church is that it is largely supported by the bishops, as Yves Congar already recognized very clearly at the time. For the bishops (who moreover had largely taken the side of Marshal Pétain's regime), the Dominicans are 'a *résistance*, in other words we are the organic force which thinks, which has an independence and which is not content with crying out, whenever the Roman idol (*l'idole romaine*) has spoken, "It is not a man, it is a god who has spoken"' (Acts 12.22: that was how King Herod, who had put on royal apparel and sat on the throne, was celebrated by the people after his speech, before the angel of the Lord struck him because he did not give God the glory, and he yielded up the spirit, devoured by worms).

And Congar continues in his *Journal* of 9 February 1954: 'The bishops have bent over backwards in passiveness and servility: they have an honest, childlike reverence for Rome, even a childish and infantile reverence. For them, this is "the church" . . . In concrete Rome is the pope, the whole system of congregations which appear as if they are this church which Jesus has built on the rock. And it is the "Holy Office". The "Holy Office" in practice rules the church and makes everyone bow down to it through fear or through interventions. It is the supreme Gestapo, unyielding, whose decisions cannot be discussed . . . So the foundation of the debate is a new conception of the church which they want to impose on us, the basis of which is first a reduction of everything to obedience and a relationship between authority and subjects; and secondly a new conception of obedience, of a *"style super jésuitique"*.'

At that time Congar made a dossier on 'papolatry', 'veneration of the pope', from Pius IX to Pius XII. In it there are some fine '*trouvailles*', like the 'three white things' in the Catholic Church: the host, Mary and the pope. Unfortunately this dossier was never published. Congar was finally content to be allowed to settle in Strasbourg at the invitation of the brave Archbishop Weber and there within modest limits even to be able to preach and give lectures again.

'If I could eliminate one person'

In the midst of the great controversies over the worker-priests I go to Fr Gustav Gundlach, with whom as president of the Social Circle I have good personal relations. As Pius XII's social expert he has beyond doubt been informed of the action against the worker-priests. I emphatically tell him that I share his and the pope's repudiation of Stalinist Communism, but can't understand the general action against the worker-priests. The great social scientist, who moreover is a convinced anti-Nazi and had become *persona non grata* in Germany as early as 1934, answers all my arguments irritably. We make hardly any progress in the conversation. 'We could have waited,' I argue. 'On the contrary,' he replies, 'we waited too long; we should have intervened very much earlier.' Finally I play my last trump card: 'Not everyone even in the Vatican thinks as you do, Fr Gundlach.' He is surprised, 'Who doesn't?' 'For example, Monsignor Giovanni Battista Montini in the Secretariat of State!' As though stung by a tarantula, the heavy man brusquely swings his chair round towards his desk, turns his back on me, and exclaims to me over his shoulder in a falsetto voice, as always when he is extremely agitated: 'If I could eliminate one person in the Vatican, it would be that Montini!'

In fact, Ottaviani, Pizzardo and their followers, together with the German Jesuits around Pius, will eliminate Montini the very next year. This man, who by origin and reading cherishes sympathies for French social Catholicism, who has reservations against doctrinaire anti-Communism, and because of his daily contact with the pope has considerable influence, keeps disturbing their circle. For example, on the suggestion of Roncalli, who is nuncio in Paris, Montini places an article praising Cardinal Suhard and the Mission de Paris in the *Osservatore Romano*. So finally, with much praise, he is 'promoted' to Milan as archbishop, but in all Pius's years is never made cardinal: he is promoted in order to be moved away. For one thing is certain: he must never become pope! I will get to know him later as Archbishop of Milan. It is John XXIII who will first bestow the cardinal's purple on him. But Gustav Gundlach has to live to see the one he would have gladly 'eliminated' elected pope. Gundlach is convinced that this is a disaster for the church. He dies two days later.

However, for me the Roman oppression of the worker-priests, whose apostolate was an important element within the wider apostolate of winning back the Christian masses, is a further fundamental demystification of the pope. Of course, as Fr Klein said to me right at the beginning of the controversy, it would have been better to make factory workers priests – on certain conditions – than to make priests factory workers; in the end priesthood is not an 'estate'. But of course this was even further from Pius XII's mind.

On a trip from Tunis to Bône (Hippo, the city of which Augustine was bishop) in Algeria in spring 1955 my fellow Germanicum student Franz Knapp and I, coming from Rome, will meet quite by chance the superior of the Mission de France, Monsignor Louis Augros. He tells us at length about the worker-priests (in 1989 François Leprieur OP presented a moving 'Dossier confidentiel' of almost 800 pages on the condemnation of the Dominicans under the title *Quand Rome condamne*). At any rate their end also marks the definitive end of the *'renouveau catholique'*, that hopeful renewal movement in religion and literature, which in the face of a rigid Roman dogmatism on the right and a positivistic deterministic laicism on the left sought to realize the values of an authentic Catholicity. It is represented at the beginning by such glittering names as Léon Bloy, Charles Péguy and Paul Claudel, then continued by Georges Bernanos and Julien Green, and is finally taken up in another way by the theological *avant-garde* of Jesuits and Dominicans, who are also involved in the resistance, and the Jesuits Chaillet, Fessard and de Lubac with the underground journal *Témoignage chrétien*.

Since I move to Paris barely two years after the suppression of the worker-priests, of this great generation I can hear in public only the voice of François Mauriac (who is strongly attacked). After his fight against Franco and Vichy he has become a supporter of de Gaulle and in 1952 has been awarded the Nobel Prize for literature. Rome's intervention is also a tragedy for French theology, which previously had been so lively, from which it will never recover. The whole biblical, patristic, pastoral, ecumenical renewal is affected by it. Since the nineteenth century, in the German-speaking world, too, a brake has constantly been applied by Rome, but in the French sphere this renewal has been totally blocked, if not definitively stopped. *'Quand-même notre Mère?'* No pope and no episcopate has yet said a *'mea culpa'* about this.

'Going my way': critical Catholicity

In the early 1950s, *Going My Way* is a famous film in which Bing Crosby, at that time the most popular American entertainer, plays a young chaplain who 'goes his way' even in the face of the resistance of his conservative priest, joyful and resolute. We are also shown this film in the Germanicum; years later in connection with a lecture I will be visiting the Bing Crosby Museum in his home town of Spokane in Washington state. Now 'going my way' has also become something of a maxim for me. I am by no means shaken in my loyalty to the Catholic Church, nor have I ever felt the temptation to join another church. But I have become critical of the mediaeval anti-modern Roman system in Rome, as a Roman insider. The reader now certainly needs to know that it is Catholic Rome which has made me a Catholic who is critical of Rome.

Before we are ordained to the subdiaconate on 3 April 1954 and commit ourselves to celibacy, by tradition we have to put on a farewell theatrical performance on Shrove Tuesday. This time our choice falls on the comedy *The Nephew as Uncle* by the French playwright Louis Picard, translated and revised by Schiller. Why always be so serious? I thoroughly enjoy the main role in this cheerful play of mistaken identity in the style of Molière, wearing French uniform and a wig. Eighteen months previously, however, I allowed myself somewhat against my will to be pressed into the modern production of a Christmas play, Karl Kramer's *The Gate of Grace*: in a dinner jacket I played the role of the Minister of the Interior in the service of King Herod. I regretted having to spare the time. Be this as it may, there is great applause for both plays and a cheerful backstage celebration by the theatre group until after midnight, which by now has become a tradition.

We from the Germanicum also visit performances at other colleges. We are enthusiastic, for example, about a production of Patrick Hamilton's *Gaslight* in the North American College, in which my friend Robert Trisco plays the main role very convincingly. A little later we go to T. S. Eliot's *Murder in the Cathedral* in Spanish in the Latin American College. It is evident that we have many kinds of international exchange, whether this is in the theatre or in sport (football in San Pastore), in the ecumenical circle or in the breaks at the Gregorian, or with students, professors or visitors, not only in our multi-national college but also outside it.

Through passing by and visiting the historic places of ancient, mediaeval and baroque Rome almost daily, and also by visiting museums and of course being taught the theology of the Gregorian with its emphasis on tradition, we live out and experience what I will later call Catholicity in time. Likewise, through study in contact with students, professors and visitors from all over the world, we live out and experience a Catholicity in space. Both distinguish me from the start from the increasingly widespread provincialism and particularism of some Protestant churchmen and theologians, whose horizon is the *Landeskirche* or at best the nation. Why be and remain Catholic? It is a question which I often have to answer later, but I already know the answer to it now: I am and remain Catholic because the whole, universal, comprehensive, Catholic Church is important to me. To the present day it has an ongoing continuity which persists in all the breaks, and a universality of faith and a community of faith which embraces all groups, nations and regions.

But from the beginning, for me this Catholicity is bound up with an orientation on the gospel. With growing experience – crises of obedience, theology, the church and the discovery and preservation of freedom of conscience in the church – this connection becomes increasingly radical. And especially since the controversy over the worker-priests this Catholicity is bound up with the demand for a reform of the church. I am no longer driven to be present in the Sistine Chapel on the day of the pope's coronation on 12 March 1954 as I was two years previously. Rather, on this day, on which there are no lectures, I eagerly read Henri de Lubac's little book on the spiritual sense of scripture. Then I have a conversation with Fr Spiritual on worker-priests and the consequences for seminary training. He thinks the church is built on the sea as well as on the rock.

The next day I then have a long conversation with the Dutch liturgist Herman Schmidt, on which I write brief notes in my Spiritual Journal: 'the most complete agreement over the liturgy and general reform in the church'. The bold articles by the German Jesuit Karl Rahner appearing at this time, which are critical of the church, strengthen me on this way. So already in Rome the foundations are laid for what I later understand by ecumenical. For me this term denotes Catholic breadth and tradition, concentrated on the gospel and church reform – an evangelical Catholicity.

In the grottos of St Peter's

Having been ordained deacon on 9 May 1954, with solemnity and joy I am now preparing for my priestly ordination. Now again there are exercises lasting eight days. Then on the day before ordination there is confession, at which the Spiritual gives me a comforting saying for ordination which stamps itself on my soul when on 10 October 1954 I lie with my face to the floor in the college church: '*In spiritu humilitatis et in animo contrito suscipiamur a te, Domine* – In the spirit of humility and with a contrite heart may we find acceptance with you, Lord.' I am moved: I have reached my goal.

In college, ordination to the priesthood is always the great event of the year: my parents, my brother and my five sisters have also come to Rome. I am happy, and we are all radiant together in the photograph taken in the college courtyard. On this day, after the service, now, as an exception, the ladies – I am very proud of my family – may come to the celebratory lunch in the refectory.

The next day each of the sixteen new priests celebrates his first mass in the church of his choice. Deep disillusionment over Pius XII has not affected my loyalty to the office of Peter in the church: I celebrate my first eucharist in the grottos of St Peter's, in the crypt under Bernini's Confessio, at what is presumed to be the tomb of the apostle Peter, though this has by no means been proved (according to assured early evidence Peter had been executed in Rome as a martyr). In this simple, silent space I can celebrate with complete concentration and without pomp my first 'mass', or better 'eucharist or thanksgiving', in remembrance of the last supper and self-surrender of our Lord. I celebrate with my family and a few friends, in the presence of my 'spiritual father' Franz Xaver Kaufmann, with my Sursee friend Otto Wüst as master of ceremonies. The Benedictine Fr Günthör is the preacher, representing Prime Abbot Kälin, who is prevented from coming at the last moment.

The joy is marred by a little incident that I hear about only after the celebration: going to the Vatican in the bus my brother Georg, who is 22, has a fainting fit. We are all convinced that he is over-tired and exhausted, and that it isn't to be taken seriously. But after three weeks recuperating with our friends in Ferrara, Georg is taken to Zurich to a world authority on brain surgery, Professor Krähenbühl. The diagnosis is a brain tumour between the cerebellum and the brain stem, inoperable. Visits to hospital with radiotherapy and chemotherapy follow – all in vain. He had always been so bursting with strength and life, and his work in banks in Sursee and Paris had been the best possible preparation for taking over our father's business. But now he is discharged as incurable. His state steadily deteriorates. One limb after another, one organ after another, refuses to work. It is a fearfully slow process of dying: an increasing burden on heart, circulation and breathing, lasting for weeks – though his consciousness always remains clear. Then finally there are days of gasping for breath until finally – almost a year to the day after the first attack – he chokes on the rising fluid in his lungs. As a motto for my brother's funeral notice I have chosen a saying from the book of Wisdom (4.13): 'Being perfected in a short time, he fulfilled long years.'

And yet: did this have to be? Is this death really 'given by God', 'ordained by God'? That is what I ask myself. No, people needn't accept all this to the end as 'God-given', 'willed by God', 'pleasing to God', 'in submission to God'. This conviction will grow stronger over the decades, so that finally with my Tübingen friend and colleague Walter Jens, in a series of lectures entitled 'A Dignified Dying' in the Studium Generale of the University of Tübingen I will make 'A Plea for Personal Responsibility'.

On the card marking my first mass in Rome 1954 (and also the card for my festal first mass at home the next year in Sursee) I have printed a sentence from the Letter to the Colossians: 'Pray for me also, that God may open to me a door for the word, to declare the mystery of Christ.' I can have no inkling in what an unexpected way this prayer will be fulfilled. I not only celebrate my first eucharist but also give my first sermon in the Vatican, at the Sunday service of the papal Swiss guard. The guards, along with their Colonel Pfyffer von Altishofen and Major von Balthasar, brother of Hans Urs, all from Lucerne, listen as a new priest makes a point to them on the feast of Christ the King. They have recently had to escort more ex-kings than usual to the pope, and they could read from Christ the crucified king the Christian reversal of all values. The monarchy of Christ means democracy (1 Peter 1.9: 'You are a royal priesthood') and ruling in Christ's kingdom means serving ('let the highest be the servant of all'). These are unaccustomed tones in the Vatican. But I mean it seriously.

Servants' chaplain

After my early 'career' in the college hierarchy – beadle of the first year, beadle of the philosophy group, president of the Social Circle, my work for the newsletter and my regular survey of the newspapers, read in the refectory, perhaps other 'higher' college offices would have been open to me. But only those who are absolutely enthused with liturgy and are born to 'higher things' – in my time Lajos Kada (later nuncio), Adalbert Kurzeja (later Abbot of Maria Laach) and Friedrich Wetter (later Archbishop and Cardinal of Munich) – become 'senior master of ceremonies'. And only those who toe the line are considered for the office of 'prefect' of the philosophy and theology groups.

But such honours are still not the goal of my longing. I think that I am remaining true to my original calling when as early as 9 November 1952 I offer to lead the prayer for the 'servants' mass', the utterly traditional Sunday worship of the Italian staff, who are called *'famigliari'* or 'servants'. I've always felt a natural sympathy for the Italians in the house and like speaking Italian with them. I've long preferred the short Italian *missa* with its melodious hymns to the stiff German or Latin college service. There I can now give the liturgical readings, rehearse hymns and say prayers. So I already exercise this little 'pastoral' service.

What is more natural than that after my ordination to the priesthood I should be appointed the 'servants' chaplain' (*'capellano dei famigliari'*). At my side is my friend Oswald Loretz from Vorarlberg, who is now concentrating wholly on Old Testament exegesis; he constantly visits the Pontifical Biblical Institute and communicates to me something of modern biblical criticism, though I can make only very basic use of this in my Italian catecheses on the first chapters of the Bible for our servants. At his wish, at the same time I am preparing with him the hundred theses for the licentiate in theology, mostly on the terrace of the seventh floor where we now live. With a few exceptions, like those on predestination and the freedom of the will, these hundred theological theses are less difficult than the hundred philosophical theses. But instead there is much more ballast for the memory: all the texts from the Bible, councils, church fathers, papal declarations, and all of it in Latin.

But now again I take the written and oral examinations contented and, to the annoyance of my contemporary André Lesch from Luxembourg, quite relaxed. With great effort I have now got through the mountains of material, and taking a matter-of-fact view I can hardly fail. So why not be cheerful? And I come out of it all most successfully. However, our repetitor Peter Gumpel doesn't at all like my 220-page licentiate thesis on the doctrine of justification in Karl Barth (and the Council of Trent), which I shall be discussing later. It's quite incomprehensible, he tells me, that a student should tackle such a large-scale theological synthesis. But at the Gregorian, as we shall see, they cannot be dissuaded from a good opinion of my work by one Fr Gumpel.

Fr Gumpel, who is predestined to become a professor at the Gregorian, will later deliberately be delegated by his superiors to work on processes of canonization and beatification. For in the meantime, along with the new Jesuit General, the Spaniard Pedro Arrupe, a new German assistant has also been chosen; Fr van Gestel, Gumpel's patron, has made himself so unpopular in his Dutch home province that no one wants him, and there is nothing left for him but to await his death, soon forgotten, in an insignificant little Roman college. However, in the year 2000, to my surprise I shall read the name of Fr Gumpel in the newspaper: he is defending, vainly, as 'postulator', the canonization of Pius XII, and in so doing is attacking the Jews who criticize Pius. This leads to the indefinite postponement of the process of the canonization of Pius XII – unfortunately in favour of the considerably 'worse' Pius IX. Here Gumpel should have listened to Pius XII's closest collaborator (with Madre Pasqualina Lehnert), Fr Leiber, as our community did: 'No, Pius XII is not a saint. He is a great man of the church.'

An uncomfortable memorandum

I had planned to spend my seventh and last year in Rome without any tiresome controversies over discipline and obedience, nature and grace, pope and church – in seclusion concentrating on the study of Karl Barth's monumental *Church Dogmatics* and the theses for the theological licentiate. In addition there is my pastoral work in the service of our 'servants', which is quite time-consuming: a sermon in Italian every other Sunday, and also the Bible catecheses on the creation of the world and human beings, temptation and fall. But the more I grow into this task and hear the complaints of our *famigliari*, the more strongly I feel that I must do more for them than engage in worship and catechesis. Or am I to shirk my responsibility for the sake of my own rest and convenience?

Our 'servants' are complaining about three things: first, about the low wages (which are by no means enough to keep a family on); secondly, about the ban on marriage (anyone who wants to marry must leave the college); and thirdly, about

the inadequate accommodation. We could in fact see how those who had previously been living usually two or three to a room were now put up by the dozen
in the former college tailor's shop: cells with partitions and curtains the height of a
person, with a view of a back courtyard and bad ventilation. Whenever I go there
for catechesis, I first always open the window.

I've considered this for long enough. One day I go to my fellow chaplain
Loretz in the next room: 'If we aren't to fail in our first pastoral task we must do
something for the poor wretches.' He agrees that I should draft a memorandum
to give to the Rector. I do so in the systematic and thorough way that I've
learned at the Gregorian: on perhaps fourteen closely written sheets of typing
paper (I was glad to see them in the college archive in 2002), on the basis of papal
social encyclicals and moral textbooks, I set out the moral principles relating to a
fair wage, respectable accommodation and the right to marry. From them I derive
irrefutably clear, concrete demands, with even an appendix on the financial
consequences for the college.

With a foreboding that this memorandum may lead to an unpleasant confrontation, I also ask our two predecessors, Bernhard Lammers and Alois Wagner,
to read and sign the memorandum. They do so without delay, so that the
memorandum now goes to the Rector, Franz von Tattenbach, with four signatures. Soon all four of us are summoned to him. He has obviously taken great
offence at our document. In fact he is in a by no means simple situation: having
got himself a Mercedes, he can hardly claim that there are no funds in the college
for social measures. Nevertheless he attempts to attack the memorandum in every
way, and in the process the man who is usually so friendly gets increasingly angry.
The situation becomes unpleasant. To begin with all four of us keep answering
him, then two, then only me.

Tattenbach vigorously criticizes the figures: 'All academic!' For example, the
use of electricity and water and suchlike hasn't been included in the calculations.
But I counter this courteously by referring to the relevant note, where these costs
are clearly taken into account. My figures are in fact firm and beyond dispute. For
– and this is something that I cannot tell the Fr Rector at this point – in order to
avoid unrealistic proposals which could be an intolerable burden on the college
finances, I have previously sent my memorandum to the Jesuit brother Johann
Kaufmann, a Swiss from St Gallen, who for years has been responsible for the
complex bookkeeping of the college and the college properties. He is an
unselfish, shrewd and fair man, whom along with the head chef, Br Dankl, I
would have postulated for canonization in preference to Pius XII and indeed Pius
IX, even without any miracles. When I have given him an assurance of con-
fidentiality, he has provided me with the necessary figures. Now even the Rector
cannot object to them, and this makes him even more angry, though he is
otherwise so friendly. For the first time in my life I see physically that the phrase
'eyes on sticks' has a very real sense: when a person is angry, his eyes can come
out so far that they really do seem to be hanging on sticks.

After perhaps an hour we are dismissed with a bad grace. I had fought and stood my ground to the end, ultimately all alone. But when I get back to my room and am all by myself, I am at the end of my strength. I lie in my cassock on the bed and weep – I don't know how long for. After the great dispute over obedience and college discipline, and then the even greater dispute over theology and truth, now there is this most vigorous dispute of all, over justice and fairness. Was this my seventh year in Rome, which I wanted to spend as quietly as possible? I feel exhausted, worn out, totally frustrated.

I'm not ashamed of my tears. I note only almost five decades later how almost at the same time another theologian felt isolated and frustrated to a considerably greater degree. This was no less than Yves Congar, who meanwhile had entered a further phase of his banishment from Rome, in Cambridge. On 5-7 September 1956 he wrote: 'Here I have endured an unfathomable feeling of emptiness and absence. No one. Nothing. Certainly the weather is also to blame . . . Caught in the rain outside and waiting under a tree for it to clear up, I begin to weep bitterly. Will I always be a *"pauvre type"*? All alone, will I be endlessly carrying suitcases around everywhere? Will I always be without anyone and anything, like an orphan? *"Dominus autem assumpsit"* (Ps. 18.17: But the Lord took me, he drew me out of many waters, he delivered me from my strong enemy, and from those who hated me . . .): these tears, will not God hear them? Will he not prove to be a Father? I weep for such a long time, perhaps an hour, and then again repeatedly, as at the end of the month of July (1956) and above all on the 25th and 26th in view of the evidence that has now forced itself home on me that I have wasted my life and do not know to what curse I am exposed.'

But no, I am far from being so alone. I have a future in Switzerland. I will not be remaining in Rome, and the hour of farewell is drawing nearer. A few days later Fr von Tattenbach comes to my room: 'I see that you're in a bad way, Herr Küng.' My answer is brief: 'Yes, I'm in a bad way, Fr Rector.' Would I like to go to San Pastore with Loretz for a couple of weeks to recuperate and continue to prepare further for my licentiate there? I immediately accept this offer. But it doesn't restore the peace. As long as I am at college, not a single one of our demands for our *famigliari* is met. *Tant pis*, I think.

Farewell to Rome

I have done well in the theological licentiate, and now the time to say goodbye has at last come. But there is no further discussion with the Rector. That's it. My Spiritual Wilhelm Klein had already said to me some time ago, 'It's no bad thing if you like the college less and less. That's normal: after all, you aren't going to be working in the college, but outside in the world.' I say goodbye with particular nostalgia to this man, already 66, but who is to live to be almost 106 with all his mental powers intact. I shall visit him once or twice in Rome, and two or three times later in Bonn, where he influences countless people as a spiritual adviser. On his hundreth birthday I will dedicate my writings on *Reforming the Church Today*, published originally under the title 'Keeping Hope Alive' (the subtitle to the English edition), 'in ever warm gratitude' to this man who taught me to do just that.

In the afternoon I go to the Gregorian for the last time, to say goodbye above all to Gustav Gundlach. After I have assured him, as I have already reported, that I've learned all there is to be learned in Rome, he gladly lets me go to Paris. But I can't bite back the observation that in college at least the Rector is very happy that I'm finally saying *'addio'*. No, Fr Gundlach thinks, that's too black a view of things; it certainly isn't the case – and he takes leave of me warmly with all good wishes. He will also mention me on his seventieth birthday as one of the presidents of the Social Circle, as he writes to me: 'Don't underestimate this, too, among your laurels.'

In order to avoid further discussion I go to Franz von Tattenbach only on the eve of my departure, at the very last moment, at 20.50, ten minutes before the *silentium religiosum*: 'Please sit down,' he says in a friendly way. 'No, Fr Rector, it's late, and I've still to finish packing.' But he presses me, until in the end I sit down in front of the very desk at which I had to defend myself to his predecessor Vorspel over my relationship to God and then to him, first over the ban on the dogmatic circle and finally over the social situation of the servants. My only thought is, 'What now?'

'I have to tell you, Herr Küng,' says Fr von Tattenbach gently, 'you were right!' I'm quite perplexed: 'Your insight comes a bit late, Fr Rector!' Again he says, 'Yes, it comes a bit late, and I regret that too.' With this introduction we now begin a discussion about the college and about our theological controversies, in which I can put much right and explain and defend the standpoint of my friends. It goes on for three full hours, long past midnight. How different might things have been if a conversation in the same spirit of openness had taken place a year or more earlier! So finally I also say goodbye to my third Rector, in peace and friendship. I don't want any enmities.

He wants to leave aside the question of the servants. Yet hardly will I have got home when reforms will be set in motion and the situation of the *famigliari* will be improved. Dario and Silvano are allowed to marry and have a family. Every time the old servants' chaplain returns to his old college they greet him with shining eyes.

A brief postlude

Now the first guest in my house in Tübingen when almost exactly five years later in 1960 I have established myself there as a young Ordinarius Professor of Fundamental Theology will be none other than Fr von Tattenbach. It is quite by chance. He comes to Tübingen and I invite him to lunch. We have a vigorous conversation. Later I listen with amazement as he tells me that now, in his sixties, he wants to transfer his activity to Central America, in order to help to improve the literacy of the Indios in Costa Rica, and then also in Honduras and Guatemala, with the help of an Institute for Adult Education (ICER), a radio school and several assistants. This is almost like a 'holy experiment' in microcosm, for which he raises considerable funds in Europe.

We will meet later in Guatemala City, and a few more times in Tübingen, before his death in 1992. In his work of teaching, upbringing and education he is concerned with the Indios in their natural environment and their adult culture, seeking to preserve their humanity in the face of external economic, social and cultural threats. In contrast to Paolo Freire, the great pioneer of educational work in Latin America, he works for education towards independent action in politics and society without a Marxist background. I shall report later Tattenbach's comforting reaction to the church's withdrawal of my licence to teach.

The brothers sing a powerful polyphonic threefold *'Vale in Domino'* in the refectory, also to 'our self-taught Hans Küng', as the farewell song comments in connection with my absenteeism from lectures and my special studies. I have the good feeling that I've withstood the seven difficult years in Rome with honour, and through all the crises have prepared for my later task with strengthened self-confidence and self-discipline. No, I shall never regret my seven years in Rome. I have preserved and deepened my freedom: an inherited civic freedom has become an acquired freedom of conscience.

I have changed completely and yet remained the same, unbowed and upright. I am cosmopolitan as a result of all the many contacts, journeys and languages, and yet I have remained rooted in my Swiss homeland. And so I look forward indescribably to my little town, my lake, my family, my friends.

IV

The Freedom of a Christian

'So, then, like Noah I look forth from the window of my ark
and salute your book as another clear omen
that the flood tide of those days
when Catholic and Protestant theologians
would talk only against one another polemically
or with one another in a spirit of noncommittal pacifism,
but preferably not at all
– that flood tide is, if not entirely abated,
at least definitely receding.'

Karl Barth

In search of a topic

'STRATEGIC thinking', if one wants to use so lofty a term and mean by it long-term and purposeful planning, came naturally to me from an early stage: studying theology and going to Rome was likewise an early decision, which then determined everything else, like my plan now to move to Paris and do my doctorate in theology there. Not only in grammar school but also in Rome people had often said to us, '*Quidquid agis, prudenter agas et respice finem –* Whatever you do, do wisely and think about the end.'

However, under the impact of the summer course on the social sciences given by Professors Johannes Hirschmann and Hermann Josef Wallraff, and of course also Gustav Gundlach, I seriously considered whether I should not do my doctorate in the social sciences. Gundlach advises me to go to the University of Münster in Westphalia. There the Germanicum alumnus Joseph Höffner, as Professor of Christian Social Teaching in the Catholic theological faculty, is head of a great institute for Christian social sciences. For example the highly-gifted Willy Weber from the Sauerland, two years ahead of me at the Germanicum and likewise a regular member of our Social Circle, is going there. When Höffner becomes Bishop of Münster in 1952, Weber is seen as his successor to the chair and to the institute. Likewise the Bavarian Anton Rauscher, who to our amusement regards himself as a second Gundlach and finally after some toing and froing through Münster becomes Professor – now very conservative – of

Christian Social Teaching at the University of Augsburg and adviser to the German Episcopal Conference.

But I am finally drawn to theology and – to Paris. Early careful planning and of course consistent work mean that my doctoral dissertation is already finished even before I begin the five compulsory special courses in Paris, in Old and New Testament, patristics, modern history and dogmatics. There is no witchcraft about it; but it is possible only on the basis of a clear scheme of the overall context and indefatigably getting down to detail every day. Often in the summer I get up as early as 4.30 a.m. and meditate alone, walking up and down the ninth-floor terrace. Colleagues who are accustomed to a different tempo will later often be amazed how an individual can write such books in a relatively short time and will sometimes attribute this – perhaps in order to excuse themselves – to the help of assistants. However, I have written not only my dissertation but all my very first books without assistance; what the help, correction and human support of good assistants mean to me will only become clear later.

'Focused', however, doesn't mean dogged, nor does 'planned' mean compulsive. As early as 3 November 1952 I outline my plan to my Spiritual (and only six months later, when everything has been worked out, to the Rector): after my theological licentiate in the autumn of 1955 I want to move to Paris. The Rector thinks that this is a good thing; however, he convinces me that I should do my dissertation not on the theology of history (I had given a well-received trial sermon on this particular subject), but on the theology of my fellow-countryman Karl Barth.

That same November 1952 I write to the Institut Catholique, the Catholic University of Paris, which since the separation of church and state has only a theological faculty, and ask for information. At the same time I prepare myself for the conversation with the Professor of Dogmatics, Guy de Broglie SJ, who teaches for a semester at both the Gregorian and the Institut Catholique, by reading his book on the ultimate goal in life (*De fine ultimo vitae humanae*). De Broglie is a cousin of the Nobel prize-winner for physics, and a member of the Paris high aristocracy. Josef Fischer, who also wants to embark on the Paris adventure, and I visit him at the Gregorian on 1 December 1952. He receives us in a friendly way and promises us help, but refers me to his fellow-Jesuit Henri Bouillard, who has already been working on a major study of Karl Barth for a long time. After lengthy consideration I write to him. Fr Bouillard replies, and proposes as a provisional topic 'The Nature of the Church in Karl Barth'. Because he too has been banned from teaching since the encyclical *Humani generis* (1950), at the same time he refers me to the Oratorian Louis Bouyer, a convert from Lutheranism and an outstanding expert in Christian spirituality, who as Professor at the Institut Catholique could supervise my dissertation as *'directeur de thèse'*. I write to him at the beginning of February, but only in April 1954 do I receive the letter in which he accepts me as a doctoral student.

That same month, Josef Fischer and I ask our Bishop of Basle, Franziskus von

Streng, under whose jurisdiction we now are, for permission to go to Paris. The 'gracious lord' (this is the courteous and ceremonial form of address to a bishop, even in Switzerland) allows this, on the one condition that we will be finished in two years at the latest. No problem for me. At the end of April I write to Professors de Broglie, Bouyer and Bouillard that everything is now in order.

Some time later, with Josef Fischer I visit Fr Jean Daniélou SJ, in the editorial offices of the Roman Jesuit journal *Civiltà Cattolica*, which are near the college; with Fr de Lubac he is editing the great scholarly series of the church fathers, 'Sources chrétiennes'. We had previously heard a quite harmless lecture on 'The Virgin Mary in the Spirituality of France' from this theologian, who was likewise suspected of the *'nouvelle théologie'*, but now is manifestly steering clear of 'innovations'. Daniélou agrees that Fischer should choose as the topic of his dissertation 'The Mystery of the Christian in the Greek Church Father Gregory of Nyssa'. However, my friend will later drop this difficult topic in favour of a historical investigation of the various concepts of reform in Cardinals Reginald Pole and Gianpietro Caraffa at the beginning of the Counter-Reformation. I shall be returning later to this topic, which at first sight seems antiquarian, but in reality has extremely important consequences.

Now study of Barth begins seriously for me. I start with the shorter writings, especially on church and theology, and of course read some of Barth's famous *Epistle to the Romans*, but then begin on selected chapters of the monumental *Church Dogmatics,* of which there are already ten volumes (for example, on the natural knowledge of God), as far as this is possible alongside my preparations for the examination (and studies on the biological theory of evolution). At the same time I make an intensive study of key works on the Catholic reception of Barth so far: whereas I find Hans Urs von Balthasar's interpretation masterly, the work of the Dominican Fr Jérôme Hamer, who attempts to accuse Barth of 'occasionalism', seems to me to be scholastically prejudiced. Of course I could have no inkling of the role that this Fr Hamer was later to play in my life.

The master of a lay order: Hans Urs von Balthasar

On my second home leave at the beginning of July 1953 I get to know Hans Urs von Balthasar personally for the first time. Born in 1905, he comes from one of those Lucerne patrician families which had either founded or upgraded their 'aristocracy' mostly through mercenary service or providing mercenaries for the French (his brother is a major in the Vatican Swiss Guard). But unlike me, he preferred the monastic school of the Benedictines in Engelberg and the Jesuit college in Feldkirch to the state grammar school in Lucerne. After studies in Vienna, Berlin and Zurich (where he gained his doctorate), the Ignatian exercises of 1927 became his key experience. He entered the Jesuit order and engaged in theological studies. In Munich he was above all the pupil of the philosopher of religion Erich Przywara SJ and then spent four years in Lyons under Henri de Lubac SJ, unfortunately without ever studying historical-critical exegesis. Since 1940 he has been a student chaplain and author in Basle. There he got to know the doctor and convert Adrienne von Speyr, wife of the Basle historian Professor Kägi, and felt called with his spiritual friend to found a lay order ('secular institute'). In 1950 this led to a break with the Jesuit order. Consequently at the end of the 1950s his call to the Tübingen chair which I was eventually to get was blocked.

Balthasar is a man with a comprehensive education, at home in both Platonism and the Greek church fathers. He is able to combine theology with classical literature in order to explain the Christian truth in a philosophical and aesthetic perspective through individual Christian figures and currents in the history of ideas. Moreover he is a master of the German language, a sensitive translator from the French (Claudel!) and the Spanish (Calderon, Loyola!), and an indefatigable editor above all of volumes of mysticism and theology, both whole works and selections (these include works by Adrienne von Speyr and his teacher Przywara). I am impressed by his rich library, in which the great theologians, philosophers and poets have peacefully found a place side by side – a model for my own library, which is now slowly beginning to take shape, and on which I spare no expense.

In his home in Basle – he lives in the Kägi's house at Münsterplatz 5 – we talk intensely about Karl Barth's theology, which he knows better than any Catholic. He shows me the great pile of the manuscript of Henri Bouillard's Barth book. But in human terms the tall man in the Roman collar seems intellectually distanced, and the atmosphere between us is somewhat cool. Balthasar, not particularly popular among the Swiss clergy because of his aristocratic bearing, presumably finds me all too self-confidently middle class. Stimulating and friendly as our conversations are and will be in the future, I don't particularly warm to him. Certainly he will always address me as 'dear friend' – usually on succinct postcards in beautiful, elegant handwriting. But I never felt the desire to open my heart to him in a friendly way. 'I get shivers down my spine when Balthasar talks of love,' I hear a young lady say after one of Balthasar's sermons in the Hofkirche in Lucerne. She is certainly exaggerating, but this is an understandable reaction to the intellectual stylizing of this man in conduct, speaking and writing.

We talk not only about theology but also about Balthasar's plans for a lay order, which have already made progress among a group of women. However, things aren't going well with the men envisaged, young academics, a leading figure among whom is my cousin, the lawyer and state advocate Walter Gut, who accompanies me to Basle. A year later, on 7 May 1954, Balthasar writes: 'Even now I am anxious about the day when I am no longer physically up to the task and when I fear that I shall look round in vain for help from the ranks of the clergy. Even in a movement and group of laity there is so much that only the priest can do – and the more zealous the people are, the more demands they make.' That this master of a budding lay order was nevertheless not prepared to give his association of men some form of legal constitution was connected with something else that was more important to him.

Only very much later do I learn how fascinated Hans Urs von Balthasar was by the figure of the high-priestly poet Stefan George, founder of a 'new alliance' of mythical aristocrats, remote from politics. Balthasar had come across George in his studies in Munich, and beyond doubt regarded George's literary circle as a model for his own. Certainly in him the aesthetic narcissism and the almost sacral veneration of his person are broken by the basic Christian attitude. But he too expects unconditional obedience from his pupils, whom – as the Swiss writer Kuno Raeber, for a long time a member of this circle, reports – he attracted in an almost magical way. Balthasar is said once to have remarked to him, 'Perhaps I am a boa constrictor', a snake which encircles its victim with its own body and squeezes it before eating it . . . At any rate he later ungraciously drops my cousin, who has proved loyal to him, when after long years he has got to know and has married his wife, with the argument that the problem of his loyal follower is not loneliness or love of his wife, but obedience. And obedience is more important to the master of the order than human relations and legal rules for his association.

Presumably at a very early stage Balthasar senses how little I am prepared to surrender the freedom I was given at home and struggled for hard enough in Rome in favour of such a personality cult and obedience to the master of an order. And the fact that because of my own career in the end I cannot commit myself to these 'plans and ideas' of a lay order will later contribute to the alienation between Balthasar and me. Even more probably, another factor will be the way in which I completely ignore the mysticism of Adrienne von Speyr. Balthasar gives me several of her more than 30 books, but much as I value his own, I cannot make anything of the freely expressed floods of thought of his soul-friend, convert and anti-Protestant, which are noted down by Balthasar at her bedside.

So I never express a desire to get to know her, although she lives in the same house as Balthasar. What am I to talk to her about? But Balthasar regards her as the greatest mystic of the century: at the age of six this Protestant girl already experienced an appearance of Ignatius of Loyola and later of the mother of God accompanied by angels! On her instructions he leaves the Jesuit order, notes down all her mystical discourses most carefully and then goes on to edit them – with much difficulty, as he complains more than once. He will even devote an admiring biography to her (*First Glance at Adrienne von Speyr*, 1968). It leads Joseph Ratzinger to remark to me in our time together at Tübingen that now all is 'up with Balthasar'. However, this won't prevent the two from later making a pragmatic alliance in church politics.

Why Karl Barth?

A few days after the conversation in Basle, on 10 July 1953, I am in Paris with Henri Bouillard. It's difficult to make personal contact with him. He thaws out only when I openly formulate my criticism of certain Gregorian theses on nature and grace. He doesn't seem to have changed his views despite the encyclical *Humani generis* and finally asks me: 'Would you say that you find de Lubac's *Surnaturel* more enlightening than the theses of the Gregorian?' When I say yes to this, I can talk better with him about my Barth dissertation. He now proposes three topics to me: 1. Justification of the sinner; 2. Man as the image of God; 3. Christian ethics. Bouillard reckons that his own book will appear in two years, in 1955, the year in which I will definitely come to Paris.

My future doctoral supervisor Louis Bouyer is returning from the USA just at that time and I only meet him on 12 July, shortly before my departure, after two failed attempts. He is now very friendly. As a topic beyond question he prefers justification, which is fine by me, since I have already been working so intensively on the Tridentine decree on justification. He recommends that I read Luther, Calvin and Newman. After a further discussion with Balthasar I am to give him my final decision in September. And that is what happens: the justification of the sinner becomes my theme. And my destiny, as I know after the event.

'Why Karl Barth?' one may ask. Spiritual Klein had already given me a first, purely external argument: Karl Barth is my fellow-countryman and like Balthasar lives in Basle, only an hour's journey from Sursee. At grammar school we had mentioned Karl Barth's name alongside those of C. G. Jung, Arthur Honegger, Le Corbusier, Friedrich Dürrenmatt and Max Frisch when our history teacher asked us who the best-known Swiss were in the world today. Above all the church struggle against the Nazis with Barth at its head had also made him very popular in Switzerland, where since being dismissed from his Bonn chair in November 1934 he had been a professor in Basle, though he did not go along with everything.

But a second argument for me is that this Swiss writes brilliant German. The years of Latin have so corrupted our German that we can hardly express ourselves on theological matters without Latin words, turns of phrase and constructions. Even in everyday language we constantly talk of *per se, per accidens, nego, concedo*. It's a real experience not just to read theological German, like that, say, of Karl Rahner, but theology in good German. In a different way from Balthasar, Karl Barth, too, is a master of language.

But what is most important for my choice of Karl Barth is of course his theology. I know that no Protestant theologian of this century has a greater authority because of his fight against National Socialism, and none has a wider and deeper *oeuvre*, given his inventiveness and his indefatigable work. After his epoch-making *Epistle to the Romans* (1919, completely changed in 1922) and many other writings, since 1932 volume after volume of his *Church Dogmatics* (*CD*) have been published: after the doctrine of the Word of God ('Prolegomena', *CD* I/1-2), three great themes: election (*CD* II/1-2), creation (*CD* III/1-4) and reconciliation (*CD* IV). When I begin to read *Church Dogmatics* IV/1 on my topic (in fact the eleventh volume), I write in my journal: 'simply magnificent'.

What do I find so magnificent about Barth's theology? Not just the conceptual and linguistic power of formulation, but above all the skilful architecture, which reminds me of Thomas Aquinas, though in Barth it is inspired by Calvin's *Institutes* and above all Schleiermacher's *The Christian Faith*. Here there is a thoroughgoing christocentricity which makes possible a new definition of the relationship between faith and knowledge, nature and grace, creation and redemption, of the kind that I have already long desired. And in the light of this radical christological foundation the great connections are rethought in an original way, right down to detail. This is done in three parallel trains of thought (a volume is devoted to each). First the lord as servant (the priestly office of Jesus Christ) – human pride, but justification through faith and the gathering of the community. Then the servant as lord (his royal office) – human lethargy, but sanctification in love and the building up of the community. And finally Jesus as a true witness (his prophetic office) – human lies, but a summons to the hope and mission of the community. After emphasis on the Godness of God, the Wholly Other, transcendence, the infinite qualitative difference between God and all creation in Barth's early years, the affirmation of the humanity of God and man in the light of the incarnation of God in Christ has become important.

I don't visit Karl Barth on my first home leave in 1953, though he lives quite near to Balthasar. I still haven't studied the *Church Dogmatics* enough. What arrogance to visit the famous man without having worked through his *magnum opus*! To the present day I feel an antipathy to explaining to unbriefed visitors (letter-writers, journalists) things about which I have laboriously written a whole book. But returning to Rome from Switzerland in the autumn of 1953, I use the last two years to get to know thoroughly the whole of Barth's work, which is now almost 9000 pages long. It is no effort, but an intellectual delight and a spiritual experience! After all, in this way I can follow Barth's large-scale and through-composed trains of thought, and at the same time gain fundamental information and orientation on the great Christian traditions, especially the Lutheran and the Reformed traditions, and on significant theological controversies of the twentieth century. Barth's *History of Protestant Theology in the Nineteenth Century* and its prehistory helps me here. I am impressed by the way in which Barth's theology, grounded in the biblical witness, constantly feels responsible to history and at the same time energetically and sometimes polemically confronts the present. Its horizon is wide and yet at the same time quite concentrated. This is no Roman theology of theses, which uses scripture only as a quarry. Rather, it is a theology completely steeped in scripture, orientated on the one centre Jesus Christ.

I learn from Balthasar's book on Barth, without which my own work on Barth would have been almost inconceivable, that the Catholic and the Protestant can be reconciled precisely where they are both most consistently themselves. I can agree with Balthasar that precisely because Karl Barth embodies the most consistent construction of Protestant theology, so too he comes closest to Catholic theology: utterly Protestant and orientated on Christ at the centre, and precisely because of that reaching out universally in a Catholic way. Here I recognize the possibility of a new ecumenical theology, in keeping with scripture and the times.

Of course I study not only Barth and not just Catholic authors like Möhler and Newman, but also Barth's great opposite number in Germany, the New Testament scholar Rudolf Bultmann, of whom Barth wrote a critical analysis under the title 'An Attempt to Understand Him'. I read Bultmann's book *Jesus* and parts of his commentary on John. Here I am helped by a long conversation with Bultmann's famous pupil Professor Heinrich Schlier, who, as I shall go on to relate, on the basis of his New Testament research into church and ministry converts to the Catholic faith in our college on 24 October 1953 – to the dismay of the Protestant theologians of Germany and the Bultmann school in particular. Schlier tells me that Barth's and Bultmann's approach to revelation and faith are right, but that with Bultmann it must be noted that everyone, including the theologians, approaches the texts of the Bible with a specific 'pre-understanding'. This is true not least for converts like Schlier (whom I shall see again later in a session of the Inquisition on the side of the Catholic bishops).

I get to know better at a dinner another remarkable convert and his wife: the Protestant pastor Rudolph Goethe, a descendant of the poet. By special permission from Pius XII he is the first Protestant pastor to remain married after his conversion, with full rights and obligations. An honourable and congenial man. But our question is: why are Protestant pastors allowed what is forbidden to Catholics?

A stimulating and annoying result

In this context I now approach Barth's doctrine of the justification of the sinner, having previously already been so intensively occupied with the Tridentine doctrine of justification, and also having worked on other church documents. It is clear to me from the start what is at stake: I have to do with the *articulus stantis et cadentis ecclesiae*, the article of faith by which, according to Luther, the church stands and falls. Thus I am confronted with the fundamental obstacle to an understanding between Catholics and Protestants. I do not venture to hope that I could succeed in going beyond demonstrating a convergence to demonstrating a consensus between Trent and Barth. I am still right at the beginning.

In any case, it seems possible to me to demonstrate a convergence only if I succeed in doing two things. First, making Barth's own intentions and perspectives even clearer without getting lost in the undergrowth of questions. And on the other hand, on the Catholic side rounding up a 'great cloud of witnesses' (Hebrews 12.1) which documents the fact that controversial doctrines like justification 'by faith alone' or the 'at once both righteous and a sinner' are also doctrines put forward in Catholic theology. But how is one to find such witnesses in almost two millennia of the history of theology? That is the adventure I faced, largely left to myself.

I get little encouragement from my professors – most from the Spaniard Juan Alfaro, with his precise arguments, who reads through some of my texts critically. When at San Pastore I once ask another person, the Hungarian Fr Zoltan Alszeghy, an informed younger professor at the Gregorian who is regarded as being open, about possible evidence, he gives me the answer: 'If you find no Catholic witnesses to certain teachings of Barth, then it is a clear sign that Karl Barth is on the wrong track' – not helpful advice. But he doesn't dissuade me from restlessly rummaging through our whole library. Later I will discover witnesses I don't find in Rome in the Bibliothèque Nationale in Paris or in the theological seminar of the University of Freiburg im Breisgau, where after my return north I shall devote several days, from morning to evening, looking for traces, and yet have time for long conversations with my fellow Germanicum student Helmut Riedlinger, now assistant in dogmatics there.

Something that I couldn't have expected to begin with now happens after all: at the end of laborious research and intellectual grappling which finally leads to a thick and detailed manuscript of around 220 pages with much small print, as early as the summer semester of 1955 in Rome I can formulate as the result of my theological licentiate work: 'Generally speaking, in the doctrine of justification there is a fundamental agreement between the teaching of Barth and the teaching of the Catholic Church.' So in the light of this there would be no basis for a schism. Its theological core and basic motive collapse. From both the Catholic and the Protestant side it can be asserted that the justification of man takes place through the grace of God solely on the basis of trusting faith, which is to be active through works of love. I begin to understand what a momentous result for ecumenism I have here in my hands in 1955.

No wonder that, as I have reported, this licentiate work stirs up my former philosophy repetitor and now hyper-orthodox theology repetitor Fr Peter Gumpel tremendously. Can a young man discuss so many themes in a single study that one could almost write a book about every page? I reply that, after all, if one wants to offer an overall solution one must treat all these problems in a wide context. However, he knows better and is firmly convinced that this work must not be accepted by the Gregorian in its present form. But there my licentiate supervisor, Maurizio Flick, Professor of Dogmatics, a delightfully matter-of-fact North Italian who is friendly in a straightforward way, will not be dissuaded from accepting it.

On 9 June 1955 I write, still from Rome, to Karl Barth that I have finished a manuscript on justification in the *Church Dogmatics* which I would very much like to send to him and then discuss with him in Basle. Because of an oversight Barth doesn't reply until 14 July, when a postcard sent to Rome is forwarded to me in Sursee. He says that in his experience it is 'much simpler to talk face to face, even when views are opposed': 'But if the manuscript is legible and not too long, by all means send it to me, and then I will see whether I can say anything to you about it.'

How will the great master react? I will always remember my first telephone call to Basle. I'm surprised when I hear straight away, 'Karl Barth.' In broad Basle German, the first thing he asks me about the manuscript which he has just read is: 'Tell me, are you really old or are you young?' My reply, that I am 27, makes him say: 'In that case something can still come of it.' I am to visit him soon in Basle. I will do that, and this will become the beginning of a great friendship.

'If you want to have praise ...'

But I am still in Rome. Would my licentiate work at the Gregorian also be accepted as a doctoral dissertation? That is more than doubtful. I can't resist the temptation to try it out. Even before I leave Rome I visit the prefect of studies at the Gregorian (no. 2 under the Rector), Fr Charles Boyer SJ, a distinguished specialist on Augustine. He is well known to me from his boring lectures on the doctrine of the Trinity, delivered in a thin voice, and as a friendly moderator of the little ecumenical circle which stands behind the journal *Unitas* in Rome. For all his commitment to France he doesn't deviate an inch from the Roman party line. And the devil prods me to want to know from him in particular what the Gregorian would have made of such a work had I ...

Fr Boyer knows my manuscript and tells me in a friendly way that Fr Flick has certainly given me a very good mark, but my 'method' is very dubious. Why? I have shown too much understanding of the Protestant Barth. I might perhaps have been allowed to show this at the end, but first of all I should have put the completely opposed teachings of Barth and the Catholic Church in confrontation (I recall his gesture of confrontation better than his precise wording). I had also quoted French theologians like Henri de Lubac, Henri Bouillard, Henri Rondet and others who, as I would know, were *personae non gratae* in Rome. A Catholic theologian should at most 'read but not quote' such suspect authors. What he means is clear to me: that *damnatio memoriae*, practised in Rome from antiquity, extinguishing contemporaries from the memory, which counts on the cowardice of colleagues and which was even to threaten me one day. Theologians are banished from the memory by silence and a failure to quote them. And then comes Bouyer's decisive remark: *'Si vous voulez avoir de louange, vous ne devez pas faire comme ça,'* he says in a friendly way: 'If you want to have praise, you mustn't act like this.'

I am struck dumb: I would never have had the idea of writing a particular theology to earn *'louange'*, praise. Isn't theology everywhere first and foremost about the truth? But I understand: that is evidently a criterion, not to say a recipe, for the success of a particular theology with which one can get on in the church. Put in a down-to-earth way, the remark means, 'If you want to have a career, you mustn't act like this.' I innocently ask whether this licentiate work, expanded as a doctoral dissertation, would pass at the Gregorian. 'No, I don't think so,' is the gentle answer. But after all, I remark, I've already had a positive assessor. 'Yes, *cher Monsieur*, you have *an* assessor,' and then laughing, 'but a doctorate needs two.' And I wouldn't find them. So I know where I am and say goodbye, also laughing, with a *'Je vous en remercie infiniment, cher Père.'* After all I had long since decided on Paris – *heureusement*.

Paris: a student's life

Forty-five years later: in the year 2000 I am again sitting in a tiny room in Paris. And I am again writing at a tiny little table, which I have been able to squeeze between the bed and the window to make use of the daylight. Again I see only the wall of the house opposite and not the sky, unless I lean out of the window. In my hotel room I am preparing tomorrow's 'débat' which I am to engage in at the 'Rencontres de la Sorbonne' with Hélène Ahrweiler, for many years Rector of the Sorbonne, and the former French ambassador in Washington, Jacques Andréani, on *'Les temps forts de l'imagination dans l'histoire des hommes'*.

I have again visited the old hallowed halls of this university, which probably has the richest tradition in the world, and which I got to know for the first time 45 years ago. The Amphithéâtre Richelieu with its three big paintings is a reminder that alongside Richelieu, the first practitioner of reasons of state, and Descartes, the first philosopher of autonomous reason, Pascal, too, the great philosopher of the heart, is not to be forgotten: he was the one who drew attention to the significance of the will, of feeling, of the emotions and the passions and thus of the imagination. I begin the debate with these observations and end them with the idea of the global ethic.

The two-star Hotel de la Sorbonne, with a room which at any rate has minimal sanitary facilities, reminds me how at that time as a doctoral student in Paris I got my little room without any washbasin, toilet or wardrobe. An eminent lady in the XVIe arrondissement had gone back overnight on her promise of a fine room because she wanted it for 'my own needs'. The priests of the nearby Spanish national church on the rue de la Pompe take in the homeless Monsieur l'Abbé in the cold November of 1956. But they put him in an unheated small chapel which is no longer used – with a stained-glass Gothic window that won't open, and no view. They never invite him even to breakfast, so the young Abbé often runs round the block to get some warmth. He is therefore glad when after two weeks he finally gets an empty room in the nearby little rue Lekain from a friend of that lady (at her shameless urging). The landlady's daughter is kind enough to carry a

French bedstead through the streets for ten minutes with Monsieur l'Abbé, who has turned up his collar. Then follow a little marble table and a mattress, which only covers half the bedstead. But that's enough for me by myself.

I've always been well looked after, but no one can tell me that I have never experienced a student's life. That was only one of my experiences in post-war Paris with its rented rooms, and I won't dwell on how previously Josef Fischer and I first fled from another room in the rue de Rennes when all the fine promises of the landlady were broken, including the use of her bath; how we then landed at Secours Catholique, at the Caritas in the rue de la Comète; how we were then glad to be in the residence of Pax Christi in the VIIe arrondissement in rue Barbet de Jouy, under the roof of the Archbishop of Paris, which was offered to priests who were studying; how we again shared a room, but with a view over the roofs of Paris, and could work on our dissertations – if not at the Sorbonne, at the 'Catho' (Institut Catholique) or in the national library, though Josef Fischer will only be able to complete his afterwards, in Switzerland.

Of course, from the beginning we enjoy the new freedom: our life in Paris is so totally different from that in Rome. We are vastly amused by the film *Roman Holiday* – soon after our arrival by chance we had hit upon a cinema – in which the captivating Audrey Hepburn as a British princess, in Rome on a state visit, falls in love with an Italian journalist (Gregory Peck is equally unforgettable) and – finally has to forget him.

However, we hardly get to know the frivolous *'Gaités parisiennes'* in the sense of Jacques Offenbach. Still, even now I love the *'gentillesse'*, the kindness and elegance of everyday French forms of behaviour. I can still hear the melodious voice of the baguette seller who greets me every morning in the little bakery with a bright *'Bonjour Monsieur l'Abbé'* (with an emphasis on the final *é*), so that my *'Merci mademoiselle, vous êtes bien gentille'*, comes straight from the heart. It's just the same dealing with the old Madame la Cuisinière in our theologians' residence. Later I will time and again be bewitched by the sparkling *'esprit de finesse'* which can easily become self-ironical, particularly as I get to know it in conversations with publishers and media representatives – quite apart from sophisticated French food.

However, my life as a doctoral student isn't led in the salons of Paris – apart from a dinner at the Swiss embassy and a tea in the Paris town palace of a French fellow student and relation of Fr de Broglie. Granted, I often pass the nearby residence of the Prime Minister on the rue de Varenne and the great and handsome bay windows of the Hotel Lutétia on the Boulevard Raspail, the name of which recalls the little capital of the Celtic Parisii, conquered by the Romans and developed as Lutetia Parisiorum, which is well known to me from the Martyrologium Romanum, read out every day in the refectory of the Germanicum. I would never have dreamed that one day I could live there. I also visit the nearby Bon Marché and other grands magasins only when I urgently need something.

But particularly in this way I get to know the city: much on foot (for example the Invalides, which is nearby, the Eiffel Tower and the Luxembourg Garden), often in the metro and above all on the bus. The almost daily bus rides from the rue de Babylone along the Boulevard St Germain to the Boulevard St Michel and the Sorbonne are unforgettable. Or past the Louvre into the rue Richelieu to the Bibliothèque Nationale, where every morning I first spend an hour going through the giant catalogue, to look out the literature of the day and the bibliographies. Usually standing on the open platform at the back of the bus, I can observe the Parisian public and life and enjoy the fast Paris traffic, where cars seem to me to be standing like greyhounds straining at the leash in front of the red traffic lights on the great boulevards, immediately to leap forward on the green with foot to the floor, hastened on by the elegant flics with their whirling batons.

My enjoyment in the evening, dead tired on my return, immediately before my night shift, is to lie on the bed and read *Le Monde*. For France is in crisis. It is true that the war in Indochina has been ended in 1954 under the government of Mendès-France after the devastating defeat at Dien Bien Phu, and under the Mollet government in 1955 Morocco and Tunisia have been given their independence. But Algérie Française is not to be abandoned, and the war there is coming to a climax, with massacres on both sides. There is a concerted attack by the Algerian underground movement on French colonial power and an army coup in Algiers – a development which finally leads to de Gaulle's presidency and the abandonment of Algeria by France (almost at the same time as that of Egypt by Great Britain).

However, I have seen the Chambre des Députés only from outside. '*C'est où l'on dispute*, that's where they argue,' my Paris friend Philippe Dubost had explained to me disparagingly as early as 1948. The Paris museums are a different matter; they can compete with those of Rome and I likewise already got to know them when I was at grammar school, as I did the great opera house and the Opéra-Comique, to which Rome has nothing comparable to offer. I visit as many performances as I can afford. *Carmen* in the Opéra-Comique or Molière's *L'avare* ('The Miser') in the Comédie-Française remain unforgettable, and in another way the Impressionists in the Jeu de Paume. I concede that for me Paris, as a sphere of life in which the political, administrative, cultural, intellectual and economic activities of the country are concentrated more strongly than in any other major European city, is still the metropolis in which I would most have liked to live permanently – had not my work sent me to a smaller and more pleasant German university town.

As I report, the fascinating period of the *'renouveau catholique'*, which seeks to renew literature from faith, is in any case past in Paris, now that Pius XII has banned the most significant theologians of France from public activity. The great Paul Claudel, whose novel Christian play *Le soulier de satin* ('The Silk Shoe') Balthasar has translated into German and whose *L'annonce faite à Marie* ('The Annunciation') I get to see in the Comédie-Française, dies in February 1955

(Thomas Mann dies a few months afterwards). The debates in the Centre des Intellectuels Catholiques, which I attend, or the famous Lent sermons in Notre Dame, are less and less the great events that they were in former years. But at any rate I can hear the Nobel prize-winner for literature, François Mauriac, in a debate – even with a heavily damaged voice he is a fiery spirit and still critical of the church; with Georges Bernanos he is the most significant French Catholic writer.

The heyday of Jean-Paul Sartre and with him existentialism is also over. For me the Sartre of the 1950s has become quite unimportant. Blind in the left eye, like so many French intellectuals he sympathizes with Communism, and this leads to a break even with friends like Raymond Aron, Albert Camus, André Gide and André Malraux. During these years he travels to the USSR and China – what a mistake for a great intellectual!

But de-Stalinization and the policy of co-existence begin with the Twentieth Party Congress of the Soviet Communist Party and a speech from General Secretary Khrushchev. It has repercussions in Czechoslovakia, Poland and especially Hungary, where there is a desire for real independence from the Soviet Union: in October 1956 there is a popular rebellion. To the dismay of all civilized people it is brutally crushed by Soviet tanks, while France and Great Britain together with Israel are entangled in the unhappy Suez affair until it is stopped by the USA. Only in the face of the Hungarian revolt does Sartre finally engage in criticism of the Communist Soviet Union. I passionately follow all these dramatic events; I cannot simply cut them off from theology.

A defensio *and a little lie*

Conscious of the boldness of my undertaking in the matter of justification, I had already opened the preface to my Roman licentiate thesis of 1955 with a *captatio benevolentiae*:

> Old wine which has settled down after long storage is more enjoyable to drink than young, stormy new wine which has not matured. It would have been better to let this work rest and mature a while until everything in it has become pure, clear and powerful. Above all we would have preferred to sink it even deeper in the fertile earth of Catholic tradition; but further digging must be put off for later. Deadlines are set, and there is also one for the theological licentiate. Young wine also has its good points: above all, it may hope to have allowances made for it.

My doctoral supervisor in Paris, Louis Bouyer, reads the 220 pages of my Roman licentiate thesis and in contrast to Fr Gumpel and in unconscious agreement with Karl Barth thinks that it is a very successful work. He also says that it would be quite sufficient as a doctoral dissertation: I could offer it to the faculty immediately. But my Roman experiences have made me cautious. I tell him that I want to work at least another year on it to increase that 'cloud of witnesses', support my statements from the Bible and the history of theology, and think them through again systematically. Already after my very first fresh manuscript on the Tridentine decree on justification, not only Fr Klein but also Hans Urs von Balthasar had admonished me not 'to theologize with the hammer'. But now I have enough time to present my statements with good evidence and in a differentiated way. I want to hit nails on the head without cutting off my fingers in the process.

But the reaction from Henri Bouillard is quite different from that of Bouyer. Bouillard's book on Barth has still not appeared in the autumn of 1955. He has just handed his work in at the Sorbonne; he has written it as a theologian for a *doctorat ès-lettres*. I innocently ask him whether I may have a look at his manuscript: I want to make my statements agree as closely as possible with his. But he makes excuses and refuses.

Only over time will I observe that this professor, who is about a generation older than me, is jealous of the young doctoral student who returns after two years and already presents a work which can compete with his own, on which he has worked for so many years: not in length (by now Bouillard's work has grown to three volumes each of almost 300 pages), but certainly in content, execution and results. In my way, for all my concentration on the justification of the sinner I have taken into consideration all the problems of Barth's *Dogmatics*: from the significance and activity of Jesus Christ, through creation, sin and death, to justification and sanctification.

I then innocently ask Fr Bouillard on what day the 'defence' (*'defensio'*, *'soutenance'*) of his thesis will take place at the Sorbonne; of course I would very much like to be there. He replies that the date isn't yet fixed and that I may read it in *Le Monde* later, where the date will be published in due time. I still have no suspicions. Shortly afterwards I am at the Dominican college of Le Saulchoir in Étiolles near Paris, where around 150 Dominicans live. There I again meet Jérôme Hamer, who has meanwhile arrived from Rome, and as ever have a lively conversation with him. 'Surely I will be at the defence of Bouillard's thesis at the Sorbonne?' he asks. Indeed, I say, but unfortunately I don't know when that will be. The Dominican says that he can tell me precisely, since he has received a written invitation. In a flash it dawns on me that Bouillard has lied to me – why? To keep me away.

The truth will out. Incensed, I appear in the relevant room of the Sorbonne on the appropriate day. A large public has gathered, since word has got around that Karl Barth is travelling from Basle to be present in person at this *'soutenance de thèse'*, though of course he may not intervene in the debate. As usual the jury is solemnly enthroned in front, at a wide table. When things get going, Basle's famous New Testament scholar, Professor Oscar Cullmann, whose course on exegesis at the 'École der Hautes Études' of the Sorbonne I attend with great profit, is prominent as a referee, picking Bouillard's work to pieces. As exegetes love to do, he points out an endless series of 'corrigenda', to which of course Bouillard cannot respond at all in detail. It is turning out that this *defensio* isn't going as brilliantly as the candidate, known as a theology professor in France (but censured by Rome), might have expected.

There's a break of quarter of an hour. Karl Barth discovers me and for the whole time talks out in front alone with the young doctoral student. Bouillard goes past us with a rigid gaze and doesn't greet me, and I am now certain that at my own *'soutenance'* I will be confronted with a heavily armed opponent who is not at all well disposed to me. I don't hear what Barth says to Bouillard afterwards. Be this as it may, Bouillard receives his *doctorat ès-lettres*, and I quickly leave the auditorium.

Karl Barth and the appearance of Christ to Pius XII

In Basle I see Karl Barth again. Now he is no longer living in Pilgerstrasse down in the city, where I visited him the first time, but in a new, friendly house up in the Bruderholzalle, though it is not really big enough for his gigantic library. However, the engravings of the great theologians and philosophers of modernity – known to me from his *Protestant Theology* – still adorn the corridors and stairwell. They are a reminder of the great tradition which the master of this house knows very well indeed.

With respect I look at the desk at which so many articles and books that have moved theology and the church have been written: I will see it later as a 'relic' in Pittsburgh Theological Seminary where his son Markus works, having remained intellectually indebted to his father all his life. But even more important, alongside the desk – though the Reformed Barth does not want there to be pictures in churches (not even the newly discovered old frescoes in Basle cathedral) – there is a fine reproduction of the crucifixion from Grünewald's Isenheim altar. When I ask, he tells me that it is a warning to theologians: how John the Baptist with his long index finger keeps pointing to the one Jesus Christ, the centre and essence of Christianity.

I get on very well with Barth, as I don't with Balthasar, both as a person and as a theologian; he already has a slight stoop and wears spectacles with thick lenses. He seems to me to be more powerful and down-to-earth than his Catholic neighbour in Basle, Balthasar, who shows little interest in politics and society, and not least because of that has problems with his group of men: Barth seems more like a tribune of the people than the master of an order. Discussion with Karl Barth, for example about the pope or Adenauer, is often argumentative. I think that one can be against Adenauer's politics of incorporation into the Western Alliance (NATO), but not necessarily because of the gospel. 'For what other reason then?' is the characteristic reply of Barth, who wants to see 'political decisions in the unity of the faith' (thus the title of a 1952 essay). In all these discussions Barth doesn't seem to me to be remote and intellectual, but for all his broad horizon and intellectual refinement always elementary and original. He is a brilliant man, with whom one can have a good argument and also, my preference, a good laugh. I prove the equal of his Basle wiles. He thinks that in theology one never knows whether 'I have him or he has me'. Because of Balthasar's Catholic interpretation Barth has 'buried' the *analogia entis* ('similarity of being' between God and man) – originally his main objection to Catholic theology.

The author of the *Church Dogmatics* is very happy with my work. Volume IV/ 3, soon to appear, of which he gives me a private summary, will substantially reinforce my theory of consensus. For Barth it is important that I wrote the first version of my study in Rome – a sign that one can after all hope for an ecumenical understanding. I report my own objections to his theology (for example about the doctrine of creation or the church and the salvation of the pagans) without any inhibitions. The Tübingen Barthian Hermann Diem will later tell me that Barth accepts this from me more readily than from his own pupils. In fact I am not a Barthian (Karl Barth does not think he is one either); I have only heard a one-hour lecture during a visit to Basle. He is now moving rapidly towards retirement, but every day works on Volume IV/4 of his *Dogmatics*. Only in the evening does he read other literature (for example about the American Civil War) or listen to Mozart ('the simpler pieces', is the smug remark of Balthasar, who rather prides himself on his knowledge of the Mozart quartets).

More than once I have lunch with Barth and his congenial, silent wife and his no less congenial, enlightened collaborator Charlotte von Kirschbaum, on whom he has been utterly dependent since his time in Bonn: she writes and corrects all his manuscripts, relieves him of much correspondence and, he comments with a chuckle, knows her way round the gigantic *Church Dogmatics* better than he does himself. The natural years of tension between the two women, much commented on in Basle, must have been overcome by the time of our acquaintance. I sense nothing of it and am not interested in 'researches' in this direction. There is also cheerful conversation between the four or us – not on justification, on which we are agreed, but on every other possible question.

We discuss the current situation of the Catholic Church a great deal, and of course the papacy, the tremendous possibilities of which fascinate Barth, though he is repelled by its concrete form and practice: 'I cannot hear the voice of the Good Shepherd from this chair of Peter,' he is accustomed to say. And by that he means Pius XII in particular. The alleged appearance of Christ to Pius XII on 2 December 1954 was made public in the illustrated magazine *Oggi* of 25 November 1955, and confirmed two days later by the Vatican press bureau and radio. Karl Barth cryptically tests me: 'What do you think of it?' 'Nothing,' I reply. However, Barth is enjoying the game and insists: 'But after all, it would be the first appearance of Christ after that to the apostle Paul. And wouldn't it be important to know what our Lord Jesus said to Pope Pius?' When I say that I don't want to know, he draws me out with the point: 'Surely Christ would have said to the pope what he said to Paul, "Pius, Pius, why are you persecuting me?"' Later I learn from a reliable source that the story of the appearance – painfully illustrated with big posed colour photographs of His Holiness with a bird on his hand, with lambs, with children, and at prayer in his private chapel by his bedroom in Castel Gandolfo, was sold to *Oggi*. By whom? By Fr Lombardi's manager, Fr Rontondi SJ, who banked at least 50 (if not 100) million lire for a 'good cause' (a building enterprise of Lombardi's 'Better World').

According to the report in 2002 by a postulator of his canonization, the well-known former repetitor Fr Peter Gumpel, Pius XII also had dealings with the devil. He several times performed an exorcism on Adolf Hitler, whom he regarded as possessed, a hitherto quite unusual exorcism at a distance of 1500 kilometres – possibly appearing to him as God's or Christ's 'representative', but of course with no success! Didn't our promoter of the process of canonization reflect that psychiatrists could diagnose an appearance of Christ or an exorcism as a sign of threatening 'Caesaromania' (= the sick exaggeration of a drive to power among rulers or dictators) *à la* Pope Boniface VIII?

Ready for the defence

However, I still have my own *'soutenance de thèse'* in Paris before me. And since my adversary will be Henri Bouillard, this may prove difficult. Certainly in a note of 15 January 1957 he confirmed the approach of my thesis with the words, 'Don't worry, *je ne serai pas méchant,* I won't be malicious.' But that makes me even more mistrustful. After all, one knows that 'One doesn't believe someone who lies, even if at the same time he is telling the truth.'

If I am not to lose, I must prepare my own 'defence' precisely: a question less of strategy than of tactics. I remind myself that the old Confederates, warned by a message on an arrow before their first fight for freedom against the Habsburgs at Morgarten, prepared up on the mountain the blocks of stone which they would then roll down on the cavalry at the narrow point between the foot of the mountain and the lake. Since Bouillard has not allowed me to look at his dissertation, and since, given all that has gone before, I must reckon with serious attacks on the basis of his own dissertation, I must provide myself with adequate defensive ammunition. So I go to the Sorbonne archive. On the basis of my doctoral student's pass, without further ado I am lent Bouillard's extensive manuscript to study in the library for the next few days.

Bouillard's methods would certainly have pleased Charles Boyer, the Roman prefect of studies: in every single chapter he first gives Karl Barth's teaching and then immediately adds his criticism, marked by three asterisks. I devote all my attention to these many critical sections. First I consider at which passage of my own work the relevant objection can be fired. Then each time on the empty page opposite my text I sum up Bouillard's objection briefly and add, in the best possible French, my own answer, point by point. No easy work. *Mais ça vaut la peine* — it's worth it.

Thus in the end, on the opposite blank pages of my beautifully bound dissertation I have set down my defence with all the counter-arguments available. At the end I have built up my defence in around two dozen closely-written and systematically ordered statements. So as to avoid long searches during the argument I make a general plan of my defensive positions with page numbers in order to be able to react like lightning. But even that isn't enough for me.

I think that an introduction to my work by Karl Barth would be worth a great deal. But Hans Urs von Balthasar, also founder of the élite theological Johannes Verlag, my future publisher, dissuades me: this could also provoke unnecessary 'counter votes'. He wants to ask Professor Feiner. His report comes on a card on 9 January 1957: 'I had a long conversation with Barth. In principle he would like to write the brief letter at the beginning of the book. He simply wants to "celebrate" the "event" of such conversations, but not take a position for or against the content. It seems to me this would be *a very great help* for the book.' Is Balthasar indicating more his or Barth's understanding of this 'brief letter'? In any case I am interested in getting this letter as early as possible, so I can send it to my professors immediately before my *defensio*. This would leave Bouillard so little time that he could not start any counter-operation.

However, Karl Barth writes anything but a 'brief letter' with no reference to content. Rather, I receive a letter of introduction dated 31 January 1957, warm, formulated in an original way, extremely substantial, addressed to 'Dear Hans Küng', and his visiting card, on which he has written, 'Avanti, Savoia!', the well-known cry of the Italian troops who stormed Rome in the Risorgimento in 1870 — unconcerned about the pope who had just been declared 'infallible' and his *'suprema potestas'* over the church and all the faithful. To my pleasant surprise Karl Barth takes a quite clear position: his 'great pleasure' in the book is 'first of all, simply because of the open-minded and resolute way you seem to have addressed yourself at the Germanicum in Rome to Catholic exegesis and to the history of dogma and theology, and then proceeded, like an undaunted son of Switzerland, to study my books as well and to come to grips with the theological phenomenon you encountered in them. Then too I admire and applaud the skill and good language . . . '

That was good, but what Barth said about the content was even better. First, he confirms the correctness of my interpretation of his teaching: 'I here gladly, gratefully, and publicly testify not only that you have adequately covered all significant aspects of justification in the ten volumes of my *Church Dogmatics* published so far, and that you have fully and accurately reproduced my views as I myself understand them; but also that you have brought all this beautifully into focus through your brief yet precise presentation of details and your numerous, apposite pointers from the particular to the larger context. Furthermore, your readers may rest assured – until such time as they themselves might get to my books – that you have me say what I actually do say and that I mean it in the way you have me say it.'

Secondly, however, Barth gives his assent to the consensus found in this question which has been controversial since the Reformation – but in the hope of a confirmation by Catholic theology: '*If* the things that you cite from Scripture, from older and more recent Roman Catholic theology old and new, from Denziger and hence from the Tridentine texts, do actually represent the teaching of your church and are establishable as such (perhaps this single book of yours will be enough to create a consensus!), then having twice gone to the Church of Santa Maria Maggiore in Trent to commune with the *genius loci*, I may very well have to hasten there a third time to make a contrite confession – "Fathers, I have sinned." ' What a remark! And later it is quoted by so many people.

In fact Barth's letter of introduction changes the approach to my book. Now the issue is no longer just specialist scholarly questions about the interpretation of Barth's theology but the fundamental ecumenical question: Catholic or un-Catholic? This 'real question – Catholic or un-Catholic? – is put to me extraordinarily sharply,' I write to Barth in my letter of thanks of 2 February 1957; 'I hope it will not be detrimental': 'My original intention was to administer the medicine to my fellow Catholics drop by drop and with a natural smile. That will no longer be possible now, for the patient, terrified out of his pre-critical sleep by your Foreword, will go rigid with mistrust at the "new" thing that people want to offer him there. Now that again makes me somewhat suspicious: not that my work will not be examined to the heart and marrow for its Catholicity – I am still convinced that my essential arguments should stand up even to the most critical eye – but in the spirit I always see the wicked pack of the hyper-orthodox this side and that side of the Alps shooting at my poor bird which has just taken wing, in order to see not so much what is Catholic about it but what could be un-Catholic about it.' So in order not to 'set the Roman bureaucracy on the march' from the start, I ask Karl Barth to make yet another reference to the 'cloud of witnesses' from the Catholic sphere that I have cited.

The same day Karl Barth accedes to my wish, which he 'understands well', and adds: 'And now, when you can, tell me how Solothurn (= the episcopal ordinariate of Basle) has spoken!' As early as 3 January 1957, on the basis of the recommendations of Balthasar ('a stupendous achievement for a beginner'), Bouyer and Feiner, I have received permission for publication from the ordinariate of Basle. On 1 February in a carefully composed letter I ask the Vicar General responsible, Dr Lisibach – a little point which is unique in the history of theology – for a separate imprimatur for the accompanying letter by the Protestant Karl Barth. Balthasar has previously left it to me whether I should send the letter of introduction to Solothurn ('without Barth knowing') in order to avoid later difficulties. I do so, but with Barth's knowledge. And I receive the imprimatur from Lisibach, who always gives a thorough answer briefly and promptly. 'In order. Karl Barth's letter is very skilful. *Salve.*' With this I have now made all my preparations to get through the examination in Paris.

A battle won

That is the position on Thursday 21 February 1957. I have translated my work into French, though this was originally not required, and had it corrected by a kind French theologian, Paul Guiberteau from Nantes, who lived with me for a few weeks in our family; we leave Barth's original texts in German. When he later discovers my book on the Council in a bookshop, he tells me how much he enjoyed being in our family – with all the walks, trips on the lake and friendly conversations about Barth's theology: *'quel merveilleux mois de Septembre . . .!'*

For a year, at the same time I have also been doing my five doctoral courses in the somewhat sad complex of buildings of the Institut Catholique on the rue d'Assas at the edge of the Latin Quarter. And just as in Rome I have already written a Latin seminar paper on 'The Concept of Grace and Justification in the Controversy with the Protestants', so now I write a French paper with an ex-egetical orientation on the words 'justify' (Greek *dikaioun*) and 'justification' (*dikaiosis*) in the apostle Paul. I also write further works on the literary genre of Isaiah 6.3, the correspondence between Cyprian and Cornelius in Eusebius's *Church History*, the brilliant painter Grünewald and the Reformation, and on Karl Barth and the Roman primacy.

On this Thursday morning at 11 a.m. my *'leçon doctoral'* on the topic *'L'éternité de l'Homme-Dieu'*, in practice my excursus on the dissertation, takes place in the Salle des Professeurs. A friendly discussion. *Pas de problèmes.* In the afternoon, in the Salle des Actes, at 14.30 there is at last my *'soutenance de thèse'*. At the front of the platform in the centre is the Rector, Monsignor Blanchet, with the status of a bishop; alongside him the dean, Joseph Lecler (author of a two-volume *Histoire de la tolérance au siècle de la Réforme*); with him as *'lecteurs'* the professors Guy de Broglie and Henri Bouillard; and finally my *'director de thèse'*, Louis Bouyer. My professors of philosophy from the Sorbonne have come, Jean Wahl, who had very kindly invited me to his house, and Maurice de Gandillac, whom I had already met when making arrangements about a doctorate in philosophy at the Sorbonne (*doctorat ès-lettres*). Hans Urs von Balthasar has travelled from Basle, curious about what will happen here, but, 'I want to remain *absolutely* in the background, so to speak incognito,' he had written on a postcard two days earlier; 'good luck and keep calm!'

Karl Barth has also been invited to my *defensio*, but it has proved difficult – another trip to Paris after such a short time and, as he tells me, he is under much pressure. His spiritual presence is much more important to me than his physical presence: by his letter of introduction to my book, which now gives me so to speak 'free rein' for all the difficult questions of interpreting Barth. In my half-hour summary exposition at the beginning of the defence, in which I explain the motives and content of my work, I moreover stress with due restraint that the author discussed in this dissertation, who is fortunately still alive, has said that he agrees completely with my interpretation.

Guy de Broglie's questions, precise and friendly, are about both Barth's teaching and my *'réflexion catholique'*. I don't find them difficult to answer. But now it is Henri Bouillard's turn. Evidently he cannot give me a list of corrigenda, of the kind that had been presented to him by Cullmann. But he begins ominously, as expected, with a question about Barth's view of the real effects of God's justification in man and accuses me of not finding fault with the decisive lack of reality in Barth. But quickly turning up the relevant opposite page in accordance with my battle plan I can prove with clear texts from the *Church Dogmatics* that Barth has throughout emphasized the reality of justification and that there is no occasion for the Catholic reprimand of 'extrinsecism'. Bouillard insists, and I reply. And so we cheerfully go to and fro.

With increasing, though concealed, amusement the other members of the jury note how a young Swiss theologian parries all the attacks of a scholar who is well-known in France, indeed sometimes ventures a counter-attack over the interpretation of Barth. At any rate, Bouillard will not budge, and finally after a quarter of an hour goes on to his second point of criticism. I thumb through my thesis again, and again begin to parry the attacks, well provided with counter-ammunition.

But now I see His Excellency, the Rector, carefully picking up his gold watch. With a charm which only the French have, he remarks with a smile to Henri Bouillard at his side, *'Je m'excuse beaucoup, cher collègue*, but your time is up. We must get on,' and with a friendly gesture he invites my doctoral supervisor Louis Bouyer to state his views. As expected, and as with de Broglie, these prove positive. After the sharp toing and froing, answering his questions is a welcome exercise in harmony.

The jury withdraws to discuss and then the Rector immediately announces the result. The dissertation is accepted *summa cum laude*. So without further ado I become *doctor theologiae*. I can hardly believe it: around twelve years have now passed – three in Lucerne, seven in Rome and almost two in Paris – since I seriously planned such a doctorate and prepared for it step by step. This is one of those joys which can only be compared with the matura, the school-leaving examination, when similarly the next morning I rubbed my eyes and asked, Was it all a beautiful dream?

No victory celebrations

No celebration has been planned for after the ceremony. Balthasar, friendly and cool as ever, speaks of the annoyance that Henri Bouillard must feel, since to his knowledge Bouillard has constructed perhaps fourteen objections (in content probably the same as those which I had constructed myself and answered on the basis of his manuscript). But Balthasar refuses an invitation to dinner: he has to go to meet Bouillard. And Bouillard definitely doesn't want to see me now. One can be suddenly very alone after winning a 'victory'.

It hadn't seemed to me to make sense also to invite my family to Paris for a discussion between French theologians; they had come to Rome eighteen months before. How glad I was when two family friends from Amsterdam had announced themselves as surprise visitors in Paris immediately before the doctorate: Ria van Stijn, in whose family I was living during my stay in Amsterdam in 1953, and her friend Inka Klinckhard, whom I discover only after the *soutenance*. Ria isn't there. That's strange, since she only had to travel from Fontainebleau, where she had taken up a teaching post in NATO headquarters, and she had visited me shortly beforehand.

So finally I celebrate my doctorate alone with Inka on the Champs-Élysees with a fine *diner à deux*, paid for by her mother. We enjoy ourselves royally and then say goodbye. The next day my French landlady shows me the front page of *France-Soir*: a big portrait photograph of Ria! Wasn't that the attractive young lady who had visited me two or three weeks previously? I discover that on the day of my doctorate she had been stabbed with a knife at her school by a North African with whom she had made friends: he had wanted to marry her, but she rejected him yet again in front of her class with a *'Non, non, non.'* She fell dead between the desks. The murderer was caught in a vineyard that same day.

As the last of the circle of her family and friends to have spoken with Ria before the brutal murder, I travel to Amsterdam soon afterwards to attempt to comfort her parents. But I will continue to remain friends with Inka for years. She is an eminent sculptor trained at the Academy in Amsterdam – her father, who owns a chemical business and was a Berlin delegate of the Stresemann party, had moved to Holland because of the Nazis. Marvellous little bronze sculptures in my living room in Tübingen ('People in Space', 'Mother and Child') and on the terrace ('Obstacle') bear witness to her.

After the first skirmishes in the Collegium Romanum over the reform of theology, the college and the church, I have withstood my first public baptism of fire in theological matters. I still have no inkling that with the first victory a 'war' has begun which has now lasted half a century, still with the outcome undecided . . .

All that comes alive before my eyes when in the year 2000 I am again living in a little room in Paris. And it all makes me so glad that on the Sunday morning before my flight I walk from the Latin quarter over to the island in the Seine, to my favourite place in Paris. It isn't one of the lecture rooms of the Sorbonne or the 'Catho', or one of the magnificent rooms of the French kings (those of us who took part in the 'Rencontres de la Sorbonne' were invited for a meal in the grandiose hall of the Palais Luxembourg). It isn't even the Louvre, where the treasures of Mesopotamia or Egypt fascinate me as much as the Mona Lisa, indeed it isn't even Notre Dame, where I can attend a service.

Rather, it is the little Sainte Chapelle, that Gothic masterpiece of transparency, built under Louis the Holy at the same time as Notre Dame in only six years and consecrated in 1248: light, colour, space, spirit, triumph here over the material, and point so overwhelmingly to transcendence that even the countless secular tourists sit down and simply look and admire. But in the silence with my whole heart I give thanks for everything that I have behind me since that year of my doctorate in 1957 – truly not in my own strength.

A theological sensation for Montini too

On this day in the year 2000, immediately afterwards I go to Charles de Gaulle airport, in order to fly to a colloquium on the global ethic at the UN university in Tokyo. That's my life these days. I would have much preferred to go back to Tübingen. But I use the time on the flight of almost eleven hours to reflect on what I've just written. I tell myself today that there need by no means have been a 'war' over my theology. And I am certainly not the only one who thinks this. For what Karl Barth had expected and wanted has now in fact happened. By now the results of my dissertation have been accepted in principle by the theology of both confessions.

My publisher Balthasar gave me brilliant advice in 1957 on all matters of publication: from the short title *Justification* (without 'of the sinner') printed in large capitals on the cover, the characterful type and the easily readable layout, to the generous number of review copies that were sent out. Since the Johannes Verlag hardly has access to a mass public – initially there was talk of an edition of only 800 copies, but finally the figure of 2500 was calculated – there is a desire to serve at least all the important European theological journals. Of course most theologians, whether Protestant or Catholic, are initially utterly surprised by the content, method and final result and, as is usual in reviews, have to object to one or the other if they do not avoid taking up a position at all – which is what happens most often. They all 'cannot stop marvelling', one reads in the *Allgemeine Sonntagszeitung* of 9 February 1958; 'that happened to many people when they read this – one is almost tempted to say – sensational comparison of the Barthian and the Catholic doctrine of justification by this Swiss Germanicum alumnus Hans Küng'. Karl Barth writes the same thing to me; he showed the book to visitors and states with biblical words: '*Et omnes mirati sunt.* And all marvelled.'

Of the many letters of thanks for a copy of my dissertation one is particularly important to me. The 'fine volume on "Justification"', it says in Italian, presents itself as 'a great novelty for the theological discussion of the fundamental thesis of Protestant theology: though reading German does not come easy to me, I will still enjoy looking at this important and very interesting work'. The letter, written in nearby Engelberg, comes from a regular holiday guest who is looked after by the Benedictine father Dr Anselm Fellmann from Sursee, a man whom I have known from my youth up: this is Giovanni Battista Montini, now Archbishop of Milan, who only five years later will be elected pope under the name of Paul VI. Soon afterwards I also get to know him personally, whereupon he again congratulates me in a most friendly way. His personal sympathy for me is manifest. We shall have to consider later how easy it would have been for me – by chance this letter from my archive arrives on my desk now in 2001 on the very day when three former German university theologians well known to me are created cardinals – to make my way into the hierarchy like these colleagues. But how happy I am to have remained true to my theology and to have gone my own independent way. Going my way . . .

'Few books which I have received have delighted me so much as this one,' the most respected Catholic dogmatic theologian in Switzerland, Professor Josef Feiner, writes to me on 15 March 1957. With the equally open Benedictine Magnus Löhrer (of Einsiedeln) he is editor of the multi-volume salvation-historical dogmatics *Mysterium salutis*. 'If all reviewers welcome it and judge it as favourably as I do, then you can be delighted at the reviews.' But I already knew previously that I couldn't look forward to the reviews by the Dominican Heinrich Stirnimann (of Fribourg) and the Jesuit Albert Ebneter (of Zurich). Whereas Feiner and Löhrer take up my fundamental criticism of the plan of *Mysterium salutis* in a very constructive way (instead of arbitrary scholastic divisions I would prefer a consistent salvation-historical approach) (cf. Löhrer's report in the supplementary volume of 1981), the correspondence with Stirnimann and Ebneter – both of whom have more of an apologetic than an ecumenical attitude – is very laborious. These two fellow-countrymen find it all too difficult to depart from their fixed views on Karl Barth. Our little inquisitor in Rome, Fr Gumpel, is delighted at this. Of Stirnimann's review he says to students, 'Devastating'. This is wide of the mark, even in the eyes of Stirnimann, who, as he tells me later, had been aiming far more at Karl Rahner; vicarious wars are also waged in theology. I answer Ebneter and Stirnimann, in a measured and matter-of-fact way, in the *Schweizerische Kirchenzeitung* (of December 1957). 'I haven't heard you speak as gently as that before,' Balthasar writes to me, 'and I hear that Stirnimann is being equally gentle with you. Excellent.'

Very pleasantly, there are two highly appreciative reviews by Joseph Ratzinger: ' . . . for such a gift Hans Küng deserves the honest thanks of all who pray and work towards the unity of divided Christianity'. Generally speaking, then, the reaction is quite positive, as my pupil Christa Hempel will establish in 1970 – the first woman to be accepted as a doctoral candidate at the Catholic Theological Faculty of Tübingen after all the resistance has been overcome – in her dissertation on the discussion of justification (*Rechtfertigung als Wirklichkeit* – 'Justification as Reality'), on the basis of many dozens of reviews in every possible language. Intensive research work has been prompted, as the Bonn theologian Johannes Brosseder will establish in an excellent account (in my 1993 *Festschrift*). In the 1960s the then Dominican theologian Otto Hermann Pesch confirms with a number of publications that a consensus in matters of justification is possible not only between Barth and the Council of Trent but also between Luther and Thomas Aquinas.

Thus it becomes even more evident that however different some perspectives and emphases of individual theologies and theologians are, the ecumenical breakthrough in this basic question may be taken to have been achieved. Precisely 40 years later Otto Hermann Pesch, who meanwhile has become the leading ecumenist, acknowledges with remarkable clarity that because of my book he himself has turned from 'pure' Catholic dogmatics to ecumenical theology: 'It can be demonstrated that this book, which went through four impressions in a short time, and since 1986 has been available in a new paperback edition, has on the one hand set theological discussion of ecumenical questions moving as never before and on the other hand has so to speak influenced the ecumenical climate in the churches in the direction of responsible expectation of ecumenical progress.'

And Rome? Rome is not grateful to the author. On the contrary. But from the start I have been anything but naïve in this matter. Immediately before the publication of *Justification*, in Lucerne I rate my chances as 50:50: either the book will be a great success despite the rigorous and authoritarian regime of Pius XII, or it will be put on the Index of Prohibited Books, something which at that time has happened to far more harmless books.

My dossier at the Inquisition: no. 399/57i

Already in the Collegium Germanicum Anno Quadt from Cologne, a contemporary of mine, had 'sharpened his knife' against me, as his archbishop, Cardinal Josef Frings, later says. And he meant that quite seriously. Quadt fought for the 'true faith', which of course he thought he had, against me and my friends from the dogmatic circle, with persistence and Thomistic weapons. He accused us of identifying nature and grace and finally ending up in pantheism. This man, who has some knowledge only of neoscholasticism, sees the roots of all evil in Hegel and Barth, whom he has never studied seriously.

So only a year after my doctorate, this theological Don Quixote, who emerged as anything but brilliant with his own dissertation at the Gregorian (insufficient knowledge of the literature, especially no knowledge of French), sends a long anti-Küng article to the *Zeitschrift für Katholische Theologie* in Innsbruck, full of this narrow-mindedness. In a covering letter his protector in Cologne, an alumnus of the Germanicum and a liturgical expert, ominously tells the editor, Professor Josef Andreas Jungmann, also a liturgical expert, of a 'rumour emerging here that Küng's book will be put on the Index'. He adds in a hypocritically friendly way: 'I hope that will not happen.' Do the hopes of our Anno run in this direction? His article could easily be used as evidence.

On 20 December 1958 Karl Rahner, who has been asked to do so by the editor Josef Andreas Jungmann, enquires in a long and anxious letter whether there really is danger and what is to be done: should the article be sent back or published with my reply? The latter course seems to me to be correct, but caution is needed. I am less afraid that I will be put on the Index than that ecumenical dialogue will be disrupted by such spanners in the works, especially since as at the same time I have to defend myself against Henri de Lubac, for whom I always have a great respect. He had replied bitterly to my criticism of Bouillard's work on Barth requested of me by the *Kölner Zeitschrift* for its 'Dokumente' – reading it even in retrospect, it seems matter-of-fact and fair. However, de Lubac himself doesn't understand German; evidently he has received a retort foisted on him by his fellow religious and friend Henri Bouillard. I again put this in a factual and fair way in a short reply in the same journal, and de Lubac answers me later in private that he is not *'fâché'*, not annoyed.

Quadt's article on my 'change of concept' in matters of 'nature and grace' is published three years later in the *Münchner Theologische Zeitschrift*, which has an alumnus of the Germanicum as editor. I ignored it and it is not noted elsewhere. Quadt himself becomes a canon of Cologne Cathedral. But in 1981 the new Archbishop of Cologne, the Germanicum cardinal Joseph Höffner, promotes this man who has been thought to be anti-ecumenical to be Chairman of the Ecumenical Episcopal Commission. Twenty years after that, in a surprising change of direction, Quadt will write a book under the provocative title: 'Protestant Office: Valid – Eucharistic Fellowship: Possible'. When I meet him at a Germanicum gathering in Freising near Munich in June 2001, he says with the gentleness of old age: 'One can always learn something more.' This statement reconciles me with much. It would have delighted me even more had he not passed over my works from the 1960s, which anticipate his thesis.

It would have been a miracle after 1957 if my book hadn't been denounced. To this extent the rumour that it would be put on the Index, which was spread from Cologne to Innsbruck and from Zurich to Tübingen by the disquieted Protestant church historian Fritz Blanke, is certainly not unfounded. Rahner, editor of the new *Lexikon für Theologie und Kirche*, complains to me in a letter: 'You won't believe how much this *LThK*, which is otherwise so sound, is being regarded with mistrust and attacked (for the moment in an underhand way)' (15 July 1958). Not only the nunciatures (which in the Council were to be called 'denunciatures' by a bishop to loud applause) can be active here, but even more the ugly little informers, as in all authoritarian and totalitarian systems. In Lucerne that moral theologian Schenker is rightly or wrongly regarded as an informer, accustomed to sending relevant reports about Catholic Switzerland to Rome. As I will later hear personally from Cardinal Ratzinger, Tübingen 'friends', probably from his former faculty, send all the important reports from the local *Schwäbisches Tagblatt* to him in Rome; I think I know at least one of the 'friends'. There is no question that this is how the 'abhorrent system of secret denunciations' functions, which, as we heard from Yves Congar, is 'the essential condition of the "Holy Office", the centre and culmination of all the rest'.

That editor of the *Münchner Theologische Zeitschrift* sends the review copy of *Justification* to our Collegium Germanicum – in case people there want to dissociate themselves from the author. It lands up at the Gregorian. But there people do not distance themselves from me even when Barth's old opponent, the Protestant theologian from Zurich, Emil Brunner, appears personally to discover whether the Gregorian has 'really gone over to Karl Barth'. The Dutchman Fr Johannes L. Witte SJ writes an appreciative critique which is directed not against my Catholicity but against that of Barth. Still, the warning comes to me from Rome that the planned second impression shouldn't be announced in advance, as this could provoke the intervention of the Sanctum Officium. *Cauti sitis*. On 23 October 1958 I receive from my publisher Balthasar the report: 'We have quietly reprinted a thousand, as Cologne (the representative of the publishing house there) advises. *Va bene*. Warmest greetings!'

Whatever may have happened there in the gloomy corridors of denunciation and inquisition, in the 'Holy Office' of the Roman Inquisition, from the year of my dissertation, I receive for life the file number 399/57i: i.e. file 399 of 1957 of the Index division for prohibited books. And once someone has earned such a file number in this 'Holy Office' he has the 'privilege' that from now on everything by him or about him is made accessible in a dossier (now of course computerized) under this number. However, this happens under the utmost secrecy: not even in the case of a process of faith may the accused see his records – just one of the reasons why the Vatican is not allowed to sign the Declaration of Human Rights of the Council of Europe.

Thanks to my teachers

It is amazing that my dissertation isn't put on the Index, though there are those who expect and desire this. The solution to the riddle is that I owe this to my Roman and French teachers, who protect me against attacks, as I later learn from Frs Franz Hürth and Sebastian Tromp, both members of the Sanctum Officium. Rome is impressed by the way in which Guy de Broglie so to speak puts his hand in the fire for my book, with a statement that we are allowed to print on the cover: '*Aucun esprit sérieux et bien informé*, no serious and well-informed person, will doubt the complete Catholic orthodoxy of the teaching presented and defended by Dr Küng, far less can one put in question the scholarship and the broad horizon against which he is able to treat such a fundamental, comprehensive and many-sided theme.' And Louis Bouyer had added: ' . . . it is important that we have been shown the convergences towards which an effort to disperse misunderstanding can already lead us'. Even today, a *grand merci* to my dead teachers.

One of those who rejoices is Karl Rahner. While he isn't my teacher, he is an important inspiration for my theology. As early as 15 March 1957 he writes to me: 'If Barth on the one side, and de Broglie and Bouyer along with the Möhler Institute in Paderborn stand to the right and left of you as patrons, then the book *must* be good and you have hit the nail on the head. Therefore such a book is a real joy. I grant that I do not always have a good word for Roman theology as it is at present; it seems to me a little fossilized (not of course in all things) and concerned only to follow the saying of Wilhelm Busch: the good man likes to note whether the other is also doing evil. So I truly rejoice all the more that someone from there has written such a book and it is evidently also recognized there.'

One thing is clear: had Rome reacted by immediately putting me on the Index, I would never have become a professor of theology. And the Catholic hierarchy would have been spared some annoyance. But as we know, things turned out differently. So within six months it is possible for my dissertation to appear in further editions. An English and a French edition will follow, later a Spanish and an Italian edition, and a German pocket book edition which is still in demand today. It is even better to have a backlist title (in this case in print for almost 50 years) than a bestseller – and a dissertation at that!

But in the Roman church the forces are in the majority which seek to hinder the already long overdue paradigm shift from the Counter-Reformation and anti-modernity to the ecumenical paradigm introduced by small ecumenical circles and by the world assemblies leading to the foundation of the World Council of Churches in 1948.

Late triumph

In fact after 1957 the churches should have translated the results of the theological reinterpretation of the doctrine of justification into church life. But it was only in 1973, almost a decade after the Second Vatican Council, that a study conference of the Lutheran World Federation and the Roman Secretariat for Promoting Christian Unity would take place on the Mediterranean island of Malta, with a highly welcome result. The Malta Report states clearly that on the question of justification the decisive convergence has taken place: 'Today a far-reaching consensus is developing in the interpretation of justification. Catholic theologians also emphasize in reference to justification that God's gift of salvation for the believer is unconditional as far as human accomplishments are concerned. Lutheran theologians emphasize that the event of justification is not limited to individual forgiveness of sins and they do not see in it a purely external declaration of the justification of the sinner . . . As the message of justification is the *foundation of Christian freedom* [my italics] in opposition to legalistic conditions for the reception of salvation it must be articulated ever anew time and again as an important interpretation of the centre of the gospel.'

So here is the confirmation from Rome on the question of the message of justification. Moreover one of the signatories was Walter Kasper, my former assistant and then colleague in Tübingen. For Karl Barth it was too late to make another pilgrimage to Trent; he had died five years previously. From the agreement reached over the doctrine of justification it was now possible to advance to the understanding of the church as the fellowship of believers which may live anew time and again by the grace and forgiveness of God as the *ecclesia semper reformanda*. Moreover there is also agreement on questions of church ministry and the recognition in practice of the Reformation celebration of the eucharist, as proposed in my 'Theses on the Apostolic Succession' (*Concilium* 1968) and in the memorandum of the Ecumenical University Institute on 'Reform and Recognition of Church Ministries' (1973).

But there of course Rome should have joined in. What will happen instead? Instead of joyfully accepting the Malta Report of that official Roman-Lutheran Commission of 1973, the Vatican strictly forbids its publication. Instead of making the liberating teaching of the justification of the sinner by faith fruitful in the proclamation of the church, the Malta Report is pigeonholed in the Vatican and eventually made public only by an indiscretion on the part of *Herder Korrespondenz*. And instead of drawing practical conclusions for the freedom of a Christian from the theological results, further progress is deliberately hindered and wherever possible freedom is suppressed.

It will take around 40 years, until 1999, for the breakthrough already achieved in 1957 to be officially sanctioned by the church. I once read in C. G. Jung that it takes around 40 years for an idea from the higher levels of the clergy to get down to the man on the street. Did the prelates also count on that? At any event, first of all there was some undesirable theological haggling: instead of taking the results of the book *Justification*, the subsequent discussion and the Malta document as the presupposition of an official recognition of the consensus, the Vatican, playing for time, set up yet another ecumenical commission with the Lutheran World Federation which for years had once again to chew through all the statements in the Tridentine decree on justification. Galley slaves' work.

It goes without saying that I remain excluded from such official discussions by commissions under the conditions of an all too eternal yesterday – at the wish of Rome and with the assent of Protestants. And I'm pleased: what a waste of time! Here of course the Roman infallibles attach importance to every single statement of Trent: these cannot in any way be false or even wrong, but were 'fundamentally' correct or were at least 'meant to be correct' (otherwise 'everything would collapse'). But of necessity Lutheran biblical scholars respond to the Roman tactics accordingly: they are concerned to demonstrate that as many formulations as possible in Luther or the confessional writings are irreformably correct and, where they can be, are to be pressed into the categories of law and gospel. In a neurosis over confessional profile, some remain caught in the mediaeval paradigm, others in the Reformation paradigm. And so they lose the opportunity of making clear to people in a competitive society in a quite concrete and convincing way how important it is that human beings as persons are not justified by God on the basis of achievements, successes, works of all kinds, but happily by God himself, who expects only trusting faith.

Be this as it may, finally in 1999, despite some shady moves and Lutheran counter-moves and after further additional declarations, on 31 October, the anniversary of the Reformation, a declaration of agreement will be signed in Augsburg. When this happens, vigorous applause spontaneously breaks out in the church and goes on for an astonishingly long time. For me – watching it on television – it is a great delight. For the applause shows those in church and those watching on TV how great the longing is for such an ecumenical agreement. A late triumph. No doubt about it. But should I conceal the fact that at the wish of Rome the name of the author of the 1957 book *Justification*, which was originally top of the list of those to be invited, was again deleted – and as so often without a protest from the Protestants involved? Certainly this pettiness niggles me a little, but I can easily get over it, and in any case I am no friend of long church ceremonies. Did my former assistant and colleague Walter Kasper, now a Curia bishop, no doubt informed about the deletion of my name, perhaps sign for me in spirit? At any rate, to conclude from several reactions, including those of Bishop Karl Lehmann, I am not forgotten by the well informed. The best sign comes a few weeks later at the 'Cape of Good Hope', on the occasion of my lecture to the Parliament of the World Religions in December 1999. On the stage, the Lutheran Bishop of Cape Town, Nils Rohwer, gives me the fountain pen, beautifully engraved by the city of Augsburg, with which he himself signed the Augsburg document: he says that I deserve it more than he does. The Lord Mayor of the city of Augsburg is kind enough later to send him another jubilee fountain pen at my request. This is practical ecumenism in small matters.

What is politically more important is that the head of the Roman inquisitorial authorities, responsible for the 'doctrine of faith', Cardinal Joseph Ratzinger, who otherwise likes to be in the foreground at church celebrations, isn't present in Augsburg, but has himself represented by Cardinal Cassidy and his *adlatus* Kasper. And what a shock: immediately after the signing, the Vatican, unrepentant and insensitive as ever, announces a new jubilee indulgence for the year 2000. As if Luther hadn't propagated his theses on justification by faith alone, specifically without such pious works, on the occasion of that scandalous jubilee indulgence for the new St Peter's! This shows some all too trusting Lutherans that the harsh Roman core has in no way been converted into honest ecumenical agreement. No, in Rome under this pontificate no one thinks of drawing conclusions for the reform of church structures from the doctrine of justification.

And those who even now still find excuses for the Roman lack of insight and unreadiness to repent – despite the warnings constantly given by me and others – are definitely taught something worse by Ratzinger's declaration of the year 2000. With an almost blasphemous reference to *Dominus Iesus*, again absolute truth is claimed for his own church, and contrary to all the intentions of Vatican II it is even denied that the Protestant churches are churches by nature. My commentary is that this document is 'a combination of mediaeval backwardness and Vatican megalomania'. At any rate the Augsburg dreams of an ecumenical heyday have flown away rapidly after this cold shock from Rome, which was only to be expected. People on the Protestant side should have been on their guard: honest ecumenism cannot be engaged in with such representatives of the Roman system at the head of the Catholic Church, smooth talkers and smooth actors. Will we ever experience it?

The foundation of Christian freedom

However, I personally will be richly rewarded by my 1957 work on justification: it gives me something decisive for my whole life, my spirituality and especially my understanding of the freedom of a Christian. In the subsequent period I get to know Karl Barth better and better. There is nothing more stimulating than to talk with a man of such character, knowledge and faith, such humanity and such humour. He will become a fatherly friend to me, something that the cool and intellectual Balthasar never is. As Barth wrote in his letter of introduction, he regards me in view of my 'whole attitude as an *Israelita in quo dolus non est* (an Israelite in whom there is no guile,' (cf. John 1.47).

It is in Basle, in Barth's study up on the 'Bruderholz', in a cheerful dispute over the papacy, that I finally say to him with an understanding smile: 'I leave the good faith to you!' To which he retorts, suddenly quite serious: 'Good faith? I would never accept that. And when one day I am called before my God and Lord, I will not come with all my collected theological works in an Älpler-Hutte (rucksack) on my back; all the angels would laugh. Nor will I say in justification of myself, "I always had good intentions, 'good faith'." No, I will stand there with empty hands and only find appropriate those words which I hope may also be my own last words: "God be gracious to me a sinner!"'

These are the words of the tax collector, right at the back of the temple. At a stroke it dawns on me how liberating and comforting this message is for my whole life. I hope that I shall always remember it: Christian trust in faith. This is the radical fundamental trust which in the light of Jesus has found its root (*radix*) in the gracious God and has no illusions about its achievements, but needn't be oppressed by mistakes either.

There is no question that the foundations of the strength of Protestant theology and also of the fearlessness, concentration and consistency of the theologian Karl Barth lies here. This will give me, too, decisive support in all the controversies and form the ultimate foundation for my Christian freedom, which is facing unsuspected tests: whether I ultimately stand there justified does not depend on the judgement of my environment and public opinion. It does not depend on faculty or university, state or church. Nor does it depend on the pope – still less on my own judgement. It depends on a quite different authority, the hidden God himself, in whose grace I, who am no ideal man but human and all too human, may put unconditional trust to the end. '*In te Domine, speravi, non confundar in aeternum*', as it says at the end of the *Te Deum*: 'In you, Lord, have I trusted; I shall never be confounded.'

A book becomes my fate

The rest of my time in Paris goes by without drama. Wherever possible I will attempt to hand on in preaching and teaching what I have learned in theology, and in so doing awaken particularly among Catholics an understanding of the good news of justification on the basis of trusting faith which otherwise is hardly passed on to them. As in Rome, so too in Paris I attempt to combine theology and pastoral work. At the wish of the Bishop of Basle I have taken on the pastoral care of the numerous Swiss *au pair* girls, most of whom have few contacts and are glad of a meeting with worship on Sunday afternoon, all in their native tongue.

Nor do I hesitate while still in my doctorate year, at the wish of the editors of the *Werkblatt*, to report on our work to the 'Girls' Protection Association' which sponsors this pastoral work. The title of this article, 'Our Girls in Paris' (I have also included it in my bibliography), will then more than once give rise at birthday celebrations to innocent jokes on the part of my colleagues. And I am grateful to 'our girls in Paris' – I have not reported this in the article – for furthering my academic work in a way which is worth mentioning.

For at that time my finances are completely exhausted: a subscription to the giant 'Corpus Christianorum' (the Christian literature of the first eight centuries in Latin) at a discounted price is a unique opportunity. However, I have to pay for the first dozen extremely expensive red volumes (every day they tempted me in the publishers' window in St Sulpice) in cash! On principle I don't approach my father for additional money. My only alternative is to scrimp and save this colossal sum. This also becomes evident in time from my appearance. So 'our girls' give me an electric cooker. Now instead of having cold dishes of rolled oats and vegetables, bread and the like, at least I can make myself something warm until my return to Switzerland, when my parents send me to the mountains to recover and go skiing because I look so wretched.

The question 'pastoral work or theology?' is beginning to oppress me. During my search for evidence in the theological seminar of the University of Freiburg im Breisgau in summer 1956 I often have discussions with another 'holiday worker', Eduard Kamenicky, a very friendly doctoral student from Vienna, from whom I will later take over in Paris that fine room from which I am then so rabidly driven by the lady I mentioned. He wants to convince me firmly that later I should embark on a university career. For me only one thing is firm: at all events after my doctorate I shall be returning to Switzerland and pastoral care. But after that? The work on 'justification' has certainly enthused me about theology and convinced me that I too could do something in theology, indeed that in this way I could also make a contribution to pastoral care.

One day, when I am engaged in discussion with Kamenicky under the window, we see a slim gentleman in black getting out of a black limousine at the entrance to the university building. This is the Catholic philosopher of religion Bernhard Welte, at present Rector of the University of Freiburg, known to me from his hotly disputed lecture at the Germanicum. Kamenicky thinks that I should ask him. Making up my mind quickly, that very morning I go to the Rector's office, have a friendly reception from Welte and explain my case to him. I say that in my spiritual training I had learned not to force anything, but to wait until I was called. 'That's right in principle,' he replies, 'but sometimes one must also raise a finger and say, I'm here.'

Certainly with my dissertation I have created a solid foundation on which an ecumenical theology can be built. And I am grateful to Hermann Häring for working out well from a later perspective in his intellectual biography of me entitled *Breaking Through* (1998) how *Justification* already announced:

a lived-out theology *capable of dialogue*, which time and again seeks new dialogue with experts and those in positions of responsibility;

a theology *intent on change*, which in comprehensible language seeks to break through boundaries between confessions, later also between religions and even between believers and non-believers;

a theology *responsible for reconciliation*, which expands the concept of ecumenism to the world religions, indeed the whole 'inhabited earth', and thus works for peace both theoretically and practically.

But how would things go on for me? In summer 1956 I visit my bishop in his residence in Solothurn. 'So, I suppose you want to extend the deadline for your doctorate,' Franziskus von Streng says to me; some time previously he had allowed a further year to my older fellow Germanicum student Anton Cadotsch. 'No, my lord, to be honest, I've already finished the dissertation. But I would like to ask you to allow me to spend the second year that I have already been given for further studies mainly in Spain and England.' This strict prelate has always been very gracious to me. And I seize the opportunity offered.

Delight in philosophy: G. W. F. Hegel

Even at school I had been interested in philosophy, and in Rome I was already intensely interested in the philosopher G. W. F. Hegel: stimulated by Spiritual Klein, informed by Professor Alois Naber's special course and important books like that by Ivan Ilijin. Sometimes I am also challenged by Edward Haible from Stuttgart, my contemporary on the course, who likes to lecture in a loud voice. He makes me aware of the name Tübingen for the first time and enthuses about the famous university there, at which a few years later he is to fail in a tragic way. But my excellent repetitors in the Germanicum, Emerich Coreth, Peter Henrici and Walter Kern – later professors of philosophy in Innsbruck, Rome and Munich – have also all worked intensively on Hegel and have had books published on him. With all due criticism, this philosopher seems to me to offer a great vision: he answers some questions about the worldliness and historicity of God more profoundly than neoscholastic philosophy and theology.

My delight in philosophy now also grows with my delight in theology. Why not work for a doctorate in philosophy at the Sorbonne after my Roman licentiate in philosophy? But Hegel – in any case perhaps the most difficult German-language philosopher to understand – seems to me by nature of his *oeuvre* again to be so tremendous a colossus that I dare not approach him directly. Rather, I think of discussing the question of the dialectic in the Godhead by means of the spiritual theology, or more precisely christology, of the humanist cardinal Nicolas of Cusa, for whom all opposites coincide in God (*'coincidentia oppositorum'*). So I visit Professor de Gandillac of the Sorbonne. He has had a book published on Nicolas of Cusa and will be glad to supervise a work on him.

But then Hans Urs von Balthasar writes to me that a theologian by the name of Rudolf Haubst, from Nicolas's neighbourhood, has just had a book published on the christology of Nicolas of Cusa, based on many studies in the archives; I immediately get hold of it. The scholarly but purely historical work impresses me, but does not satisfy me, because it has no consequences for present-day theology. Nevertheless it is a clear indication to me: don't turn to Nicolas but directly to Hegel. Gandillac agrees, and so I 'set down' as subject for a *doctorat d'état*: *'L'incarnation de Dieu. La christologie de Hegel'*. I also achieve the very rare acknowledgement of the *'équivalence'* of my philosophical licentiate by a *'décision du Ministre de l'Éducation Nationale'* of 18 April 1957, on the basis of reports by Professors Wahl and de Gandillac, and go to courses in philosophy at the Sorbonne for doctoral students.

Hardly have I finished my Barth dissertation when, still in Paris, I throw myself with verve into the new work. I also seek conversations with experts like Jean Wahl and Jean Hyppolite about Hegel. I myself apply a novel historical-systematic method which requires much study and discipline. I rein in my curiosity and always read only those works by and about Georg Wilhelm Friedrich Hegel from the relevant phase of his life: first only about the schoolboy in Stuttgart, then about the theology student in Tübingen, then about the tutor in Berne and Frankfurt, then about the philosopher in Jena and school rector in Nuremberg, and only now about the university professor in Heidelberg and Berlin. So I range from the diaries of the schoolboy, through the printed opuscula and opera, to Hegel's lectures on the philosophy of history of which notes were taken by pupils. In every section, first comes the biography, then the development of thought generally and the slowly developing system, and then the christology (first of the man of the Enlightenment, then of the Kantian, and finally of the speculative philosopher), and finally everywhere the philosophical and theological discussion with Hegel, which I undertook on my own responsibility.

Thus in the end, after several revisions of each chapter, five intertwining strata run through the work – mostly in the form of a narrowing spiral, resulting in an initiation into Hegel and a discussion with him which both brings things out and penetrates them. Here it becomes clear how Hegel the theological student, repelled by Protestant dogmatics and its rigid picture of God, becomes a philosopher. He then sets out to reflect on God's 'career' between Enlightenment deism and Romantic pantheism. He goes on to attempt to describe the Absolute in its changeability and identity – 'presented' on the religious level, represented in the life and suffering, death and resurrection of Christ, the deity himself – and then finally he 'sublates' ('transcends and abolishes') everything in the history of philosophy (as the philosophy of philosophy).

But now to be quite practical: why, I said to myself at a very early stage, continue my Hegel studies only in Paris, which I already know well? After all, I can pursue Hegel's life and thought from very different places in Europe. I have the opportunity to extend not only my philosophical and theological field of interest but also my knowledge of the concrete world, the various countries, peoples and languages. I've long wanted to learn Spanish: not only for reasons of tourism but Spain, the only country of Western and Central Europe that I don't yet know, seems indispensable for an understanding of Europe and Christianity (and also Islam).

Madrid: fascinating Spain

I set out at the end of February 1957. I always take Hegel literature and my manuscript with me from place to place. My big leather suitcase is so heavy that the porter on Sursee station, who wants to swing it up on to the rack despite my warning, falls flat on his belly, while the bag hardly moves. Even the dry Hegel would have been amused at this . . .

It's a long train ride to Barcelona, my first stop, Spain's biggest industrial city. Time for Spanish lessons. A Catalan paediatrician explains the difference between Barcelona and Madrid just as any Milanese would explain the difference between Milan and Rome: they earn the money and it's spent in the capital. One day a Catalan arrives at a Madrid ministry on a Monday morning. But it's shut. 'Don't they work here, then?' A porter behind a barred window replies, 'That's in the afternoon!' The Catalan says to me, 'Claro? That's Madrid: holidays in the morning, loaf about in the afternoon.' I had understood. But clichés are there to be corrected.

One can immediately understand why the Catalans are proud of Barcelona when one falls under the spell of this combination of mediaeval old town and modernity. But I don't want to talk about the Ramblas or about Gaudi's Catalan-Gothic-Modernist cathedral which remains unfinished, or about the 'Gothic quarter' with the Gothic town hall, where many years later, after a lecture, my name is entered in the Golden Book of the City. However, I won't conceal the fact that here I went to a bullfight for the first – and last – time. For this show fight between man and bull, which takes place pompously according to strict rules and certainly with very artificial moves, alienates me. Not that afterwards I would have attempted to dissuade my Spanish friends, in the name of protecting animals, from what – reaching to mythical depths – has been depicted by Goya and Picasso and written about by Hemingway and de Montherlant on a grand scale. *Chacun à son gout* – it's a matter of taste. But I can find little pleasure in this fight, in which the animal, maddened by various methods, has no chance, finally collapses from the 'hero's' dagger blow between the shoulder blades and is then dragged out. For those who like to psychologize: I am a fighter, but certainly not a hunter.

Still, after a stop in the capital of Aragon, Zaragoza on the Ebro with its grandiose cathedral, my destination is Madrid, where I hope to spend March and April. 'From the provinces to Madrid and from Madrid to heaven' runs a well-known proverb, certainly not invented in Catalonia but in Castile. I immediately feel at home in Europe's highest capital, which may not be as varied and fascinating as Paris, but in spring because of its altitude of over 600 metres shows its best side in bright light and good air: an Arab foundation. Arabic is still present throughout the country under the cover of Spanish, not only in architecture and ornaments but also through the 1500 Arabic loanwords and the thousands of Arabic names for places and stretches of water – not to mention the mosques, which have been transformed into Christian churches. All this is very important for me and the 'dialogue of cultures', which is particularly lively again in Spain.

A peaceful room has been found for me in Madrid, in a small residence at the top of the modern Mutual del Clero in the Calle San Bernardo, where it is already pleasantly warm enough for occasional study on the big terrace. From there I go most days by the metro to the Biblioteca Nacional in the Paseo de la Castellana, the overburdened central north–south traffic axis through the capital. There I steep myself in Hegel's works from his time in Jena; here after the first outlines of systems he writes his first *magnum opus*, *Phenomenology of Spirit*. It seems strange against this backcloth: Hegel in Spain; the Jena period in Madrid.

One has to be able to combine opposites: every morning I learn Spanish for at least an hour. I had already begun in Rome to study the third most common language in the world after Chinese and English. It is a daughter language of Latin which is very like Italian in grammar but very dissimilar in tone and character. Whereas Italian can as it were be sung with long and short, open and closed *e* and *o*, Spanish is spoken amazingly quickly, staccato, without long and short vowels, even in solemn speeches. I love this language, which manages with a very reduced sound-system of only nineteen consonants (as opposed to thirty-six in Italian) and five vowels, so that writing and pronunciation almost match. This would make any reformer of the German language go green with envy. But despite all the passion Spanish seems to me to be both disciplined and restrained in pronunciation, especially where the *s* hisses as a fricative, the double *r* rolls and the initial *v* becomes *b*, so that in Spain one does not drink *'vino'*, as in Italy, but *'bino'*.

Nor do I want to speak here of the Prado, of El Greco, Velasquez, Murillo and the late Goya of the enigmatic and spooky *'pinturas negras'*; in my book *Credo* I will paint a little literary-theological portrait of El Greco's unique picture of Pentecost. A German historian who becomes a friend urges me to go to the Teatro de la Zarzuela, the 'Singspiel', which is unseemly for Spanish theologians. Fascinated, I follow the richly varied and colourful folk dances and folk music from the regions of Spain, which are so different. After my visit to Mexico my favourite folk music will later be the Mariachis (probably from *'mariage'* = wedding feast), in which wind, string and plucked instruments, Spanish, Mexican and even Austrian (from the unhappy time of the Mexican emperor Maximilian), unite.

But nothing enthuses me more than the flamenco, which in fact has fused together Arab-Indian, Jewish and gipsy elements. A dancer (or a couple) stamps out the rapidly changing rhythms with the feet to guitar accompaniment and accompanies it with handclaps or castanets, gloomily dramatic or often lightly and happily; the flamenco sings artistically of love, death, guilt and atonement! That could inspire even a German 'political theologian', who later became well known. Despite initial 'moral' inhibitions, he visits an intimate Flamenco Bar after the traditionally late Spanish dinner. The great *bailarina* only enters shortly before midnight, when the beginners have danced. Now this political theologian loses all inhibitions and, buoyed up by Rioja, gets on to the stage and offers the fair lady a flower from the table. And what in fact is more 'moral'? Once again, for those who like to psychologize: I admire this combination of passion and discipline, pride and surrender, earnestness and cheerfulness, overpowering beauty and sometimes grotesque comedy.

If later – in the Council or on lecture tours – I make contact with people amazing quickly, it is often because of my knowledge both of the language and also of the land, which I have acquired at an early stage. Toledo, the church centre of Spain, Segovia with the Alcazar and the Roman aqueduct; and more important for me Avila, its well-preserved mediaeval city wall and more than 80 towers: the Middle Ages 'live'! How well I can empathize with the time of the great mystic Teresa, persecuted by the Inquisition, the subject of our reading at table in Rome!

Seeing things will be important for my later analysis of the epoch-making paradigms (macro-constellations) of Christianity: no reading can simply replace it. Thus for example I visit the lonely, grey, cool monastic palace of the Escorial in the hill country of Castile, built by Philip II: for me it is abidingly the symbol of the great Spanish sixteenth century (*'siglo de oro'*), a monument to the struggle and victory of the Counter-Reformation. How different from that is the splendid château of Versailles, built by Louis XIV, surrounded by a gigantic garden landscape: a cult place of the absolutist monarchy and its paraliturgy, responsible with all its excesses for the outbreak of the French Revolution!

Spain seems to me to be very different from Italy – more serious, if you like, because of its history and character. No one ever waged in Italy a civil war so painfully long and at the same time so terrifyingly fanatical as the three-year Civil War in twentieth-century Spain between the progressive Republican govern-ment, supported by Communists, Socialists and anarchists, and the authoritarian nationalist movement, supported by the Catholic Church. By contrast with the 'Guerra civil' (1936-9), the Italian 'Risorgimento' in the previous century seems almost like a stroll: in Rome the Germanicum students always mocked what is perhaps the biggest single war memorial in the world, on which the gigantic Italian soldier, swinging his rifle, runs into the city gate instead of defending the city. Now in Spain under the victor General Francisco Franco a centralist-authoritarian state with a conservative and military stamp has firmly established itself. As a foreign visitor one sees relatively little of his dictatorship in public, apart from the police presence and the strictly censored and therefore unin-teresting media. And if one asks questions: The church? Privileged by the state. The bishops? Chosen by Franco, with virtually no contact with the modern world. The priests? Trained in seminaries. The faith of the people? Mixed with superstition.

Through Carlos Santamaría, organizer of the Conversaciones Catolicas Internacionales of San Sebastian, I gain a true friend in these two months: the knowledgeable church historian Ignacio Tellechea, a Basque, who did a doctorate on the important Dominican theologian Bartholomé de Carranza, an archbishop of Toledo accused by the Spanish Inquisition – of 'Lutheranism' and above all of defending the reading of the Bible by the laity and theology in the vernacular. For a whole seventeen years, almost until his death, this great man of the church languishes in the prison of the Inquisition. Tendencies towards Reformation are suppressed in Spain at a very early stage.

With theologians in Spain I talk a great deal about Rome, the Spanish church and the rich fascistoid Catholic secret society Opus Dei, which is hitherto unknown to me. Here it is often called 'Octopus Dei', because it stretches its tentacles into banks and businesses and the Spanish government: the majority of the last Franco cabinet will be members of Opus Dei. Even in 2003 the 'Work of God' disseminates so much fear among people that my main informant at the time is unwilling to recall any such conversation and forbids me to mention his name. In 1957 we would really never have dreamed that its founder, the Spanish priest José María Escrivá de Bálaguer y Albás (1902-75), regarded by many witnesses as vain, arrogant and ambitious, would be canonized by a Polish pope as early as 1992 in record time, bypassing the regulations, and in the year 2002 will even be beatified. Nor that the same pope, six decades after the Civil War, will at a stroke cumulatively canonize 2302 Catholic 'martyrs' – without even mentioning the failure of the Catholic Church over social questions, without mentioning its one-sided position in the war, and without mentioning the socialists 'martyred' by the nationalist troops.

Strange Lourdes (and Fatima)

After about two months I travel with my leaden case of books in the train through northern Spain in the direction of Paris, but then detour from the main line. I want to spend at least a day and a night in Lourdes, the scene of the appearances of Mary in 1858. In Rome we had listened to Franz Werfel's world bestseller *The Song of Bernadette* in the refectory and had also been allowed to see Henry King's filming of the novel: the Jew Werfel's vow should he be saved, when in June 1940 he found shelter in Lourdes on his flight from the Germans. I was impressed not so much by the story of the girl Bernadette as by the provocative incomprehensibility of the miracle brought out by Werfel.

But in the course of my own reflection during my years in Rome on knowledge and faith I have become increasingly sceptical about reports of appearances and miracles, though I am far from that enlightened arrogance that Werfel illuminates in ironic and amusing scenes. Werfel, too, is certainly aware of the craving for miracles among the faithful, who do not venture the risk of faith but only want to enjoy security. I simply want to 'experience' Lourdes for myself and do not neglect to ask for grace. May I be shown it if it is important for my spirituality.

As ever, having arrived at some small hotel, in Lourdes I wander through the countless shops and stalls. I am not particularly disturbed by the commerce, since one can find the same sort of thing in Einsiedeln in Switzerland. I had often been there with my parents and my grandfather as a child and a young man. But no particular messages of good news or threats and no miracles of the Madonna were associated with Einsiedeln, which goes back to the hermit Meinrad in the ninth century. There was always a touch of festivity about Einsiedeln. Since the baroque period, in which the grandiose rebuilding of church and monastery along with the square was done, the monastery has also served as the powerful backcloth to impressive theatrical performances, for example of Calderon's *Great Theatre of the World*. Many healing miracles are also reported in Einsiedeln. However, I could never forget that it was on a pilgrimage to Einsiedeln that my grandmother lost her life through a car accident. I couldn't reconcile the journey to the 'place of grace' and the gracelessness of this death.

But in Lourdes I am theologically disturbed by the fact that Mary, Queen of Heaven, is presented alone, without her Son, distributing grace herself with both hands. So it is here that 'the Lady' who finally made herself known as 'the Immaculate Conception' is said to have appeared to the ignorant girl Bernadette Soubirous – interestingly enough, precisely four years after the proclamation of the controversial dogma by the 'Marian pope' Pius IX in 1854, who also promptly has the first statue in Lourdes crowned by his nuncio. There is always the same statue of Mary at the front of the square, in the centre, up on the church, in the church. No room for the *'solus Christus'* as mediator.

However, 'the Lady' not only called for a sanctuary, procession, prayers and penitential exercises but also made a wonderful fountain spring up. Over the decades many thousands of healings are reported of it and some dozens at any rate have been recognized as 'miraculous' – inexplicable by science. Lourdes was finally 'authenticated' by the beatification of Bernadette in 1925 by Pius XI: Werfel concludes his 'historical epic' with this celebration. My French colleague, the Mariologist René Laurentin (I will get to know him more closely at the Council), has published several books and two dossiers of *'documents authentiques'* on Lourdes. But what is really authentic here? Doubts arise. I try to pray earnestly, but from the beginning I note how ill at ease I feel. And the sermons about Mary at the masses, which I necessarily have to listen to on the fringe, annoy me more than they help me. Thankfully, indeed praise God, the prayers of the official liturgy are still always concluded with *per Dominum nostrum Jesum Christum* . . .

Doubts increase when I think of the second famous case of appearances of Mary, Fatima. Later in Lucerne Dr Otto Karrer, a specialist in mysticism, and I are given through the mediation of Karl Rahner the possibility of reading a summary of the original protocol of the appearances of Mary to the children of shepherds in Fatima. For a long time these documents were unknown, and now have been rediscovered in Spain. They were composed by the Lisbon professor of theology Nuñes Formigão and published in 1927 under the pseudonym Visconde de Montelo (414 pages of them!). It is immediately clear to me that I needn't go there as well. With my 'logistical' help Otto Karrer sends this summary with a warning letter to various cardinals (including Montini) and bishops. For many indications (two different Madonnas at the same time, an appearance to other people as well, foreknowledge of what is revealed) convince him that at least Fatima, though likewise confirmed by popes, is a pious and in some respect contradictory projection by the children (more precisely by the oldest of the three). It is all easy to explain: their mother had previously told them of other appearances in La Salette, where the Queen of Heaven had already appeared to shepherds' children in 1846. Karrer's critical analysis has completely convinced me. However, the pilgrimage trade in Fatima continues as if there were no doubts. Indeed Paul VI (Montini) and John Paul II (Wojtyla) will enhance the place further by personal appearances. Since the nineteenth century, papalism and Marianism have gone hand in hand.

And La Salette? On the advice of my cousin Walter Gut, who is enthusiastic about Mary, I will also visit this place once on my journey while passing through:

a very beautiful location in the department of Isère in the French Alps, modest, congenial and far less commercialized than the other great scenes of appearances. But what am I to make of the message from Mary that was already disseminated by these children, which threatens punishments, calls for submission to the authority of God and the church, and offers the intercessory mediation of Mary between her divine son and sinful humanity? Veneration of Mary under the title 'Reconciler of Sinners'? It is practised by the brotherhood founded here. For me it is utterly impossible in the light of the New Testament, which speaks explicitly of the one and only mediator, Jesus Christ.

But in Lourdes I am impressed by the eyes of the countless sick, in the evening also brought on stretchers and wheelchairs. Now in the light of the hundreds of candles they receive the blessing of the Madonna and hope for healing. Eyes full of trust and longing. On this occasion I recall more intensely than before how in the early summer of 1955 at the request of my mother I travelled from Rome to southern Italy to ask for help from the miracle-worker Padre Pio (1887-1968) in San Giovanni Rotondo (Apulia). How am I to refuse her request to ask for the healing of my brother, in the last stage of a terminal illness, with a brain tumour, from the popular saint who as early as 1918 was marked by bleeding wounds in his hands, feet and side? In vain. Was faith lacking? In 2002 Padre Pio, too, is canonized by the self-same pope who visited him around the time that I visited him as a student, and was given the prediction that he would become pope and survive an attempt on his life. Padre Pio didn't prophesy anything for me, but I didn't ask him anything for myself either.

I'm not a rationalist. Later, in a long chapter of my book *On Being a Christian* I have indicated in a historical–critical account that one may by no means interpret out of the Gospels all the healings of the different kinds of sick people. And today's medicine, recognizing more than ever the psychosomatic character of many illnesses, knows of amazing healings on the basis of extraordinary psychological influences or stimuli, on the basis of an infinite trust, on the basis of 'faith'. I can take the healing stories of the New Testament seriously as stories of faith. And of course what happened there can in principle also happen in Lourdes. It is a matter of the powers of self-healing stimulated by faith.

However, the 'nature miracles', where natural laws are directly abolished and the unbroken causal connection is said to be violated – a horror for any natural scientist – have a rather different character. Am I to allow Werfel to convince me that reason must capitulate before such miracles? No, they can be explained by historical criticism as the formation of legends or as taken over from other traditions; they by no means need simply to be 'believed'. Is miracle the dearest child of faith, as Goethe's *Faust* puts it in the Easter night scene? The New Testament says that love is faith's dearest child, love in the sense of unshakable self-surrender. This must also be the meaning of the love that the Jew Franz Werfel wanted the girl Bernadette to sing – without 'ogling with Rome', as Thomas Mann mocked. Real miracles do not happen visibly but in the human heart.

156

London: English democracy – Anglican Church

After my visit to Lourdes I have another brief stay in Paris. But I want – and all this is by train and boat – to go on to London, where I am thinking of spending the next two months, June and July 1957. London is the most cosmopolitan city in Europe; it may not have been planned and built as rationally as the Paris of the grandiose boulevards and squares, but it has a historic centre with own grandeur, the City and Westminster north of the Thames. There is an indescribable mixture of people from very different nations, regions and religions which indicates to me that I am in the capital of the British Commonwealth. I have no inkling how important London will become for my efforts for the world religions and world peace.

A private pleasure, but not to be despised: here I again meet my cousin Liselotte, who had been with me in Paris ten years previously, and her husband, a lawyer in the city. In 1956 I had married them in Paris against the will of her father, my godfather. Now in London they're expecting their first child. At a cheerful dinner the three of us laugh so heartily that that same night a daughter is born. The Lord gives his own in laughter. 'Lovely day, isn't it?' In London people reply with political correctness, 'Isn't it lovely?', even when the skies of England are lowering, but also often when it has cleared up again. In the land of Eliza Doolittle with her 'the rain in Spain stays mainly in the plain' there is no more important topic of conversation than the weather.

In London, too, I sit daily at 'my Hegel'. Most days I go in a heatwave from the rather boring north of London where I have a little apartment, by bus and underground to the British Museum. I have never found a more beautiful and more comfortable place – the circular reading room under the dome, which is 50 metres high, with every chair covered in blue leather. I work here intensively, as did Karl Marx long before; he regularly wrote his *Das Kapital* in this place. Did Marx go over in the lunch break, as I do, to the other part of the 'treasure house of the British nation', to the unique Parthenon sculptures, the 'Elgin Marbles' taken by Lord Elgin from the acropolis in Athens and subsequently purchased by the British state?

I had already walked historic London when I was at grammar school. I don't necessarily want to see again from within the Tower of London, which reminds me of the dark sides of the British monarchy, especially the beheading of his Lord Chancellor Thomas More ordered by Henry VIII. Here while on the scaffold, with humour More moves his beard aside with the words 'That has not committed treason.' Today at any rate this great humanist, over whom for a long time there has often been silence in the Anglican church and in literature, is commemorated with a memorial plaque in the Tower and in the English Parliament as one of the greatest Englishmen in history. I will later devote a little work of my own to him and be warden of a student hostel named after him.

The crown jewels on display in the Tower, above all those of Queen Victoria, Empress of India, in the diamond jubilee of her reign over the world's greatest empire, remind me of how as a twelve-year-old I marvelled at the British empire in pink on my small map of the world and of how meanwhile the political situation of the world has fundamentally changed. Decolonizalization began with the independence of India and Pakistan in 1947; it continues with the Suez War which is lost in 1956 and now in 1957 with the independence of the British Gold Coast (Ghana) in Africa. Great Britain is losing its leading position in the Commonwealth and is falling back into second place as a great power. Instead, America, the coming superpower, is newly present everywhere.

For me the British Parliament, the 'mother of all parliaments', is important. Not because, as I observed at a session of the House of Commons (pleasantly small and modest by comparison with the coming German Bundestag), here no long speeches are read out from prepared texts; arguments go to and fro in free discussion (moreover my newspaper is taken away, as newspapers are taken away from all visitors: not even members can have them). It is important because here, after much turbulence, the rights of the people against the absolutism of rulers – still the dominant system in the Roman Catholic Church – were established earlier than elsewhere (1688/9) without guillotining the king, in a 'Glorious Revolution'. For centuries there has been a 'constitutional' monarchy in England: in 1948 I watched the British royal couple George VI and Queen Elizabeth (later the 'Queen Mother') go from Buckingham Palace to the Opening of Parliament in their golden coach. But now, in 1957, already five years after the death of her father, Elizabeth II is on the throne of Britain, and with her husband Prince Philip, Duke of Edinburgh, enjoys the utmost respect. One day he will write the preface to the English edition of my *Global Responsibility*. And with him in the chair, I will give the St George's Lecture in 1986 in St George's Chapel, Windsor.

In Westminster Abbey, where the kings of England are crowned and buried, I attend Sunday worship. In contrast to the nearby Roman Catholic Westminster Cathedral, a Neo-Byzantine domed building, where an extremely boring Latin service is celebrated with much Gregorian chant, here I experience a moving, simplified and concentrated service in English, which in the liturgy according to the Book of Common Prayer sounds particularly beautiful, accompanied by joyful festal hymns by Handel and other classical composers. However, the fact that the church is anything but full makes me think. What is missing?

I gladly concede that from the beginning (quite apart from my high esteem for the English way of life which I got to know in Cornwall in 1948, conscious of tradition yet relaxed and unconventional) I have always had a great empathy with the Anglican Church – of course without any desire to be converted to it and with all the reservations about any form of state church. In the Church of England I can study what the Catholic Church on the continent of Europe could have looked like had not Rome and the German episcopate excluded Luther's concerns from the start. Would the break between England and Rome have been prevented if at that time the pope had declared null the marriage of Henry VIII, a Renaissance man, to a Spanish wife, Catherine of Aragon (it was uncanonical, and entered into only on the basis of a papal dispensation), without fear of her nephew, the German emperor Charles V, and allowed him to marry Anne Boleyn, the lady of the court? No one knows.

At any rate in this Anglican service I have a vivid experience of how the Church of England is a Catholic but Reformed church down to its liturgical vestments, images and crosses. Reform of doctrine: including the justification of the sinner. Reform of the liturgy: the vernacular. Reform of discipline: the marriage of priests and bishops. But all without giving up the traditional structure of ministry: the episcopate. Thus there is a good English middle way (*via media*) between the extremes of the former Roman authoritarianism and the subsequent Calvinist–biblicist Puritanism.

How will this church hold together? After all, it is distributed all over the British empire. By loyalty to the Archbishop of Canterbury, though unlike the pope he does not claim any kind of legislative and executive power. So the unity of the church doesn't need any dogma of primacy and infallibility. I will always believe that Rome and Canterbury can be reconciled. But on one condition, namely that Rome retracts its claims to power and right – which are in no way based on the Bible and the first millennium of Catholic tradition – and returns to the *communio* model of the Christianity of the first millennium. So I know why a decade later I will dedicate the English edition of my book *The Church* to the Archbishop of Canterbury, Dr Michael Ramsey, and will call Archbishop George Carey my friend.

Amsterdam: Catholic tradition and renewal

I should now note with gratitude how much I can carry in my memory of the art of the English cathedrals and English painting: with all due respect to Gainsborough, J. M. W. Turner remains the most interesting painter for me. Right at the beginning of the nineteenth century, with his visionary paintings he is a forerunner of Impressionism; he dissolves his motifs, even objects of industrial society, in floods of light and colour, sometimes shining brightly, and sometimes also uncannily dark, so that the atmospheric effect aims at the almost metaphysical impression of a boundless world.

Back in Amsterdam after my months in London, I often talk with my friends about art and religion. For me as a theologian – for all my admiration for Rembrandt – my favourite Dutch painter remains the tormented and thwarted preacher Vincent Van Gogh. Combining the Dutch tradition with the new artistic currents in France, he becomes the pioneer of expressionism and twentieth-century art. Even at school I have acquired two or three reproductions of his paintings. With thick rapid stokes, ignoring many details, the late van Gogh can suggestively express what seems essential to him – until he breaks down and takes his own life.

I am particularly fond of the Netherlands – so totally different from my mountainous Swiss home. Granted, in the Swiss Mittelland one by no means feels imprisoned by the mountains. But I like the broad open horizon, the wide panoramic view which in Switzerland one gets only on the high peaks. I like the water that is present everywhere and the play of clouds which often changes rapidly. If the mountains, in a mythical exaggeration, are a symbol of freedom from external influence, so too in another way is the sea, which links all the coasts of this earth. And with over-powerful neighbouring nations on their frontiers, the Dutch, like the Swiss, have developed an unbounded will for freedom. In many characteristics the matter-of-fact, pragmatic, thrifty, reliable Dutch, intent on independence, are not dissimilar to the Swiss, though to me they also seem open to the world and humorous – as an old seafaring nation with colonies. They can subsequently cope more easily with the consequences of the loss of their colonial empire – in 1956 Indonesia has abolished the union with the Netherlands – than the British and the French.

In Amsterdam I live with the family of our friends, the van Stijns, in one of the typically Dutch narrow houses with steep steps and curtainless windows, which are brightly illuminated in the evening. I make an effort to read, to understand and to speak Dutch, so like German and yet in many respects so unlike it: later I will also be able to give some lectures in 'Dutch'. For in the coming decades I often return to the Netherlands, not only because of personal relations but also because the Catholic church of the Netherlands will become the spearhead of the Catholic renewal. In the middle of the 1950s I got to know it as still traditional, yet very lively. In Amsterdam's great Rosary Church, which I visit, as everywhere else there is active participation: during one service often five or six collections are made – all for different causes. The Dutch Catholics finance their work themselves, without any church tax: even the biggest newspaper in the country, *De Volkskrant*, and the Catholic radio network KRO, whose studios in Hilversum I visit, as I do much else. Not only this is organized here on a confessional-ideological basis.

But in the course of the centuries, the small Catholic minority, which after the Reformation dared only to worship in secret, had become probably the most powerful church in the land with a competent clergy, a lively theology and an active laity. This church with its episcopate is predestined to play a special role in the coming Council. The future Roman Secretariat for Christian Unity and the future international theological journal *Concilium*, the *New Catechism* and renewed Catholic synodicality have their roots in the Netherlands. It would never have occurred to me that one day I would be able to give a lecture (on the global ethic) in the royal palace in Amsterdam (at the invitation of Queen Beatrice).

A wise German once said that the shortest way to oneself is a journey round the world. An Englishman said, perhaps even more wisely, 'Those who know only England do not know England.' This can be applied even more to little Switzerland, to which I now return after nine years of absence – apparently permanently. It is here that a new era will begin both for me and for the Catholic Church.

V

✺✺✺✺

The Church Sets Out for Freedom

*'You will never write such a book
when you get older.
So publish it now!'*

Counsellor Prelate Josef Höfer

A practical test: Lucerne

In July 1957 back in Sursee: at last, undisturbed on our terrace, I can dictate the first draft of my study on Hegel's christology chapter by chapter to my younger fellow-student from the Germanicum, Leonz Gassmann, also from the diocese of Basle, as he sits at the typewriter. The title is *The Incarnation of God*. In due course it is meant to be revised from beginning to end and presented to the Sorbonne as a philosophical dissertation. But because of many unexpected developments, that will never happen. The study will appear in print only in 1970 – a good twelve years later – on the 200th anniversary of Hegel's birth, having meanwhile been worked through two or three times and expanded.

And what a twelve years! In 1958 Pius XII dies and John XXIII is elected. In 1968 Paul VI publishes the encyclical *Humanae vitae* on birth control, which in 1970 is the occasion for my book *Infallible? An Inquiry*. What lies in between? A dramatic history, but for me it begins quite harmlessly. I am not quite 30 and spend the next two years back in Switzerland, which with some effort has worked its way out of its isolation after the Second World War. It is true that the country has not joined the United Nations Organization because of an exaggerated principle of neutrality – a mistake which will burden Swiss foreign policy for decades. But at any rate there is participation in other international organizations. During the 1956 rebellion in Hungary there are protest demonstrations and 10,000 Hungarian refugees are accepted. Just over a decade later, in 1968/9 the acceptance of 12,000 Czechoslovakian refugees shows solidarity. Political neutrality does not mean moral neutrality; neutrality and solidarity belong together.

On my return, in Sursee I receive news from the Bishop of Basle: I have been appointed assistant priest (*Vikar*) at the Hofkirche in Lucerne. I am delighted: my new place of work is barely twenty kilometres from Sursee. From my time at the grammar school there I have felt at home in Lucerne, which in summer and during the weeks of the international music festival is a cosmopolitan city. And the main church of Lucerne, with its two pointed towers the hallmark of the city, seems to me to be an ideal field of activity.

In fact I am lucky with my first parish priest and his whole team. Dr Joseph Bühlmann is doing all he can to renew the pastoral care of this great parish, which stretches from the famous Kappell Bridge to the boundaries of the city. He faces the opposition of the old canons of St Leodegar. Provost Joseph Alois Beck from Sursee – as he once tells me – had required him to take the traditional oath to observe the existing statutes and rules of the canonical foundation on being appointed. The new priest said that he couldn't do that; in particular in matters of liturgy – the choral singing of the canons – he had to act firmly against existing practices. The provost's answer was in good Roman style: 'It isn't really very complicated. Do what you want. But you have to take the oath!' So he did. And now he does what he thinks is pastorally right. This is an anecdote which characterizes him, but it is also a particular way of surviving spiritually in Catholicism as it actually exists.

I am likewise lucky with my two fellow assistant priests, Anton Studer and Franz Xaver Schwander: they take the same line on the church and theology; we keep having discussions but hardly ever have a serious dispute. Both are capable helpers when at that time a striking article of mine on 'A Lack of Priests in Switzerland?' is published under the sign of three asterisks *** in *Civitas*, a journal of the Swiss Student Association, which opposes the employment of ordained priests in functions alien to their calling. This results in an enormous discussion. With satisfaction, together we edit the reactions, and I write the concluding reflections, almost 50 pages in all. Our good relations prove themselves in the clergy house, when a small clique in the parish tries to involve me in intrigues against the parish priest because I 'obviously have the right ideas'. My boss thinks highly of me, because in this affair, which lasts for weeks and in which even the episcopal ordinariate intervenes, from the beginning I lack neither truthfulness nor loyalty.

Our priest is also always open to suggestions. And he gratefully allows me to invite friends as visiting preachers, especially for Holy Week or the great festivals. So in my time cycles of sermons are given not only by Otto Karrer and Hans Urs von Balthasar, but also by Wolfgang Seibel and Oswald Loretz; Karl Rahner has to decline because he can't spare the time.

What an assistant priest has to do

We alternate over baptisms, marriage instruction and funerals. Two or three times I also write short articles for the parish magazine, above all about the renewal of the liturgy and Latin ('It was always so! Was it always so?'). And every day during this period, sometimes quite alone, we celebrate our eucharist. The silent masses of the many priests – a custom which first began in the Middle Ages, against which Karl Rahner is the first to make successful theological objections ('The One Sacrifice and the Many Masses', 1951) – will then in fact be abolished by the Council in favour of concelebration.

I especially enjoy the sermons: normally one gives a sermon four or five times (Saturday evening until Sunday evening). At the youth service I often preach in 'Schwyzerdütsch', which communicates a special feeling of homeland and fellowship. I will continue to use it when occasion demands to the present day, even if later I argue resolutely for high German in the media as opposed to the popular wave of dialect – so that the media can be understood within Switzerland by Romands and Ticinesi and even more by the millions of foreigners who are settled in Switzerland or passing through. My simple experience in preparing sermons is, however, that the scholastic theology of the Gregorian is virtually no help to me. I hardly ever open my Latin textbooks, which I've had beautifully bound, for a sermon. Barth's *Church Dogmatics* already help me more: I give a whole series of evening addresses on the individual attributes of God, and here Karl Barth's accounts are a great inspiration.

Religious instruction in the schools is more difficult. There are few catechetical aids that can be used in teaching children. However, the youth of the 1950s isn't particularly rebellious. But it isn't always easy to maintain discipline and provide teaching that will hold the attention of boys and girls of twelve and thirteen, who are already showing signs of being at different stages of puberty, are excited, and protest. I like those of ten or eleven most; unlike the even smaller ones, they do very well in spiritual matters, but aren't yet at a rebellious age. The girls in particular are so devoted that sometimes a little group meets me at the door of the clergy house: some want to carry my briefcase and others want to hold my hand, which earns me good-natured mockery from my fellow assistant priests, who use terms like 'Pestalozzi'. But I'm glad that with few exceptions I get on well with all the pupils, boys and girls. Later I will often meet grown men and women who tell me with pleasure that they attended religious instruction that I had given.

People are amazed how, as president of the 'Blue Ring' of Catholic girls, with all the leaders' meetings and group meetings, with forest Christmases and parents' evenings, and a successful holiday camp in the Valais which lasts for several weeks, I still have time for scholarly work: two big articles on 'Justification and Sanctification according to the New Testament' (*Festschrift* for O. Karrer) and on 'Karl Barth's Doctrine of the Word of God as a Question for Catholic Theology' (*Festschrift* for G. Söhngen). But as always I make use of every free minute, and above all the free day that we have every week.

The Congregation of Marian Virgins, which has similarly been handed over to me, poses particular problems. I've already heard a lecture in the Collegium Germanicum about these communities composed of clergy and laity in the spirit of the Ignatian exercises for service in the church and the world; they were initiated by the Jesuits in the Counter-Reformation – ten years after the foundation of the college. But the Roman General Secretary of the Marian Congregation, the Dutchman Fr Paulussen SJ, who seems a bit of a fanatic, can't convince me or others that they are still 'fellowships of Christian life' (as they were renamed after the Council), in keeping with the time. Many of the conversations in which I've sought information in Holland and Belgium about the organization of pastoral care – especially the JOC (Jeunesse Ouvrière Catholique) of Canon Cardijn, who also spoke to us in Rome, which has quite a different stamp – have reinforced me in this.

But what is to be done now in Lucerne? This is a test case for reforms. Do I abolish it and in so doing reject some older unmarried ladies, who are the backbone of the group? I don't want to and mustn't. Do I keep everything as it is? I don't want to do that either. First of all, it seems to me important to do away with the old-maidish flavour of the Congregation. Preparing everything carefully by individual conversations with those concerned, contrary to all previous custom I accept the resignation of the members of the committee which is offered as a matter of routine and have no problem in replacing them with younger members.

So we now form a 'core' made up of a rejuvenated committee and youth leaders. Alongside this there is a Dragonfly Club for younger people with voluntary membership: on Fridays it usually offers a theme evening with an artist, jazz musician, psychologist, theologian or whatever. In this way there is at any rate new life in this sector of pastoral care, and I certainly don't forget the older members of the community. With them, as always after a thorough explanation, and long before official permission is given, I celebrate a simple eucharist in the vernacular, no longer looking towards the altar wall but to the assembled community, and in a way which is certainly far more spontaneous than what I once found in Westminster Abbey. People are enthusiastic. Our priest welcomes that. The bishop knows nothing about it. And Rome is a long way away.

The considerable amount of work associated with this pastoral care of girls and women couldn't have been done without the help of women. Maria Merz, the housekeeper of the clergy house, is important as a calming influence in the building; the parish secretary and the pastoral worker are responsible for the administration, but the people who are particularly important for me are Hildegard Meyer, the newly-elected leader of the Congregation, and Odette Zurmühle, who helps me to look after the Dragonfly Club. Later she will become my first helper in Tübingen (1961-7) in place of my youngest sister – until it proves that the double burden of secretary (formally a part-time job) and housekeeping, which I completely underestimate, is simply too much for one person, however capable and generous.

Leading theological figures

When I report to my priest that I would tell married couples who accused themselves in the confessional of the sin of contraception that this was not a 'mortal sin', and that they need no longer accuse themselves of it if they already have a responsible number of children, because birth control is a matter of personal responsibility, he argues seriously: 'Do that if you want. But if you're denounced to the bishop you must expect severe sanctions.' I continue to do it and am not denounced. At the same time Franz Böckle, around seven years older than me, well known to me and now visiting us, has a similar experience in the confessional. Initially Professor of Moral Theology in Chur, he speaks on the crisis in morality and moral theology and boldly takes a public stand on matters of birth control. From 1963 professor at the university of Bonn, he becomes the leading Catholic moral theologian ('Law and Conscience', 1964). More than anyone else he takes on the topics of sexuality, marriage, the family and medical ethics.

However, I have few connections with one institution in Lucerne, the theological faculty, although it is located just behind the Hofkirche. Unlike the ecumenical circles of Zurich, Berne, Basle and Lucerne, with one or two exceptions the faculty is little interested in a renewed theology or even in the topic of justification. The dogmatic theologian is interested only in the theology of the Eastern Church, and the moral theologian (the Schenker who 'sniffs out' heretics) and the canon lawyer (of the same spirit) are opponents of my ecumenical ideas.

I am invited as a visiting lecturer not by Lucerne, which is nearby, but by Regensburg Theological College, which is a long way away. There, from 29 January 1959 onwards, I have the honour and joy, at the initiative of Professor Georg Englhardt, who had paid me a visit in Lucerne, of being allowed to give my first series of lectures at a German college, on justification.

In Lucerne I can console myself with the fact that the same faculty also has no interest in relations with the famous Otto Karrer (1888-1976), whose wide theological horizon, ecumenical openness and warm humanity impress me greatly; he immediately suggests that we use the informal *Du* with each other, and I am invited to share his seventieth birthday in the Fürstensaal of the monastery of Einsiedeln. Perhaps no German theologian in his life and his work so anticipated the coming *aggiornamento* as this Jesuit, who left the Jesuit order: his biography of Franz von Borja, the third General of the order, had met with the disapproval of the Jesuit General, nor had he been willing to go on to write an apologia for the controversial anti-Reform theologian Bellarmine. On an impulse, he joined the Evangelical Lutheran church for some months. After his return to the Catholic Church he was punished for that with a penitential year and sanctions until his seventy-fifth birthday.

In 1935 this anti-Nazi German whom many people treated with hostility became a Swiss citizen; he worked indefatigably as a preacher and pastor in Lucerne and was the inspiration behind the various ecumenical circles. In his publications he devotes himself especially to spirituality and mysticism, and particularly to the revered English theologian John Henry Newman. In 1942, in the middle of the war, the Vatican (which kept extremely quiet about the Nazis) had nothing better to do than to place Karrer's book on 'Prayer, Providence and Miracle' on the Index of Prohibited Books. He had put in question the immediate, visibly physical consequences of prayer in the form of miracles (e.g. rain, blessing on the harvest and the like). Otto Karrer doesn't allow himself to be deterred from his way. He lives wholly by the Bible and translates the New Testament into comprehensible German. At a very early stage he engages in constructive argument with the world religions and devotes himself intensively to the Christian ecumenical world. He seems to be the first to have spoken of a 'Petrine service' (orientated on the Bible) rather than the 'papacy' (with its historical ballast) – for him this isn't just an exegetical-historical question but a psychological and political one.

This great theologian has never been invited to give a lecture by the theological faculty of Lucerne, but has often been denounced to the bishops and in Rome. My friendly relationships over the years (including our joint action against the credibility of Fatima) are simply kept quiet about in the biography of Karrer entrusted to the church historian of the faculty (and given financial support by me). This is just throwing Catholic church history together.

Another important Lucerne theologian, Herbert Haag, no less congenial a person than Otto Karrer, had lasted only three years in the Germanicum. He wanted above all to study exegesis and in his day this lay in the shadow of the erroneous decrees of the Pontifical Biblical Commission under Pius X. Even Fr Bea, Rector of the Pontifical Biblical Institute, advised Haag to continue his studies in Paris. He then gained his doctorate in Freiburg and went on to study in Jerusalem at the École Biblique, whose founder, M.-J. Lagrange OP, had fought more than any other Catholic exegete for the introduction of the historical-critical method which was vilified in Rome, and had suffered under the Inquisition.

Very few exegetes can have acquired such comprehensive linguistic equipment (five ancient and five modern languages), knowledge of literature and archaeology as Herbert Haag, an indefatigable worker. Now in Lucerne he has produced his historical-critical 'Bible Lexicon' in several fascicles (1951-6). Just two years later he becomes my colleague on the Tübingen faculty and my most loyal friend. But like Otto Karrer, he too is never invited again by his own Lucerne faculty. In the Lucerne faculty does mediocrity fear extraordinary lucidity?

Since in any case I am overburdened, it doesn't bother me that over the next five decades I too am never once invited to give any form of teaching, although I have good relations with one or two professors: 'No prophet in his home town.' But unfortunately the 'ban' is also extended to my pupils, and this troubles me:

'No pupil of the prophet, even if he comes from Lucerne, in his home town.' Professor Urs Baumann from Hochdorf/Lucerne deserves honourable mention here; his publications need fear no comparison with those of his Lucerne colleagues, and he has been passed over for two professorial chairs.

Ecclesia semper reformanda: *an explosive theme*

Ten days before Regensburg an event took place which was far more important for me – in Basle. In Lucerne, some time in autumn 1958, I receive a telephone call from Karl Barth: he invites me to give a guest lecture at his own faculty, the Protestant theological faculty in Basle. I am to talk on justification. But I don't want to do this in Barth's presence: I say that my book is better known there than I am; people can read it and I don't want to repeat myself. 'Then perhaps another topic?' Karl Barth reflects for a moment: 'It would be extremely interesting to hear from you as a Catholic theologian what you had to say on *Ecclesia semper reformanda* – "the church always in need of reform".'

This is not only a highly interesting topic but also a highly explosive one. Will I be able to cope with it on top of all the pastoral work? Two weeks later I accept. I feel well prepared. First, on the practical level, by all the experiences that I have had in Rome, which have been tested in various countries of Europe. Secondly, theologically: by the Gregorian theology which has clearly taught me the limits of the 'Catholic', and on the other hand by the works of Barth and Congar (on church and reform), of Lortz (on the Reformation), and the conversations with Josef Fischer (on a possible 'third force' between the Reformation and the Counter-Reformation), and much more.

On Sunday 18 January 1959, to introduce our world Week of Prayer for Christian Unity, I give all the sermons in the Hofkirche on the topic 'Christians on the Way to Unity'. Then on Monday, 19 January 1959, there follows in Basle my lecture on *Ecclesia semper reformanda*. A 'dangerous topic,' I explain in the introduction, 'for which very few Catholic theologians must envy one'. The very title of this lecture is unacceptable to many Catholic theologians. Basically, every single word is disputed.

Semper? To be reformed 'time and again'? The well-known Zurich ecumenist and Jesuit Ebneter tells me on a visit to Zurich that no Catholic could possibly say this; it is typically Protestant. I listen to his arguments, but they don't convince me.

Ecclesia? 'The church'? According to the traditional Roman view (warmed up again by Cardinal Ratzinger in the year 2000) this doesn't need to be reformed at all. Only its 'members' need to be reformed. The church itself is 'holy', *immaculata*, immaculate. Only its members are 'sinners'. Therefore the church is *immaculata ex maculatis*. While it consists of sinners, it is not itself sinful. Even Yves Congar, who has written the most comprehensive book on church reform, follows the traditional line on this basic question. Only Karl Rahner points out how completely abstract this distinction is and consequently wants to talk not only of a church of sinners but also of a 'sinful church'. Accordingly the issue is also the reform of the church itself and confessions of the church's guilt, and not just (as John Paul II still thinks in the year 2000) the guilt of 'its sons and daughters' (of course the 'holy fathers' are not mentioned).

Reformanda? There is especially a dispute about what authentic reform is. Congar's book may have the title *Vraie et fausse Réforme dans l'Église*. But what for him is *'vraie réforme'*, 'true reform'? His answer is: only a reform of the 'life' of the church: for him only this is a Catholic reform. What then is *'fausse réforme'*, 'false reform'? Amazingly, for Congar it is reform of the 'teaching' of the church. And according to him Protestant reform is precisely this. So is the Reformation false reform?!

Unfortunately this sharp basic distinction runs right through Yves Congar's book, rich as its material is. But all my experience with the basic problem of the doctrine of justification shows the opposite: that Catholic theology too is quite decisively concerned (like Luther, Barth and also the Council of Trent) to achieve a reform not only of the life of the church but particularly also of its doctrine. Often Congar seems to me to be all too indebted to the Thomistic system and Thomistic categories. Is this perhaps a purely theoretical discussion? It was suddenly to become a topical and practical issue in a quite unexpected way.

A council!

I know what I now have to argue for as a Catholic theologian in Protestant Basle, even if it is difficult to bring the mass of problems together in a paper which will take a full hour to deliver. As I read through the 24 closely-written pages once more, it becomes a high-speed lecture in three parts, with a systematic construction and divided up to the last detail:

Is reform *possible* in the Catholic Church? As a visible church consisting of sinful people the church itself needs constant reform.

How far is a reform possible in the Catholic Church? We may suffer and pray, but we must also criticize and ask: there must be not just a reform of the heart, not just a reform of abuses, but a creative reform of the situation, in accordance with the norm of the gospel.

Is reform *real* in the Catholic Church? A connection has to be seen between the reform before the Reformation, the repudiation of the Protestant Reformation and the Catholic restoration. Catholic reform today, Catholic approaches to the positive realization of Protestant concerns for reform and many other positive points of contact have to be discussed, above all the reform of doctrine.

I can base all this briefly and clearly both on Holy Scripture and on church history and also go into practical demands for reform in detail. A good part of it has already come home to me in Rome. However, my central demand would hardly be subscribed to even by a Congar: Catholics must realize the justified concern of Protestants in life and teaching, and conversely Protestants must realize the justified concern of Catholics – both in the light of one and the same gospel.

After almost an hour and a half I reach the conclusion. Here it is, word for word:

We are on the way! No more. We are on the way and still far from our destination. We still have many wishes for our church and for yours. We must expect resistance, disappointments and setbacks; they are part of the human church. The faithful are not discouraged by them. Four centuries show them that Catholic reform is going forward in earnest. We are on the way! We, the old church, the church with the many wrinkles, but still the old church: a living church which attempts to take the *ecclesia semper reformanda* seriously. Kierkegaard said that Protestantism was a 'corrective' to this church, which must never become 'regulative'. But what will happen if what needs to be corrected slowly goes on correcting itself? If a church which, while remaining to the end of its day *ecclesia reformanda*, one day in the course of the concern for reformation became *ecclesia reformata? Ecclesia catholica reformata?* Suppose that things got this far. What should happen then? I would like to conclude my all too long lecture with this question to you, my dear audience.

Tumultuous applause. Karl Barth in complete agreement. But in the ensuing discussion, by tradition in the restaurant next door, comes the question of a Protestant student: 'Aren't you all too optimistic about the future of the Catholic Church and its capacity to reform itself?' There is murmuring. I reply: 'Since 1 October of last year we have had a new pope, Angelo Roncalli, John XXIII. He has already given many stimuli towards reform. I don't believe that they were the last ones.' That happened on Monday 19 January 1959.

Six days later, on Sunday 25 January 1959, comes one of the strangest strokes of providence in my life: at the end of the Week of Prayer for Christian Unity, which had been concluded in our parish with seven lectures (on the Eastern Churches, Protestantism, Anglicanism, Old Catholicism and also on Judaism and Islam) and with an ecumenical collection for a Protestant community (proposed by Oscar Cullmann, my teacher at the Sorbonne), on this Sunday, precisely 90 days after his election, John XXIII announces the Second Vatican Council! What a tremendous surprise for the whole church, indeed the whole world! With my Basle lecture I already have prepared the detailed basic plan for a book on the Council. Karl-Josef Kuschel has rightly said that it is my 'biographical good fortune' to be theologically in position 'at a moment in church history when the Catholic Church began to reassess its theological foundations' for the first time since the Reformation. At this point a brief retrospect on the change of pontificate from Pius to John is necessary.

Pius XII: the greatest pope of the twentieth century?

During the previous October 1958 I spend two weeks with a group of people from Lucerne on a study trip in the footsteps of the apostle Paul in the Aegean. In Athens on 9 October we receive news of the death of Pius XII. With my knowledge of ancient Greek I attempt to read the Athens newspapers, written in modern Greek. But only later, after a long train journey through the Balkans, can I finally study extensive reports and commentaries in the Italian press on the death of Papa Pacelli. It is strange that the *'Pastor angelicus'*, previously so highly praised and flattered, is commemorated with highly critical obituaries.

Pius XII – the greatest pope of the century? Now some journalists dare to write about the autocrat Pacelli, his triumphalism, dogmatism and nepotism, which previously they had anxiously kept silent about. Indeed the pope's personal physician (an ophthalmologist!) Dr Riccardo Galeazzi Lisi (his name was advertised in large letters in the Piazza Barberini, which we crossed every day on our way to the Gregorian), greedy for money and fame, shamelessly sells to the media the photographs of the dead pope which he has been highly indiscreet in taking. In addition there was his unappetizing diary on Pacelli's agony and finally, in a press conference, the technical details of the embalming. Since this goes wrong, it has to be 'corrected' by night in St Peter's – there are reports of a ghostly scene at the giant catafalque under Michelangelo's dome. One feels reminded of Innocent III, allegedly the 'greatest pope of the Middle Ages', who was found after his death in the cathedral in Perugia, forsaken by all and completely naked, because he had been robbed by his own servants. It is in keeping with this macabre scene that immediately after his death Pius XII's powerful confidante, Madre Pasqualina Lehnert, is curtly ejected from the palace.

Of course the whole world now waits expectantly for the election of the new pope. Pius XII, increasingly isolated and incapable of making decisions, had created virtually no new cardinals and in his last years had filled hardly any new Curia posts. Thus of the college, which intrinsically consists of 70 members, only 51 take part in the conclave. Having returned to Lucerne, I too follow every new vote with burning interest on the radio in our clergy house. Only on the fourth day, Tuesday 28 October 1958, after ten votes with no outcome, does white smoke finally rise from the chimney of the Sistine Chapel. Who has been elected? The name of Ruffini is called out from the colonnades below. I am horrified: Cardinal Ruffini of Palermo – one of the most reactionary cardinals from the orbit of the Sanctum Officium, who has attacked the doctrine of evolution and modern interpretation of the Bible in publications? But soon afterwards the real name is proclaimed in the loggia of St Peter's: Angelo Roncalli, Patriarch of

Venice, who to everyone's surprise has chosen for himself the name John: John XXIII.

I am one of the few who aren't completely surprised by this choice. A long time previously my doctoral supervisor Louis Bouyer had predicted to me on a visit to our family in Sursee that the next pope would be Roncalli. Why? Because he was 'jovial, pious and not all that intelligent'. So I took notice of a report in the press in small print that on entering the conclave, Cardinal Gerlier of Lyons had answered the question who would be the candidate of the French cardinals with the word 'Roncalli'.

But, people all over the world are asking, can this have been the right choice? After the tall, slim, hierocratic Pacelli, now this rotund, not very spiritual Roncalli? An amusing quasi-prophecy goes the rounds in the Vatican in this connection: the rotund popes (with an R in their name) alternate with slim popes (without an R in their name). One can in fact follow this rule back from Roncalli and Montini at least to the middle of the nineteenth century: Pius XII (Pacelli), Pius XI (Ratti), Benedict XV (della Chiesa), Pius X (Sarto), Leo XIII (Pecci), Pius IX (Mastai-Ferretti). However, the superstition is to be interrupted after John XXIII (Roncalli) and Paul VI (Montini) with John Paul I, who will die after 33 days. One could become superstitious.

With the best will in the world I cannot say that I am particularly enthusiastic about the choice of the Patriarch of Venice: but at least Roncalli isn't a fanatical reactionary. It is known that as apostolic delegate in Turkey during the Second World War he saved thousands of Jews, especially children (through blank baptismal certificates), from Rumania and Bulgaria. And that as nuncio in Paris, despite diplomatic hitches he was able very skilfully to help 30 bishops who had been compromised by collaboration with the Vichy regime, so that in the end only a few of them had to give up their episcopal sees at the demand of de Gaulle. During his time in Paris he met the shrewdest head of the French episcopate, Cardinal Suhard of Paris, who was not particularly popular in Rome, around 50 times. Only after his move to Venice did the Curia act against the worker-priests.

But for most people Roncalli is still an enigma. Is he a good Vatican official and a friendly pastoral diplomat – or more? It is usually said that, always full of curiosity and enjoying his travels, he has learned openness to alien cultures and religions in Bulgaria and in Turkey. But Roman Catholic church historians like to ignore or play down the fact that in his years of study in Rome he was close to the most important Italian 'modernist', the church historian Ernesto Buonaiuti (this can be read in a dissertation by my pupil Bernardino Greco, *Ketzer oder Prophet?* ['Heretic or Prophet?'], 1979, on Buonaiuti).

Only after Roncalli's death will I go to Sotto il Monte near Bergamo, there to visit the simple farmhouse where Angelo Roncalli was born in 1881. Beyond question, even as pope he was a countryman of traditional faith with his feet on the ground. According to his *Journal of a Soul* he grew up in the same church piety and self-discipline, with the same post-Tridentine exercises and cultivation of the moral virtues, as we did in the Germanicum, but developed further spiritually by integrating different strands of spirituality.

In the split conclave Roncalli was obviously the compromise candidate who finally seemed electable to both conservatives and moderates. After the all-too-long pontificate of Pacelli the desire was for a man of advanced age with a kind face. But don't some of those who voted for Roncalli all too much confuse his simplicity and peacableness in thought and action with simplistic kindness? Don't they considerably underestimate his intellectual and spiritual substance, watchfulness, purposefulness and resolution? It is not Pacelli but Roncalli who is to become the greatest pope of the century – this becomes evident at a very early stage and can also be taken to have been confirmed in retrospect. In his five-year pontificate he achieves more than the popes before and after him, whose time in office is four times as long.

John XXIII: a different understanding of the papacy

The old 'transitional pope' becomes a pope of the great transition. The first pointer in a new direction is the choice of John as the papal name; here, with his good education in church history, he clearly dissociates himself from the Pius popes. Granted, some church historians like Karl August Fink of Tübingen, beyond doubt one of the greatest experts on the subject, are annoyed that Roncalli hasn't chosen the name John XXIV. After all, one of the three feuding popes in the period of the Western schism of three popes in the fifteenth century was called John XXIII. He shouldn't be disqualified as an anti-pope, since neither the Council of Constance (1412-15) nor Pope Martin V, chosen by that Council, later wanted to decide who had been pope in the decades of the schism. Angelo Roncalli didn't want to pass judgement on the disputed question of legitimacy (as he said in his brief address on accepting the election). He wanted to honour the patron of his father, his parish church and the Lateran basilica, and in his office, like John the Baptist, to prepare the way of the Lord and like John the beloved disciple be near to the Lord.

Very soon it becomes clear that the new pope wants to be Bishop of Rome really and not just symbolically, and to practise a different understanding of the papacy from that of his predecessor – not through a new theory but through a new style.

Whereas the Pius popes styled themselves 'prisoners of the Vatican', Pope John affably makes private and public visits to the city and issues invitations to dinners: he is a man more of spontaneous encounter than of great ideas and schemes.

Whereas Eugenio Pacelli gave himself aristocratic airs although he wasn't an aristocrat at all, Angelo Giuseppe Roncalli quite deliberately shows a simple desire to be a brother also to the Jews, indeed to all people ('I am Giuseppe, Joseph, your brother').

Whereas Pius had himself photographed in set poses with children or animals, at prayer and at the typewriter, and in group photographs always shows his best side, John mockingly says – with a healthy self-confidence capable of healthy irony – that with his ample body he isn't at all photogenic. However, through his face, which is guileless, humble and kind, he shows utterly without distortion a compelling kindness and hidden power.

Whereas his predecessor, as an expert on every possible question from astronomy to midwifery (twenty volumes of speeches), gave great discourses on social questions, the new pope keeps a 'spiritual journal', and having grown up in the social Catholicism of his home town of Bergamo, in one of his first official actions raises the shabbily low wages of the Vatican officials, including their child allowances.

Whereas Papa Pacelli, in the style of the Renaissance and baroque popes, makes his three middle-class nephews Giulio, Carlo and Marcantonio 'princes' (*'principi Pacelli'*) and powerful men in the Roman financial world, Papa Roncalli rejects any family politics and any nepotism and instead, as bishop, is concerned about his diocese of Rome and its clergy; he visits the parishes, particularly in the suburbs; he is a great communicator who awakens trust through direct contact with a great variety of people.

Whereas the lofty and mistrustful autocrat Pacelli, who rules as the last absolute monarch of the West, where possible without the Curia, is marvelled at, wondered at and feared, Roncalli, the unpretentious and unconventional friend of his fellow human beings, is loved. He abolishes kissing the feet and the three prescribed genuflections at private audiences, along with the most verbose honorific titles and forms of expression in the *Osservatore Romano* (this is accustomed to 'pluck the words from the majestic lips of the Elect'). Soon Pope John creates new cardinals, at their head the Archbishop of Milan, G. B. Montini, 'eliminated' by Pius.

From the beginning the real problems of this pontificate do not lie, as later will often be supposed, in foreign policy, but in domestic policy; not in the question of international détente but in renewal within the church. And since I wouldn't dream of being sparing in praise for John XXIII, I must formulate the criticism just as clearly.

The failure to reform the Curia

Even the hagiographies of the pope of the Council were not to keep silent about one great dark shadow which from the beginning lies over the whole pontificate of John XXIII and thus also falls on the coming Council: the pope concerned for reform rules over a Curia unwilling for reform. And certainly the pope is the one who is mostly to blame for this, though he certainly does not stand alone.

In former centuries the announcement of a council would by no means have been such a surprise; formerly councils were often called for. However, in the church of previous decades, while there had been calls for many things, there had been no call for an ecumenical council. Not even Fr Lombardi did so publicly. Outside the Catholic Church the widespread view was that the process of centralization of the Catholic Church had come to a climax in Vatican I in 1870, and that this council had to have been the last Catholic council, since the fullness of authority attributed to the pope here made a further council fundamentally superfluous. Outside the Catholic Church, too, people no longer really believed in ecumenical councils; at any rate, they didn't reckon with them as a concrete possibility. In the handbooks of Catholic dogmatics the treatises about the pope had grown longer and longer and those about the council shorter and shorter; indeed sometimes – in the thickest ecclesiologies in particular – they had disappeared altogether. Councils were no longer asked for in the life and theology of the church.

Against this background it is an incomparably bold act to convene an ecumenical council. For Roncalli, contrary to some claims, it is by no means an ill-considered spontaneous act. Planned from the beginning of his pontificate, it is his wholly personal initiative and decision, with a basis in his pastoral and papal sense of mission. Had Pius XII (at that time under the influence of Fr Lombardi) finally decided on a council, this would have become a papal synod, largely pre-programmed in its content and decision, as under Gregory VII or Innocent III in the Middle Ages; in the definition of the new Marian dogma by Pius XII in 1950 the bishops, consulted previously *pro forma*, had in fact been forced into the role of mere onlookers. But John XXIII wants a gathering of the college of bishops focused on shared responsibility which, certainly under his guidance, is meant to read the 'signs of the time' for itself, and in the spirit of Jesus Christ achieve an *'aggiornamento'*, a renewal and ecumenical understanding: a 'new Pentecost'.

At the very point of announcing the Council, the pope hopes for, indeed particularly requests, the co-operation of his most important colleagues in this great event involving the whole church. But the cold silence of the cardinals present in San Paolo and then also of most of those who are absent (38 don't reply at all), together with the playing down of the announcement of the Council by the *Osservatore Romano*, the vehicle of the Curia, shows the pope that he will have to reckon with serious opposition from his own officials rather than with collaboration. These see their power seriously threatened by the Council, although in all their administrative actions (which are often arbitrary) they constantly appeal to the pope.

In view of the 'deafness of some circles in the central administration', as the sensitive interpretation in a biography of the council pope by the Italian church historian Giuseppe Alberigo has it, 'John applies his characteristic methodological principles: above all the rule to emphasize more that which unites, and similarly to be ready for the greatest possible degree of indulgence; to see everything, to ignore a great deal and to correct little. This basic rule had always been dear to him, and he liked to observe it. At the same time, however, he was convinced

The Küng family at my ordination to the priesthood, Rome 1954

First mass in the grottos of St Peter's, 1954

1960: Professor at Tübingen at the age of 32

Hans Urs von Balthasar, Basle

Otto Karrer, Lucerne

1963-96: Institute for Ecumenical Research. Assistants: Hermann Häring, Karl-Josef Kuschel, Urs Baumann; Secretaries: Margaret Gentner and Annegret Dinkel

With Karl Barth on his eightieth birthday in Basle, 1966

With the Old Testament scholar Hermann Haag

The New Testament scholar
Ernst Käsemann

The dogmatic theologian Hermann Diem

Pope John XXIII Roncalli (1958-63)

The Second Vatican Council, 1962-5

Seminar with Dr Hermann Häring

In Africa for the first time, as a student (Oasis of Touzeur, Tunisia)

that he could not depart from the plan he had announced. Possible resistance goaded him on to explain it even better and more precisely.'

But is such a 'method' adequate in the face of the massive resistance of leading circles of the Curia? Is it enough to show 'the greatest possible degree of indulgence' and simply to explain the plan for the Council 'even better and more precisely'? That is my question to Giuseppe Alberigo, the director of the Istituto per le Scienze Religiose in Bologna, an outstanding expert on the history of Vatican II, whose papal biography ultimately becomes a hagiography, and has no critical overtones. Did Papa Giovanni really have no political alternatives? It seems to me that with the best intentions, precisely because of his 'method' – perhaps it would be better to say his mentality, upbringing, education, attitude to life – he missed an opportunity at the beginning of his pontificate.

There are some who say that the pope would certainly have wanted a thorough reform of the Curia had he been able to carry it through in the face of opposition from the Curia. But for what purpose did Vatican I in 1870 solemnly (and against the tradition of the first thousand years of Christianity) attribute to the pope a legally binding power of jurisdiction over every local church and each individual Catholic Christian? And surely he also has this jurisdiction over his own Curia cardinals? The pope is the only absolutist prince of Europe after the French Revolution, something like a 'sun king' in the church ('L'état – c'est moi' of Louis XIV and 'La tradizione sono io' of Pius IX, the pope of the council at that time, correspond); so is the pope helpless in the face of his own 'creatures'?

History can also teach church historians. When Louis XIV at the age of only 23 made himself prime minister after the death of Cardinal Mazarin, to the anger of some in his 4000-member court state he nominated a very few highly qualified, effective and all bourgeois departmental ministers to his 'cabinet' (originally 'small room'). Yes, people say, a king can do that, but surely not a pope? My reply is: popes too could do that at decisive turning points in time. For when in the eleventh century the Lothringian pope Leo IX in a pontificate lasting only five years was able to initiate the 'Gregorian Reform', which was then carried through under Gregory VII, this was only because (with the greatest personal involvement) he made the cardinals a kind of papal senate and also appointed to this body prominent advocates of reform from the other side of the Alps (including Hildebrand, the coming Gregory VII). And when in the sixteenth century the Farnese pope Paul III, though himself a Renaissance man, helped towards a breakthrough of Catholic reform, he did so only because he appointed the leaders of the reform party, a series of capable and deeply religious men (including the lay Contarini), to the college of cardinals. And what about examples to the contrary? There are, of course, plenty of these and they too prove my thesis. Why did Pope Martin V (after the great Western schism and the Council of Constance) and Pope Pius IX (after the 1848 revolution) completely fail as reformers? Because after initial goodwill they again conformed with the curial system. And now in the twentieth century, 1958/9?

Weakness in leadership

I am certainly not the only one to be disappointed that Pope Roncalli doesn't make better use of the unique chance offered him to renew the Roman Curia. He pursues a completely misguided personal policy – measured by his great aims: instead of nominating fresh reform forces he confirms dry reactionaries. He makes one wrong decision after another, and this betrays a dangerous weakness in leadership.

Wrong decision I. The post of Secretary of State and many important key positions in the Curia are vacant: to win over the Curia the pope nominates as Secretary of State Domenico Tardini, one of its members, who though experienced is abrupt and unecumenical. After Tardini's death on 30 July 1961, however, he is replaced by Cardinal Amleto Cicognani (previously delegate in Washington for 25 years), who is also a member of the Curia but more conciliatory. Then the pope confirms all the cardinals of the Pius Curia (Ottaviani, Pizzardo, Micara . . .) who are against reform, and finally he even fills all the free posts with conservative curial functionaries. He will pay a high price for these apparently shrewd tactics: instead of gaining control over the Curia he flatters it.

Wrong decision II. The new pope can fill fifteen vacant cardinals' seats and should have nominated another eighteen cardinals over and above the number of seventy, which was established in the sixteenth century after the time of Sixtus V. Since the church has spread to all the continents, this is a quite legitimate expansion. But despite some good men (headed by Montini) and some new members from Asia, Latin America and Africa, the new Sacrum Collegium looks even more conservative than the old. The result is that instead of surrounding himself at least in the Curia and the college of cardinals with a circle of men ready for reform (apart from his private secretary Loris Capovilla and Cardinal Augustine Bea), he is now under constant pressure from his former superiors and colleagues who are against reform. In other words, John XXIII keeps the Curia of Pius XII, whose exponents are resolved to show allegiance to the new pope only so far as is absolutely necessary and otherwise practise 'damage limitation' and obstruction in order to be able to preserve the previous power structures. Thus the new pope, who doesn't want to dominate, but doesn't really want to rule either, manoeuvres himself into the impossible situation of a head of government who wants to carry out a policy of renewal with the cabinet of his conservative predecessor which is not very well disposed towards him and indeed is largely incompetent. That is inconceivable in Washington and other seats of government. Why then in the Vatican?

Wrong decision III. At the wish of the Curia he 'consecrates' all the secretaries of the individual dicasteries (ministries) – hitherto simple 'Monsignori' – archbishops, now 'Eccellenze'. In so doing he not only increases the number of court bishops (with the names of non-existent dioceses) who have no real diocese, but also gives these Monsignori an even higher status and authority by comparison with the simple diocesan bishops, who have to make humble *'ad limina'* pilgrimages to them. This is a tremendous burden for pope and episcopate to the present day. Who will ever again free the church from these court bishops and court archbishops? The situation is like that in ancient Byzantium.

Wrong decision IV. The nomination of the Curia cardinals of the Vatican dicasteries as heads of the preparatory Council commissions inevitably proves paralysing. Conciliar reform commissions now have as their presidents (and also secretaries!) curial officials of the style of Ottaviani and Pizzardo, who want to obstruct any serious reform and cement the status quo with the help of the Council. 'Parliamentary' commissions of investigation with the minister himself and his secretary of state at their head? It would be unthinkable elsewhere. Yves Congar calls this the *'péché originel'*, the 'original sin', of the Council. Opponents of reform as the presidents of the reform commissions: how can that turn out well?

But fortunately at that time, in 1959, I needn't preach about all this. I'm still active in pastoral care in Lucerne and never misuse preaching for church politics. The Council and the church have to bear the consequences of the papal weakness in leadership. And now I must make decisions about my own life.

At the parting of the ways: practice or theory?

Hardly had I taken up my pastoral work in Lucerne when I received from Innsbruck an invitation to a conference of the Association of German-Language Dogmatic and Fundamental Theologians, which was to meet there in October of that year, 1957. I owe this invitation to none other than Karl Rahner, who at that time is teaching dogmatics in Innsbruck. He is very concerned to bring fresh blood into this body, which has become all too venerable. However, I don't like having to ask my priest for three or four days leave soon after accepting my pastoral work in Lucerne. Still, my boss, with a doctorate in theology and interested in the renewal of theology, immediately agrees: I must certainly make use of this opportunity.

So I travel by train through the Arlberg and take part in the conference, which is led by Michael Schmaus, Professor of Dogmatics in Munich, as its youngest member. The papers and contributions to the discussion give the impression that Karl Rahner and Bernard Welte, who is likewise present, play more of an outsider's role in this body. In October 1957 of course there could as yet be no talk of a council. Pius XII was still alive. I meet the fundamental theologian Heinrich Fries, formerly at Tübingen and now in Munich, who wrote an excellent review of my book and reports on a seminar on it by the Tübingen Protestant professors Hermann Diem and Hanns Rückert. He is interested in my future. What do I plan now? I say that after spending some time in pastoral work I would like to return to the Sorbonne to get a doctorate in philosophy there.

Fries thinks that this is a waste of time: it would be better for me to come straight to Germany and work for a habilitation there so that I would be able to lecture. That is also Karl Rahner's view. I allow myself to be convinced, although given my education hitherto the German university is quite alien to me. Habilitation at a German university is a complicated matter, since no faculty needs to accept a habilitation student (unlike a doctoral student). Moreover one can't apply, but has to be asked by a professor. But now I had been 'asked' and could even choose.

So habilitation with whom? Rahner is out, because I don't want to do my habilitation in Austria or with the Jesuits, but in Germany, and at a state faculty. And there are two dominant figures there: in the south, Professor Michael Schmaus of Munich, and in the north, Professor Hermann Volk in Münster. Schmaus, author of a five-volume 'Catholic Dogmatics' which I have already procured for myself in Rome and have studied as a supplement to my reading, because it is more orientated on scripture, the church fathers and the history of dogma, is quite well-disposed towards me ('But he is certainly impudent', he is said to have remarked about me with a knowing chuckle). However, I hear from Rahner that Schmaus is surrounded by something like a 'fan club' (many of its members are adoring young women). So why not go to Professor Volk, who in any case knows Protestant theology considerably better than Schmaus and Rahner? After all, he had done his doctorate on Karl Barth's view of creation and his habilitation on Barth's rival Emil Brunner ('The Image of God and Sin').

So having made up my mind quickly, while I am still in Innsbruck I ask Professor Hermann Volk whether he would accept me as a habilitation student. He agrees in principle and holds out the prospect of the post of academic assistant as a way of earning my living. Thus in principle the decision over the next fork in the road has been made. As early as 23 December 1957 I receive from Professor Volk the good Christmas news that after a discussion in the faculty (which also covers my nationality and the pattern of my education) he sees no obstacle to my habilitation. In January 1958, as always handwritten, there follows, in a brief and friendly way, his promise of the post of an assistant with the handsome monthly stipend of DM 700. In March 1958 I can send him my provisional 320-page manuscript on the christology of Hegel, which I want to develop into my habilitation thesis. I prepare my priest and colleagues for a 'long farewell'. I don't want to end my work as assistant priest in Lucerne too early. At my request, my start in Münster is fixed for 1 May 1959. By agreement with our generous Bishop von Streng I am allowed to end my practical pastoral work in the diocese of Basle on 31 March 1959, so as to move to Münster for the summer semester of 1959.

I've become fond of Lucerne, the parish and the people here and it is with tears that I finally say goodbye. 'His colleagues and everyone in the parish will sorely miss him,' remarks the parish magazine on 1 May 1959, 'we are deeply grateful to him for his initiatives and his untiring work . . . We hope that we will all continue to experience the inspiring power of his words and his pen, and do so again very soon.' My experience in practical pastoral work – leaving aside my activity as chaplain to the servants in Rome and pastor of the young women in Paris – now amounts to eighteen months. But these were so intensive and constructive in every respect that they shape the whole of my life. I will always be able to assess very accurately how one or another doctrine or reform measure will work out in practice. And I tell myself that in an 'emergency' I can always return from the university to pastoral work and come home from abroad. Indeed I have no inkling how things will turn out for me in Germany.

The way to scholarship

In spring 1959 Germany now looks very different from the way it did in summer 1947. The currency reform has led to an unparalleled 'economic miracle'. And this time I am not in Cologne but in Münster in Westphalia, where I arrive on 24 April, full of amazement: the old city, likewise almost completely destroyed in the war, has largely been rebuilt in traditional form. As well as the cathedral and other Gothic churches, above all the characteristic Prinzipalmarkt with its gabled houses, arcades and the splendid Gothic town hall with its filigree stepped gable represents one of the most outstanding achievements in the city architecture of the post-war period. But the university largely consists of fine new buildings and gives the impression of modernity. The Catholic theological faculty is still lodged in an old, renovated teaching building, but also has an adequate library and some space. A new Theologicum is already being built. Generally, things are on the up and up.

There I am now to be appointed academic assistant and to 'habilitate' myself for teaching dogmatics. At the same time I again take on a pastoral task: warden of a student hostel, which likewise has just been built, the Thomas Morus College. It's a pleasant task to have to look after about 50 students from all the faculties here. In the same hall as them I have two small rooms; I am assisted by an excellent tutor, Wilhelm Wemmer (later a department head in the federal chancellery), and work with student chaplain Werners, a true Westphalian and a skilful, committed pastor. Later he will be the Münster clergy's candidate for bishop, but not that of Rome, because he is too independent. I get on very well with the students, for whom once a month I hold a joint service with a sermon and once a week a study group on the church and socialism – the topic chosen by them. As Dr Wemmer recently wrote to me, the inhabitants of the hostel 'were very pleasantly surprised how unprejudiced, open to suggestions and in every respect ready for collaboration' the new warden of the hostel proved to be from the beginning: 'This was felt to be very good and liberating.'

I celebrate Shrove Tuesday and the summer festival with the students. The Old Testament scholar Professor Hermann Eising, warden of another hostel, the Marianum, in another wing of the complex of buildings, is a somewhat senior counterpart; the students sometimes chafe under him, but get on very well with him too. At my recommendation he later allows Oswald Loretz, my fellow-student and friend of many years, who had lived in my Tübingen home for some weeks, to come to Münster to do his habilitation in Old Testament. But Loretz has problems with Eising, later marries, devotes himself completely to Ugarit and Ancient Near Eastern studies and hardly bothers at all with the church and theology. What a disappointment after all the friendship, proven collaboration and hospitality!

In Münster, between the old city and the new university quarter, I quickly feel at home. As with my first boss in Lucerne, a kindly pastor, so too in Münster I have particular good fortune with my second (and last) boss, a likeable professor, Hermann Volk, Ordinarius Professor of Dogmatics. I meet him there on 27 April for the first time; in the following days I also meet other professors, including the social scientist Joseph Höffner, not suspecting that as Archbishop of Cologne this friendly colleague from the Germanicum will later become my most bitter and dogged opponent. Volk is a man with a good, open face and often youthful smile, which makes it difficult for one not to like him. His many human and scholarly qualities made him a focal point within the Catholic Theological Faculty (at this time as their dean), the university (he was formerly its Rector) and the city of Münster (a member of its culture committee). With his sense of poetry and his love of the theatre (Paul Claudel!), with his delight in flowers and passion for the mountains (he has taken photographs of the snow-covered peaks he has climbed), he is a scholar who practises theology not only with his head but as a whole person, and moreover as a Christian and pastor with a deep faith.

It goes without saying that such an academic teacher can captivate his students. With impressive rhetoric this tall man often walks up and down the platform of the largest auditorium, his gestures telling and his language impressive, never denying the Hessian accent of his homeland. During the war he was a chaplain, and he lives by a realistic piety which is averse to empty phraseology and does not fail to note the difficulties of faith in today's church. His strength as a theologian is a lively and intuitive grasp of the situation, especially the reality of creation and redemption. 'Unity' is one of his central themes: unity of theology, of the mysteries of faith, and of the church; not, however, as uniformity but as the interconnection of different things.

Hermann Volk helps me with the somewhat unusual formalities: because I am a Swiss citizen I need permission from the interior minister of the state of North Rhine-Westphalia to be admitted to an official position. At the same time my Paris doctorate has to be 'nostrified' ('made our own') by the University of Münster. So Volk accompanies me to the late-baroque former prince bishop's castle, likewise beautifully restored, to go to see the curator of the university, Freiherr von Fürstenberg. Finally, on the significant date of 1 August 1959 he formally appoints me academic assistant, without tenure (initially I had been appointed only to an ordinary assistant's post).

My activity as assistant is modest: the custom in German faculties of humanities is for the assistant to spend roughly half his time on his duties and otherwise devote himself to his own academic work, in my case the habilitation thesis. My main task is to look after the dogmatic section of the theological seminar library which is still in the process of being rebuilt: ordering books, signing for them and cataloguing them, and otherwise being at the disposal of my boss for small scholarly or administrative matters.

Time and again I accompany him – he doesn't drive a car – for a good quarter of an hour from the Theologicum to the door of his house. Two or three times I am invited to lunch with him at his house with his sister. It's a congenial little scene: the professor looks at the big salad bowl which has been emptied, hesitates, finally picks it up, and with the observation, 'I always do this, you can pass it on!' drinks the dressing. Of course I never tell anyone this during his lifetime. My second boss can rely on my loyalty, discretion and natural commitment as much as my first, so I have an untroubled relationship with him, too, for a second time disproving the gloomy prophecy of my former Rector Vorspel. In Münster, too, I had unproblematical relations not only with my boss but also with my colleagues and the secretaries, and have happy memories of the excursions of both the seminar heads and the theological faculty into the countryside around Münster. Nor will I ever forget the afternoon when I clamber with Dean Volk in the framework of the new faculty building up to the roof ridge. It still hasn't been covered, because he wants to get a picture of the whole structure.

Volk is always generous. He has no objections to my lecturing on justification in Krefeld or going to a Germanicum meeting in Osnabrück or Cologne. Moreover in Münster's super-modern theatre I have the opportunity to see Shaw's *Pygmalion*, the *Urfaust* and Handel's *Julius Caesar*. However, it is more important to me that through August Nitschke, a historian with broad interests whom I know from my time in Rome, I get to know as colleagues a whole series of open-minded assistants in other faculties who will later play a public role in Germany: Ernst-Wolfgang Böckenförde (later a federal judge), Arno Borst (later Professor of Mediaeval History in Constance), Golo Mann (previously a lecturer in the USA, soon Professor of History in Stuttgart), Günter Rohrmoser (later a conservative Professor of Philosophy, likewise in Stuttgart) and Robert Spaemann (a skilled but unfortunately later an increasingly reactionary Professor of Philosophy in Munich with an honorary doctorate from Opus Dei). We live in a time when fundamental decisions are being forced on philosophers and theologians.

A German theology put to the test

I needn't attend Professor Volk's lectures, but instead of course I go to his colloquium for doctoral students. My special assistance is required only for the seminar, where as usual I have to keep the register and make contact with those giving papers. The topic of the seminar is confirmation. Why confirmation? Because its administration is a privilege of the bishop? Hardly. It is because receiving confirmation is the particular mark of the laity, and in his theology Volk is pre-eminently concerned with the laity, and in university practice especially with the lay theologians. Confirmation as a sacrament of spiritual strengthening seems to him to be very important.

However, the more closely I get to know this theological thinking, the clearer it becomes to me that such dogmatics has an inadequate exegetical and historical foundation. This is certainly a defect not just in Volk, but in neoscholastic theology generally. I am making great efforts to catch up with my own back-wardness in exegesis, particularly by studying research into the historical Jesus, which has just got going again. And in the light of historical-critical exegesis I am struck by something that has been claimed in Catholic theology since the Middle Ages, but disputed by Luther, and since the Council of Trent defined against the Reformers, though unfortunately little examined, namely that confirmation as a sacrament has been 'instituted' by Jesus Christ himself.

And here, after all, it cannot even be demonstrated that from the beginning confirmation was an independent sacrament, distinct from baptism. For the New Testament writings clearly attest that baptism already communicates the Holy Spirit and therefore there is no foundation for a separate sacrament of receiving the Spirit. In fact the remarkable second anointing at baptism (signing with chrism), initially known only in Rome, was reserved for the bishop, and developed into a self-contained 'rite of confirmation' only in the ninth century. This then served in the twelfth century as theological justification for a second sacrament, which was meant to be 'for strengthening' (ad robur).

In my somewhat rare contributions to Volk's seminar I cautiously attempt to point out that on the basis of the exegetical-historical evidence, confirmation cannot make sense today as an independent sacrament but is a development, confirmation and completion (con-firmatio) of baptism – and justifiably so, in view of infant baptism. However, the seminar leader doesn't follow up the suggestions made by his assistant – which are somewhat uncomfortable for him. And why should there be a theological confrontation and possibly a burden on good personal relations on his part over this point?

So one session after another takes place – and this is often the case in seminars on neoscholastic theology in Germany – undisturbed by exegetical and historical difficulties. At the end of the semester (and indeed at the end of yet another semester) no substantial progress has been made: for all the new reflections, the tradition of a separate sacrament instituted by Christ seems to have been con-firmed. Dogma is infallibly true and both the Bible and history are domesticated.

Although I find Hermann Volk so congenial and recognize his indefatigable activity far beyond the university, I simply can't get round these substantive differences. Of course I far prefer Volk's living theology to the dry theology of the Gregorian. But for me, even Volk's responses to Barth and Brunner move all too modestly in a neoscholastic framework. More precisely, this is a largely Roman theology, prepared in German, which does not ask any critical and constructive questions.

A professor as bishop?

Hermann Volk seems to me somewhat exhausted after 35 years of teaching, with no great theological perspectives on the future. And somehow he also seems to sense this himself. Couldn't that office to which the privilege of administering confirmation is entrusted, the office of bishop, bring rescue from the burden of academic routine?

I don't want to be misunderstood: I think it by no means reprehensible that a professor of theology like Volk (and after him Höffner, Wetter, Ratzinger, Lehmann, Kasper, Koch) should aim at the episcopate, because presumably he hopes to achieve more for the church in that role than in theology. In the end, at one time even the great Hegel in Heidelberg accepted the call to the University of Berlin with the incidental thought that 'in advancing age he might move from the precarious function of teaching theology at a university to another activity and be able to be used'; here he was probably thinking of a post in administration or government, perhaps even that of Kultusminister. A professor of theology can be allowed what is right for a professor of philosophy. However, what matters is what the person who gives up his professorial chair in favour of the episcopal chair makes of his episcopate: whether the mitre, as the saying goes among the clergy, acts as the 'snuffer' of theology or as a stimulus to translate good theology into better church praxis.

Of course Hermann Volk sometimes wants to hear details about 'Rome' from me; since he was educated wholly in Germany and has been professor in Münster since 1946, he knows it only at a distance. It dawns on me in a flash how anxious even an important theologian and well-established university professor can be about this Rome when he initiates me into his plan to found an Institute of Ecumenical Theology in Münster. He asks me whether such an institute wouldn't come under Cardinal Ottaviani's Sanctum Officium, which as is well known claims to keep all 'ecumenical theology' under its control. Couldn't I ask Augustin Bea, whom I know well, and who has now been promoted to cardinal under John XXIII, how he, Volk, should proceed in this matter? I advise him not to trouble Rome but simply to establish a 'Catholic Ecumenical Institute' instead of an 'Institute for Ecumenical Theology' and in so doing to ignore the Sanctum Officium. He does that, and there are no problems.

For meanwhile preparations for the Second Vatican Council are advanced and are claiming all the Vatican's energy. And this Council in particular has prompted reflections by Professor Volk's academic assistant which could finally lead to a certain tension with him. For in his briefcase this assistant still has the lecture on the *Ecclesia semper reformanda* prompted by Barth. In view of the coming Council, about which no one has any precise ideas, it cries out to be developed and published soon.

The Council and Reunion

Since my lecture in Basle in January and the announcement of the Council I have become strongly focused on the problems of church reform. Conversations with leading theologians who come to Münster confirm me in many of my views. There is Hans Urs von Balthasar, who as we walk together across the cathedral square in Münster cannot cease to wonder that the Romans have taken no action against my book on justification. Yves Congar, previously condemned and exiled, has been promoted to Council adviser and now speaks on the Council and the ecumenical movement. And Gérard Philips, professor at Louvain, gives a lecture on the laity in the church; he is later to become the influential second secretary of the Theological Commission at the Council.

Even more important for me are the Dutchmen Monsignor Jan Willebrands and Dr Franz Thijssen, who come to Münster on Friday 10 July 1959 to talk with Hermann Volk about the Sixth Catholic Conference on Ecumenical Questions, fixed for the end of September in Paderborn. I am included in the conversation. For at the desire of my fellow Germanicum student Franz Thijssen – a loud character with as much ecumenical passion as strength of voice – I had already got to know Dr Willebrands on my early visits to Holland at the seminary of Warmond, where at that time Willebrands was regent. In contrast to Thijssen he is a quiet, shrewdly diplomatic and always friendly man, a classic 'prelate'.

This Dutchman has achieved the feat of building up since the early 1950s an international network of theologians with ecumenical interests (supported by bishops). In personal conversations in Rome they convince first the influential Jesuits Bea, Tromp and Leiber and finally even Cardinal Alfredo Ottaviani, whose Sanctum Officium has in fact strictly supervised all ecumenical operations in the Catholic Church after the anti-ecumenical instruction *Ecclesia catholica* of 1950, that such a Catholic Conference on Ecumenical Questions is doctrinally innocuous as a platform for mutual contact and the exchange of information; indeed it is helpful to the Catholic Church. The Vatican normally mistrusts international Catholic associations in which it doesn't have the say. The conference, which met for the first time in Fribourg in 1952, cannot use the name 'Catholic Ecumenical Council', which Willebrands originally wanted. Many of the respected ecumenical theologians known to me, like Boyer, Congar, Dumont, Höfer, Rahner and Rousseau, belong to it.

It would have been impossible for a Secretariat for Christian Unity, whose Spiritus Rector under Cardinal Bea will be none other than Jan Willebrands, to be formed so quickly without the preliminary work above all of the courageous

Catholic ecumenist Willebrands – a friend of Holland's greatest Protestant ecumenist, Dr Willem Visser 't Hooft, General Secretary of the World Council of Churches which was founded in 1948. For me it is an honour and a challenge that Willebrands, who from the beginning has addressed me with the familiar 'Du', accepts me immediately as the youngest theologian in this international Catholic Conference on Ecumenical Questions.

A few days after the visit by Willebrands and Thijssen to Münster, on 16 July 1959, I can go away on vacation – back to Sursee. It is a long but by no means boring journey, with plenty of time for reading. I wanted to use the free weeks in the summer to write a book on the Council and reform on the basis of the Basle lecture. It was intended to be a short book, a 'pocket book', in a format now making triumphal progress as a novelty, well produced and cheap, for a mass public. At all events it wouldn't have the tremendous scholarly apparatus of *Justification*. I am well equipped for this task, and the Basle lecture on *Ecclesia semper reformanda* represents the framework, which now has to be developed consistently up to the roof beam.

So in Sursee I immediately begin writing section after section, with a hot heart and a cool head, rapidly, but considering every sentence carefully. Everything is written out at least twice by hand, at home or whenever possible by the lake; then every day in the late afternoon I read what I've written into a hired dictating machine (likewise a technical novelty), from which that same evening it is put down on paper quickly and virtually without a mistake by my school-friend Marlis Knüsel, a perfectly trained and skilful secretary. The result is a manuscript 'all of a piece'. And the best compliment that I was later to get from an English theologian was that the book is a combination of 'German depth, Latin clarity and Anglo-Saxon pragmatism'. That is also my ideal for books in the future: to achieve 'depth' by penetrating through the surface to the essentials, but without mystifying theological profundity; to aim at 'clarity', at simplicity, logicality and comprehensibility yet without any enlightened rationalism; and to show 'pragmatism', related to the subject-matter, orientated on application, related to action – to argue, but without an ideology which measures the truth of ideas solely by their use and success.

But how will the church react to this book? I know only one thing, that I have begun a second highly risky theological undertaking: for how can an individual 32-year-old theologian develop a comprehensive programme for reform for the Second Vatican Council? I personally, however, have the opposite question: why shouldn't I do it if I can do it now and perhaps no one else can? The Council needs precisely this, a programme.

An overall vision

In this book I can give a theological foundation to the fact that there is a renewal in the church in a concrete and differentiated way which is quite different from my Basle lecture – making many references to historical developments which indicate that the church of God is a church of human beings in this world. And there are many references to key theological witnesses (after Augustine and Thomas Aquinas especially J. H. Newman and Karl Adam) who emphasize that this church of human beings is also a church of sinners, indeed a 'sinful church' (as Karl Rahner puts it), and thus needs constant 'reform' or 'renewal'.

On the basis of many personal experiences I can describe in four statements how the church is to be renewed: for a renewal of the church as Christians we may *suffer* under its defects and sins (no self-satisfied superficial apologetic); *pray* for deliverance from evil and for the Spirit of God which renews everything (no reform activism without the Spirit); *criticize* the church, which needs criticism and is worthy of criticism (according to Thomas Aquinas a *correctio fraterna*, 'brotherly correction', even of the prelates); and *act*: neither revolution nor restoration, nor a mere reform of the heart or a mere reform of abuses but rather a creative reform of the situation! According to John XXIII one of the great programmatic words of the coming Council is *renovatio* or *aggiornamento*: 'bringing up to date'. I point out the stimuli that I have received particularly from Congar's book *True or False Reform in the Church*, deliberately going against the advice given in Rome to read, but not to quote, suspect authors.

But to make it clear that all these principles aren't just fine theories, I refer back to church history and sketch out a brief history of church renewal: in the first millennium, then before the Reformation, in the Reformation and also in the Counter-Reformation. A good 30 years later I will follow this course once again in my book *Christianity* with infinitely more effort and analyse the five epoch-making paradigms of Christianity – the mediaeval Roman Catholic paradigm only as the third after the apocalyptic paradigm of primitive Christianity and the Hellenistic paradigm of the early church. And instead of the 40 pages here it will then take me more than 1000 pages to describe the whole history in a far more precise and differentiated, concrete and colourful way. For example, I shall become considerably more negative about the Gregorian reform, but evaluate the Reformation of Luther and Calvin far more positively. I will incorporate Anglicanism and make more marked differentiations over the achievements of modernity.

But I will always be able to identify with the 1960 history of church renewal seen as a whole, and above all with the aim already clearly formulated in Basle, how Catholics and Protestants can find one another. Not through an inactive summons back to the unity of the Catholic Church. Not through individual conversions in one direction or the other. Not through merely moral 'reform of customs'. But rather through the renewal of the Catholic Church by means of the realization of justified Protestant concerns, in hope of a realization of Catholic concerns by the Protestants – in accordance with the norm of the same gospel.

Is all this sheer utopia? On the contrary. Different approaches to a positive realization of Protestant concerns can already be noted in the Catholic Church of the present. I have already attempted to realize some of them myself in community work in Lucerne: revaluation of the Bible in theology and piety; the development of a Catholic popular liturgy, with the vernacular and singing by the people; a sense of the universal priesthood of the laity in theology and practice; an increased assimilation of the church to the cultures; an understanding of the Reformation as a religious concern; a concentration of popular piety. In addition there is need for a de-politicizing of the papacy and the beginning of a reform of the Curia.

As for the reform of doctrine, if I am to be given the imprimatur, the church's permission for printing which is still necessary, I have to have a lengthy discussion with the very understanding censor, Johannes Feiner of Chur, a professor of dogmatics whom I know. For initially Feiner, too, maintains Congar's misleading distinction: yes to the reform of church life = true = Catholic reform, but no to the reform of church doctrine = false = Protestant reform. But in the end, Feiner, too, doesn't dispute that there is a development of dogmas and a polemic against dogmas. And he concedes that the dogmas of the church also have their theological limitations and therefore must be seen against the background of the normative revelation of Old and New Testaments and reinterpreted time and again. I am able to convince him that there must therefore also be renewal, reform of doctrine.

From the start we are agreed that in addition a reform of popular piety is necessary, in the face not only of all the mediaeval superstition but also of the 'Marian maximalism' which overflowed under Pius XII. In my criticism here I can refer not only to the Tübingen fundamental theologian Heinrich Fries, but more recently also to Giovanni Battista Montini, who has finally been made a cardinal. But what is the main difficulty for the reunion of separated Christians?

The rock as an obstacle

In my experience and in the judgement of all the experts the main difficulty is the concrete organizational structure of the Catholic Church, the problems of which are crystallized in the question of church office (apostolic succession and the recognition of ministries) and culminate in the question of the papacy (primacy and infallibility). In order to make clear to Catholics the whole urgency of the papacy, which for Protestants has no credibility in its present form, I quote at length three testimonies from such Protestant theologians, who unlike others strive to achieve a positive understanding of the Petrine office and yet have strong objections to the present-day form of the papacy (H. Dombois, M. Lackmann and H. Asmussen). For me these culminate in Karl Barth's critical question whether a Protestant Christian can really hear the voice of the Good Shepherd from Peter's chair.

Beyond doubt the problem of the lack of credibility of the papacy in these days has not been presented by a Catholic theologian with such clarity. Will it be accepted? But as a great argument for a new credibility of the Petrine service I can now point to the hope embodied in the new pope, John XXIII, who in his striking words and actions is explicitly concerned not to be a spiritual autocrat or dictator but to be a good shepherd after the biblical example.

Of course these words and actions of the pope are not enough, which is why he has convened the Second Vatican Council. I know that there is still widespread scepticism about the Council: the church is not prepared for it, the theologians will block everything, the assembly of bishops is far too big, their members would largely come from 'Latin' countries with no great delight in reform. I attempt to give a brief answer to all these points, combined with positive proposals like the creation of a separate Roman congregation for ecumenical questions with competent specialist advisers. This was soon to come about in the form of the Secretariat for Christian Unity.

But the big question remains: what should and can the Council achieve? The pope doesn't want to specify its content in advance. And so far neither a cardinal nor a bishop has dared to circulate comprehensive proposals for reform. The theologians mostly concentrate on comfortable historical or formal questions: a whole series of books appears on the ecumenical councils of the past. Why should I be the one to expose myself with concrete proposals for reform over and above fundamental statements on reform of the church?

But it is clear to me that if Vatican II is not to fail, then concrete proposals for reform must be made. I am convinced that the Council is meeting in a 'transitional situation of an unprecedented extent in which all the directions must be changed – the beginning of a new era of the world' (later I will speak of a 'paradigm shift') and 'our responsibility arises' from this. Will our corrections be too slight, our reforms too superficial, all our actions finally ineffective? No, if the Council is not to be a great disappointment but the fulfilment of a great hope, then it will have to make a great stride forward.

So I venture, cautiously and modestly, to formulate a comprehensive programme of reform: granted, it is not the theologian's task to set up a plan of renewal for the Council and to make proposals directly, but at any rate he can point to concrete possibilities about which the bishops may then decide. If one thinks of what people want from the church government, the results of surveys also indicate that there is a 'disturbing litany' of widespread Catholic anxieties and complaints: 'the wretched state of preaching and religious instruction, the way in which the liturgy runs wild or has become rigid, the Index and Roman centralism, episcopal bureaucracy, damage to the training of priests, monastic training, political conformism, a moral theology which is alien to the world particularly in respect of atom bombs and sexual questions, Latin as the language of worship, scandals over priests, a fuss about managers and meetings in organization, Thomism, rationalism, Marianism, the pilgrimage business . . .' And so on and so on.

In view of this 'disturbing litany' it seems to me that if the Council is to achieve great deeds it must concentrate on a little and what is essential. However, evidently also in the view of the pope, from the start further dogmas must be excluded: the further definition of traditional controversial questions of theology and particularly new Marian dogmas would clearly be a hindrance rather than a help towards the reunion of divided Christians. But if there are to be no new dogmas, what then? What is possible and what isn't?

Reforms: what is theologically possible?

All possible proposals for reform are discussed among the Catholic and non-Catholic public without an overall scheme becoming visible. Above all: where should the Council begin? Directly with the reform of the papacy and the Roman Curia? This has no prospect of success because of the supremacy of the Curia. That is confirmed two years later by the case of the Jesuit Fr Lombardi. In his book *Un concilio per una riforma nella carità* ('A Council for a Reform in Love'), conjuring up an apocalyptic background and with a reference to the pope himself (which is not justified), he speaks broadly about the structural defects of the Roman Curia and the sins of the clergy. The pope can hardly cope with the telephone calls from the Curia about this 'scandalous' book. And drops Lombardi.

In my estimation, before the Council one shouldn't appeal to the pope, who is restraining himself, far less to the dominant Curia, but directly to the bishops, who are at last assembling again. They will have the say in the Council. So strategically I concentrate all concrete proposals on the revaluation of the office of bishop. This is also close to the heart of the present Bishop of Rome, who has great respect for the episcopate of his brothers. The issue here is of course the greater independence not just of the individual bishop but also of the local church concerned. The federative principle, the principle of subsidiarity which was already affirmed by Pius XII for the church as well, but only in an abstract theoretical way, is important: what can be achieved by individuals themselves in their own strength should not be foisted on the community, and what can be carried out by the smaller community should not be foisted on the higher and superior community.

But in this situation it is not enough merely to appeal to the personal responsibility of bishops to exploit to the full the rights they have already been given and not constantly to ask the Curia for answers and action where they themselves should respond and act as bishops. New concrete possibilities must be formulated for the Council – truly not my 'personal inventions' but concerns which are in the air and are being discussed in the Catholic press. The issue here is the call for reform both on the theoretical level of dogma and also on the practical level of organization.

What is possible on the theoretical dogmatic level? The Council could lay down new dogmas without a definition, as a declaration by the German episcopate on the position of bishops in relation to the pope (approved by Pius XI after Vatican I) stated against Chancellor Bismarck. This was first of all negative: the pope cannot alter the episcopal constitution of the church instituted by Christ; the bishops are not the pope's instruments and officials; their rights are not claimed and absorbed by the pope; their authority is not a substitute for the papal authority; the pope is Bishop of Rome and not Bishop of Cologne or Breslau. Then it was positive: the bishops are the successors of the apostles appointed by Christ; the episcopate just as much rests on 'divine institution' as does the papacy; its rights and responsibilities arise from there.

From here it is possible to go deeper theologically into the indispensable importance of the episcopate and once again assimilate the relationship between bishops and pope to the biblical relationship between the apostles and Peter. So the Petrine office is not identical with a papalism which ignores the divine right of the episcopate throughout the church but is the supreme arbiter for the sake of unity.

Reforms: what is practically possible?

What is possible at the practical level of organization? The old church order certainly can't just be restored. But given the greater areas involved, there is need for a revaluation of the episcopal conferences of a country, a language area or a continent. In keeping with the principle of subsidiarity they could resolve many questions which hitherto have all fallen under the Roman Curia. So the bishops are bound not only to the Petrine office but also to one another: *communio* in the old sense! It would make sense to have fundamental conciliar frameworks of legislation for reforms which the bishops of the various countries, language-groups or continents could carry through themselves and adapt to their situation.

But all this still seems to me to be too general. What are the great concrete reforms which with the revaluation of the episcopate could also represent steps towards the renewal of the Catholic Church and thus towards the reunion of the separated churches? To be more convincing, I refer back to the traditional distinction between the episcopal office of priest, pastor and teacher.

First, in the sphere of the episcopal priestly office there is a need above all for a reform of the mass which brings out anew what must unconditionally be expressed in any Catholic celebration of the eucharist: a liturgy of the word in a comprehensible form with scripture reading and a homiletic explanation, as a central part a comprehensible eucharistic prayer with a simple and clear structure, and finally the eucharistic meal. The individual episcopates should themselves decide on the details, above all on the vernacular, which at least in the German-language area is the most important question, but also on communion under the forms of bread and wine for particular occasions, on the possibility of the con-celebration of several priests, and on liturgical dress and gestures. At the same time, by simplification and concentration there needs to be a reform of the rites of baptism, confession and marriage and a reform of the breviary, the all too long obligatory prayer for secular priests (a specific time of prayer instead of a specific quantity of prayer).

With reference to the abolition of the obligation to celibacy in the case of the ordination to the priesthood of Protestant pastors who are already married, which has already been practised by Pius XII in individual cases – purely a matter of canon law and applying only to the Latin church – I propose that given the ongoing conflict in the Latin church, in cases of extraordinary harshness a solution which is legally and humanly tolerable should be sought (possibly by making laicization easier): to ask for more would have been folly before the Council. Only for the diaconate do I argue that obligatory celibacy should be abolished and the rule of the early church should be introduced: the diaconate not only as a transitional stage to the priesthood but married deacons as a supplement to the heavily overburdened priests.

Secondly, in the sphere of the episcopal pastoral office a reform of marriage law is urgently needed: a decentralization and acceleration of the processes of marriage, a simplification of the laws of marriage and the demolition of unnecessary bureaucracy, the abolition of outdated obstacles to marriage and a positive rule for confessionally mixed marriages. A reform of church administration needs to be carried through at the same time: here too there should be simplification and decentralization along the lines of the principle of subsidiarity, a reduction in the requests for dispensation and an absolute minimum of church penalties; stronger representation and more possibilities for the local churches to engage in dialogue with the Roman Curia; a clear distinction between the legislative and the executive and the introduction of a church administrative court.

Thirdly, in the sphere of the episcopal magisterium there is an urgent need for a reordering of the censorship of books, in which Rome should be only the final authority. To protect authors who have been denounced the legal principles applicable in any fair disciplinary proceedings should be observed: the author should be given a hearing and an opportunity to defend himself; there should be no condemnation without a reason being given; no involvement of the higher authority without the inclusion of the lower. In addition there should be a fundamental reform or abolition of the Index of Prohibited Books (which is useless and counter-productive); a warning on a solid basis is better than a ban on reading, and a free discussion to clarify the problem is better than a hasty condemnation. But above all there is a need for positive measures to raise the quality of preaching and the study of theology. There is a need for emphasis on the saving significance of the Bible as the word of God for liturgy, instruction, theology, pastoral care and spiritual life.

However, to avoid a new centralization on the bishop in all this, which no one wants, a strict application of the principle of solidarity in favour of the priests is necessary: the bishop should maintain close personal relations with the priests. But above all there is an urgent need for a declaration of principle on the importance of the laity in the church; after all, they do not just belong to the church in some way but *are* the church: not simply in the passive and receptive role of objects to be looked after, but in the active and initiating role of subjects who share responsibility for the church. And the granting of the chalice to the laity is an impressive sign of this.

Even more important, however, for the Council would be a word of repentance for all the failure of the church and a word of faith: a cheerful and strong confession of faith in the living God, who is unchangeably near even in the age of satellites and space travel and who has not forgotten us in the distress of two world wars and in the threat of nuclear death. At the end of the book a reunion in stages is proposed: in accordance with the words of John XXIII first approach (*'avvicinamento'*), then coming together (*'riaccostamento'*), and finally perfect unity (*'unità perfetta'*).

The more I formulate concrete proposals for reform, the clearer it becomes to me that my overall vision does not attack anything that is inalienably Catholic and in some of its statements is also being advocated by others. However, in a concentrated summary it will appear to many people to be bold, perhaps all too bold. Certainly I am convinced that bold measures are necessary today. But I am not one of those who don't know what they are doing. And in the face of the denunciation and condemnation which doubtless threaten, of the kind that in fact happened two years later to the book on the Council by Fr Lombardi mentioned above – it was disowned in a leading article in the *Osservatore Romano* and prevented from being distributed and translated on the instructions of the Curia – in 1959/60 I do everything possible to prevent condemnation and suppression. But here I need help. Will I find it?

'It won't do!'

My hope is pinned in the first instance on Julius Döpfner. Like me he is a Germanicum alumnus; he then became Bishop of Berlin at a relatively young age and has recently been made cardinal. He is a congenial and open man, as I know from his visits to the Germanicum, and carries great weight within the church. On Monday 10 August 1959 there is a Swiss Germanicum meeting in Niederuzwil in the canton of St Gallen. I travel there above all to ask Julius Döpfner for an introduction or preface by way of support. My short and compact book contains so much that is explosive, and although it makes no direct attacks, it is so far from the position of the Curia that it needs the support of a cardinal if it is not to be denounced, banned and suppressed right from the start.

So I sit all alone with Julius Döpfner on the veranda of the clergy house at Niederuzwil. I show him my manuscript and tell him its content; he listens attentively, with approval on his face – until I ask him for a preface. Then comes his surprising answer: he would rather not. Why? Now he is a bishop, and it is 'not the task of bishops but of theologians to rush in'. I think to myself that this is a remarkable distribution of roles: although the bishop is in a much stronger position in church law, he is to keep out of the conflict, whereas the theologian is to sacrifice himself so to speak for better or for worse. I am insistent, but am quickly made to realize that nothing can be done. It is the first but unfortunately not the last time that I have to note that Döpfner, outwardly an experienced Bavarian, is simply afraid. But at any rate he has shown understanding for my concerns and has at least declared his readiness to read the manuscript.

Disappointed, I travel back to Sursee. That same week a visit to Hans Urs von Balthasar, who has been staying in Montana to recuperate, does not help either. In any case a commendation from him would have been no use to me, for since he left the Jesuit order he has been one of those who have been ostracized in Rome. So what is to be done? In the second half of September 1959 I finish my manuscript and return to Münster. On 26 September I write to Cardinal Döpfner that the manuscript will be sent to him in Berlin by Herder Verlag. The Bishop of Basle is at present engaged in an unpleasant business with Rome and therefore would rather not burden himself with this imprimatur as well. At the same time I renew a restrained and indirect invitation to Döpfner: 'Herder also wrote to me that "cover" from a foreword will be necessary. We shall see.'

In Münster my manuscript is now in the hands of my boss, Professor Hermann Volk. As planned, I take part with him in the Catholic Conference on Ecumenical Questions in Paderborn. It meets from 27 September to 1 October under the leadership of Monsignor Willebrands. The topic is the tensions between 'unity and mission' and 'our expectations for the Council which has been announced'. It is interesting for me to be present: the most important Catholic ecumenists from all over Europe discuss keenly, with the public excluded (I even meet Avery Dulles from the USA in the train on the way there).

On 30 September, the penultimate day of the Conference, Hermann Volk asks me to take a walk with him in the park. There we walk for a few steps in silence and then he hisses out: 'It won't do!' This very emotional outburst shocks me. I am somewhat perplexed, 'Not at all?' Whereupon he repeats, 'It won't do.' At any rate we now have a serious discussion. However, it wouldn't be worth investigating his precise objections for these memoirs. Not a single one of them was so telling that it has etched itself on my memory. Evidently not only does he not like this or that detail; the whole thing seems to him to be a dangerous, probably impertinent enterprise. While there is no dispute between us, it has become clear to me that like Cardinal Döpfner, Professor Volk is afraid, afraid of being personally compromised by his assistant's book.

But am I to not take this anxiety seriously? Is it really not on? Have I gone too far? Would it be better for me not to go ahead with this publication? Or rewrite a good deal? But what should I change? What should I leave out? Deeply uncertain, that same day I go to a man whom I likewise know from the Germanicum and in whom I have great confidence, Professor Dr Josef Höfer, the shrewd counsellor at the German Embassy to the Vatican and together with Karl Rahner the editor of the ten-volume *Lexikon für Theologie und Kirche*. He too has come to the conference and I bring him the manuscript. 'Herr Prelate, I know that it's asking the impossible of you, but I really don't know what to do and your advice would be a decisive help for me. Would you please look at this manuscript this evening? Then tomorrow, as you know, we all separate. And I have to make up my mind.'

The next morning Monsignor Höfer comes to me and now I walk with him through the same park. His answer? It comes without a long introduction: 'You will never write such a book when you get older.' So is he too against it? But Höfer adds, 'So publish it *now*! Later you won't have the courage because you'll hesitate.' What a remark! Thank God (and Höfer!).

I make use of the next few days to decipher Professor Volk's questions and observations and to correct my manuscript as best I can. I am then to keep the manuscript with his observations: evidently he wants to be safeguarded against any difficulties that may arise. Ah, I think, how little he risks and how much I risk. Now firmly resolved on publication and aware of the risks, I certainly want to get further information. On 6 October 1959 I travel to Passau. There the Association of German-Language Catholic Dogmatic and Fundamental Theologians is meeting again from 7 to 10 October. Of course there too the Council is much talked about – how could it be otherwise? The views of Heinrich Fries and Bernhard Welte are particularly important to me. However, one can't rush this great and varied gathering of professors into any statement or initiative. Who wants to burn his fingers at this stage? And from the start my real destination was not Passau, but Rome.

Rome before the Council – Cardinal Montini

In St Peter's, precisely five years to the day after my own first mass, on 11 October 1959, I preach a sermon at a first mass; not however, below in the grottos but above in the big left-hand choir chapel: it is for my fellow Germanicum student Leonz Gassmann from the diocese of Basle. The theme picks up the Johannine saying of Jesus to Peter: 'And take you where you do not want to go' (John 21.15-19). Previously without ties, now with ties, not knowing where our way is leading. And on it only one thing matters, 'Follow me!'

I visit my old professors at the Gregorian: Boyer, now replaced as prefect of studies by Dhanis (a very critical specialist on Fatima), the liturgist Schmidt, and the dogmatic theologian Alfaro, always more open. He encourages me. They contrast with the somewhat morose Tromp, still with a picture of Pius XII and not of John XXIII on his desk. In the spirit of Pius, as Secretary he will become the most important man on the Theological Commission of the Council alongside Cardinal Ottaviani. No one expects that Fr Augustin Bea will become a cardinal so soon.

On the roof terrace of the Gregorian, Fr Franz Hürth tells me with a note of friendly warning that before any call to a chair in a Catholic theological faculty in Germany the local bishop has recently had to make enquiries of the Roman Congregation of Studies, but that this hands on the enquiry 'to us', by which of course he means the Sanctum Officium. This is doubtless a gentle hint about the boundary post; at least it isn't the stake. So in fact decisions as to who will occupy Catholic chairs in the German state faculties are made in the 'Holy Office' of the Inquisition – a good prospect! Rather later I hear that Hürth has recently extended his activity as 'Zion watcher' to the Gregorian and in so doing is increasingly getting on the nerves of his closest colleagues. Happily the rumour that the more liberal moral theologian Josef Fuchs is to be dismissed proves wrong. Hürth, too, becomes a member of the Theological Preparatory Commission of the Council, responsible for the schemes on moral theology.

I am all the more interested in the views of the Archbishop of Milan, Cardinal Giovanni Battista Montini, about the coming Council. I hoped to visit him in Milan, but he lets me know that at this time he is in Rome. All the better. I meet him in the Domus Mariae on the Via Aurelia. I saw Montini only rarely during my seven years in Rome, since while the substitute for the Secretary of State, a tireless worker, signed countless letters and telegrams in the pope's name, he almost never appeared in public. When I spied him once during a solemn entry of the pope into St Peter's he struck me because he didn't inspect the public, like the Curia cardinals, giving a jovial nod to those whom they knew all too well, but marched along with tightly folded hands, sunk in prayer, his head bowed in devotion.

With rapid strides (as Pius XII liked to do in St Peter's, rushing along the prelates behind him), the 63-year-old enters the big room, his body leaning slightly to one side. Here is the one who is regarded as *papabile* should Angelo Roncalli die: slender limbs, friendly, with watchful eyes and big ears, inspecting me in a benevolent way. I am not unknown to him. Unlike most members of the Curia, Giovanni Battista Montini is something of an intellectual: he is well aware of the importance of Karl Barth and of my dissertation on the doctrine of justification. I will get to know him personally at the summer villa of the bishops of northern Italy in Gazzada near Milan, in the framework of the seventh Conference on Ecumenical Questions, on 'Unity in Difference' and the problems of the Council, which will meet there from 19-23 September 1960.

Now the cardinal is sitting in front of me *con dignità*, with one hand on the other; he isn't a man of spontaneous and hearty chat, but of dignified addresses and statements. I speak with him about various controversial matters of reform. He answers in a considered and cautious way. He sees the problems and recognizes the necessity of reform. However, with measured speech and gestures he always has his 'but':

Introduction of the vernacular into the Latin liturgy? In principle yes, but: only in the liturgy of the word; the *'missa sacrificiale'*, the sacrificial worship with the canon is better left in Latin.

And the need for a decentralization and shift of the competences of the Curia to the bishops? In principle yes, but: '*i servizi della Curia sono molto svelti*', the service of the Curia today is very prompt, so that it is easy to ask for permission or a dispensation in a telephone call to Rome.

Reform or abolition of the Index? As early as 1925 Montini was a co-founder of the progressive publishing house Morcelliana in Brescia, which drew fire from the Sanctum Officium for its publication of Karl Adam's *Essence of Catholicism* (all translations of Karl Adam's books were withdrawn from the Roman bookshops). In 1942 he had secured from Pius XII in the face of opposition from Ottaviani permission to reprint a work by the northern Italian Aristocrat Antonietta Giacomelli, a champion of liturgical renewal, which had been put on the Index in 1912. From his youth up he has known the problems of the Index ('May I read Renan? That is the question which arises every day' is the beginning of an article that he wrote at the age of 23). However, as a cardinal his view now is that the prohibition of books should remain, but the penalties imposed by the church should be abolished and permission to read them should be given more easily.

I look at him: impenetrable to the end, he keeps his secret to himself. Is Montini a real reformer or only half a reformer? I try to look into his heart: at any rate he is considerably more open than most Italian cardinals. Should I perhaps ask him for the preface that I want? No, I may not expect that of him in his exposed position. In any case, because of his political and social attitude he is regarded as dangerously 'progressive' by the conservative Curia and I still have Fr Gundlach's outburst ('eliminate him!') ringing in my ears.

But I know that I have Montini's sympathy and will send him my book on the Council the next year. On 4 October 1960 he will express his warmest thanks: 'I express to you my most sincere pleasure in your excellent study, which is full of useful information and is highly topical.' Montini's tacit agreement is now expressed in his Lent pastoral letter to the Council in 1962, which likewise sees the Council as wholly focused on the question of the church and the episcopate. His starting point is 'that the Second Vatican Council will also include the question of the episcopate among its topics, in order to describe its evangelical origin, its sacramental gifts of grace, its authority in teaching, pastoral work and jurisdiction, whether in respect of the individual bishop or in respect of the college of bishops . . .' In the process the 'royal priesthood of the laity' must be strengthened and the ecumenical task of the Council must be taken seriously. He doesn't go into much detail. But what more could I want?

Of course in the Germanicum, where I am staying, I discuss everything with my former Spiritual, Wilhelm Klein, who encourages me in every way. I tell him of Cardinal Döpfner's refusal, which doesn't surprise him: since Döpfner has received the 'red mantle' from the pope, he is so infinitely grateful that he thinks he can't allow any criticism of the Roman system. But undeterred, I am to write to another Germanicum cardinal and refer gently to him, Fr Klein: my letter is to the Archbishop of Vienna, Cardinal Francis König.

On 18 October, at 23.15, I return to Switzerland by the night express, spend a few days in Sursee, and meet Karl Barth again. He has read the manuscript about the Council and reform and is enthusiastic about it. But he says that the title of the book, *The Council, Reform and Reunion*, smacks too much of 'Protestantism'. The next day he sends me his proposal to Sursee: *The Council and Reunion* with the precise sub-title 'Renewal as a Call to Unity'. Imprimatur!

In Sursee I also receive from Berlin a reply from Cardinal Julius Döpfner dated 24 October: 'Your manuscript has been sitting here for a long time, but because of urgent daily work I didn't get round to reading it in peace. Over the last few days, thank God, I have succeeded in letting it make its impact on me as a whole. The main lines may seem bold, but the statements are made with Catholic responsibility and a good knowledge of the subject-matter. So the work can be presented with a good conscience, and particularly at the moment performs a very valuable service. I really have read the pages with keen interest and have been much stimulated. So I want to encourage you over the book out of full conviction.'

Then follow half a dozen suggestions on details: I am to avoid 'unnecessary annoyance', for example by omitting the expression 'confessional bigotry' or statements like 'If we were to see the return of the primacy of Peter, the modest fisherman of the lake, would this primacy be the problem that it is today?' It is better not to say 'historical mistakes *of* the church are usually covered up' but '*in* the church'. Instead of 'other churches' one should speak of 'our Protestant fellow Christians' and in so doing not emphasize so strongly the 'need for Luther to act like this'. There is also a lack of 'a positive but differentiated account of church obedience'. He, Döpfner, feels that the accounts of the priestly office go 'too far'. 'The other proposals are sometimes bold and unusual, but, it seems to me, one can make them with a good conscience.' 'Finally, should it seem advisable to say a word of commendation to the ordinarius who gives the imprimatur I am ready to do so.' Here he is saying in a diplomatic and unambiguous way what he is not prepared to do even after reading the manuscript, despite my repeated request: write a preface or even give the imprimatur. What am I to do?

On 30 October I again go to Münster, report back to Professor Volk, and tell him some of my experiences. The winter semester is beginning. In the Thomas Morus college there is the introduction of the new students to the hostel, the beginning of regular services and the study group. At the university there is Volk's second seminar on confirmation and of course the colloquium for doctoral students – all the usual business. The topping-out ceremony for the new building of the Catholic theological faculty takes place on 26 November. That same evening I have another long conversation with the well-known moral theologian Professor Herbert Doms. Already long retired, but still deeply wounded, he tells me the story of the suffering he had to endure, simply because in a book on marriage he put the two purposes of marriage – procreation and loving devotion

– on the same level, instead of subordinating the second to the first. What will later even find its way into Pope Montini's encyclical *Humanae vitae* was at that time reason enough to put the book on the Index of Prohibited Books and thus to outlaw the Catholic theologian Doms for ever. One more reason for me to avoid a condemnation as far as possible.

Much effort over a preface

As early as 20 October 1959 I have written to the Archbishop of Vienna, Cardinal Dr Francis König, a Germanicum alumnus, who enjoys high respect both as a bishop and as a scholar on the religions (he is the editor of three big volumes on 'Christ and the Religions of the Earth'). I refer to the many important Catholic theologians (Volk, Feiner, Hirschmann, Lortz, Klein, Seibel, Witte) and the few Protestant theologians (Barth, Kinder) who have read the manuscript in the meantime and to my conversations with Cardinal Montini and the professors of the Gregorian. I say that several of the persons I cite had advised me to have a preface. 'They said to me: 1. a book like this certainly needs the protection and the support of the relevant hierarchy; 2. it must be made clear that this is not the arrogant opinion of a young theologian but also an expression of the problems of the senior pastors in authority; 3. it is of the utmost importance for people in Rome itself – where only the authority of a cardinal makes any impression – to become clear about the earnestness and the difficulty of the questions; 4. this is particularly necessary, as the pope himself is hardly sufficiently orientated on the problems of Protestantism, is planning the Council more as an external mani-festation of Catholic unity, and wants to call it very soon (which would make a thorough preparation impossible); 5. your person is particularly suitable for a word of introduction not only because of the place of publication but above all because of your scholarly reputation, which is also well known to the Roman Curia.' I add that I would not hesitate to travel to Vienna should this be necessary.

Cardinal König's reply comes dated as early as 27 October 1959: 'I read your work on the doctrine of justification with great interest and I am therefore in principle positively disposed to your concern.' Of course he wants to read the manuscript before he finally agrees.

My definitive manuscript goes to Herder Verlag in Freiburg in the first half of November. On 8 January 1960 I again write to Cardinal König. I get the galley proofs on 26 January. I immediately have them sent to Cardinal König. But for a long, long time there is no reply. In such a case one doesn't want to press. Finally I learn from the paper that our colleague from the Germanicum, Cardinal Ste-pinac, who was arrested by Tito and then interned, died on 10 February 1960 and the Cardinal of Vienna is travelling to Zagreb for the funeral. Then a few days later comes a second report: Cardinal König has been injured in a serious car crash on the return journey. It is understandable that no news has come from Vienna about a theologian's book. But now I already have proofs. I have to learn patience.

Finally on 27 February I again write to the residence of Cardinal König in Rotenturmstrasse, near St Stephen's Cathedral in Vienna, although the cardinal himself is still in the General Hospital. Now I receive from his secretary the news that the cardinal is ready to write a word of introduction. But he asks me to come to Vienna. A journey from Münster in Westphalia to distant Vienna is no small matter, but it is necessary.

I telephone Herder Verlag in Freiburg. Some time previously I had made the by no means easy decision to change from Balthasar's élitist theological Johannes Verlag to Herder Verlag, the representative German Catholic publishing house. A conversation with the head of the biggest university bookshop in Münster had convinced me that the publicity of the little Johannes Verlag and its distribution system were minimal; my dissertation certainly had an amazing success, but that was despite the publishing house rather than because of it. For the book on the Council maximum distribution, also among non-theologians, must be a priority. So I have a pocket book in mind, and think of a publishing house like Herder, which has an excellent distribution network and its own pocket book series.

In a carefully considered letter I again express my gratitude to Hans Urs von Balthasar and attempt at the same time to explain to him what from now on will be my maxim for publishing policy: the publishing house which guarantees the best distribution will get the book; everything else, including the financial aspect, is secondary to that. Only later, when I am hit by another publisher with a lump sum royalty for all editions of my little book *Freedom in the World*, will I refuse and firmly establish a separate series of 'Theological Meditations'. However, Prelate Höfer has dissuaded me from immediately having the manuscript published as a pocket book; he thinks that in this format it wouldn't be taken sufficiently seriously, quite apart from the fact that for example the German embassy at the Vatican normally cannot give away pocket books. Of course Balthasar is not exactly delighted by my letter, but his answer is not unfriendly and he now links his Johannes Verlag even more closely with Benziger Verlag. But as a man who in any case reacts in a highly sensitive way, presumably he took this decision worse than I as an inexperienced author had thought.

Herder Verlag – I think in gratitude of my long collaboration with the editor, Dr Robert Scherer, and the publisher, Dr Hermann Herder – is generous enough to pay for the assistant Dr Küng, who as yet has no car, to fly from Düsseldorf to Vienna. There a representative of the Vienna branch of Herder Verlag takes care of me. The next morning I go to the General Hospital, where I find Cardinal Francis König: he is lying on the bed, his whole head in plaster and bandaged up, so that he can only speak with difficulty through his teeth.

But what he says is clear: he is ready to write the introduction; it can surely be short. 'Yes,' I reply, 'a few words are enough.' So I am to sit by his bed and write down his words. Here is the complete published text as dictated and written down at the bedside: 'It is a happy omen to find a theologian responding to the stimulus provided by the Holy Father when he announced the holding of an Ecumenical Council; to see, with his help, in all loyalty to the Church, the perspectives that are opening before us concerning the divisions in Christendom and the hopes offered by the coming Council. I hope that this book, and the challenge which it presents, will be received with understanding, and spread far and wide. Francis, Cardinal König, Archbishop of Vienna.'

It was and is clear to me that these sentences by the cardinal, highly esteemed for his learning, shrewdness and diplomatic capabilities, are the reason why with my book on the Council I did not come up against the same difficulties as Fr Lombardi later did with his. Rather, it's just the other way round: whereas the distribution and translation of Lombardi's book was prevented by the curial authorities, my book goes through three impressions in seven months and wins much approval. The French edition soon appears with a preface by the highly respected Cardinal Achille Liénart of Lille. An English–American edition will soon follow. But caution is needed: a quite different, in part opposite story, runs parallel to the long history of the publication of this book.

The mysteries of an academic procedure

At an early stage in my time in Lucerne, one day a Tübingen professor named Joseph Möller, Ordinarius Professor of Scholastic Philosophy, had come to visit us in our clergy house. He is known to me from my time in college as one of the very few Germanicum alumni who managed to find his way into one of the German theological faculties which were not particularly friendly to Rome. After lunch he wants to speak with me alone, and so we go to my bed–sitting–room on the second floor.

Here Professor Möller asks me quite abruptly whether I am interested in a chair of fundamental theology at the University of Tübingen. I feel like someone who is asked whether he would like to take part in the next space flight. 'Yes,' I say a little perplexed, 'yes, certainly!' Granted, I've never been to Tübingen and have hardly any experience of the German university system. But why shouldn't I take on such a task if other competent people think me capable of it? However, Möller emphatically tells me not to say a word to anyone about this conversation. Of course I don't, indeed I forget the whole matter completely, as if it were a dream. Later on occasions I see this as an encouraging example for those ambitious for a career: don't think about it and speculate on it, but let it be given when the time comes. Or, in the words of the Bible: 'The Lord gives it to his beloved in sleep.' This isn't an invitation to doziness but to waiting in trust.

At any rate, I am completely surprised when – by now I am already in Münster – one day I hear from the said Tübingen professor. A handwritten card arrives in which he reports to me that meanwhile progress has been made with the procedure for a call, but I am to continue to keep quiet. Through a fellow assistant in Münster, the historian Dr August Nitschke, I receive confidential information about the state of the proceedings in the Great Senate of Tübingen.

The average person has hardly any idea of the complicated procedure of a call to a university chair in Germany, with all the negotiations, sessions, opinions, reports and votes. The call of a Catholic professor of theology must be the most complicated of all, since in addition to the three weighty authorities – faculty, university, ministry – there are two others: the bishop and the Vatican. The whole process of the call is surrounded with the utmost secrecy: from the 'faculty secrecy' through the 'ministerial secrecy' to the 'Secretum Sancti Ufficii', a violation of which can be allowed only by the pope personally. So how did the procedure work out in my case? At least without any intrigue. I knew the most important phases at the time. I shall limit myself to essentials: Walter Jens has described phases I–III in an inimitable way in his lecture at my farewell in February 1996.

Authority I: the Catholic Theological Faculty. The chair of fundamental theology has long been vacant, and one of the reasons is spoken of openly: an ongoing dispute among the professors between Swabians and non-Swabians. Three calls in autumn 1958 proved fruitless: first the call was rejected by the first person chosen, Professor Bernhard Welte (I have related my meeting with him in Freiburg). Then the second person to be called, Dr Hans Urs von Balthasar, refused; Balthasar explained to me that he refused because of his lay order. I later hear from Rottenburg that Rome would never have consented to a call of the ex-Jesuit. And because two other candidates, nominated in somewhat half-hearted way, likewise dropped out, now the name of Küng has arisen in the faculty discussion. The Germanicum connection with Möller is important only in so far as he can inconspicuously make contact with the assistant priest in Lucerne. Finally people in Tübingen agree on the person of the one who has meanwhile advanced to become an assistant in Münster, although he has not yet 'habilitated' for teaching, as is otherwise customary.

As early as November 1959 I had to send my manuscript on *The Incarnation of God. The Christology of Hegel* (around 400 pages), revised in Münster and enlarged with new sections, to Professor Möller in Tübingen along with my philosophical licentiate thesis on the existentialist humanism of J. P. Sartre. At the same time I tell Professor Möller that during the long summer and autumn months I have devoted all my energy to a new book on *The Council and Reunion*, a manuscript of 200 pages. This has prevented me from finishing my work on Hegel, but I expect to complete it very soon.

Authority II: the University. The list of the Catholic Theological Faculty on which only the name of Dr Küng stands (*unico loco* instead of the usual *terna*, list of three) goes from the faculty to the Rector of the University. He appoints the classicist

Professor Ernst Zinn to make a report to the Great Senate, to which the around 100 ordinarius professors belong. Along with my work on Sartre, my book on the Council and my habilitation thesis on Hegel, Zinn's report to the Senate praises above all my book on justification, which has 'so to speak with a jerk advanced the conversation in controversial theology between the confessions by a quite unusual achievement of interpretation and thus not only aroused widespread respect but also found the assent of key theologians'. It is 'to be expected that the youthful power to penetrate central problems which has been shown so far and which makes Küng's whole appearance so promising will in the future prove itself in the historical sphere or in fundamental theology in the narrower sense'.

The discussion in the senate on 19 December 1959 goes positively; the only complaint is about the lack of a habilitation. At the age of 31 one hardly ever advances from assistant to ordinarius without a habilitation. But the decision of the Great Senate to call Dr Küng to the chair of fundamental theology finally follows after eleven votes with no opposition. At the same time it is resolved to call the outstanding Lucerne exegete, Dr Herbert Haag, editor of the *Bibellexikon*, to the chair of Old Testament exegesis: 'His countryman in manner and career – Lucerne, Paris and Tübingen! Practical ministry and learned dealings – a colleague and friend related in many ways' (as Walter Jens was to put it).

Authority III: the Kultusministerium. On 6 February the Tübingen list with the reports by the faculty and senate arrives at the Kultusministerium of Baden-Württemberg in Stuttgart. The Kultusminister Dr Gerhard Storz sees no difficulties over forwarding the list with the enclosures to the Bishop of Rottenburg, Dr Carl-Joseph Leiprecht, so that he may give the *nihil obstat* ('nothing in the way') to the call as soon as possible. According to the concordat law the *ordinarius loci,* the local bishop, and not the Curia (the Reich government of the time would never have accepted that) is responsible for the *nihil obstat*; the bishop is also beyond doubt the best informed person in the relevant diocese and state.

Authority IV: the Bishop of Rottenburg. Dr Leiprecht has no objection whatsoever to the teaching and way of life (according to the Reich concordat he does not have to decide on anything else) of the two to be called. So the episcopal *nihil obstat* could be given without further ado and the procedure over the call which had lasted so long could be brought to a rapid conclusion. But the actual circumstances are not the same as the legal regulations: under Pius XII the Curia succeeds by a simple internal directive – contrary to the letter and spirit of the concordat – in taking upon itself the *nihil obstat*; to my knowledge no German bishop and no ministry has ever protested against this undermining of the concordat. Formally Rome now declares unilaterally that the Congregation of Studies is responsible. But in fact, as I heard from Fr Hürth, the decision is made in the Sanctum Officium, which has control of all the dossiers of those who are suspect or unpopular.

Authority V: the Vatican. The procedure takes considerably longer than expected. For two years now there has been a dossier in the Index division of the Sanctum Officium under my name with the protocol number 399/57i. The obscure situation makes me write on 25 January 1960 to Counsellor Professor Dr Höfer at the German Embassy to the Holy See: 'Since you are sufficiently aware of the resistance which there was not all that long ago to the call of H. U. von Balthasar to Tübingen, you will understand if I ask you cordially to keep something of an eye on the course of these calls. Granted, I do not fear any serious resistance, since on my various visits in Rome last October I had a very friendly reception not only from his eminence Cardinal Bea but also from Frs Hürth and Tromp. Professor Haag is highly valued as an exegete by Cardinal Bea, to whom he has been known personally for many years.' I also mention that my book *The Council and Reunion* has not yet appeared and that in the circumstances it could cause difficulties, but that the page proofs have already been sent by Herder both to me and to Cardinal König for the imprimatur and introduction.

As early as 3 February a short message comes from Prelate Höfer: 'The following in absolute confidence: Herr Cardinal Bea is prepared if need be to intercede for both of you; Secretary Staffa and Reporter Romeo (of the Congregation of Studies) told me that such a proposal from the Most Venerable Lord of Rottenburg would receive the *nihil obstat*. I have just reported this to His Excellency Leiprecht *ad informandam conscientiam*. In my view your work on the Council would better remain unpublished. And you must keep absolutely quiet. Warmest greetings, Höfer.'

I report this correspondence to Professor Möller, who meanwhile has been elected dean for the next academic year. At the same time I ask Herder Verlag to delay publication of the book on the Council. But things go on and on and I do not know now whether I should be preparing for habilitation in Münster or for a professorship in Tübingen. At the same time I am urgently asked by Monsignor Willebrands to come to an important confidential meeting of theologians at Warmond in Holland from 25 to 29 April 1960, together with some representatives of the high-church ILAFO (International League for Apostolic Faith and Order) which is canvassing particularly for Catholic concerns – apostolic faith and apostolic succession – within the World Council of Churches. But what happens if I suddenly get the call to Tübingen? Some letters go to and fro between Münster, Rome and Tübingen.

A call and a book

Finally, on Easter Tuesday, 19 April 1960, the situation is this. In Sursee, where I am spending Holy Week and Easter week, I receive the call to Tübingen through a letter from Kultusminister Storz dated 12 April: 'The Great Senate has proposed you in agreement with the Catholic theological faculty for the occupation of the ordinarius chair of fundamental theology. I allow myself to notify you of this and ask you to indicate whether in principle you are willing to accept the call to Tübingen.' Three days later I travel back to Münster. When I can now inform Dean Volk about my call he is literally speechless. Three times in succession he remarks in his inimitable way: 'Donnerwetter' – pause – 'Donnerwetter' – pause – 'Donnerwetter!'

Now things really get moving. From Sursee I had already asked my bishop, von Streng, for consent to my permanent move to Tübingen: 'Even in Tübingen I hope to maintain links with my home diocese, and especially my bishop.' I take part in the ecumenical conference in Holland as planned, from 25 to 29 April, there to discuss the sacrifice of the mass, the need for the office of bishop and the expectations for the Council. On Tuesday 3 May I travel to Tübingen, where I arrive at 18.25 by the proverbially slow Swabian railways, to have negotiations that same evening with Dean Möller and the next day in the Kultusministerium in Stuttgart.

As the summer semester has already begun, I am firmly resolved not to take up my chair until the autumn, since otherwise I cannot prepare for my teaching in any way. I attempt to make clear to the dean that I have never run a seminar nor ever given a series of lectures at a university apart from two or three guest lectures. But I have come to the wrong man: since I have been praised to the skies in all the reports, the dean implores me not to postpone the beginning of my teaching to the autumn. The chair of fundamental theology has remained vacant for so long.

My first night in Tübingen is very restless – they have put me up in the ancient Hotel Lamm in the marketplace (later pulled down and replaced by the Protestant parish centre). What am I to do? On the morning of 4 May I have decided: I mustn't disappoint my future faculty. So I will begin my teaching in Tübingen in the summer semester, on 1 July. In Stuttgart I negotiate with the competent, friendly and fresh director Dr Hoffmann. We quickly agree on the conditions. Since I am only an academic assistant I may hardly make any special demands – as well as an assistant I am also to have a part-time secretary; that is more important to me than the highest possible salary. I am subsequently informed of the amount: a basic salary of DM 1150 per month (plus additions and almost as many subtractions). That isn't much. Will I now be able to afford a car? A friendly couple from my former Lucerne community relieves me of this anxiety and gives me my first car, a VW beetle, which in future will transport me from Tübingen to Sursee in three hours.

My farewell to Münster is both cheerful and nostalgic: after all, I have felt extremely happy in the city and the university and have had the best possible relations with both professors and students. All goes without a hitch on 27/28 May 1960: farewell celebrations of the theological seminar, farewell dinner with Professors Eising and Volk, with whom I have particularly close relations, and my colleagues Nitschke and Spaemann . . . and at the same time the arrival of the first copies of *The Council and Reunion*, not too early and not too late. 'Now go confidently to Tübingen' I am cheerfully told by the director of the theological seminar, the congenially blunt church historian Professor Bernhard Kötting, who is a great force in the faculty, 'but after three years we will call you back to Münster!'

Does Kötting already know that Professor Volk is being discussed as an episcopal candidate in his home diocese of Mainz? 'What is the bishop?' is one of the theological questions often repeated by Hermann Volk, in which he always emphasizes that the pastoral office of bishop does not mean rule over the church but only service to fellow human beings. Volk had already been a prelate for a long time: he never made anything of himself; he loved neither title nor adornment. Without any vanity he remained simple, humble and natural.

A few months later, when our Catholic Conference on Ecumenical Questions meets in Gazzada, that villa of the bishops of northern Italy, I will ask my former boss directly in a quiet lunchtime in the hall of pillars: will he become Bishop of Mainz? All the world is talking about it, he replies, but he himself doesn't know. Moreover with his right hand he makes a gentle caricature of the episcopal blessing which is usually given to the right and the left in sequence: 'I can't do that!' 'Then don't do it' is my quite natural reply. It causes him to shrug his shoulders in an uncertain way.

The next year the announcement is made of Hermann Volk's call to Mainz, to a German see which is one of the richest in tradition (in the time of Luther the occupant was the most powerful churchman in Germany). At Volk's invitation, on 5 June 1962 I and Karl Rahner attend the consecration along with the dogmatic theologian Michael Schmaus and the canon lawyer Klaus Mörsdorf. We sit at the front of the choir and see everything: at the end of the long ceremonial service it is customary for the new bishop to give the threefold episcopal blessing, to the right, forward and to the left. That should really be enough blessing, I think, and now watch expectantly to see whether, as he goes out, Hermann Volk finally does what, as he said, he 'can't do', contrary to his convictions. And he does: he goes down the long nave to the porch and keeps blessing to the right and also to the left. What a pity. Certainly Hermann Volk will be a well-meaning bishop and pastor. But a great reformer and bold ecumenist? Moreover, what is to be expected of the social scientist Joseph Höffner, who becomes Bishop of Münster the same year and whose theology, unlike that of Volk, has notoriously remained at the level of the Gregorian in the 1930s?

In my homeland people are only half delighted at the 'call away of our Swiss theologian'. The 'central organ of Swiss Catholics' says of Franz Böckle, Herbert Haag and Hans Küng: 'They are the best three theologians. Open to the world, dynamic, thorough in their professional knowledge . . . It is certainly a joy and an honour for little Switzerland . . . But on the other hand we are filled with a feeling of nostalgia and regret that our best theologians have to emigrate' (*Vaterland*, 26 April 1963).

Freedom in the world

On Monday 30 May I leave Münster in the evening to be in Stuttgart next day at 6 a.m. For on the afternoon of 1 June I have to give my first lecture in the University of Tübingen. I have the most deeply moving farewell surprise at the station. Almost the whole Thomas Morus College is there, and they wave to me until the train disappears. Here, too, as in Lucerne I have to say goodbye too soon and with sorrow in my heart. Someone who was there writes to me that at the end of my last sermon at the Thomas Morus College I had said, 'Pray for me, I have a hard balancing act ahead of me.'

Quite apart from the students, one or other of whom I will see again in later decades, one last souvenir of the Thomas Morus College in Münster has remained with me to the present day: the simply framed print of the portrait of the man who gave his name to this college. It hangs at the entrance to my Tübingen home and greets me every morning: this fine, strong face; the eyes, quietly thoughtful, critical, almost sceptical, yet not hard but kind; the nose and mouth, marked by discipline and moderation, unforced certainty and steadfastness; all in all features which are natural and simple: that is Sir Thomas More, at the age of 51 the first lay Lord Chancellor of Henry VIII of England and first statesman of the realm. Later I will be shown Hans Holbein's original painting in Windsor Castle when I am allowed to give the St George's Lecture in St George's Chapel, a jewel of English Gothic.

This Thomas Morus, as his Latinized humanist name runs, impresses me; from my time at the Germanicum he raised the question for me how I can and should live as a Christian in keeping with the gospel, not only in a Roman college but outside in the world. For I too did not want to enter an order; I did not want to retreat into the cloister, where in any case it is difficult to escape the world. Not even in the Curia of the Franciscans up above the Vatican, which I was allowed to visit after its rebuilding, can one live in the poverty that Francis of Assisi required; as a matter of course people there claim all the conveniences of modern life in accommodation, food and hygiene.

This Sir Thomas lived in the world, indeed he was even what is called a man of the world, self-confident, superior, with good manners. A worldly diplomat and scholar, he was the first author of a social critique, *Utopia*, in outstanding Latin. But this man of the world, with towering intelligence, iron resolve, a high sense of justice and a fearless approach, at the same time had a bewitching modesty, friendliness and kindness. He is 'a man for all seasons' (a play was written about him under this title) in whom deep earnestness is coupled with irony and humour and noble *humanitas* is grounded in a completely hidden way in the discipleship of Christ.

It is reported that Sir Thomas had 'no antipathy to innocent pleasure'. He enjoyed his property but wasn't addicted to it. More, the man of the world, was not a *bon viveur*; his everyday life was simple, and he knew neither avarice nor greed, but was ready to let others share his riches. He didn't set his heart on money but on God the Lord alone, in an inconspicuous way, without making a fuss about it. Here it becomes clear that the decisive thing for Christians is not to give up the goods of the world but not to lose oneself in them either, whether in wealth or power or sex. The considered detachment of the free man from the things of this world ultimately makes him indifferent to superfluity and lack. Freedom in the world.

A period of my life has come to an end. So far I have lived as a student; I have seldom been hungry, but also seldom lived in superfluity. Now this time will be over. I too will occupy a position in the world, will ultimately own a house with a library and a garden, and will have to see how in the new situation I remain the same and preserve my inner freedom.

However, I can have no inkling that Sir Thomas — a martyr not for the papacy but for the unity of the church 'to relieve his conscience' and thus for 'consensus' (Council!) and 'conscience' — will be my model in yet another situation. *Omnium horarum homo*, a 'man for all hours', as his friend Erasmus named him, who stands by his own convictions not only in periods of fine weather but also in bad and gloomy times. One against the powers — if it is a matter of preserving freedom even in confrontation with a supreme authority in 'civil' disobedience: by force of argument deciding by one's own conscience and paying the price.

VI

ଶୁଓଷ୍ଟୋଷ

The Struggle for the Freedom of Theology

'Duly assembled in the Holy Spirit, forming a general council,
and representing the Catholic Church, the synod has its authority from Christ.
Thus everyone of whatever estate or dignity, even the papal dignity,
has to obey it in all that concerns the faith,
the overcoming of the said schism
and the reform of this church, head and members.'

Ecumenical Council of Constance, 1418

Looking for hot potatoes?

A KEY scene from my first two years in Tübingen: 'An exciting book, this *Structures of the Church*. It can deprive one of sleep. But if you always choose the hot potatoes in theology, one day you'll get your fingers burned.' That's Cardinal Julius Döpfner's comment on the new book by the young Tübingen professor, made in the courtyard of the Collegium Germanicum on the eve of the Second Vatican Council at the beginning of October 1962. And the professor replies to his episcopal colleague with a smile: 'How do you imagine theology? Do you see a whole series of potatoes lying there, hot, lukewarm and cold, and me audaciously looking for the hot ones? After all, I've only taken up topics which are formally important for a theologian in view of the Council and the church.'

Hardly anyone now knows the information that went into a book like *Structures of the Church*, which appears a few months before the beginning of the Council, the discussions and conflicts that are associated with it. But with this book too, the dramatic history of which must now be told, along with that of my first two years in Tübingen, I think that I was simply doing my theological duty. After the programmatic work *The Council and Reunion* it was absolutely necessary to reflect on certain forgotten or neglected structures of the church which could again be brought into view by the announcement of the Council, theologically, historically and in terms of the present. Not in a superficial and enthusiastic way, or in a speculative and remote way, but in a sober, matter-of-fact, yet at the same time passionate way. The new problems raised here may have robbed the Archbishop of Munich of his sleep, but previously they had tormented the author of the book day and often night.

Even certain Roman Catholic historians of the Council like Giuseppe Alberigo, who has already been mentioned, editor of a history of Vatican II at the end of the twentieth century, would rather not deal with these 'hot potatoes' – and the story of the conflict associated with them, with the options that were suppressed and denied; instead they occupy themselves circumspectly with the 'lukewarm' and the 'cold' ones. Earlier things were different: as early as May/June 1962 the same Alberigo invites me in two letters to give a critical interview on Vatican II for a series on the Council by Televisione Italiana. In March 1963 at his request I send him my publications on the Council and my collected lectures on the Council (published in the USA as *The Council in Action*; in Britain there are two editions, *The Living Church* and *The Changing Church*). He recommends the book I send to him, *Structures of the Church,* to the Milan publishing house Mondadori for an Italian edition (unfortunately in vain). In the *Tübinger Theologische Quartalschrift* I have thoroughly discussed and praised Alberigo's valuable new edition of all the decrees of the twenty ecumenical councils with its advantages over the tendentious selection of decrees by Heinrich Denzinger. So we become friends, see each other after the Council every year in the week after Pentecost at the meeting of the journal *Concilium,* and share many experiences.

But *'tempora mutantur, et nos mutamur in illis* – times change, and we change with them'. In 1993 Alberigo wants to have nothing to do with hot potatoes. He doesn't mention my name in his composite volume *Verso il Concilio Vaticano II (1960-1962).* In the first two volumes of the *History of the Second Vatican Council* edited by him and Klaus Wittstadt (1997/2000), even my printed contributions to Vatican II and the public reaction to them will be almost completely ignored, although I was the only German-speaking Council *peritus* to give a lengthy, albeit very critical, report of my experiences in the international symposium organized by the two professors on the 'Contribution of the German-Language and East European Countries' (Würzburg, 17 December 1993). Indeed I don't appear at all in the discussion of the *'periti* of a theological renewal' (Wittstadt). It doesn't matter – I'm comforted by the thought that almost four pages are devoted to Karl Rahner. It is worse that certain problems are ignored and that the failure of the popes – an essential cause of the ambiguities and half-heartedness of Vatican II – isn't clearly worked out. It is even worse that the lack of a solid exegetical foundation for important statements of the Council isn't perceived at all. Worst of all, though, there is an over-abundance of superficial information; the basic dilemma of Vatican II over the understanding and reform of the church isn't worked out perceptively. Alberigo declines the 2000 Herbert Haag Prize, 'For Freedom in the Church' (as previously did the good Catholic German Bundestag President Rita Süssmuth), with an eye to the Vatican. He wants to present the first volume of his history of the Council to John Paul II in a private audience, and this is in fact hardly compatible with a freedom prize. The author of these memoirs congratulates him on such an honour, and in the chapters to come allows himself by personal insights to open up the 'semi-official' history of the

Council a little: this is something like an 'alternative' history of the Council 'depicted from within' (like that by Ullathorne-Butler-Lang for Vatican I). My personal sources for Vatican II are my experiences and encounters, my diaries and correspondence, my personal notes on the Council and some publications, and finally the many volumes of press cuttings concentrated on my name – all supports of a memory which happily still functions well.

Looking for hot potatoes? At the beginning of the 1960s one thing has become clear to me. In contrast to my student days, I cannot simply plan my life as a theologian, given all the strategic considerations. However, now that happily I have been appointed ordinarius professor with tenure (the document, dated 20 July 1960, is signed by the prime minister of Baden-Württemberg, Georg Kreisinger, who later becomes federal chancellor), I can work with the feeling that I have almost unlimited time. But I have no inkling how vital this document will prove twenty years later for my academic survival at the university.

Looking for hot potatoes? My question was: what scholarly project should I give preference to in this first decade? I decide in accordance with Arnold Toynbee's slogan 'challenge and response': if a serious challenge of the time – and the Council is such a challenge – comes to me, I will not back off. I will approach it as a theologian and attempt a response. In this sense – not conforming to the changeable 'spirit of the age' – for me 'the voice of the time (*vox temporis*) is the voice of God (*vox Dei*)'. And so instead of completing my study on Hegel's christology I decide to work out a theology of the ecumenical council. This is certainly a hot potato, which must also be tackled in any serious definition of historical position.

Fundamental problems

There are only three weeks left for me to prepare my Tübingen lectures. No joke, I say in the introduction to the first series of lectures on 1 June 1960, for a theological stripling who can't take well-prepared manuscripts out of a pigeon-hole, and who literally has to produce his lectures on fundamental theology out of thin air. One could suffer the same fate as the writer Mark Twain, who had to give a historical lecture and began as follows: 'Alexander the Great is dead, Julius Caesar is dead, Napoleon is dead; I'm alive, but I'm not in very good shape either.'

My first Tübingen students – the Catholic Theological Faculty numbers 167 students, the university as a whole 9192 – are mostly candidates for the priesthood and therefore male; there are just three women students. The students largely belong to my generation and I enjoy the sympathy of shared youth. This can confuse older persons: 'What course are you taking, then?' I am asked kindly by Wilhelm Sedlmeier, the suffragan bishop of Rottenburg, in the courtyard of the Tübingen theological hall of residence (the 'Wilhelmsstift'), where in the first semester I occupy two rooms. 'I'm the new Ordinarius Professor of Fundamental Theology,' I answer with satisfaction. This was not to be the last perplexity that I was to cause the lords of the episcopal ordinariate of Rottenburg – it is only a dozen kilometres from Tübingen, but another world.

So I teach 'fundamental theology' in these first years and am very happy to do so. What finer task could there be – an eminently pastoral task, I explain to the members of my first semester – than as a young theologian to build the theological 'foundation' for their later pastoral work: to offer the fire of the Spirit to those who are ready to hand it on? There are no empty phrases when I ask them to work with me intensively and also ask for their prayers – in the sense of Colossians 4.3, which five years previously was printed on the card for my first mass.

I see two opportunities in 'fundamental theology': first, in their first four semesters I can introduce the students, who have not yet been corrupted by any scholastic theology, to the fundamental questions of revelation, God, Jesus Christ and the church, in other words to the foundations of faith. I would never have dreamed for reasons of prestige of making fundamental theology an overarching theology, as my successor was to strive to do in years of faculty wrangles, thus robbing the students of a fundamental introduction to theology.

Secondly, in 'fundamental theology' I can discuss those very topics which have occupied me in the personal experience of my student years as a basis for my faith and thought. What a delight it is to think through in quite a new way what I experienced and learned in Rome, expanded and deepened in Paris, and assimilated in practice in both Lucerne and Münster, to work it out in historical perspective and to pass on the results to the Tübingen students. I no more want to 'celebrate' or 'pontificate' loftily in my lectures than I do in preaching – Protestant theologians can also do that. I want to inform critically and argue convincingly, and to be understood without any German academic fussiness. Nor do I want to raise endless problems 'hermeneutically', but to give answers that are helpful for praxis in life and the community.

In retrospect I ask myself whether I didn't overestimate my audience with my demand for 'intensive thinking and skilful writing'. I assumed that they could acquire the elements of traditional theology for themselves in their own study, as I did as a student, and write down my lectures for themselves, guided by the clear structure of the lectures on the blackboard (projectors are as yet hardly in use). Evidently they haven't learnt this at school, and working the textbook material into my lectures was probably beyond the capacities of most of them.

On the other hand, the revolutions of 1968 would never lead me to the illusion that long series of lectures belong to an authoritarian past, as they do my Protestant colleague Ernst Käsemann. Under the impact of a cultural revolution which also embraced pedagogy and didactics, this extremely successful academic teacher replaces his lectures on Romans with group work (using a variety of commentaries) and comes to grief. He resigns – lamenting the 'old' university which will never return. In my very first series of lectures, long before 1968, I offer 'colloquia depending on time and opportunity', to give the students the possibility of asking questions – not to mention personal contact after lectures and before discussions. That for a long time students will not make as much use of these opportunities as I had hoped is another matter.

Faith or knowledge?

In 1960 it is certainly extremely unusual to begin the regular series of lectures on 'the doctrine of revelation' with a long first part on 'the question of human existence'. Granted, I am also concerned to clarify the question of 'revelation', but on the basis of a different starting-point and method. As it were from below upwards, starting from the uncertainty of human existence I investigate a fundamental certainty which can support everything. Only after that do I pose the question of faith and revelation. So my procedure is quite different from that of Karl Barth in his *Church Dogmatics* (starting from the Trinity!): questions are to be asked about God and his revelation from the depth of human existence which is so doubtful.

And I discuss these problems not in the context of the Middle Ages but in that of modernity. Not like 'progressive' fundamental theologians of the same age who follow Maréchal, Rahner, Bouillard and others with the help of Thomas Aquinas, now reinterpreted so that he becomes an 'anthropocentrist' (J. B. Metz) or a 'theologian of history' (M. Seckler), but so to speak in a modern 'classical' way, starting with the founder of modern philosophy, René Descartes, and his opposite, Blaise Pascal, in controversy with the idealism of Hegel, the nihilism of Nietzsche and the existentialism of Sartre, and advancing to positive answers for men and women of today.

However, I don't take this difficult way in my lectures simply by abstract analysis and reflection, but as far as possible through narrative, starting from the life and fate of the great leading figures of modernity. There are no purely theoretical questions, no philosophical or theological systems which only give rise to yet other systems. Rather, there are the existential questions of living people, who have assimilated and thought through their experiences, disappointments and successes; who have not only devised their answers but experienced them and often endured them. Later I can only smile at the way in which the demand for a 'narrative' theology is suddenly made by theologians who prefer to fabricate theological placards or treatises about narrative rather than narrate themselves.

So step by step I develop the most neglected basic question of 'fundamental theology': faith or knowledge? Is there a foundation which theology knows from elsewhere, for example from philosophy? Or a foundation which theology lays for itself in faith? What is the 'foundation' of what?

Does reason provide the foundation for faith? But if faith is grounded in reason, faith seems to come to grief on it. In that case faith is fundamentally no longer faith, but knowledge.

Or is faith its own foundation? But if faith has a foundation in itself, then faith appears groundless and irrational. In that case, in the end faith has no foundation outside itself.

'Problems about problems' I say in my introduction. Anyone who is interested in how I attempted to solve them through narrative, analysis and argument, starting from Descartes' *cogito* of reason ('I think, therefore I am') or from Pascal's *credo* in the God of the Bible ('I believe, therefore I am'), may read this in the first chapter of my book *Does God Exist?* (1978): fifteen years later I thought through, deepened and expanded my first series of Tübingen lectures. But the subject-matter remained the same: working out a way from the fundamental uncertainty of human beings to their inescapable basic choice between fundamental mistrust and fundamental trust, and then comparing this fundamental trust with those statements in the Old and New Testaments which also presuppose a kind of 'faith' among the pagans. By this approach I can finally distinguish different 'stages' of revelation and thus different 'forms' of faith, all of which have their own dignity: the faith of the one who believes in the good, of the one who believes in God, of the one who believes in Christ, of the one who believes in the church.

But, it might be asked, wasn't this a theology very much in accord with the spirit of the time, with an individualist and existentialist narrowness? Looking through my handwritten lecture manuscript 40 years later, I am amazed how already in my very first Tübingen lectures series of 1960 I set the question of human existence against the wider background of society: 'We are in a transitional phase of world history of unprecedented dimensions: "the end of modernity", "the atomic age", "the cosmic age"! Signs of this are the artificial satellites, space rockets and space ships; the anxieties, fears and needs of highly technologized peoples; the problem of the masses, technology and the economy; the newly awakening peoples of Asia and Africa and the rapid elaboration of a global civilization and a global economy; the unprecedented and often chaotic unrest in present-day art, literature and philosophy, which manifest a large-scale intellectual revolution.'

An epoch-making paradigm shift – a global horizon and global problems – a fundamental trust and fundamental ethic which are possible for anyone: already at that time those central elements are appearing which decades later are to become fundamental to the global ethic project. In 1960 I likewise state that in this transitional phase of world history the church faces giant tasks: the gathering together of separated Christians and the unification into one church of a Christianity which has been torn apart; a positive discussion with the world religions, which are converging ever more closely; a 'leavening' of the old Christian world, which has again become pagan. For theology this means that now is perhaps not the time to set up big systematic structures. It is the time to look for a new viable foundation. Where – this is my expectation – will this be more possible for me than in Tübingen? I set to work.

The free air of Tübingen

'Tübingen – gateway to heaven!' This saying, coined by some theologian whose name I no longer know, is of course true only for theologians and for those who still believe in a heaven. But certainly I very soon feel at home in Tübingen, if not precisely happy. This is first of all because Swabians and Swiss – quite apart from their common need to learn High German as a first foreign language – have the same virtues: a zeal for work, conscientiousness, a love of order, straightforwardness, common sense, reliability, tenacity. And the same vices: a certain narrowness, hesitation, pettiness, stubbornness. At a very early stage I no longer feel that crossing the narrow frontier between Germany and the confederacy is a transition into another world – not least because of the German 'economic miracle'.

The main reason why I quickly feel at home here is the congenial Swabian town. With its barely 60,000 inhabitants I like it more than the great cities of the world in which I've lived for most of the past decade. It may not be by the lake in front of the Swiss Alps, but it is by the Neckar in front of the Swabian Alb, in an attractive landscape on more or less seven hills. However, I can't swim in the Neckar. During the war, because of its many clinics and the planned French headquarters, Tübingen remained virtually intact, and has only a little industry; it is essentially a mediaeval, typically German university town. People do not say that it 'has' a university but that it 'is' a university.

The university, already almost 500 years old, was founded in 1477 by Count Eberard im Bart on the basis of papal privilege: how could I ever have dreamed that I would be asked to give the Jubilee speech in 1977 in the Protestant Stiftskirche as a Catholic theologian? The university has retained its original buildings in the romantic old town. Later these came to include the Schloss Hohentübingen, from which there are splendid views all over the city. In the nineteenth century the university extended in front of the gates of the old town for lack of space, and in the twentieth century with its clinical and scientific institutions increasingly took over the heights. There is no need to draw a veil over the fact that once, say in the time of Goethe – he stayed in the home of his publisher, Cotta – the city was dirty and the university provincial. For a long time that has ceased to be the case. No German university can boast a history which is so exciting to read. Walter Jens, a distinguished philologist and man of letters – in 1963 the Great Senate will resolve that he should be given the first professorship of rhetoric in the Federal Republic of Germany – will describe it in his *Eine deutsche Universität. 500 Jahre Tübinger Gelehrtenrepublik* ('A German University. 500 Years of the Republic of Tübingen Scholars').

And what is the attraction of Tübingen for me as a theologian? First of all there is the famous Evangelische Stift, which has produced and still produces the majority of Protestant Swabian pastors, and on the other hand there is the Catholic Wilhelmsstift, which performs a similar function for the Catholic clergy of Swabia, of the diocese of Rottenburg-Stuttgart. And as well as the two Stift libraries there is the university library, one of the best libraries in the world for theology and oriental studies, which can well compare with Washington's Library of Congress or the British Museum Library. That is because for more than 400 years the university has been collecting all published works of theology. It is understandable that Tübingen in particular was selected after the Second World War from among the German university libraries as the main catchment area for theology and oriental studies. As a result of extraordinary federal funding, almost every theological work from all over the world can be bought, and subscriptions can be maintained to hundreds of journals of theology and oriental studies.

But another reason why for theologians Tübingen is the gate of heaven is that here, despite all the fits of inquisition, Catholic and Protestant, in the end academic freedom has been maintained. Not only because at the time of the French Revolution Hegel, Schelling and Hölderlin, who were disciplined in the Evangelische Stift, which at that time had an authoritarian rule, are said to have danced round the freedom tree, but because in Tübingen, first of all a Protestant and then also a Catholic 'Tübingen school' became possible, of a kind that no other German university can boast.

The history of the two faculties needn't be reported here. But the fact that with Ferdinand Christian Baur, Tübingen became the birthplace of historical-critical exegesis has governed my development more than I assumed to begin with. And the Catholic Tübingen school, too – the faculty was only founded in 1817 – has an important name in the Catholic world. In Germany it was the first Catholic faculty to stand alongside a Protestant one: it was almost the only one to engage in constructive critical discussion with contemporary Protestant theology. It was a pioneer in its efforts to unite historical and speculative theology.

Independent theology

For me personally it is important that here I am coming to a faculty with its own tradition: Catholic, but not neoscholastic and Roman; open to reform, but not without a profile. It is a place of freedom where, after my Swiss homeland, I can presumably live and breathe theologically better than anywhere else in Germany. And who knows what lies ahead of me as a young theologian? From Vienna Cardinal König sends me his heartfelt congratulations that I have been 'given the chair in Tübingen in so short a time': 'Times have changed. A generation ago such a career would have been impossible for a "Roman".' In fact my call – and the fact that I don't exactly behave like a 'Roman' – is understood as a signal that the 'anti-Roman spell' in German state faculties has been broken. On 1 December 1963 it is reckoned that at the seven German theological university faculties there are 50 students doing their habilitation, a fifth of them from the Germanicum, all of whom were at the college with me. In the coming years they also become professors: Casper and Hünermann in Freiburg; W. Weber in Mainz; Gleissner, Seybold and Wetter in Munich; Lengsfeld, Loretz, Schulz and H. Weber in Münster.

In the first weeks, still without a car, I cross the town on foot to pay my inaugural visits to different colleagues, Catholic and also Protestant: Diem, Käsemann, Michel, Rückert. There isn't one of them from whom I don't have a very friendly reception. These contacts help me to gain information on all sides and to develop an independent theology. I want nothing to do with the clashes between Swabians and non-Swabians in the Catholic faculty. Rather, I say clearly that I don't want to be burdened by the earlier controversies and don't think that I belong to any party. Indeed I succeed very well in this in the first years, so that four years later I am unanimously elected dean – by far the youngest in the university – and after a year am even re-elected unanimously, though this was to cause me serious difficulties with one of the two parties.

The Great Senate, in which all ordinarius professors, around 100, have a seat and a vote, is a prominent institution in the University of Tübingen. During the semester it meets once a month on a Saturday morning. Here at an early stage I get to know the eminent authorities in all the faculties. The lists of appointments must be discussed and approved, and this provides a varied insight into the problems of the faculties and the positions of colleagues. Soon regular reciprocal invitations establish private links between me and some colleagues (quite apart from the theologians, the legal historian Elsener, the dermatologist Schneider and the odontologist Fröhlich). And already after a year I feel completely accepted by these Tübingen colleagues. Later as dean, but also as a member for many years of the Commission for Scholarly Development and more briefly also of the Buildings Commission of the university, I quite naturally make closer acquaintance with many colleagues in other faculties. What a difference in climate there is between the university of Tübingen, which reflects the real world, and the Gregorian, which represents clerical Rome! I don't have the slightest longing for Rome.

From the start I understand my lectures and seminars as ecumenical teaching occasions. 'The seminar is proving all too much of an attraction: more than 80 people, which is surely too many,' I write on 2 December 1960 to Karl Barth; 'of the twelve people giving papers – one could volunteer – seven are Protestant. What a *communicatio in sacris*.' Moreover twice a day I will go past Neckargasse 10, where Barth lived for a semester in 1908, and often think of him: 'Because you asked me about my date of birth – the year 1908 was twenty years *ante*.'

Sessions of the senate and the faculty, often time-consuming, are initially academic routine for me, until later I am drawn into conflicts which can hardly be avoided. The church historian Karl August Fink becomes important for my theological development. He has hardly any published work, but has done much research, and in many conversations he makes me see the conciliar movement in a completely new light and with it the ecumenical reform Council of Constance, which defines the superiority of the council over the pope. Two exegetes with whom I can discuss all the questions about the Bible in confidence are also important: the New Testament scholar Karl Hermann Schelkle, whom I regularly meet for longer or shorter discussions after celebrating early mass at the same time (pre-conciliar silent 'private masses' are also customary in Tübingen), and then of course the Old Testament scholar Herbert Haag, my Swiss compatriot, who is treasured on all sides. More undeterred than any other exegete in Germany, he is able to break open biblical questions which have been encrusted in dogma – until his death in 2001 he is my closest and most faithful friend among the Catholic professors of theology.

Immediately after becoming professor, Herbert Haag, likewise called to Tübingen for the summer semester of 1960, has bought a plot and built a grand house in which the professors of the faculty meet countless times after the faculty session for 'post-mortems'. Because of the noble hospitality of the host and his housekeeper Julie's highly-prized skill in entertaining, he makes an important contribution to good relations within the college.

As previously, in the first semester I live like a student in the Catholic Wilhelmsstift. In search of my own home, because of the scarcity of accommodation in Tübingen I find this at the place to which I went first simply for the sake of formality: the town housing office. I am offered the house of Mayor Weihenmaier, who has just been promoted to Landrat of Freudenstadt – Gartenstrasse 103 on the Neckar. It looks bigger than it is from outside and below, but its three floors each with two rooms suits me well. For practical reasons I want my personal secretariat in my house, and this will remain the case in the future. On 10 October 1960 I move in.

I have kept a desk, much furniture, and the Scandinavian style to the present day. I love this kind of consistency in externals, which makes it easier for me to be mobile in spiritual matters. And now demands are made on me there. 'Hermeneutics', the art of understanding, particularly biblical texts, is also at the centre of theological interest in Tübingen in these early 1960s. And there is no dispute that many questions of substance are decided by this fundamental question – not only for theologians, preachers and catechists, but also for every reader of the Bible.

How to understand the Bible – literally, spiritually, or . . .?

How, for example, are the stories of the creation and the fall in the Old Testament to be understood, or the healing and nature miracles in the New Testament? Word for word in a fundamentalist way or in a spiritual allegorical way – or realistically and historically? This is a question which occupied the church fathers, mediaeval scholastics, Reformers and men of the Enlightenment, and it has again become controversial since the appearance of the Protestant exegete Rudolf Bultmann. I am glad that I have got to know all three methods of biblical exegesis in succession.

First the fundamentalist method, which takes everything word for word. I practised it at the Gregorian: the Bible as a quarry for the prefabricated school theses of neoscholastic dogmatics. Our Roman exegetes, Spaniards for the Old and New Testaments, concentrate on refuting the laborious efforts of 200 years of critical (above all German) scholarship, for example, that the 'Pentateuch', the 'five books of Moses', derives from various sources several centuries apart. 'Saltem non probatur': that this new modern theory about the sources of the Pentateuch is 'at least not proven' is said time and again of each pericope. The same is said of the similar theory about the New Testament, which attempts to explain the genesis of the Synoptic Gospels from Ur-Mark and a source Q that can be reconstructed.

Then there is the spiritual-symbolic interpretation: I got to know it from my Roman mentor Wilhelm Klein. His original exhortations and perspectives, which were never boring, aimed at seeking the living spirit behind the killing letters of scripture, in other words at understanding it more deeply, more widely, more comprehensively than is suggested by the 'superficial' discourse of the particular biblical author. The head of the 'nouvelle théologie', Henri de Lubac SJ, and his pupil Hans Urs von Balthasar, both of whom were inspired by the symbolic allegorical method of exegesis of the Hellenist Origen and the Latin Augustine, also propagated such a spiritual interpretation at that time. De Lubac's little book on the spiritual sense of scripture – the deeper spiritual content is to be interpreted from behind the historical and moral content – deeply impressed me then, just as I also learned a great deal from Fr Klein's interpretation of scripture.

Only in time did it dawn on me that this approach sets virtually no limits to the personal caprice of the biblical exegete, particularly when in my last years in Rome my highly esteemed Spiritual began to look for the 'truth about Mary' (Mary as 'the mystery of a creation which has remained pure') everywhere from Genesis to the Apocalypse, and to find it in ingenious ways. At the time that convinced only a minority in the Germanicum; others spoke of 'gnosis', secret 'knowledge'. When for example Wilhelm Klein identified a word like 'grace' ('charis') with Mary the immaculate ('created grace'), of course he could discover his 'truth about Mary' even in the Letter to the Romans. He could do this especially in the apostle Paul, who knows nothing of a virgin birth of Jesus – for him Jesus is simply 'born of the woman' – far less of an 'immaculate' conception of Mary! No wonder that in this way our skilful Spiritual also justified priestly celibacy as a quasi-sacramental sign of the relationship between creator and creation as bride, between Christ and Mary – unfortunately without going into the questionable nature of the mediaeval law of celibacy. I find something similar later in Balthasar, for example in his theology of the three main days of Holy Week, especially in detail about the mystery of the night of Holy Saturday. This is an interpretation, influenced by Adrienne von Speyr, of the death, forsakenness and descent into the abysses of the world hostile to God which has no support in the New Testament texts. Could this way of 'spiritual' interpretation be mine in the long run?

Finally, historical-critical interpretation: certainly I also went to the lectures by critical exegetes at the Pontifical Biblical Institute who had firmly distanced themselves from the reactionary tendencies of its founder, Fr Leopold Fonck (also a Germanicum alumnus, after whose example Fr Klein had become a Jesuit!). This was no longer rescuing the literal sense of the texts of scripture, nor reading a random 'spiritual' meaning into them, but understanding the biblical writings as historical documents: scriptural interpretation is to be 'ex-egesis', 'reading out', not 'eis-egesis', 'reading in'.

I am most indebted for this understanding to two professors of the Biblical Institute who now even under John XXIII are the targets of attacks from the Curia right. This emerges from a brashly impertinent but dangerous article in *Divinitas*, the journal of the Pontifical Lateran University, written by that Monsignor Romero who was responsible for the *placet* to my call in the Congregation of Studies. The German Max Zerwick, who investigated the historicity of the infancy stories of Jesus and often gave lectures in our college, is denounced. So too is the Frenchman Stanislas Lyonnet, whose lectures about biblical theology put in question traditional positions on original sin and the understanding of redemption. But the article is generally aimed at the critical exegetes – in the 'misty north' or the 'northern mists' they evidently lack the clarity of the Latin sun. During the summer holidays in San Pastore, Franz Knapp and I drove Lyonnet for a whole day through the Abruzzi in a small borrowed Fiat to our mutual contentment – as far as the castle of Fumone near Frosinone, where Celestine V, the only pope ever to resign from office, was held prisoner by his successor Boniface VIII. What constantly repeated nonsense it is to claim that a pope can never resign! Remember Pietro del Morrone, the saintly Celestine V, who was helpless in the face of corruption in the Curia. Remember 1294!

Whereas Wilhelm Klein, wholly brought up in neoscholasticism, rejected historical-critical exegesis in principle, Karl Barth, brought up in liberal theology, accepted it in principle. But in practice he neglected it wherever it put in question his initial dogmatic theses, for example in matters of the Trinity, the Incarnation and the Virgin Birth. Barth, who became famous as a young pastor as a result of his brilliant prophetic reinterpretation of the Letter to the Romans in 1919 – a critique of liberal culture Protestantism – and in 1921 at the age of 35 had been called to Göttingen as an honorary professor of reformed theology without a habilitation and even without a doctorate, had later time and again concerned himself anew with precise exegesis of the Bible. He initially impressed me deeply by his biblical theology, so that I even added a highly speculative excursus to my dissertation, on 'The Redeemer in God's Eternity' (in Paris the subject of my *'leçon doctorale'*); I can no longer identify with it today. But when Karl Barth had to teach dogmatics in Göttingen with no preparation, helped by a textbook on dogmatics by Hermann Heppe (1861), he rediscovered old Protestant orthodoxy and thus also scholasticism and the church fathers: his decisive shift was thus to something like a 'neo-orthodox' dogmatics – Karl-Josef Kuschel has given a precise analysis of this in his work on the 'Dispute over Christ's Origin' (*Born Before All Time*, 1990) – a step in which the Bultmann school certainly did not want to join him.

However, coming from orthodox Roman-Catholic and Barthian dogmatics I had already learned at the 'École des Hautes Études' of the Sorbonne from Professor Oscar Cullmann, the author of important books on *Salvation in History*, *The Christology of the New Testament* and *Peter*, what it means to work in a thoughtful way with precise philology and an awareness of the importance of the study of religions. Then in Münster and even more in Tübingen I make an intensive study of the methods and results of historical-critical exegesis. I find the question of the historical Jesus, which has arisen again, particularly exciting. No less exciting is the historical view of the New Testament church, the constitution of the church and its ministries. In all these questions I must now find my own way – not only over against my neoscholastic Gregorian professors, but also, it grieves me, over against Wilhelm Klein and Karl Barth, those inspirers and mentors whom I so venerate. For all my gratitude, *'iurare in verba magistri* – swearing on the words of my teacher', will not be for me. Even theologians have their time.

Great theologians in their last phase: Barth and Bultmann

'I've been overtaken,' Karl Barth complains to me on one of my visits to Basle in the 1960s. Is he fishing for a compliment? Does he want me to contradict him? I do contradict him, since I am and remain convinced that the great theological intentions with which Karl Barth so successfully attacked the liberal theology of the nineteenth century aren't out of date, and may not simply be abandoned. But – I also cannot overlook the fact that a change is taking place in the theological landscape which Barthian theology can no longer cope with.

Karl Barth's great rival Rudolf Bultmann, who has allegedly overtaken him, was in fact very much a fellow-fighter from the beginning. Coming from the historical-critical school, but at an early stage under the influence of Heidegger's philosophy of existence, he affirms Barth's basic intentions (the Godness of God, God's word, the preaching of the church and human faith). Against a liberal theology which threatens to dissolve the Bible in history, Bultmann too demands that the message of scripture must be taken seriously again as revelation for faith. But is the historical-critical method, which Barth now largely ignores in favour of orthodox dogmatics, to be given up? No, Bultmann is convinced that the New Testament can be understood as a 'message' ('kerygma') for men and women of today only if it is critically interpreted and 'demythologized'. That means that the mythological 'framework' of the biblical message – a three-storey picture of the world with all the miracles and demons – can no longer be accepted in the age of science. However, it cannot just be eliminated, but has to be interpreted in terms of the existence of men and women today ('existentially'). It is emerging that in the great demythologizing debate Bultmann's position is in principle proving the stronger; his pupils have forced those of Barth on to the defensive.

After a serious illness which kept him in the clinic for weeks, on 17 April 1964 Barth makes his first journey outside Basle – to Sursee, to see me in my lake house, where we talk theology excitedly before and during lunch. On 19 April 1965 we meet again in Basle. It's a blow for me when Barth reveals that he has stopped work on his *Church Dogmatics*, which have by now grown to twelve mighty volumes, after 9185 pages. They are almost twice as long as Thomas Aquinas's *Summa Theologiae* (likewise broken off) and nine times as long as Calvin's *Institutio Religionis Christianae* (which was constantly expanded). Now, after completing a fragment on baptism, he tells me that he has turned to family history. He thinks that if one no longer has the intellectual strength to cope with the tremendous material of Christian ethics and then the doctrine of the 'last things', it's better to stop. There is no absolute need for him to complete his dogmatics, as did his other former companion in battle, Emil Brunner in Zurich, who then became an opponent and finally once again a reconciled friend. However, Brunner had presented his dogmatic *summa* in only three volumes of very much more modest extent. Karl Barth won't get beyond the beginnings of his family history, begun on a broad scale with his grandparents. He has only three more years to live.

'That's my last book,' Rudolf Bultmann, only two years older than Barth, tells me on my visit to him on 15 June 1967 in Calvinstrasse 14, Marburg. And modestly with both hands the great theologian hands me his commentary on the Johannine Epistles. That sounds unspeakably sad and makes me say: 'But it must be very satisfactory for you to be able to look back on such a tremendous scholarly life's work, dear Herr Bultmann. One only has to think of your *History of the Synoptic Tradition*, the Jesus book, all the articles on *Faith and Understanding*, the great commentary on the Gospel of John, and finally this commentary on the letters of John.' Bultmann's answer is just: 'But it's my last book.' He has eight years more to live than his contemporary Karl Barth, which he has largely to spend in blindness. Which is better?

Strangely moved, I travel back from Marburg to Tübingen. So now this second great representative of twentieth-century Protestant theology is at the end of his academic activity. After my call to the Tübingen chair of fundamental theology Barth had certified a 'meteoric rise' for me. But after this visit to Marburg I reflect on what will one day be an 'unavoidable decline' and feel confirmed in my attitude to dying, which has developed following the slow dying of my brother: one day I want to be able to die at the right time. 'There is a time for everything ... There is a time for being born and a time for dying,' we read in the Old Testament, in Koheleth, the preacher of transitoriness (3.1f.).

Now I am sitting at my memoirs; soon I will be the same age as Barth and Bultmann, and I ask myself how long I can continue to work at this intensity and to this extent. I also think of the fate of a contemporary of Barth and Bultmann, Karl Adam, one of the leading Catholic theologians in the first third of the twentieth century, from 1919 Professor of Dogmatics in Tübingen. Adam compromised himself by his positive attitude to National Socialism in 1933 (this was corrected in 1934). Yet Pope Paul VI will himself mention him to me as an exemplary theologian in so far as Adam, as Montini already experienced in his youth, reached people today 'beyond the walls of the church'. In Rome I too had enjoyed studying Adam's books on *The Essence of Catholicism* (1924) and *Jesus Christ* (1933), which were translated into all the major languages of the world. After all, they were an expression of his self-confident reform Catholicism, quite unlike the Gregorian theology rooted in Christian life, addressing not just the intellect but the whole person. When I and faculty colleagues visit him in 1961 on the occasion of his eighty-fifth birthday, Karl Adam points to me and asks, 'And who is that young man there?' My colleagues say, 'That's your successor.' Karl Adam simply smiles in a vacant, meaningless way. It was clear to all of us that the dementia of old age had already made terrifying progress in him. The transitoriness of life.

In a big panel discussion at the University of Tübingen in 2001 I will address this terrifying scenario quite personally and speak, supported by my colleague and friend Walter Jens, on the topic: 'Am I as a Christian obliged to let things get that far? Is this only the question of people who have grown old?' One of my last official actions as dean is to pay a compassionate visit to Karl Adam's house, 'Im Schönblick', on 1 April 1966, after his death; it is only a few steps from my present house.

Karl Barth 'overtaken'. Whereas the Barth school is increasingly losing significance, the Bultmann school is dominant. But the discussion produces contradictory positions on central questions even in the Bultmann school.

Becoming Catholic because of the Bible? Schlier and Käsemann

Bultmann's pupil Hermann Schlier had already explained to us at length in a lecture given on the occasion of his conversion, which took place in the Germanicum in 1953, why because of the insights of historical criticism into the New Testament he had resolved to become a Catholic. His reason was that Catholicism is not to be found, as present-day Protestant theology thinks, only after the New Testament. As the liberal exegesis of the nineteenth century was already aware, it is already to be found in the New Testament.

Protestant exegesis in particular must take seriously the fact that we already find 'early catholic' elements both in the Acts of the Apostles (written a generation after Paul) and in the 'Pastoral Epistles' to Titus and Timothy attributed to Paul. These are the understanding of the church's ministry, ordination by the laying on of hands, the presbyterate and the monarchical episcopate. Thus, Schlier concludes gently and at the same time provocatively, on the basis of the Reformation any Protestant theologian who feels obligated 'to scripture alone' has no alternative but also to accept this 'early catholicism' in the New Testament. Consequently, of course, he also has to accept 'late catholicism', and then formally to become a Catholic, as he, Heinrich Schlier, has now publicly attested.

For Protestant theology this is an unparalleled challenge. Moreover it comes from the Bultmann school. It is my Tübingen colleague, the Bultmann pupil Ernst Käsemann – as a pastor of the Confessing Church in the Ruhr, supported by his miners, a man of unyielding resistance – who resolutely and eloquently builds up and extends the opposite position to Schlier, his former ally but now a Catholic. It is correct, Käsemann says, that the writings of the New Testament canon already embrace early catholic elements, tendencies, indeed whole writings like the letter of James, which praises works instead of faith, as Paul does. But is that a reason for becoming a Catholic? By no means. For Käsemann this is a reason for selecting the writings, tendencies and elements in the New Testament which are truly in accord with the gospel, in a Protestant, critical way. That means criticizing the subject-matter, even the foundation documents of the New Testament, in order to shed light on the foundation itself, the gospel.

What is Käsemann's alternative to becoming a Catholic? A Protestant Christian may not simply accept the whole canon of the New Testament writings as binding. Rather, he must accept a 'canon in the canon': apply a criterion within the New Testament and resolutely engage in 'discerning the spirits'. For the Lutheran Käsemann, beyond question only the apostle Paul can provide this criterion. And that is the authentic Paul (as distinct from the Acts of the Apostles and the Pastoral Epistles), with his message of the justification of the sinner by grace alone on the basis of faith. This, according to Paul, is the gospel. Käsemann once again boldly goes on to conclude that the New Testament canon is not the foundation of the unity of the church, as is commonly accepted in Christianity. Precisely because of its different elements, which also include early catholic elements, it is the foundation of the multiplicity of confessions. This is a position which enlightens Käsemann's numerous hearers in Tübingen.

Ernst Käsemann, fearless and of a radical disposition, on the left wing both theologically and politically, then makes use of the forum of the Fourth World Conference on Faith and Order in Montreal 1963 to develop his view of unity and multiplicity in the New Testament doctrine of the church in the presence of all the representatives of the Protestant and Eastern Orthodox Churches: is the New Testament the basis not only of the unity but of the division of the church of Christ? Such a view is rejected as completely unecumenical not only by the conservatives but also by the moderate progressives. But Käsemann stands by his conviction. It is incomprehensible but – in view of the ignorance of exegesis even among many Protestant churchmen – to some degree understandable that in Montreal evidently no one is able to formulate a generally convincing 'response' to Käsemann's 'challenge'. People there content themselves with incomprehension and indignation.

Be this as it may, for me in Tübingen at the beginning of the 1960s this represents an explosive and unresolved problem of ecumenical dimensions, which will also have to feature at the coming Council. Ignore it, evade it, fearfully talk round it, as is usually the case in Catholic theology? No, I must take a stand. And I do so by entering into discussion with the Tübingen representative of the Bultmann school, Hermann Diem, like Käsemann a member and pastor of the Confessing Church during the Third Reich, and only after the war Professor of Protestant Dogmatics in Tübingen in the spirit of Barth. But unlike Barth himself, Diem had grappled with the new exegetical questions of the Bultmann school.

Triangular discussion about the Bible and the church: Käsemann and Diem

Report a local discussion in little Tübingen? That's not worthwhile. But it is worthwhile reporting to readers a discussion of the fundamentals of the Christian understanding of scripture. This is a topic which was to become my destiny as a theologian, though unfortunately it was bracketed out at the Second Vatican Council. With a little effort it can be understood even by non-theologians. I can now also apply what I practised in critical discussion with Barth in Rome and continued in Paris with the interpretation of Hegel in grappling with the historical-critical exegesis of the New Testament: first of all read the texts in an unprejudiced way and respect the facts! It is never right, as in neoscholastic and often also in Protestant theology, to conceal, twist or ignore them for the sake of the dogmatic system. More than once in lectures I tell my students in the form of a 'truism' that 'What is true is true!' Comfortable or not, one mustn't twist texts or deny facts. What one does with this fact, this text, this truth is a secondary question. However, already at the Gregorian I am warned that with such a love of truth one cannot expect 'louange', 'praise', a 'career' in the framework of a church system which is primarily interested in the status quo and in maintaining power, and therefore simply doesn't want to face uncomfortable facts, texts or truths.

But isn't the Bible 'always right'? Like many Christians, I too initially took it for granted that there are no real errors in the Bible. And when in my first seminar a Protestant student put the infallibility of the Bible in question I gave him the terse apologetic answer: 'In that case everything goes down the drain!' But I've learnt important things particularly in arguing with people like Ernst Käsemann and Hermann Diem. However, here it wasn't the sword but the rapier that was required. It was an exciting intellectual fight, which I still enjoy reading decades later in the *Tübinger Theologische Quartalschrift* of 1962. This is no shadow-boxing, but a serious dispute over the understanding of the Bible, the church and ministry which still has not been settled in the relevant churches and theologies. What position am I to take? For me as a young theologian this is a difficult question, involving much study.

Is the Bible free of error? Ernst Käsemann gives me many instances which I can no longer overlook: because of its multiplicity, fragmentary nature and complexity the New Testament does not offer any uniform inerrant doctrinal system, as is still assumed by Lutheran and Reformed orthodoxy in its defence against the Catholic principle of tradition. The various writings of the New Testament are stamped by the extremely different situations for proclamation in which the various authors and their communities stand. In other words, I have to concede that there are tensions, inconsistencies and contradictions in the New Testament: already between the three Synoptic Gospels (of Mark, Matthew and Luke) and between these and the Gospel of John; and also between the authentic letters of Paul and the inauthentic letters, between Paul and James . . . all this must be taken seriously, and not glossed over by imposing a dogmatic conclusion. But that's only one side of the problem.

For Hermann Diem convinces me against Käsemann that we need not immediately give up the unity of scripture and the New Testament canon of scripture simply because of all the differences. Granted, we can no longer provide a theological justification for this canon in principle. But we can accept this criterion even today, as something which has in fact existed since the first Christian centuries. I agree: none of the New Testament writings which have been recognized in the church for so long, not even the letter of James with its emphasis on works, may a priori be thrown out as no longer binding today. Thus there is no 'canon in the canon' with which one a priori discredits individual writings of the New Testament which are uncomfortable, above all the 'early catholic' writings, in the light of Paul and his understanding of justification, as if the gospel of Jesus Christ cannot be heard in these writings. Rather, it dawns on me that a reshaping, development and revision of the original message, depending on the changing situations in which the authors preached and of their communities, was absolutely necessary. This in particular gives us today the right once again to translate the original Christian message into a new situation of preaching instead of merely repeating it word for word, to interpret it in a way which accords with the time.

So do I simply back Diem? By no means. For my decisive question to my Barthian colleague is: how will he avoid the trap laid by the early catholic elements, passages and writings in the New Testament? I ask Diem whether, if he wants to avoid Käsemann's selection of the writings which are truly in accord with the gospel, he mustn't take the way of Schlier and likewise convert to the Catholic Church? But Hermann Diem, a wily Swabian, attempts to jump over the trap or avoid it. Certainly he recognizes the early catholic New Testament writings in principle, theoretically – but in practice? There he has no trouble in ignoring them: neither in the first nor in the second volume of his 'Theology' does the 'catholic' – i.e. ordination, apostolic succession, episcopate, sacraments, even the Petrine office – play the role that according to the New Testament it should. So far, not so good.

Ignoring the catholic like this is unacceptable to me. Should I dispense with the catholic in the New Testament and give up my own catholicity? No, to become a Protestant isn't a responsible option for me, precisely because of the new exegetical results. What then?

Catholicity instead of 'heresy': but only a programme

Really only the Catholic, I argue in my own now almost provocative solution to the problem, can take the catholic in the New Testament completely seriously and give all the New Testament writings a fair interpretation in context. It is important for me that before the New Testament canon there was the New Testament church. It recognized this canon in a long-drawn-out and complex process of selection in which a mass of factors played a part (especially real or supposed apostolic authorship and the authority of the apostolic churches, not least that of Rome). For the church all these writings – including the early catholic writings – are binding testimony to Jesus Christ: they had to be read out and expounded in worship and must still be.

The question remains: why then is there a contradictory multiplicity of confessions? At this point it seems to me that I must give a clear answer. It is because one doesn't approach the New Testament writings with a comprehensible and in this sense 'catholic' understanding (Greek *katholikos* = 'that which forms a whole'). Rather, one makes a 'selection', Greek *hairesis*, 'heresy': this is practised in principle by Ernst Käsemann but in fact also by Hermann Diem in his reading of the New Testament. To use a metaphor: a flammable beam is the presupposition for a burning building; however, the reason for the fire or its cause is not the beam with its many layers, but the arsonist. In plain terms: with its material, which does not form a unity, the New Testament can be the occasion, the presupposition for a contradictory multiplicity of confessions. But it is not their basis or their cause. This is, rather, the selective *hairesis* which dissolves the unity of the church into the different confessions. If it is understood in a 'catholic', all-embracing way, the New Testament canon is the presupposition not of the multiplicity of confessions but of the unity of the church.

This may be said to be a palpable hit in a sharp fight. So am I being the lucky bystander? No. This controversy doesn't damage my good personal relations with Diem and Käsemann only because with intellectual honesty at the same time I reveal the great weak point of my own Catholic position, which others could hit.

I explain that in the Catholic Church and in Catholic exegesis unfortunately such 'catholicity' in the interpretation of the New Testament is only a grandiose programme and not a reality. Is such a 'catholic' freedom and openness to the whole New Testament really being lived out credibly for other Christians in Catholicism as it actually exists? No, instead of the atmosphere of fear, totalitarian supervision and therefore hypocrisy and cowardice of the kind that prevails particularly under the anti-modern Pius popes, in both Catholic exegesis and dogmatics there now has to be an atmosphere of freedom: sober theological honesty, undeterred matter-of-factness and only in this way loyalty to the church.

So I don't understand Catholicity simply as the assertion of a fact, but rather as an imperative to be realized. But the more time goes on, the clearer it is to become to me what a difficult way I have to take as a theologian with my proposal. I mustn't dissociate and reduce the contradictory statements of the New Testament about the church in a Protestant way. But I mustn't harmonize them and level them down in a Roman way either. Rather, everywhere I have to practise the high art of differentiation and nuancing. Specifically this requires understanding all the derived New Testament witnesses, which are chronologically later and also often more remote from the subject-matter, in the light of the more original and central testimonies. And what really is the centre of scripture? This question was to occupy me for a long time.

Be this as it may, at the end of this controversy, which is fundamental to my interpretation of scripture, I maintain that the only way in which a reunion is conceivable is if Catholic theology attempts to take the New Testament seriously with a concentration on the gospel, and conversely Protestant theology attempts to take the same New Testament seriously in its catholic breadth. So this is a joint ecumenical task, which the ecumenical Second Vatican Council (though in fact it is Roman Catholic) will have to face. Of course one can wonder whether this isn't asking too much of a council. But I have also grappled in depth with the theology of the Council before this controversy. And now a first-class forum is offered me to which to present the results. What a sleepy semi-official history of the Council keeps quiet about must be related in detail here.

What is an ecumenical council?

My public inaugural lecture is now fixed by the Rector of the University of Tübingen, the constitutional lawyer Otto Bachof, for 24 November 1960, the afternoon of the matriculation ceremony. But for some reason the Auditorium Maximum, the planned location for it, isn't free. Dean Möller gives me the choice: a smaller auditorium which could prove too small, or the big Festsaal, which might possibly be half empty; normally inaugural lectures aren't given in the Festsaal. I consider briefly, venture and win: every seat in the Festsaal, including the gallery, is filled.

Originally I had planned to devote my inaugural lecture to the debate on the historical Jesus, which has revived. But I know my limitations. I have certainly occupied myself with much of the more recent research into Jesus that has likewise been sparked off by an article of Käsemann's, a lecture given to the 'old Marburgers'. But I am well aware that I am still far from the end of my reflections. So I had better keep clear of this topic. The topic of the Council is now no less burning. Of course I don't want to go into the problems of church reform described in *The Council and Reunion* again. Rather, I must attempt to advance in 'honest theological reflection on the nature of the ecumenical council itself' – not least in order to revalue the council over against the universal authority of the pope as defined one-sidedly at Vatican I. So my topic is 'The Theological Understanding of the Ecumenical Council'.

In the very first sentences I point out that 'the inner success of the ecumenical council is not given a priori' with the fact of an ecumenical council: 'An ecumenical council can be held, and yet seen as a whole can be a catastrophic failure – like, for example the Fifth Lateran Council in Rome, planned as a reform council and closed six months before the outbreak of the Lutheran Reformation. For all its imposing external solemnity and all the proclamation and excommunication, it can miss the decisive demands of the time and the church.'

My starting point is the blatant contradiction between church law and church history. According to Canon 223 of the existing *Codex Iuris Canonici* all the rights to convene, to lead, to abolish and to confirm an ecumenical council lie with the pope. But the history of the seven ecumenical councils of Christian antiquity which are fundamental and recognized by all the churches of both East and West unambiguously attest the opposite: it is not the pope but the emperor who convenes these councils, defines the subjects to be discussed, establishes the order of proceedings, moves, adjourns or concludes the council, and who leads it and approves the decrees either in person or through legates.

So am I comfortably to content myself, like most authors before the Second Vatican Council, with an account of the status of an ecumenical council in canon law or church history? No, I must attempt to arrive at an authentic theological starting point for a definition of the essence of a council. The semantic affinity of roots between *con-cilium* (from *con-calare* = call together), i.e. assembly, and *ec-clesia* (Greek *ek-klesia,* from *kalein* = 'call', 'summon'), and therefore likewise 'assembly' or 'church', puts me on the right track. What in fact is the church of Jesus Christ according to the New Testament other than the assembly of those who believe in Christ, summoned by God through the gospel, the New Testament people of God (Hebrew *qehal yhwh*)?

So I can formulate as the first principle of a theology of the ecumenical council that the church itself is an ecumenical council. It is the assembly of the faithful called together from the 'whole inhabited earth' (*ecumene*), which God himself has called through Jesus Christ in the Holy Spirit. But what then is what is commonly termed an 'ecumenical council', i.e. the ecumenical council as humanly called?

The second principle of a theology of the ecumenical council gives the answer to this: the ecumenical council as humanly called is the representation of the ecumenical council as divinely called, that is, the church. Is this a new insight? No, this answer already appears in the earliest writer of the Latin church, Tertullian, around 200, and in the age of the late mediaeval reform councils, in the face of papalism, and so too today it takes on new importance: 'In the Greek lands, at particular places those councils representing all the churches are held by which more important things are dealt with in common and the whole of Christianity is represented in an impressive way.'

Council = representation of the church: those two principles are so illuminating that they convince not only my Tübingen audience but also a theologian of the same age who, as Professor of Dogmatics at the University of Bonn since 1959, will soon be an expert at the Council with me: Joseph Ratzinger. In an article on the ecumenical council he adopts as his first basic thesis: 'The whole church appears as the one great council in the world.' However, for that he doesn't cite my inaugural lecture but an article of his own which doesn't speak of the church as 'council'. Still, this is less important than the clericalistic narrowness with which Ratzinger concentrates the collegiality of the church directly on the collegiality of the bishops, for whose ordinary and universal magisterium he strictly demands infallibility, with an appeal to Vatican I. Here the structure of the early church is formed both by the college of apostles *and* the community.

This (after his fine review of *Justification*) is a somewhat disappointing theological encounter with Ratzinger, whom I will meet personally for the first time at the beginning of the Council in Rome in a café on the Via della Conciliazione. He seems to me very friendly, though perhaps not completely open, whereas to him I possibly seem all too spontaneous and direct. For me he is more a *'timido'* with an invisible spiritual anointing, whereas to him I perhaps seem audacious, with more worldly charms. But all in all he is a very congenial contemporary, with whom one can argue on the same level about all the questions which have arisen. In my inaugural lecture another aspect of the Council is already important to me: the collegiality of the whole church, the communities and thus also the laity.

Laity at the Council? Martin Luther's concern

That second, harmless-sounding principle in fact includes a critical relativization: is the ecumenical council only a representation of the church? In that case, in principle the church can exist even without councils humanly called. And in fact for three centuries it existed without ecumenical councils until the emperor Constantine, a pagan who still called himself Pontifex Maximus, convened the first ecumenical council in his residence of Nicaea in Asia Minor to serve his state political interests. Is the ecumenical council only a representation of the church? In that case this 'ecumenical council humanly called' can also assume very different historical manifestations: and in fact the person and office of those who were called, those who presided and those who approved, those who took part and the subjects they discussed at the various councils of the first and second millennia, were very different indeed. So, particularly with a view to the reunion of separated Christians, in the light of church history questions of changeable church law may not be made demands of unchangeable dogma.

Even more important for me, however, is the positive and constructive form of that principle: that the ecumenical council humanly called is now to be a real representation of the church. In concrete, that the 'one, holy Catholic and apostolic church' – to mention its classical dimensions – is represented in a truly credible way. I explain that, for example, the 'one' church would not be represented credibly if the council were only an external manifestation of unity (however imposing), say, like a well-organized totalitarian party congress, where the uncritical *placet* to the plans of the leader is regarded as a sign of loyalty. The 'one' church will be represented credibly only if an inner unity of faith and love gratefully embraces the multiplicity of the different individual views and individual churches and allows them to exist.

The same is to be said of the representation of the 'holy', the 'catholic' and finally the 'apostolic' church. On the explosive point of apostolicity I quote the Reformer Martin Luther for the first time. As is well known, right at the beginning of the Reformation, in his writing *To the Christian Nobility of the German Nation* (1520), he appealed from the (ill-advised) pope to a future free council. Luther thinks that, on the basis of the universal priesthood of believers and the experiences of church history, others, not just the pope and even the emperor, could convene and lead a council. He too took it for granted that not only the Byzantine emperors but also the German kings and emperors summoned councils, as did Henry III, who at the epoch-making Synod of Sutri in 1046 made the rise of the reform papacy possible by removing three rival popes. Likewise, laity and those who were not bishops could always be found at councils. I conclude from this that no dogmatic objections can be made to a direct representation of the laity at the Council. Rather, their representation should become the object of earnest consideration for Vatican II – aren't people always talking of the 'hour of the laity'?

Does that mean that the ministries of the church may simply be glossed over at a council? No, Ratzinger is right here: representation of the 'apostolic' church means that a council has to be in accord with the apostles, with the apostolic testimony of Holy Scripture, as Luther rightly emphasized in his late work *Of the Councils and Churches* (1539), but also with the apostolic ministry of preserving the apostolic faith and confession. This means the office of the bishops, without whom an ecumenical council, which is to represent the individual local churches, had never been possible.

And the role of the papacy?

In my lecture, which lasts almost an hour and a half, I can only indicate that here questions open up for ecumenical conversation which are as difficult as they are full of hope. Here of course I point out the importance of 'conciliar theory' and its utterly orthodox origins in the canon law of the twelfth century. At all events the central difficulty for an ecumenical understanding remains the papacy as it has developed in history. Following the Bible I prefer to speak of the Petrine office and emphasize two things: the pope must certainly be able to perform his special function even at an ecumenical council, namely to represent the unity of the church in the service of love. But he can be present in very different ways, as the history of the councils proves. Therefore a distinction has to be made between the necessity of a centre in the church and papal centralism, between the necessity of a Petrine office and – here happily I can likewise refer to Joseph Ratzinger – papalism. What sacrifice the removal of a schism can require of the Petrine office in the service of unity was shown in particular by the ecumenical Council of Constance, which deposed three rival popes and elected a new one.

My concern is that the one-sided definition of primacy at Vatican I should be given a 'supplementary correction' in theory and practice at Vatican II, by emphasis on the collegiality of all bishops. These would not come to the Council to advise the pope. Rather, they would come to make authoritative decisions themselves, on important concerns of the church as a whole, as the highest serving authority, together with the pope, and so play their part in the universal governance of the church. I clearly state that the Council has not been convened for 'the church to reflect on itself', but for 'Christians to reflect on themselves': 'for the bold and generous renewal of the church in the light of the gospel of Jesus Christ'.

The persistent applause after this inaugural lecture encourages me, but colleagues warn me. Germany's most important Catholic pastoral theologian, Franz Xaver Arnold, comments as we go out: 'Formerly people were burned for saying such things.' And the well-known liberal criminal lawyer Jürgen Baumann, who in good time abandoned his plan to become a Benedictine in favour of jurisprudence, remarks, 'Little monk, little monk, you're taking a difficult course!' But who could have known that better than I did? If I am not to remain unfaithful to the truth, I have to continue on the way I have taken.

On 5 March 1961, I write to Cardinal Bea, who has sent me an article on ecumenism: 'In connection with the theological understanding of the ecumenical council I have attempted to describe openly and honestly difficulties and solutions which here are pressing so hard on the "front".' Somewhat later I receive encouragement from Rome: Monsignor Willebrands, now the number two in Cardinal Bea's Secretariat for Christian Unity, writes to me that he has 'read with amazement' my inaugural lecture, since 'this is the most profound statement on the theology of the ecumenical council I have yet read'. He sees difficulties only over apostolicity and ministry. So do I.

Committed to the Council without euphoria

It doesn't occur to me for a moment that I could take part in the Council myself. In what capacity? In any case I am far too young for this gathering of church 'fathers'. And how could I enjoy immersing myself again in the clerical milieu of this Rome, possibly now in a black cassock instead of a red one? No, not that. *Videant consules!* Let the bishops see to it!

But I want to devote myself fully to the Council, both theologically and in writing about it, precisely because I won't be taking part in it. All too many theologians hesitate: scepticism, lethargy and cowardice are widespread. The very first reaction that I hear after the sensational announcement of the Council on the evening of 25 January 1959 in the sacristy of the Hofkirche in Lucerne from a respected Swiss theologian is: 'The Council is coming too early!' But the pope, who called on his church to read the 'signs of the time', has fortunately carried out no survey about his plan for the Council either in the Roman Curia or among the theologians north of the Alps.

Precisely because I am more aware than others of the tremendous difficulties and obstacles which face the Council, I begin to accept invitations to give lectures very soon after I become professor in Tübingen. The questions which form the titles of my lectures are 'What do Christians expect of the Council?', or 'Is the Council coming too early?' My view is that it is coming 400 years too late! On a later occasion I write to Karl Rahner (on 3 February 1962): 'It is sad enough that as youngest of the German university professors I am about the only one (along with the church historian Jedin) to have committed himself positively to the aims of the Council in public. Almost nothing but depressed scepticism can be found in our circles.' It was hardly pure pleasure going on whistle-stop tours, sometimes lasting three or four days, usually by car, travelling through the various regions of Germany and Austria, and time and again talking about the problems of the Council realistically yet in an encouraging way. In January 1961 I am in Hanover, Hamburg and Würzburg; in October 1961 in Vienna, Leibnitz, Graz, Salzburg and Dillingen; in January 1962 in Lubeck, Bremen and Bremerhaven. Then again to Münster and back to Tübingen – more than 1100 kilometres. There are still hardly any traffic jams.

I attempt to campaign for renewal and ecumenism especially among the *young*: at the assembly of the Federation of German Catholic Youth in Frankfurt Cathedral, in a course for youth leaders from all over Switzerland in the Collegium Schwyz, and at the general assembly of the Swiss student association in Sursee. Everywhere there is much applause, a hopeful mood, and no serious opposition, except, for example, from a clergyman, the editor of a parish magazine in Basle, whose article stirs up much dust, even provokes the bishop to engage in correspondence, and preoccupies church bodies. It should be remembered that at the time of John XXIII there are *no* polarizations in the church: this pope is a pastor who goes forward and awakens trust. Among both

Catholics and Protestants people are waiting for a renewal of the Catholic Church and welcoming the ecumenical convergence. 'I can assure you,' a school friend who organizes a lecture in rural Beromünster with the canons' foundation writes to me in a letter, 'that I have heard enthusiastic echoes from all sides: even older clergymen – who perhaps are no longer keeping up with everything – later expressed their full approval to me.'

I also like speaking and discussing in smaller groups, in the more immediate surroundings of Tübingen and Sursee, in chaplaincies and student associations, in ecumenical circles and theological study groups, in Catholic (Wiesbaden, Königstein) and Protestant (Bad Boll, Boldern/Zurich) academies. At the same time I have my 'Letters to Young People' published in journals for Catholic young people in the Federal Republic and in Switzerland; they are then collected and appear as a short book under the title *That the World May Believe*. I will enclose this with my book *Structures of the Church* when it is sent to bishops like Döpfner and Volk. It may make clear to them that for all my historical-critical research I am at the same time concerned with pastoral instruction and help.

I give my first lecture in English (which is still very halting) in the headquarters of the American Seventh Army in Stuttgart-Vaihingen. In Vienna, I am horrified to see my name quite suddenly in large letters on a poster in the city. But I quickly get used to giving interviews for the newspapers and engaging in conversations on the radio. Thus once with my friend Otto Wüst on Swiss radio, where I get stuck only at one point, because I may possibly have got the century wrong, I say, 'I don't exactly know, but you can cut it out afterwards!' in Swiss dialect. However – we are in Berne – they promptly forget, to the delight of listeners who tell me about it. My only worse experience is later in a recording by the Austrian radio station ORF in Tübingen. There is a whole hour of intensive questioning on the group of problems surrounding *Eternal Life?* At the end the tape is checked. Not a single word can be heard. Bad connection. I have to repeat it all bit by bit between other conversations – other visitors had already arrived for the next hour. At the end I no longer know what I had or hadn't said. Nevertheless it may have helped belief in eternal life in the midst of human fallibility.

One question is asked, and not just by envious colleagues, among whom in the meantime the *invidia accademica* has multiplied with the *invidia clericalis*: am I seeking publicity? No, it's required of me. But I don't refuse it when it helps the cause. I certainly feel the responsibility, but I'm not anxious. I don't get stage fright when I have to advocate my cause. However, I say no to broadcasts which have nothing to do with my cause, like the series put out by the Basle studios, 'What Do You Think, Professor?', where one is asked every kind of possible and impossible question, and the chat-shows which become popular later: one has to travel for a couple of hours to be able to speak for a couple of minutes, and then has to fight with other more or less pleasant contemporaries to get a word in.

It is also pleasing that even the critical news magazine *Der Spiegel* deals as benevolently with me as it does with John XXIII. A sympathetic article appears, written by Werner Harenberg. After the event the editor, Rudolf Augstein, an ex-Catholic, who was away at the time, indicates that he would have preferred to see it as the lead story. Of course I am honestly grateful for any possibility of openly expressing my views, which often don't correspond with those of the official Roman church: on German-language stations (on NDR four successive Sundays), but also on foreign radio and television stations, on the Dutch KRO, the Italian RAI, and already since my time in England time and again on the BBC (the BBC World Service is particularly important).

My question in the face of all too many enquiries is: why do people want so much to talk with me? There are surely plenty of other theologians. The answer usually goes roughly like this: in the media we need scholars who speak in an expert but understandable way, and don't waste time beating about the bush. These relations with the world of the international media will be very important to me for future discussions in and after the Council. The 'globalization' of theology will be forced on me at an early stage.

However, my commitment has meanwhile gone so far that I even accept invitations like that to a small Catholic church community in Reutlingen. I am asked to give on 26 February 1961 in a pub in Pfullingen the lecture that I gave on 20 January in the Auditorium Maximum of the University of Hamburg. I think that the 'little ones' shouldn't be neglected either, and so have to put up with a good deal. The chairman refuses to believe that I really am already an 'ordinarius' professor; the pastor has never heard of my book *The Council and Reunion*; the fooling around of some choirboys will disturb me; at the end the chaplain who chairs the meeting asks me to make a small detour in my car to take him home, and finally says a fond farewell with a sealed envelope: the honorarium is DM 20, including travel expenses. 'You would have done better to have gone to the cinema . . .' my colleague, the vivacious Christa Hempel from Berlin, says to me later, when I tell her the whole story with amusement. And in fact on this day I began to weigh up the invitations so as not to take on too much. After all, as an ordinarius professor I can't cope with countless extraordinary obligations. Even so, I hardly have time for the cinema.

The Council can fail

The invitations to the International Catholic Publishers Association on 14 May 1961 in Lucerne and to the Society of Catholic Journalists in Germany on 2 July 1961 in Bonn/Bad Godesberg are important for me. Both events go well, but the second has unpleasant consequences. I speak on the topic 'Can the Council also Fail?', and am not told that a tape is being made which may possibly be circulated afterwards. Anyway, I speak my mind openly and freely, asking whether despite all the good intentions of the pope, all the goodwill of those preparing it, and all the varied work of the ten preparatory commissions, the Council being held at this decisive hour in the world will have the desired internal success.

In so doing I refer openly to a number of disturbing facts, without directly criticizing the weakness of the pope's leadership. The Roman diocesan synod called by John XXIII was disappointing. Moreover the anti-modernist campaign of the Curia (Holy Office, Congregation of Seminaries) with like-minded allies (the Lateran University) against the Pontifical Biblical Institute is continuing. It is being said that there scripture is being put above tradition and too much importance is being attached to the study of the literary forms of the ancient Near East and the form-critical methods of Bultmann and Dibelius. This campaign is directed not least against the former long-serving Rector Augustin Bea, but now affects the present Rector, the Swiss Ernst Vogt, and Professors Zerwick and Lyonnet. They are all banned from teaching and are to leave Rome. The pope stops the inquisitors too late and only to a limited degree: Lyonnet remains at the Biblicum as vice-dean and Zerwick as Professor of Biblical Greek.

Renewed inquisitorial measures are also taken against other distinguished Catholic theologians. The life of Jesus by the French theologian Jean Steinmann is put on the Index. Later there is a warning against reading the work of Pierre Teilhard de Chardin. The Apostolic Constitution *Veterum sapientia*, prejudging the Council, quite unrealistically attempts to establish Latin as 'the language of the church' in the liturgy and in academic instruction: of course it is also meant to guarantee the control of the Curia over the Council. Then there is the confiscation of the Italian translation of the pastoral letter of the Dutch bishops on the Council. German university theological faculties like that at Tübingen are passed over in obtaining opinions for the Council. The preparatory commissions, quite one-sidedly composed of Romans, produce little that gives any pleasure. A large-scale controversy is in the making.

In view of these disturbing developments I recommend to the journalists that instead of adopting the customary course of superficial Roman Catholic apologetic ('already – but') they should take the way of honest reflection and unambiguous admonition: in the interest of the church and the Council they should call black black, white white, and grey grey. Of course I never forget to point to positive developments, above all the establishment of the Roman 'Secretariat for Christian Unity' under the outstanding leadership of Cardinal Augustin Bea and the programmatic combination of the reunion of separated Christians with the self-reform of the Catholic Church, proclaimed by the pope himself. In view of this ambivalent situation, I argue that what is needed is: first, honesty with no illusions; secondly, courage to make oneself unpopular to the point of danger; and thirdly, a readiness all round to achieve the aim of the Council.

Always with a reference to the Fifth Lateran Council of 1512-17, on the eve of the Reformation, which was a complete failure, I warn against ineffective reform decrees and above all ineffective doctrinal definitions. There is a real danger of these. For the president of the Preparatory Theological Commission is none other than the feared Grand Inquisitor Cardinal Ottaviani. In my own teacher in fundamental theology, Fr Sebastian Tromp, the secretary of this commission, he has a practised and efficient drafter of papal doctrinal texts. The Sanctum Officium and the majority of the Curia are interested in presenting as many conciliar definitions as possible. I hear from Rome that all the questions which the First Vatican Council could not go on to discuss because it was broken off in 1870 will at last be settled definitively, a century later, as Rome wants. Please God!

By contrast I point out to the Catholic journalists that in the history of the councils many definitions pass by the real requirements of the age and the church. Simply for reasons of time it is utterly impossible for a church assembly of more than 2000 bishops to discuss all these pre-prepared definitions or declarations seriously and to endorse them. Moreover John XXIII is happily less interested than others in the Vatican in conciliar definitions, condemnations and new dogmas, even Marian dogmas. He has prohibited the real condemnations (*'anathema sit!'*) which were still customary at Vatican I. And I had heard from a cardinal how the pope had told him that he had just measured with a ruler one sentence in a council decree that had been prepared. It was about 75cm long. Impossible!

A first exchange of blows

'I still often hear journalists talking about your lecture in Godesberg,' Dr Otto Roegele, Chairman of the Society of Catholic Journalists of Germany, writes to me in a letter. 'For all of us it was a memorable experience.' However, my often ironically witty and perhaps also sometimes angry remarks to a benevolent audience of Catholic journalists who were ready to assent with a smile hadn't exactly been aimed at readers of church papers. Yet after that conference tendentious extracts had soon been presented at least to readers of church papers in the diocese of Aachen, word for word in five long articles, and at the same time 'refuted' as un-Catholic. This was the work of a not very popular figure: Canon Heribert Schauf, Professor of Canon Law in the Priestly Seminary of Aachen, a Germanicum alumnus who got on our nerves every time he visited the Germanicum because both in college and at the Villa San Pastore he kept going on about the 'old spirit'. In the meantime he has advanced to become a member of the theological preparatory commission and a loyal servant of its secretary, Fr Sebastian Tromp. He helps greatly in preparing the long decrees on doctrine which are finally to bring the dogmatic structure of the Roman Catholic Church to its crowning conclusion. Precisely what I have spoken out against.

He says that I have 'disturbed and unsettled' wide circles. It is quite dangerous to be attacked in a whole series of articles by this man of the 'old spirit' with the best connections in Rome. Schauf himself sends them to important personalities. From Lucerne people report to me that a German bishop, probably a Germanicum alumnus, has descended on the moral theologian Alois Schenker and made him read a photocopy of my lecture about the Council. My intimate enemy Schenker has this copied out by his housekeeper that same night, so that he finally has something tangible. The bishop will thoroughly pull this text to pieces in Rome, and things will go on from there. These two prelates are agreed in their verdict: '*haeresim sapiens* – it reeks of heresy'. I then also find Schauf's counter-articles on the desk of Cardinal König when I visit him in Vienna for my lecture, just as they have doubtless also landed on the desks of Fr Tromp and Cardinal Ottaviani and other dignitaries. Indeed I hear that Schauf is handing them round in person in Rome.

What am I to do? I decide – with some reluctance – on a public answer. People will later often describe me as a 'combative' or 'pugnacious' (but not 'quarrel-some') theologian. In fact often I have to stir myself up to fight and do so only after taking advice from colleagues and friends. However, once compelled to 'dispute', I fight with 'pleasure': 'joyful to fight', as the old Swiss national anthem has it. And my '*frater maior*' from the Germanicum will realize that.

With wordy excuses the Aachen church paper refuses to allow any reply to Schauf's articles – how often I will experience the same thing with church papers! But Dr Otto Roegele, also chief editor of the *Rheinischer Merkur*, gives me a page and a half in his weekly magazine of 27 October 1961. The headline is 'Can the Council also Fail?' My direct manner of answering makes the theologian Schauf, hitherto unknown to a wider church public in the Federal Republic, known and notorious at a stroke: people don't like inquisitors. He will never forgive me this, and will not offer me his hand at the Council, where we will meet again.

In my reply I first point out the differences between a talk given in a particular situation and a style intended for a wide public, and correct misunderstandings. But essentially I concentrate on the question of the success or failure of a council. Schauf claims that 'the truth knows no failures'. Referring to the Fifth Lateran Council, I maintain that there have been completely ineffective doctrinal defi-nitions. Schauf asserts that there would be a disturbing inadequacy 'if the church were to keep silent *where* the situation and the truth required speaking and clear speaking'. In my view the opposite is also the case: there would be a suspicious inadequacy 'if the church or the Council were to speak where the situation and the truth required silence and no definition'. I refer above all to the doctrinal questions in dispute within Catholic theology and the new Marian dogmas. For those in the know, my answer amounts to no less than a frontal attack on the pretentious production of doctrinal documents by the theological preparatory commission of Cardinal Ottaviani under the command of Tromp and his henchman.

Rumour upon rumour

As the editorial on 1 December next remarks by way of introduction to a two-page discussion, my article has 'met with an unusually strong response among the readership'. Apart from a short comment by a church historian 'the only voice against Küng' has been a response by Professor Schauf. By contrast I am supported above all by a warm Open Letter from Dr Otto Karrer, who refers to my pastoral work with the parish priest and assistant priests in Lucerne and grants me the right to a 'prophetic testimony'. This controversy ends with my reply, which is at the same time a final plea 'for a reform council of a practical kind', the demand of Josef Frings, Cardinal of Cologne. It is also the subject of an article in *Der Spiegel* and – at the proposal of Bishop Leiprecht – of a harmonious conversation with the apostolic nuncio Corrado Bafile in Rottenberg on 12 November 1961. My article also appears during 1962 in English, French and Dutch, and strongly influences the atmosphere before the Council. And didn't our council historians Alberigo and Wittstadt want to take any notice at all of this controversy? Ignorance, lethargy, conformism?

The Gregorian ecumenist Johannes Witte, a Dutchman, writes to me at that time from Rome that I spoke 'from a different world from that of Schauf and he will never understand you'. Schauf told him: 'How can Küng say that my spirit is different from that of the pope? I'm only saying what any lawyer has to say.' Yes, that is 'the other world'; today I would say 'the other paradigm'. And a conversion of the heart is needed to move from a legalistic-mediaeval paradigm to a modern, even a post-modern, one. After all, what was being asked for? Bernhard Casper, later professor, who is seeking the post of assistant with me, writes to me that my Bad Godesberg remark about the 'canon of the mass whispered against the wall' has shaken the Würzburg chapter to the core. And what else?

Rumour upon rumour – happily only a fragment of them comes to my ears. A friend from my student days, the musicologist Helmut Hucke, writes from Rome: 'You know that you aren't popular here. The sparrows are almost piping from the rooftops that Cardinal Döpfner has written you a letter in which he reproaches you for having drawn cardinals into the *Rheinische Merkur* discussion (with Schauf) . . .' Simply because of Frings' remark 'for a reform council of a practical kind'? Be this as it may, I have received no such letter from Döpfner. My Sursee friend Otto Wüst, now general secretary of the Swiss Catholic Volks-verein, who has connections with Germany, reports to me his anxiety and that of others: 'You could make enemies in the German episcopate'; he hears 'that Cardinal Frings of Cologne doesn't have a good word for you. So look out.' That is probably connected with the Schauf controversy, but perhaps also with my fellow Germanicum student in Cologne, Anno Quadt. A friend who is an assistant priest in Switzerland writes to me anxiously: 'It would be a bitter blow for me if the spokesman of the "suffering church" in the German-speaking world which is in need of reform were hit by spiteful snipers.'

People ask me whether I'm not anxious sometimes. My heart beats faster, but *Angst* (later regarded as being typically German) isn't my basic mood. Of course I worry often, and my worries sometimes pursue me into the night. I am no block of ice, but a human being with strong emotions which I can usually control with my reason. And there is no question of my being deterred by fear or worry from a course or an action which after long consideration I have recognized to be right. By origin, temperament, upbringing and education I take a healthy self-confidence for granted and, where necessary, civil courage. So I will not allow myself to be made fearful and anxious by either cardinals or colleagues.

But how things can go is shown soon afterwards by the above-mentioned case of the brave Fr Riccardo Lombardi SJ. Peter Nober SJ, the librarian and bibliographer of the Pontifical Biblical Institute, gives me a scrupulously accurate report. On 11 January 1962 there is an unsigned article on the front page of *Osservatore Romano* against Lombardi's book on the Council. Then on 24 January there is an article by Monsignor Giuseppe de Luca against 'great men' and in favour of 'de-Stalinization' (implicit criticism of Pius XII, Lombardi's protector) followed by a vigorous direct attack on the religious as a 'false prophet'. According to Nober, the book 'was rapidly sold out in the few days of the booksellers' "lifetime", e.g. ALCI (in the Via dei Lucchesi) sold around 100 in one day. Big newspapers, then illustrated journals, praised it.' But after the verdict the book disappears from the Roman bookshops; now it is no longer praised. Nober hopes that 'Lombardi escapes the *fulmen dium* (divine thunderbolt)': 'In the whole matter I also think of you, and of other ecumenists. Perhaps Lombardi has merely collected and (with great love for the church) "prophetized" what others, too, said before him in books and lectures . . . Prayer for "firm faith" for those who have to be concerned with ecumenical matters . . . and many greetings, also to colleagues Schelkle and Haag, your fellow champions in Christ, Fr Peter Nober SJ.'

My former over-cautious boss, Professor Hermann Volk, tells me from Münster that for him 'Schauf's positions are intolerable in their naivety – it seems that crooked things are being done here; also in the KNA (Catholic news agency). But you too have a responsibility not to provide more grist to the mill unintentionally. We can't have that. I hope that Schauf will finally go quiet . . .' What a storm in the teacup of the anxious! The controversy with Schauf must be the basis of my reputation of not being a person to cross swords with (though I am basically friendly and peaceable). Kennedy's maxim is also mine: 'Don't look for conflicts, but if you are forced to, be thorough in them.' In retrospect the first public exchange of blows with Heribert Schauf will seem to me to be child's play compared with the initially quite private controversy with the theologian whom I value more than any other, Karl Rahner. It is connected with the publication of what – after *Justification*, *The Council and Reunion*, and *That the World May Believe* – is my fourth book, under the title *Structures of the Church*.

New–old structures of the church: three ways to the ministry

My inaugural lecture, 'The Theological Understanding of the Ecumenical Council', is published, as is customary, in the *Tübinger Theologische Quartalschrift*. In its 141st year, this journal, the oldest theological journal still existing in Germany, edited by the professors of the Catholic Theological Faculty at the University of Tübingen, appears under the names of the emeriti Karl Adam and Joseph Rupert Geiselmann, with me in last place. The lecture comes out in the first issue of 1961, together with the very interesting inaugural lecture by Herbert Haag on 'Homer and the Old Testament'.

The plan to work my lecture up into a book is quickly made. After all, there is no real theology of the ecumenical council. But the two principles about the ecumenical council as a representation of the church need to be much better attested from the theological literature and thought through with all their consequences for the problems of Vatican II. I find more material than I expected and go into more problems than I intended. So at the end of the day a book of 356 pages comes into being with a wealth of bibliographical information and evidence in around 400 sometimes very long notes. As an appropriate title I choose *Structures* (not *The Structures*) *of the Church*.

My main concern, over and above conciliarity as a basic structure of church reality – totally forgotten in an age of papal absolutism and triumphalism – is to advance the discussion of the two main difficulties for an ecumenical understanding between the Christian churches. The main point of dispute is now no longer the doctrine of justification, nor basically is it the relationship between scripture and tradition or the seven sacraments generally. The points of dispute are rather the question of church ministry, important for the validity of Protestant celebrations of the eucharist, and especially the question of the papacy.

Over around 100 pages I take the trouble to describe Martin Luther's complex view of ministry and community in its historical development objectively and critically on the basis of the sources, in a way that no Catholic theologian has ever done before. Then I investigate the more recent Protestant views: the Declaration of the United Evangelical Lutheran Church of Germany on the apostolic succession (1954) and the controversy between Schlier, Käsemann, Diem and me with its consequences. Then it is above all the Protestant systematic theologian Edmund Schlink from Heidelberg who helps me to get a clearer view through his reflection on the apostolic succession, with its good exegetical foundation. He is able to combine loyalty to the basic Lutheran concern with real ecumenical openness, and already does so in the preparatory phase of the Council as an observer for the Evangelical Church in Germany.

Like Käsemann and others, Schlink understands the church in Pauline terms as a community of charisms and services. But at the same time he takes seriously the early catholic view of the pastoral ministry on the basis of a special mission. More sharply than other Lutherans he emphasizes the positive significance of the laying on of hands for the apostolic succession. He also works out more sharply the three possible ways into the pastoral ministry. On the basis of the New Testament writings I think that I cannot deny that alongside the call to office through those who hold office there is secondly a mission through those who have received no special mission (in the Acts of the Apostles, for example, the laying on of hands by prophets and teachers). And thirdly there is the human charisma, which breaks out freely, of people who in a community of believers recognize a call to the ministry of leadership (1 Cor. 12.28; 16.15) or of presiding (Rom. 12.8).

Understandably, in the church of the post-apostolic period the first-mentioned way into the ministry – on the basis of a special mission with the laying on of hands – becomes established; this is finally called 'apostolic succession'. But mustn't the church in principle remain open to the possibility originally given in the Pauline communities of charismas of founding and leading the community? And this not only in extreme situations, for example in a situation of persecution or a prison or concentration camp, but also in renewal movements within a church which has grown weary and self-righteous? In fact, only by recognizing this free charismatic call to leading the community can the schism be overcome with those Reformation churches which, because of the unwillingness of the hierarchy of the time for reform, attached, and still attach, little importance to a valid 'apostolic succession' by the episcopal laying on of hands, and which have developed ministries that function well.

My question is: if on the Lutheran side the apostolic succession by the laying on of hands is accepted as the norm which is desirable today, may not the Catholic side be expected to re-examine the decrees of the Counter-Reformation Council of Trent, at least with regard to 'emergencies' in matters of the eucharist and ordination? These Tridentine decrees were certainly imperative, given the decadence of church and ministry in the sixteenth century. But in the twentieth century there is a whole series of reasons from scripture and tradition why at least in particular emergencies, as is generally conceded, according to Catholic doctrine, too, an 'emergency baptism' can take place. Indeed, in the end of the day not only the task of preaching and baptism, but also the task of celebrating the eucharist, have ultimately been given not just to individual office holders but, as my New Testament colleague Karl Hermann Schelkle also thinks, to all disciples of Jesus, to the whole church.

Beyond question, in this chapter on the structures of the ministry I have stuck my neck out a long way. 'This is what I am teaching here in the treatise on the church,' the Dominican Bernard Dupuy will write to me some time later from Paris (24 January 1964), 'but with great power you produce many new arguments. It will take ten years for your work to be "assimilated" by Catholic public opinion, but this will be a datum in the history of ecclesiology. I found nothing to censure; perhaps the discussion with J. Ratzinger might be continued . . .' But what am I to say first about the cardinal problem of a theology of the ecumenical council, about the papacy, and the highly problematical relationship between the pope and the Council?

The Council above the pope? Constance and Vatican I

With the same precision with which I have described Luther's view of church ministry I go on to analyse the Vatican I doctrine of the papal primacy and its limits, which I know very well from Rome. Even after Vatican I (1870) the papal primacy is not said to be absolute and arbitrary. It is a priori limited by the existence of the episcopate, the ordinary exercising of their office by the bishops and the aim of the papal leadership itself, which is meant to serve not the destruction but the building up of the church. However, I begin from the traditional canon 228 of the *Codex Iuris Canonici* on the Council: 'The ecumenical council has the highest authority over the universal church.' This *suprema potestas* of the church stands in a so far undefined rivalry with the authority of the papal primacy. So there is a need for clarification.

In order to make people aware of the problem I initially turn to the not all that rare case of conflict between the pope and the church – about which more recent Catholic dogmatics is silent. This is not resolved by canon 1556, which is frequently cited, *'Prima sedes a nemine iudicetur.'* For that 'the first see is to be judged by no one' clearly goes back to a forgery in the sixth century. The historical truth is that from earliest times until the fifteen century, as my Tübingen colleague the mediaeval historian Harald Zimmerman has shown in an extensive investigation, there has been a whole series of 'papal trials'. The pope was summoned to them as the accused and was usually deposed – especially in the case of heresy or illegitimate seizure of office.

The justification for the depositions of popes in the conciliar era of the fifteenth century, which ultimately brought the end of the Western Schism with its rule of three popes and the restoration of the unity of Western Christianity, was therefore that the ecumenical council stands above the pope. This doctrine was formally defined by the ecumenical Council of Constance (1414-18). Its decisive definition runs: 'Duly assembled in the Holy Spirit, forming a general council, and representing the Catholic Church, the synod has its authority from Christ. Thus everyone of whatever estate or dignity, even the papal dignity, has to obey it in all that concerns the faith, the overcoming of the said schism and the reform of this church, head and members.'

In a thorough historical excursus, based on the most recent research, and advised by my colleague in church history, K. A. Fink, I explain how the decrees of the Council of Constance must in principle be given the same authority as the decrees of other ecumenical councils. Indeed according to the investigations by the American Brian Tierney, the decrees of Constance are the results of utterly orthodox mediaeval ecclesiology. I will also argue this emphatically in a lecture celebrating the 550th anniversary of the Council on 10/11 January 1964 in the council building of Constance – focused on the present.

Of course it is clear that the decrees of Constance form the opposite pole to Vatican I in church history. I point out how, after Vatican I, leading canon lawyers cite various cases in which the pope loses his office. As well as death and voluntary resignation from office, which is always possible, there are above all three of these: mental illness, heresy and schism. Even in the case of schism? Yes, schism arises not only if a person or group separates from the pope, but also if the pope separates from the church: this is the view of the Jesuit theologian Francisco Suárez, the most important representative of Spanish baroque scholasticism. But who passes judgement in the case of a heretical, schismatic or mentally ill pope? According to the self-same Suárez the church, the council! But what if such a pope refuses to convene a council? In that case corresponding provincial or national councils could be sufficient. Otherwise the college of cardinals or the episcopate would have to convene an ecumenical council against the will of the pope. And what if the pope were to want to prevent this? He should not be obeyed, because in such a case he would be misusing his supreme authority as a pastor against the just action and the common good of the church. How clearly people were able to speak about such questions in former times – and indeed were allowed to! And how understandable it is that our conformist council historians at the time of an authoritarian and senile Polish pope prefer to keep quiet about these problems and a key book about *Structures of the Church*, and instead disseminate page after page of unimportant historical detail!

Through these accounts attested by cases from canon law and from history, I want to make one thing clear for the present time: that the Catholic Church is by no means for better or worse in the hands of a pope who acts against the gospel. Church members and particularly bishops and theologians cannot therefore release themselves from responsibility for their own action by an inactive, excessive trust in the Holy Spirit, as if this functioned like a *deus ex machina*. Resistance can be offered. But with the discussion of the relationship between the council and the pope I have not yet reached the most difficult question in the understanding of the church.

Doubts about infallibility: bishops of Rottenburg

In the last chapter of *Structures of the Church* I cannot avoid going at least briefly into the tricky question of infallibility. My starting point is again the view of Luther and Calvin on the fallibility of councils. But I likewise report Karl Barth's criticism of the definition of infallibility at Vatican I and of the Catholic Tübingen school (J. S. Drey, J. A. Möhler, J. Kuhn and F. A. Staudenmeier). Here too I attempt to clarify what has to be clarified.

On the basis of the acts of the council I first investigate how far the vigorous opposition of the leading German and French bishops at Vatican I did in fact lead to a limitation of papal infallibility: the pope has no absolute infallibility and he may not act separately from the church. For here already on the basis of the dispute between a pro-infallibilistic majority and an anti-infallibilistic minority I must unambiguously state that despite such limitations, according to the dogma of Vatican I there is in fact no possibility of effectively preventing the pope from making definitions which may be true, but in the circumstances are highly detrimental to the church. Catholic theologians are always reluctant to note that if the pope really wants to, in the end he can define anything by himself, without the church. Why? Because he alone as the supreme interpreter interprets how, when and for what he will use his magisterium, and does so *sine consensu ecclesiae* – without the assent of the church.

It was this formula in particular which led the majority of French and German bishops to protest and leave the Vatican Council even before the definition of infallibility. They included the Bishop of Rottenburg, a former Tübingen church historian and author of a seven-volume history of the councils, Karl Joseph Hefele, who more than anyone else fought against this form of definition with a reference to erring popes. Hefele was almost the last bishop in the world – only after a nine-month delay! – to write a pastoral letter to his clergy saying that for the sake of 'peace and harmony in the church . . . great and demanding personal sacrifices' had to be made, and that therefore he submitted to the Vatican decision. And in this way he continued to remain Bishop of Rottenburg.

My first assistant in Tübingen is a doctoral student from the diocese of Rottenburg, Walter Kasper, an intelligent, friendly and co-operative Swabian. I can't expect too much work from him, as I have to share him with my colleague in dogmatics, Professsor Leo Scheffczyk, and he also has other duties in the Wilhelmsstift. At any rate it is worth a good deal to me that Kasper can also give me some help. He is a pupil of the Tübingen dogmatic theologian Geiselmann; he didn't do his theological studies in Rome but is now finishing off his dissertation on the doctrine of tradition in the Roman school. Even now I can see him standing in front of me in my study when, working on this very chapter on infallibility, I put to him the question about infallibility which is decisive, however many qualifications may be made: 'Is it sufficient that, in a church history of thousands of years, only one pope at a particular time can express with absolute certainty a principle of faith which alone is binding on the church as an a priori infallible pope? This poses in all its acuteness the problem: is a man, who is not God, infallible?' Kasper can't answer. Isn't God alone infallible?

I will later have to describe the possible solution already indicated in this chapter in a separate book, and Walter Kasper will then be the one who will put forward my solution – 'the church is maintained in truth despite any errors' – word for word without quoting my name. But he will also immediately reject it again when there are serious difficulties, and this time quote my name. On 16 February 1961 I examine him for the doctorate in fundamental theology. Three years later he will gain his habilitation with us and in 1964 will become Ordinarius Professor of Dogmatics in Münster. I am among those who propose him. Then, again at my suggestion, in 1970 he will become my colleague in the same discipline in Tübingen. However, in 1980, after initial protest against the shady Roman action, with six other colleagues, the majority of them from the diocese of Rottenburg, he will speak out against me and support the implementation of the Roman compulsory measure, my exclusion from the faculty. Later he deservedly becomes Bishop of Rottenburg and then – after a public statement against the demand by the Catholic Theological Faculty for my reinstatement (1996) and a pastoral letter against his own lay theologians on the question of lay preaching – become curial bishop (1999) and later Curia cardinal. Here he must have attained his goal on earth.

A similar Rottenburg clerical career likewise begins in 1962. On 1 May I am visited by a student chaplain to make further arrangements for his doctoral examination. I examine him in fundamental theology from 10.10 to 10.30, and the same day he gets his doctorate in theology. He is a jovial man and a good pastor, this Georg Moser. Later he will become director of an academy, suffragan bishop and finally Bishop of Rottenburg, Kasper's predecessor. As such, on 18 December 1979, in the dispute over infallibility, he deprives his professor and examiner at that time of the church's permission to teach – on the orders of Rome and against his inner convictions. This too is a separate story, which will have to be told at length in the second volume of these memoirs.

Also in connection with infallibility, I have never failed to refer clearly to the positive possibilities of the papacy: if a pope is really there for the church, if he fulfils his task to preach as unselfish pastoral service to the whole church, then he can do many great things and avoid some evils. To this degree, from the beginning I was an 'apologist' for the papacy, albeit a critical one. Of course I am not thinking of the way in which the Pius popes exercised their office but of John XXIII. And his representative for ecumenical affairs is now to come to Tübingen.

A Curia cardinal at the university: Augustin Bea

I hear from the ecumenically committed Catholic student chaplain Hans Starz that he wants to invite Cardinal Augustin Bea, the president of the Vatican Secretariat for Christian Unity, to Tübingen. Sometimes Augustin Bea in fact comes to Riedböhrigen, a little village near Donaueschingen, which I regularly pass in the car on the way from Tübingen to Switzerland, but without ever stopping. He was born there on 25 May 1881: since my years in Rome he has been well known to me as a leading exegete and Rector of the Pontifical Biblical Institute (1930–49), as a college visitor, the confessor of Pius XII and also as a confessor to the Germanicum. What is more natural than to invite him, when he visits his birthplace, to the university town of Tübingen, which is only an hour away? I then do that quite naturally, in the consciousness of preparing an honour and a joy for my faculty and university. Since I don't know what the cardinal's answer will be, I don't inform anyone about it officially in advance. Bea's answer is positive.

The good news of the visit of a cardinal to our university prompts more dismay than rapture among my Catholic colleagues: 'How could you invite a Roman cardinal to Tübingen without saying anything to me? Nothing like this has ever happened since the foundation of the university more than 400 years ago! A Curia cardinal at this university stamped by Protestantism? Think of the developments and complications that might lead to.' I take the objections calmly and promise to sort everything out with the Rector of the university.

His Magnificence, Theodor Eschenburg, State Counsellor and Professor of Political Science, with whom I have been on the same wavelength from the beginning, proves highly delighted at this initiative. Of course the cardinal is welcome, and he himself will do everything he can to make the visit run smoothly. Eschenburg, the scion of an old patrician family from Lübeck, is very familiar with the right protocol. The visit of a cardinal is rather different from the annual visit of the Prime Minister of Baden-Württemberg, at the time Kurt Georg Kiesinger, for the matriculation ceremony. The Rector has always refused to receive the prime minister down at the gateway, because this isn't required by protocol, and he shouldn't present himself in this way as the subject of the local ruler. But a cardinal of the Holy Roman Church is rather different. According to the diplomatic protocol which has held since the Congress of Vienna in 1815, the cardinal has to be treated as a 'prince of royal blood'. So as a matter of course the Rector will receive him down below at the gateway and then escort him to the Rector's Office and from there to the Festsaal.

Cardinal Bea arrives in Tübingen on Saturday 10 February 1962, at 9 a.m. First there are personal discussions in the Wilhelmsstift: at 9.15 with the Catholic Old Testament scholar Fridolin Stier (demoted to honorary professor in the philosophical faculty because he has an illegitimate daughter); at 10.00 with me; at 11.00 with the Protestant systematic theologian Köberle; and at 11.30 with the director of the publishers Katholisches Bibelwerk in Stuttgart, Dr Knoch. Then in the afternoon in my house in Gartenstrasse 103 there is a discussion for more than two hours to which I have invited the exegete Käsemann, the patristic scholar Eltester and the Reformation historian Rückert. Not exactly the most comfortable Protestant conversation partners! But the conversation is fair and constructive. The Protestant theologians are impressed by the ecumenical attitude of the cardinal.

On Sunday 11 February, in fine winter weather, Rector Eschenburg receives the cardinal at the main gate, and at 11 a.m. precisely escorts him, to the friendly applause of the public – including Prime Minister Kiesinger, many professors and representatives of public life – into the Festsaal, every seat in which is occupied. After a warm greeting from Rector Eschenburg and Bishop Leiprecht, Cardinal

Bea speaks on the topic 'What is to be expected from the Council?' It is not a union council, but it is meant to further the unity of separated Christians, which Rome is striving for, neither out of a desire for power nor for reasons of prestige. However, the Catholic Church cannot be expected to deviate from the truth that has once been recognized. But in external questions like those of liturgy, the language of the liturgy, canon law and piety, changes and accommodations are quite possible. In all these areas theological conversations are desirable and helpful.

This certainly isn't a sensational lecture, but the person giving it is: a cardinal of the Roman Curia, and not just any cardinal but the influential president of the Secretariat for Christian Unity, known to possess the ear of the pope and evidently full of respect for Protestant piety and the search for truth. Moreover, he is a prince of the church who does not seem at all hierocratic but is a modest, likeable scholar – smiling, slim, but slightly bowed under the burden of years. So the enthusiastic applause is certainly even more for the speaker than for the speech.

I will not deny that I am relieved when the purple-clad figure gets back into his black limousine and with a friendly wave returns to Riedböhringen. I can now return encouraged to theological research, which for me is increasingly to feel like walking a tightrope. The same day I write to Karl Rahner my quite personal assessment of Cardinal Bea's visit: 'Today, too, personally he has made a very good impression, and it also has to be said that his lecture was very much above average by comparison with the usual Roman theology. Nevertheless, his theological remarks, which related above all to ecclesiology, caused deep disappointment here. And much as the cardinal personally gives hope that all will go well, I am now depressed when I see the direction that this means. None of this is understood by the Protestants. Beyond doubt Bea has the best will in the world, but you know the kind of theology which is largely associated with his best will. At all events my fears for the Council and for the statements to come, particularly on ecclesiology, have been increased rather than diminished ... All this shows me again how important it is to describe how complex the ecclesiological problems are.'

Later, however, I hear of the double pressure on the president of the Secretariat for Unity. On the one hand this is theological: from Cardinal Ottaviani, who stands by the anti-ecumenical decree *Ecclesia catholica* of 1949 and the encyclical *Mystici corporis*, which denies non-Catholics any participation in the 'mystical body of Christ'. And on the other hand political: from Cardinal Secretary of State Tardini, who for example on the first visit of an Archbishop of Canterbury, Dr Geoffrey Fisher (in the statements of the Secretariat of State always given only the title 'Dottore'), was able to prevent any meeting with Cardinal Bea. So a first meeting between Cardinal Bea and the General Secretary of the World Council of Churches, Dr Willem Visser 't Hooft, has to take place in secrecy in almost conspiratorial conditions. Only after Tardini's death on 30 July 1961 do the ecumenical visits increase, and are Catholic observers allowed to take their place in the Third General Assembly of the World Council of Churches. That is how the weakness of the pope's leadership works out in practice.

But Augustin Bea still has this pope completely on his side. Through lectures, articles and personal contacts, the 80-year-old attempts in an admirable way to campaign for his great aims. As we shall see, three epoch-making reorientations will put him to a hard test in the Council under another pope: the ecumenism of the Christian churches, the new relationship to Judaism, and freedom of religion and conscience. But the freedom of theology generally is an indispensable precondition for coping with these tasks.

A champion of freedom in theology: Karl Rahner

After all my previous experiences and insights I am well aware that the publication of *Structures of the Church* is extremely risky. What worries me? I am not so much afraid of condemnation afterwards as of obstacles to publication. For every book of a Catholic theologian still needs an imprimatur, the church's permission for it to be printed. No Catholic publishing house can dare to publish a theological book without an imprimatur, not even the powerful Herder Verlag (which after all wants to go on printing mass books, catechisms and similar official literature).

Now every episcopal imprimatur, usually given by the relevant vicar general, needs a church censor appointed by him, who with his name endorses the Catholic orthodoxy of the content. As I have already related, *Justification* received the imprimatur of the episcopal ordinariate of Basle dated 3 January 1957 (the censors were Hans Urs von Balthasar, Louis Bouyer and Johannes Feiner). *The Council and Reunion* received the imprimatur from the archiepiscopal ordinariate of Vienna dated 12 March 1960 (the censor was again Professor Johannes Feiner of Chur). 'Letters to Young People' under the title *That the World May Believe* (soon translated into more languages than the two previous books) received the imprimatur from the episcopal ordinariate of Rottenburg responsible for Tübingen, dated 17 April 1962. I also hope for the imprimatur from Rottenburg for *Structures of the Church*. But who could be the theological censor for this difficult book? I puzzle for a long time over this and discuss the matter with friends and also with Fr Klein in Rome. Finally the choice falls on the highly respected Jesuit Karl Rahner, whose positive opinion will represent a favourable prejudgement both for the episcopal ordinariate and for the wider Catholic public.

I have the highest respect for Karl Rahner, since 1949 Professor of Dogmatics at the University of Innsbruck, one of the great inspirations of my years of theology in Rome. When later I get to know him personally I also like the unpretentious, human way in which on my first visit to Innsbruck, during a lengthy explanation of a theological point, he simply lies back on his bed and goes on teaching, or how on another visit to Freiburg, though 24 years older, he helps me to carry my heavy suitcase of books to the station. He has written a critical-constructive article on my book *Justification* in the *Tübinger Theologische Quartalschrift*, many pages long, and this was a substantial help to the reception of this book in the theological world. ('The book on which a few observations will be made here justifies further attention because of its importance . . . ') He had also been the one who had invited me to that fateful conference of dogmatic theologians at Innsbruck, at which the direction was set for my academic career. And finally, in my book on the Council, he was the chief witness to the concession that there is a 'sinful church' and to the need for radical reform. I am full of gratitude; could I find a more understanding 'censor'?

I know that as a dogmatic theologian Rahner had himself incurred criticism under Pius XII for his affirmation of concelebration ('The Many Masses and the One Sacrifice') and a non-biological interpretation of the 'virgin birth'. At the same time he had made bold and pioneering statements on questions of the structures of the church. His publications on *The Dynamic Element in the Church* (1958) and – together with Joseph Ratzinger – on *The Episcopate and the Primacy* (1961), which were not sparing with critical observations, attracted attention. Both are published in a new series by Herder Verlag with the politically shrewdly chosen traditional title *Quaestiones disputatae* ('Disputed questions'), which is open to the future. The editor is none other than Rahner himself. In 1958 he had opened the series with bold thrusts on the inspiration of scripture and the theology of death. I hope that my book on structures can also be published in this series and that with Rahner's positive opinion I will kill two birds with one stone: winning over both a church censor who is well-disposed towards me and also the editor of the already respected series. So with the name of Rahner a good deal is at stake for me.

Rahner had spoken in Tübingen on the Council as early as 14 January 1962 – and was enthusiastically received by our students, who noted very clearly the agreement with their theological teacher. At that time we also already considered plans for thwarting the curial strategy on the Council. On 3 February I now ask Rahner in a letter to include *Structures of the Church* in his series *Quaestiones disputatae* – in the hope that he will read through my manuscript carefully: 'For there is no doubt,' I write, 'that in the present state of preparations for the Council the book will encounter a very tense situation: the effects are unpredictable and everything should be done to avoid unnecessary difficulties. On the other hand it is important that now in particular some things are said which in some circumstances could be a positive influence on one-sided doctrinal declarations like those in prospect. One publisher has already expressed interest in the French edition and another in the English.'

For me beyond any question Rahner is 'the leading figure in German-language Catholic theology', a quotation from the *Neue Zürche Zeitung* which I confirm for

Der Spiegel. However, the more time goes on, the less I can overlook the fact that Rahner's theological method is increasingly different from mine, as it is now developing in Tübingen. Rahner is a 'speculative mind', a brilliant systematician. Even Hans Urs von Balthasar has to concede, when on one occasion I am driving him from Basle in the Black Forest to visit the philosopher Gustav Seiwerth, that he, Balthasar, is really more a man of letters, and Karl Rahner is the real theologian. In fact Rahner is a profound thinker and an extraordinarily acute dialectician, trained on Hegel and Heidegger, who by arguing in oppositions arrives at amazing 'reconciliations'. That is his strength, but also his weakness. So while he brings the 'charisma' into play in opposition to 'ministry' in a way which makes the hearts of the renewers beat faster, he ends up with a 'synthesis' within the system in which the office has a charismatic structure and the charisma seems to be controlled by the office. It is the same with episcopacy and primacy, where he puts great stress on the collegiality of the bishops but at the same time also affirms the papal primacy unchanged in the framework of Vatican I. I ask myself, 'Can this be my way?' In *Structures of the Church* I have already continued by means of historical criticism the way indicated in *Justification*.

However, it is understandable that Rahner's dialectical method also does not meet with approval in the Roman Sanctum Officium: it is felt to be dangerously subversive. But they can never really get at Rahner, because for all his alleged 'heresies', in the end time and again he lands up with the wording of the dogma and can finally 'rescue' the wording even of such remarkable (Jesuit) exercises in piety as veneration of the Heart of Jesus or the (mediaeval) indulgence, by a theologically elegant reinterpretation. Thus in Pius XII's wave of purges after *Humani generis* – which, I hear from Balthasar, also suggests that he should make some 'blurrings' in his own book on Barth and leads him to call off a joint visit to Rome with Karl Barth – Rahner is merely put under the censorship of the General of the order. Unlike his French fellow-Jesuits he is not punished with the loss of his chair and a temporary ban on speaking and publishing. But it is precisely for that reason that Karl Rahner, more than any other theologian in Germany, is an acknowledged protagonist of freedom in theology for those of us who are about a generation younger. What would I have to fear from him?

A dispute over dogmas

The publication of *Structures of the Church* is a pressing matter. The opening of the Second Vatican Council has now been fixed for 11 October 1962 in St Peter's. I have steeped myself in the problems and – despite working day and night – have taken more time than I planned. On re-reading my correspondence with Karl Rahner I am still moved today by how this man, who works hard and travels a great deal, finds time to read a manuscript which is now much more extensive and reaches him only at the beginning of April instead of the beginning of March.

He would like to publish it in his series even before the manuscript by the Jesuit Overhage which has already been handed in, and that of Professor Geiselmann which has been announced, and urges Herder Verlag to be quick about it. My anxious question is: what will his verdict from Innsbruck be?

On Thursday 3 May he asks me to meet him half-way, in Munich. There we now sit in the Jesuit house in Kaulbachstrasse, in a relatively big room at the end of a table which is yards long. I immediately sense that Rahner is tired and in an extremely ungracious mood. He certainly doesn't attempt to turn the manuscript down as unsuitable for publication, as Hermann Volk once turned down the manuscript for *The Council and Reunion* with his apodeictic 'It won't do!' But evidently in hours of work he has taken the trouble not only to study my remarks page by page but also to correct them according to his Roman Catholic orthodoxy. *Correctio paterna* (fatherly correction), not the *correctio fraterna* (brotherly correction) that Thomas Aquinas called for.

Now contrary to my public image I am one of those who likes to be corrected, as all those who have close dealings with me will confirm – if there are convincing reasons for the corrections. Indeed even now I let my assistants and other competent people read my manuscripts to correct and supplement them; this helps me a great deal. So I had nothing against Rahner rewriting, sometimes in a very arbitrary way, my article on 'Christocentricity' for the new *Lexikon für Theologie und Kirche* (1958), of which he was chief editor (with Prelate Josef Höfer).

But in the case of my *Structures of the Church* it is now more than a matter of details. My historical-systematic method of treating the question of ministry, in which I largely have to concede that Luther is right, and above all my description of the relationship between the ecumenical Council of Constance and Vatican I, has evidently infuriated Rahner. He doesn't seem accustomed to being contradicted. But I can't simply first treat the Council of Constance historically and demonstrate the legitimacy and abiding validity of the decrees of Constance with respect to the superiority of the council over the pope, and only then describe Vatican I and its doctrine. No, contrary to the historical order I must first discuss Vatican I (1870) and its definition of the primacy and infallibility of the pope, and then investigate the decrees of Constance (1415!). I think of my argument with Rector Tattenbach over the Gregorian theses and retort to Rahner that this is a completely unhistorical, prejudiced procedure. He feels that my way of proceeding – in a word – is completely undogmatic and un-Catholic in his sense. Where does this contradiction stem from?

A fundamental defect of Rahner's theology suddenly dawns on me: a manifest lack of consistent historical thinking. He evidently has little inkling of the problems of the Council of Constance. In fact its decrees were often passed over in neoscholastic lectures (not only at the Gregorian). As of course they are in the quasi-official collection of doctrines by Heinrich Denziger (also an alumnus of the Germanicum), although the legitimacy of all the popes since Martin V, who was chosen by this council, hangs on the decrees! If these decrees were invalid, so too would be the papal election of the pope of the time and his successors. Although he speaks contemptuously of 'Denziger theology', still under Pius XII, Rahner had edited Denziger's highly tendentious collection of documents, in a practically unchanged 31st edition (the 1991 37th edition is revised, expanded and translated into German by the Tübingen dogmatic theologian Hünermann, who hides the fundamental decree of Constance in his preliminary remarks: more than 1700 pages and weighing more than two kilos – so heavy have the Roman Catholic dogmas of faith become in 2000 years).

But what am I to do now, here in Munich, so to speak between Tübingen historical criticism and Innsbruck dogmatics? I know that I am a priori in a weaker position over against my church censor and the editor of the series. The conflict gets more pointed, Rahner becomes more pressing: evidently my investigation behind the Tridentine decrees formulated against the Reformers seems to him to be even more dangerous than my affirmation of the decrees of Constance. The Council of Trent, which in the first session of 1547 had laboriously worked out a carefully planned decree on justification against Luther, contented itself in later sessions with a superficial and little-thought-out confirmation of the mediaeval doctrine of the seven sacraments (and allegedly already at the Council in Florence decided against the Orientals), especially the sacrament of ordination. Yet for Rahner the controversial question of the apostolic succession seems to have been decided once for all by Trent.

On the basis of the results of New Testament research I have ventured to claim that just as according to the New Testament any Christian may baptize, so in principle any Christian may also celebrate the eucharist. I argue that 'Do this in remembrance of me' is ultimately just as much addressed to all the faithful as 'Go and baptize'. Of course I don't mean by that that any Christian can celebrate his 'private mass' at home, as the Sanctum Officium later claims in a declaration which caricatures my position. By its nature the eucharist should always be a community celebration. But if the priest who should normally preside at the eucharist isn't there, the community can celebrate the eucharist without celibate ordained priests, at least in an emergency (one example is the underground church in China), just as according to 1 Corinthians, in the absence of the apostle Paul the community of Corinth had celebrated the eucharist completely without ordained ministers. This is a fact which has never been reflected on even by progressive theologians (not to mention historians of the Council) in Catholic dogmatics, as I will note at the Council.

A second fundamental defect in Rahner's theology also becomes evident to me: the lack of historical–critical exegesis. Rahner once laughingly advised a student known to me that it was enough to go to lectures on exegesis for one or two semesters; but in the end dogmatics was decisive. Is it surprising that my view of the celebration of the eucharist (in some circumstances even by those who have not been ordained), which is supported by exegesis, seems unacceptable to him?

Karl Rahner has now got up, but this time not to lie on a sofa. The master walks up and down like a lion in a cage and lectures me long and loud. He tells me that as a Catholic theologian I should have accepted the dogmas of the church as defined and why I should have done so. He continues for perhaps ten to fifteen minutes in a roundabout dialectic, as is his nature; he seems to me to be going on for ever. But I already learned how to control myself in the Germanicum among the Jesuits. So I sit there in this room in Kaulbachstrasse in Munich, controlled and silent, just as I once did with Fr Vorspel, and patiently listen, without interrupting, but also without being convinced. Finally this magisterial lecturing becomes too much for me. 'Enough,' I exclaim loudly, full of holy wrath, and beat my fist so powerfully on the heavy table that afterwards all my knuckles hurt. 'Enough, either these dogmas are true, in which case I accept them. Or they aren't true, and to the devil with them!' Plain speaking, and it helps.

Imprimatur?

Rahner observes that he's gone too far for his young but not unknowledgeable colleague. He calms down. Finally he suggests that I should now study all his corrections and incorporate them as far as possible. Then we will meet again in ten days at the same place, on Sunday 13 May. I agree, and we part in a not unfriendly way.

I return in my VW from Munich to Tübingen deeply depressed. Indeed, this is the only time that I think, 'The best thing would be for you to hit a tree! For what are you going to do in theology if even the theologian who could best understand you doesn't understand?' I succeed in controlling my emotions through my reason. Had I already read Charles Darwin's Foreword to his classic *The Origin of Species,* I would possibly have been spared such gloomy thoughts. For there Darwin writes that he doesn't expect that experienced colleagues in biology, who all their lives have put forward another view, will ultimately change their views about the theory of evolution. He only hopes that a few young scholars will read his book and continue his ideas.

Happily, in my house on the Neckar I find my colleague Christa Hempel, a convert from the Evangelical Lutheran Church. What I tell her agitates her tremendously: 'How can this Rahner want to dictate to you what you have to write? That's unbounded arrogance and you certainly shouldn't yield to it!' I readily concede that it's done me good to be strengthened in such a direct Lutheran and Berlin way. But how am I to get my book through the church censorship and to a Catholic publisher? Without an imprimatur the book would be disqualified from the start.

And I can't get the imprimatur without Karl Rahner. So there is nothing for it but to study closely the objections, changes and new versions which he has written on the opposite pages to mine, to see what I can do with them. But from the start I am clear that the truth will in no way be sacrificed, and that the historical structure of the book will remain unchanged: Constance before Vatican I! Where I can correct, modify or make things more precise, of course I do so. I really do take a good deal of trouble, and in a few places the expert will be able to discover Rahnerian formulations.

On 9 May I send Rahner a long express letter and attach my corrections, where I have not taken them over from him word for word. 'I don't know whether you will like all this. I quite understand that you take your responsibility as editor seriously. But I would beg you with all my heart – since after all I am the author – to put yourself in my position. It is certain that I am running incomparably greater risks. But it seems to me to be a demand of the hour to perform this service for the church (for me it is nothing else). I have done what I could. You will recognize my good will from the improvements. But it must remain my book, which I must be able to be responsible for to the last word; you will surely understand this and not ask the impossible of me.' Rahner confirms receipt two days later: 'A first rapid run through (I haven't been able to do more yet) gives me the hope that we will be able to come to an agreement on Sunday. I myself long very much for this.'

So on Sunday 13 May 1962 I again drive to Munich at crack of dawn and Rahner again comes from Innsbruck. At 9.00 a quite different Rahner meets me at the same place. Amazingly he is no longer grumpy, unfriendly and angry but jovial, smiling, conciliatory. Have just my corrections led to this? I have never discovered what has made him, as they say in Switzerland, a 'glove turned inside out'. Has he meanwhile spoken in Munich with his good friend the writer Luise Rinser, who will later explain to me at length that Rahner has told her that he wants 'basically the same thing as Küng, but . . . the dogmas'?

Rahner thumbs through the whole manuscript from beginning to end and reads the new version. But he does it obviously fast and in a benevolent way. There are no objections. He will give a positive opinion for Rottenburg and accept the work as Vol. 17 in *Quaestiones disputatae*. I breathe a sigh of relief. I thank him most warmly and we part great friends. Now I definitively conclude the manuscript at 336 pages. The book receives the imprimatur from the Vicar General of Rottenburg, Dr Knaupp, on 15 May 1962. On 25 May I thank Rahner for the 'Editor's Preface' which has just arrived: 'I am truly delighted that in our second Munich conversation we reached agreement so quickly.'

But what happens then? Strikingly, a few days later, on 5 June, Rahner and I, as I have reported, are reunited at the consecration of Hermann Volk as bishop in Mainz: our Dutch friends Willebrands and Thijssen are there. It's a happy party. But eight days later I get from Rahner 'in utter confidence' the following disturbing report: 'A few days ago I received an official communication that from now on everything that I write and is subject to the censorship of the order must in my case, unlike others and contrary to the normal course of things, be submitted to censorship in Rome. No reason for this measure is given. Though it, too, comes formally from the leadership of the order, I believe that I have every reason to assume that it has been decreed on the instructions of higher places. In these circumstances it is impossible to retain my preface to your book . . . Given my reputation and yours in Rome, I have no prospect of getting this preface past Rome.'

I reply to Rahner at length: 'I can imagine all too well what it means for you, as a man who in all his activity wants only to serve the church, to be disciplined in this unjustified and un-Christian way by his church superiors. I think that this measure is a downright scandal, particularly now, immediately before the Council . . . Certainly men like König and Döpfner will also be outraged at such intrigues.' I can find no satisfaction in the sudden reversal of roles – the censor censored. Against the background of all these controversies it is at any rate easier to understand that Cardinal Döpfner will then find my book *Structures of the Church* – the first copy reaches me on 7 July 1962 – 'exciting' and that it robs him of his sleep. But is that because of the author? Isn't it rather because of the historical facts and the problems, which are treated in an unprejudiced and honest way?

The person who immediately recognizes this is the first Protestant theologian to receive the manuscript from me, at the same time as Rahner: Professor Edmund Schlink, observer from the Evangelical Church in Germany at the Council, whom I have already mentioned. He reads it immediately and praises not only the thorough biblical foundation but also the 'resolution, maintained to the last chapter, to give a precisely historical treatment of church history, especially of the councils and popes', which otherwise is 'largely reinterpreted in the light of its final canonistic conclusion'. In this way 'the dividing walls between our churches become transparent in a way that is seldom the case'. But, I ask myself, will such a consistent biblical and historical view also have a chance at the Council?

The bishop's expert

In my academic life I have quickly learned that despite all my strategic planning I must constantly reckon with surprises, which have a considerable influence on my life. On 17 June 1962 I had given a lecture on the Council to young people in the cathedral in Frankfurt. The very next Friday, 22 June, I receive a telephone call from the secretary of the Bishop of Rottenburg: Bishop Leiprecht would like to visit me that afternoon in my home. May I ask why? Yes, he wants to ask me to accompany him to the Council as his personal *peritus*, expert.

I really didn't expect this, and I'm by no means enthusiastic. In fact I'm disturbed. I've directed all my efforts towards helping to prepare for the Council in a good spiritual and theological way. But then, as they say, *'videant consules'*, the bishops are to see to the rest. Why should I, who know the 'eternal city' inside out, return for many months, if not years, to that 'black' Rome on which I've turned my back with gratitude, but with relief? Why more of this whole clerical business of cardinals and prelates at the papal court, where the *persona grata* prevails instead of the principle of competence, and where the individual bishop counts little and the theologian even less?

So I seriously hesitate about saying yes to the bishop. But everyone whom I consult in these few hours – as always, Herbert Haag has important things to say – firmly advises me to accept the bishop's invitation. After all, it's the event of the century in the church. They're right. So at 4 p.m. the bishop comes to my house, as friendly and persuasive as ever. And when he asks me to become his theologian at the Council I say yes. How am I to suspect that this yes will determine my fate for almost a decade and beyond? On 26 June I put in a request to the Kultus-ministerium for leave for November/December. Where I cannot fulfil my duty to lecture, my assistant Dr Walter Kasper will represent me.

On 17 July I receive a letter from Karl Rahner that Cardinal König has invited him to accompany him to the Council, and Cardinal Döpfner manages to get the pope to nominate Rahner personally as an official *peritus* at the Council – not, however, for the Theological Commission (where the Sanctum Officium rules), but for the Commission on the Sacraments. Rahner writes to me: 'I hope that the Bishop of Rottenburg will stand by his invitation. As Ratzinger and Semmelroth also seem to be coming, with Congar, Schillebeeckx, etc. we can set up a very nice club.'

Yves Congar? As early as 15 January 1961 he had spoken in Tübingen on 'Council and Ecumene' – like Rahner, taking our common line. In the evening we sat together in my house with Herman Diem and others. We discussed theological problems, not so much the problems of the hermeneutics of the Bible and dogma as those of church order and the papacy, in which Congar is the supreme expert. In Bonn, Congar tells me, after his lecture they had sat with the church and council historian Hubert Jedin (Alberigo's teacher) and talked only about wines, which bored Congar, this born monk and ascetic scholar, to tears. 'Small talk' – another 'Roman Catholic way' of getting round uncomfortable problems even as a historian, but contrary to the saying *in vino veritas*! I want to look up Yves Congar in Strasbourg after the summer holidays, to arrive at a joint strategy at the Council.

Catholic theology re-formed

So I will take part in the Council as a theological novice, but to my great sorrow two highly regarded 'elder statesmen' in theology and ecumenics, Otto Karrer and Hans Urs von Balthasar, won't be there. On 21 August 1961 I had travelled with both of them to a new meeting of the Catholic Conference on Ecumenical Questions in Strasbourg from 22 to 25 August, there to discuss 'the renewal of the church'. But suddenly this conference on ecumenical questions no longer has the same significance as before. On the one hand it now has more weight; on the other it risks losing importance. For since that same month, August, the Secretariat for Christian Unity has been working in Rome, initially only with four members: under Cardinal Bea as executive secretary there is Monsignor Willebrands with two assistants, the Frenchman Monsignor J. F. Arrighi and the American Paulist father Thomas Stransky. These are excellent people, who, having now and again been present at our conference, will work very constructively at the Council. Of the sixteen members of the Secretariat for Unity entitled to vote, six come from our conference, and of its nineteen counsellors (*consultors*) as many as twelve.

Thus this conference has gained considerable influence on the work of the Council. At the same time, though, it largely overlaps with it and makes itself increasingly superfluous. Granted, we have another conference from 26 to 30 August 1963 in the Villa Caglione in Gazzada near Milan to discuss 'The assessment of the ecumenical situation in various countries during the Council'. But Cardinal Montini is now pope in Rome, Cardinal Bea cannot come, and while Willebrands is present, he is overburdened by the new secretariat.

So no further conference will take place. Since in any case the conference has a purely informal and minimal organizational structure, it can peacefully go to sleep without a formal resolution to dissolve, and even without a worthy obituary. Only a good 30 years later will a newly appointed Professor of Church History and the History of Theology at the University of Tilburg in the Netherlands, Dr J. Y. H. A. Jacobs, give his inaugural lecture on 'The Catholic Conference on Ecumenical Questions. A School and a Leader, 1951-65'. But this is a laboured archive work, which gives no glimpse of the lively experience of those involved and their inner passion. In truth we were no 'school', and Jan Willebrands, who published hardly anything theological, was no 'leader'. We were a fellowship of the most original and obstinate minds in Catholic theology, and Willebrands was the shrewd initiator and co-ordinator. For me and the other participants he remains the bold and understanding pioneer of Catholic ecumenism, who despite resistance from Rome was able to build up a network of ecumenical theology before the Council. As secretary, later president, of the Secretariat for Unity and cardinal, he will be able to perform only a few major services.

And Balthasar and Karrer? Although theologians from the start and academically better qualified than most others, they don't become consultors to the new Secretariat for Unity. Their fellow-Jesuits in Rome still do not forgive the two of them for having left the Society of Jesus. The serene Otto Karrer, in any case over 70, takes it lightly. But Hans Urs von Balthasar, almost two decades younger, and still fighting for his lay order and for recognition, feels humiliated. Moreover our Bishop of Basle, Franziskus von Streng, doesn't take the famous but uncomfortable Balthasar with him to Rome as his personal expert, as many expect, but the less well known but more open Otto Wüst from Sursee.

Doesn't that explain why Balthasar follows the Council from the start not just at a geographical distance but also at an inner spiritual distance? And the fact that neither the theology of the Greek and Latin church fathers nor German or Spanish mysticism play a great role there, indeed that quite different problems and solutions of the modern and post-modern world stand in the foreground, only strengthens his reserve. Soon some of the things that happen in the Council seem to him, an utterly apolitical aesthete, to be false accommodation to the dominant spirit of the time. With his mordant commentaries and invective, at first not noticing it, he becomes a reactionary who in the end fatally comes closer to the Curia than to the Council. Withdrawn and misunderstood, in the next 25 years he erects his gigantic three-aisle theological cathedral in which he brings together the most varied saints, mystics, poets and speculative spirits in order to give God's trinitarian revelation an aesthetic (*Herrlichkeit/The Glory of God*), dramatic (*Theodramatik/Theo-Drama*) and theological (*Theologik/Explorations in Theology*) interpretation. On his sixtieth birthday on 12 August 1965 I dedicate my theological meditation 'Christianity as a Minority. The Church among the World Religions' to him. Unfortunately he knows little about the world religions and thinks little of interfaith dialogue.

At the same time as the demise of the Catholic Conference on Ecumenical Questions, another group forms as the *avant garde* of Catholic theology. And again – here I am thinking not only of Jan Willebrands, but also of the great Willem Visser 't Hooft, the first General Secretary of the World Council of Churches – it is a Dutchman who gives the decisive organizational impetus: the publisher Paul Brand. On 14 April 1962 he visits me in Tübingen, and with Karl Rahner and Edward Schillebeeckx we develop the plan for an international journal of theology. It is to be given the name *Concilium*, and it will be described at length later.

The Curia's preparation for the Council and counter-actions

As early as Pentecost, 5 June 1960, the pope had charged the eleven preparatory commissions and the three secretariats with working out the draft decrees = 'schemata'. On 9 July the substantive briefings on content, prepared by members of the Curia and presented to the pope by the alert General Secretary Pericle Felici, had gone to the chairmen of the commissions – unfortunately all Curia cardinals. Initially the world, and people in Tübingen, hear about the work of the commission only through indiscretions. It's kept a strict secret, and is more Roman than Catholic. When I see a photograph of the Preparatory Theological Commission I know most of the members by sight: at the top of the table is Cardinal Ottaviani with the commission secretary, Fr Sebastian Tromp, my teacher in fundamental theology; on the left are the Jesuits Hürth, Bidagor and Dhanis and the Dominican Garrigou-Lagrange, and on the right the Dominican General Fernández.

In other words, it's the old Roman curial team (of course there is no trace of any women) of the Sanctum Officium. The two bishops I recognize who aren't members of the Curia, our conservative Germanicum alumnus Schröffer from Eichstätt and Bishop Wright from Pittsburgh, make little difference to it. All this suggests the worst. Are such people going to renew the church? What interest will these men, who so far have prevented reform, suddenly have in it? They all think in a typically Roman scholastic way, no matter what nation or order they belong to: they think that one gets the correct view of the Catholic Church and orthodoxy only from the centre, so it is important to preserve what one has and resist all centrifugal tendencies.

My fears are confirmed. By summer 1962 more than 70 schemata have been worked out – more than 2000 big printed pages, which no council will ever cope with. However, only seven finished printed schemata can be sent to the bishops strictly 'sub secreto' as a 'prima series'. There are four theological schemata: on the sources of revelation, on the preservation of the faith that has been handed down, on the moral order, and on chastity, virginity, marriage and family. In addition there is a fifth on the liturgy (the best of them all), a sixth on means of communication (utterly innocuous), and one on the unity of the church (ecumenical only to a limited degree). The very first schema, on the two sources of revelation, particularly alarms us Council theologians. Why?

With the Counter-Reformation statement that the Christian revelation is contained only 'partly' (partim) in scripture and 'partly' (partim) in oral tradition, the commission evidently also wants to refute the view of the Tübingen scholar J. R. Geiselmann, one of my predecessors in dogmatics. In a 1956 article on the relevant formulation of the Council of Trent he had found that the Council of Trent did not assert the incompleteness of the content of Holy Scripture (the 'partly-partly' had been replaced by a simple 'and', i.e. scripture 'and' tradition); this was very important for my method in Justification (1957). Evidently Rome now once again wants to prescribe the undifferentiated equivalence of scripture and tradition along the lines of Trent – to the detriment of Holy Scripture. Tromp's confidant Schauf had already betrayed this to me in his article, to which I replied with question marks: 'Alongside (?) Holy Scripture (?) stands the oral tradition which in content (?) goes beyond (?) Holy Scripture.'

Of course it is also easy to derive the basis for new unbiblical Marian dogmas from some 'tradition', as the Croat Carlo Balić, Rector of the Roman Franciscan Antonianum College and president of the International Mariological Society, is energetically doing. In February he sends suggestive Latin questions about a 'Marian movement' at the Council to Rahner and to me, among others. In my response I tell Balić bluntly that 'the sharpest protests will be made by key bishops, theologians and laity against any attempt to orientate the Council in the direction of a "Marian maximalism"'. On 8 March 1962 Balić 'expresses deep gratitude for your letter of the 4th inst. And wishes all the best and God's richest blessing.' Rahner tells me that he, too, writes 'quite a crude letter' and gets 'a subdued-friendly answer that his question had not sought to indicate that there should be any mariological definition at the Council'. Rahner: 'We hope so, but there are plenty of other points where we do not know what Tromp et al. are planning.'

I visit our Tübingen emeritus Geiselmann, who a little later sends me three handwritten pages of criticism of the revelation schema to the effect that it is 'mistaken even in approach'. I pass on Geiselmann's reaction to other Council theologians, especially to Congar and Rahner. They too are dismayed at just how backward-looking the four doctrinal schemata of the Theological Commission are. The first two betray the hand of Sebastian Tromp, the other two largely that of my moral professor Franz Hürth. Here are all the outpourings of that neo-scholasticism which we heard in our lectures at that time, but then in a far fresher and more differentiated way. The overall impression given by these schemata is that they are alien to the world and church, with no historical thought and no pastoral approach. They are legalistic rather than theological, essentialist rather than existential. I am personally oppressed above all by the lack of an exegetical basis. The critical opinion I ask for from the Tübingen New Testament scholar Karl Hermann Schelkle – more one of the quiet men in the land of theology – leaves nothing to be desired in the sharpness of its judgement and the clear personal disappointment over the lamentable way of treating the Bible. On 29 September 1962 Schelkle writes to me in his very neat script: 'I have repeatedly read the pages of the schema on the Old and New Testament that were sent to me. If anyone were to ask me my comment on them I could only say that I am utterly depressed. I have to assume that not a single German Catholic exegete of the New Testament as far as I know them can assent to the scheme. We hold completely different convictions both on many details and also in principle. This is not because we are not loyal to the church but because of the insights that we have laboriously gained.'

After a series of critical individual observations comes Schelkle's final judgement: 'It is sweepingly asserted that the church has been entrusted with the interpretation of scripture and has to watch over it. Here the Monsignori are evidently confusing themselves with the church in order to attach strings to it. Aren't we others the church (we others, not as a little club of arrogant professors, but as those who for better or worse also want to be Catholic Christians)? *Sufficit. Dixi.* Let's turn to better things, either to the New Testament or to going for a walk.' A PS follows: 'It is impossible and nonsensical to want to force against the evidence of the text the assertion that the Bible of the Old (!) and New Testaments is absolutely inerrant.'

But untouched by these controversies, my book on the Council makes its way behind the scenes.

A bestseller contrary to expectations

Even publishers can make mistakes – especially Catholic publishers, if they are all too conformist. In 1962, two years after its appearance, the house of Herder in Freiburg is already bringing out the sixth edition of *The Council and Reunion*. It's amazing where and by whom the book is not only being read but also reviewed, usually in a friendly way, from parish magazines and church papers, through the daily press, to the technical theological journals. Around 150 reviews have found their way into our archives. And today I grieve a little when I see how many of the journalists and theologians so well known to me are no longer alive. How often was I to be dependent on them in the time to come!

So in view of the success of the German original, what was more natural than that the book should also be published in other languages, and above all in English? But Herder and Herder in New York turns it down: such a book in 1960 – too early for the USA! The Catholic Church here hasn't got as far as this. This is a grotesque error of judgement, evidently governed by the milieu: for conservatives, reforms always come 'too early'. In this way Herder and Herder loses some income. At that time I still have no international publishing link (at first Herder Tokyo is similarly negative over a Japanese edition). In any case, only a few German books are brought out in America; even my *Justification* is so far known only in theological circles. But here an English gentleman, Robert Sencourt, with the remarkable address 'The Royal Automobile Club, Pall Mall, London SW1', comes to my aid. He has got hold of *The Council and Reunion* and is tremendously enthusiastic. Despite his defective knowledge of German he sets to work and quickly translates some chapters into English. With these he goes to Sheed and Ward, at the time the most popular Catholic publishing house in England. Sencourt's translation is quite unusable, but his enthusiasm is infectious. Sheed and Ward acquires the rights, and in Cecily Hastings, sister of the well-known theologian Adrian Hastings, finds an excellent translator.

In the English-speaking world, too, the book doesn't come out 'too early' and becomes a bestseller! At least the Roman Catholic church historians of the Second Vatican Council in the 1990s couldn't keep completely quiet about this. J. O. Beozzo (of Sao Paulo) devotes half a page to the book and states that its 'extraordinary success' led to an 'explosive dissemination of Küng's idea of a necessary and sufficient link between reform and unity' (1997). Is that all? Be that as it may, even now some theologians think that one can plan a bestseller strategically. However, that requires not only the ingenuity but also the *kairos*, the given moment, the favourable point in time, the historical hour: not too early and not too late. And also the right content and the right form. The Canadian Jesuit theologian Elmer O'Brian made the following amusing comment on the latter: he doesn't know who has described 'the German theological mentality as the deep-down-divingest, under-water-stayingest, mud-up-bringingest ever accorded to man by a beneficent providence'. But such a person happens along: 'He is the major theological talent to appear in this decade. He is a German among Germans, as only a native-born Swiss, it would seem, ever properly manages to be. He dives deep. Yet in a book now available to us he thinks as clearly as a Frenchman and . . . speaks with the directness of an American. This, I would suggest, is suitable cause for rejoicing.' Also for the author, Fr O'Brian!

At the end of July 1962 I travel with my youngest sister to London for the publication of *The Council and Reunion*. With my publishers Sheed and Ward, on 3 August for the first time I experience an English 'party' of a kind that is still unusual on the continent. 'What would you like to drink?' I am asked by Neil Middleton and Rosemary Middleton-Ward, daughter of the founder of the firm, who are now in charge. 'Something specifically English' is my answer. In that case a gin and tonic? This is still my favourite drink.

Time Magazine: *Between Luther and Pope John*

The book will also be a sensational success in its English edition, and in the Catholic milieu, too. The respected *Clergy Review* writes: 'This book with all its sweep and detail rises incomparably to the heights of the pope's challenge and the world's needs.' The editor of the *Clergy Review* is England's most important Catholic theologian, Professor Charles Davis, with whom I have a long con-versation in London on 5 August. He too supports the Council with all his might, and will even take part in it for a time, but without ever being nominated *peritus*. Later he will be the first well-known Catholic theologian to give up his ministry and the church as a public protest, out of disappointment at developments after the Council. That is understandable if one knows that in England he has to deal with hierarchs like Archbishop John Heenan of Liverpool. Under too much pressure, and annoyed, as the bishop responsible for ecumenical relations Heenan declares bluntly and unashamedly that my book on the Council is useless and is meeting with approval only among non-Catholics. I write to him, but the Irish-born churchman refuses to correct himself, though he knows better: he will soon become Archbishop of Westminster and a cardinal. 'A very honest man . . .' I hear from well-known Catholic intellectuals like John Todd, Norman St John-Stevas, the Earl of Longford, the Benedictine abbot Christopher Butler and the former Archbishop of Bombay, Thomas D. Roberts, how it is only since John XXIII that the Catholic intelligentsia of England have been able to get an effective hearing in the face of the Irish-English episcopate, which is imprisoned in anti-modernism.

One thing is correct. The book is even more a success among Anglicans than among Catholics: 'You should all look at it!' exclaims Lord Fisher, Archbishop of Canterbury. 'I have never read such a book in my life!' And the *Church of England Newspaper* says: 'It approaches the almost cosmic cleavage between Rome and the Rest with a frankness and shining honesty which must be without precedent or parallel . . . The cause of reunion will substantially advance if this little work becomes a bestseller.' From the English-speaking world around 150 reviews of this little book find their way into our archive: most are an invitation to read the book, often described as 'a must' for Catholics, and at any rate as the one book that one should read if one wants to read anything about the Council.

And America? A contract is immediately signed with the American branch of Sheed and Ward in New York. I am to delete and initial anything that I don't like says Sheed's son-in-law, the director Neil Middleton, with a laugh. Since then I always read contracts for books carefully, even if this is a tedious business. Amazed, Tom Burns, among other things editor of the influential Catholic *The Tablet*, passes the news on to other publishers. *The Council and Reunion* appears in New York on 28 March 1962 with the even clearer title which I originally had in mind, *The Council, Reform and Reunion*.

A few weeks later *Time Magazine* publishes a full-page article on the book under the title 'A Second Reformation, for Both Catholics and Protestants' (8 June 1962). There are also three portrait photographs: between Luther and Pope John XXIII, Hans Küng with the caption 'Reuniting is not necessarily returning or capitulating'. I am somewhat afraid that this arrangement of pictures could arouse sleeping dogs in the Vatican; after all, with good reason I have not yet allowed an Italian edition of the book. But at the same time I am enormously delighted. For anyone who appears like this in *Time Magazine* has received the highest accolade of American journalism – which is important for the future. Respected representatives of both Catholic (Gregory Baum, Avery Dulles, Andrew Greeley) and Protestant theology (Robert McAfee Brown, Claude Nelson) express themselves at length and approvingly on the book.

What impresses *Time Magazine*, the paper of Henry Luce, whom I will also get to know personally during the Council? Three sub-headings indicate this: the admittedly 'fallible infallibility', the 'sympathy for Luther' and the 'forgive us our sins'. The following demands for reform are emphasized:

- a doctrinal statement on the role of the episcopate that would restore the office of bishop 'to its full value' and limit the tendency towards 'Roman centralism';
- liturgical reforms that would allow bishops and diocesan councils wide liberty to create rites suitable for local needs;
- reform or abolition of the Index of Prohibited Books;
- a declaration of principle on the role of the laity in the church and restoration to the laity of the use of the chalice at holy communion on certain occasions;
- and above all a declaration of repentance: 'It would be a truly Christian act if the pope and the Council were to express this truth: forgive us our sins, and in particular our share in the sin of schism.'

It will be 40 years (remember Jung) before there is a solemn public confession of sins by the pope and Curia in St Peter's, Rome, and even then there will still only be hierarchical talk – and singing – around the point (for example the Inquisition and the Holocaust). Nevertheless, quite a number of these reform demands of 1960/62 will already be met at the Council. The president of one of the most important Protestant colleges in the USA, Union Theological Seminary, New York, Dr van Dusen, will be correct when he writes: 'If this volume were to be taken by the determinative leadership of Roman Catholicism with only one-half, one-tenth of the seriousness it deserves, one could be safe to venture this bold forecast: the forthcoming Ecumenical Council would become the most important event in Roman Catholicism since the Protestant Reformation.'

Soon there are soundings in an attempt to lure me for a guest semester to Duquesne University in Pittsburgh (by Leonard Swidler, who did a licentiate in theology at Tübingen) or possibly even to a new chair for Catholic Studies at Yale University in New Haven (by Dean Julian Hartt). And after the faculty had 'unanimously and enthusiastically' voted for it, President van Dusen invites me to New York for a year as visiting professor. What fascinating possibilities! But not only do I have a chair in Tübingen, from the summer semester of 1964 I am also appointed dean. A lecture tour between Tübingen semesters would be more feasible.

The book is noted in important places not only in the American but even in the Communist world, in the Roman Communist party paper *Unità*, which emphasizes the call for greater autonomy in the local churches and the internationalization of the Roman Curia. And also in the key Moscow journal *Nauka i Religija* ('Science and Religion') of September 1962. The internal Vatican press service (Rassegna Stampa Internazionale) of 18 September 1962 rapidly passes on the gist of the Soviet article to all nuncios: according to the Soviet journal, the current tendency of Catholic theologians is well expressed in Hans Küng's book *The Council and Reunion*, which develops ideas that 20 or 30 years ago would have been condemned as heretical. Despite his traditional orthodox views on the timelessness, immutability and fixed nature of the teaching of the church, the author comes to the conclusion that the church must adapt and needs criticism: 'After the Soviet author has once again recalled that in the past the slightest "criticism" of Catholic doctrine has been condemned, now the dissemination of Küng's theses bears witness to the deep dissatisfaction of believers with the attitude of the church to the problems of the world.' Somewhat disturbed, I ask myself what the reactions to such an article will be in the Curia and the papal diplomatic service? Much is uncertain.

A link with John XXIII

From London, on 6 August I travel on to Oxford, England's oldest and, along with Cambridge, most famous university, to polish up my English before the

Council. In Oxford I stay with some vacation guests in the Old Palace, which belongs to the Catholic chaplaincy, under the leadership of the congenial and skilled chaplain Michael Hollings, who like chaplain Werners in Münster would surely have become a good bishop – had he been more conformist in his behaviour. I am a guest in the Jesuits' Campion Hall, in the Dominicans' Blackfriars – and also go to stay in the Benedictines' Downside Abbey (near Bath). I not only enjoy the big parks, which are always green, but also go punting on the Thames or the Cherwell: there is also punting on the Neckar in Tübingen.

Opposite our Old Palace is the grand college Christ Church, presided over by Dr Henry Chadwick as Dean and Regius Professor of Divinity, Oxford's highest ranking professor. With this extremely learned Anglican theologian I can easily arrive at an understanding on every possible ecumenical question. I also play an active part there in a eucharist and enjoy Chadwick's invitation to the splendid Christ Church hall: he will later often be my guest in Tübingen. The bonds of friendship remain.

My knowledge of English makes progress with the help of my Scottish friend Peter Nelson, a Catholic theologian, and I am finally capable not only of giving an extended interview for the BBC but also on 30 August a half-hour lecture, 'Has the Council Come too Soon?', which is broadcast by the BBC on the Sunday before the Council. One day my friend Peter tells me with a mock-threatening laugh that soon we will have a Vatican Monsignore to stay with us, so I should watch out. I reply that I have no fear of such contacts. In fact soon an Italian prelate does appear, by the name of Antonio Travia, one of those shrewd, modest and congenial Curia officials who quietly do their duty in the Vatican. For a long time Travia was the substitute Montini's right hand in the Secretariat of State. He is highly delighted to find in me someone educated in Rome with whom he can carry on a conversation in Italian without difficulty. *Vedremo*, we shall see what comes of that.

Our conversations show me that the Monsignore is not in principle anti-pathetic to reform. So I go all the way; in a bookshop I buy the French edition of my book on the Council – which is easier for him to understand – and present it to him with a friendly dedication. Because of a single translation mistake in the French edition (the laity are said to be 'part of the hierarchy') it had caused a great stir in the French media, and this has extended right down to the 'quite important church milieu' of the Vatican, as the chief editor of *Civiltà Cattolica*, Roberto Tucci SJ (later a member of *Concilium* and Director of Radio Vaticana, then the papal travel marshal and finally a cardinal), warns me in a friendly way. I brush it aside and reassure my two excellent French translators, the Benedictines Dom Evrard and Dom Rochais, with whom I am engaged in a friendly correspondence.

But how will Monsignor Travia react? He reads the book at a sitting and proves enthusiastic about it. He thinks that it must certainly reach the hands of John XXIII, since I have developed his programme precisely. We are together for only a few days. On 25 August I invite the prelate to dinner in a stylish Oxford restaurant. Previously I have bought another copy of my book for the pope himself, again in French.

I write a letter in Italian in the curial style, dated 1 September 1962, to John XXIII, the 'Beatissimo Padre'. Cardinal König has in fact spoken to him about my book some time ago, telling him that it has already been translated into a variety of languages. I allow myself to send a copy to the one who had the inspiration for a Council: 'My modest work is in fact meant to do no more than bring out the programmatic line which Your Holiness has drawn for the Second Vatican Council, orientated on the renewal of all Christians through the renewal of Catholic life.' Monsignor Antonio Travia takes the book and letter with him back to Rome, where he is now Consigliere of the Vatican Embassy to the Italian Republic, but has all the necessary links with the Palazzo Apostolico.

'His Holiness . . . has read it'

On that 1 September I travel back from Oxford and England across the Channel with my sister Irene, who meanwhile has been staying with English friends: we spend the night in Béthune in northern France and then return to Sursee via Arras, Reims, Nancy and Basle. September 4 is the official publication day for *Structures of the Church*. There are now only four weeks to the opening of the Second Vatican Council.

And Monsignor Antonio Travia? He writes to me on 21 September giving me the news *in via riservatissima* that John XXIII has already commented favourably on my book *The Council and Reunion* some time previously: 'His Holiness acquired a copy for himself some months ago and of course has read at least part of it.' Now the copy I sent has come into the hands of Fr Ciappi OP, Maestro of the Palazzo Apostolico, for him to read and express his personal view on. I will then get an official word of thanks for my gift to the pope. Moreover Monsignor Travia hopes that during my stay for the Council I will give a paper to his Gruppo Romano Laureati di Azione Cattolica. This meeting can take place as early as 14 October, immediately after the beginning of the Council. I am to telephone after my arrival in Rome.

In a letter dated 13 October the Bonn nunciature then informs me on behalf of the Vatican Secretariat of State that the book sent to the pope has 'met with his high approval'. 'The Secretary of State informs Your Worthiness of the satisfaction of the Holy Father for the expression of your obedient respect and communicates to you his apostolic blessing as a pledge of divine grace.'

Attached anonymously are 'some remarks which have been made on your work by the Secretariat of State of the relevant place'. So they come from the Dominican Luigi Ciappi, the pope's highly conservative court theologian. At any rate general 'advantages' of the work are praised: 'a valuable contribution to clarifications, deepenings and stimuli in respect of the problem of unity between the Christian confessions, through "the return to unity" which our Lord wills, after a previous renewal of all confessions not excluding those of the Roman Catholic Church'.

However, defects which I am warned about are that the book emphasizes the responsibilities and the obligations of the Catholic Church, 'while in some respects passing over the responsibilities and obligations of dissidents or showing a degree of consideration for them more than is appropriate'. Hence 'the not unfounded impression that there is a certain levelling down between the Catholic Church and the dissident churches and therefore an eirenism which is not completely orthodox'. Then come some detailed observations along the lines of Roman scholastic theology, not dissimilar to the objections that Cardinal Döpfner expressed earlier.

More to the point is what Monsignor Jan Willebrands had already written to me on 18 July 1962: if Archbishop Heenan says that my book on the Council has met with little attention and approval among Catholics, that makes it 'quite clear that it arouses the most understanding and goodwill for the Council among non-Catholics, and to no less a degree also represents a call to the conscience of Catholics about the true significance and task of the Council. Indirectly this book has also become very important for the work of our Secretariat.'

However, he is still not 'convinced that it has been good for the real success of the book that it has not been translated into Italian'. The Sanctum Officium has always made efforts to protect the faithful from the truth, particularly in Italy. Only at the end of the Council, in 1965, does an Italian edition appear.

Meanwhile, however, as I suggest, my new book *Structures of the Church* has already been sent to important figures in Rome. Cardinal Bea expresses his 'best thanks for the book' with the handwritten addition 'See you soon.' Fr Tromp also replies that because of much urgent work he has not yet had time to read the whole book, but he has read enough to note: '*multa fecit tulitque puer, sudavit et alsit.* The boy has done and brought together much, has sweated and frozen.' This Fr Tromp, who always greeted me as a student in the corridors of the Gregorian with friendly waves and 'Ciaò', has a sense of humour. His letter ends, 'warmest greetings, Arrivederci'. We are in fact to meet again soon, under not such a happy sign.

Prelate Höfer, from whom I have not concealed my fears about *Structures of the Church,* writes at almost the same time: 'Your writings will not fall under any official censorship: 1. because there is no occasion for this in respect of the subject-matter; 2. because the pope would have to give his personal approval; 3. because you perhaps do not have as many unknown private enemies as my friend Karl Rahner.' Unfortunately Prelate Höfer, in other respects always well informed, was to prove mistaken.

VII
ೞಽೞಽ

The Struggle for the Freedom of the Council

'As President I would not take orders from any
Pope, Cardinal, Bishop or priest . . .
If any Pope attempted to influence me as President,
I would have to tell him it was completely improper.'

John F. Kennedy

A pessimistic mood before the Second Vatican Council

4 OCTOBER 1962, time to leave for Rome. It's a long drive with overnight stops in Sursee and Florence. Time to reflect. My mood is somewhat gloomy. On the journey I listen on the radio to a long report of John XXIII's pilgrimage to Assisi. It's the first rail journey by a pope from the Vatican (and its little neo-baroque station) since 1870, celebrated everywhere by enthusiastic crowds. What a brilliant idea, and how wretchedly it is implemented and reported! Papalistic waffle, a holy fuss – there is none of the urgent reference to the gospel and a renewal of the church which Francis of Assisi should have prompted. All this could have happened under Pius XII. And of course the pope also travels on to Loreto where, according to a mediaeval legend, after various intermediate stops the 'holy house' of the 'holy family' from Nazareth, borne by angels, was set up in 1219 in a laurel grove (Lauretum); the 'Lauretian litany' to the Madonna commemorates this. Is such mediaeval credulity perhaps to be the spirit of the new Council?

I arrive in Rome on 6 October and drive to the Villa Francesco in the attractive Parioli district, run by sisters. I shall be living here in the Via dei Monti Parioli for the next few weeks, taking meals with the Bishop of Rottenburg, Carl-Joseph Leiprecht, and the Apostolic Nuncio in Germany, Corrado Bafile – provided that they have no commitments elsewhere. A pleasant atmosphere: of course the conversations constantly revolve around what is happening at the Council; they're always friendly, but never go very deep. Serious theological controversies? This isn't the place for them. Be this as it may, I have evidently proved myself sufficiently for the two gentlemen jointly to propose in the Secretariat of State that I should also be an official *peritus* of the Council. So far I've been just the *peritus* of the bishop. As early as 20 November 1962 I receive the nomination from the pope along with the valuable Vatican *peritus* pass issued by the Cardinal Secretary of State. So I am once again right back in the clerical Roman milieu. As always, I don't need much time to get used to it. I am simply open to the people I meet. I pay visits in the first few days to my old professors at the Gregorian: Alfaro, Boyer, Tromp and Witte. And to my old friends: Feiner, Lengsfeld, Seibel, Thijssen and Willebrands.

The whole world is now talking about the Council. In Rome at the beginning of October 1962 no one has any inkling that at this very moment the most dangerous confrontation between the superpowers of the USA and the USSR is building up: the secret stationing of Soviet fighter planes and long-range rockets on Cuba. Here is a direct threat to the United States. Then on 22 October comes President Kennedy's famous television broadcast ordering a total sea blockade of Cuba. Finally the dangerous game is broken off by Khrushchev. Meanwhile the Council goes its way undisturbed.

On 10 October, the day before the Council opens, there is a first meeting of the German bishops and theologians, and in the evening a reception at the German embassy. The mood ranges between uncertain and bad. All the conversations centre on the excessive leadership role of the Curia, the draft texts for the Council decrees ('schemata') prepared in its spirit, and above all the lists it has made for elections to commissions, which contain mostly bishops subservient to the Vatican. Even theologians like Chenu, Congar, Daniélou, de Lubac, Rahner, Ratzinger and Schillebeeckx, whomever one meets, are worried, indeed pessimistic. There is virtually no trace of *'aggiornamento'*, of a pastoral attitude, of ecumenical openness, in the prepared texts. How will the elections and the schemata go? Aren't the open and active ones among bishops and superiors of orders a tiny minority – what can they achieve? Hasn't everything been signed and sealed by the manipulative preparation of the Council and its decrees over the past three years? Evidently the discussions are to run along safe tracks, as suggested by the Curia. The spectre of the unsuccessful Roman diocesan synod is going the rounds. People speak of a *'concilio lampo'*: a ceremonial 'lightning council' without any serious discussions. General Secretary Felici talks in terms of two months. But there must be no centrifugal processes, warn the men from the era of Pius XII, no 'confusing' of the faithful and the bishops by dangerous theologians.

In the end we abandon the 'call' by leading Council theologians to the Council fathers, prepared in Tübingen and agreed with Congar and Rahner, to postpone the completely inadequate dogmatic decrees in favour of the schema on the liturgy. We do this because our view is in any case widely known in the episcopate. But subsequently I will refer openly on every possible occasion to the doubtful character of conciliar dogmatic formulae and church structures. After all, I've done my theological 'homework'. The *Frankfurter Allgemeine Zeitung* of 28 November 1962 reports under the headline 'Dogmatic Theology at the Council': 'Hans Küng has been singled out for particular attention because of the undeterred objectivity and unprejudiced honesty of his book *Structures of the Church*, which has appeared recently. It is one of the most successful publications in the literature of the Council.'

Discord at the opening of the Council

Then comes that memorable morning of 11 October 1962. It is the eighth anniversary of my first mass in the same basilica. A grander scenario for an assembly of the Council is hardly conceivable. The procession of around 2600 Council fathers with their white mitres and liturgical vestments, from the Vatican Museums across St Peter's Square into this basilica through the crowds of people, is long and impressive, and takes almost an hour. Its grandeur and splendour are incomparable. For the first time, thanks to transmissions by Eurovision and Telstar, the event of the Council, which in earlier centuries was experienced only by a small intimate group, can be shared from beginning to end by millions of people in free Europe and North America. What an unusual sacral drama it is too for the 86 special government delegations and the 700 journalists who have come, many of whom have felt a new sympathy for the Catholic Church since John XXIII and the announcement of the Council. The photographs of the giant raised platforms on both sides of the nave (in Vatican I only a transept was needed) with all the bishops – and in addition, in the galleries, the raised platforms for the theological experts – find their way into countless journals and newspapers in the free world.

However, now the millions see from very close up not only much that is gripping but also much that is disturbing. And like me, many fellow Christians and non-Christians feel repelled by the completely outdated baroque pomp of this ceremony. So much faded splendour, so much empty religious solemnity – and because it's in Latin, it's in any case incomprehensible to almost everyone. Even many bishops – and not just those from Central Europe – find it sad that those in charge of papal ceremonial evidently haven't yet detected even a breath of the liturgical renewal blowing through the church.

But the decisive element lacking in this 'Mass of the Holy Spirit' celebrated by Cardinal Tisserant, the Dean of the College of Cardinals, is the real concelebration of pope and bishops, who only 'assist' instead of 'concelebrate'. It is a 'dry' pontifical mass – quite incomprehensibly – with no communion. All the bishops have had to celebrate their private masses beforehand, and the laity aren't admitted. In fact there are old formularies for the joint conciliar worship of the bishops with the Romanus Pontifex – but in the Curia this has deftly been overlooked. Once again the great Catholic tradition is passed over by the Roman traditionalists – in favour of some *'idées reçues'* – received ideas, which aren't actually very old. The Counter-Reformation confession of faith with the new addition about papal primacy and infallibility is in keeping with this. The pope pronounces it, but happily it is barely understood by the bishops and not at all by the non-Catholic observers.

270

Pope Paul VI Montini (1963-78)

Cardinal Josef Frings (Cologne)   Cardinal Franz König (Vienna)

Council moderators: Cardinal Léon Suenens (Brussels), Cardinal Giacomo Lercaro (Bologna), Cardinal Julius Döpfner (Munich)

General Secretary of Vatican II: Pericle Felici

Cardinal Secretary of State:
Amleto Cicognani

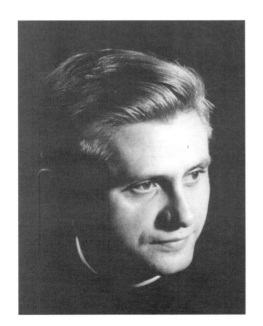

Council theologian Joseph Ratzinger
(Bonn – Münster – Tübingen)

Bishop Hermann Volk (Mainz)

Henri de Lubac SJ (Lyons)   M.-D. Chenu OP (Paris)

Discussion with Karl Rahner SJ (Innsbruck)

Yves Congar OP (Strasbourg)

Edward Schillebeeckx OP (Nijmegen)

Cardinal Augustin Bea with Professor Oscar Cullmann (Basle and Paris)

Cardinal Alfredo Ottaviani, Sanctum Officium

Cardinal Emile Léger (Montreal) Cardinal Achille Liénart (Lille)

Press conference at the Council with Bishop Carl-Joseph Leiprecht (Rottenburg)

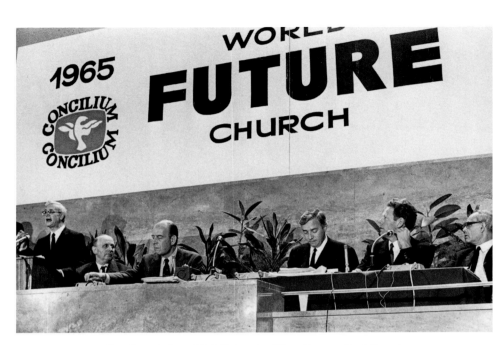

Concilium: Edward Schillebeeckx, Yves Congar, Paul Brand,
Antoine van den Boogaard, Hans Küng, Karl Rahner

Gregory Baum (Toronto)

Bishop Léon-Arthur Elchinger (Strasbourg)

The actual act of opening the Council isn't meaningfully incorporated into the celebration of the eucharist but follows as an appendage. What I, like many Christians inside and outside the Catholic Church, miss above all is a clear confession of guilt at the beginning: a confession of guilt by the Catholic Church, which is an essential accomplice in the splitting of Christianity and the misery of the world. The German episcopate made an impressive confession of this kind in its pastoral letter on the Council:

Since now in our homeland we face such a great spiritual wilderness, we cannot be content with a cool statement, but as members of the one body of Christ we feel partly to blame that so many brothers and sisters have gone astray. So we penitently say before God our *Confiteor* and *mea culpa* for all that we have failed to do to keep these Christians with Christ and his church or to win them back again. Our *Confiteor* before the Council also should not pass over the centuries-long stumbling-block of the split in Christianity. In Germany in particular, where the Western schism has its origin, we suffer especially painfully from these deep wounds in the mystical body of Christ. We cannot simply be content with them as an unalterable happening. Rather, we feel entangled by a thousand threads in the great tragedy of the church in our fatherland.

However, would such a confession of guilt have been in keeping with this triumphalist baroque framework? Even the gospel, a precious fifteenth-century codex of the Bibliotheca Vaticana, brought in solemn procession with candles to the altar by the grave General Secretary Felici and 'enthroned', is presented in a pompous way: it has been brought to be venerated, not to make a demand. What will be the *norma normans*, the supreme norm for this Council? Holy Scripture itself or all the many Roman traditions?

In any case there is much that is superfluous in this service, above all the 'obeisance' at the end, the show of obedience by the Council fathers, who have to kneel before the Pontifex sitting on the throne. This is the old Byzantinism: the cardinals and patriarchs kiss the pope's ring. Two archbishops as representatives of the episcopate kiss his stole. The two representatives of the superiors of religious orders even kiss his feet. As if they weren't all already utterly sworn to obedience to Rome! But they aren't at all accustomed to collegial, even parliamentary collaboration. This is particularly necessary for a council.

However, there is one ray of light in this ceremony, which lasts almost seven hours: Pope John XXIII. No one makes him responsible for the outdated pompous framework. We had heard beforehand that this time too the *sedia gestatoria* (portable throne) would be forced on him. But those at the end of the festal procession who see this man of over 80 slowly coming down the Scala regia on foot and only then mounting the throne borne by eight courtiers immediately get the impression that this humble and modest pastor of the church is completely indifferent to all the goings-on. He looks at the assembled Council in surprise: when he arrives in the nave of the basilica, he gets down from the sedia. He wants to go through the double line of his brothers in the episcopate on foot – as an act of respect. And then kneeling down he joins in the '*Veni Creator Spiritus* – Come, Holy Spirit' with a firm voice.

I hear later from Protestant observers – the ostentatiousness of this inauguration initially puts them off – how the earnest, inward-looking, prayerful face of the pope, never distracted by the liturgical 'business' around him, helps them to get over some of the incomprehensible aspects of the opening ceremony. Only when Papa Roncalli exchanges a few easy, friendly words with each of the cardinals who prostrate themselves before him (often laboriously) does the well-known smile of the farmer's son from Bergamo appear on his face. Simplicity, kindness, benevolence. If there is any good omen for Vatican II at all, it is that it is taking place under this pope, who radiates so much more of the gospel than some of his predecessors. And then there is his speech at the opening of the Council, which has extraordinary consequences and dynamics for the coming negotiations there.

The leap forward

I am excited at the prospect of this speech, which will perhaps indicate a direction for the Council. Pope John XXIII, on whom the Curia has recently pressed an 'Apostolic Constitution' in favour of Latin, is preparing it in Italian! '*Non mi parli di questa maledetta costituzione* – don't speak to me about this accursed constitution' – the pope had previously said to a cardinal close to me, 'but now I'm delivering the opening speech at the Council, and I'm writing it myself!'

Those who don't listen with Roman ears and can distinguish between what is important and what isn't will find long passages of this speech, which takes up the great conciliar tradition of the church, somewhat innocuous. There is no precise programme and there are no concrete instructions of the kind that Pius XII would doubtless have given. Instead, there is the demand for a particular basic attitude and the commendation of a basic approach. As John XXIII confided to his then secretary Loris Capovilla, 'Time and again I have looked across attentively to my friend on the right (Cardinal Ottaviani).' Seen from the pope's study, the Sanctum Officium is down on the right.

However, when looked at more closely, this opening speech adopts a bold and unmistakable position – against the doctrinalization of the Council intended by Ottaviani, Tromp and their allies. This is immediately recognized by most bishops and by the Curia. The pope is taking up a position against such reactionary tendencies. As we know from the reports of his secretary Monsignor Loris Capovilla, he has worked out this speech himself, bit by bit; as he himself said, baked 'with meal from my own sack'. In the key passages beyond doubt the Italian text is original; the Latin text betrays individual instances of orthodox toning down.

What, according to the pope, is the 'salient point' for the Council in the face of the ever greater gulf between the official proclamation of faith and the modern world? Is it perhaps a new dogma, perhaps a new declaration of faith? No, it is something that the Preparatory Theological Commission must regard as forthright criticism of its work: 'The salient point of this Council,' says John, 'is not therefore a discussion of one article or another of the fundamental doctrine of the church which has been repeatedly taught by the fathers and by ancient and modern theologians, and which is presumed to be well known and familiar to all. For this a Council was not necessary.' I hear Ottaviani, Tromp, Parente and Schauf gnashing their teeth – truly, this pope is taking our line! According to John, the salient point of the Council is the contemporary proclamation of faith and thus an exodus from the intellectual, terminological and religious ghetto: 'a leap forward (*un balzo innanzi*) towards a doctrinal penetration and a formation of consciousness in faithfulness and conformity to the authentic doctrine, which, however, should be studied and expounded through the methods of research and the literary forms of modern thought'.

'Modern thought'? Tromp later objects in the Theological Commission: 'We speak of modern man. But there is no such thing!' Isn't such a reshaping and renewal of doctrine blatant 'modernism'? The pope's clear answer is: 'The substance of the ancient doctrine of the deposit of faith is one thing, and the way in which it is presented is another. And it is the latter that must be taken into great consideration with patience if necessary, everything being measured in the forms and proportions of a magisterium which is predominantly pastoral in character.' However, the Secretary of the Theological Commission counters this once again: 'We want to be pastoral, but the first obligation of pastoral work is the doctrine of faith, to which the pastors then have to conform!' But my teacher in fundamental theology cannot prevent the bishops from time and again in the coming Council debates emphasizing the 'pastoral' character of the Council over against the doctrinaire curial party. And the pope has definitively also introduced the term for renewal and modernization, *'aggiornamento'*, into the official language of the Council.

But aren't there also errors, even today, and mustn't errors energetically be fought against? This at any rate is the centuries-old teaching and praxis of the Inquisition, its 'Holy Office'. Still, according to Pope John, a church which stands under the abiding truth of its Lord need not be stirred up by human opinions which rapidly change. It may counter the errors of the time with calm relaxation: 'At the outset of the Second Vatican Council it is clearer than ever before that the truth of the Lord will remain for ever. We see, in fact, as one age succeeds another, that the opinions of men follow one another and exclude one another. And these errors often vanish as quickly as they arise, like mist before the sun.'

But in view of the many errors of the time isn't the method of strict condemnation as indispensable as ever? No, Papa Roncalli commends the method of helpful mercy rather than any anathema (condemnation): 'The church has always opposed these errors. Frequently she has condemned them with the greatest severity. Nowadays, however, the spouse of Christ prefers to make use of the medicine of mercy rather than severity. She considers that she meets the needs of the present day by demonstrating the validity of her teaching rather than by condemnations.'

How can I fail to feel my views confirmed when the pope himself time and again declares that new dogmatic condemnations and moralizing admonitions are superfluous: 'Certainly there is no lack of fallacious teaching, opinions and dangerous concepts to be guarded against and dissipated. But these are so obviously in contrast with the right norm of honesty, and have produced such lethal fruits, that by now it would seem that men of themselves are inclined to condemn them, particularly those ways of life which despise God and his law or place excessive confidence in technical progress and a well-being based exclusively on the comforts of life.'

I feel my views even more confirmed by the pope's demand for ecumenical breadth: 'That being so, the Catholic Church, raising the torch of religious truth by means of this Ecumenical Council, desires to show herself to be the loving mother of all, benign, patient, full of mercy and goodness towards the sons who are separated from her.' The speech, delivered in such a hopeful tone, culminates in the demand for the unity of Christians, indeed of all men and women – contrary to the fear of catastrophe current among the 'prophets of doom', above all in the Curia, who 'in the most recent past and up to the present day note only abuses and false developments' and 'who always predict only doom, as if the end of the world were imminent'. At any rate this Council – unlike former councils – can be held without 'the illegitimate interference of state authorities, free from many worldly hindrances of the past'.

All these are truly new tones. In the new world situation which is developing this is no more and no less than what I would now call a paradigm shift, a change in the overall constellation. First, it is a clear rejection of a purely defensive and polemical anti-Protestantism. But secondly, it is also a rejection of a moralizing anti-modernism which is stuck in the negative. And in fact it is also, thirdly, the rejection of a sterile anti-Communism – the silence of the pope in this respect causes a stir far beyond Italy. There is a general awareness that Communism in Italy and France has not been introduced under pressure, as in the East, but has been chosen in free elections! Anti-Communism attempts to fight it by tolerating horrifying social abuses, along with great speeches, negative defensive measures and decrees of excommunication which can't be implemented – and all in vain – instead of overcoming it positively by a self-critical analysis of its causes and a constructive economic and social policy.

I ask myself: won't all this set not only the hard core of the Curia but also the whole of the Italian right wing in politics, economics and journalism against this lovable 'revolutionary' Papa Giovanni? Be this as it may, what is at stake is more than the *mondo piccolo*, the little world, of the militant priest Don Camillo, who in Giovanni Guareschi's cheerfully satirical novel deals in a friendly yet artful way with the Communist mayor Peppone.

Openness towards the ecumenical world

What a tremendous change too in the perspective on the ecumenical world: until recently! On the instructions of Pius XII the other Christian communities and particularly the World Council of Churches in Geneva were ignored as far as possible: no official relations. After all, these were 'heretics and schismatics'. Even now under John XXIII, who speaks of 'separated brethren', there is resistance from the Sanctum Officium, which previously had sole responsibility for all ecumenical matters, to the presence of non-Catholic observers. Tromp isn't the only one to think that ecumenism encourages 'minimalism'. But now work is being done towards the foundation of an independent Secretariat for Christian Unity under the wise and efficient leadership of Cardinal Bea and Monsignor Willebrands: both Orthodox and Protestant observers, mostly delegates of their churches, will in the end be invited to the Second Vatican Council. The previous narrow-minded practice of Catholic churchmen all over the world in avoiding representatives of non-Catholic churches as far as possible is thus ended once and for all.

However, even on the eve of the Council the Secretariat for Unity doesn't know where in the basilica the observer delegates will be placed – this is more a symbolic question than one of organization, and one for which there is no precedent. But now, at the opening ceremony, they aren't hidden in an inconspicuous corner of the gigantic basilica, as some expected. They are given a place of honour right next to the papal altar, for all to see. Nor will things be different at the sessions of the Council: when after the celebration of the eucharist General Secretary Felici proclaims the '*exeant omnes* – all (non-members) may go out', the observers may remain in their seats. This raised platform where observers sit is the best place in the aula (the name used for the space in which the Council meets) – right next to the presiding body of the Council and the Council secretaries and immediately opposite the College of Cardinals. From here, where necessary supported by translators from the Secretariat for Unity, they can often follow the whole event of the Council better than the bishops, and see and hear everything: the good speeches and the bad, the progressives and the conservatives, the unrestrained mutterings and the liberating laughter, the good Latin of those who fight against ecclesiastical Latin and the bad Latin of those who defend it.

The observers will be present when, to the applause of the assembly, a Curia cardinal is prevented from speaking because he has exceeded his time, when a draft decree is timidly praised or vigorously attacked, when it is accepted or rejected. And they can form their own opinions. They enter and leave the basilica with the Council fathers and the theologians. They are with us in the famous Council coffee bar in a big side chapel of St Peter's which has been suitably fitted out and immediately gets the name 'Bar Jonas' – in memory of Peter, the 'son (Hebrew *bar*) of Jonas'. It is here in particular, as in the broad aisles and the transept of the basilica, that so many opinions are exchanged and important contacts are made. Like the Council fathers and the experts, the observers also receive the schemata to be discussed and have a sight of all the Council documents. And unlike them, they may even report the proceedings of the Council to their own brothers in the faith. However, as observers of course they cannot vote.

Naturally I develop numerous contacts with the observers. The Heidelberg theologian Edmund Schlink, whom I have already mentioned on a number of occasions, and who represents the Evangelical Church in Germany, is important for me. Then there is my Swiss fellow-countryman Dr Lukas Vischer, representative of the World Council of Churches in Geneva, whose call to Tübingen is sadly later prevented by an intrigue in the faculty. And there are also Pastor Herbert Roux (Paris) of the Reformed World Alliance and Professors George Lindbeck (Yale) and Kristen Skydsgaard (Copenhagen) from the Lutheran World Federation: I will draw on the Danes in particular for advice about a speech (these speeches are called interventions) at the Council – on the abiding sinfulness of the church and the need for its reform. The representative of the Archbishop of Canterbury, Bishop Dr John Moorman (Ripon), and the two representatives of the Moscow patriarchate (after the ecumenical patriarchate of Constantinople had all too thoughtlessly declined because of the opposition to observers in its own camp) are also, of course, important. I talk with the two latter, Archimandrite Vladimir Kotliarov (Jerusalem) and Archpriest Vitalij Borovoj (Leningrad), about the situation of the church in the Soviet Union.

There are those who aren't representatives of the churches, but guests of the Secretariat for Unity: my Paris teacher Professor Oscar Cullmann, who has a high reputation in the ecumenical world; the Reformed systematic theologian G. C. Berkouwer (Amsterdam); Archpriest Alexander Schmemann (New York), probably the best theologian on Eastern Orthodoxy; and finally the two Taizé brothers, Prior Roger Schutz and Max Thurian. When they ask me during a dinner what they should be doing at this particular historical moment, I reply, 'Remain good Protestants', an answer which isn't meant entirely to please them. For all my admiration of their work for the young, which is so important, I have the well-founded anxiety that the founders of Taizé, pampered by the Vatican, are all too conformist to Rome and for example are suppressing the freedom of the call to remain unmarried in favour of the Roman law on celibacy. In fact they will later endorse Paul VI's encyclical on celibacy unreservedly and thus betray a central concern of the Reformation, which is backed up by the Bible. The fact that a few years before his death Max Thurian is ordained a Catholic priest completely confirms the fear that I've harboured from the beginning.

The observers certainly cannot agree with all that is said in the Council aula by Catholic bishops from all over the world. But there cannot have been one among them who didn't praise the confidence placed in them. And the fact that now the whole of non-Catholic Christianity – at any rate approaching half of all Christians are not Catholics – is represented in the Council aula is a permanent admonition to the Council fathers: in all that they do and accept they mustn't forget the unity of Christians but encourage it by every means. The course of the debates shows to a growing degree that the presence of the observers, who regularly hold their own meeting, is worthwhile. After all, they lighten the task of the Council fathers by following their deliberations not only as outsiders, but also with inner understanding combined with discretion, and often even advice. They are well aware that Rome was not built in a day, nor will it be renewed in a day. They note defects and weaknesses, but don't overlook the tremendous ecumenical awakening and the rapid progress which is already made during the first weeks of the Council. The Catholic Church now has an ecumenical orientation. That can no longer be reversed. Or can it? That is what I ask myself after the event.

The Council – a personality of its own

It had generally been feared that the Council would be just a great appendage and that the bishops would be puppets of the Roman Curia, completely dependent on the preparation by the Curia and subject to its rule. I had spread the slogan, 'The beginning is important!' From the time of our arrival in Rome we theologians and many bishops work energetically to resist the curial spoon-feeding, primarily in connection with the election of the ten Council commissions which will determine everything. The Curia hasn't provided for discussion about the members of these commissions. The Council fathers simply receive the lists of the ten curial preparatory commissions with the request to fill in sixteen names in each of the lists for the Council commissions. The wily members of the Curia hope that, for want of other realistic possibilities, the bishops will simply write out the names of the Roman preparatory commissions: $10 \times 16 = 160$ names! For many bishops this is an unworthy procedure. But what can be done about it? Intensive conversations behind the scenes and the preparation of an alternative Central European list!

On 13 October 1962 a small miracle takes place. In the first hour of the first session (General Congregation) the Council takes on a personality of its own. Against the will of the Cardinal Dean Tisserant and the Council Secretary Felici, who don't want any discussion, the highly-respected Cardinal Achille Liénart of Lille speaks from the table of the ten-member Presiding Council. In a short request relating to the order of proceedings, read in Latin, he asks for the election to be postponed for a few days so that the bishops can prepare for it better. He is interrupted by a long burst of applause. Then we hear the high, penetrating and clear voice of the Archbishop of Cologne, Cardinal Josef Frings, just as highly respected, who asks for a postponement, also in the names of Cardinals Döpfner and König, so that the Council fathers can get to know one another and the bishops' conferences can find time to work out their own lists. Even louder applause from the world episcopate. Only individual Italian cardinals exclaim, '*Scandalo!* What a *spettacolo* before all the world!' From the very beginning the great personalities of the Council make themselves known, and a German–French alliance which plays well together becomes visible as the core of the non-curial tendency. After a short discussion in the Presiding Council Tisserant announces that the cardinals' proposal has been accepted and that the Council is postponed until Tuesday 16 October to give time to prepare for the elections.

The Council has become itself! In amazement the Council fathers note that in fact what is maintained in *Codex Iuris Canonici* canon 228§1 as ancient Catholic tradition and since the announcement of the Council has seemed to me to be so important has been put into practice: '*Concilium oecumenicum suprema pollet in universam ecclesiam potestate*: the ecumenical council has the supreme authority over the whole church.' The strategy of the Curia, to safeguard their power over the Council from the start by means of the elections to the commissions, has misfired: the episcopal conferences, which are not much liked by the Curia but have now become indispensable in preparing for the vote, have been given a tremendous boost; even the Italian bishops, so far completely overshadowed by the dome of St Peter's, have to establish a conference of their own. And in the sight of all, the Curia has degraded itself to being the 'Roman party', which primarily advocates its curial interests, that are by no means necessarily the interests of the church.

This has an effect only two days later. On 15 October the Presiding Council decides by five votes (Tisserant, Liénart, Frings, Alfrink and even Ruffini) to four (Gilroy of Sidney, Pla y Deniel of Toledo, Spellman of New York and Tappouni of Beirut; the Argentinian Caggiano is absent) that instead of the dogmatic schemata the schema on the liturgy will be discussed, since fewer difficulties are to be expected there. This is a great victory over the decree-makers of the Sanctum Officium. From now on the Council more or less resolutely goes its own way, even against the resistance of the Curia. At any rate, from now on no quotations from the Codex or from papal encyclicals or from disciplinary decrees of former councils or of the Curia (for example '*Veterum Sapientia*' for the monopoly of Latin) may stop the bold discussions of the fathers on the needs and expectations of church and world – at worst they can put a brake on them.

The first document is passed on 20 October 1962 after around 40 speeches. It is a 'Message to all Men and Nations'. This derives from the initiative of the French Dominican Marie-Dominique Chenu. He had asked me to translate the draft into German. Congar, Rahner and I, utterly dissatisfied with the abstract and theoretical inner-church schemata prepared by the preparatory commissions, had already circulated it before the Council among cardinals and bishops: Liénart,

Alfrink, Döpfner, Suenens, Léger and Marty were the first to approve it. This *'Message au monde'* makes the goals and inspirations of the assembly clear to all the world: in the language of today the openness of the church to the world is to be proclaimed, the fears and hopes of men and women, Christians and non-Christians, are to be recognized, and their longing for peace, brotherhood and the advancement of the poor is to be taken seriously. But some French bishops, above all Guerry (Cambrai) and Garrone (Toulouse), had worked over Chenu's draft and 'baptized it with holy water', as Chenu critically observed. Thus the declaration unanimously approved by the Council is a text with an all too pastoral tone, substantially different from that of the prophetic Chenu, so that the message meets with relatively little response in the church and the world. Chenu himself will never be nominated *peritus* because he is too 'dangerous'. At any rate this message indicates that the church of the Second Vatican Council no longer wants to rule over the world but to serve it. I ask myself whether this will be put into practice, and if so, how.

But John XXIII respects the episcopal college of the church and generally protects the freedom of the Council, on occasion even with wise interventions which are welcomed by the Council. Linked to the Council aula by television, he is delighted at the lively discussion and in public he chuckles: *'chi va piano, va sano e lontano* – Those who go slowly go soundly and go a long way!' Is it any wonder that this pope – unlike the authoritarian Pius IX at Vatican I – enjoys the sympathy of the whole assembled Council? Except, of course, for the hard core of his Curia, which is firmly resolved to thwart any decisions of the Council that it doesn't like.

Since the construction of an absolutist system of rule in the eleventh century Rome has been interested in every bishop having the closest possible direct relations with the centre but not particularly close relations with his own fellow bishops. *'Divide et impera* – divide and rule' was already a slogan of the Roman emperors. 'No little councils (*conciliabula*) alongside the great council (*concilium*)' was initially also the Curia's cautious slogan for Vatican II. But the improved preparation of the elections has necessitated gatherings of bishops in which the bishops, who previously hardly knew one another, get to know and learn to trust one another.

Thus it becomes clear that the Catholic Church isn't just a universal church dominated by Rome but consists of local churches. The gatherings of bishops and episcopal conferences are important throughout the Council in many ways. Here the questions are talked through. Here numerous personal contacts are made. Here we theologians give lectures on the problems under discussion. Contrary to all the curial prophecies of doom, this doesn't lead to nationalistic encapsulation or federalist separatism. Quite the contrary. Only in this way does the comprehensive catholicity become concrete reality. It is not the Curia but the episcopal conferences which make possible a truly Catholic representation of the different national churches in the commissions and in the plenary sessions.

However, the Curia does feature in the commissions in yet another way: according to the rules of procedure which it has formulated itself, in all ten commissions a further eight nominees 'of the pope' are added to the sixteen elected by the Council (in fact contrary to the rules of procedure there are even nine on each). That wasn't even the practice at Vatican I: it is in fact a 'blocking minority' of one-third. This will make the work of the commissions, which in any case are all under the direction of curial presidents, vice-presidents and secretaries, extremely difficult; it will often block them and result in ambiguities and compromises on numerous important questions in the decrees. In this way a constant clash of Council versus Curia is pre-programmed and institutionalized in the Council commissions.

A Catholicity which embraces the world

However, it is good that the West–East conflict, which overshadows everything that is happening in the world, can be kept away from the Council. During the Cuba crisis John XXIII develops an inconspicuous peace diplomacy which wins him above all the sympathy of Khrushchev; this finally leads to the release of the Roman Catholic Metropolitan of the Ukraine, Josyf Slipyi (Lemberg). But national rivalries play hardly any part at the Council. It is especially welcome that French and German bishops in particular work together from the start. It is even more welcome that the episcopates of Germany, Poland and Yugoslavia, whose states maintain no diplomatic relations, can even agree on a joint Central European commission list. My bishop, Carl-Joseph Leiprecht of Rottenburg, receives the second highest number of votes among the sixteen members for his mandate in the Commission on the Religious Orders, after Bishop Gérard Huyghe of Arras.

Thus at least within the framework of the Roman Catholic Church a Catholicity is being practised which spans the world. There is an impressive representation of the different continents and countries, skin colours and rites. In the Presiding Council the cardinals of Cologne, Lille, Utrecht, Palermo, Toledo, Beirut, New York, Sydney and Buenos Aires follow one another in succession. The lists of the bishops who speak cover the whole globe. Countless links between every country and continent are made in this church assembly; anxieties and interests, problems and solutions, theories and experiences are exchanged. As in ancient times, the world episcopate really does seem like one great college in the solidarity of the local churches. But – in contrast to ancient times – this college is unfortunately still confronted with the tremendous power of a central Roman administration which has overgrown it since the Middle Ages. 'How will it all develop?' I keep asking myself.

The experience of freedom

Anyone who has experienced the oppressed mood in church and theology during the last years of Pius XII is amazed at the freedom to express opinions which has now broken through. Everyone makes use of it, and not just in the official statements in the Council aula. It is also found outside the aula in the countless conversations, discussions and encounters which make up the everyday life of the Council fathers and the theologians. The most incidental but probably the most amusing element of this freedom of the Council consists of the Council jokes which those taking part in the Council tell, or which circulate in the aula and rapidly also go the rounds all over Rome. For example, Cardinals Ottaviani and Ruffini summon a taxi: 'To the Council!' The taxi goes north. 'Wrong way,' they exclaim. 'Oh,' says the driver, 'I thought the gentlemen wanted to go to Trent!' Even better is the limerick:

> Rahner and Congar and Kung,
> Their praises are everywhere sung.
> But one fine domani
> Old Ottaviani,
> Will have them all properly hung.

The following 'prayer' circulates against Ottaviani in the aula: 'Dear God, open the eyes of Cardinal Ottaviani. And if your mercy does not succeed, then in your omnipotence close them for ever.' However, it is no joke that already in the Central Commission before the Council – allegedly after a speech by Montini – Ottaviani is said to have remarked: 'I pray to God that I can die before the end of this Council – in that way at least I can die a Catholic.' And if we are already at the 'life hereafter': Küng – the story goes – in 'purgatory' doesn't want to get out of the pool assigned to him as punishment for his theological sins in order to enter heaven. Why not? Because he's standing on Ottaviani's shoulders. However, the joke attributes to me a personal aversion to the head of the Sanctum Officium, and that isn't my nature.

In fact, though, of necessity my position becomes the opposite pole to this champion of the Roman view of things as the only true Catholic view. For a front against freedom in the church becomes visible: in the aula Ottaviani is regularly supported by Cardinals Ruffini (Palermo, a former collaborator with the Sanctum Officium) and Siri (Genoa) and the Irish Dominican Cardinal Browne. This front is also supported by most of the cardinals from the congregations, tribunals and offices, many Italian bishops and the newly nominated court bishops, together with their following all over the world: in the USA Cardinals Spellman (New York) and MacIntyre (Los Angeles), and Vagnozzi, the Apostolic delegate in Washington. Under the banner of the rights and privileges of the pope, this party of the Roman 'zealots' ('zelanti' and at the same time 'politicanti') is in fact fighting for the rights and privileges of the Curia. They defend their power over the church with the utmost vehemence and refinement, without shrinking from crass partisanship, Machiavellian manipulations and open breaches of the rules of procedure. Isn't the Council too much under the thumb of these people? That is my constant question.

Some of the Council fathers resort to ridicule to help them to cope: Cardinals Ottaviani, Ruffini and Siri are in a boat on the sea. A storm comes up and the boat capsizes. Who will be saved? Ottaviani? Wrong! The right answer is: the church. Despite the Roman party, the freedom of the Council is an unforgettable experience for all who take part in it. So many people experience it here for the first time in their lives in the free fellowship of the bishops. What someone often felt instinctively is clearly formulated here. What someone thought that he was alone in daring to think is shared by many others in the church. What someone only whispered quietly to his friends is here stated in the face of the whole church. Instead of the usual diplomatic caution and wisdom another virtue again comes to be respected which had long been forgotten in the church: the proverbial apostolic boldness. And everyone senses how this boldness brings freedom from anxiety, hypocrisy, inactivity. This freedom, fearlessly perceived in the Council, is now the presupposition both for a renewal of the church and for a reunion of separated Christians. There is no negative carping or destructive rebellion, but courage for constructive proposals.

What a change of fronts, a *'renversements des alliances'*! At the First Vatican Council in 1869 the leading bishops of Central Europe (who were by far the best educated) from the great dioceses of France, Germany and the Danube monarchy formed an isolated minority which made no mark on the mass of bishops from the little dioceses of Italy and Spain. So, resigned, they departed in silent protest before the definition of papal infallibility by the majority, which was overwhelmingly inclined towards Rome. Now, a century later, in 1962 at the Second Vatican Council the Central European episcopate, and with it Central European theology, have the leading spiritual position: they form the 'Central European block' (Belgium, Germany, France, the Netherlands, Austria, Switzerland). However, a new progressive majority can form only because the great majority of the bishops of North and South America, Africa and Asia, and even many from Spain and Italy follow the same line. The Central European block quickly develops into a world alliance.

That is the only explanation of the results of some votes: the French and German bishops in particular get the largest number of votes in the elections to almost all the commissions. So some of us Europeans have to revise our verdict on the church, say, of South America and the 'mission countries' in a highly positive direction. The openness of the well-organized episcopates of the continents beyond Europe for bold reforms is one of the great and welcome surprises of Vatican II. In this way what seemed at the beginning of the Council to be the 'tiny minority' has now proved to be the 'vast majority'. So some representatives of the progressive wing of theology, hitherto looked on with suspicion by 'Rome', note with amazement that their theology is significantly more representative of the church as a whole than they themselves had thought. Now it also becomes clear to some Protestant theologians that these Catholic theologians are not individual borderline outsiders but the representative advance party of the whole church, which is following slowly behind, and deserve more 'evangelical' support. But, I ask myself, in view of the leadership and composition of the commissions and the Curia-inspired rules of procedure, will the progressive majority and its theology be able to establish itself in the long run?

The monopoly of Latin as an instrument of power

From ancient times Rome has ruled, dominated and also manipulated with laws. The *leges*, the regulations, the order of procedure of the Council are thus extremely important for the outcome of Vatican II. This is particularly true in view of the numerically great imbalances which still exist: the Roman Curia alone has 115 Council fathers (in addition to the 30 Curia cardinals there are the dozens of titular bishops, some of whom have been newly nominated), Italy 379 (with those from the Curia and missions there are far more), while France has only 171 and Germany only 72 Council fathers. Formal rules of procedure can predetermine important decisions on specific material questions. Depending on the rule, a matter can be treated in one way or another, or indeed not treated at all.

There is widespread discontent about this: the rules of procedure worked out for Vatican II are more appropriate for a Roman diocesan synod than for an ecumenical council engaged in serious discussion. In any case, many bishops from colonial countries or countries with authoritarian regimes have virtually no experience of democracy. The rules for the Council urgently need to be supplemented. So far there is no possibility for putting direct questions about the rules of procedure. And how are those Council fathers who are not members of the Curia to formulate impromptu statements in Latin in perhaps a dramatic situation?

The reasons for Latin as the language of negotiation are traditional. For the Curia the monopoly of Latin is a question of power, because Rome rules over the Catholic Church not only with laws but also with language. It should be remembered that with the help of Latin and its terminology Rome defines and dominates the liturgy (Latin Mass), theology (neoscholasticism), church law (*Codex Iuris Canonici*), indeed the whole mentality of the 'Latin' Catholic Church. Is Latin the language of the church?

That's a myth. Regardless of the Eastern churches which speak other languages, above all Greek, the universality of the church is identified with Latin.

After all, the Romans tell themselves, what would be the primacy of Rome in the church without the primacy of Latin?

But it has to be asked: isn't it the will of the pope that Vatican II should explicitly involve itself in adapting to the new time? Shouldn't it be working towards developing a contemporary preaching (and liturgy) in contemporary language? And doesn't the use of Latin as the language of the Council also have considerable practical disadvantages? It can be foreseen that Latin will seriously hinder the discussion in terms of:

Comprehensibility: the state of many Council fathers' knowledge of Latin and their very different modes of pronunciation make it very difficult to follow the discussion with the necessary precision;

Liveliness: the statements to the Council prepared in Latin can hardly refer to one another and often become a series of wearisome monologues;

Freedom: in unforeseen developments, those who have not mastered curial Latin with curial deftness are decidedly at a disadvantage over against the members of the Curia. That is particularly true of the Council presidents and the cardinals, the only ones who are also allowed to make direct spontaneous interventions. Even the pope doesn't speak in Latin when he speaks impromptu, but – to the joy of many – in Italian or French. However, once, when devoutly addressed in Latin by the spokesman of the German episcopal conference, he translates the prepared Italian or French answer into Latin – it's terrible. Papa Giovanni remarks as he goes out: '*Oggi abbiamo fatto brutta figura!* – We've cut a bad figure today!' Even the Curia circulates many official Council documents (lists, voting cards, letters, etc.) in Italian.

But neither the public demands of the Melkite patriarch Maximos nor the interventions of Cardinal König behind the scenes achieve a change. Even the pope himself doesn't dare to allow other languages, except for the commissions. The practical solution would be a system of simultaneous translation. Cardinal Cushing of Boston, who doesn't understand a word and soon departs, declares himself ready to pay for its installation. But on one pretext or another the curial authorities manage to delay this until the end of the Council. Only the notices given by His Excellency General Secretary Felici are time and again repeated in different languages – why? So that they're understood. A Roman paradox – or rather a Roman power play.

Other improvements in the running of the Council are finally conceded:

Conciliar secrecy, an invention of Vatican I, is later restricted: the dry communiqués are preventing the interested public from sharing the experience.

Applause in the aula, initially said by the authoritarian General Secretary to be undesirable, but which breaks out again and again, is allowed; spontaneous applause is the earliest conciliar tradition, in which the unity of the Spirit is manifested.

The schemata to be discussed will in future be printed in good time, distributed in good time to those taking part in the Council, and put on the agenda in good time. Only when the discussion of a schema can be thoroughly prepared in peace is the success of the discussion guaranteed. This is particularly true of the great debate on the liturgy.

Why reform of the liturgy first?

Already in Trent and at Vatican I the Roman Curia was more interested in (its) dogmas than in reforms (relating to them). Even in the first volume of the draft decrees which have been prepared, initially there are four theological dogmatic schemata and only in fifth and penultimate place the schema on the liturgy! But as I have reported, already during the preparatory period, for Congar, Rahner and me and an increasing number of theologians and bishops the slogan that crystallized was: the liturgy first! And now, after the fiasco of the commission elections, the members of the Curia can no longer prevent it: by the decision of the Presiding Council the schema on the liturgy takes first place.

I'm happy about this decision for two reasons. First, because of the concentration on the pastoral and practical aspect: from the start I've energetically fought against a 'doctrinalization' of the Council. Then because of the concentration on the centre: in this way an 'externalization' of the Council is avoided, at least for the moment. The liturgy is and remains the centre of the life of the church. If this can successfully be renewed, won't that also have effects on all the areas of church activity? If it can successfully be given an ecumenical form, won't this be of fundamental significance for the reunion of separated Christians?

Reform of worship has been a central concern of mine since my studies in Rome. It has been said that the Reformation came because the Germans were pious and wanted to speak with their God in their mother tongue. From my youth I was influenced by the movement for liturgical renewal. With its roots in the German Enlightenment, and developed further in the nineteenth century by representatives of Romanticism in Germany and the restoration in France, in the twentieth century it is taken up by the Catholic youth movement. When I was at school I read Romano Guardini's little book on 'Holy Signs'. I grew up with the German 'pray-and-sing mass'; I was proud of my big 'Latin-German People's Mass Book' with gold leaf and ribbons (edited by that congenial Fr Urbanus Bomm OSB who then gave a liturgical summer course for us in San Pastore). In the Germanicum we discussed the liturgy a great deal – many of us found it all too stiff – with its countless bowings, genuflections, signings with the cross and other complications. At an Italian 'pray-and-sing mass' I attempted to involve the servants at the Germanicum more closely in the celebration. And as I have already related, the lectures on the liturgy by the Dutchman Herman Schmidt were the only interesting lectures in my unpleasant seventh year in Rome. Already at that time I made a thorough study of the standard work *Missarum solemnia* by the Innsbruck Jesuit Josef Andreas Jungmann, now a *peritus* with me at the Council.

This 'genetic explanation of the Roman mass' (to quote the subtitle) in two volumes is certainly a learned academic work for specialists. But those who know how to use it theologically have here an instrument for reform with an explosive force for church politics. Thus already in Lucerne Jungmann enabled me to work out something like a paradigm analysis of the mass for my sermons. One can help even ordinary churchgoers to understand the far-reaching changes in the celebration of the 'eucharist' ('thanksgiving') over the course of two millennia. Everything wasn't always 'like that' in the 'mass', which seems so eternally valid. And now I present this paradigm analysis at the Council in various addresses to gatherings of bishops. For I note that in this respect the state of knowledge of an average bishop isn't very much higher than that of the ordinary churchgoer.

However, since the time of the Reformation the Curia has vigorously contested reform of the liturgy, the vernacular and the people's liturgy. Even in the 'Central Commission' before Vatican II it opposed any decentralization to the conferences of bishops of competence to regulate the liturgy, and even more the introduction of the vernacular, concelebration and the chalice for the laity. Isn't enlightenment needed if one wants to gain majorities for reform in the Council? This is best achieved by lectures on the history of the mass. It is above all the lovable Brazilian archbishop Dom Helder Camara (Recife), secretary of the Latin American Conference of Bishops (CELAM), a man fully committed to the Council, who invites me to address such gatherings. Thus I speak in the Domus Mariae, in the Brazilian College or in the Chiesa Argentina. The unofficial meetings at which bishops, theologians and journalists from all over the world may speak openly and freely in their own language are just as important for the formation of opinion in the Council as the ritualized Latin sessions in the Council aula. During this time I also speak on liturgical or ecumenical questions to the Anglophone and Francophone episcopal conference of Africa. My contacts here are the secretary of the Anglophone conference, Bishop Joseph Blomjous of Mwanza, Tanganyika, and the secretary of the Francophone conference, Archbishop Jean-Baptiste Zoa of Yaoundé, Cameroon. He later sends me as a doctoral student Jean Amougou-Atangana, who becomes Tübingen's first African doctor of theology with a dissertation on confirmation; unfortunately he will be granted only a short life.

Coaching for bishops

The American Council reporter John Cogley writes me the pretty verse:

> I hope the Council won't decree
> that all that was will ever be.

In fact while I was an assistant priest I had already written: 'It was always like this. Was it always like this? And must it always be like this?' Is the authority of the bishops in matters of liturgy, the vernacular, concelebration, communion with the chalice an innovation? No, all this was also the case in former times, but it fell into disuse. Let's look, I tell the bishops, at four characteristic images of the mass from different centuries: a house mass in the second century, a basilica mass in the fifth/sixth century, a mass in the Middle Ages and a mass after the Tridentine reform of the sixteenth century. There are no poetic inventions here; everything is attested by the most recent historical research.

What is the 'mass' (a later name) originally? A thanksgiving (*eucharistia*) with a meal (*coena*) in memory (*memoria*) of Jesus Christ. I now pass on what for me was the decisive insight of my studies: originally the celebration of the eucharist had a very simple basic structure which was easy to understand: it is the celebration of a meal with thanksgiving = *eucharistia*, at the centre of which stands the account of Jesus' last supper. Its whole form is very loose, and only the essential outlines are laid down. Every bishop or priest shapes his liturgy largely as he thinks good, of course in the language of the people. So the earliest Roman liturgy is not in Latin at all, but in the then vernacular of the Roman empire, *koine* Greek.

So can't the 'mass' again become a family community celebration, in which all join in the prayers and sing psalms and hymns? Of course anyone who was present at the meal communicated, under the forms of bread and wine. Several masses side by side? Unthinkable. And if several priests (presbyters) are present? In that case they all celebrate a single eucharist together with the main celebrant: concelebration. Only in the magnificent Roman basilicas did everything become bigger, longer, more solemn: intercessions are inserted into the old simple prayer of thanksgiving. At the beginning of the eucharist there is an introductory hymn (*introitus*), at the preparation of the gifts an offertory hymn (*offertorium*) and at the end a communion hymn (*communio*). Only now are there the many genuflections, bowings, signings with the cross and kisses; only now are there also objects like incense and candles; only now are there special distinguishing marks like stole, ring and much else. Only since around 240 has the liturgy in Rome been in Latin and no longer in Greek.

But what have we all been celebrating up to this Council? The mass of the Middle Ages! It was Charlemagne who transplanted to France the liturgy previously used in Rome. Until then there had been no 'silent mass'. All the prayers, including the thanksgiving prayer with the account of the institution, were of course spoken aloud. Now numerous quiet prayers are added by the religiously emotional Germans. In time the priest even begins to pray the thanksgiving prayer and the account of the institution quietly. In any case the people do not understand Latin.

And what is the result? A disastrous alienation between altar and people which lasts to the present day: an incomprehensible liturgy; yet further ceremonial with an increase in genuflections, signs of the cross, incense; and finally even a spatial separation of the clergy in the choir from the people in the nave, often by a dividing wall (rood screen), later a lattice choir screen. The altar table, which stood close to the people, has become a 'high altar' as remote from them as possible, pressed right up against the wall of the apse. To the present day the priest no longer celebrates the 'mass' (more wondered at than understood) facing the people, but in part whispering to the wall. It is understandable that in the thirteenth century for the first time (initially against vigorous episcopal resistance) the sacred elements were elevated and venerated with genuflections. Out of sheer anxiety about sinfulness and the pressure of the confessional, receiving communion had become an exception, and then only in the form of bread. People wanted at least to look at this – now instead of ordinary bread increasingly an unleavened, snow-white, mysterious 'host' hardly resembling bread, often displayed in a 'monstrance'. And whereas in the early church all the priests celebrated one and the same eucharist together, now in our day each priest 'celebrates' his own mass and gets a 'mass stipend' for that. Alongside the sole altar, more and more side altars, even side chapels, have been built in churches for these 'private masses' which were paid for.

The mediaeval mass: the reform of the Council of Trent (1570) had indeed removed the worst abuses and excesses, but at the same time it specified all the details with instructions printed in red (rubrics) – down to the last word and the precise way in which the priest has to hold his fingers, which we had also had to learn in the Germanicum. But the people had no possibility of actively joining in the celebration! 'No wonder, dear bishops,' I say, 'that private personal popular piety with its emotions increasingly finds its way into the ever more numerous devotions: to the saints, and above all to Mary, behind whom the one mediator Jesus Christ often retreats completely into the background.' As they say ironically in Italy, '*Se non c'è Dio, c'è almeno la Madonna*' – 'If it isn't God, at least it's the Madonna.'

Return to the origin: am I going too far?

In the light of this paradigm shift through two millennia I can easily demonstrate what the celebration of the eucharist has to look like in the future. I attempt to convince the bishops that the Second Vatican Council faces an epoch-making task: a more marked assimilation to the binding example of the last supper celebrated by Jesus and the apostolic church, and thus increased concentration on the essentials and a more comprehensible rite. 'Do this in memory of me!' Do *this* – not something, however beautiful, however solemn, however accustomed! Hasn't what according to the Gospels Jesus celebrated and commanded at the last supper been almost completely concealed over the course of the centuries? Had the apostle Paul happened to have come to a Catholic high mass, wouldn't even he have had difficulty in understanding that this mysterious action was an enactment of the Lord's saying 'Do this in memory of me!'?

So my '*cantus firmus*' is that the present reform of the liturgy must once again make clear the original structure of worship given in the light of the New Testament. Hence two things are necessary: in the celebration of the meal itself audible, comprehensible praying of the simplified eucharistic prayer and proclamation of the account of the last supper. And in the preceding liturgy of the word a meaningful, shared praying and singing of the faithful along with audible comprehensible proclamation and (at least a short) explanation of the biblical texts which takes closer notice of the whole of Holy Scripture. For this it is necessary both to use the vernacular from beginning to end and to celebrate facing the people.

Surely that's all clear and consistent!? Yet as early as February 1959 Fr Josef Andreas Jungmann, who with *Missarum solemnia* had set the liturgical movement on a firm historical basis, responded to my article in the *Schweizerische Katholische Kirchenzeitung* which argued for the introduction of the vernacular: 'Content very good, full of compelling logic . . . But it seems to me also to be rather too sharp in some formulations (e.g. Latin – Esperanto), and sometimes also to go rather far in what it calls for, e.g. the vernacular for all mass texts spoken aloud. The first thing that is attainable and therefore is a priority is simply the readings . . . Perhaps I am too cautious. But I have already had some experience.' I too had my experiences: at that time the aforesaid article brought me a handwritten warning from Bishop von Streng of Basle (and a long effusion from a conservative Lucerne classmate). So are my proposals too 'radical'?

Even liturgical experts of whom I have a high opinion also think this, for example the leading German experts from the Liturgical Institute of the German Bishops in Trier, Prelate Johannes Wagner and Professor Balthasar Fischer, both eminent church diplomats, whom I had already heard more than once in the Germanicum. The Monsignori of the Vatican Congregation of Rites have already extracted some concessions, not least over the vernacular. They hope to achieve more through the Council, always starting from the German pray-and-sing mass. They had explained this to Professor Volk and me on the eve of the Council, when we were together in Gazzada in northern Italy at the Catholic Conference on Ecumenical Questions.

But now? Now in Rome, I object, it's no longer a matter of petitions to a Vatican authority. Now it's a matter of proposals for an ecumenical council. And this is superior to all Vatican offices. How long are we to go on waiting for reforms which Martin Luther quite rightly called for more than 400 years ago? Certainly not everything should be changed; the basic structure should remain. But people of today, increasingly under the pressure of secularization, need the whole liturgy in the vernacular now and not at some future time; they need the restoration of the simple, comprehensible, primitive Christian eucharistic prayer ('canon'), as far as possible without too many later additions, now – before the exodus from Catholic worship goes even further.

When I look him up in the Jesuit Curia during the Council, Josef Andreas Jungmann still thinks that would be going too far. I attempt to persuade him, as the expert with the greatest authority, to make a last moment intervention in the commission, since he is a member of the sub-commission for Chapter II on 'The

Mystery of the Eucharist'. After all, the morning Council services had shown how many non-Latin Catholic liturgies had preserved the eucharistic prayer very much more clearly than the Latin Roman one. All the Council fathers had been impressed by the fact that in some of these Catholic liturgies the eucharistic prayer and the account of the institution was prayed aloud, even sung, and ended with the people's Amen. So shouldn't all this be an encouragement not to let the reform of the Roman mass stop where it was needed most of all – at the centre? Our worship would be infinitely more meaningful, comprehensible, impressive, if the original unitary eucharistic prayer were restored: prayed aloud and of course adapted to the seasons of the church year. Isn't that in fact 'very good in content, full of compelling logic'? But Jungmann won't be persuaded to make an intervention.

Even during the first session of the Council I write an article of my own for the Vienna journal *Wort und Wahrheit* on 'The Eucharistic Prayer' – very much along the lines of Fr Jungmann – and also send it to the director of the Liturgical Institute in Trier, Johannes Wagner. He replies: 'In my view it is out of the question for the Council formally to concern itself with the matter. The Council debate is finished. It really has not touched on the point. Perhaps in the Liturgical Commission in formulating the *emendanda* (improvements) it will be possible to keep the doors open more systematically. Perhaps it will then be possible to ensure that the *Postconciliaris* (the post-conciliar liturgical commission) sees the problem.' I ask myself: why was and is nothing to be done on this central point even in the much-praised Liturgical Commission?

The Liturgical Commission on the Curia's leash

Here is a political lesson of the first order. In the struggle over the Constitution on the Liturgy – the best experts in the world like Jungmann, Martimort, Wagner, Lengeling, Diekmann, McManus and Vagaggini have shared in the work – I observe for the first time precisely how the Curia attempts to dominate with every means and to thwart the reform. The pre-conciliar 'Central Commission' to which all the schemata of the ten preparatory commissions go, and in which the later champions of the Council (Alfrink, Döpfner, Frings, König, Liénart, Suenens) are more restrained despite their criticism, had already given curial support to the schema on the liturgy in relation to the competence of bishops and the vernacular. Then in the Council Commission itself the president, the Spanish Curia cardinal Larraona, the new prefect of the Congregation of Rites, surprises the members right at the beginning of the first session with the arbitrary nomination of two insignificant but pliable members of the Curia as vice presidents. At the same time the outstanding previous secretary, Monsignor Annibale Bugnini, is dismissed (a ban on teaching follows for him!) and replaced by a conformist Franciscan. There is no protest. It's all a prearranged game on the part of the Curia, guided by Ottaviani and his Office, supported both in the commission and also in the Council aula by the phalanx of the Roman party.

So from the start the conciliar Liturgical Commission was on the Curia's leash. Often the members of the commission and the bishops in the aula had the impression that they were wasting time on the squabbles of the 'Romans' and on every possible dogmatic, legal and linguistic detail. Above all the brave Archbishop of Atlanta, Paul Hallinan, who knew that he had the vast majority of the US bishops and their signatures behind him, fought against this and both orally and in writing urged speed and concentration.

But each of us will always remember one event in the aula: the spectacular defeat of Cardinal Alfredo Ottaviani in this debate. The man who thinks that he embodies the truth of the Catholic faith talks on and on and ignores the bell. After ten minutes, as usual, there is a warning from the president; on this day it's the Dutch cardinal Bernard Alfrink. Ottaviani goes on talking. Another warning. Ottaviani goes on talking. Now Alfrink abruptly turns off the microphone. Ottaviani goes on talking but is no longer heard. This is an unprecedented humiliation, and even more humiliating for the Grand Inquisitor whom formerly even the pope hardly dared to challenge. Tumultuous applause for Alfrink! Ottaviani must have felt like the later Stasi chief Mielke facing the Volkskammer after the 'change', when for the first time he is shown how unpopular he is and then desperately exclaims, 'But I love you all.' Deeply depressed, Ottavini leaves the aula and shuts himself up in the Palazzo del Sant' Uffizio. Indeed, to begin with he won't even see friends, and boycotts the Council sessions for two full weeks. But he isn't missed. Then, unfortunately, he returns, resolved to fight on. A true Roman from Trastevere doesn't give up as quickly as that.

There is tremendous tension before the first major vote on the acceptance in principle of the schema on the liturgy, which has been opposed so vigorously by the members of the Curia. And what a surprise on 14 November: 2162 votes for and only 46 against! So the curial party doesn't even have 3 per cent of the Council behind it. Yet it could and can continue nevertheless to block or impose a great deal. Consequently some passages of the Constitution on the Liturgy, down to specific formulations (for example, the eucharistic meal is time and again called *'sacrificium'*, 'sacrifice', contrary to the Bible), simply represent compromises laboriously arrived at. That remains the decisive weakness of this reform of the liturgy: the church community doesn't have sufficient explanation of the ultimate issue, namely the assimilation of the liturgy to Jesus's last supper. It doesn't get as far as the renewal of the original eucharistic prayer and the consistent introduction of the vernacular. Like me, some bishops and theologians are convinced that the vast majority of the Council would have been quite ready 'to go still further'. Nevertheless:

Realizing Protestant concerns

Despite all the compromises and half-measures, the Constitution on the Liturgy represents a tremendous step forward in realizing the concerns of the gospel, particularly from an ecumenical perspective. In fact there are at least the beginnings of a greater assimilation of the Roman mass to Jesus's last supper. The proclamation of the word of God is again heard in a comprehensible way. There is active worship by the whole priestly people. The liturgy is adapted to the different peoples. And the three great controversial questions which arose with the Reformation have in principle been decided along the lines of reform: in future, at least in principle, there will again be communion with the chalice, concelebration and the liturgy in the vernacular, even in the Latin church of the West. Certainly everything is often unnecessarily restricted, but the spell has been broken. This is a first breakthrough at the Council. Later, further reforms will be carried through by a post-conciliar commission. There will be a revision of all rites, which are to become simpler and more understandable. There will be a revision of the rite of the mass which brings out the essentials and makes it possible for the faithful to participate; a revision of the priestly prayer (breviary), which is tightened up, simplified and abbreviated; a new rite of concelebration; new cycles of scripture reading for the celebration of the mass and the breviary. And there will also be regulations for the reform of the other sacraments.

So at any rate no doors have been shut in the face of further developments in the spirit of renewal – not even in the face of a further introduction of the vernacular, which according to the decree remains limited to particular readings, prayers and hymns. In fact because of the many compromises the new liturgical regulations are so complicated and inconsistent that even at the Council I adopt the pragmatic standpoint: the greater the confusion now, the more quickly there will be a consistent resolution after the Council. And that is in fact what will happen: all the reasons which are now cited for the celebration of some parts in the vernacular can also be cited 'with compelling logic' for the others. And quite specifically for the eucharistic prayer, the 'canon' with the account of the last supper. So in the end I am content with the outcome of the struggle. The unusual effort has paid off.

All this will have a grotesque sequel in Tübingen. In my regular Sunday celebration of the eucharist (11 a.m.) in the Johanneskirche, in the centre of the city, I have already put my liturgical principles into practice and seen that as far as possible everything is in German, audible and understandable. That is, apart from the canon of the mass, which I still say only in Latin – until finally after the Council this seems to me to be literally too dumb, and one day I also proclaim the account of the eucharist in German.

'Did I doubt inwardly, even tremble?' I am asked. Not at all. I had studied the question all too thoroughly, had already followed the German canon all too long. Even in Lucerne as an assistant priest and then and time again in more intimate circles I had practised what seemed to me to be both legitimate and pastorally right according to the example of Jesus, the apostles and the early church. So I acted in Tübingen – though now in the wider framework of a parish service before a congregation which I knew well – without any doubts, in the firm conviction that all this soon had to come back not only here but everywhere. In other words, I acted, as Catholics say in a humorous but serious way, in 'anticipatory obedience'. And this certainly pleased my congregation, which always also included many academics and students.

However, as I discover after the service, I meet with the utmost disapproval from the parish priest, Dr Fridolin Laupheimer, who was installed fairly recently, in June 1964. He is a pillar of the pre-conciliar Marian-Latin-Roman-orientated Catholicism in the diocese of Rottenburg. In the sacristy, in unholy wrath he presents me with the alternative: either the canon (eucharistic prayer) in Latin – or no more services in 'his' church! Whereas as always I celebrated the eucharist in a great inner peace, I too am now extremely annoyed, at such stubbornness and arrogance. But since legally as pastor he has the whip hand over me and regular Sunday worship is very important to me, I choose Latin. But I warn him that I will report this to the congregation, though he doesn't take me seriously. The next Sunday, after his sermon, I explain briefly and concisely why on the previous Sunday I prayed the eucharistic prayer (canon) in accordance with old tradition in the vernacular. And why I am no longer allowed to do this. Loud hissing runs through the church.

But even worse is to come for the parish priest: a week later Paul VI formally allows the canon in the vernacular. At the latest from this point in time this pious pastor and venerator of Mary, who regards those of different opinions as heretics or worse and loves to ply them with letters seeking to convert them ('I am praying for you'), does all he can to make Sunday worship in his church impossible for me. He will finally even abolish 'my' 11 a.m mass as unnecessary, and lose some faithful churchgoers in the process. Backward-looking in his whole attitude, he becomes more and more rigid. That reminds me of the great American liturgist Godfrey Diekmann, who nailed to the door of his Benedictine cell the warning 'Remember Lot's wife!' As we know, Lot's wife looked back, contrary to God's instructions, and turned into a pillar of salt. Godfrey himself will die in 2002 at the age of 93, without ever having looked back.

Turning away from the Counter-Reformation

We are in an ecumenical Council, an event of prime importance in church history, and for a long time the story of my life has been bound up with the story of the Council. So here again I must inflict some theology on the reader. Nothing had caused so much unrest in the preparatory period of the Council as the work of the then Preparatory Theological Commission under Ottaviani and Tromp.

And if I and others who knew the documents were in such deep gloom immediately before the Council, it was because of the schemata presented by this commission. As I had always feared, these were meant as far as possible to dogmatize along the line of the Councils of Trent and Vatican I and definitively decide all questions of faith that were still open, so that what 'Catholic teaching' is and is not should finally be clear to all. Of course Catholic teaching is identified with the teaching of the Roman Curia. That is why now the commission proposes a new form of oath. That is why there is a draft decree on the two sources of revelation, scripture and tradition. That is why there is another decree on keeping the tradition of faith pure (from God the Creator to spiritism and the fate of children who die unbaptized). That is why there is a further schema with eleven chapters on the church. That is why, finally, in addition to all this there are three more schemata on Mary, on the moral order, on virginity and marriage. In practice these are all without exception products of a school which is not representative of the whole church, namely the Roman curial school in which I was brought up.

What is the background? Modern exegesis was not taken seriously in the drafts that were prepared: the specialist exegetes were a negligible force. Nor could ecumenical perspectives prevail. The Preparatory Theological Commission did not feel responsible for this; nor did it consult the Pontifical Biblical Commission (which was too progressive for the Sanctum Officium), or the Secretariat for Christian Unity (which the Sanctum Officium thought dangerous). After all, it regarded itself as the 'supreme' commission, although neither the pope nor the regulations of the Council had given it this status. But it was spiritually and to a large part also personally identical with the *Suprema Congregatio Sancti Officii*, which fights for its 'supremacy' with every means. True, the Theological Commission, too, is newly appointed at the beginning of the Council, but it remains under the control of Cardinal Ottaviani, Tromp, the secretary of the commission, and members well disposed to the Curia who are directly appointed by the 'pope' – in other words a Roman blocking minority.

However, unlike the Liturgical Commission, the Theological Commission, the composition of which is by contrast completely partisan, has no luck in the first session, as is dramatically shown at the presentation of its first schema on 'the sources of revelation'. Is this an abstract-theoretical question? No, in fact it is of extreme practical relevance, though only over time does this become clear to the bishops with a Roman Catholic training. From where do we know what God has revealed to us? The Reformers are unanimous that the answer is Holy Scripture. And also from sacred tradition, Rome stubbornly asserts. After the general attack by the Reformers on the countless mediaeval traditions in piety, liturgy, theology and church discipline, Rome was extremely interested in protecting 'the tradition' and using it as an authority to defend the status quo (from the Latin translation of the Bible, the Vulgate, to the unbiblical law on celibacy). It is therefore no coincidence that at that time the Council of Trent had already devoted its first decree to the relationship between scripture and tradition. But even this Counter-Reformation council had guarded against speaking of 'two sources' of revelation and an 'inadequacy of scripture'. Rather, it spoke of the gospel as the one 'source of all saving truth and moral order' (*'fons omnis et salutaris veritatis et morum disciplinae'*).

Now at the Second Vatican Council there is a widespread conviction that a new concentration on scripture as the word of God is pastorally necessary. Since those meticulous investigations by my colleague Josef R. Geiselmann (1956), it has been clear that it was the post-Tridentine controversial theologians Canisius and Bellarmine, both Jesuits, who first circulated the *'partim-partim'* as the view of the Council: revelation is to be found 'partly' (*partim*) in scripture and 'partly' (*partim*) in tradition. So of course all Roman Catholic traditions, dogmas and practices which are not found in the Bible can be justified by the 'oral tradition' which allegedly likewise goes back to Jesus, and which has a greater bearing on faith and morals than the Bible.

As early as the summer of 1962, when I was able to look at the first volume of the Council schemata sent by the Vatican, as I said earlier, I immediately consulted our emeritus Professor Geiselmann on the draft on scripture and tradition and prepared a paper which then went above all to Congar and Rahner. This first schema on the sources of revelation also alarmed critical French-speaking theologians like G. Martelet and C. Moeller. During the first session of the Council especially the critical remarks (*'Animadversiones'*) by Karl Rahner and (anonymously) Edward Schillebeeckx, widely circulated in the Council, are essentially responsible for the fact that more and more bishops ask whether they can accept this schema at all as a basis for discussion. Numerous conversations and conferences with bishops take place, and also among us German-speaking experts, who meet a day or two before the general debate. We are convinced that this schema must be brought down. However, my view was that it made no sense to propose an alternative schema, as Rahner did on the basis of his specifically 'transcendental' approach – without gaining much backing. Even Ratzinger didn't want to join in that.

Only Fr Tromp's faithful follower Heribert Schauf takes a different view from us and later asserts that the whole meeting of German-language theologians was 'more a conspiracy and a political gathering than a theological conversation'. In fact the theological question had already long been clarified. But a Protestant theologian from Harvard University engages in intrigue with the Sanctum Officium against the conciliar majority (not the last Protestant theologian to curry favour with it): the Dutchman Heiko A. Oberman sends his fellow-countryman Tromp a confidential message (which of course Tromp immediately announces triumphantly to the Theological Commission) that he will write an article against the Tübingen scholar Geiselmann's interpretation of the Council of Trent. However, we are to learn of this only very much later in Tübingen, for Oberman will never write this article. After the Council, in 1967, he has himself called to Tübingen as Professor of Protestant Church History – of all things. There I will hold a peaceful joint seminar with him on the Tridentine decree on justification, but will have to correct his often very imprecise knowledge of scholastic terminology.

In the Secretariat for Unity it is above all the interventions of Cardinal Augustin Bea and the Swiss theologian Josef Feiner, who is always pleasantly clear, which lead to an amazingly clear rejection of the schema by the Secretariat for Unity. In the Theological Commission itself there is a vigorous argument on the eve of the debate: Cardinal Ottaviani, Fr Tromp and the assessor from the Holy Office, Archbishop Pietro Parente, crudely attack the critics of the schema and want to commit all members of the commission to the curial commission's draft. But Cardinal Paul-Émile Léger (Montreal) – by nature a gentle and aimiable man, whom on one occasion I drive back to his residence after a reception – threatens to resign from the Commission if he doesn't have freedom of speech in the aula, and finds widespread support for his stand. Ottaviani and the Roman party have to realize that they can't win the day: the session comes to an end without any consensus. And the first session of the Theological Commission in the first session of the Council was initially also the last.

A vote against the two-thirds majority

Of course in St Peter's on 14 November we are now all tremendously tense. How will the debate go? The impulsive Ottaviani is unwise enough, contrary to the agreement, to speak even before the official spokesman of the Commission, Garófalo. This leads to repetitions and impatience. He doesn't discuss the basic question of 'in part – in part', but engages in polemic only against the requirement that such a constitution should be 'pastoral' and thus implicitly against the pope's opening speech. But immediately after that the cardinals Liénart, Frings, Léger, König, Alfrink, Suenens, Ritter and Bea formulate their rejection of the scheme. Ottaviani finds few allies on the first day. He finds a few more on the second, when the Roman party speaks out more strongly.

What will be the voting on the scheme, which is set for 20 November? I recall how Congar asked me in St Peter's whether it hadn't struck me that in complex questions basically the bishops don't primarily want precise technical theological information but simply to know whether a theologian they trust is for or against the scheme. And the vote? According to article 39 of the Council rules, two-thirds of the votes of all the fathers present are needed for a final decision in the general congregations and Council commissions (apart from the elections).

In fact on this day the question has been turned upside down by a manipulation on the part of the Curia which is hard to see through in the dramatic moment of the vote: those *for* (not the schema, but) breaking off the discussion should vote '*placet*'; those *against* (not the schema, but) breaking off the discussion should vote '*non placet*'. Many bishops have not understood this: someone who is against the schema and for a continuation of the discussion must vote *placet* (there are 1368 of these); someone who is for the scheme and for carrying on the discussion must vote *non placet* (there are 822 of these). What was the fatal result of this perverse way of putting the question? Instead of those in favour – which would have made sense according to article 39 of the rules of procedure – now the opponents of the draft must have a two-thirds majority. Because of the misleading way of putting the question, the article on the two-thirds majority led to a paradoxical outvoting of the almost two-thirds majority by a one-third minority. The result is that to the delight of the Curia the completely inadequate schema on revelation remains on the agenda for want of 105 votes.

There is a tremendous stir in the Council. John XXIII is at first perplexed and then at his wits' end. Various objections follow, above all from Cardinals Bea and Léger. The pope considers and prays – it is said – far into the night. The next morning, during the Council mass, Cardinal Cicognani gives the flabbergasted General Secretary Felici a document with the pope's decision. The vote is in fact annulled, the schema is removed from discussion and not referred on to the Theological Commission. Rather, it is completely revised by a new Mixed Commission consisting of members of the Theological Commission and the Secretariat for Christian Unity with which the Preparatory Theological Commission had strictly refused previously to engage in any constructive collaboration. Felici hesitates for a moment, and then is forced to read it out. There is jubilation in the aula, and agitation and embarrassment among the members of the Curia. But in no way do they accept defeat.

By his wise and moderate behaviour during this debate John XXIII has given concrete evidence of the usefulness of the pastoral primacy in the church. Rightly understood, this doesn't consist in legalistic–absolutist dictatorship but in a supreme act of mediation and arbitration in favour of the unity of the church. On the basis of a mode of voting which has been made quite precise, in future it will no longer be possible to reverse a majority by reversing the question. The two-thirds majority is retained for the acceptance of schemata. But an absolute majority is sufficient to reject a schema or to postpone the discussion. However, isn't the new 'Mixed Commission' under Cardinals Ottaviani and Bea and secretaries Tromp and Willebrands a commission with a Janus head? How will things develop? When I pass Fr Tromp in St Peter's in front of Bernini's Confessio he no longer greets me jovially, but with a tense face. For him I now belong in another theological camp.

Conciliar theology gets organized

That same evening of 21 November 1962, when the two-source scheme is withdrawn on the intervention of the pope, the Dutch publisher Paul Brand visits

Karl Rahner at the Gregorian and again discusses with him the pet idea which he has cherished and nurtured for years: the foundation of an international Catholic scholarly theological journal. He had put this idea to Rahner as early as 1958 and had met with a refusal: 'We wouldn't be able to write what we wanted to write!' I too wasn't immediately enthusiastic when Brand visited Tübingen in April 1962. But now, after this successful vote, since large parts of the episcopates of Italy, Spain, North and South America and Africa have voted against, together with the episcopates of Central Europe, the situation has changed. Rahner agrees. The very next morning, 22 November (there are no sessions of the Council on Thursdays), Brand visits me in the Villa San Francesco and in the afternoon Edward Schillebeeckx in the Dutch College. Now both of us are definitely in favour.

Paul Brand has published *The Council and Reunion* in the Netherlands – he then goes on to publish all my later books. This publishing success has reinforced the publisher in his view that there can be a market for scholarly theology which is also comprehensible to educated laity and has an ecumenical orientation. Paul Brand is one of those rare publishers who can combine idealism and realism, a scholarly level and commercial interest, theology and the public. Since his early visit to Tübingen close personal relations have bound me to this Dutchman. It is he who advises me that because of my name and my knowledge of foreign publishers I can now make contracts directly, without the German publisher as an intermediary. And that is what I've done since then. He receives a manuscript of each of my books at the same time as the German publisher, so that the Dutch edition, like the English edition later, appears almost at the same time as the German. With the theological trio of Rahner, Schillebeeckx and Küng behind him and with the help of the Belgian Dominican Marcel Vanhengel, a capable organizer who has been recommended by Schillebeeckx, Paul Brand thinks that the new journal can definitely be launched. On the evening of 22 November 1962 our trio meets at the invitation of Paul Brand for dinner at Ernesto's in the Piazza Dodici Apostoli, with Bishop de Vet of Breda as guest of honour and the theologians Daniélou and Ratzinger, together with Berkouwer, Groot and Haarsma from the Netherlands.

Around six months later, on 20/21 July 1963, we meet in the Hotel Alfa in Saarbrücken with the liturgist Johannes Wagner (of Trier), the musicologist Helmut Hucke (of Frankfurt), and a good dozen other theologians who aren't Council theologians. They include my assistant Walter Kasper, proposed by me; Johann Baptist Metz (Münster), proposed by Rahner; and then P.-A. Liégé (Paris), T. Jiménez Urresti (Bilbao) and Anton Weiler (Nijmegen), all of whom are candidates for becoming *'directeurs adjoints'* to the directors of the various sections. Congar and Ratzinger, the Louvain church historian Roger Aubert and the American ecumenist Gustav Weigel have declined. Our purpose is clear: we want to found a journal which makes the central European theology that has been so successful at the Council also known in the other parts of the world, a journal which is addressed to bishops, pastors and laity. Rahner and Schillebeeckx give inspiring introductions about the significance and course of the new journal. Good proposals about the committee of directors and the various editorial committees, about audience, technical implementation and internal organization, lighten this constitutive session of the *Revue Internationale de Théologie Concilium*. *'Concilium'*? This attractive name was a suggestion of Brand's friend, the leading Catholic Swiss publisher, Dr Oskar Bettschart (publisher of my series 'Theologische Meditationen'). We certainly don't want to be the semi-official journal of the Council, but to work resolutely in the spirit of the Council.

When I ask whether instead of a journal in three languages (German, French and English) we couldn't publish a journal in several different language editions, Brand replies that this is possible in principle: in fact his publishing house has finally also brought out a big five-volume work on church history in international co-operation with publishers and authors in various languages. So it is decided to produce a journal in several languages (there will eventually be seven). In addition to Bettschart (Benziger), a key role is played by Dr Jakob Laubach (Grünewald), the Italian publisher Dr Rosino Gibellini (Queriniana) who was with me at the Gregorian, and then the publisher of the English *Tablet*, Tom Burns (Burns and Oates), mentioned earlier, and the Spaniard Sanmiguel (Guadarrama). But the Americans with Paulist Press form the strong financial backbone of the joint work.

A unique experiment is in the making: a journal which not only appears simultaneously in German, Dutch, English, French, Italian, Spanish and Portuguese, but which in ten numbers a year is also to cover the ten disciplines of theology, each with its own editorial committees: dogmatics, pastoral theology, moral theology, spirituality, exegesis, church history, canon law, borderline questions, liturgy and ecumenical theology. Only a Polish edition will be suppressed by the Polish hierarchy after a few issues. It is important for the future that here lasting friendships form which extend beyond disciplines, countries and continents. But back from *Concilium* to the Council.

Impulses for the reform of the structures

Only on 23 November is the long-awaited Draft Decree on the Church (Schema *De Ecclesia*) finally distributed. Cardinal Ottaviani's proposal to delay it by giving priority to the schema on Mary is rejected in the Presiding Council. The discussion begins only in the last week of the Council, on 1 December. Ottaviani himself as president of the Theological Commission introduces the schema briefly – with grim gallows humour: it is probably not pastoral, ecumenical, contemporary enough. The Cardinal's fears are confirmed: 77 ask to speak, most of them expressing sharp criticism.

Meanwhile Monsignor Gérard Philips from Louvain – I have got to know him in Münster as someone who can speak very well on the laity without attacking the mediaeval privileges of the hierarchy – has a compromise scheme circulating among the Council fathers. But above all the damning criticisms of the commission's scheme distributed among the bishops by Edward Schillebeeckx and Karl Rahner have their effect. Whereas Philips wants to mediate between Curia and Council, in arguments covering many pages Rahner and Schillebeeckx argue for rejection. On all sides there is criticism of the concentration on the visible juristic-social dimension and the neglect of the inner mystical dimension. To tumultuous applause attention is paid to the pungent criticism, right at the beginning, by Bishop de Smedt (Bruges) in the name of the Secretariat for Unity: he denounces the legalism, the clericalism (the church as a hierarchical pyramid) and the pompous Roman triumphalism of the schema (and indirectly of the Curia). There is then no less applause on 4 December for the forward-looking speech by Cardinal Suenens. This is about the orientation of the whole work of the Council on the church, in two directions: on the one hand the *ecclesia ad intra*, concentrating on the inner nature of the church, and on the other the *ecclesia ad extra*, the relations between the church and the world and the dialogue with its own faithful, the other Christian communities and the modern world generally. It is striking that the day after, on 5 December, Cardinal Montini, who hitherto has constantly remained silent, explicitly joins Cardinal Suenens and thus by distancing himself *de facto* from the Curia commends himself as a *papabile*, a papal candidate, for the progressive majority. Finally, on 6 December another *papabile*, Cardinal Lercaro of Bologna, speaks out along the line of Francophone and Latin American theologians for a 'church of the poor' (with practical consequences), but finds relatively little response in the Council.

But now there is a further bold ploy by the curial power block: immediately following Lercaro's speech General Secretary Felici reads out an ordinance issued by the pope on work to be done between the sessions. 'Because, remarkably, that is how the timetable turned out,' remarks G. Ruggieri cryptically and typically in his teacher Alberigo's history of the Council – an almost grotesque cover-up of the Curia's coup. Why? In this way the whole work of the Council is abruptly ended without any draft resolution – and thus a devastatingly negative vote on the commission schema is avoided. What is the consequence? This a priori prevents a clear rejection of the schema on the church that has been presented and the production of a radical new version. But in the period between the two Council sessions the duo of Ottaviani and Tromp in particular, who will not hesitate to employ any trick and manoeuvre (not even the policy of the empty chair in the Commissions) to block renewal, ensure that their old schema on the church (like other schemata believed to be 'settled') stays on the commission's table and thus remains a constant point of reference. However, at the moment of this conclusion without a vote and draft resolution on 6 December we cannot all see the whole scope of the manoeuvre, nor do we see the significance of the papal ordinance that the commission for revising the *Codex Iuris Canonici* is to have Cardinal Secretary of State Cicognani as its president and thus to be firmly in the hands of the Curia. In any case the bishops are more concerned about the giant mass of Council texts which haven't been coped with and the pope's terminal illness. And of course we are all looking forward to our longed-for return home.

On 8 December the end of the first period of the Council is celebrated with a solemn *sessio publica*. The closing service seems to be a substantial improvement on the opening service: the bishops not only 'assist' but join in the prayers and singing. Even Rome proves to be capable of learning. And yet – how glad I am, having often been plagued with homesickness, when after a long journey I again reach our winter Gotthard and drive under it to the Vierwaldstätter See, to Sursee. There is a happy reunion with family and friends and there are nego- tiations with the Lucerne authorities for a building permit for a little house by the Sempachersee. This permit is issued, and my uncle Josef from Zofingen helps with the financing. He is given permission to live in the house in my absence: the building can begin. Then back to Tübingen and two lectures here on 19 December on the results of the first session of the Council. At the same time I prepare all my articles and lectures before and during the Council for publication in a Herder pocket book: the English title will be *The Living Church. Reflections on the Second Vatican Council* (in the USA *The Council in Action*). I complete the manuscript on 23 December 1962, immediately before Christmas. The book will appear in Spring 1963 – in the middle of an exciting time for me.

Am I content with the Council? Not even the Constitution on the Liturgy was definitively passed. There were no sensational decisions. Nevertheless, I emphatically argue that despite the lack of decisions we can be content with the first session. A new freedom has broken through, much good has been set going, and strong impulses towards the renewal of the church can be detected. The church which is assembled and represented at this Council no longer gives the impression of being absolutist or totalitarian. However, the absence of the laity (present only in the persons of the non-Catholic observers!) is more than just a slight drawback: the representation of the laity as the people of God is part of a Council meeting in 'the hour of the laity'.

Nevertheless, the Council assembled here showed the Catholic Church in a new light. Not only was a world-embracing Catholicity represented in an impressive and colourful variety of rites and languages, races and cultures, nations and continents. Not only had a sum of individual bishops come together, feeling themselves to be the recipients of commands; this was truly the episcopal college of the church which, late enough, became aware of its own dignity, responsibility and authority. The connection, the cohesion, the fellowship, indeed the unity between the bishops, a unity which hitherto had been taken seriously only in a single dimension, in their orientation on Rome, is here experienced existentially in a completely new dimension. The unexpectedly strong activation of the college of bishops at the same time represents an activation of the local churches standing behind these bishops. Some statements were made in the name of a whole country or even a continent!

Of course the unexpectedly strong activation of the college of bishops and the local church resulted in a marked retreat of the central administration, whose subordinate executive function of implementing human law was emphasized at the Council as never before: a Curia cardinal with his vote was only one bishop among many. Finally, it was then above all the exercise of the papal primacy at the Council which made this credible in a new way: not as a quasi-dictatorial power of jurisdiction but as a restraining service to the church and to the college of bishops in the function of a supreme mediator and arbitrator. It is now evident that the church owes to John XXIII more than a new 'style': he is modestly exercising this highest service in the church in a way that is orientated more on scripture, on the example of Peter himself. And what is the result of this newly awakened sense of the church? It is the highly increased credibility of the Catholic Church, both inwardly and outwardly!

Between the first and second sessions of the Council I was now to be given a greater opportunity than any other theologian to work for the Council, renewal and the ecumenical movement: after all the lectures in the German-language countries I went on a big eight-week lecture tour through the United States of America and through England. But not all the Catholics there liked this.

A historic debate and a ban on teaching

It was a great shock: the headline over a long article in the Saturday edition of the *Washington Post* of 23 February 1963 – two weeks before my flight to the USA – was: 'Ban on Theologians Dramatizes Debate'. The university authorities had banned lectures at the Catholic University of America in Washington DC by the two best-known Jesuits in the USA, Gustav Weigel, the leading American Catholic ecumenist, and John Courtney Murray, the theoretical founder of a modern democratic relationship between state and church (he therefore appeared on the cover of *Time Magazine* and was publicly attacked by Ottaviani). They had banned the Benedictine Godfrey Diekmann, whom I have already mentioned, the most important liturgist in the Anglo-Saxon world and the editor of *Worship*, the leading US liturgical journal. And fourthly, they had banned the author of the book *The Council, Reform and Reunion*. I was in the best of company: Murray, Weigel and Diekmann in the USA, quite comparable with Congar, Rahner and Schillebeeckx in Europe.

In fact in the September issue of the *American Ecclesiastical Review* my book had been more vilified by invective than refuted by arguments. The author of the article regarded this bestseller as 'pure nonsense' and 'a ridiculous hodge-podge'. He stated: 'The time has not come, and the time will never come, when any "renewal" of this doctrine (revealed through Christ), in the sense of a reformation or modification of it, will be either permissible or requisite.'

Who was the author? Monsignor Joseph Fenton, 'a cleric of considerable weight, physical and mental', the *Washington Post* states – who has already been editing this journal for twenty years; for a long time he has been Dean of the School of Theology of the Catholic University and is so to speak Ottaviani's representative in the USA. It is this local inquisitor who engages in polemic first against Murray's support for freedom of religion, then against biblical criticism, and now against me. He is supported by another friend of Ottaviani, the Vatican ('apostolic') delegate Excellency Egidio Vagnozzi, whom individual bishops fear more than God himself. What does the 'historical debate now being carried on in the Catholic Church' turn on? According to the *Washington Post*: given that the Catholic Church is departing from the way which it has been pursuing since Trent and together with the Protestants is combining the full power of spiritual forces against scientific materialism, the question arises: What will win through in the human spirit: materialism, which takes no note of the fundamental mysteries of life, or religion, which believes in the revelation of these mysteries and an ultimate integrity of a supernatural spiritual power?

Whether or not that is a precise description of the question to be decided, certainly the analysis of the two camps by the *Washington Post* is correct. Most of the Catholic bishops of France and Germany, most of the Jesuits under the leadership of Cardinal Bea, the most influential Catholic laity, very many American and other bishops, and of course Pope John XXIII are positively for renewal. This camp has been able to establish itself in the first session of the Council and represents the majority.

But Cardinal Ottaviani and the Holy Office are against renewal, supported by the Roman Curia, conservative bishops around the world (including between three and five American cardinals), and people like Monsignor Fenton, who with the support of Rome is still capable of preventing lectures by distinguished colleagues at the Catholic University. But the authorities of the Catholic University, under strict episcopal supervision, show themselves to be 'embarrassed' in view of the countless protests, even from Catholic church papers, and consider how they can prevent further damage to the Catholic University and its academic credibility. However, it has now been made clear to me what a minefield I am entering if as a young European theologian I venture to tread on American soil. At any rate the United States hadn't yet entered directly into the Vietnam war, which three years later was to hurl American society into crisis. Only then will Senator William Fulbright's warning book *The Arrogance of Power* (1966) appear, a book which is again becoming topical in our day.

The United States: a remarkably happy set of events

The decision had been made for me at an early stage: at that Sheed and Ward party in London on 3 August 1962 on the appearance of my *The Council and Reunion*. An American Jesuit wanted to talk with me for five minutes alone. I am only just beginning to feel at home in the United Kingdom when this unassuming, kind Fr Francis Sweeney surprises me with an invitation to Boston. He has talked about my book with no less a figure than Sir Alec Guinness, who is enthusiastic about it; Alec Guinness had asked to be accepted into the Catholic Church in 1956, and in 1959 inspired the whole world as a British major in the film *The Bridge on the River Kwai*: 'a most profound and devout man', Sweeney writes to me later. Unfortunately there is no time for the personal meeting that Sweeney hoped to arrange.

So I am to give a lecture at Boston College, the Catholic university in Boston, in the framework of its centenary celebrations. For a European in 1962 America is still quite a long way away – for a theologian and a public lecture at any rate it is another world and therefore a tremendous challenge. But, I think to myself, if this American has the courage to invite the young inexperienced man, then this man must also have the courage to accept the invitation.

So on 9 March 1963 I fly from Stuttgart via Frankfurt to New York. Unfortunately I am then laid low with a foul cold, so that I have to stay in bed in the Brooklyn home of my hosts, Wilfrid and Missie Sheed. But for purely technical reasons it's quite impossible to call off a party given by the publishers in New York, invitations to which have been accepted by an unprecedented number of people. What is to be done? With a high fever I am driven to the Plaza Hotel on Fifth Avenue. In a big room I greet countless people whom I don't know, but who are extraordinarily kind. Then I give a brief talk. On the advice of the doctor I keep drinking Coca Cola and sweat profusely. When we return to Brooklyn I note that the fever has gone. Now I know what 'sweating it out' really means.

On 17 March I fly to Boston. With its four universities, Boston is the intellectual centre of the New England states, where now a change in structure is slowly being prepared for, from the traditional branches of industry like shipbuilding and heavy engineering to high technology and the service industries. My first public appearance in America is to take place in this city, first of all at a press conference, where moreover there are two or three dozen journalists and three television cameras. No one has ever told me how to deal with the media; indeed, though I am now 35, I have never given serious thought to the matter. I do just one thing: I concentrate completely on what I have to say. I have considered this, 'my cause', really well and now advocate it, though in often clumsy English, with conviction and power, with arguments and humour. Above all I am honest and direct, without academic fussiness and clerical unctuousness. When, decades later, one day Irish Television gives me a little film of a conversation with the press dating from that time, I cannot but be amazed and smile at the natural self-confidence with which the 'young theologian' – for many years that continues to be my title – advocates his cause. '*Rem tene, verba sequentur* – hold to the cause, the words will follow': decades later my friend Walter Jens, Germany's only professor of rhetoric, interprets the phenomenon with this saying by the Roman statesman Cato (Major).

But in the spring of 1963 in America I am speaking in a situation which is favourable in two ways. On the one hand I know that I have the backing of the reform spirit of John XXIII and appear with the experience and authority of a Council theologian. Later some of my opponents think that, 'combative' as I am, I need opposition, and that it is the dispute with the Vatican which has made me famous. The opposite is the case: my books and their cause have made me well known, and I find it most inspiring to speak with the pope and the Council to some degree 'behind me'. Like Thomas Mann, I could say that I was born more to represent than to oppose. And I have no desire at all to assume the role of martyr (which Thomas Mann had in view).

On the other hand, however, I also feel a bond with the then new President of the United States, John F. Kennedy. As a 35-year old Catholic European I would never have found so much of a response on the American continent without this first Catholic and second youngest President of the USA. Kennedy is only around ten years older than I am. He has taken office about a year previously: with the slogan 'new frontiers' and a memorable inauguration speech. I am to be deeply moved when I watch it again as it were live almost four decades later at a television showing in the Kennedy Library in Boston. Here an era of hope, new beginnings and reforms is being announced – after the Eisenhower years, which were sluggish in domestic politics and in foreign policy monotonously orientated on the East–West context. All this was in harmony with our intentions at the Second Vatican Council.

Finally, the Archbishop of Boston is important for my start in the USA. 'My name is Cushing,' is his warm and simple greeting in a rasping, smoker's voice. Cardinal Richard Cushing, who comes from poor South Boston, is an extremely popular figure in all circles because of his character and his beneficence. He lets me see that 'Hääns' has his full sympathy. I go with him, in purple cloak and biretta, and the Orthodox Metropolitan Athenagoras, all in black, to the gymnasium of Boston College. An audience of around 3000 claps as soon as we go in. Without any experience of America, where in any case everything is on a bigger scale than it is at home, I hardly know how to assess what kind of a reception awaits me there. And my theme could hardly have been more challenging.

The church and freedom?

'Very interesting,' a congenial colleague from Yale University, Professor of Jewish studies, had said to me in Tübingen before my trip to the USA: 'I know that there is the church; I know that there is freedom, but I didn't know that the church and freedom go together!' This remark already states the whole problem. May we honestly use the 'and' at all here? 'The church *and* freedom'? May we use it as a true conjunction, not as when one often speaks of 'Communism *and* freedom' and in fact means 'against freedom'? That American colleague was not a

Christian; presumably he would express his doubts not only about the Catholic Church but also about any Christian church. 'The intolerance that spread over the world with the advent of Christianity is one of its most curious features', remarks Bertrand Russell in his book *Why I am not a Christian* (1957).

In the face of this, only unconditional honesty helps. As realistically as possible I describe the phenotypic similarities between the Roman system and the Communist system. Then I go deeper with Dostoyevsky's accusation voiced by his Grand Inquisitor that the church has betrayed the gospel of Jesus Christ and the freedom that he brought. This is an accusation which also applies to the churches of Luther and Calvin: they too burned heretics and witches at the stake and practised or tolerated every possible form of unfreedom and capriciousness, authoritarianism and totalitarianism, though this doesn't of course in any way excuse the Spanish and Roman Inquisition.

My counter thesis is that everything that indisputably manifests itself as un-freedom in the church is not a revelation of the good, clear essence of the church but a revelation of its dark, evil perversion. In the light of the message on which it bases itself, the church in its inner being should be a sphere of freedom. A church which proclaims the gospel of Jesus Christ shouldn't bring people servitude but freedom: 'For freedom Christ has set us free' (Gal. 5.1). In all this I don't allude to personal experiences, though as a Catholic theologian I know what I am talking about. I am aware from my own experience that this freedom must be fought for time and again in the church. So I go on to speak of freedom as a gift and task, a notoriously difficult task: for the threat to freedom from within is in fact far more dangerous than the threat from outside. In the threat to freedom from the outside world the Christian can find protection, refuge and freedom in the church (this was soon to prove itself very clearly in the churches of the embattled German Democratic Republic). But in the threat to freedom in the church from within Christians can find protection, refuge and freedom only in solitude within themselves – in the refuge of their free consciences.

Here I am by no means thinking only of extreme cases like Galileo and John of the Cross in the prison of the Inquisition, or Joan of Arc at the stake. I am also thinking of the countless scientists, philosophers, theologians, politicians, known and unknown, who have been involved in severe conflicts of conscience – why? Because representatives of the church didn't keep to the boundaries set for them by the freedom of all the children of God. Because they confused God's rev-elation with an ideology. Because they exceeded their competences and involved themselves in pure questions of science, philosophy, politics and economics. It is infinitely tragic that particularly in modern times countless people have fled from the church, the original sphere of freedom, to seek freedom in the world. Here only one thing is of any use: more than ever, the church today, where freedom is threatened so severely from outside and from within, must try once again to be a truly hospitable home in freedom for all those who are well-disposed to it. I am surprised and encouraged that my speech is often interrupted by applause.

Freedom of conscience, speech and action

Certainly capriciousness shouldn't prevail in the church, but ordered freedom. But the manifestations of freedom in the church mustn't be suppressed. That begins with the freedom of conscience which is so often scorned and condemned; it is first recognized unambiguously by John XXIII in his encyclical *Pacem in terris* and, I say clearly, holds even in the face of dogma, which must never be accepted if it goes against the conscience.

But in addition to freedom of conscience there must also be freedom of speech, and in this connection there now follow words which immediately find their way into the media. They hasten ahead of me wherever I go and will make Rome annoyed with me: 'It would be a magnificent manifestation of freedom to take those repressive institutions which the church got on very well without for 1500 years, and which are unquestionably out of date today, and boldly and confidently abolish them: the Index of Prohibited Books; advance censorship of religious books and Roman inquisitorial proceedings in which denunciations are accepted, in which the accusers, the evidence of the charge, the order of procedure and all the acts are kept secret; in which the accused is not given a hearing, those who defend him are not admitted, and sentence is passed without stating the grounds for the judgement. Such methods surely offend against the gospel, not to mention the natural law we hear quoted so often. It is urgently necessary that the church today should clearly repudiate the methods of the totalitarian state. If in many fields, such as exegesis, history of dogma, comparative religion, etc., the Catholic Church has lagged far behind Protestant theology, this lamentable fact is not due to a lack of intelligence or unreadiness for work among the Catholic theologians, but to a lack of freedom.' The news will reach even as far as Rome: tumultuous applause regularly greets my words.

Finally, freedom of conscience and speech culminates in freedom of action. The principle of the totalitarian systems which violate human freedom runs: 'Freedom as far as is necessary, constraint as far as is possible!' Conversely, according to the principle of subsidiarity, the principle of Catholic church order should be: 'Freedom as far as is possible, constraint as far as is necessary!' Unity, not uniformity; a centre, not centralism: for the Catholic Church this is the demand of the hour. It is a programme orientated on praxis:

Freedom first in the liturgy: one God, one Lord, one baptism, one eucharist. But different titles, different languages, different peoples, different communities, forms of piety, prayers, hymns, vestments, styles of art.

Freedom secondly in church law: one God, one Lord, one church, one government. But different church orders, different legal orders, different nations, different traditions, systems of administration, customs.

Freedom thirdly in theology: one God, one Lord, one gospel, one faith. But different theologies, different systems, different styles of thought, conceptual apparatuses, terminology; different trends, schools, universities, different theologians.

I close with these sentences: 'When, in recent centuries, has the world had such great anxieties and problems as it has today? When, in recent centuries, has Christianity had such great chances as today? Only a free church, the church as the free community of the free sons of God, is capable of fulfilling these chances. Freedom in the church is not a theory; freedom in the church is a reality and a challenge. How much freedom shall be made real in the church depends – on you, on me, on all of us.' For the first time in my life I experience a standing ovation. It goes on until I've left the gigantic hall with the Cardinal and the Metropolitan. How relieved I am: I've passed the first test. I can confidently fly to Chicago, where 5000 people are waiting in McCormack Place. And then further, first of all westwards.

My discovery of America

Sometimes during my series of lectures in the United States I am asked whether I would like next to write a book about the situation of the church in America. It's an extremely attractive prospect, but not one for me. Even if one travels all over the country for eight weeks with open eyes and ears, from the East Coast to the West Coast, from the Canadian frontier to Mexico and back to the Midwest; even if one talks with countless people, with Catholic and non-Catholic Christians, with bishops, priests and women religious, with theologians and laity, in gigantic halls and small groups, in universities, seminaries, colleges and parishes, I think one has to be modest and recognize that at best one knows this great land and its great church only superficially. It would be presumptuous to write a book about it.

I had arrived in the United States with no fear, but waiting to see what it was like and perhaps a little mistrustful. I go away full of invaluable experiences. First of all I was impressed by the colourful variety of landscapes and cities. There are some pictures that I will never be able to forget: the view over Manhattan during a lunch in the roof restaurant of the Time-Life Building with the founder and head of *Time* and *Life*, Henry Luce and his staff. Luce asks me about the Council, the pope and Teilhard. Then there are Chicago's imposing lakeside; the hills and highways of Los Angeles; the plains of the Midwest and the lakes of Minnesota; Pittsburgh's Golden Triangle, renovated with amazing energy; Seattle, which with the sea and mountains is so very like my Swiss home town of Lucerne; Washington's dogwood and its gleaming white memorials. And finally – for me as for many perhaps the most beautiful city in America – San Francisco . . . and an audience of 6500 at the University of San Francisco. I can only guess what this experience in the USA may mean for my future. First I feel above all gratitude to the many friends who have made this possible for me and shown it to me.

But my special discovery of America is the experience of a church which after the beginning of the Second Vatican Council is awakening to new hope, new life and new energy. I speak of *new* life and *new* energy. For there have always been life and energy in the church of the United States. Time and again European visitors have to marvel at the amazing things that have been achieved here in just a few decades. For me it is a special honour at the end of my series of lectures in Washington to speak in the oldest Catholic University in the United States, founded in 1791. How surprised I am to hear there that the founder of this university, John Carroll SJ, the great organizer of the young Catholic Church of the USA, became the first bishop of the United States only a year before the university was founded. What a short time – only 170 years – and what tremendous progress! In 1790 a Catholic bishop and perhaps 35,000 Catholics. In 1963 around 250 bishops and 44,000,000 Catholics.

Those are dry figures, but one can recognize what it means just to found a church in the gigantic territory of North America when one is shown the first simple colonial church of St Louis on what was then the 'new frontier' of the Midwest and compares it with today's strong and dynamic archdiocese of St Louis in the heart of America. Or if one can admire the tremendous buildings housing the schools and charitable institutions of the archdiocese of Boston (1.7 million Catholics) and the splendid work of the Catholic organizations of Chicago (2.3 million Catholics). What, after all, does it mean in a city like Los Angeles, which goes on endlessly for mile after mile (perhaps 60 miles across, boulevards with numbers in the 16,000s), simply to establish the parishes that are needed, train priests, build churches and open schools?

And the same rapid development that I can observe in California (between 1940 and 1950 its population has increased by 59 per cent) and experience in Texas (in twenty years its industrial population has increased fivefold; Texas alone produces more oil than the USSR) had taken place previously in the Midwest and even earlier in the great centres of the East. It had become necessary everywhere with tremendous energy first of all simply to 'establish' the church in the parishes and dioceses. Only Europeans who haven't seen how much work, toil and money had to be invested here will be surprised that there isn't always enough time and energy left for theory and reflection, for theology and research.

Europeans may prefer the European state schools with religious instruction to a Catholic school system. They may find an officially regulated church tax better than the system of voluntary giving and collections, which consumes a great deal of energy. They may think that the integrated theological faculties in the great state universities are more effective than the diocesan seminaries segregated from the intellectual centres; but if they want to be fair, they will first of all recognize with respect and admiration the tremendous achievements of the American church with its countless universities, colleges, schools, hospitals and churches together with the often heroic dedication of the people who have given shape to all this. The Catholic Church with its more than half a dozen universities and almost twenty colleges is now accepted.

Three things in particular have struck me in connection with my lectures in the USA in 1963: 1. the quite extraordinary size of the audiences, even for America, on average perhaps 3000 (if there was sufficient room for them), but rising to 5000, 6000 and 8000, among them often hundreds of priests and women religious; 2. the enthusiastic approval of the audiences, which surprises me; 3. the echo in the media, extending far beyond the Catholic Church into the other churches and into secular circles. I am encouraged that my ideas for reform, which truly aren't just mine, are beginning to spread all over the giant country – in particular in the face of the obstruction by circles subservient to the Curia, which can be detected again and again.

For no one can be surprised that critical voices are also raised about my lectures. As well as Monsignor Fenton, for example there is Bishop George Ahr of Trenton, New Jersey; he is also an Ottaviani man, and his verdict 'nonsense' is quoted in all the church papers. The criticism comes most of all from people who haven't heard a word of my lectures and have read only one-sided press reports. As so often, the newspapers quote statements about more freedom in the church or against the Index and pass over statements about the need for order, respect for authority and the significance of the ministry in the church. Passing remarks made to journalists on problems which still need quite a lot of reflection (as, for example, on mixed marriages) are blown up into basic standpoints (one is amazed at how short the way is from San Francisco through agencies to a Swabian church magazine). But would one ever get to an end if – almost every day in another city – one were constantly to keep refuting and correcting?

By contrast, the not very benevolent criticism by Rabbi Arnold Jacob Wolf of Chicago in *The Christian Century* seemed to me to be partially correct and at any rate important. He argued that in my book on the Council I had not paid sufficient attention to the question of Judaism. My book, which clearly censures the persecution of Jews by the church and praises John XXIII's corrections to the Good Friday liturgy, in fact concentrates on the agreement between Catholics and Protestants. But I plan to make an intensive study of the history of the relationship between the church and Jews as soon as possible. As a theologian I make public statements on important topics only after thorough study.

The first honorary doctorate

One thing which particularly strikes me is the ecumenical revival. In Central Europe we have a lengthy tradition of ecumenical encounters, and for various reasons the church in the United States took a long time to get started. But now things are moving forward more quickly in the USA: with greater spontaneity, with more energy and with fewer traditional prejudices and exaggerated doctrinalism. Countless discussion groups and working parties have sprung up all over the continent in a very short time. There are countless new contacts between Catholic, Protestant and Orthodox Christians and theologians, and also increasingly between Christian and Jews. The Catholic newspapers and journals are full of articles with an ecumenical slant. The radio and television have an increasing number of joint religious broadcasts by Catholics, Protestants and Jews.

The growing number of ecumenical books (like *Christianity Divided*, *Dialogue for Reunion*, *The Layman in the Church*, *Looking toward the Council*) shows that a feeling for ecumenical theology has grown by leaps and bounds. It is also evident in the scholarly theological *Journal of Ecumenical Studies* planned in Pittsburgh and prepared by a very good international and interconfessional staff under Professor Leonard Swidler (an old Tübingen student) (it was later to be based in Philadelphia). I become one of its associate editors. The new interest of the laity in theology and theological study and the new initiatives by Catholic universities (like the University of San Francisco, Notre Dame, Marquette, etc.) is particularly welcome; this interest is being met by graduate studies and the possibility of equivalent academic degrees.

For a long time in Europe there have been ecumenical conferences in a small framework. But I have hardly ever seen so impressive an ecumenical gathering as that in the archiepiscopal seminary in St Louis, where Cardinal Joseph Ritter has invited me in his own name to lecture on 'The Church and Freedom' not only to all his clergy and all his seminarians, but also to all the Protestant and Orthodox clergy from the area of the archdiocese. I am more impressed by the fact that the kind, highly-educated cardinal sits in the midst of all these Catholic and Protestant clergy in simple priest's clothing than by some solemn entries of European hierarchs.

The annual congress of the National Catholic Educational Association is taking place at the same time at the University of St Louis. Around 8500 participants have found their way into the giant Kiel auditorium of the Opera House, where I am now being given a special academic honour: my first honorary doctorate. A counterpoint is deliberately to be set to the punitive action by the Catholic University of America in Washington, DC, immediately before my departure for America. Cardinal Ritter or one of his colleagues is said to have suggested this honour. Be this as it may, I am very happy when in a black robe and wearing the flat American doctoral beret I have the scarlet gown of the faculty of law thrown over my shoulders by Paul Reinert, the Rector of the university, and as a 'man of vision' I am nominated an honorary Doctor of Laws (LLD). For me such an honour is not primarily a personal ornament but a political symbol which is important for my task.

Of course people in the Vatican do not see it like this. They are enraged at this elevation of my person and all that I stand for. The Prefect of the Congregation of Studies and Universities, Cardinal Giuseppe Pizzardo, to whom I owe the silver medal for my philosophical licentiate, decrees as early as 25 May 1963 – Pope John is on his deathbed – a *'lex Küng'*, illegal because there has been no previous plenary session nor the approval of the pope: in future Catholic universities may not bestow honorary doctorates without the approval of Rome. And there is a new restriction on academic freedom to teach, which is defended by the Secretary of the Congregation, Archbishop Dino Staffa, in a press conference with the reason: 'There are so many *periti* who talk stupidly. If we were to give him (Küng) an honorary title it would look as if we approved of his ideas.' According to *Time Magazine* (20 September 1963), however, this also has to do with the publication of my critical lectures on the Council in a pocket book, *The Council in Action*. Translated into other languages it has had quite a wide influence. Fortunately fears of being put on the Index or being prohibited from teaching aren't confirmed.

There is also a strong response to the public interconfessional theological dialogue on church, scripture and tradition arranged by the Catholic University of Boston, Boston College, on 15 April 1963, in which with the French Jesuit Jean Daniélou I am allowed to represent the Catholic side, while the brilliant Americans Jaroslav Pelikan, historian of theology in Yale, and Robert McAfee Brown, a Reformed, but also politically active, systematic theologian in Stanford, speak for Protestant theology. Perhaps 200 Catholic and Protestant theologians from all over America (Protestants above all from Harvard and Yale) take part in these two days. Against the background of the Council debate I defend the primacy of scripture, the original tradition, for theology and the church, but on the other hand also the conscience, which according to Thomas Aquinas himself is the subjective criterion, even if objectively it goes astray. By comparison with the situation in Europe it is also an extraordinary sign of ecumenical convergence that regardless of questions of prestige, quite naturally on the first day the Catholic Bishop of Manchester (New Hampshire), Ernest Primeau, is in the chair and on the second day the Episcopal Bishop of Massachusetts, Anson Phelps Stokes. In this theological dialogue Cardinal Cushing gives a very constructive closing speech on the relationship between the Catholic and the Orthodox Churches: 'The Church as a Bridge between West and East'.

Of course there are strong nests of resistance in both the Protestant and the Catholic spheres. *The Wanderer*, edited by the Matt brothers (St Paul, Minnesota), supported by the theologically naïve former regent Monsignor Rudolph Bandas, is typical of the reactionary 'Roman Catholic hole-in-the-corner papers' which are now developing in some countries. The loyal Swiss-American Benedictine Placidus Jordan, who attended the Council for the Religious News Service of the USA, defends me against this friend of Ottaviani. At first encouragingly with a strong commitment to social justice and paradigm renewal, but left behind in the paradigm change that is developing, *The Wanderer* now in every number vilifies not only me but all the 'progressive' bishops and theologians as 'heretics' or 'modernists' with false and wrong arguments and character assassination. If these gutter journals were not taken so seriously in the Vatican (as were later *Der Fels* in Germany and *Timor Domini*, 'Fear of the Lord', in Switzerland – the clergy called it *Tumor Domini*), and supported generously by gifts of money from conservatives, they would have had no significance.

Cardinal Richard Cushing, a 'roughie', unlike the 'smoothie' Cardinal Spellman of New York, who has become important in the Roman Curia, observes that after eight weeks of speaking every day and travelling right across the United States I have become rather tired. He has maintained his sympathies for me, even after all the official turmoil over my person and my cause. When I ask him for an imprimatur and preface for the English-American edition of my book *Structures of the Church*, he immediately agrees. And I am encouraged when he adds that he will immediately put in an order for 1000 copies for his clergy and his friends. His preface with imprimatur of 27 November 1963 is also worth documenting, because it preserves something of the basic mood which has supported my first visit to the USA:

> I do not necessarily agree with every conclusion and every proposal that this priest and scholar makes; I do not doubt for a moment, however, his scholarly integrity or priestly dedication. My meetings and conversations with him in Boston and in Rome have convinced me of these. Christians in America are familiar with his former works on the Council. Indeed, in the American mind the name Hans Küng has been linked as few others have with the Council and Catholic theological renewal. He has done us a great service in this country – by his writings, by his visit, by his lectures. He has not always met with unanimous approval and agreement; but he has always won overwhelming admiration for his scholarship and his humility – the true marks of the Christian scholar.

It can easily be understood that such statements are also precious to me personally in view of all the criticism from the Ottaviani camp.

'An unusual visitor to Washington'

One of the most promising signs of the new time – I experienced it in Harvard, Yale, the University of Chicago, the University of California in Los Angeles and Rice University in Houston, Texas – is the marked interest of the great non-Catholic universities in Catholic theology, to which now increasingly also Catholic professors and students are finding access. No one will be surprised that here theologians like John Courtney Murray, George Tavard and Gustav Weigel, liturgists like Godfrey Diekmann, church historians like John Tracy Ellis, canon lawyers like Stephan Kuttner (he gets the new chair for Catholic Studies in Yale), sociologists like Andrew Greeley and also educated Catholic politicians like Senator Eugene McCarthy (Minnesota) and the Kennedy brothers (Boston) are held in high respect.

Moreover I may also count Eugene McCarthy, Democratic Senator of the State of Minnesota – not to be confused with the fanatical Communist hunter and

Republican senator Joseph McCarthy of Wisconsin (removed from office in 1954, died in 1957), among my friends. Together with his wife Abigail he has invited me as guest of honour to an unforgettable welcome dinner in 'the nation's capital'. Contact has been made by a mutual friend and *peritus* at the Council, the journalist Monsignor Vincent Yzermans, of the small but very lively diocese of St Cloud, Minnesota. In passing he has also told the senator the often repeated story which in his memoirs *Journeys* (1994) he later shifts to Rome: on an almost empty dead-straight highway in Minnesota I was allowed to try out his new Chevrolet and to his horror quickly got up to 110 mph: 'I drive as I do theology,' was my laughing reply, 'fast but safe!' However, I learned to drive in Rome, where at roundabouts rapid reactions are more important than traffic rules.

Senator McCarthy is a refined, highly-educated man and professor, perhaps a little too academic at a later date (1968) to win the presidency for the Democrats in an electoral struggle against the Republican Nixon. Among the guests are the German and Swiss ambassadors and the Spanish ambassador Garrigues (later a companion of Jacqueline Kennedy through Spain). Garrigues gives the best speech on Spain's greatness and terror, art and Inquisition, that I have ever heard or will hear. I too have by now become accustomed to saying a few words at every dinner and of course use every opportunity to canvass for my cause without Teutonic heaviness and where possible with humour.

The lecture at Georgetown University, where I am commissioned to bring greetings from the universities of Berlin, Bonn, Heidelberg and Tübingen, goes better than ever and lasts longer than usual. The tense silence lasts until the end. That afterwards, surprisingly, the professors and students of the Catholic University of America, whose authorities had imposed a 'ban' on me, give a reception, seems to me to be a late victory over the administration, which is orientated on Rome and the Curia. The canon lawyer Fred McManus, well known there, subsequently writes to me that this administration is now at least 'infinitely more fearful that its suppressive and oppressive actions may become known publicly', and Monsignor John Tracy Ellis, America's leading church historian, openly criticizes 'a decade of suppression at the Catholic University'. But I would have liked to have given the many people standing there in a long row more than a word of greeting and a handshake. The eucharist which I was allowed to celebrate in the family circle at Sacred Heart College gives me no less joy. A son of Robert Kennedy, the Minister of Justice, is the server, and a daughter of McCarthy's and a little Kennedy receive their first communion from me.

After the blockade with which the 'Roman party' seeks to prevent my appearance in Washington and elsewhere, my appearance at Georgetown University and the Catholic University is a double triumph. Mary McGrory, an important Washington columnist, catches the mood of the time well in her article 'A Theologian is an Unusual Visitor' (*America*, 8 June 1963). It's strange to read this again:

Hans Küng, youngest, most famous and perhaps most controversial 'expert' of the Vatican Council, was a recent visitor in Washington. His appearance caused a deep stir in a city which is accustomed to many guests. Never before has a theologian received such a welcome . . . 3000 people went out to hear him and sat in rapt silence while, for an hour and forty minutes, the 35-year-old Swiss theologian defined his message of 'Freedom in order'. He was given a standing ovation when he finished.

If one – it goes on – reads not only the press reports about the abolition of the Index of Prohibited Books and advance censorship of religious books, which had hastened ahead of him, but the message of freedom which delighted so many, this is 'not so much revolution as return – a restoration of "the royal freedom" which Christ has brought to the children of God'.

John F. Kennedy's new frontier

I have been interested in the politics of the United States since my youth; there is a great similarity between the Swiss democratic system and the American, to which it was assimilated in the nineteenth century. During my eight weeks in the USA, at every opportunity I try to make myself better informed. In Washington I am shown the Capitol and people are surprised that I know the function of, say, the House Rules Committee and the conservative–liberal composition of the Supreme Court. It is in political Washington that the climax of my long tour through the United States awaits me. On 30 April 1963 I am personally welcomed at the White House by President John F. Kennedy.

Ralph Dungan, since the 1950s a friend and assistant of the then young senator of Massachusetts, and present at the dinner given by Senator McCarthy which I mentioned earlier, manages the 'audience' for me at the request of Monsignor Vincent Yzermans. Early in the morning, accompanied by him and Joseph Selinger, the Dean of Georgetown University, I am taken to the White House and finally into the 'holy of holies' of the American administration, the Oval Office with Kennedy's rocking chair and the cabinet room, where on the individual leather seats I note all the famous inscriptions: 'Secretary of State, Secretary of Defence, Secretary of the Treasury . . .' Very much later I will get to know the Secretary of Defence, Robert McNamara, personally – then with completely changed views on the Vietnam war, which is now assuming ever more threatening proportions.

Now at the Council every day I had to do with 'authorities', with senior clerical 'dignitaries', distinguished by the purple – a former sign of dignity for emperors and kings – or at least violet, with a ceremonial ring and pectoral cross. These were gracious, friendly, usually rotund, in their long robes often seeming somewhat effeminate figures, but at the same time sacrally exalted 'by the grace of

God', since according to the current Roman view they have received their authority personally from Jesus Christ. But now in the White House I meet a quite different authority: the most powerful man in the world in a beige everyday suit, slim, smart and tanned, with no distinguishing marks, no medals, no ring, his left hand casually in his jacket pocket. Here is a democratic authority, grounded in personal qualities and supported by the will of the people. With a friendly smile John F. Kennedy extends his right hand to me. He has come from the traditional Wednesday breakfast with the leaders of Congress and introduces me. 'This is Mr Johnson, Vice President. And this Senator Humphrey, Leader of the Senate, and Senator Mansfield, and this the Speaker of the House of Representatives, John McCormick.' And he introduces me to these gentlemen with the words: 'And this is what I would call a new frontier man of the Catholic Church.'

Indeed, I stand for the 'new frontier', the renewal of the Catholic Church, and in my lectures applause breaks out every time I come to mention the new frontier of the Catholic Church. Here is an echo to which Kennedy alludes. A regular churchgoer, he has never concealed his Catholic convictions; time and again they have been the subject of electoral clashes. But unlike Al Smith, Governor of New York, the first and only Catholic candidate for the office of President at an earlier time (in 1928, the year of my birth), Kennedy succeeded in demolishing the resentment of the Protestant and the Jewish population. Not by quoting papal encyclicals and church dignitaries, as Smith did, but by referring to his previous conduct in Congress. As President, too, he practises shrewd restraint on confessional questions. He doesn't like being photographed in the White House with Catholic clergy. Doubtless the understanding of a new relationship between church and state of the kind that had been developed by my friend John Courtney Murray has helped him here, but even more the new understanding of papacy and church embodied in John XXIII and the Second Vatican Council. However, the Democrat Kennedy too has the impression that the sisters and priests are more behind him than the bishops and monsignori, the majority of whom are Republican sympathizers.

A free man with a free mind

Even if at a later critical distance some aspects of Kennedy's life and political activity may seem ambiguous, hardly any statesman has impressed me so far as much as John F. Kennedy. And even now the little bronze bust which his sister Eunice gave me on my second visit to Washington stands on my bookcase. At that time we visited the Kennedy Centre, where the giant original dominates the whole of the long corridor, though not in an oppressive way. And I didn't remove the head even when years later I read the unpleasant stories of the President's womanizing, which don't do much for his moral integrity. Why?

Even now I am still impressed by Kennedy's style: unaffectedly sovereign, natural, inconspicuously elegant, always retaining his dignity. And I am also impressed by his rhetoric: clear, direct, factual, appropriate, never too pompous, melodramatic or silly. And finally I am impressed by his mentality: a disciplined and analytical mind, at the same time thoughtful and bold, marked by self-confidence, openness and humour. When he was once asked by a schoolboy how he became a hero in the Marines, with many decorations, he replied: 'It was easy – they sank my ship.'

I also like the way in which Kennedy would not be impressed by generals or admirals and was sceptical about military indoctrination. But he also preserved a respectful, never devout independence of bishops and cardinals. Indeed in the election campaigns he kept stating that as President of the United States he would never accept any instructions even from the pope, even in matters of birth control. Kennedy is a liberal in the best and original sense of the word, who rejects a doctrinaire and aggressive liberalism.

That is so very different from what is customary in the Vatican court, where people are afraid of changes: '*pensiamo in secoli* – we think in centuries'! And where it isn't professional competence but the grace of the ruler (*persona grata* or *ingrata*) and personal relations that are decisive. Here for me Kennedy embodies a new style of competent, reflective and active government. A Harvard graduate with no fear of professors, from the beginning, more than any other president before him, he called in eminent scholarly advisers from the universities. Only the best are good enough for him as colleagues and conversation partners. And only with new forms of the decision-making process can the responsibility of the President of the principal Western power be exercised effectively.

At the same time Kennedy knows how to enthuse the young generation, not only of America but also of Europe. So at a very early stage he founds the Peace Corps under the leadership of the capable Sargent Shriver, the husband of his sister Eunice, with whom I will become friends a little later. Ralph Dungan himself is especially involved in outlining an 'Alliance for Progress' with Latin America, based more on reciprocal partnership, and then becomes ambassador in Chile. I will later read the biography of another close colleague of Kennedy, Theodore C. Sorensen, from the first to the last of its 880 pages, and mark important passages. It is to him that I owe the characterization of Kennedy as 'a free man with a free mind'. But there are also some parallels which I delight in: a great intensity of work and a rapid tempo, inspiring leadership and great demands on his team, the capacity to be able to sleep briefly at any time, even in a plane, a car or an hotel. Not a hunter nor an angler, but always fond of the fresh air and best of all of the water.

I am fascinated by the Kennedy phenomenon, the mixture of charisma and competence, personality and effectiveness. I am interested – in view of the weak leadership and structural problems in my own church – in the question of leadership and the possibility of changing great apparatuses and adopting new standpoints: how he deals with power in a skilful way, not, however, simply for power's sake and out of personal ambition, but as a duty for the nation: in this way something happens which benefits the whole commonwealth. At the beginning of his political activity, of course, he was simply out to win. But the more he grew into responsibility, the more important ideas and ideals became to him. As his great inaugural speech on 20 January 1961 shows, at a time of tremendous challenges both in foreign policy (the competition with the Soviet Union) and domestic policy (civil rights for the blacks) he wants to usher in a new era of hope: public service before private interest, fearless negotiations instead of fearful wars, new constructive relations between East and West, black and white, businessmen and trade unions.

Kennedy successfully fights inflation, boosts the economy and reduces unemployment. Of course he also experiences failures: he immediately takes responsibility for the unsuccessful invasion of Cuba planned under his predecessor (April 1961). However, in a sovereign way – simply by a sea blockade without a military confrontation – in October/November 1962 he compels the removal of the Soviet medium-range rockets from Cuba, thus resolving the Cuba crisis and at the same time leading to arms control. What, in the face of strong conservative forces in Congress, could he have realized of his far-reaching programmes in four or eight years in office? Who knows? As President, Kennedy wasn't granted even three years.

Just before my visit to the White House the President has to send in federal troops against white fanatics at a demonstration of blacks in Birmingham, Alabama. An ill omen. In foreign politics he has dangerously increased US involvement in Vietnam – with fatal consequences. When I objected, at a later date his sister Eunice thought that he would probably have quickly found the way back to disengagement. In his book *Profiles in Courage*, which won him the Pulitzer Prize, Kennedy writes: 'A man does what he must, in spite of personal consequences, in spite of . . . dangers – and that is the basis of all human morality.'

What could have become of his presidency? In deep sorrow I ask myself this, for that same year 1963, on 22 November, John F. Kennedy is murdered in Dallas. 'What was most characteristic about your brother Jack?' I later ask Eunice on a long drive from her splendid residence in Virginia to Washington. 'He just liked people!'

A pleasant stocktaking – with shadows

It isn't until the evening of 30 April 1963 that I fly back to London from Washington, overwhelmed by all that I have experienced in America. The summer semester begins in Tübingen on 3 May. However, I hadn't wanted to turn down three very important invitations from England. So on the next two evenings, 1 and 2 May, I speak on 'Church and Freedom' to a packed King's College in London and on 3 May to the University of Oxford. On Saturday morning, 4 May, we go by car to Cambridge – significantly there are no reasonable connections either by train or by road between the two famous rival university cities. Contrary to the expectations of my kind chauffeur Fergus Kerr OP, the journey is tense and time-consuming, because there are markets everywhere. We arrive late, and run over the lawn to King's College. I cool my face with cold water and immediately begin my lecture in the auditorium, where the audience are even sitting in the window seats. There too there is great applause at the end. So on the Sunday, 5 May, happy in every way, I can take the last flight from London to Frankfurt and Stuttgart and finally return to my beloved Tübingen.

What had I achieved? The young Dominican Thomas Riplinger of Chicago, later my doctoral student in Tübingen, describes the mood when people in Chicago were reading my book on the Council in their house of studies and this led to an intellectual explosion:

> No themes were any longer taboo. For the American church, Küng's book and the simultaneous lecture tour under the topic 'Freedom in the Church' detonated an explosion which is still reverberating through the church and its organizations. 'Freedom' was the last thing we American Catholics associated with the Roman Catholic Church. Suddenly it was a programme. Küng's book opened up the floodgates for Catholic theology in America. The clouds which had hung over the heads of theologians like Chenu, Congar, de Lubac, Daniélou, Bouyer, Courtney Murray, Rahner and Schillebeeckx dissolved instantaneously into thin air.

That is what is now called a change of consciousness. By far the majority of my demands at that time will find their way into the Council decrees. But this is by no means the only criterion for judging what was achieved. Even the demand for the abolition of the Index of Prohibited Books, an institution which had stamped the whole Counter-Reformation era (since 1564), not made by any leading theologian or bishop before 1960, will in fact be met under John XXIII. Not because the abolition is discussed in the Council aula and will be followed by some Council resolution, but rather because the Index, which I shall be discussing later, will tacitly be buried by Paul VI at the end of the Council in the framework of the reform of the Curia.

A catalyst was needed for the abolition. In the article on me in the well-known *American Current Biography* of July 1963 special emphasis will be placed on the abolition of the Index. And conversely, I will be vigorously attacked in my homeland specifically because of my 'theological attack on the Index', which is also hawked around in the Swiss press. The main critic is the Lucerne moral theologian and Germanicum professor Alois Schenker, already known to us, who – having finally been dismissed as editor of the *Schweizerische Kirchenzeitung* by the bishop after a verbose attack on Hans Urs von Balthasar – now attacks me in several articles in a pamphlet entitled *Schildwache. Herold des Königtums Christi* ('Sentinel. Herald of the Kingdom of Christ'). He can refer to his colleague

Charles Journet of the University of Fribourg, who has written an article on my proposals for reform under the title 'Too much is too much'. Journet is one of those theologians who may have written a great work on the church but now no longer goes along with innovations and as a reward will succeed in being made cardinal in later years.

Peter Hebblethwaite, perhaps the most knowledgeable and intelligent observer of the Council, an English Jesuit and biographer of John XXIII and Paul VI, writes about this time:

> The Curia was furious about the way in which this jumped-up young man was denouncing the Holy Office and waving his personal programme for the coming Council in the press and on television while sound theologians and serious-minded persons like themselves were exchanging decent Latin memos on the limits of religious 'exemption'. It was intolerable.

But the young scholar now had a mass of support: Cardinal König, Cardinal Liénart and also some in the Curia were delighted to see that 'Ottaviani had finally met his match'. Hebblethwaite goes on:

> It was reasonable to conclude that whatever the Preparatory Commission might be doing, Küng had provided the real agenda for the Council, and drawn up the battle lines for its first session. Never again would an individual theologian have such influence.

Hebblethwaite's assessment indicates that in church and Christianity, people and clergy, there is in fact great readiness for the renewal of the Catholic Church, the reunion of separated Christians and a more constructive attitude to the secular world envisaged by the Second Vatican Council under the inspiration of John XXIII. The time is ripe for the realization of the programme laid down in *The Council, Reform and Reunion* and discussed openly in my lectures under the key concept of 'freedom'. And it may be added that never in all the centuries was the credibility of church and papacy so great as it was in these years of John XXIII and the first session of the Council. And – unfortunately – it will never be as great again. No, the dispute of the century over the form of church and Christianity is still undecided.

The danger of failure

Peter Hebblethwaite also indicates that despite all obstacles and difficulties, it is possible for an individual to achieve something in this church without schism if he is well-informed and motivated, promotes his 'cause' resolutely and consistently and at the same time is also prepared to take considerable risks. And of course there is also the danger of failure.

Quite by chance, on the Easter Day afternoon on which I am writing these lines, I again watch the beginning of the great 1962 film *Lawrence of Arabia*, directed by David Lean. I really only want to see Alec Guinness once again, that enthusiastic reader of my book on the Council and probably the greatest quick-change artist in the history of film, now in the role of the Arab Prince Faisal. But immediately I am once again captivated by Peter O'Toole's portrayal of this young, headstrong English scholar, officer and then guerrilla leader Lawrence, which keeps so close to history. On 6 July 1917, after a two-month march through the desert, Lawrence captures the town of Akaba at the north-east end of the Red Sea with a small group of Arab warriors. He then fights with his Arabs for independence and the vision of a single Arab nation. Then with the British General Allenby he takes part in the parade in Jerusalem celebrating victory over the Turks and afterwards also captures Damascus with his warriors. But at the same time Lawrence is cheated of his vision by the political establishment of his country: by the pernicious secret agreement between the British and French governments which betrays the Arabs by giving Syria and Lebanon to the French and Palestine to the British as mandated territories, so that Lawrence, promoted to colonel at the age of 30, resigns his commission at the age of 34, returns to England and in protest even returns his royal honours.

1963: I am now 35. How will things go with me? Truly, I am no professional optimist and don't suppress the doubts and suspicions which constantly arise; I am shrewd in my reflections and cherish no illusions. Even on this first lecture tour of the USA, for all the successes, I experience just how far the hidden arm of the Roman Curia and its 'Holy Office' reaches. The Roman old boys' network still functions, and large parts of the episcopate are just as subservient to Rome as all the clergy who seek careers and titles (one example is the Archbishop of Denver, who prevents me from lecturing at the University of Colorado). They have mostly voted for Nixon rather than Kennedy. Talk has gone the rounds that the Vatican delegate Egidio Vagnozzi is also continuing to do all he can to deter Catholic colleges and seminaries from issuing invitations to this dangerous young theologian. And this chapter should also mention that with his support the Archbishop of St Paul, Minnesota, Leo Binz (theologically narrow-minded), and the Archbishop of Los Angeles, Cardinal McIntyre (a former Wall Street executive with a strong will and a narrow horizon), both friends of Ottaviani, even cancel the public lectures which have already been organized at their Catholic institutions. I would prefer not to describe my various painfully long telephone negotiations from San Francisco with the Chancery Office in Los Angeles, struggling in vain with perverse arguments. How much mendacity (even worse than lies) there still is in our church! The American theologian Ronald Modras notes in retrospect: 'And when the highest echelons of power in the Catholic Church sought to marginalize Küng and discredit his theology, they only succeeded in making him a symbol of the Council for hundreds of thousands of Catholics throughout the world and certainly in the United States.'

But 'symbols' in particular live dangerous lives. Peter Hebblethwaite was only too right: the reports of my activity in the USA alarmed the reactionary circles in the Roman Curia. These have so far not been disempowered either by the pope or by the Council. Rather, they defend themselves against the loss of power threatened by the Council, with their usual thoroughness, Machiavellian refinement and increasing resolve. And they practise this between the Council sessions as they have done before. The very week of my return I am asked by Bishop Leiprecht to come to Rottenburg. He has received mail from Rome, evidently not a letter of thanks. As early as Monday 13 May 1963 a conversation takes place in which he informs me of three warning letters from Rome: one from the Holy Office, one from the Congregation of Studies and one other – which he does not hand over to me. I am relaxed about all this and attempt to explain my positions and actions. But I have been warned.

I had asked a great deal of myself with my eight-week American–English lecture tour – was it perhaps too much? Constantly in a plane and in city after city; wherever I went greeted on my arrival with interviews and conversations, short speeches at receptions and dinners; then the big lectures and small discussion groups. It is understandable that people used every opportunity to ask the young Council theologian from Europe about God and the world, the church and the Council, the pope and the Curia. So – except on the days round Easter in Mexico with my Gregorian friend Bob Trisco, now a church historian in the Catholic University of America – I have usually been on duty from breakfast until deep into the night. But when it is a delight and one detects the sympathy of others, everything is easier.

'Have I never really been ill?' I am asked. No, apart from the usual childhood illnesses (measles) and occasional chills or stomach upsets, I have never had a serious illness and will not have one for decades. I have never been in a hospital or in bed for more than two or three days. Nevertheless, on my return I go for the first time for a check-up at the Tübingen Medical University Clinic. The new head, Professor Hans Erhard Bock (who in 2002 still attends our university lectures at the age of 93), says that my health is robust, but that I have a 'fragile neuro-vegetative system'. That frightens me – until he explains that without the sensitivity that this guarantees I couldn't write such books at all.

The death of the Council pope

At the end of November 1962, towards the end of the first period, talk was going around the Council that Pope John XXIII was incurably ill of stomach cancer. In the Vatican there is malicious talk of the 'hand of God'. He is given only another six months to live. The 81-year-old doesn't appear personally in the basilica in the closing ceremony on 8 December 1962. He announces that he will give his blessing to the Council from his study in the Palazzo Apostolico. So all of us, bishops and theologians, leave St Peter's a quarter of an hour early and assemble by the obelisk between Bernini's colonnades.

I am sadly aware that I am seeing the face of this pope, who has become a great hope and encouragement to me, for the last time. He speaks some encouraging words, still with a firm voice, and then gives his blessing. But as if he cannot tear himself away, after the blessing he speaks again and then finally says: '*E adesso, ancora una benedizione* – And now, another blessing!' With a pontiff more concerned with formalities one would probably have asked critically what a second blessing could be, whether the first was perhaps invalid or whether it would now be duplicated. But with Pope John such legalistic questions are more than out of place. The *'papa buono'* – as he is now lovingly called by the people – simply wants to give a spontaneous expression of his good will. He is a pope who radiates Christian love instead of ecclesiastical domination.

His testament, more important than any private statements, proves to be his last encyclical, *Pacem in terris*, of 11 April 1963. This is not, as is customary, in curial language but in modern language; not addressed, as previously, only to the bishops, the clergy and the Catholic laity, but explicitly 'to all men of good will'. In it he calls for a lasting peace on the basis of a just world order. But whereas former popes condemned human rights, he sees them – though always combined with human responsibilities! – as the basis of the new world order. And whereas former popes always spoke only of the 'freedom of the church' to work and speak without hindrance, he clearly acknowledges the 'freedom of Christians', indeed freedom of conscience and religion for each individual. The decisive draft for the encyclical evidently no longer comes from Tromp but from Monsignor Pavan (of the Lateran University).

Former popes had called on Catholics to fight against or at least to keep themselves apart from those of other views (Protestants, Jews, liberals, socialists, Communists), but John calls for collaboration in service of the common good. The United Nations, viewed with mistrust by the Curia, and the 1948 Universal Declaration of Human Rights, ignored by Pius XII, are recognized as 'signs of the time' willed by God. The participation of women in public life, the rights of minorities, the autonomy of developing countries, the repudiation of high levels of armament and nuclear weapons and pleas for negotiations and treaties: these and others are the themes which prompt a powerful positive response in the church and the world. They alarm the Sanctum Officium and the Italian right. And when on 28 April 1963, despite clear orders from the Italian conference of bishops and even threats of excommunication from Ottaviani, the Communists in Italy gain more than a million votes (25.3 per cent), the right-wing press blames the silence of Pope John. As if the Communist share of the vote hadn't risen under Pius XII from 19 per cent (1946) to 22.7 per cent (1958)! But it is not only the head of the CIA, John McCone, who thinks that he has to warn the pope against the Communists in Moscow and Italy. Cardinal Ottaviani also alarms senior military figures by pointing out the disastrous consequences of the private audience granted to the atheist Alexei Adjubei – Khrushchev's son-in-law and chief editor of the official government paper *Isvestiya* – and the dangerous distinction between errors and the erring. Only President Kennedy gives the pope encouragement through Cardinal Cushing.

John XXIII now has only a few weeks to live, and his powers are ebbing away. For all the weakness in leadership of the all too good pope, which I couldn't pass over, during the brief five years of the pontificate of Papa Roncalli the situation of the Catholic Church and the ecumenical world has improved more than in the past 50, indeed almost more than in the past 500, years. It has been confirmed that this pope was not a transitional pope but the pope of the great transition. Is it surprising that all men and women of good will are grateful to him, and before Pentecost 1963 tremble for his life? In the evening, in St Peter's Square, the chief rabbi with a group of Roman Jews has joined Christians in praying for his life. All these people have understood that here is a man who understood his ministry as service: for the Catholic Church, Christianity, Judaism, indeed for all men and women of good will. Up to the three-day agony before his death, which he had already known about for a long time, he had persisted in this service – without any solemnity and without stylizing himself like two of his successors as a second Christ, the 'man of sorrows'. Precisely three weeks after my conversation with Bishop Leiprecht in Rottenburg, on the eve of the Monday after Pentecost, 3 June 1963, like all the world I hear the news of the death of John XXIII, the pope of the Council. Certainly I am not the only one with tears in my eyes.

A pope who was a Christian

Unlike his great predecessor, John XXIII didn't want to be a great churchman, orator, diplomat, scholar and organizer, as he already said in his coronation address. Just a good shepherd. Following the example of the biblical Peter, he wanted to comfort, strengthen and motivate his brothers and sisters. The more time went on, the more he proved his greatness in serving; here he had the backing of the words of another who makes his greatness unassailable: 'Whoever among you will be the greatest, let him be your servant.' He didn't teach a new papacy but lived it out, and precisely in so doing introduced an epoch-making paradigm shift for the papacy: instead of an absolutist Roman primacy of rule, as had been the practice from the time of Gregory VII and Innocent III to Pius IX and Pius XII, a pastoral primacy of service. A papacy with a human, Christian face.

No wonder that Karl Barth had already once said to me: 'Now I can hear the "voice of the good shepherd" from the chair of Peter – which I could not in the times of the monarchical popes.' Now, however, after John's death, this contrast between him and Pius is not popular everywhere: above all because my obituary makes an 'allusion to the nepotism of Pius XII', the semi-official Parisian *Docu-*

mentation Catholique refuses to publish it. 'One cannot describe the figure of John XXIII better,' but, as the editors tell me, '*Toutes les vérités ne sont pas toujours bonne à dire* – It is not always appropriate to tell the whole truth.' *Voilà* – is it better to gloss over, veil, lie, even posthumously?

Is Papa Roncalli a saint? No doubt about it, he appeared to people to be not only a good man but also a true Christian. For all its ingenuousness, time and again his *Journal of a Soul* keeps showing the wisdom of a wide heart: he is deeply concerned with the discipleship of Christ. In a quite normal way he wants to be the 'image of the good Jesus' and as pope 'servant of God and servant of the servants of God'. He is no extraordinary human being, but already during his lifetime a saint. There are no appearances of Mary or even Christ, no mysteries of Fatima and pious play-acting. 'Pius X was a saint and didn't know it, Pius XI wasn't a saint and knew it, Pius XII was a saint and knew it' was the mocking talk in the Curia. And John XXIII? A pope who needed no 'canonization', even by Council historians, who keep quiet about his fatal wrong decisions. What is the meaning of the constantly misused word 'saint'? What is the meaning of the Roman 'canonization' which is used as a political instrument (and associated with great financial gain for the Curia)? A pope who is a Christian – that's the sensation!

Instead of miracles there are works of mercy. Which of his predecessors as pope ever made personal visits to the poor, comforted the sick in hospitals, sought out priests who had suffered shipwreck in their lives? Papa Giovanni makes his way to the Roman state prison with its around 1200 inmates. And there he finds the right words – where even great orators can so easily fail. He tells these prisoners and criminals, who could never have dreamed of such a visit, that prison has oppressed him greatly ever since he was a boy, since at that time his own uncle had gone to prison for poaching. The *Osservatore Romano*, which often suppressed the best parts of the pope's addresses, replaced the 'uncle' by 'relative', which was apparently less of an insult to the pope's dignity. Whenever Papa Giovanni spoke, his words, inspired by the gospel, found their way to people's hearts. He always lived out his pastoral commitment from the Bible as he had got to know it every day above all from the mass book and the breviary. It was precisely in this way that in the silence he had freed himself from certain traditional Roman stereotypes and clichés. As pope he read the writings of the Italian reform theologian Antonio Rosmini, which had been put on the Index. And he always spoke with respect of his fellow-student, the three times excommunicated Italian arch-modernist Buonaiuti, who had died on Easter Day 1946 *excommunicatus vitandus* (excommunicated and to be avoided), a victim of the Jesuits and the Fascists, using his priestly name 'Don Ernesto'.

Despite the failure in the leadership of his Curia, which cannot be overlooked, by his gentle humanity and the simple Christian nature which he radiated, John XXIII quite spontaneously and without any spiritual violence, threats and sanctions, created that great new consensus in the church (*consensus ecclesiae*) which he thought to be so important – and did so far beyond the Roman Catholic Church.

A change in church politics: the first ecumenical pope

'Giovanni ventritresimo' was also the first ecumenical pope. Indeed he became a figure of hope for all humankind. As it were overnight he had torn the church away from the reserve towards ecumenical efforts practised by his predecessor and given it an ecumenical orientation. Certainly there had already been an ecumenical movement in the Catholic Church before this, but it was the concern of a small, often marginalized, advance guard of theologians and laity. Pope John made the reunion of separated Christians, and also openness towards Judaism and the other world religions, the concern of the whole church, the episcopate and, to a limited degree, also of the centre. Certainly before him – as they are accustomed to say in Rome – 'arms were opened wide' to the other Christians. But usually things stopped at this invitation to return. John XXIII was the first to show that opening the arms isn't enough: one must first boldly and resolutely touch hands: each must make his own contribution towards preparing for the reunion from the Catholic side and drawing near to the other churches.

Finally, another historical turning-point is that John XXIII tacitly buried the sterile anti-Communism of Pius XII, who excommunicated all members of the Communist party. He was the first pope since the foundation of the state to keep completely aloof from Italian domestic politics and elections and to maintain a distance from all political parties, even Democrazia Cristiana. However, the milieu of the Curia, formerly largely fascist, and now conservative, proved for the most part to be dismayed – and with it the conservative circles of Italy. This pope introduced that change of style, method and mentality in the Vatican in global and ecclesiastical politics which issued in a cautious liberation from entanglement in Italian politics and a *modus vivendi* with the states of the Eastern block. Only later will it bear fruit, as finally even the German bishops have to realize.

Monsignor Agostino Casaroli, responsible for *Ostpolitik*, worked in a systematic and constructive way. After the culmination of the East–West conflict in the building of the Berlin Wall in 1961, in a now deliberate 'active neutrality' John XXIII issued calls for peace and warnings against nuclear war. To his surprise, on his eightieth birthday on 25 November 1961 he received congratulations from the party leader Nikita Khrushchev as a 'man of peace' – the first feeler to the Vatican from the Soviets since the October Revolution of 1917, though now provoked by the pope himself, who had earlier confidentially indicated his interest in better relations in Moscow through Togliatti, the Italian Communist leader (whose 'testament', critical of Moscow, will encourage 'Eurocommunism'). Khrushchev promised the bishops of Eastern Europe that they could travel to the Council. After the renewed climax of the East–West conflict in the Cuba crisis in October 1962, when the Council had already assembled, an appeal from the pope, again to both sides, helped to set in motion the process of *détente* that was now beginning.

But wasn't that too much of a good thing? This was the question asked by Roncalli's opponents in the Curia, and not only after his death. The pope even allowed a Communist who had left the church (because of its support of Fascism), the great sculptor Giacomo Manzù, likewise from Bergamo, to visit the Vatican to make a sculpture of him, and to design the extreme left-hand portal of the seven great portals of St Peter's (*'la porta della morte'* for the dead cardinals). He crowned the spectacular visit by Alexei Adjubei and his wife Rada to the Vatican with a private audience. All this seemed to the (formerly fascist) old guard in the Vatican to be politically stupid and dangerous. In his encyclical *Mater et magistra* (1961) John XXIII no longer identifies the 'social question' with the question of European workers. He also discusses at length the problems of land, agriculture and farming. More clearly than any pope before him he condemns colonialism and under-development. For *Time Magazine* he becomes the 'man of the year'. This, too, is no commendation for the right wing in the Vatican. Nor is the highly-endowed Balzan Peace Prize, which he accepts despite the resistance of the Curia.

Yet never since the Reformation, indeed never since the schism between the Eastern and Western Churches in the eleventh century, has a pope met with such wide approval. In this case all the official announcements of sympathy in fact express what countless people feel. As the General Secretary of the World Council of Churches, Dr Visser 't Hooft, states: 'The essential thing is the fundamental change in relations between the Roman Catholic Church and the other churches, which has marked the beginning of a true dialogue.' And the same can also be said with reference to Judaism, and all the other religions and peoples in the secular world. Even the Soviet warships in the harbour of Genoa have their flags at half-mast.

The reactionary forces in the Curia see themselves confronted with a plebiscite of the world public which amazes and annoys them. Only one qualification must be made. The indications of the trust of all the world in this pope as a person do not mean an acceptance of the papacy as an institution. With the unreformed mediaeval claim to absolute rule in the church and infallibility in doctrine, for other Christians and even more for all secular people this remains as unacceptable as ever. Unfortunately, despite all the concern for change, the core of the papal Curia hasn't gone along with the paradigm. It hasn't liked the Council pope or the way in which he has held office, which is governed more by the gospel. People there say it will take 100 years to correct his mistakes. Here is a symptom of this. Twice, in November 1964 and October 1965, some bishops in the Council will attempt to propose that Pope John should be canonized *per accla- mationem* and not, as is sometimes customary, by a bureaucratic procedure. Both times the Curia is able to prevent this. So be it – but who could have guessed that the same Curia would succeed on 11 September 2000 in canonizing John XXIII (to tremendous approval of the assembled mass of people) and at the same time (!) (to their almost complete silence) his complete opposite, Pius XII, that authoritarian enemy of human rights, antisemitic, egocentric and a propagator of his own infallibility? So once again: what is the significance of 'saint' and 'canonization' here? *Corruptio optima pessima*: the corruption of the holy is the most unholy of all.

Neither the hesitant Paul VI nor John Paul I, who lived for all too brief a time, nor even the authoritarian yet divided John Paul II will succeed like John XXIII, together with the Second Vatican Council that he convened, in addressing the deepest longings of people inside and outside Christianity – the longing for understanding, peace, fellowship, the longing for a renewed church in a better world. Papa Roncalli wanted to open the windows of the church and he did open them. Truly, he is the greatest pope of the twentieth century.

These five brief years between 1958 and 1963 were a 'window of opportunity'; an extremely hopeful pontificate came to an end with John XXIII. Everything that has so far been achieved by the Council is only a beginning. The task is enormous and the outcome uncertain. And then on 22 November of the same year, as I have reported, comes the second disaster: President Kennedy's assassination. The world is now poorer by another hope. The twin star of a constellation of hope, a new paradigm of 'Catholicism' – the 81-year-old pope, the symbol of a goodness which embraces humankind, and the 47-year-old president, the symbol of youth and the new frontiers – has set. 'It is always the wrong ones who have to go early, while others remain.' I am no stranger to such quarrelling with God's guidance and dispensation.

One observation at the end of this chapter. Easter 2002. Once again I read through my hopeful pages on the church in America and on John XXIII to check them. But beside me lies the Easter issue of *Time Magazine* (1 April 2002) with the shocking main headline, 'Can the Catholic Church Save Itself?' As previously in *Newsweek* there are pages of terrible reports of child abuse by Catholic clergy, but also reports of the catastrophic decline in the number of priests, nuns and ordinands, and the 27 per cent increase in parishes without priests (the situation is similar in Europe!).

How, many even more traditional Catholics, priests and bishops now ask, could this greatest crisis in the history of the Catholic Church in the United States and elsewhere come about in the last four decades? The next chapter will describe how at a very early stage, despite all the correct decisions, a whole series of false moves were made: problems suppressed, abuses concealed, reforms prevented and the façades of the church's power and pomp maintained.

VIII

❧☙❧☙

Power against Freedom

'We must accept with humility
the criticisms that surround us,
with reflection, and even with gratitude.'

Pope Paul VI, speech to the Roman Curia

A Paul instead of a John

IT is a papal election without surprises: on Friday, 21 June 1963 – in the sixth round of voting – the 67-year-old Giovanni Battista Montini is elected pope. The election had been conducted by Cardinal Aloisi Masella as Cardinal Chamberlain; by now he is 85. Twenty-five years previously – is it already as long ago as that? – he had paid me a sick visit in San Pastore with a 'Bravo, bravo'. Pope John himself had given clear signs. He immediately chose as cardinal his friend from Lombardy, who had fallen out of favour with Pius XII in 1958; indeed he even had the man who had been driven out of the Vatican staying in the Vatican as a special guest for the first session of the Council. The Curia doesn't love Montini, the inscrutable sympathizer with the 'left'. It would have preferred to see the election of the Curia cardinal Antoniutti, previously a nuncio in Spain and popular with Franco, and if need be even Cardinal Lercaro of Bologna. However, Cardinal Suenens persuaded Lercaro's supporters to vote for Montini. Finally, in the sixth round of voting, there was a compromise between the majority favourably disposed towards the Council, around Bea and Suenens, and the curial minority around Ottaviani and Cicognani, who could easily have blocked the two-thirds minority needed. Montini got 57 votes, only two more than the two-thirds majority required. So even at the end, between 20 and 25 cardinals didn't vote for him – the core of a future conservative opposition? Montini's election, hoped for by the progressive majority at the Council, is widely welcomed. This man is also my desired candidate – *'omnibus bene perpensis*, all things considered'. But now that he is in office, will he live up to my desires, the desires of the Council – or will he go along with the Curia?

The choice of the name Paul is a great surprise – this choice of name is always a first indication of the will of a pope. No reasons are given. No pope has chosen this name since the Borgia pope Paul V (1605-21), whose name 'adorns' the façade of St Peter's in excessively large letters. According to recent tradition he couldn't choose the papal name John, since he already has John as his own name. And clearly he didn't want to choose the name Pius, since he had notoriously become increasingly alienated from Pacelli. But Paul surely isn't named after that Paul V who wanted to implement once again the mediaeval paradigm of the church with the papal claim to supremacy over the republic of Venice, using ban and interdict? It was in his pontificate that the first trial of Galileo took place. Rather, as Cardinal König at once rightly explains, Montini is following the apostle Paul and Paul's worldwide activity in the service of the gospel of Jesus Christ. This is also matched by the new pope's saying on his election: '*In nomine Domini* – in the name of the Lord'.

Strongly influenced in my theology by the apostle Paul, already as a student I had wanted a pope by the name of Paul. But my professor in church history at the Gregorian, Freiherr Ludwig von Hertling SJ, a relative of the conservative philosopher Freiherr Georg von Hertling, later to become Chancellor (1917/18), practised as his speciality a number game with popes' names (and set examination questions on it). One of the 'results' of his research was: '*Omnes Papae cum numero sexto erant papae infelices* – all the popes with the number six were unlucky popes.' At that time the thought immediately occurred to me that a new pope with the name Paul would be a '*Papa infelix* – an unlucky pope' simply by virtue of his number.

But now, on the morning of that 21 June 1963, I say to myself as a rational human being: why should this rule, for which there is no rational justification whatsoever, apply? Why shouldn't there for once be a lucky pope in a series of sixes? Meanwhile, at the request of the Vatican, Fr von Hertling had written an article for the edition of the *Osservatore Romano* on the election of the coming pope and in it developed his thesis about the number six. These pages of the *Osservatore* had already been printed at the time of the election. So the copies on sale in St Peter's Square after the election also contained this article – until the *faux pas* was noted and the whole issue was reprinted without Hertling's contribution. To his great delight Hertling got hold of an issue containing his article, but could never discover whether Paul VI ever saw it. At any rate he wouldn't have changed his name.

At that time no one could suspect just how unlucky this pope was in fact to become. However, in respect of origin, development and mentality one could have some doubts about how this man would in fact shape his pontificate. Despite all my personal sympathy for Giovanni Battista Montini, I too cannot completely suppress my reservations. For Fr Gundlach, who would most have liked to 'eliminate' Montini, his election as pope must have been a shock. Two days later, on 23 June 1963, he dies, and even now in circles in the know people puzzle as to whether this was *post hoc* or *propter hoc*. But Montini is 'crowned' (in fact he is the last to be so!) pope with a modernized tiara newly made in accordance with his own ideas, the triple crown of the ruler of the world – placed on his head by

Cardinal Ottaviani, the head of the Sanctum Officium. What does such an ambivalent gesture mean for the new pontificate?

'Our Hamlet of Milan'

As a student in Rome I had always observed Monsignor Montini with special respect on his rare public appearances. As I have said, when he entered St Peter's, unlike the other lofty Roman prelates he did not look to right and left for acquaintances, but was concentrated, his eyes sunk in prayer, his hands firmly folded. I find it congenial that Montini comes from a good middle-class democratic family from Brescia – without the good middle-class Pacelli's thing about aristocracy. As we saw, Pacelli made his three nephews princes ('principi Pacelli') and financial magnates (for example, Giulio was president of the supervisory body for the Banco di Roma). Montini's father, a lawyer, was editor of the Catholic paper and a parliamentary delegate of the Catholic people's party until it was dissolved by Mussolini. His mother was president of the Catholic women's association of Brescia, and in the 1960s one of his two brothers is still a parliamentary delegate of Democrazia Cristiana. Of course the Montini family was loyal to the church and the papacy; however, it didn't take part in the anti-modernist campaign but also maintained links with Italian authors suspected of modernism.

Later, friends in Brescia tell me how the little Giovanni Montini, in poor health, had to break off his secondary education in the Jesuit college and complete it privately. He also had to do his theological studies at the priestly seminary as a day student, 'a 'Lord's little boy', who came only for the lectures, greeted everyone in a friendly way, and left again immediately afterwards. So the new pope is from the start a very serious type, but perhaps he isn't very communicative?

At the Gregorian people are proud of the ex-alumnus Montini, though he began his lightning career not in Rome but in Milan. Ordained priest at the age of 23, he gained his doctorate in canon law that same year. Without any doubt he had a strictly traditionalist training in scholastic theology and canon law. Just a year later the doubtless highly-gifted young man completes this rapid course, lacking any modern exegesis, church history or history of dogma, with his theological doctorate, only now at the Gregorian. He doesn't have theology in view, but the Curia. That same year he is accepted into the Accademia dei Nobili, the papal diplomatic school, and after six months at the nunciature in Warsaw, at the early age of 27 enters the Secretariat of State, where he will remain from 1924 until he is promoted to be Archbishop of Milan in 1954. So the new pope is a model priest of absolute integrity, but for all his reading of modern theological works (Karl Adam!) he is orientated above all on church politics, with no thorough theological training and with no experience of being a parish priest.

When Vorspel, Rector of the Germanicum, was negotiating at that time with Montini in the Secretariat of State about the building of the new Vatican transmitter on our large college estate of Santa Maria di Galeria, he went on to express amazement at Montini's acute intelligence and precise knowledge of the documentation: he was a tireless worker. He had matured into a doubtless perfect church diplomat, who with a high legal knowledge of the facts and political skill as early as 1937 – at the time of the growing threat from Fascism and National Socialism – rises to become one of the two 'substitutes' ('representatives' for 'ordinary' or domestic church matters) of the Cardinal Secretary of State, Eugenio Pacelli, along with his colleague Tardini, responsible for 'extraordinary', predominantly political matters. When Pacelli is elected pope, both are confirmed in their offices, but neither is made Secretary of State, since Pius preferred to be his own Secretary of State and remained so until his death. So apart from six months in Warsaw the new pope has never worked abroad; instead, for three decades he has constantly been in the Secretariat of State and in daily contact with Pacelli, who has long been admired. Despite some travels he necessarily regards the world completely from a Roman curial perspective – which at the same time means against a very limited Catholic horizon.

As I reported, I also got to know Montini personally for the first time at the summer villa of the bishops of northern Italy in Gazzada. As a young official (*minutante*) of the Secretariat of State he had already shown his pastoral commitment among the young intellectuals of Rome and then as spiritual adviser to the union of Catholic students for Rome and finally for all Italy; now, as Archbishop of Milan, he showed great zeal for the administration, pastoral care and liturgical renewal of this diocese. He sought contact with all classes, and preached in churches, hospitals and prisons, even factories. So the new pope beyond doubt is a bishop with a social concern and interested in people – not an absolutist ruler like Pacelli, nor just a first colleague among all his episcopal colleagues like Roncalli, but a hierarch who is always concerned for his dignity. In his pastoral letters, sermons and writings he quotes progressive French theologians like Congar, de Lubac, even Teilhard, and German theologians like Rahner and even me, but it's hard to see how deeply he has appropriated their ideas. At all events, his education and development hardly allow him to see the historical relativity of the mediaeval hierarchical structures (clericalism, absolutism, celibacy).

On the basis of his origin, career and mentality it is easy to understand why Giovanni Battista Montini is very soon seen as a Hamlet figure: '*il nostro Amleto di Milano*'. This remark is even attributed to Papa Giovanni, himself a father figure. Montini is so very different from Roncalli with his humour, his all-embracing warmth, his carefree attitude rooted in believing trust; like Shakespeare's prince of Denmark, Montini shows more of a tendency to brood and hesitate than to be decisive, more melancholy than cheerfulness. However, he also shows more of a tendency towards self-doubt and reflection, a gift which one will again rightly learn to treasure in view of his all too self-confident successor from Poland. Montini is perhaps the only pope of the twentieth century who deserves to be called an 'intellectual' in the broadest sense. I am glad to know him personally and hope in sympathy that despite all the reservations he will impose himself with his great gifts. And I look forward eagerly to his first decisions, which as pope he now cannot avoid.

Controlling the power of the Curia?

One welcome sign is that Paul VI immediately has it announced that he wants to continue the Council. And both bishops and theologians hope that he will do so in a more resolute and purposeful way than his predecessor. For all its romanticism, his inaugural encyclical on dialogue indicates that he wants to show more strength in leadership and reinforce the great movement towards renewal within the church and the constructive grappling with the pressing problems of the world which has been pioneered by the Council.

So it is with great expectancy that I await Montini's first personal decisions. It is with these that every head of government sets his course, and with them Montini's pontificate at this decisive hour of church history will stand or fall. Unless, as is asserted time and again, far-reaching corrections are made to the highly complicated mechanism of the Roman Curia he is doomed to failure from the start. As I have already indicated in the case of John XXIII from earlier examples of reform popes, the one thing that is certain is that a pope cannot implement reform by himself, but is dependent on competent, strong and unconditionally loyal fellow-fighters.

And now Paul VI is given a unique possibility which not even Pope John had: with the death of his predecessor all curial offices are now vacant and new appointments depend entirely on the new pope. That is the case with every change of pontificate. But Montini has a greater knowledge than anyone else in the church of the church as an institution, the Curia personnel and literally each individual bishop. What is even more important, he himself has noted many weaknesses in the curial system; he has personal experience of the excesses of the papal absolutism under Pacelli, indeed he was sent off to Milan with elegant violence. Now he has returned to the Vatican as victor, and both his enemies and his friends await the consequences.

In addition there is an almost historic opportunity for a reform of the Curia: this pope has the backing of the ecumenical Council, the overwhelming majority of the bishops who will meet again in the autumn. There had been loud calls for a reform of the Curia in the first session of the Council. And now there isn't the slightest doubt that a resolute personal new beginning, feared by many in the Curia, would be particularly welcomed by the Council fathers. Like Leo IX or Paul III – and I am truly not the only one to think this – the pope would only need to appoint some prominent advocates of church renewal among the cardinals and bishops to the few central posts and carry through with them the reform desired by the Council, above all internationalization and decentralization.

In fact it would be basically simple for Paul VI to appoint generally recognized, trustworthy and well-known leaders (also personally well known to me) of the conciliar majority (during the second session of the Council I will collect their speeches for publication) to the Curia and to commit them to his programme and to collegial collaboration. For example? In the view of many people Cardinal Suenens, primate of Belgium, the *uomo ascendente*, the 'coming man', would make an excellent Secretary of State. Cardinal König, Archbishop of Vienna, an extremely learned theologian with years of pastoral experience, would make an excellent head of a radically reformed Sanctum Officium. Cardinal Léger, the friendly, sovereign Archbishop of Montreal, would make an understanding head of the Congregation of Bishops. Cardinal Silva Henriquez, the socially open Archbishop of Santiago de Chile, would be a good head of a congregation for the laity. And of course there are also archbishops who have shown their stature at the Council: for example Elchinger of Strasbourg for the Congregation of Studies; Eugene D'Souza from Bhopal, India, for the Congregation of Mission 'Propaganda Fide'; Dennis Hurley of Durban, South Africa, for Justitia et Pax. And of course Cardinal Bea shouldn't be replaced as head of the Secretariat for Unity.

What a grand, loyal 'cabinet', with which the pope could collaborate in an admirable way and efficiently guide the renewal of the church! But what happens? At the very first homage Paul VI inconspicuously confirms not only Cardinal Bea as president of the Secretariat for Unity but also the 82-year-old Amleto Cicognani as Secretary of State, although the replacement of this skilful, stubborn church lawyer who thinks entirely along curial lines (by no means a Hamlet!) was generally expected. Monsignor Angelo Dell'Acqua, certainly a very capable member of the Curia, remains at his post as substitute in the Secretariat of State. As a result the control centre in the Palazzo Apostolico – the Secretary of State on the third floor is in daily contact with the pope on the fourth – is again completely in the hands of the Curia. But the pope makes an even more disastrous wrong decision: contrary to expectations he confirms as head of the even more important curial institution, the Sanctum Officium, that Cardinal Alfredo Ottaviani who with his authority represents the centre of resistance to conciliar renewal, firmly resolved to obstruct what has to be obstructed. He also leaves the prefect of the Congregation of Studies, Ottaviani's friend Cardinal Giuseppe Pizzardo, in office. The curial power block, the Vatican Pentagon, remains intact – not to mention lower offices. No, this sixth Paul who was greeted so hopefully will hardly ever become a great charismatic leader of the church. So will he perhaps be a *'papa infelix'*?

This occupation of key positions is my first great disappointment, and not just mine. Had Montini, as is rumoured, entered into an electoral capitulation to Cicognani and Ottaviani: the Council, yes, but with the same leadership? But are

electoral capitulations at papal elections admissible? And doesn't the papal primacy of jurisdiction also apply to the members of the Curia? I am convinced even
more than others that by the same basic strategic mistake as John XXIII – wanting
to carry through a reform with a 'cabinet' of those opposed to reform – Paul VI
has fundamentally obstructed a radical reform of the Curia and the church, if not
already made it impossible. For the curial bureaucrats will make use of the
positions of power graciously granted to them by the pope to thwart his best
intentions of reform by unscrupulous methods. This is particularly true of
Archbishop Pericle Felici (Montini's former opponent), whom Paul VI now
likewise confirms as General Secretary of the Council; according to experts he is
said to believe only in two things: the Nicene Creed and the cardinalate. His
general secretariat quickly develops into the control centre for the manipulation
of the Council: Felici, Cicognani and Ottaviani work very well together.

This is unfortunately the way in which this pope resembles Hamlet: he wants
to and yet he doesn't want to. By his personal nominations he delays and blocks
precisely that reform of the Curia which he wants, but at the same time fears. For
Montini, already prone to anxiety, is really anxious: he fears the Vatican
potentates and cliques, his former colleagues, to whom he owes much and who
don't always deal graciously even with a pope – as long as he lets them. But he is
also anxious about a somewhat uncertain future if he agrees to a serious reform of
the Curia and the church. So what will the pope do in this situation? It is also
characteristic of Montini that instead of acting immediately, he will first, as we
shall see, give a speech on the reform of the Curia. I spend the time between the
first and second sessions of the Council in my university town.

A 'laboratory' of freedom?

On the evening of 21 June 1963, the day of the papal election, a torchlight
procession of dozens of theological students is waiting for me in Tübingen. 'Im
Minschter isch's finschter,' they chorus in Swabian – 'It's dark in Münster.' They
want to prevent me from accepting a call there. My colleague Hermann Diem of
the Protestant faculty gives a speech in which he begs me to stay in Tübingen:
'It's never been like that before,' a Protestant pastor writes to me. How quickly
those three years in Tübingen had gone! Shortly before Christmas 1962 a telephone call from Münster indicated to me that the call mentioned when I left
there would soon materialize. And indeed the call does come through a letter
from the Kultusminister of North Rhine–Westphalia, Professor Paul Mikat, dated
16 May 1963, together with the information that he hopes to welcome me
personally in the negotiations over the call. This is extraordinary, a clearly positive
sign.

So I turn my attention towards Münster, which seems to me simply to have the
better cards. At the time I felt very happy in this city and university, rebuilt

quickly after the war, and I got on with the Westphalians just as well as now I do with the Swabians. Beyond doubt it would be a special honour for me to take over the chair of my teacher Hermann Volk, now Bishop of Mainz and soon to be cardinal. The Catholic theological faculty, the biggest in Germany, has perhaps three times as many students as the Tübingen faculty. And much as I enjoy dealing with the basic questions of fundamental theology in Tübingen, after three years I am keen to change over to dogmatics, where I can teach and do research on all areas of theology. The far greater distance of Münster from my Swiss homeland needn't prove decisive.

The morning after the torchlight procession – a little nostalgic because of this declaration of sympathy, but nevertheless resolved – I do go to Münster and there, as is to be expected, am welcomed in an extremely friendly way. In Münster everything is more generous than in Tübingen, not simply because of the thrift of the Swabians, but also because of the pettiness of Tübingen faculty politics. 'One theological discipline – one ordinarius professor': in Tübingen that is regarded as a dogma which excludes any duplication of a chair and artificially keeps the faculty small at the time of a general expansion of the universities. In the end it is all done so as not to endanger the existing constellation of power in the faculty.

In Münster it is precisely the opposite: 'The more you extract for yourself from the ministry,' Kötting, the director of the seminar, explains to me, 'the better others can do after you.' As well as having the first chair of dogmatics and the Ecumenical Institute, Münster already has a second chair in dogmatics: its occupant since the summer semester of 1963 has been Joseph Ratzinger. He had written four months previously from Bonn that he would accept the call to Münster for the second professorship of dogmatics and the history of dogma. And as I am first on the list of the faculty proposals for the first professorship of dogmatics, he wants to tell me 'that I would be very pleased if we could attempt to tackle the dogmatic work at the university of Münster together'. At the same time he proposes to me 'a new type of differentiated work in systematic theology', in which 'for example in rotation one gives the main series of lectures and the other a special lecture series'. I replied to him that I would enjoy such collaboration very much: 'I very rapidly noted in Rome that we are on the same wavelength, and that's the decisive thing.'

On my visit to Münster we could now agree without friction on a division of the material. So far Ratzinger has two assistants. 'If you could get three assistant posts, that would be very good,' says Kötting. Soon agreed on the course of action with the Münster faculty, on 24 June 1963 I go to Düsseldorf, the capital of the state of North Rhine–Westphalia. Mikat, the Kultusminister, an open Catholic in the spirit of Vatican II, tells me that this faculty is rock-solid, but a bit too bland. Theology there needs new blood, and he assures me of his support. So I drive back: everything seems to be in favour of Münster. Back in Tübingen I get yet another letter from the student representatives of the Catholic Theological

Faculty in Münster: they want to leave 'nothing untried to win' me 'for Münster'. Since I know Münster, I don't have to contradict what they say: 'Surely you know the line from the Münster song "Fair city in the garland of lime trees"? "Whoever called you dark was a darkling."'

However, meanwhile people have also been thinking about me in Tübingen. I am informed that it is quite possible to create a second chair in dogmatics: the occupant of the chair, Professor Leo Scheffczyk, would have no objections. They could create a new chair for dogmatic and ecumenical theology. And since in Düsseldorf I have been assured of three assistant posts, the idea occurs to me that with these three posts it would be possible after all to found an Ecumenical Institute, of the kind that Münster already has. This now leads to a small quarrel with my colleague Scheffzyk, whose view is that with such a plan I would be doing too well for myself. Independently of this he will soon accept a call to the more conservative Catholic theological faculty in Munich, where he feels spiritually more at home, as he replies when I urge him nevertheless to remain in Tübingen.

Thus the Tübingen faculty changes its spots and now resolves on its first institute, which to the present day – I shall have to talk about this later – remains its only one. Since in this institute my concern is really to clear up the differences which have existed between Catholics and Protestants since the sixteenth century, I choose for it the unusual name 'Institute for Ecumenical Research'. People like this name so much that it is soon adopted by the Strasbourg institute of the Lutheran World Federation. Unfortunately we aren't invited to the baptism, as Catholic godfathers customarily are.

On 3 September 1963 I inform the ministry in Düsseldorf and the Münster faculty that unfortunately I can't accept their call; however, I add that my assistant Dr Walter Kasper, who is about to finish his habilitation, is a qualified candidate. Joseph Ratzinger writes: 'I personally had looked forward to working with you, but I can understand your decision . . .' and later: 'I was very glad to have your news about Herr Dr Kasper. He is in fact in serious discussion with us . . .'

Now a great reshuffle is in process in the sphere of fundamental theology. Some lecturers are available for chairs: Bernhard Casper, Peter Hünermann, Walter Kasper, Peter Lengsfeld, Johann Baptist Metz. But in my faculty the successor people want is an old Tübingen alumnus, recently professor at the Theological College in Passau. For a while Max Seckler was my next-door neighbour in Paris, but so far he has made his mark only by his knowledge of Thomas Aquinas. I write to Seckler not as dean but as a former fellow-student: 'I would now like to clarify some basic questions for the faculty, together with Professor Möller, in a personal conversation. Would it be possible for you to come to Tübingen for that as soon as possible?' The conversation takes place in my home on 26 January 1964. My reservations (a fixation on Thomism, etc.) are dispelled, and there is no longer anything in the way of Seckler's call; two days later it is decided on by the faculty.

The foundation of a new chair in Tübingen and the institute associated with it is sealed with me by a contract with the state of Baden-Württemberg (this legal confirmation was endorsed by a senate decree of 18 January 1964). Fortunately I have no inkling how important this document will be in guaranteeing my academic position when only five years later the 1968 revolution shatters the traditional structures of the German universities and their institutes, and even more when in 1979 the intervention of the Vatican will put in question my academic position at the University of Tübingen generally. In 1963 the world still seems to be in order: that of the university and the church. But the freedom of theology is by no means guaranteed, even in the extraordinarily favourable conditions of Tübingen. Paradoxically it isn't threatened by the state, as formerly, but now by the church.

The spirit of true and false freedom

It seems to me important that from the beginning our Institute for Ecumenical Research should be presented to the public effectively. How better could this be done than by my USA lecture on 'Church and Freedom'? So I give it for the first time in German, at 5 p.m. on 12 February 1964, in the Festsaal of the university. Once again the hall is packed. I am introduced by the dean, Herbert Haag, with interesting historical references to the Tübingen theologian Johann Adam Möhler, who initiated ecumenical research with his early work on 'The Unity of the Church' (1825). A reception in the rooms of the Institute in Nauklerstrasse follows. The bookshelves are still empty, but they fill up rapidly in the following months. And with the library we also start on a catalogue of bibliographical research.

My programmatic inaugural lecture meets with enthusiastic approval. Ernst Müller, the publisher and chief editor of the local paper, the *Schwäbisches Tagblatt*, who has an honorary doctorate from the Mainz faculty, reports individual parts of the lecture at length and ends by writing: '. . . an almost evangelical (not Protestant) mode of pastoral concern with people in a happy faith which does not work with safeguards and controls but trusts in the efficacy of the Spirit . . . The Protestant reviewer (Müller) expresses warm thanks to the Catholic theologian Küng and thinks that he would feel happier in the church outlined by Küng than in his present state church, if one day Küng's manifesto became reality: "Unity but not uniformity, a centre, not centralism."' Finally comes the reporter's big 'but' – against a church dominated by an authoritarian Roman primacy: 'But then in Küng's thesis he would again lapse into Protestantism if one church and one leadership were required. God and Christ are the leaders of the church, but scripture does not mention the primacy of the Bishop of Rome above all bishops, prescribed in an authoritarian way.'

Here the chief editor is in fact addressing the 'new Roman question' which has not in fact been resolved even by the Council, as can also be heard from the congratulations of the dean of the Protestant sister faculty, Professor Hermann Diem, who speaks about the controversial theology in Tübingen after 1825. For Möhler with his book *Athanasius* (1827), his writing on celibacy (1828), and especially with his bestseller *Symbolik* (1832), which appeared in twenty editions – he works out one-sidedly the differences between Catholics and Protestants – fell back on traditional Roman positions and founded in the faculty the party of 'Möhlerians' ('Romans') which in 1848 would be victorious over the critical men of the Enlightenment. This is a process which was to repeat itself in a different form in our lifetime. Ernst Müller ends his article with the question: 'When will the reunion of the two churches take place?' And he replies: 'A Swabian professor with a sense of humour thinks that this will be on the Last Day, but for the Alt-Württembergers and arch-Protestants it will not be until the evening. In no way should the old apologia be renewed; new rules must be found for the controversies. It is proposed that no argument may be used against the other which no longer stands up to one's own self-criticism.'

That is said to both sides. For the pendant to the often spoilt freedom of the arch-Protestants is the spoilt freedom of the liberal Catholics. Earlier I had once spoken within the circle of my Catholic Tübingen colleagues of the 'church as a sphere of freedom'. At that time I earned roars of laughter without any substantive commentary, which alienated and hurt me. The scepticism of the philosopher and the cynicism of the church historian combined in mocking laughter with the conformism of the canon lawyer and the harmlessness of the moral theologian. This is a typical example of how colleagues often express criticism of theology in cheerful conversation and behave 'freely', but in public hardly ever risk a free, undeterred word in order 'to proclaim from the rooftops what is whispered in the ear' (cf. Matt. 10.27). Our language knows church law alongside civil law, but why not church courage, even Christian courage, alongside civil courage? I usually agree with my colleagues' criticism of the church, but as by far the youngest in the faculty – the average age of the others is almost 55 – am I always to be the one who calls for civil courage, indeed the courage of a Christian? Truly, I want to make at least my Institute for Ecumenical Research a place of work, a 'laboratory' for freedom – freedom to seek the truth. However, what this will cost me one day is by no means clear – though in my lecture on freedom in the church and theology I always have Rome and the pope in view. I am also thinking of Karl Barth, always a model for me in matters of civil courage and church courage.

Karl Barth visits the pope

I receive a letter from the Vatican, from Monsignor Johannes Willebrands, dated 17 September 1963 and marked 'confidential'. He had already discussed a certain plan with me in Gazzada, but had meanwhile been in Serbia. The question is whether Karl Barth should be invited to the Council. Willebrands now writes: 'When I put to His Eminence (Bea) the possibility of inviting Karl Barth to the Council as a guest of the Secretariat he was in principle in agreement. So may I ask you to sound Karl Barth out over this possibility?' The guests of the Secretariat for Unity would have virtually the same rights as the observers/delegates representing the churches. They would enjoy the same trust and in turn would be asked for trust. 'As soon as you have spoken with Karl Barth about the possibility of an invitation, report to me. Of course it is not a matter of "winning him over": you should describe the possibilities quite freely and exclude any egotistic element on our side. With best thanks for your service and in the hope of seeing you again soon in Rome, Yours, Johannes.'

I telephone Basle from Tübingen. I tell Karl Barth that this is a confidential preliminary enquiry: would he accept an invitation from the Secretariat for Christian Unity to take part in the Second Vatican Council personally as an 'observer'? An immediate answer isn't necessary. I observe that this is an unusual recognition on the part of Rome of his theological activity. In this way he could bring his voice directly to bear in the Council; there are many possibilities for doing that.

Karl Barth, by now a proud 77, wants to consider the matter. But he must finally 'decide to say no, prevented by *force majeure*, because of frequent visits to hospital'. Only eighteen months later, in 1966, when he has recovered, does the plan mature in him 'perhaps also stimulated by the glorious Catholic church music of Mozart, with which I and many others were refreshed shortly before my eightieth birthday, for the moment to put aside the plan to work on my autobiography, which had occupied me the previous winter, and once again turn to the theological present' (*Ad limina apostolorum*, 9).

Barth studies the sixteen Council documents thoroughly in Basle. He formulates ten schemata of questions, with requests for clarification and critical questions on the most important of them. Now in September 1966, accompanied by his wife and his Catholic physician, he is in Rome, and in five working days discusses these questions, which can be read in his account *Ad limina apostolorum* (1967). Always accompanied by a member of the Secretariat for Unity, he carries on conversations with the Jesuits on the roof terrace of the Gregorian, and also with the members of other religious orders. He has discussions with Cardinal Ottaviani and Archbishop Parente in the Sanctum Officium, and with Cardinal Bea in his residence on the Via Aurelia, and finally, 'in the innermost sanctuary of the Roman Catholic Church', with the pope.

Karl Barth also puts some of his questions to the pope, especially about the status of the 'separated brethren' and about mariology. But first of all the pope, unlike his predecessor always attaching importance to papal dignity, makes a little speech in praise of Barth's theological work and is then equally effusive about himself. He says that it is a very heavy task to use the keys of Peter entrusted to him by the Lord: *'Les clés de St Pierre sont très lourdes.'* In his account Karl Barth represses the thought which flashes through his head on hearing these papal statements and which he confides to me afterwards: as Molière put it, *'Tu l'as voulu, Georges Dandin, tu l'as voulu* – You wanted, you wanted to be representative of Christ. So you mustn't be surprised that this task is a heavy one, perhaps all too heavy.' He tells it with an implicit point: the pope could in fact take back some of his exaggerated titles and claims. If he doesn't, he deserves no sympathy.

But is it at all possible for him to take them back? I say yes. For in the first centuries things were different. In fact it was only after the power-conscious Leo the Great in the fifth century that the popes advocated a kind of Petrine mysticism, as if Peter were speaking and acting personally through them. And only since the power-obsessed Gregory VII, the former monk Hildebrand, in the eleventh century did the popes heighten to a superhuman degree not only their external power and authority within the church, but also their titles. In contrast to the 'representative of *Peter*' which was customary previously, at the climax of papal power Innocent III prefers and monopolizes the title 'representative of *Christ*' or even 'representative of *God*', used up to the twelfth century of any bishop or priest: only the Bishop of Rome is *'vicarius Christi'*, even *'vicarius dei'*.

Isn't it a step in the right direction here when Paul VI, at least in the introduction to the Council documents, terms himself *'Episcopus, servus servorum Dei'*, 'Bishop, servant of the servants of God', following Gregory the Great? However, the Roman Curia still does all it can to go on maintaining the absolute authority and power of the pope and thus also its own authority and power. Paul VI does nothing about that. Indeed, the pope who sighs so bitterly under the weight of the keys of Peter will soon also go on to cultivate a remarkable mysticism of suffering in his self-chosen isolation – as if with his office he had personally taken upon himself the heavy cross of Christ, and other men and women no longer had to suffer. Soon he will be the first pope constantly to present himself to the public with the Crucified Christ on his staff instead of the episcopal pastoral staff: the pope – a 'second Christ', a 'second crucified'? That seems to me to be blasphemy. I am slightly reassured by the fact that Paul VI's confessor is my former highly-revered and sober professor of metaphysics and Rector of the Gregorian, Fr Paolo Dezza SJ, now a *peritus* with me. And in the end Papa Montini does also surprise me as a reformer.

A papal call for the reform of the Curia

An unprecedented event for the members of the Curia takes place in Rome immediately before the second session of the Council, on 21 September 1963. Paul VI summons the whole of his Curia to a special audience, punctually at 10 a.m. in the Hall of Benedictions above the narthex of St Peter's. What for? He calls for a reform of the Curia. How times have changed despite all the obstacles! After all, we remember the fate of Fr Riccardo Lombardi, who likewise had ventured to make a quite matter-of-fact criticism of the Roman Curia in loyalty to the church and was bitterly punished for it even under John XXIII. But now Paul VI himself takes the well-intentioned critics of the Roman Curia under his wing, indeed he puts forward significant proposals for reform. After the first bitter disappointment over matters of personal policy, for me and many others this is again an occasion for hope. And in view of the balance of power, which unfortunately he hasn't changed, this enterprise is by no means without danger for the pope.

The speech is then published: the pope isn't sparing in praise for his officials, much criticized and humiliated in the Council, and on this occasion also approves the increase in all Vatican stipends and salaries announced by his predecessor and proclaims a day's holiday. A *captatio benevolentiae*. In fact even critics of the Roman Curia recognize, as I do, what specific work has been done by some people and how much the Catholic Church owes to the organizational power of its central organs over the last century, despite all the abuses.

But happily the pope also doesn't conceal the deficiencies of the Curia; indeed he recognizes the justification of the criticism: 'It is a prod to watchfulness, a recall to observance, an invitation to reform, a ferment to perfection. We must accept with humility the criticisms which surround us, with reflection and also with gratitude. Rome has no need to defend itself by making itself deaf to suggestions that come to it from honest voices, especially when they are those of friends and brothers.' Unfounded accusations will certainly be responded to, but without evasions, circumlocutions, polemic. However, it is possible to note 'today that the resolution to modernize the juridical structures and deepen spiritual consciousness not only finds no resistance in the centre of the church, the Roman Curia; it finds, rather, the Curia itself in the advance guard of that perennial reform of which the church itself, in so far as it is a human and earthly institution, has perpetual need'.

'Finds the Curia in the advance guard'? In the curial style the indicative (denoting a fact) is often used where the optative (denoting a wish) or the imperative (denoting a command) would be appropriate. At any rate it is now clear to the Roman Curia, too, that the *ecclesia semper reformanda* is not un-Catholic! It is easy to see that the pope thinks that reforms must be carried through even in the Curia itself. As is well known, the last reorganization of this old and multi-level organism goes back to Sixtus V in 1588; it was supplemented by Pius X in 1908 and in this form was incorporated into the 1917 *Codex Iuris Canonici*: 'Many years have passed. It is understandable, therefore, how such an establishment would have grown ponderous with its own venerable age, how it feels the disparity of its organs and of its practices with respect to the needs and customs of new times, how at the same time it feels the need of being simplified, decentralized, and of being broadened and made fit for new functions.' But obviously, I tell myself, Paul VI doesn't think back further than the sixteenth century, to the decisive eleventh century.

'Various reforms' will be needed. 'These reforms will certainly be weighed. They will be drawn up according to the venerable and reasonable traditions on the one hand and according to the needs of the time on the other. They certainly will be functional and beneficial, because they will have no other purpose than that of dropping what is ephemeral and superfluous in the forms and norms that regulate the Roman Curia and of putting into being what is vital and serviceable for its efficient and proper functioning. They will be formulated and propagated by the Curia itself!'

'Formulated and propagated by the Curia itself'? Was the Curia thought to be in a position, in the present situation, to reform itself? Isn't that equivalent to Baron von Münchhausen's effort to pull himself out of the morass by his own hair? And what about the Council? At any rate the pope is now demanding resolute internationalization and ecumenical development of the Curia: this will 'not be afraid to be composed in accordance with further supra-national and ecumenical development'. It will 'therefore not be jealous of the temporal prerogatives of former times, of external forms no longer suitable for the expression of high religious meanings. Nor will it be miserly of its faculties which the episcopacy, without damaging the universal ecclesiastical order, can today exercise better by itself and locally.'

Pope Paul deserves full praise: by these bold words he has put himself at the head of those who call for a *'reformatio'* not only *'in membris,* in the members' but also *'in capite,* in the head', to use the formulations from earlier reform councils. In so doing he is making himself the spokesman of the bishops and theologians, indeed of countless among the clergy and the people who have few things closer to their hearts than the reform of the papacy and the Roman central administration ('Vatican'). As things are, the success and persistence of the renewal movement depends on this.

What is needed here is a real agreement between the organs of the Curia and the pope, and this was by no means there in the time of John XXIII. Hence Paul's undisguised insistence on the obedience of the Curia: 'We are certain that no hesitations regarding the chief desires of the Pontiff will ever come from the Roman Curia; that the Curia will never be suspected of any differences of judgement or feelings with regard to judgements or feelings of the pope.' Again the indicative instead of the optative, even the imperative!

Evidently Papa Montini is by no means wholly 'certain' that his Curia will follow him. For at the end it is not by chance that he appeals to them 'to acknowledge' their reform 'firmly and openly': 'Now if ever the assent on the part of the Curia to what the pope ordains or wishes must be quite clear (*rigorosamente univoca*); indeed, if this assent is its law and its honour, now in particular is the moment to acknowledge this firmly and openly.' Does this agreement between the pope and his Curia apply 'only in great historical moments'? No: 'This agreement applies in perpetuity and to every papal decision; that is seemly for an organ which stands immediately below him and owes him absolute obedience, an organ of which the pope makes use to express his universal mission.' Here it is stated quite clearly that the Curia is not to claim the pope for itself; the pope claims the Curia for himself as his organ which owes him 'absolute obedience'.

And what is the reaction of the Curia to this papal admonition, which is so bold and urgent? Where is the 'firm and open acknowledgement' of Curia reform from this audience of dignitaries? One hears amazingly little of this, and I am disturbed when I think back to the passive resistance of the Curia cardinals to the announcement of the Council by John XXIII. At the beginning of the second session of the Council I ask one of the members of the Curia who were present at Paul's reform speech, 'How did you react to the pope's speech?' His answer was: 'We kept silent, and we all left the room in silence.' 'Why keep silent?' I ask. He smiles: 'Anyone who had spoken in favour of reform would have made himself unpopular with many of his colleagues. And anyone who had spoken against would have had to reckon with a denunciation to the pope.' So they all keep silent and – wait: *pazienza,* let's see whether this Paolo Sesto follows up his bold words with bold actions. What does the pope plan? From the beginning he is concerned to strengthen the presence of the Vatican in international organizations (UNO, UNESCO), to continue the *'Ostpolitik'* and to build up a collection of modern art in the Vatican. And what else? The reform of the church itself and the Curia, which is so urgent?

Paul VI's programme for the Council

On Wednesday, 25 September 1963, I drive from Tübingen via Basle to Sursee. On Friday 27 September I leave Sursee at 6 a.m., and at 8 p.m. arrive in Rome. I have now been officially nominated an adviser to the Council by the pope, and as such am no longer under Bishop Carl-Joseph Leiprecht of Rottenburg. That's fortunate: having asked me a year previously in a conversation in his house to be his personal *peritus,* and having proposed me as an official Council *peritus* in the first session of the Council, a short time before the beginning of the second session he gives me an unpleasant surprise with a cool official letter: for his Council Commission on the Religious Orders he has brought Fr Friedrich Wulf SJ as *peritus* and therefore is dispensing with my services. This time there is no personal conversation. He is 'dispensing' with me; among 'brothers' that's that. In cases like this should I keep describing my conflicting feelings, which readers with perhaps similar experiences can easily imagine for themselves? At any rate he's released me so now I have more freedom. It seems to me counter-productive to inform the public about Bishop Leiprecht's step. The bishop isn't interested in doing so either, and is at least prepared to bear my hotel expenses for the second session of the Council.

But I have to look for new accommodation. I find it in the little Hotel Rivoli, not far from the Villa San Francesco. The next morning I visit the bishop there. He is as friendly as ever and talks of his work in the Commission on the Religious Orders. But he still keeps his real reasons to himself. And to this day I haven't discovered what made him act like this. Was his 'dispensing' with my services a price demanded by the Curia for my visit to America? Had I been all too bold for his taste? Did he simply want to safeguard himself over against nuncio and Curia for the future? Did he want to, did he have to? Enquires would have got nowhere.

For the rest of the day, with increasing reservations I begin to study the revised schema on the church which is now printed and available. At 5 p.m. I meet Karl Rahner in the Collegium Germanicum and then invite him to Rivoli for supper. We discuss in detail the by no means simple situation before the second session and many pending theological questions. We both eagerly await the new pope's opening speech at the second session. It will doubtless be programmatic and indicate something of the future course of this pontificate.

When we all stream into St Peter's on Sunday 29 September 1963 for the opening of the second session of the Council, there is a mood of hope and a new beginning. The improvement of the Council rules by Paul VI and the pope's address on the reform of the Roman Curia have met with a positive response in the episcopate and the church. And so we theologians, too, on the two raised stands of experts, listen to his important programmatic speech on the opening of the second session with great attention and sympathy. Nor are we disappointed: it stands out for its courage and clarity. I am reassured: Paul VI will continue John XXIII's course at this Council powerfully and resolutely.

There are passages in this speech about which I can be quite personally pleased: the Council itself is seen theologically, just as it was described in my Tübingen inaugural lecture, as a representation of the church. The pope also clearly states that in the Council those four classical marks of the church – unity, catholicity, holiness and apostolicity – are to be used as imperatives. Has the pope himself, or perhaps Monsignor Carlo Colombo from Milan, his personal Council theologian, who is sitting directly beside me in the front row on the platform of experts, taken note of *Structures of the Church,* or at least my inaugural lecture? In fact Carlo Colombo looks at me with a happy smile which confirms this when with greater clarity than any pope since the Reformation the pope expresses the christocentricity which is so important to me in *Justification*: 'Christ is our starting point. Christ is our leader and our way. Christ is our hope and our goal.' Karl Barth will doubtless be delighted at these programmatic statements, and I myself will put them at the head of the collection of pioneering 'Council speeches' which I assemble with the American Jesuit Daniel O'Hanlon. I translate some of them into German, and then edit them with the French Dominican Yves Congar at the end of the second session of the Council.

In the light of this christocentric starting point the pope then puts to the Council the following four main tasks, to which I can subscribe completely: 1. a deepening of the self-understanding of the church; 2. the renewal of the church; 3. the restoration of unity between all Christians; 4. dialogue between the church and the people of our time. So finally the Council has a clearly formulated christological foundation and a coherent concept, and this largely corresponds to that laid down in *The Council and Reunion*. The pope makes further important programmatic statements on points of detail, but if one reflects on them more closely they seem to display a certain ambiguity and raise questions for me.

We all listen with approval to emphatic words about the papacy as service: 'The least one among you, the Servant of the servants of God,' wants 'to show you in act that he wishes to be with you, to pray with you, to speak with you, to reflect with you and to work with you.' 'At this first moment of the second session of the great synod we declare to God that in our mind there is no intention of human predominance, no jealousy of exclusive power, but only the desire and the will to carry out the divine mandate which makes us, of you and among you, the supreme shepherd.' I ask myself: certainly there should be 'no intention of human predominance', but in that case what is the 'divine mandate to be the supreme shepherd'? Does that still mean the mediaeval primacy of papal rule?

Of course bishops are glad to hear the clear words about the episcopate as college, as a fellowship of brothers: 'You yourselves are the successors of the apostles and their true heirs.' He awaits the discussion on the position of bishops 'with great expectations and confidence'. 'Taking for granted the dogmatic declarations of the First Vatican Ecumenical Council regarding the Roman pontiff, this discussion will go on to develop the doctrine regarding the episcopate, its function and relationship with Peter.' But, I ask myself again: to what extent does the college of bishops go back to the apostolic college? And does 'regardless of' perhaps mean that the 'Roman pope' does not seriously want to restrict the claims to absoluteness defined at Vatican I in favour of a collegial leadership of the church?

Of course I am also pleased at the end by the way in which the pope understands the task of the church as service to the world: the church has 'the sincere intention not of conquering it but of serving it, not of despising it but of appreciating it, not of condemning it but of strengthening and saving it'. The pope gives a positive assessment of the young rising nations and the great world religions, 'which preserve the sense and notion of the one supreme transcendent God, Creator and Sustainer, and which worship him with acts of sincere piety'. 'In such religions the Catholic Church sees omissions, insufficiencies and errors which cause her sadness. But she cannot exclude them from her thoughts and would have them know that she esteems what they contain of truth and goodness and humanity.' Nevertheless, I ask myself: where does the church stand on their fundamental 'omissions, insufficiencies and errors', and can 'what there is of truth and goodness and humanity' in the other religions also be the way to salvation?

My overall impression is that Papa Montini, beyond doubt a man of good will, well-read and concerned for reform, but thinking in scholastic and ecclesiastical terms and with little experience of modern exegesis and the history of dogma, seems all too little aware of the historical background to the present controversy. For what is the present great conciliar process of renewal about? It can be summed up in the following formula:

Is the church a pyramid or a community?

Here I must again inflict some theological background information on readers; without it they will hardly be able to understand my own struggle in matters of church reform. Later I will often be annoyed that people with little or no knowledge of the Catholic Church, above all from the world of business, politics and journalism, keep wanting to argue that it has to be as it is: hierarchical, centralistic and absolutist. They say that it has always been like this and must always remain like this. We reformers shouldn't expect the pope to stop being the pope. Indeed, anyone who criticizes papal absolutism puts the papacy itself in question. But if I may be allowed to say so, in the light of history all this is sheer nonsense.

In later years I shall provide very much better historical evidence in connection with my paradigm analysis and also conceptualize it: here basically we have the replacement of the model of the church (paradigm) which has been dominant since the Middle Ages. And that is of course a question of the first order about power. Up to the Council the Catholic Church has given the impression to many people that it is absolutist, and to some even that it is totalitarian. Is this only the result of its strict, and for many people disturbingly effective, external organization? No, it is likewise the result of a hierarchical and pyramidal system of the church of the kind that I have known since my youth! The 'real' church rises from a broad base in the people: priests and religious, then the bishops and archbishops and cardinals, and right at the top the pope.

In the legalistic-scholastic ideology of the church which I have known all too well since my time at the Gregorian, this model is deduced theoretically right from the top: from the pope as the source of power. Since the mediaeval dispute between the pope and the emperor – only now are there treatises on the church! – the longest and most impressive chapters have been devoted to him. The bishops (who had already been treated much more briefly) and the priests (only peripherally) appear as the subordinate organ of the pope, who as 'head' ultimately alone has the initiative; from him all the authority in the subordinate ranks derives. Is it surprising that such an 'ecclesiology' devotes at best brief chapters to the 'ecclesia' itself, the 'church' as community, the people of God, and that these above all emphasize obedience in doctrine and discipline? And what about the freedom of a Christian (*libertas Christiani*)? This isn't a theme. The only theme is the freedom of the church as institution (*libertas ecclesiae*) – freedom from the state. Such a static model of the church is characterized by authoritarianism, centralism and absolutism; by the neglect of the episcopal college and the local churches; by the supremacy of the curial apparatus in doctrine and life; by a lack of initiative and creativity at all the lower levels.

But what all too few people know is that this hierarchical model of the church isn't the traditionally Catholic model! Though of course it was already prepared for in Rome in the first millennium, it was implemented in the eleventh century by that Pope Gregory VII (Hildebrand) and the men of the 'Gregorian Reform' by means of excommunication, the interdict and the Inquisition (directed above all against German emperors and theologians, against the episcopate and the clergy). And this was done on the basis of the claims made by crude forgeries (above all that of pseudo-Isidore), which presented the Roman innovations of the second millennium as Catholic traditions of the first millennium. In *The Catholic Church: A Short History* (2001) I have sketched out extremely briefly the development which I described broadly in *Christianity. Its Essence and History* (ET 1995). According to all the researches of serious church historians, what happened here is not just a preservation of the tradition, as is claimed in Rome, but also an invention of the tradition, or more precisely a suppression, a narrowing and in part even a falsification of the Catholic by the Roman. Here was a new 'Roman Catholic' model. It was fought for in the eleventh century by a revolution from above – at the cost of the schism with the Eastern churches and later the Lutheran Reformation. It was accentuated and cemented by the later polemic, apologetics and politics, all directed against the Reformation and modernity.

What we hardly ever heard in Rome as students, but what I have already worked out in my Tübingen inaugural lecture, is that the New Testament, patristic and in part even the early mediaeval understanding of the church had a different orientation: not on a monarchical head but on the community of believers – the *communio fidelium*, and the ministries in the service of the community. People are now reflecting on this again in the Council, as one of the best speeches at the Council, made by Léon-Arthur Elchinger, Archbishop-coadjutor of Strasbourg, points out. Yesterday the church was regarded above all as an institution; today it is experienced as a community. Yesterday people above all looked to the pope; today they see the bishop united with the pope. Yesterday people looked only at the bishop; today they look at the bishops as a college. Yesterday theology emphasized the importance of the hierarchy; today it is discovering the people of God. Yesterday it spoke above all of what divides; today it speaks of what unites.

Everything is clear both historically and theologically, but now I am anxious: what model of the church will become established at the Council? The reform of the liturgy is only the beginning; it has to be followed by other reforms, above all a correction of the mediaeval Counter-Reformation understanding of the church. Here in particular the tricky question of the exercising of power in the church arises. As could already be foreseen in the debate during the last week of the first session of the Council which was broken off by the Curia without any vote and final decision, the planned decree on the church (*De ecclesia*) is now increasingly coming into the centre of interest. And what does the schema revised in Rome between the first and second session now look like? Here the issue is the central Roman position of power. Who, according to the Council, ultimately has the say in the Catholic Church? Is it still the pope (= Curia) as the absolute infallible ruler, or the pope with his place in the college of bishops (= collegiality), where possible represented by an episcopal council which decides with him? It is crystal clear that the hard core of the Curia will defend itself with all its means against any threats to a loss in power.

'Mediation' from Louvain

Even now, 40 years later, I get extremely angry when I once again pick up my original Council documents and begin to thumb through the large-format volume of the revised draft of the Constitution on the Church, bound in grey. The questions that I raised at the time are in the margin: objection after objection. How could such a deeply contradictory second draft decree come into being between the sessions? And what were the disputed points? Today I recognize even more clearly than at the time that the issue was not and is not the finer points of theology but the basic question whether the *communio* model of the church orientated on the Bible, or the mediaeval absolutist pyramidal model, would again win through. A look behind the scenes shows how this contradictory Council constitution came about.

The new draft is a compromise product. The responsibility for this lies with a sub-commission of the Theological Commission under the Curia cardinal Browne as Ottaviani's representative: seven bishops and seven theologians, the majority of them progressive but all of them still imprisoned in neoscholastic ecclesiology – at any rate there isn't a single specialist exegete or historian of dogma among them. Of seven alternative drafts, that by Monsignor Philips of Louvain prevails – why? Alongside the dogmatic theologian Philips, who then produces the draft, here the fundamental theologian Moeller, well-versed in literature, has been active, together with the ecumenist Thils and the church lawyer Onclin. I may regard all of them as my theological friends. I hope that they will forgive me here if for the sake of the cause I have to go on to offer a very critical analysis. The small 'Belgian working party' (*'squadra belga'*) from the University of Louvain, very efficiently supported by the Rector of the Pontifical Belgian College, Monsignor A. Prignon, have collaborated admirably. And in their primate, Cardinal Suenens, they have probably the best strategist and orator of the Second Vatican Council, who moreover is responsible for the schema on the church in the Co-ordinating Commission between the two sessions.

But Gérard Philips has made the main contribution, problematical as it is. I know him from my time in Münster: he is an open theologian, but at heart a conservative, who has gone along with everything in Ottaviani's Preparatory Commission. Philips has a foot in both camps, but precisely in so doing commends himself to his archbishop Suenens as a man of the *via media*, who also gets on well with Ottaviani, Parente and Tromp. Of course Philips won't say a word about his trading with the Curia in his commentary on the Constitution on the Church published after the Council by Herder, and the later historians of the Council won't see through him either. Here he now increasingly plays in the Theological Commission the role that Tromp played before the Council. Though far from having the theological stature of a Congar, Rahner or Schillebeeckx, the short friendly prelate surpasses them all as a tactician and formulator of consensus texts (tested by long years in the Belgian Senate). He skilfully takes up all the suggestions, works on them, and invisibly draws the threads together. Monsignor Philips sees himself as the indefatigable mediator between Curia (called 'minority') and Council (called 'majority'), between 'integrists' and 'progressives', old schemata and new efforts.

But at whose expense? Today more than ever I am convinced that this is at the expense of the truth – above all the truth of the Bible, the foundation document of the church. For one thing unfortunately escapes even the learned and wily Louvain dogmatic theologian: a solid knowledge of the current state of discussion in New Testament exegesis. He uses biblical texts dogmatically, supported by one or two traditional exegetes. He has no serious knowledge either of the problems of a 'founding of the church' by Jesus, of the charismatic constitution of the Pauline communities, or of the questionable nature of the classic biblical texts about Peter. In more than one conversation I attempt to make him more sensitive to the explosive nature of these questions.

Once in an aisle of St Peter's I put to Philips the test question: 'Who really celebrated the eucharist in the community of Corinth when the apostle Paul was abroad (say in Ephesus)?' Philips – unfortunately like Congar and others later – proves perplexed, and innocently asks what I mean. I tell him that it is clear from 1 Corinthians (and this isn't just the Tübingen perspective but that of critical exegesis generally) that in Corinth there was no bishop or presbyter (Timothy or Titus) whom Paul could have addressed when abuses at the celebration of the eucharist were reported to him: some, probably slaves, arrived late, and others were already drunk. In his letter to Corinth Paul doesn't address any official but the community as a whole: 'Wait for one another' and so on. What does that mean? It means that the community of Corinth celebrated the eucharist even without the apostle, and even without a bishop or presbyter. And what follows from that for today? It follows that according to the New Testament, Catholic communities, say in Communist China, indeed if need be any group of Christians today, can celebrate a eucharist which is theologically valid even without a priest, even if perhaps it is also illegal according to church law! And Protestant communities with pastors who don't stand in the apostolic succession of ministry can celebrate the eucharist in a quite valid way. 'Do this in remembrance of me', like 'Go, baptize and teach', is said to all the disciples of Jesus and not just a hierarchy. Everything is set out at length in my book *Structures of the Church*! And our schema on the church? It completely ignores such fundamental problems. And because these have never been tackled officially, the recognition of Protestant ministries and the eucharistic fellowship of the Christian churches is still blocked as I write in the year 2002.

Philips? I get the impression that he isn't clear about the scope of these questions. Paradoxically, the reactionary cardinal Ernesto Ruffini is. As early as 6 October 1963, with a precise reference to my book *Structures of the Church* (187ff.), he will state in the aula: 'Beyond doubt, not even the best of the laity may ever be given the capacity to celebrate the eucharist or to forgive sins, which as a *peritus* of this Council recently asserts in a book with the church's permission for publication, probably could have been granted in a changed time.' This particular question should at least have been discussed seriously in the commission – and historical-critical exegetes should have been involved!

The disastrous compromise

On 17 April 1963 *Der Spiegel* publishes a long and very well informed article by Werner Harenberg – also containing photographs of Cardinal König, Bishop Volk, Karl Barth and Michael Schmaus – on my theological activity from *Justification* to *Structures* in Germany, Rome and the USA. The editor of *Der Spiegel*, Rudolf Augstein, absent at the time, later thinks that this would have proved a better lead story than the story about Rainer Barzel, Minister for All-German Affairs and later leader of the Christian Democratic Party. Of course *Der Spiegel* emphasizes the critical passages of my book in connection with the structures of the church: above all, that according to the dogma of Constance the ecumenical council is above the pope, that the pope can resign, and in particular cases like heresy, schism or mental illness even automatically loses office. These qualifications to papal absolutism are also well known in the Curia, but are normally kept quiet about. Only Pope John is occasionally threatened by the Rector of the conservative Lateran University, Monsignor Piolanti, of course without any names being mentioned, that in the case of heresy he would *ipso facto* lose office.

But now, in the discussion of the document on the church, people in the Sanctum Officium do not dream of reviving the overgrown primitive Christian collegial and democratic structures of the early church. They have long grasped the explosiveness of these questions and want to subject the author of the book *Structures of the Church* to an inquisitorial process. A first warning: according to a press agency report of 1 October 1963, on the basis of an oral instruction by the Roman vicariate (the Officium is behind this), my books, and those of the bright American journalist Xavier Rynne (*Letters from Vatican City*), a pseudonym for the

Redemptorist Fr Francis X. Murphy who also writes for the *New Yorker*, and Robert B. Kaiser, the brilliant correspondent of *Time* (*Inside the Council*), are to be removed from the shop windows. In future they may be bought only by Council fathers and 'reliable' theologians. 'Pope bans 3 authors' is the headline of the London *Daily Express* and other papers. As soon as this inquisitorial action gets into the media, it is withdrawn. And Bob Kaiser's extremely informal and informative Saturday evening parties can continued undisturbed. There I find the leading exponents of the English-speaking progressives: *periti* like Gregory Baum, George Higgins, John Courtney Murray, Gus Weigel, Vincent (Art) Yzermans and bishops like Paul Hallinan (Atlanta), Mark McGrath (Panama), Thomas Roberts (formerly Delhi), and many others.

Quite unconcerned by the admonition which Pope Paul has just given to the Curia to accept well-meant criticism in humility, meanwhile the assessor of the Sanctum Officium, Archbishop Parente, is raging on against the young reformers as the '*sans-culottes* of theology': 'Many shameless things have been written during these months against the Roman Curia, its bureaucracy, its dogmatism and its disciplinary rigidity. This has happened above all at the expense of the Holy Office, which represents the pinnacle of the Roman Curia. This youthful iconoclastic shamelessness gives us occasion to remind the *sans-culottes* that in the light of their history their arrogance is to a great extent the daughter of a deception.' Everyone in the Council knows to whom that mainly refers.

But how does the revised draft on the church look, as it is presented to the Council at the beginning of the second period by the 'Mixed Commission' (made up of Ottaviani's Theological Commission and Bea's Secretariat for Unity)? Prematurely, the joke had been told in the Council that the palazzo of the Holy Office now bore the advertisement 'Fly BEA'. What is my overall impression of this second scheme? A tremendous disappointment: it is Ottaviani rather than Bea who has won on the key points! Beyond doubt some progress has been achieved. At first glance the reformers can rejoice: the schema now no longer begins with the hierarchy but with two new chapters, the first on 'The Mystery of the Church' and the second – a good proposal by Suenens – on 'The People of God', to which pope and bishops, priests and religious also belong. Here in fact the biblical patristic *communio* model has come into its own, and here wishes of the Council have been fulfilled.

But has this 'rebuilding' of the schema 'quite clearly put an end to the pyramidal notion of the church'? That is what Jan Grootaers, the correspondent of the Brussels *De Maand*, who was quite well disposed to me, later writes in Alberigo's history of the Council. What an illusion! The third chapter, 'The Church is Hierarchical', shows this blatantly: here the Curia has clearly won. Instead of the biblical structure of service, again the mediaeval structure of rule is cemented: the all-dominating hierarchical pyramid is again established over the people of God! There is no attempt to put the whole ordering of ministries on a biblical and historical basis –

appointed to serve rather than to rule. There is no critical examination of the Roman ideology of primacy and infallibility which has been built up and extended in the course of the century by tendentious use of the New Testament texts about Peter. The result is that the traditional conception of hierarchy in Chapter III in fact degrades the previous Chapter II about the people of God so that it becomes a harmless prelude. For Chapter III decides who alone has the say in the people of God: the hierarchy, and ultimately everywhere solely the pope.

Of course we reformers are glad that there is a new passage in the third chapter about the collegiality of the pope with the bishops and another about the consecration of bishops, through which the bishop becomes bishop (and not through papal nomination). But these passages are in fact covered up by the uncritical and complete confirmation of the Vatican I definition of primacy. And while the fact that the confirmation of the infallibility of the pope is further supplemented by a paragraph on the infallibility of the episcopate flatters some bishops who are theologically uninformed, it is an 'emendation for the worse'. In future, say for the coming encyclical *Humanae vitae* against contraception, the pope can quite simply appeal to the allegedly infallible consensus of the episcopate. But by referring to the infallibility of the college of bishops (the 'ordinary' magisterium) Rome will skilfully veil the increasingly obsolete papal magisterium.

Hence I can by no means agree with the verdict of Jan Grootaers when in his very informative article he highlights the revised schema on the church, seen through Louvain spectacles, as the 'masterpiece of the interim session 1962/3', and sets Philips' compromise off against the 'maximalism of certain radical currents which argued for a complete replacement of the old schemata with new texts'. Who is meant here? Must I understand from this that Grootaers will finally after all think it unnecessary to come to Tübingen for information, a visit which he announced to me more than once? In truth, why should he have his justification of the fatal compromises, which is rich in words and facts, unmasked by some 'radical' questions from Tübingen?

In October 1963 my own conclusion is quite a different one: Ottaviani, Parente, Tromp and the Roman party have clearly established themselves at the centre of the schema on the church. How? By assenting in principle to the compromise forged by the Louvain people in the best of faith between the biblical orientated *communio* model (Chapters I and II) and the mediaeval absolutist pyramid model (Chapter III) (and calling for many corrections). For in this way the Curia ('minority') with its pyramid model has forced its will on the Council ('majority'). Yves Congar also clearly sees it this way when on 23 September 1965 he writes in his journal (also with reference to de Lubac): 'The tiny minority will achieve its aims, at least in part. In the end people will give in to their cry (about Chapter III) like parents who finally have to give in to their rebellious children to have peace . . .' The church after the Council will pay dearly for this. Reading this whole document at the beginning of the second session already depresses me deeply. My only thought is: how can one even now break open this new old schema on the church at least on some important points? Just what can one do?

Join the Commission – yes or no?

I talk with Karl Rahner more than anyone else during these days. As adviser to Cardinal König he has been invited on to the Theological Commission and was one of the seven theologians of the sub-commission between the sessions. Nevertheless he shares many of my objections and says: 'You speak Latin well and are impertinent enough, why don't you simply come into the Theological Commission?' For me this is perhaps the most difficult and momentous decision at the time of the Council.

I don't lack the courage. But the reasons for and against make me hesitate and ask Rahner for time to reflect.

Certainly I am now an official Council theologian nominated by the pope, and on my *peritus* pass the Cardinal Secretary of State asks 'all civil and military authorities to grant the bearer of this document, who is one of the experts of the Second Vatican Council, free passage, and if necessary any help and support required'. But should I just go into the Theological Commission without having been formally invited? Since I am all too well known to Tromp, the secretary of the Commission, Parente and others, should I risk being politely shown out of the session room?

Certainly I am undeterred if the cause requires it. But what chance do I have as the sole, presumably the youngest, expert, of achieving anything in this body made up of cardinals, archbishops and bishops, who are the real members of the Commission? As an adviser am I constantly to intervene in the debates? Am I to explain my fundamentally different standpoint on Chapter III in particular by a brief report, as I have done in this retrospect? Not a chance.

Basically, a completely different draft is needed for Chapter III. But would Ottaviani, Tromp and their supporters allow a new debate on principles ('maximalism') on this *'articulus stantis et cadentis Curiae'*? That is inconceivable. Certainly I could achieve some corrections of detail in the Commission. But in the circumstances I can make these more effectively through interventions by bishops in the Council aula.

And what are the further consequences for me personally? If I join the Commission, in the end I shall either have to be among the signatories or protest. So am I not threatened with a 'go along and become a prisoner', which will make it difficult for me later to adopt a critical position in public? Am I not putting my personal credibility more at risk, which so far has been perhaps my strongest trump in public?

After two or three days I meet Rahner again and explain to him why I don't want to slip into the Theological Commission. I tell him that I have other possibilities of active collaboration: I can compose speeches for bishops, can give lectures to gatherings of bishops, and have spoken not only to the Latin American and African bishops but also to those of India, Canada, the USA and Belgium. By conversations inside and outside the aula I can offer suggestions, and if necessary I can have an influence through the media. Gain access to this Commission? Later, too, in similar cases, it will be my principle to use the main entrance, not the side entrance.

Of course, it will be possible for people to play my negative decision off against me after the Council. And in retrospect it will be precisely those German bishops who did not want my critical involvement at all who spread the rumour that I refused to collaborate with the Commission from the start. In fact at no time during the whole Council was I ever asked for any kind of service by a single bishop from the German-language area. For these 'gentlemen' – they always greeted me in a very friendly way – I am doubtless too much the man who uncomfortably grasps 'hot potatoes': young, fresh, 'radical'. Bishop Hengsbach of Essen knows the explanation: 'Küng got a chair too early!' Cardinal Döpfner remarks in his typical 'yes-but' style: 'Küng is right in everything, but he's too soon.' And Bishop Leiprecht? He at any rate knew that I wasn't *persona grata* in the Sanctum Officium.

So I am invited by various episcopal conferences to give lectures, but never by a German-language one. Both in the Germanicum, and in the Campo Santo to the Goerres-Gesellschaft, I speak about early Catholicism in the New Testament and the consequences of the charismatic Pauline constitution of the church for the present day. But no German-speaking bishop ever indicates any interest in such problems to me. Conversely, I hear from various sources that episcopal ordinariates (on the instructions of Rome) are increasingly deterring theological students from doing their doctorates with me. In four decades of teaching in Tübingen I never have a single doctoral student from our diocese of Rottenburg: one (my first server) who is already firmly resolved to study there is lured away from me again and sent to Kasper in Münster (where this priest marries – what if that had happened under me!). To this extent the negative attitude of the German conference of bishops to my theology after the Council will hardly come as a surprise.

Instead of working on the Commission, which in other conditions I would have been quite prepared to do, now, however, possibilities in journalism open up for me which few others have. For on the basis of my knowledge of languages, many translations and earlier journeys, I have contacts with every possible journalist. I have a particularly high regard for Henri Fesquet of *Le Monde,* Michel van der Plas of *Elzevier's,* Amsterdam, Joseph Schmitz van Vorst of the *Frankfurter Allgemeine Zeitung,* Ken Woodward of *Newsweek,* John Cogley of *Commonweal* and Bob Kaiser of *Time Magazine.* I would like to express my thanks to all of them here. Whereas the reporters of the *New York Times* have to maintain strict impartiality, Bob may adopt positions on the basis of comprehensive information – in favour of the 'conciliar majority' concerned with reform which is time and again blocked by the 'curial minority' (perhaps numbering 10 per cent). And I am also grateful to the Jesuits of *Civiltà Cattolica* (Tucci), *Stimmen der Zeit* (Seibel), *America* (Campion, O'Hanlon and Graham) and *Études* (Rouquette). Leo Alting van Geusau from Holland (his information centre 'doc' publishes many important texts), Tom Stransky from New York (later General of the Paulist Fathers) and Jorge Mejía from Buenos Aires (in 2001 together with Roberto Tucci he will become a cardinal and prefect of the Vatican library) are also active in a welcome way.

Time and again I receive invitations from radio or television stations. An historic date for television generally is 15 October 1963, when at tremendous expense the first 'Telstar' transmission takes place, broadcasting a live conversation carried on over three continents: in Princeton the leading American Protestant Dr James McCord, in London Bishop Lesslie Newbigin, architect of the church union of South India and president of the International Missionary Council, in Rome the African cardinal Laurean Rugambwa (Tanzania) and me. A worldwide dissemination of our conversation on the Council and the ecumene was guaranteed. What an occasion!

When on one occasion I meet the Louvain theologian Charles Moeller at a *'ricevimento'* (reception) given by the Americans and discuss with him the basic problems of the 'hierarchical constitution of the church', he finally remarks: *'Cher ami*, when I hear you talk about the problems I feel that I should really resign from the Theological Commission.' *'Pas de tout*, by no means,' is my reply: 'There must be those who remain outside and those who work within. We must both attempt to achieve what we can for the Council.'

The struggle for power

For me by now one thing has become more than clear. Under the leadership of this head of the Sanctum Officium and his equally authoritarian loyal assistant Tromp, no thoroughly revised schema on the church can be worked out. The Dutchman was capable of banging his fist on the table during the session and exclaiming: 'This is a question which is decided by the encyclical!' Of course he meant the encyclical *Mystici corporis*, which he himself had written. There is widespread dissatisfaction with the work of the Council commissions, and especially the Theological Commission. Shouldn't an attempt be made to replace Cardinal Alfredo Ottaviani as president of the Commission with someone who has had a better theological training and is less authoritarian? Many bishops explicitly want a thorough renewal of the commissions and their presidents. And many suggestions have already been made about the personal renewal of the central authorities of the Council.

Should I write to the pope about Cardinal Ottaviani and use the way known to me through his private secretary, the helpful Don Pasquale Macchi? This seems to me to be all too ambitious, and to have little prospect of success. But I win over the most important representative of the Eastern churches united with Rome, the Melkite Patriarch of Antioch, Maximos IV. His personal spokesman Orest Kéramé (Beirut) serves as his middleman. So I compose in French a well-considered letter to His Holiness, which asks for the dismissal of Cardinal Ottaviani. And Kéramé confirms to me that the patriarch has handed on this letter to the pope in his private audience.

And what is the reply of Paul VI to all the many demands and requests for a reform of the work of the Commission? A typical Montinian both-and. On the one hand the curial presidents and secretaries of commissions are to remain in their posts; in this way the pope can avoid a new conflict with the Curia. On the other hand, the Council is graciously allowed to hold a new election of four new members for each commission (in addition to which there is again one nominated by the pope); moreover it can itself elect a second vice-president and a second secretary for each commission. And the result? Certainly the weight is shifted in favour of the Council, but not decisively. The Curia keeps the lever of power in its hands, and the system of conciliar-curial compromises remains, slightly improved. It is cause for despair.

On 22 October 1964 I have a lengthy conversation with Cardinal Augustin Bea. I complain in clear words about the manipulation of the Council by Cardinal Ottaviani, other Curia cardinals and General Secretary Felici. As president of the Secretariat for Unity, he himself also has to suffer under these members of the Curia. The wise old man replies with a gentle smile: 'You're quite right. But you can't shoot everyone.' It is said that no one goes away from Cardinal Bea without being comforted by him. But how, I often ask myself, is one to change an absolutist system like that of the French kings without the guillotine, which of course is not an option for Christians? The alternative to be thought about would be a non-violent 'glorious revolution' in the English style.

The pope appoints four moderators to co-ordinate the Council better: Cardinals Suenens, Döpfner and Lercaro (called 'the three synoptists') represent the progressive 'majority' of the Council. But the Armenian Curia cardinal Agagianian, more Roman than the Romans, is attached to them as a chaperon. Their task will be to guide the discussion in the general congregations, to examine the suggestions and petitions of the fathers and to hand them on to the relevant commissions. But will they be able to assert themselves? Here too there is a Montinian half-measure: the pope immediately weakens what was originally meant to be their strong position over against General Secretary Felici. In any case he finds it difficult to delegate power: in this he remains a disciple of Pacelli. Paul VI simply doesn't approve the internal regulation urgently desired and worked out by Suenens, to guarantee a confidential collaboration of the moderators with the pope and their independent role over against the Council. Indeed he smoothly has the secretary appointed by the moderators, Fr Giuseppe Dossetti, formerly a well-known left-wing politician and now a confidant of Lercaro, kicked out when Felici objects. He deliberately leaves unclear the demarcation of competences between moderators, Presiding Council and General Secretariat – in so doing he deliberately accepts countless frictions and conflicts.

The most significant success of the cardinal moderators will be the trial vote on the five questions relating to the consecration of bishops, collegiality and diaconate. This had already been announced for 15 October 1963 and can at last finally take place on 30 October despite all the delaying actions by the Curia. It was the first and last time that the moderators dared to seize such an initiative; subsequently they seem largely to be degraded into nice figureheads – in favour of General Secretary Felici, who, with Cicognani and Ottaviani behind him, skilfully and stubbornly fills the power vacuum allowed by the pope.

Only the complaint by the Eastern churches that their patriarchs, who go back to the first centuries of the church, were being put after the cardinals (originally Roman city pastors), who in the present form derive from the Middle Ages, finds a hearing with the pope, as it costs little: the patriarchs now no longer have their places alongside and after the cardinals, as in the first session, but facing the cardinals.

What is very much more important to me is that this Council still lacks first-class critical exegetes who could put the picture of the church on a thoroughly biblical basis: I can't get Professor Schelkle's angry opinion on the revelation schema out of my head. I raise this question at a dinner at the British embassy with Bishop Moorman, the representative of the Archbishop of Canterbury, and my friend Jan Willebrands, secretary of the Secretariat for Unity. Willebrands replies that after all the well-known Louvain exegetes Beda Rigaux and Lucien Cerfaux are both on the mixed commission. I have nothing against Louvain, I say, but despite their undisputed knowledge these professors (who have already done great service to the Curia in the preparation of the Council) are neither critical nor strong enough.

My suggestion – if people can't or won't bring in Fr Lyonnet or Fr Zerwick from the Roman Biblical Institute – is to add two or three internationally known German exegetes like Schelkle (Tübingen), Schnackenburg (Würzburg) or Vögtle (Freiburg), who are experts in the current discussion on church and ministry as this is being carried on in Tübingen and elsewhere. Willebrands replies, 'No, they're too heavy.' So historical-critical exegesis will in fact remain absent from the Second Vatican Council. And what remains to be done in these circumstances? An attempt must be made at least to expand and improve this completely unsatisfactory Chapter III on the hierarchical constitution at least in some important parts. At any rate I want to work on that with all my might.

Correcting Council definitions

In a small group of German-language *periti*, right at the beginning of the second session we discuss the topics on which we want to work out interventions by the bishops. Happily Karl Rahner says that he is prepared to work out with me an intervention on the traditional doctrine of three offices, which is meant to correct the Tridentine definition. We meet once more in the Germanicum, where among the students I also get to know Karl Lehmann; already with a doctorate in philosophy he is preparing for a doctorate in theology, is active as senior librarian and is later to become Rahner's assistant. Karl Rahner wants to type the intervention himself. A third party is Fr Otto Semmelroth, a good ecclesiologist, author of the thesis of the church as 'primal sacrament', who in the break wonders in an amused way at how I dare to contradict Karl Rahner. I had only ventured to observe that one does not need to begin every sentence with *'cum'* (Rahner's equivalent of 'Well').

The condemnation by the Council of Trent which needs to be corrected runs like this: 'Whoever says that in the Catholic Church there is no hierarchy instituted by divine ordinance, which consists of bishops, priests and deacons, let him be excluded' (Denziger 966). Our correction relates to three points:

- Trent: 'hierarchy'. We propose 'ecclesiastical ministry' (*ministerium ecclesiasticum*).
- Trent: 'divine ordinance', referring to the division of the ministry into bishops, priests and deacons. We propose 'divinely instituted', relating only to the ministry of the church as such.
- Trent: 'hierarchy which consists (*constat*) of bishops, priests and deacons'. We propose: 'The divinely instituted ecclesiastical ministry is *exercised* (*exercetur*) in different degrees by those who even *from ancient times* (*ab antiquo*, but not from the beginning) have been called bishops, priests and deacons.'

All this is probably a bit difficult for non–theologians to grasp, but it is very important. Why? Unlike the Tridentine dogma which presupposes that the three ministries had existed and functioned in this way from the very beginning, our new formulation avoids certain unhistorical statements. Only thus can it be justified in the light of the present situation in exegetical-historical research, and possibly bring about a new order. Precisely as it has been prepared, it is finally presented in the Council aula in the name of the German episcopate by suffragan bishop Eduard Schick of Fulda, himself originally an exegete, and is included, hardly changed, by the Theological Commission in article 28 of the Constitution on the Church.

At this point it becomes unmistakably clear that in its chapter on the hierarchy Vatican II doesn't claim to be giving an account which is substantiated from the beginning, and is exegetically and historically solid. What the Theological Commission writes about our reformulated sentence can be written without further ado about the whole hierarchy in Chapter III: 'Whatever may be the historical origin of the priests, deacons and other ministries and the precise sense of the terms which are used in the New Testament to denote them . . .' In other words: at that time the Council described only a very time-conditioned historical form of the ministries, a theological and pastoral description of the nature, order and function of the various ministries orientated not on the origin but on the present order of the church. The consequence is that such a description need not be binding for the future. Have the Catholic theologians of the period after the Council drawn sufficient conclusions from these insights?

The Theological Commission makes it easier for itself in other condemnations which were stated wrongly or in a distorted way by Trent. The Commission simply leaves open the question whether only the bishop (and not also the priest) can ordain priests. And the Commission resolves the question whether the bishop (and not also the priest, as in the Eastern churches) can be the 'ordinary dispenser' of confirmation by the hardly perceptible alteration of two letters in the constitution: for Trent the bishop was the 'minister *ordinarius*' – the 'ordinary administrator' of confirmation; that excluded priests. For Vatican II he is only the 'minister *originarius*' or the 'original dispenser'; that also allows confirmations by priests.

Unfortunately these aren't honest acknowledgements of mistakes and responsible corrections, but theological tricks, which aren't meant to be noticed. Or, as I will put it more vividly after the Council at a colloquium of leading German church historians in honour of the 80-year-old Reformation historian Joseph Lortz in Mainz in 1967, in a contribution to the discussion of the authority of ecumenical councils: they 'cheated'. But this will so enrage the famous historian of the Council of Trent, Professor Hubert Jedin, that he bangs his notebook with both hands on the desk in front of him and roars in a quite unacademic way: 'I protest, I protest, that isn't the way to talk about an ecumenical council.'

I quietly retort that he has probably spoken not as a historian but as a dogmatic theologian: I at any rate wouldn't speak against the authority of the Council but for it, but such dubious methods of correction damage it. Yet the allegedly infallible authority of the Council is evidently another of those 'hot potatoes' that even Roman Catholic Council historians don't want to grasp. Which is why even in Alberigo's four-volume history of the Council there is hardly any critical account of the problems of the order of three ministries and suchlike. But these volumes also have amazingly little to say about the background of other important statements at the Council either.

The laity and their charisms

I have never had such an experience with a German-speaking bishop throughout the Council: on 15 October 1963 Cardinal Léon Suenens invites me to come to him at the Domus Mariae conference centre on the Via Aurelia. And he asks me quite directly what I think he should make another speech about at the Council. I mention two or three important concerns to him. Immediately he firmly chooses a theme: the charisms in the church, the gifts of the Spirit. This corresponds to his previous commitment to the laity and represents a new dimension in the understanding of the church for the Council. So he asks me to work out such a speech for him – 'but not in good Latin,' he adds with a chuckle, 'otherwise the bishops won't understand'.

Suenens is convinced by my biblically-based sketch, completely built on the Pauline understanding of the church. Presented in his clear sonorous voice with a slight French accent, the speech makes a strong impression. Alongside the hierarchical structure of the church there is a charismatic dimension. Not only the pastors but all Christians have their own charisma, their spiritual gift, their personal calling. Alongside the charisms of the apostles, the charisms of the prophets and the teachers are particularly to be valued in the church. Indeed, in pastoral praxis the inconspicuous charisms of the laity, say in catechesis, proclamation, social and charitable action, are to be taken particularly seriously.

It is the task of the pastors – whether they are pastors of the local and individual churches or of the church as a whole – to discover and further the charisms of the Spirit in the churches with a kind of 'spiritual instinct' and allow them to develop. It is the task of the pastors of the church to listen attentively and with an open heart to the laity, who individually and together are rich in their own gifts and charisms, and thus often have a greater experience in the life of today's world, again and again to carry on a lively conversation with them.

Conclusions are drawn from this on the level of doctrine (this charismatic dimension is worked into the Constitution on the Church) and also on the practical level: the number and universality of the lay audience at the Council is to be reinforced. And of his own accord the cardinal has added the demand: 'Women may also be invited as hearers; unless I am mistaken they make up half of humankind.' There is tumultuous applause, particularly at this point, but also at the end of the speech.

Peter Hebblethwaite calls this the 'most influential speech of the Council so far', and it found its way into Article 12 of the Constitution on the Church. Nowhere in the proceedings of the Council is there any indication of who the original author of a particular intervention is. Thus in 2001 an ignorant English Dominican, extremely annoyed on reading my book *The Catholic Church: A Short History*, which first appears in English, accuses me of passing over the charismatic structure of the church. His mistake is that he unknowingly quotes against me the very text from the Vatican II Constitution on the Church which the Council owes to me ...

I always enjoy being in St Peter's for such great speeches (and of course not only when I have written them!); otherwise the many repetitions and trivialities often bore me and I prefer 'homework' to being present in the basilica. For the first time, in the second session lay people are also admitted as hearers (*auditores*);

few in number and completely passive, their presence is only a symbolic, minimal representation of the laity. But it leads to communion being given every morning at the Council mass. On the penultimate day of the second session two lay people, Jean Guitton, my former professor of philosophy at the Sorbonne and a friend of the pope (I see him again at a reception given by our Paris publishers, Desclée de Brouwer), and the advocate Vittorino Veronese, who also has a long association with Montini, are allowed to speak in the aula. One can be quite certain that neither of these will say anything unconventional. Moreover what they say makes no impression whatsoever on the Council fathers.

But a woman may not speak. I gladly concede that the burning topicality of the question of women in the church only really dawned on me at the Council, when I was given an energetic reminder by the bold ladies of St Joan's Alliance for Women's Rights in the Church. It is still a long way to my 2002 book *Women in Christianity*!

Against legalism, centralism and triumphalism

Despite the lack of a schema, the month-long debate of October 1963 signals a strong leaning towards the church as community, as *communio* – against the dominant hierarchical system advocated by the members of the Curia and the General Superior of the Spiritan missionaries, Archbishop Marcel Lefebvre, who after the Council becomes head of the traditionalist sect with its headquarters at Ecône in the Swiss Valais.

So where an opportunity offers itself, I engage intensively in working out episcopal Council speeches in Latin. This is by no means easy. It's quite a *tour de force* to state in precisely ten minutes all the essentials on what can be quite complex questions. And then a bishop always has to be found to deliver the speech in the Council aula, usually with only slight alterations. Relations with Karl Rahner, Otto Semmelroth, Aloys Grillmeier, Max Zerwick and others are very helpful here. The Munich 'pope of the dogmatic theologians' Michael Schmaus had departed at an early stage because his neoscholastic theology was manifestly not called for; he remarked that here only 'the teenage theologians', by which he meant Ratzinger and me, had something to say. But the Aachen neoscholastic Schauf collaborates on the curial side as Tromp's minion. And the historian of the Council of Trent, Hubert Jedin, also doesn't feel completely at home in this clearly no longer Counter-Reformation Council: he thinks that here the 'dogmatic theologians' have the say. At any rate in this way I can express various of my concerns and eventually introduce them into the Council texts.

My opposition in principle to the legalistic, clericalist and triumphalist understanding of the church, which is shared by many others, has nothing to do with the 'anti-Roman feelings' which Balthasar and others later impute to me. That's nonsense: as a result of my seven years at the Germanicum I love the city of Rome, I move with great ease in the Roman milieu and have fewer anxieties than others about contact with representatives of the Vatican establishment. My argument isn't emotional but rational, and I am not for the abolition of the Roman Curia but for its fundamental reform (my *ceterum censeo* is '*Romanam curiam esse reformandam*' – 'Otherwise I think that the Roman Curia must be reformed'). I talk to the apostolic delegate Egidio Vagnozzi in St Peter's with slight irony about his activities against me in the USA (I tell him that he simply made propaganda for me) and likewise with Cardinal Ruffini after a session in front of the basilica (I tell him that his speeches against my books have done me no harm in the Roman bookshops).

As well as Monsignor Antonio Travia, Archbishop Emanuele Clarizio, the former nuncio in Santo Domingo, is a real friend to me. I meet them both now and then for meals, since they are as seriously interested in my views on the church and theology as I am interested about theirs on the Curia and the church. At Clarizio's request I even get Yves Congar, Henri de Lubac and Charles Moeller to come to supper with him and Travia in his apartment. Particularly through personal contacts one can both support the forces favouring reform in the Vatican and also provide a little satisfaction for those previously persecuted by the Inquisition.

However, things are less forced and easier at the '*ricevimenti*' which American bishops and *periti* give, usually at the weekend, either at the Hilton or at the home of the *Time Magazine* correspondent Bob Kaiser. I also regularly meet my numerous American friends here. Here, where bishops, experts, observers and journalists mix in an unhierarchical and friendly way, the church is visible and tangible as communion, *communio*. There are visitors to the Council like the leading American journalist Walter Lippmann, who invites me for a conversation in his hotel; or Professor Ralf Dahrendorf, whom I have already mentioned and with whom I spend almost two days in the Council aula, on the Palatine, in the Castelli Romani, and finally in the evening in Trastevere. They are all pleasantly surprised at everything that has become possible in the Catholic Church, which hitherto has been so authoritarian. And yet – how many fundamental problems are still unresolved!

Collegiality, diaconate, celibacy?

One of the questions which excites the Council most is the common, collegial responsibility of the bishops together with the pope for the whole church: strong forces in the Curia turn against the better balancing of the Vatican I definition of primacy which is urgently required in the light of the Bible, old Catholic tradition and the present situation; they even want to go back behind the revised schema. Supporters and opponents of the collegiality of the episcopate are almost balanced in the debate, as the curial party throws all its forces into the battle. I have worked out the speech in favour of collegiality, which is given by Bishop Rusch (Innsbruck) in the name of the Austrian episcopate.

Like everyone else I wait tensely for the trial vote on 30 October 1963: in it the following question (laboriously wrung out of the Curia word by word) will be circulated to the Council fathers by the moderators for a written and secret vote: 'Do the fathers wish the scheme to be drafted in such a way that it is said that the corpus or college of bishops is the successor of the college of apostles in the office of preaching, sanctification and the pastoral office, and that together with its head, the Roman pope, and never without this head (whose primacy over all pastors and all the faithful remains unassailed and undiminished) is endowed with full and supreme authority for the whole church?' The question is answered in the positive with 1808 votes for and 336 against. Great applause breaks out in the aula. The true balance of forces in the Council has become visible. This historic trial vote – there is a similar result on the decisive significance of the consecration of bishops – is now called the peaceful 'October Revolution' of the Catholic Church. A battle has been won, but what about the war? By no means; after all, the papal primacy of jurisdiction remains 'unassailed and undiminished' and the Curia still holds the levers of power.

And what about the celibacy of priests, which in view of the lack of priests in many countries on earth represents a problem of the first order for church structure? There is no vote on this, indeed it isn't even talked about. Why? Because people aren't allowed to talk about it in the Council aula. Bishop Sergio Méndez Arceo of Cuernavaca (Mexico), with whom I have made friends, tells me that he put his name down on the list of speakers in the General Secretariat of the Council with an indication of the topic, as required there: 'Celibacy'. This is a dramatic problem, particularly for the church of Latin America. But shortly afterwards he learns from the General Secretary of the Council, the jovial but brutal Curia bishop Felici, that Felici has struck out this entry, since speaking on the topic is not allowed. 'And why?' asks the bishop. As so often the snooty answer is: '*Ex auctoritate superiore*, on higher authority.' By this impressive phrase the members of the Curia mean the pope – whether they've asked him or not. One must then ask in curial jargon, '*ex ore ipsissimi* – from his own mouth?' For the members of the Curia, regardless of the collegiality of bishops, the pope is still the absolute ruler, high above the Council; and every member of the Curia thinks that he represents the pope. This authoritarian curial censorship explains the amazing phenomenon that not a word is said at the Second Vatican Council about the problem of celibacy, which is central to pastoral care all over the world, and which will burden the period from the Council to the present day. Only the Eastern Churches united with Rome finally manage to ensure that the married status of their clergy is mentioned in the Constitution on the Eastern Churches – to some degree positively, without any censure.

But there is a third vigorously disputed question which, while not very important in itself, is contested by the curial party with the same intensity because of its effect – the possible weakening of priestly celibacy: the possible introduction of a permanent office of deacon in the church. However, here too the progressive majority has already made two disastrous concessions in the very way in which the question is put: the decisive question of married deacons is left open, as the Curia requires. The question of women deacons, although these are clearly mentioned in the New Testament, is simply passed over (it is incompatible with the character of church ministry, which in principle is male!). At any rate the introduction of the permanent diaconate is approved by a vote of 1588 to 525. So this is a battle won (but only half won).

I am glad that after all the debates and votes an interval in the General Congregations is announced for the period from 30 October to 8 November (the feasts of All Saints and All Souls). Many bishops and theologians go home. Making up my mind quickly, on the 'first day of the holidays' I fly via Zürich to Stuttgart and over the next few days in Tübingen can clear up much of the work waiting there. Before I fly back to Rome on 6 November I make a brief intermediate stop in Sursee – and look forward not only to seeing my family again but also to being able to approve the building of my little house on the lake. The very next day a dinner is planned in Rome with Yves Congar and Charles Moeller, and two days later one with Charles Moeller and Monsignor Philips of Louvain, especially to talk about the unsatisfactory sections of the schema on the church – all in a pleasant and friendly atmosphere. But will these discussions have any practical consequences? On one question at any rate it is less easy to speak; it is taboo:

The suppressed question of the infallibility of the church

It is evident that the church magisterium has very great difficulties in publicly conceding errors of whatever kind, although such errors are known to any well-informed Catholic: from the condemnation of Galileo and the Chinese name for God and rites through the condemnation of freedom of religion, human rights and the doctrine of evolution, to all the historically erroneous decrees of the Biblical Commission under Pius X. The 'Vatican' doesn't err! The members of the Curia like to give the impression that they are speaking with the (infallible) authority of the pope. Did any of them ever reflect that the infallibility promised by Vatican I to solemn decisions of the pope is sharply repudiated both by the Orthodox Churches of the East and by the Churches of the Reformation (not to mention the Old Catholics)? In *Structures of the Church* I pointed out the problems of this Roman Catholic special doctrine which was first defined in 1870 by Vatican I, but at the same time also indicated the direction for a theological solution. On various occasions I've tested this out in lectures to experts (also in the Tübingen Wilhelmstift and at a Swiss meeting of Germanicum alumni). On 26 November 1963 a widely-noted article by me appears in the *Frankfurter*

Allgemeine Zeitung on the historical contingency of Council decrees under the title: 'Our knowledge is in part'. It ends up by pointing out the deeply fragmentary character even of 'infallible' formulations of faith.

As a Council theologian I now feel a special responsibility to mention the taboo problem of infallibility at the Council itself, even if this isn't talked about openly even in the Secretariat for Unity, although it is of prime importance for both Catholic and non-Catholic Christianity. I am constantly tortured by the question whether I should write a speech on this dogma of all dogmas. Of course I'm clear that the question of the infallibility of the church and the pope is as tricky for the Vatican as the infallibility of the Communist Party and the General Secretary is for the Kremlin: those who err can also be criticized and corrected. This affects the structure of power at a central point.

Imagine my inner torment. Whenever I consider the question of an intervention, the result is negative on every point:

- It is impossible to discuss these problems in ten minutes.
- Many Council fathers will find them hard to understand in Latin.
- No bishop will be prepared to give such a speech.
- Presumably the General Secretary won't allow the topic.
- The Curia (and also the pope?) will react immediately.
- Finally, the Theological Commission will ignore or domesticate such an intervention. This has already proved to be the case with other less explosive questions.

Infallible Bible?

Would it be ignored? The Council can certainly do that. For example it has ignored such important interventions as that of the Eastern bishops on divorce or mixed marriage – which are treated in the Eastern churches in a very much more humane way. The brave speech by the Swiss missionary Bishop Ammann OSB on the nuncios and their police supervision of the bishops – nunciatures as denunciatures – is also ignored.

Would it be domesticated? Certainly. For example the bold speech by Cardinal Franz König of Vienna on the infallibility (inerrancy) of the Bible on 24 September 1964 is domesticated, though positive comments on it are made by a variety of further speakers. I have prompted this speech, too, in the circle of German *periti,* and then worked it out with Professor Zerwick of the Pontifical Biblical Institute. Paradoxically, one can talk more openly about the infallibility of the Bible than one can about that of the pope, although this in turn is said to be grounded in the Bible. One can simply start from indisputable concrete errors in the Bible.

Cardinal König explains that oriental studies demonstrate 'that in Holy Scripture the historical and scientific information sometimes deviates from the

The university town of Tübingen with the Stiftskirche and Schloss Hohentübingen

President John F. Kennedy, died 1963

First USA lecture in Boston, 1963, with Cardinal Richard Cushing (Boston) and
Athenagoras, Orthodox Metropolitan of Canada

Four prohibitions on teaching in Washington (from the left) for Gustav Weigel, Godfrey Diekmann (host Monsignor Vincent Yzermans), John Courtney Murray, Hans Küng

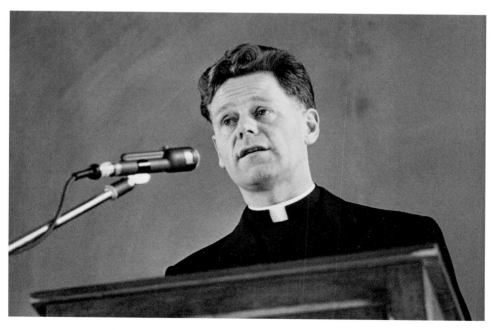

First honorary doctorate, University of St Louis, Missouri 1963

University of San Francisco, 'The Church and Freedom', 1963

My daily place of work

'Lake house' by the Sempachersee

The first books, 1957-67

Index division protocol no. 399/57i

My sisters Hildegard, Irene, Marlis, Margrit, Rita

Holidays in Sursee with my nieces Sonia, Carmen and Sibyl

truth'. For example, according to Mark 2.26 David entered the house of God and ate the showbread under the high priest Abiathar; in fact, however, according to 1 Sam. 21.1ff. this didn't happen under Abiathar but under his father Abimelech. Matthew 27.9 reports the fulfilment of a prophecy of 'Jeremiah'; in truth it is a prophecy of Zechariah (11.13), and so on.

So according to the cardinal it is necessary 'to speak honestly, unequivocally, straightforwardly and fearlessly' on the question of inerrancy. An unhistorical approach in these matters doesn't save the authority of the Bible, but robs exegesis of its credibility. A deviation from the truth in historical and scientific questions in no way endangers the authority of scripture today. Here, rather, theologically the condescension of God becomes visible. God takes the human author with all his weakness and his mistakes – and yet achieves his goal with him: teaching people the 'truth of revelation'. The Council theologian Aloys Grillmeier later remarks on this as a commentator: 'Thus the Cardinal of Vienna also implicitly abandons those premises stemming from aprioristic and unhistorical thought which have played a role in the doctrine of inerrancy since the patristic period: anyone who concedes any error in a hagiographer necessarily imputes an error to God himself.'

But what now emerges from the whole discussion in the Commission? A compromise, as I am told by Joseph Ratzinger in an aisle of St Peter's. Unfortunately it's a lazy compromise. Apart from the constant pressure of the Curia on the Council and the Theological Commission, 'the new view and motivation of the doctrine of inspiration and inerrancy' was 'unfortunately too little prepared for in theological writing and therefore unfamiliar to the majority of the fathers' (Grillmeier). What would have been the clear solution? To omit the expression 'without any error' (*sine ullo errore*) and instead to provide a positive formulation, that the biblical books 'teach the truth integrally and unshakably (*integer et inconcusse*)'. That is precisely what Cardinal König had proposed – but Grillmeier doesn't mention this in his commentary.

And what happens? The Commission gratefully adopts two positive words 'firmly and faithfully' (*firmiter et fideliter*) but at the same time allows 'without any error' to stand. Except that instead of 'without *any* error' the statement now reads '*without error*'. This solution has a lot to do with politics and nothing to do with theology. The completely ambiguous text of the Constitution on Divine Revelation now reads: 'Since, therefore all that the inspired authors or sacred writers affirm should be regarded as affirmed by the Holy Spirit, we must acknowledge that the books of Scripture *firmly, faithfully and without error* teach that truth which God wished to see confided to the sacred scriptures for the sake of our salvation' (Art. 11). This domesticated Cardinal König's speech, and the problem of the inerrancy and inspiration of the Bible and the definition of the relationship between scripture and tradition generally remained unresolved – after a whole series of manoeuvres by the Curia and massive interventions by Paul VI in the Theological Commission. And unless I am mistaken, this unfortunately happened with the assent of Cardinal König, the chairman of the sub-commission responsible for inerrancy; in such controversies he prefers diplomacy to fighting.

Had I been present in the Theological Commission, would I have been able to prevent this compromise in favour of an honest statement? Perhaps with the support of Cardinal König? But in any case, this would have led to a serious dispute with the members of the Curia, with Ottaviani and especially with Tromp, whose Gregorian treatise on the inspiration of the Bible (according to Fr Bea a 'vivisection' of inspiration) had been our examination material. And I could hardly have managed more than one such controversy if I didn't want to make myself quite impossible in this Commission. In short, all this unfortunately confirms the decision I made at the beginning not to take part in such commission work, which was so tied up by the Curia.

This is a heavy burden for theology and the church after the Council: in his later commentary Fr Aloys Grillmeier rightly thinks that the traditional view of the literal inspiration and inerrancy of scripture has to be abandoned after this discussion in the Council: 'It is left to theology to think inerrancy through completely in the light of this new approach.' But Fr Grillmeier doesn't do that. Otherwise, in the controversy a decade later over my book *On Being a Christian* (1974), he would not be in the phalanx of a counter-publication organized by Balthasar (on the prompting of the German episcopal conference): against my christology, built up on a solid historical-critical basis which generally finds assent among exegetes, he uncritically sets the christology of the Hellenistic church fathers, which he had researched thoroughly, but with dogmatic prejudices. And it was precisely these church fathers who, as he himself says, had provided 'those premises stemming from aprioristic and unhistorical thought' of the 'doctrine of inerrancy since the patriarchal period'.

Here the Frankfurt Jesuit – later deservedly nominated cardinal at the age of 84 (and thus without the right to elect the pope!) for his work and his perfect Roman orthodoxy – would only have to draw conclusions from Article 5 of the Constitution on the Church: after the highly dogmatic trinitarian opening, happily it after all begins in a sober way with the preaching of Jesus of Nazareth, the content of which is not the foundation of a church but the coming of the kingdom of God.

Important concerns introduced

In the presence of Grillmeier I myself proposed a draft on Jesus's proclamation of the kingdom of God (Article 5) in the group of German *periti* and worked it out together with Fr Zerwick. My second text – of decisive importance for Reformation theology – on the sinfulness of the church and the constant need for reform of it (Article 8), which the Copenhagen Professor Skydsgaard, an observer from the Lutheran World Federation, checks carefully for me, is presented by

Bishop László (Burgenland) in the name of the Austrian conference of bishops. My third concern is the local church (Article 26), which since the Gregorian reform has been neglected in favour of the 'universal' (= Roman) church. The speech which I have prepared is delivered by Suffragan Bishop Schick (Fulda) in the name of the German episcopal conference. In this context mention should also be made of the not very intellectual and apologetic description of the act of faith which comes from me and is presented by Cardinal Döpfner: instead of 'giving full obedience of the intellect and the will to the God who reveals' (Vatican I) there is now an obedience of faith 'by which man freely commits his entire self to God' (Vatican II, Revelation, Article 5).

Charles Moeller of Louvain, who as adviser to the Theological Commission plays a decisive role in the redaction of the new draft, knows the real author and therefore asks me where in my view the passage on the local church ought to be inserted. My answer is: 'Because in New Testament usage the church is originally the local church, it should come in the first possible section of the first chapter!' To this he replies: 'Unfortunately that's no longer possible – we've completed the redaction of Chapter I on the mystery of the church and Chapter II on the people of God.' This is the explanation of the strange fact that the statement about the church as local church, which is so central in the light of the New Testament, is hidden in the section on the bishops in Chapter III on the hierarchy – immediately after the paragraphs on episcopal and papal infallibility! One shouldn't see the Holy Spirit at work everywhere in the Council texts.

From all this the reader will easily understand why in retrospect I am at the same time both happy and unhappy about the Constitution on the Church which will finally be proclaimed in the third session of the Council (1964). Happy, because I have succeeded in introducing many of my concerns into the Constitution through speeches by bishops at the Council: Jesus's proclamation of the kingdom of God, the church as local church, the charismatic dimension of the church, the historical relativity of the order of three ministries (bishop–priest–deacon), the sinfulness of the church and the abiding need for its reform, and finally, along with many other interventions, the collegiality of the bishops with the pope – the basic notion of the church as people of God being presupposed everywhere.

But I am unhappy because all this hasn't been developed consistently in the light of the New Testament. Because the biblically-orientated texts on the church as mystery and the people of God have been countered by legalistic reflections on the hierarchy. And because finally everything has been overshadowed by a now irreversible compromise between the biblically-orientated *communio* model and the mediaeval papal-absolutist pyramid model. And which, I ask myself, will dominate in the period after the Council? I hope the first; I fear that it will again be the second. Unfortunately I'm right here, as can be demonstrated after the event: this is one of the main reasons for the post-conciliar wretchedness mentioned in the Easter 2002 issue of *Time Magazine* to which I referred earlier.

So what is to be done? What can I do as an individual theologian – apart from episcopal speeches to the Council, lectures and work with the media? On mature consideration I feel that the break in the coming Constitution on the Church produced by Chapter III on the hierarchical make-up can no longer simply be mended. All the conciliar statements about primacy, episcopate, presbyterate and diaconate need to be re-examined in the light of the New Testament and put on a new basis. And because not very much may be expected from the Council discussion on this issue, since the majority of theologians are not specialist ex-egetes and the few specialist exegetes aren't critical enough, after tortuous toings and froings in head and heart I decide on a fundamentally different way: on the matter of the church I will present my own draft, consistently and stringently, without the pressures of conciliar commissions and the painfulness of theological compromises with the Curia. I resolve to write a book on the church.

How a book comes into being

I no longer know precisely what day it was in October 1963 (at all events, towards the evening I am sitting with the Canadian ecumenist Gregory Baum over a coffee on the Via Vittorio Veneto and putting him in the picture). After perhaps two weeks of brooding and fretting over what evidently cannot be achieved at the Council in the Constitution on the Church it has suddenly dawned on me that I should formulate the new theological synthesis myself. Given the circumstances, it can't be expected from the Council. After the Council people will be glad of a wider interpretation of the Council constitution – to work on further in the church and the ecumenical world. In practice this means that instead of wasting my energy in the Theological Commission I should invest it in an ecclesiological synthesis in the spirit of the Council.

It's a bold plan: no boring commentary on individual chapters and sentences in the Constitution on the Church; after the Council sufficient conformist scribes will be found to do that. Nor a detailed critique of individual statements; this bores me and is unfruitful. Rather, an overall view of what the church is in the light of its origin and should be today, grounded step by step in scripture and backed up by history.

Be this as it may, that same day I sit at my desk in my little hotel room. In perhaps two hours of complete self-forgetfulness I draft for myself a coherent, consistent and transparent conception of the book. It is to have the simple yet demanding title 'Essence of the Church' or 'The Church'. There will be five long chapters, which don't begin with the pope, as the first treatises on the church in the Middle Ages do, but end with him. Each chapter will be in three or four sections and these in turn will be divided into several sections. All as basic as possible:

- Belief 'in' the church? Local church or the whole church?
- Basic structure: people of God, creation of the Spirit, body of Christ.
- Dimensions: the one, holy, catholic and apostolic church.
- Ministries: offices and community – the Petrine office.
- Church and world.

What looks simple here is extremely complex when worked out, and what looks harmless is highly explosive. On the same small sheet I scrawl below in the margin the literature to be used: for Catholic exegesis Cerfaux, Schnackenburg and Schlier; for Protestant exegesis Bultmann, Campenhausen, Käsemann and Schweizer. For Catholic dogmatics Adam, Balthasar, Congar, de Lubac, Möhler; for Protestant dogmatics Barth, Brunner, Diem, Ebeling, Elert, Prenter, Schlink and Weber. I already know all the authors well (and also know most of them personally) and they are generally recognized. But – how am I to take up their countless suggestions, work out the differences and the convergences, and present my own view convincingly? None of this is an easy task.

And will I be able to finish this book by around the end of the Council? I have no illusions about the tremendous amount of work to be done. For this will be no relatively short book which can be read through rapidly, like the 250 pages of *The Council and Reunion*. It will be more like *Justification*, a work of certainly several hundred pages (in the end it will be 600 pages, despite all the abbreviations and much text in small print). This isn't the kind of book that scientists sometimes write, summing up the detailed investigations of colleagues. Nor will it be collective work or teamwork; despite all the inestimable secretarial help I shall have to make my own way through the jungle of problems, do the real thinking myself. Only in this way will it become a book which is all of a piece in thought and language, a credible synthesis that can be followed.

Now composition is more an art than a craft. I like comparing a book with a great symphony: first I have the themes in my head or have even noted them down; they are usually based on intuitions. I already have some preliminary work (in this case two books) behind me. But only now does the real work of composition and orchestration and an extremely complex score begin, so that I can achieve as complete a 'sound picture' as possible. And even with the utmost effort – since so much else must run in parallel – I won't be finished until a year after the end of the Council, utterly exhausted.

Of course I am ready to accept as far as possible all the suggested corrections and comments, above all those of my colleagues. For my book will be examined not only by well-disposed readers but also by hypercritical professional colleagues and by quite different authorities, not least the Roman Sanctum Officium, which still wants to have the say in the church. If the conflicts which are now to come are to be put in context, it is necessary to understand the power and the mechanisms of this curial authority.

The power of the Roman 'security headquarters'

The headache for any reform of the Curia is the reform, indeed some think even the abolition, of the 'Holy Office', which as is well known has a fatal history going back centuries in the form of the Inquisition. Since the anti-modernist campaign at the beginning of the twentieth century it has proudly given itself the title *'suprema'*, 'supreme' congregation of the Curia: it is the real power centre of the Vatican. The average Catholic clergyman can hardly have any idea of its possible influence. For nothing at all goes in the Vatican without the Sanctum Officium:

It is responsible for all matters of the doctrines of faith and morality – and what in the Vatican doesn't come under that?

It works in absolute secrecy and can annul, block, change or replace any decision by another congregation.

It controls the most powerful ministries quite directly, and exclusively members of the Sanctum Officium stand at their head: for the bishops and dioceses the Consistorial Congregation (Cardinal Antoniutti); for the discipline of the clergy and faithful the Congregation of the Council (Cardinal Ciriaci); for education, training and church teaching institutions the Congregation of Studies (Cardinal Pizzardo); for political and religious questions in the church (foreign policy) the Congregation for Extraordinary Ecclesiastical Affairs (Cardinal Cicognani). This is the 'Vatican Pentagon', consisting all in all of notoriously narrow-minded men whose representatives likewise have a seat in the Sanctum Officium and whose theological advisers all come from one school, namely the Roman neoscholastic school.

Now in 2002, as I write these lines, the persons and the names have of course changed, but not the system, and only to a limited degree its modes of procedure: Vatican bullying has replaced the stake. Recently, again three distinguished German-language theologians – Willigis Jäger, the German Benedictine and mystic; Josef Imbach, the Swiss professor of theology in Rome; and Paolo Suess, the Brazilian liberation theologian – have all had church penalties imposed on them. This had previously happened to the much-read theologians Eugen Drewermann (Paderborn), Jacques Dupuis (Gregorian) and Tissa Balasuriya (Sri Lanka). In the jargon of the Curia the dry bureaucratic command goes out from the ex-Sanctum Officium ('Congregation of Faith') 'in order to protect the faithful', without the slightest human, let alone Christian sensitivity, that they are to 'refrain from any kind of public activity (lectures, publications . . .)'. Religious superiors or bishops usually pass on the commands against their will. My God, will we ever be rid of the evil cancer of the Inquisition?

As pope, Angelo Roncalli, typically of him, contented himself with getting hold of his own Inquisition dossier. He wanted at last to know who had denounced him in his early years: a pastor from Bergamo, long since dead. But now, immediately after the first session of the Council, and still in the time of

John XXIII, a report goes through the world press that the Catholic student chaplain at the Free University of Amsterdam, Fr Jan van Kilsdonk SJ, is the object of a *monitum* (admonition) by the 'Holy Office' to the Bishop of Haarlem, J. van Dodewaard. The order is that the popular student chaplain should be dismissed. Why?

In a lecture to an association of Catholic intellectuals in Rotterdam van Kilsdonk had ventured to criticize the Curia and the Sanctum Officium quite directly. He said that the Curia limits the freedom of the pope, dominates the bishops and as a result prevents fruitful contact between the pope and episcopate. The 'Holy Office' has gained the reputation of being a bastion (an allusion to Ottaviani's book *Il baluardo*, 'The Bastion'), which allows no criticism of itself whatsoever from outside. The proceedings against Fr Lombardi, who in his book on the Council had called for the quite justified reform of the Curia, are one example of the 'spiritual terror' of the 'Holy Office'. The admonition against the great work of Teilhard de Chardin in summer 1962, who is persecuted beyond his death, is another. Not least for this reason, in the journal *America* the American Jesuit Robert A. Graham had called for 'civil rights' and a 'charter for Catholic intellectuals' over against the Sanctum Officium, which in practice had arrogated to itself the directives for all research work in the church. So at the end of his lecture the brave Dutch Jesuit calls for 'loyal opposition' to such proceedings. Clearly, after all that I have said in my own lectures, I can only rejoice at such confirmation.

In the Netherlands the Roman repressive measure provokes a storm of indignation: numerous protest letters and furious newspaper articles which show the Vatican that Catholics, Reformed and Socialists are united in this matter – against the violation of human rights and the disruption of the new hopeful ecumenical climate. A whole series of prominent theologians of both confessions impress not only the initially timid bishops, including Cardinal Alfrink, primate of the Netherlands, but finally also the Roman Curia and Pope Paul VI. Only a few readers' letters from conservative Catholics call for the submission 'to the supreme authority' which has previously been customary, and is allegedly still the most important thing in the life of a Catholic. This controversy has a welcome outcome. The 'Holy Office' beats a tactical retreat and leaves further measures to the local bishop, who of course keeps the student chaplain in his post. On this one occasion the church of the Netherlands has defeated the Curia.

Painful parallels

But the question remains topical for the Council. Is it to go on in this style? Was the talk of 'spiritual terror' really exaggerated? In France, where the word *'terreur'* is associated with Robespierre, already in the last years of Pius XII who, having become old and ill, no longer controlled the Sanctum Officium, people spoke of a *'terreur intellectuelle'*. In the twentieth century the term 'terror' was elsewhere used above all for Stalin's Soviet inquisition. Some Catholic insiders, however, are convinced that despite all the differences, the Roman Inquisition authority is something like a spiritual counterpart to the political secret police in the Soviet empire. In the spiritual Roman empire, too, there is a worldwide organization working in as much secrecy as possible with far-reaching authority to guarantee the 'security of the state' and to stabilize its own system in an inexorable fight against the 'enemies', deviants, dissidents and revolutionaries – real or alleged. The Vatican authorities, like the political police of the Soviet empire, which on various occasions altered its hated names (Cheka, GPU, NKVD, MGB and since 1954 KGB), is in fact above the law; and the *Congregatio Sancti Officii Romanae et Universalis Inquisitionis* also changes its name (simply Sanctum Officium, later Congregation for the Doctrine of Faith) but preserves its methods. The Catholic Church owes the best-known catastrophic wrong decisions to this 'spiritual' security authority, already more than 400 years old: from the case of Galileo and the Chinese Rites dispute through the indexing of the most important thinkers of Europe (Descartes, Kant, Sartre, etc.) and the condemnation of freedom of religion and human rights, to the case of Teilhard de Chardin, the ban on the French worker-priests and the inexorable purges of theologians under Pius X and Pius XII.

So it is no exaggeration to say that just as the KGB understands itself as the 'sword and shield of the Party' in order to safeguard its rule, so too according to a statement which he himself makes, Cardinal Ottaviani understands himself in a disparaging way as the 'old *carabiniere* (policeman) of the church' who with his organization has to ensure the safeguarding of the ideological order ('the Catholic truth') in the church. In fact he also argues in the Council time and again with the Roman knock-down argument: 'That is the will of the Holy Father.' And the Vatican police also supervise as far as possible academic and cultural life, the important posts of the ecclesiastical apparatus and the diplomatic representations abroad; they are also responsible for 'celibacy cases'. The Sanctum Officium has secret direct recourse to nunciatures, bishops and superiors of religious orders in all nations. Every day the head of the 'Holy Office' receives 'top secret information' from all over the world and reacts to it daily in a top secret way. Bishops, religious superiors and nuncios have to show unconditional obedience to the supreme guardian of the faith and its 'Holy Office' (Politburo). And all this is under the seal of the 'secrecy of the Holy Office', which is protected by the highest level of excommunication: only the pope personally can give absolution from its violation. Thus power is safeguarded in a 'spiritual way'.

Only in the case of better-known victims does one hear something in public. Granted, no one is physically burned any more; instead they are psychologically and professionally annihilated, wherever this is necessary for the 'well-being of the church'. One might recall the cases of Teilhard de Chardin and Congar. But in the Roman system too the well-known names and 'great' cases mentioned in these memoirs are only the tip of the iceberg. No less bad than the public condemnation of the few, to which recourse is had only in the case of wider public resonance, is the secret blocking of countless people who are called to 'order' through a bishop or religious superior and in some circumstances are given short shrift, being ostracized, dismissed, transferred, put under special censorship or having a ban on publications and speaking imposed on them. On such an occasion the official letter of the Sanctum Officium (or another Roman congregation) is not usually handed over by the person's own superior but at best is read out, so that the one being disciplined has the least possible evidence in his hands. The indirect and completely intentional result of all these measures is fear: constant pressure especially on bishops and theologians, who on the publication of a book or article must prophylactically exercise 'caution' and therefore do not dare to write anything bold at all. Even the Secretariat of State and the pope hesitate to intervene once a matter is in the hands of the 'supreme congregation'.

I have to concede that I too have a quite personal interest in the reform of the Office. As is well known, there I have the file number 399/57i, under which since the year of my doctorate in 1957 evidence has been gathered about my writings and my speeches in Europe and the USA, especially against preliminary censorship and the Index. I must also reckon with proceedings against my *Structures of the Church*. Will the Council change anything here in time?

A cardinal against the Inquisition

How widespread the fear of this institution of the Inquisition is, even in the Council, is evident from the fact that only one bishop dares publicly and directly to attack the inquisitorial practices of the Sanctum Officium, though hundreds think the same thing. The 76-year-old Archbishop of Cologne, Cardinal Josef Frings, intellectually very with it, again has this glory. With his light, high and penetrating voice, speaking Latin with a German accent, in the debate on the schema 'On the bishops and the leading of dioceses' on 8 November 1963 he immediately attracts the special attention of the Council assembly. And when bishops and theologians observe that he is clearly attacking that institution which is by far the most unpopular of all curial institutions, one can hear a pin drop in the Council aula.

Cardinal Frings criticizes above all the fact that the Sanctum Officium stands above church law generally: he demands that the Sanctum Officium too be subject to the norms of the *Codex Iuris Canonici* and that a clear distinction be made between administrative and legal proceedings. And he adds: 'In many respects the mode of procedure of the Sanctum Officium is no longer in keeping with the present time; it does damage to the church and for many is a scandal.' Now applause breaks out in the Council aula. *'Plausus in aula'* is briefly noted in the official proceedings of the Council. Remarkably enough, on the next page of the printed proceedings is a later written version of the speech, where by way of qualification it is said that the practice of the Sanctum Officium is 'a scandal to non-Catholics (*acatholicis*)'. Who is responsible for this manipulation? At any rate in this version, too, the cardinal's conclusion is given rightly; one day it is to be extremely important to me: 'The demand must be made that in this congregation, too, no one is accused, judged or condemned with reference to the true faith without a previous hearing being given to him (and his bishop); without his previously knowing the arguments against him or the book which he has written; without his previously having been given the occasion to correct himself or his book.'

A further popular reform demanded by Cardinal Frings relates to the Vatican inflation of bishops: the number of bishops in the Roman Curia needs to be reduced, and no one should be consecrated bishop who is not really a bishop: 'The episcopate itself is an office and not an honour and decoration for another office. Let anyone who is bishop be bishop and nothing else . . . So I propose that it be resolved that the number of bishops and priests in the Roman Curia be reduced and that laity too should be admitted to the Curia. I have spoken.' How many Vatican dignitaries would have to put their mitres in the Vatican museums – and how many would get no mitres at all?

These were all clear words. It could have been added quietly that the procedures of the Office are also contrary to the United Nations Universal Declaration of Human Rights of 10 December 1948. Article 10: 'Everyone is entitled in full equality to a fair and public hearing by an independent and impartial tribunal, on the determination of his rights and obligations and of any criminal charge against him.' And Article 11.1: 'Everyone charged with a penal offence has the right to be presumed innocent until proved guilty according to law in a public trial at which he has had all the guarantees necessary to his defence.'

There is tumultuous applause in the aula after the speech by the Cardinal of Cologne, not noted in the proceedings. Shortly afterwards Cardinal Alfredo Ottaviani replies, red and quivering with anger: 'I hope I may be allowed to protest most solemnly (*altissime*) at the words that have been spoken against this Supreme Congregation of the Holy Office (*Suprema Congregatio Sancti Officii*) whose president is the pope himself . . . (applause from the curial side). These words arise out of ignorance, to use no worse a word . . .' He praises the work of his congregation, whose *consultores* are the best people from the Roman universities. And conceals the fact that with one exception all members of the Office are Italians and that while the *consultores* come from different nations, they all belong to the same conservative tendency. And after the pope's reform speech can he still simply be identified with the procedures of his subordinate organization?

There is no doubt about it: the criticism of the Cardinal of Cologne has hit the mark and, as might be expected, the chief target has cried out. The need for a fundamental reform of the Office has been demonstrated to all by this clash between the two cardinals, which has been reported and commented on in all the world press. And in Paris the elderly physician Marc Oraison, who became a theologian and priest and was put on the Index by the Holy Office as early as 1955, uses Frings's speech to uncover the Kafkaesque methods of this Roman institution in *Le Monde* by means of his own proceedings. For Ottaviani this is a PR catastrophe.

But who is the theological adviser of Cardinal Frings, who must have done him a major service over this statement? It is none other than my esteemed colleague Joseph Ratzinger, now still professor in Bonn, soon to be in Münster and finally in Tübingen. During these years he writes statements which sound prophetic and likewise uses the word scandal, not just for 'non-Catholics':

It is a secondary, self-caused and thus culpable scandal if under the pretext of defending the rights of God, only one particular social situation and the positions of power gained in it are being defended. It is a secondary, self-caused and thus culpable scandal if on the pretext of protecting the unchanging nature of faith only one's own past is defended. It is a secondary, self-caused and thus culpable scandal if on the pretext of safeguarding the whole of the truth the opinions of schools are perpetuated which have asserted themselves as a matter of course at one time, but have long needed the revision and reinvestigation demanded by the authentic original. But the danger is that this secondary scandal will time and again be identified with the primary scandal (of the gospel itself) and thus make it inaccessible, will conceal the real Christian claim and its seriousness behind the claims of its messengers (*Das neue Volk Gottes*, 1969, 302-21: 318).

That could also have come from the 'combative' critic of the Inquisition, Hans Küng.

Yes, this is indeed the same Ratzinger who one day will himself become head of the Inquisition authorities and who then according to his own testimony 'every day receives top secret information from every continent' (and of course also sends back top secret instructions to every continent). He will be the one who himself time and again gives rise to the same 'self-caused and thus culpable scandal'. Some will accuse him of having betrayed the legacy of Council Cardinal Frings. I would rather accuse him of having betrayed his own legacy. Be this as it may: shouldn't the pope and the bishops now have looked for justice over the Office of the Inquisition? In quite practical terms: shouldn't there be a supreme council of the episcopate instead of the 'supreme congregation of the Holy Office'?

A supreme council of bishops?

In fighting for more rights for bishops and local churches the Council is engaged in a power struggle – perhaps comparable to the earlier struggle of the English

Parliament with the absolutist king for its rights. Will the Council rouse itself to a 'glorious revolution'? The Summus Pontifex is never criticized directly in the Council, but there is criticism of his relationship with the bishops, particularly as it is expressed in the Council schema on the pastoral task of the bishops. The programmatic word is collegiality: this is experienced in the Council. A man who is bishop by 'divine right' ('brother' of the bishop of Rome) can certainly resist a man who is cardinal ('son' or 'creature' of the pope) only on the basis of papal nomination. Here bishops find that most others also reject the spirit which rules in the Curia. And they all feel members of a college characterized by collegiality. The demand is now made openly that the pope's court, an institution by human right, must not replace the college of bishops in the universal leadership of the church. The title bishop is not to be bestowed *honoris causa* in the Curia. The curial officials are to be the servants of the bishops and not act as their masters. The Curia must not be dominated by a single nation. And there are many other demands.

Of course I too am convinced that Paul VI personally is a highly motivated and humble Christian. The claim to primacy is not his personal problem, but an objective problem which has come down to him from history. Moreover the Council fathers do not want to force him to reform his own administrative apparatus. However, they do want to make constructive proposals for the pope to take up. Like any administrative apparatus and any functional hierarchy, the Vatican, too, tends to become isolated and petrified, to perpetuate its own time-conditioned forms and functions, to hold on to power and to accumulate competences. What specific practical proposals for reform are the bishops concerned with? For me too an elected council of bishops alongside the bishops' conferences is an important concern.

Various bishops have said in their speeches that simply taking some of their number into the Roman congregations is not enough for a reform of the church. With good reason they fear that such bishops, who aren't always steadfast, will be Romanized and curialized. Rather, what is demanded by many cardinals and bishops from a great variety of countries and continents is a representative supreme council of bishops: composed of representatives of episcopal conferences chosen for a period. Periodically – twice or three times a year – they will meet with the pope in Rome to discuss the most important problems of the church as a whole and to make decisions. This isn't a new curial congregation above the others but rather a senate of the church independent of the Curia. It is to be an episcopal college which together with the pope has legislative competence over the whole church – and the Roman Curia along with the Holy Office is again to be a purely executive, subordinate administrative organ. Will that be accepted?

The theory of a shared collegial responsibility of the whole episcopate (with the pope) would be put into practice by a supreme senate. The participation of the world episcopate in the leadership of the whole church would – at least to a certain degree – be guaranteed, as would an authentically Catholic representation of the different nations and problems at the centre of the Catholic Church. As I put it at a very early stage: it is time for the Catholic Church – *mutatis mutandis* – to be transformed from a Roman 'empire' into a Catholic 'commonwealth'. The centralist and absolutist structure of administration and law in the Roman church, the foundations for which were laid down in the eleventh century, has become obsolete in today's democratic times. Even more, it contradicts a picture of the church orientated on the Bible. It does immense damage to the church in fulfilling its task. So it is high time for a church leadership in brotherly solidarity, more orientated on the apostolic church, which as in the first millennium respects the particular importance of the individual local and particular churches in an open catholicity! But will the pope, the absolutist monarch of the church, be prepared to surrender power, at least in the spirit of a 'constitutional monarchy'? The Curia can be expected to produce every possible obstacle. In 1870 the popes renounced worldly power only as a result of military and political force. Will this pope in 1970 perhaps voluntarily renounce spiritual power – in the spirit of the Sermon on the Mount?

An age limit for the pope?

As well as the Curia and the council of bishops, other very practical questions are discussed. For example, should there be an age limit for bishops? It is again the primate of Belgium, Cardinal Suenens, who on this question, too, presents a brave, clear proposal for an age limit of 75. Not only pseudo-dogmatic objections to such an age limit (the 'mystical marriage' of the bishop with his diocese) but also great figures who are exceptions are cited, though these tend more to prove the rule. However, in our time, with the swift pace of life, it is vital not to be content with admonitions to retire at the right time but to aim at legal regulation. A gulf between bishop and people and an ageing of the episcopate is for various reasons more dangerous today than it used to be. The office of bishop should always appear to be a service to the people of God from which one retires when one no longer has the full energy required for the service. But shouldn't that also apply to popes?

On the occasion of a lecture to bishops in the Belgian College, on 23 October 1963, I ask Cardinal Suenens confidentially why he has made the pope an exception. Is clinging to the 'holy see' more holy than clinging to other sees? His answer is disarming: without excluding the pope in this way there would certainly be no majority for an age limit. Neither Suenens nor I at that time have any inkling that one day a pontificate of now 25 years would be granted us by a pope who thinks that he (and no other) 'must' lead the church into the third millennium even as a seriously ill and handicapped man. Shouldn't one at least think of an age limit for the pope, too, if the pope will not accept even the possibility of voluntary retirement prescribed in canon 332§2 of church law?

The principle of subsidiarity is also discussed in the second session. Of course this applies not only to the relationship between the pope and the bishops but also to the relationship between bishops and pastors and between clergy and laity (this is not clear to all bishops). To this degree decentralization must also be carried through at diocesan level. For collegiality must also be realized at that level. Just as the concept of the episcopal college has faded and been forgotten in the course of time, so too has the concept of the college of presbyters. It should be renewed by a council of priests or by a pastoral council – in keeping with the time, together with the laity.

There are many questions and proposals but so far few decisions. I am very glad that I can really relax with two genuine, completely unclerical laity over the weekend of 16/17 November 1963. With the musicologist Dr Helmut Hucke – with whom I have been friends since my time at the Germanicum – and his wife, in brilliant weather I drive to Caserta, Naples and Salerno. There I very much want to visit the tomb of the unfortunate but blessed and beatified pope Gregory VII, who in the eleventh century had struggled for the absolutist papacy with every possible means. Besieged for weeks in Castel San Angelo by the troops of King Henry IV, whom he had excommunicated (Canossa!), and freed by the Normans who were plundering the city, this 'holy Satan' (thus his fellow cardinal Peter Damiani) died in Salerno. Here one can read what were allegedly his last words: 'I loved righteousness and hated iniquity, therefore I die in exile.' Is that the real reason? Of course we also talk about politics, above all Italian politics, where dramatic developments are taking place which also affect the pope.

Political crisis in Italy

Everything could have continued to go well with the Council – but what about Italy? Since 1960 there has been talk in this country, particularly to reduce votes for the Communists, of an *'apertura a sinistra'*: an openness of Democrazia Cristiana towards the Socialists. A 'centre-left coalition' under Prime Minister Fanfani with the parliamentary acceptance of the Socialists had been formed on 21 February 1962, even before the opening of the Council. But this is already in crisis as early as April 1963 as a result of the electoral gains by the Communists (despite Ottaviani's threats of excommunication). After tortuous months Leone's transitional cabinet has to resign as early as 5 November 1963, in the middle of the second session of the Council.

A government crisis – what will happen next? The Communists at the gates? Italy, and perhaps also soon France, socialist, even Communist? Italy's conservative circles in politics, business and journalism are extremely alarmed. So too are the conservatives of the Vatican, for whom likewise considerable financial and economic interests are at stake. Doesn't the *'Giovannismo'* of the dead pope – this is how people in the Curia now speak about John XXIII's talk of Christian love, understanding and co-operation – manifestly have devastating consequences? Of course there is no agreement between the Christian religion and materialistic atheism, but practical co-operation at a social and political level between the Catholics and Communist governments can and must be achieved: for Ottaviani and his followers this *'sinistrismo ecclesiastico'* which supports a *'sinistrismo politico'* is a self-destructive policy.

And in addition to all this, they complain, there is this Council, at which people sympathize with the left-wing tendencies. On 30 October the opponents of the Curia have answered 'yes' with overwhelming majorities to four questions of the moderators; a major attack is being made on the Congregation of the Holy Office (more than 500 Council fathers are calling for its reform in a petition!); with the help of pernicious 'collegiality' the primacy of the pope is being undermined (more than 100 Council fathers are calling for a council of bishops!); the Council fathers are even making peace with the Jews, the old enemies of the church. Indeed they want to proclaim a universal freedom of religion and conscience which on many occasions has been condemned by the pope. Isn't all this un-Catholic, indeed politically suicidal?

There is no doubt that since the vote on 30 October – which for the Curia is the height of unacceptable 'conciliarism' – Paul VI has come under massive pressure. However, people at the Council initially take very little note of this. The pope is being pressurized by Italian politics and business and by the potentates in the Curia, with the exception of Cardinal Bea, if not to break off the Council at least to abandon the *'Giovannismo'* of all-embracing love to 'all people of good will'. In other words, he is being pressurized to put a stop to the modernizing *'aggiornamento'*, the pernicious *'aperturismo'* towards Protestants, non-Christians (there is now also a Secretariat for Non-Christian Religions), Jews, socialists and Communists. This must be done for the sake of the church, indeed for the sake of Italy, Rome and the papacy, which mustn't be further weakened. The 'Catholic tradition' – Trent, Vatican I, *'Romanità'* – must take the place of 'conciliarism'. In the Roman Congregation people have already been long lamenting *'questo maledetto concilio che manda in rovina la chiesa* – this damned Council which is ruining the church'.

With the Italian governmental crisis it seems to the conservatives in the Vatican that the time has come for the open counter-offensive which they have long since planned. Cardinal Siri and the Italian conference of bishops attack with the utmost force the threat of a first government made up of Christian Democrats and Socialists. Curia cardinals now put pressure on the pope with theological and political arguments to think back to the well-tried Roman line which had previously been prepared for by a congress on Trent and the Tridentine reform. Moreover on 4 November the pope has a letter on the 400th anniversary of the Council of Trent and seminary education read out which has been composed by the conservatives. This amazes the Council fathers by its retrogressiveness and alienation from the world. In the Council and the city, anonymous pamphlets circulate on 'The Council and the Threat from the Central European Block' and 'The Jews and the Council in the Light of Holy Scripture and the Tradition'. Cardinal Ottaviani publicly states that an obligatory corporation of bishops supporting the pope would restrict the pope's primatial power.

On 5 November Paul VI receives State President Segni, who is looking for a prime minister for a new cabinet. But on 7 November the Council greets Cardinal König's demands for collegiality and a senate of bishops and on 8 November Frings's speech against the Sanctum Officium with applause. This is followed by that vigorous reply from Ottaviani who is still convinced that as the extended arm of the Holy Office – after all this is still the 'supreme' congregation! – in matters of faith and morality his Theological Commission is also superior to the Council. The same day, rumour has it, Cardinals Ottaviani, Antoniutti and Siri have persuaded the pope to revise his standpoint.

And it is striking that on 10 November Paul VI visits the Lateran church and there emphasizes most strongly his status as successor to Peter, representative of Christ and supreme pastor of the universal church ('recognizes in our person the greatness of our exalted and pontifical task'); like a mediaeval pope he makes a bombastic speech in praise of the splendour, the glory and the infallible pre-eminence of Rome ('We greet you, Rome, See of Our Honour, with a grateful and loving heart . . .'). That same day the pope receives the news that Aldo Moro will form a centre-left government with the socialists.

The pope on a course against the Council

Only in the period of the second session does the Secretariat for Unity come up with its schema on ecumenism. But as early as the middle of November, under pressure from conservative circles, Paul VI seems to have decided that the explosive Chapters IV of this schema on ecumenism on Judaism and V on freedom of religion do not qualify for a vote (moreover, after a further delay, the latter will not get into the hands of the Council fathers until 19 November). However, Bea, called on by the pope to show restraint, doesn't mobilize his friends, but is silent. As a Jesuit he is accustomed to obedience, and he orders his secretariat to show the same restraint. So the conservatives in the Curia gain the upper hand, and over time the Curia increasingly takes charge of the Council.

Much that I didn't yet realize in the second session of the Council in 1963 will become clear to me in the third session in 1964: there are links between the feverish activity in the Council and Curia from the end of October to the middle of November 1963 and Italian domestic politics, though these are largely left in the shade at the end of the century by our Council historians under Alberigo. Yet they had been precisely analysed by a knowledgeable and perceptive author under the pseudonym Michael Serafian (*The Pilgrim*, New York 1964), whom I know from one or two meetings. The Council historian Alberto Melloni, a friend of

Alberigo, refers to this highly uncomfortable book in only two footnotes. Instead of investigating the dramatic and disastrous ecclesiastical and political tangles and possibly correcting Serafian, he discredits the book, though it is teeming with facts and worth considering (it is able to put itself in Papa Montini's position), out of hand as 'blackening the pope', *'denigrazione antimontiniana'*. That means that instead of working out Paul VI's own responsibility for the growing alienation between pope and Council, Melloni attempts as far as possible to exonerate Papa Montini.

Certainly Melloni and Alberigo know the true author of *The Pilgrim* by name and also know that the name 'Serafian' conceals more than, as they cryptically write, 'an Irishman, at this moment a Jesuit in Rome'. He is none other than Fr Malachy Martin SJ, a personal colleague of Cardinal Bea, professor at the Pontifical Biblical Institute and a friend of Bea's secretary, Stephan Schmidt SJ, a man with unique insider knowledge of both the Council and the Curia. This brilliant Jesuit, though something of a split personality and of sometimes doubtful credibility, gives up his post with Cardinal Bea as early as 1964, after the publication of his book, and unfortunately also his membership of his religious order and the priesthood. One may speculate: is this as a consequence of his book, done in despair at all the developments in church politics, or the result of an affair with the wife of the *Time Magazine* correspondent Bob Kaiser? This is a truly tragic 'true story', all the details of which are described only in 2002 (three years after Martin's death in New York) by Robert B. Kaiser, in his book *Clerical Error* (namely of Martin and the clergy who conceal him). At the time Kaiser didn't say a word to me about it. So Kaiser gives up reporting on the Council after the second session, but almost four decades later recalls how 'appalled' he was during that session 'when the old entrenched powers (though they were in a tiny minority) seemed to be reversing the tide'. 'The victories of the first session and the defeats of the second meant more to me than they would have to an objective reporter.' In his 1993 biography of Paul VI Peter Hebblethwaite calls *The Pilgrim* 'by far the best' of Martin's books; he quotes it on various occasions but likewise does not go into its uncomfortable and highly political aspects.

What went on in October/November 1963 behind the Vatican's Portone di Bronzo? Without knowledge of the archives, that is difficult to check, but a couple of decades later post-conciliar historians would have been able to establish on the basis of the reported facts (as I did at the time) that whereas with his addresses on the reform of the Curia and the opening up of the Council Paul VI initially clearly put himself behind curial renewal, favoured collegiality, appointed progressive moderates and allowed the Council every freedom, now, although in principle above the parties, in fact he adopts a fundamentally anti-conciliar policy. What I, like most of those involved in the Council, will grasp the whole scope of only towards the end of the third session of the Council in the 'black week' of November 1964 has manifestly already been prepared for in the second half of the second session in 1963. Paul VI has clearly become a partisan supporter of the

Curia and now largely goes along with its ploy. Until the archives are opened up, I must leave open the question whether this is a real 'conversion', as Martin thinks, or a Montinian toing and froing between the fronts, a desire to do everything right which finally yields to the stronger pressure (and beyond doubt that now comes from the 'right wing' in the Curia and the state).

The fact is that in the second session of the Council in 1963, to the annoyance of the Council, and especially the Americans, Papa Montini allows only the first three chapters of the Decree on Ecumenism to be discussed. Time and again, in shameful delaying tactics, the bishops will be denied a vote on Chapters IV (Judaism) and V (Freedom of Religion!) until it is too late. Early in the morning of 2 December, Cardinal Bea receives the papal command through Cardinal Secretary of State Cicognani: he, Bea, has to state in his speech to the Council announced for that same morning, contrary to the truth, that for insuperable reasons of time a vote is unfortunately no longer possible. Before the end of the speech – Bea also wanted to mention Pope John – the moderator Cardinal Agagianian switches off the microphone. For the Council, and also of course for me, the blatant thwarting of a statement on Judaism and the freedom of religion is an enormous disappointment, but it is accepted without a protest. At any rate, people say, we may now vote on the first three chapters of the Decree on Ecumenism. They are accepted by an overwhelming majority. A bird in the hand is better than two in the bush, certainly, but for me it is too little.

Ecumenical openness

With his opening address to the Council, Paul VI had initially also given important stimuli to ecumenism. For him, outside the church there are not only individual Christians but 'venerable Christian communities'. Not only do they share a common religious heritage with the Roman Catholic Church but they have also developed this heritage in a positive way. He explicitly praises the efforts of ecumenically minded theologians on both sides, who also attempt to see the truth of those on the other side.

However, the confession of guilt, which Paul VI was the first pope to make since Hadrian VI at the time of Luther, is combined with a Montinian 'if – referring to his own guilt but not the 'injustice done to the church': 'If we are in any way to blame for our prolonged separation, we humbly beg God's forgiveness and ask pardon too of our brethren who feel themselves to have been injured by us. For our part we willingly forgive the injuries which the Catholic Church has suffered and forget the grief endured during the long series of dissensions and separations.'

That sounds very paternalistic. But that the reunion of separated Christians is being discussed at the Second Vatican Council at all is itself an important fact of church history. The way in which highly impressive voices, not only from

Central Europe but also from Italy, Spain, North and South America, Africa and Asia, speak out in favour of 'ecumenism'– in terms not so much of theory and doctrine as of pastoral action and movement – must have horrified the conservative circles of the Curia. The discussion lasts from 18 November until towards the end of the second session.

The revised schema on ecumenism presented by the Secretariat for Unity on 18 November 1963 (the one prepared by the Commission on the Eastern Churches had been rejected in the first session) doesn't set out to offer a comprehensive discussion of the preparation for the reunion of separated Christians, but just a few pastoral principles and instructions which are needed to introduce serious preparation: they are primarily intended for Catholics. A comparison of the new schema with the earlier one shows me that, as I had been informed by Jan Willebrands, among other things a reading of *The Council and Reunion* has had its effect in the Secretariat for Unity: the reform of the Catholic Church – liturgical, biblical and pastoral renewal – is strongly emphasized as a presupposition for reunion. So too is the need for inner conversion and a life truly in keeping with the gospel – also for Catholics. Practical guidelines then follow: for the whole prayer of Catholic Christians and others; for better mutual acquaintance and ecumenical dialogue; for the ecumenical training of ministers and laity, theological students and missionaries; for an ecumenical account of Catholic faith; for practical collaboration with other Christians. For the Catholic Church all this represents progress towards ecumenism unimaginable at the time of Pius XII.

Yet many observers from the other Christian churches find the schema still very unsatisfactory in the form in which it is presented: it is too legalistic and static. How is the Catholic Church to argue that all the other churches present only parts of the truth, and that it alone possesses the totality of truth? After all, the Catholic Church has for a long time forgotten, overlooked and neglected important truths of the gospel like the justification of the sinner or the freedom of a Christian. And are only the Orthodox churches, and not the Protestant churches, to be called 'churches'? That would put off many evangelical Christians. The criterion of episcopal succession and church order (and the celebration of the eucharist associated with it) seems arbitrary. It is not in keeping either with the biblical (Pauline!) evidence or with the problems of the Protestant Reformation. But there are no expert exegetes and historians of dogma even in the Secretariat for Unity: and goodwill alone is no substitute for solid knowledge.

In the Council debate on the schema it is now formally demanded that the Protestant churches should also be called churches. For that an unequivocal confession is needed of the Catholic share in the blame for the schism, and a critical confrontation with the truth, which hasn't always been given sufficient space and freedom in the Catholic Church. Finally, the positive salvation-historical significance of the schism is important. God's gracious providence can be recognized even in human schisms. 'Conversion' to Christ is required of all, including Catholics. So there is a need for intellectual humility towards other

Christian communities and the free work of theologians – a presupposition for ecumenical understanding . . . Not a 'return' to the Catholic Church but – as the title of the decree will finally run – the restoration of unity, *'Unitatis redintegratio'*.

There is a vote as early as 21 November 1963: but only on whether the first three chapters of the scheme on ecumenism (guidelines for the ecumenical movement, the practice of the ecumenical movement, the attitude to Christians separated from the Catholic Church) can be accepted as a basis for discussion. This is endorsed with the amazing majority of more than 95 per cent. The vote shows just how much ground has been covered in the last five years. However, there is no mention in this decree of what could still be read in Paul VI's accession encyclical *Ecclesiam suam*: the papacy with its claim to a primacy of honour and jurisdiction is an 'obstacle' to Christian unity.

Fortunately, however, a second important obstacle isn't introduced at all: despite all the emotional agitation by Marianists, there is no new dogma on Mary and no separate document on Mary. With a narrow majority of only 40, on 29 October 1963 the Council votes for a chapter on Mary to be integrated into the Constitution on the Church, which is also to warn against exaggerated veneration of Mary. In any case, more recent theology is going in a different direction, as is becoming clear in the international project *Concilium*.

For and against Concilium

During the second session of the Council in 1963, Rahner, Schillebeeckx and I have various opportunities to discuss the content and structure of the planned international theological journal *Concilium* and also to recruit other co-directors and colleagues from among the Council theologians. Our Dutch publisher Paul Brand has set up a small secretariat in a hotel in Rome. On 19 October 1963 the committee of directors meets to fill the vacant posts in the various sections. On 28 November this committee then meets with all the collaborators and many sympathizers in the Unitas centre in the Piazza Navona. Schillebeeckx opens the session in French. Karl Rahner presents *Concilium* in Latin and the Louvain church historian Roger Aubert in French, and I explain the internal organization of the ten editorial committees in English.

Over the next few days the section directors meet with colleagues from their disciplines, for example in the dogma sections Schillebeeckx with B. Dupuy (Paris), P. Fransen (Louvain), J. Neuner (Poona, India) and J. Ratzinger (Münster). In the ecumenism section I meet with the ecumenists A. Fiolet (Netherlands), B. Lambert (Canada), M. Le Guillou (France), J. Mejía (Argentina), E. Vogt (Norway), W. de Vries and J. Witte (Rome). The same happens with the other eight sections. In this way, brought together by the Council, an international network of theology is built up, which embraces a large number of leading figures in the various disciplines. Congar will be the author of the first article and

Ratzinger the author of the second article of the first issue. Because of the extremely complex preparations in the various languages, however, this issue will not appear in January 1964, as first planned, but only in January 1965.

One of the few who had not accepted our invitation to be involved is the French Jesuit Jean Daniélou, at one time exponent of the *'Nouvelle théologie'*. Spared from condemnation (although according to Rahner the author of perhaps the most questionable article), the skilful, nervous little father is now concerned for Roman orthodoxy and fulminates against our planned journal everywhere. When at a private dinner I talk to his fellow religious and former ally Henri de Lubac about Daniélou his brief answer is: '*Oh, vous savez, il était toujours comme ça* – he was always like that.' Daniélou develops into the main agitator against *Concilium* and trumpets everywhere: 'This journal will be dead in a year. The Curia will not allow it to live.' At any rate he manages to dissuade the French Jesuits from joining in, and de Lubac, a generous man, has to withdraw. But even without Daniélou our journal remains alive. Deservedly made a cardinal as early as 1969 because of his conformity with Rome (when an important theologian becomes toothless he is ripe for the cardinalate), he is to die in 1974 in mysterious circumstances – in a stairwell on a 'pastoral visit' to a prostitute. He did no harm to me personally. *Requiescat in pace.*

Of course Daniélou immediately saw the point. In the Roman Curia our enterprise is regarded with the utmost mistrust, and since it cannot be torpedoed, attempts are made at least to domesticate it. A member of our team, the Milan dogmatic theologian Monsignor Carlo Colombo, Montini's house theologian and soon to become bishop, makes himself the spokesman of the Curia. He, too, likes to refer to 'higher authority', avoiding anything in writing and never making it quite clear whether he has the pope personally or the Secretariat of State or the Sanctum Officium behind him.

In November 1963 Colombo invites Rahner, Schillebeeckx and Brand to the Café San Pietro at the Vatican and reveals to them: 'On higher authority I have to tell you that it is impossible to nominate Hans Küng as director of the section on ecumenism.' Instead Monsignor Willebrands may be accepted. Normally such a reference to 'higher authority' is enough, and all resistance collapses. Not in our case. My three friends unanimously back me and insist that as a competent man Küng must lead the section on ecumenism. They don't accept Colombo's compromise proposal that I should be made *directeur adjoint* (a post which Walter Kasper is to hold).

Once again it is a matter of whether individuals have the civil courage to resist. In gratitude I will dedicate the American and English edition of *Structures of the Church* to Karl Rahner 'who spared himself no effort in helping me with his authoritative advice'. 'I am very touched and grateful,' Rahner replies, 'that you have also dedicated the English edition to me.' But of course the episode in the Café San Pietro was only the prelude to further machinations in the shadow of the *cupelone di San Pietro*. That is clear to all of us.

Concilium *resists the Curia*

On 24 February 1964 Carlo Colombo writes a letter to Edward Schillebeeckx, the director of the dogma section, to the editorial committee of which Colombo himself also belongs, in reply to the redactional schema for the first issue of *Concilium*. It contains new demands, which are now more precise. After a conversation with *'les plus hautes autorités'* (the pope? Ottavani?), on the basis of a verbal instruction from the cardinal Secretary of State he has to report that the journal *Concilium* may appear on the following three conditions: (a) the editorial committees of the individual sections must be expanded by representatives of Roman theology; (b) a committee of bishops must be appointed which can follow the editorial activities, in order 'to guarantee perfect doctrinal certainty and the opportune time for publication'; (c) the title of the journal *Concilium* must appear in such a way that it does not seem to be an organ of the Council or even a semi-official organ.

On 24 October 1964 at 9.00 a.m. there is the first annual meeting of the Committee of Directors of *Concilium* in the Foyer Unitas of the German national church Anima under the chairmanship of Schillebeeckx. Again Monsignor Colombo formulates his demand for a 'committee of bishops'. This time happily it is Yves Congar and Monsignor Neophytos Edelby of Damascus who reply to him with the utmost clarity: Congar emphasizes the distinction between the 'pastoral authority' of the bishops and the 'scholarly magisterium' of theologians, which has its own independence. Edelby, a representative of Eastern Orthodoxy, supports Congar and says that in no way is a *'supervision romaine'* acceptable. This will also in fact be the journal's line in future. Unimpressed by all this, we finally concentrate on the many questions of organization. Around 10.30 the publishers of our various editions join us, and at 11.30 there is a gathering with other theologians present in Rome who are interested in *Concilium*.

At a very early stage Fr Vanhengel, now secretary of *Concilium*, had made contact with the Dutch businessman Antoine van den Boogaard. The two of them, with the assent of Schillebeeckx, propose to Paul Brand that *Concilium*, hitherto Paul Brand's publishing undertaking, should be made a registered foundation. Brand, who is by no means enthusiastic about this idea, allows himself to be persuaded by me that a foundation could be an advantage in the case of a multilingual edition of a journal with different publishers, which is now a really international enterprise. The Concilium Foundation based in Nijmegen is established on 5 June 1965 and with van den Boogaard on 7 August in my house by the lake I draft the basic lines of its *'règlement interne'*. On 23 October in Rome, now under my chairmanship, the second meeting of the editorial committee takes place with 48 theologians from all over the world. In accordance with this *règlement* Congar, Rahner, Schillebeeckx and I are the four theologians elected to the Foundation.

In the future, work for *Concilium* will demand a good deal of time of me each year: on the one hand I am responsible for the section on ecumenism (as Rahner is for pastoral theology and Schillebeeckx for dogma); on the other there are the meetings of the Foundation, which discuss matters of finance and organization and at the same time prepare for the annual meetings and decisions on personal policy. For me as a young man it is a great enrichment to work in a small group with some of the most important Catholic theologians of the day – with Congar, Rahner and Schillebeeckx. My experience in the faculty that one gets on better with strong partners than with weak ones is fully confirmed. Together we withstand the pressures from Rome and together we plan new actions, including the famous 1968 'Declaration for the Freedom of Theology', which will finally be subscribed to by 1360 theologians from all over the world.

I am to suggest and prepare this declaration. And not least because of this there has often been talk in Rome and among Catholic theologians of my personal influence on *Concilium* – in praise or in blame. There is no doubt that for decades I am fully to identify myself with this journal. But *Concilium* is never to be the journal of an individual theologian or individual theologians who have put forward their special ideas in it. Rather, it is a journal based on teamwork in mutual trust and on international co-operation and friendship, and for all the criticism of it orientated on the common good of the church. The annual meeting, in the week of Pentecost each year, is a unique place for theological ideas to be expressed.

However, I will not deny that I have presented my position very firmly, in particular when warding off Roman interventions; always, however, as I think, in the interest of the common cause. My key witness is the founder and first publisher of *Concilium*, Paul Brand:

> From the beginning Hans Küng was able to outline programmes, work out drafts and develop proposals which were then discussed, developed further and reshaped in general discussions. He could and can lead discussions, if need be, in a controversial way and exercise a decisive influence on them – deep into the night. But all who had taken part in them could soon also discover that these controversies were in the service of the journal and always aimed at consensus.

He is to contribute this to the book published on the occasion of my sixty-fifth birthday. 'Loyal and unconditional commitment': that is a compliment which I can repay to Paul Brand and which moreover is the basis of our friendly relations to the present day.

Papal contempt for theology

'In Moscow they don't know, but they understand everything. In Rome they know everything but they understand nothing.' I hear this comment from the writer Luigi Barzini, former Moscow correspondent of the *Corriere della Sera*, who wrote the critical bestseller on the manners and morals of the Italians (*The Italians*, 1964, advisedly first in English), when he invites me to his fine villa on the Via Cassia. 'They understand nothing,' I say, 'because they don't want to understand anything. The Roman Curia still thinks nothing of serious academic theology. Just as formerly philosophy was treated as the handmaid (*ancilla*) of theology, so now theology is treated as the handmaid of the magisterium.' They simply attempt to ignore the fact that traditionally alongside the pastoral authority of the bishops there is the scholarly magisterium of the theologians, as Congar argues against Colombo. More than once we Council theologians were lectured at by Cardinal Dean Tisserant to be good and not to distribute papers in the Council aula. Basically people are afraid of theology, indeed, of a 'council of theologians'.

We Council theologians, who are in fact the authors of by far the majority of the speeches by bishops, have a prime example of this authoritarian attitude in the audience for *periti* which is granted to us by Paul VI – towards the end of the second session, on Saturday 30 November 1963, in the Palazzo Apostolico. Certainly the pope praises us and thanks us, but only as the good aides of the bishops. And what he expects of us is not an iota of independent thought, honest criticism or constructive proposals, but simply and solely obedience, subservience to the hierarchy: servility. Right at the beginning of the papal address I see which way the wind is blowing and allow myself a mental experiment. How would the whole speech sound if it were not being given to Council theologians but to the bishops' chauffeurs? Truly, every statement could also have been made to the chauffeurs.

No, we needn't have been invited to a papal audience for such an address. Ottaviani too could have spoken like that. '*C'est une honte*, it's a scandal,' says Yves Congar under his breath when leaving the audience chamber. Three days later, in the afternoon of 3 December, the pope does in fact grant an audience to the bishops' chauffeurs. It doesn't seem to me worth the trouble to reverse the mental experiment and discover whether the address to the chauffeurs could also have been given to the council theologians. It certainly had the same content and the same level.

Of course this not very pleasant experience doesn't prevent us from fulfilling our theological obligations. Daniel O'Hanlon, a Jesuit from California, and I work intensively during the last days of the second session of the Council to prepare our volume of episcopal speeches to the Council in English, German, French, Spanish and Dutch editions. We get Yves Congar as a third editor. That same 3 December we are able essentially to finish our work. The translations will follow.

An extremely friendly young American by the name of Michael Novak, whom I have previously got to know, together with his wife, a painter, helps us on the technical side. During our editorial activity he indicates a desire to do a doctorate in Tübingen, and I listen to this request sympathetically. But confidential investigations among American colleagues indicate that Michael has already previously sought in vain once or twice to do a doctorate at Harvard: I am told that he would do better to aim at a doctorate with a second-rank American university than under the more difficult conditions of Tübingen (not least in terms of language). I attempt to explain all this to Novak – for his own benefit – in a friendly way. But he is bitterly disappointed. After the Council he will take his revenge on me with an ugly lead story in the *New York Sunday Times Magazine*, originally with just a caricature of me on the title page. And Novak? The 'left-wing' Catholic reformer does his doctorate at some American university, then rides the wave of ethnicity for a while with reference to his Polish origin and finally finds firm ground under his feet at the well-endowed 'right-wing' Enterprise Institute in Washington, where in the light of papal encyclicals he then canvasses for a 'Christian capitalism'. Thus he is comfortably off in every respect. I will not see him again for 30 years, at the World Economic Forum in Davos in 1997 – on my side nothing is forgotten, but all is forgiven.

Back to the Council aula: instead of a vote on Chapters IV (Judaism) and V (Freedom of Religion) of the Decree on Ecumenism, for which allegedly there is no time, on the morning of 3 December 1963 in the presence of the pope there is a commemoration of the Counter-Reformation Council of Trent – which in the view of most bishops is quite superfluous. This is an unmistakable answer by the pope and the Curia to the *de facto* departure of the Council from the Tridentine mentality. On this occasion two men are allowed to speak in the Council; they are the first laity to do so: Montini's friends Jean Guitton and Vittorino Veronese, whom I have already mentioned. The Curia bluntly calls these speeches 'attestations of reverence'.

The Council fathers of Vatican II allow what the pope and the Curia have forced on them to pass over them uninvolved, but also without contradiction. Again we hear the Council joke about Cardinal Ottaviani on the way to Trent, but we don't find it as amusing as we did at the beginning of the Council. Ottaviani, having had his fingers burnt once, is this time shrewd enough and doesn't give the commemorative speech on Trent himself. Cardinal Urbani, who is designated to do this, doesn't of course say a word about any historical relativization of the decrees of Trent; nor is there a word about John XXIII's invitation to translate the 'substance' of the old doctrine into a modern time and language. The whole ceremony is a farce with no value as information, in favour of the mediaeval Counter-Reformation system. And it is a warning to bishops and theologians: an attitude to this Council of the Counter-Reformation which differs from the traditionalist one can have serious consequences, as I myself learn the very next day.

First Inquisition proceedings in Rome

That the 'Holy Office' has by no means been paralysed by Cardinal Frings's speech, which was greeted with great applause, is already demonstrated to me the next day, 4 December 1963, the last day of the second session of the Council. On it the Constitution on the Liturgy is finally passed with only four votes against because of the countless compromises, as is the harmless moralizing Decree on the Means of Social Communication, which gives no indication that we live in a media age. This is the very meagre result of a whole session of the Council lasting many weeks. But that is disguised by the pope's announcement that he is making a pilgrimage to the Holy Land, there to meet the ecumenical patriarch Athenagoras of Constantinople. For a reconciliation with Eastern Orthodoxy? At all events there is great applause from the Council fathers: is a new era dawning between the Western and Eastern churches? The kiss of peace between pope and patriarch, above all the shared reading of the gospel, alternately in Latin and Greek, will have great symbolic value.

However, for the same day at 5 p.m., through the Bishop of Rottenburg, I have received an invitation from the 'Holy Office' to discuss my book *Structures of the Church*. It is – graciously – to take place in the Villa San Francisco, where the bishop is still staying. As well as Bishop Leiprecht, the Bishop of Basle, Franziskus von Streng, appears, along with two Gregorian professors, the German church lawyer Wilhelm Bertrams and the Dutch ecumenist Johannes Witte. All is under the chairmanship of Cardinal Augustin Bea – and that is a good omen.

In the course of the discussion I am confronted with eight questions, most of which turn on church order and the church's ministries: on the consensus in the church, the verdict of conscience, faith and the formulations of faith, the Council of Constance, the laity and the Council, the validity of polemical council definitions. I answer them all without any nervousness. Bea is always very kind: 'Surely you mean . . .' Or: 'Surely you don't mean . . .' I don't find it difficult to answer the questions from the Sanctum Officium to the satisfaction of the gentlemen. I think back to the public disputation at the Gregorian a decade previously; at any rate I needn't answer in syllogisms, as the secret 'Inquisition' is in German. At the end the cardinal also asks me when I return to Tübingen to respond briefly in writing and in Latin to the eight questions which I have answered verbally in German. I gladly promise this, since this hearing has evidently gone positively for me.

The next morning, 5 December, I make an early start at 5.30 a.m. and drive undaunted in the direction of Bologna, Milan and the Gotthard; fortunately by 6.30 p.m. I am in Lucerne, where I always pay my old clergy house a visit, and drive on to Sursee, where I celebrate a happy reunion with parents and sisters. Finally I reach Tübingen, where I take part in a session of the faculty and a session of the Great Senate to elect a new Rector, and give a two-hour lecture on the results of the second session of the Council. Back home again – thank God!

On 16 December I drive with the brothers Kurt and Walter Helbling, two Lucerne theology students, to Strasbourg. There Yves Congar is to be proclaimed '*Maître en théologie*, master of theology' – a kind of recompense on the part of the present Dominican General, since this is something that had been refused him in his earlier years. What a paradox: the *'Maître Général'*, no great theologian, nominates the great theologian Yves Congar, long recognized as a master by all theologians, 'Master of theology'. Of course I accept the invitation of the prior, who writes to me that Congar – known as the *'marcassin* (young wild boar) of the Ardennes' – would prefer no official ceremonies and big speeches, but a gathering with friends. And I want to be counted among those long-standing companions who have shared work, hopes and trials with him. It is a great delight for me to take part in the lunch in the Dominican residence and in the symposium that follows, where we all keenly discuss the history and perspectives of the 'ecumenical movement'.

On Tuesday 17 December I have another conversation with nuncio Corrado Bafile. On 10 January 1964 I sent the explanations required of me to Rome: *'Explicationes quaedam auctoris librum suum* Strukturen der Kirche *spectantes'* (9 pages). The proceedings of the Sanctum Officium against *Structures of the Church* are thereupon terminated. On 20 January 1964 Bishop Carl Joseph Leiprecht of Rottenburg sends me 'warmest congratulations' on my election as dean of the Catholic theological faculty: this will 'further increase' my 'burden of work'. He would therefore like to release me 'for the next session of the Council . . . So you can use the next semester without being claimed by me for the Council.' After the release the unburdening? With this letter the bishop, who had released me as his personal *peritus* the year before, is simply releasing himself: he need no longer make a financial contribution to my stay in Rome. It's laughable: in any case, in the past session of the Council he hasn't claimed me for the Council at all. Not for a minute.

How much people in Rottenburg still think and act in the Roman style follows from the highly solemn *decretum episcopi* that the bishop sends to the members of the cathedral chapter, the professors of the Catholic Theological Faculty, the senior clerical teachers of religion and others in positions of responsibility. For what purpose? To free them from the church's prohibition on reading books on the Index. All those mentioned are now freed from the ban on books *per decretum* of the authorities. As if they would have been observing it! Wouldn't a brief note in the diocesan magazine have been enough? However, I am now to note to my sorrow that the Inquisition continues to be at work not only in Rome, but unfortunately also quite near by, in Rottenburg.

An Inquisition also in the episcopal city

I didn't even note in my diary my election to be dean of the Catholic theological faculty, on which the bishop congratulated me. I took this event in a businesslike way; at first I firmly refused it because of my involvement in the Council, and in any case I would have preferred to have waited two or three years and accumulated experience. But it was impossible to evade it. Elected in January 1964, in the summer semester I succeed Dean Herbert Haag, who had performed his office to the great satisfaction of the faculty for a second year. I quickly note that one only really learns how the university functions from within, as a dean. And I find it very interesting to come into close contact with the Rector, the deans of other faculties and some elected senators in the sessions of the Little Senate, in order to discuss the problems of the university and the other disciplines. In 1964 we live in a time when one can achieve something in the university in terms of persons and buildings, because of the good financial situation financed by the public purse.

As well as all the academic business, twice a year feasts take place: the rectoral feast in the winter in the main building, the Neue Aula, and the summer feast up in the Schloss Hohentübingen. The theologians of both faculties usually shine by their absence. I take part in these feasts whenever possible. I am not one for feasts, but in a cheerful mood one can refresh old acquaintances and make new ones. Normally I am always assigned a nice lady to sit next to. But since my youngest sister is studying Romance languages and literature for a semester in Tübingen and is living in my home, I take her with me, marvellously attractive in a flowery white dress, into the Rittersaal of the castle, to greet the Rector. All eyes are on us. There is amazement all round: 'Has he got married now?' And then whispering: 'It's "only" his sister . . .'

My commentary: 'Were I to arrive tomorrow morning at the Sanctum Officium at about 8 a.m. to get a dispensation from celibacy, I could guarantee to have it in my hands by noon, because people there would be afraid that I might have changed my mind by 6 p.m.' According to the view there, a marriage would also put paid to my theology. But I cannot and will not give the Vatican this pleasure. With Rector Theodor Eschenburg I have a breath of fresh air under the gateway around midnight: 'Magnificence, I'm always impressed by the way in which you exercise your office without the usual sighing and shrugging of the shoulders: you really seem to enjoy it.' His reply is brief and typically Hanseatic, 'It's crazy, isn't it?' In a way I can also say that of myself.

But my first test as a dean comes soon. The duplication of chairs in dogmatics is to be followed by a duplication of chairs in church history. The call process has already been going on since December 1962. Number 1 on the list for early church history and patrology, by the unanimous resolution of the faculty and the Great Senate, is Professor Alfred Stuiber, extraordinarius at the University of Bonn, who held a chair with us in the winter semester of 1960 with no objections and gained considerable respect. He is a very solid but very dry scholar, certainly critical, but at all events different from our church historian Fink, whose witty mockery and jokes are notorious in the episcopal ordinariate of Rottenburg. Beyond question people don't want to have a second Fink, but we don't expect any objections to Stuiber.

However, then comes the surprise: instead of the *nihil obstat*, Bishop Dr Carl-Joseph Leiprecht of Rottenburg issues a veto against the call – in accordance with the concordat against Stuiber's teaching (not his way of life). But, in good Roman style, not the slightest reason is given. And this in a democratic constitutional state, although Stuiber has the *venia legendi* (permission to teach) in Bonn with no objections. Our faculty cannot accept something like this – for the sake of its own credibility and the good reputation and advancement of a distinguished scholar. From the beginning it is clear that resistance is necessary: as dean I will firmly fight for Stuiber and academic freedom in research and teaching.

Since the bishop constantly refuses to offer the Kultusminister or the faculty any reasons for his attack on Stuiber's teaching (how can a church historian, of all people, become heretical?) and he refuses to grant Stuiber a legal hearing, the faculty turns to the Great Senate. There I make an urgent plea for Stuiber's call and ask the senate in the name of the faculty to make a clear protest against the action of Rottenburg. Nothing of this kind has ever happened before: a unanimous vote of the Great Senate against the local bishop for violating the law of the concordat. For Bishop Leiprecht in public this is highly unpleasant, for the faculty a plus – clearly these Catholic theologians have recently become capable of resisting 'the Inquisition' if the freedom of teaching and research guaranteed by the constitution are at stake.

Politicians back out

This is the beginning of a long tug-of-war involving many letters and telephone calls: the forces are roughly of equal strength. It is a stalemate for the Kultusminister Dr Gerhard Storz and his successor, the Protestant (!) theologian professor Dr Wilhelm Hahn, who is 'very glad' that he can avoid a dispute with the bishop and leave the decision to the Prime Minister of Baden-Württemberg. Politicians prefer not to get involved with the churches. 'According to my information from the nunciature in Godesberg, people there want "peace with the state at any price" ', Professor Stuiber writes to me on 9 November 1964: 'So the minister could announce the call without needing to fear that there would really be a conflict relating to the concordat; it would have to begin in Rottenburg and the nuncio would divert it . . . Many thanks for your efforts; if with my case the Tübingen faculty is fighting for everyone I must be very grateful. Many greetings, too, to colleague Haag. All best wishes for Wednesday evening . . . '

On Wednesday evening, 11 November, Prime Minister Kurt Georg Kiesinger, who had signed the document appointing me ordinarius professor in 1960, invites me as dean along with pro-dean Herbert Haag for a personal conversation in his home in Tübingen. In this way I get to know from within the house which a few years later will be offered for sale to me when Kiesinger moves to Bonn as chancellor or, rather, outside the city to Schloss Bebenhausen. However, I will then prefer a house higher up the same street, because it is lighter and gives me a wonderful view of the Swabian Alb.

Prime Minister Kiesinger, already at that time named 'King Silvertongue' for his aesthetic speeches, doesn't want to spoil things either with the church or with the university. The dilemma is that the state shouldn't make any calls without the assent of the church – but the faculty for its part refuses to present a new list. For to be dissatisfied with the church, because Stuiber allegedly spoke disparagingly about church authorities in a lecture, as is subsequently claimed by the bishop – really wasn't an objection to 'teaching and way of life'. Kiesinger wants to decide the matter 'by strictly constitutional criteria'. His way out is to ask two recognized legal experts for opinions, and that takes time. A month later he asks only the Cologne lawyer Professor Hans Peters, who on 16 January 1965 sends him an opinion which is negative for Stuiber. It is immediately attacked by the faculty, because still no reasons are given against Stuiber. Cardinal Frings of Cologne, who is responsible for Bonn, explains to Stuiber in an audience that there are no objections to his teaching (and way of life) and that he will intercede for him with the Bishop of Rottenburg. But Kiesinger goes on waiting. In this way one can put off a decision – until it is unnecessary.

Only many months later is this stalemate ended from outside: on 6 August Stuiber has received a call from the new university of Bochum and will accept it. There, too, there is no talk of church objections to his teaching. I don't know what went on behind the scenes. Certainly people in Rottenburg are also 'over the moon' that in this way a solution has been reached with which both sides can save face. At any rate we have maintained academic freedom also against an inquisitorial church government, and since then my library has been adorned with the 'seventh, fully revised edition' of the classical *Patrology* by Altaner, dedicated to me by the new editor, Professor Dr Alfred Stuiber, with à simple visiting card: 'Warmest greetings! 23 November 1966'.

And Rottenburg? The bishop, who is also a politician in his own way, wants to sort out the whole matter with the faculty. This affair, which has also been discussed in public, has damaged his prestige, but not that of the faculty. Who now 'unburdens' the bishop? The one who has 'relieved' and 'unburdened' me as a *peritus* invites me to coffee. I am not vindictive, but I won't accept such an invitation as dean without the formal assent of my faculty. In fact there are those in the faculty meeting who speak in favour of rejecting this invitation, especially the church historian Fink, who otherwise has slyly kept in the background in this controversy. But I am against maintaining 'fraught relations' between the bishop and the faculty. As the one who has been the leader in waging the academic 'war' against the bishop, I now argue resolutely for peace and can achieve an almost unanimous vote.

We have coffee in the new cool and modern episcopal palace of Rottenburg in a pleasant atmosphere. I receive from the bishop, to pass on to the faculty, the assurance that nothing of this kind will happen again. A success. What would the same bishop have done, I ask myself afterwards, if one day an intervention was ordered by Rome against the one to whom he had once given such an assurance? But Bishop Leiprecht, who ultimately remained personally well disposed towards me, despite all our differences, as I did to him, will then unfortunately have long ceased to hold office and will no longer be alive. I hear from Rottenburg that when he left office he took the whole Küng dossier with him – and later destroyed it. Why? What for?

With the best will in the world I cannot reconstruct the various conversations with him, most of which turned on some Roman complaints. That letter from the Roman dicasteries was also read out to me without my being given a copy. Basically the details are uninteresting, since everything always revolved around the same thing: 'teaching of the church', 'magisterium', 'not sufficiently Roman Catholic'. And then as often as possible I try to make it clear that nevertheless, and precisely in this way, I am truly Catholic and will remain so. I hear from the Vatican that on his birthday, the first day of Christmas, Cardinal Ottaviani had said to his assessor Archbishop Parente, 'Today I am giving a pizza to all the captives in prisons – except for Küng, Rahner and our venerable brother!' By the latter he meant none other than Cardinal Bea.

How, I keep asking myself, will the great dispute over the further course of the Catholic Church in the twentieth century turn out? As yet nothing has been definitively decided, nor has it been decided for me personally. However, I don't want to land up in the prisons of the Inquisition or to be dependent on Roman pizzas. That makes it all the more important for me to concentrate on my work and be my own man in theology.

Work – and leisure?

Every free moment – at the Council and even more between the sessions – I sit at my book *The Church*. Only two important things have changed since the overall draft of 1963: for substantive historical reasons it seems to me necessary to insert after the first chapter on the church and faith another on the question of 'Jesus and the foundation of a church'. How am I to be able to talk about the church of Jesus Christ without knowing precisely what this Jesus of Nazareth himself wanted or did not want? This chapter in particular demands an unexpectedly large amount of work because of the New Testament studies which are necessary. Then for reasons of time I will abbreviate the last chapter on church and world so that it becomes an epilogue. Much has already been said about that in the main text, the tolerable number of pages has already been reached, I am totally exhausted, and in any case the political problems, a year or two before 1968, are fluid.

I am often asked later: how was it, how is it, possible to write such long and complex books in a relatively short time? As an answer to this question for *The Church*, but also for some of the books which follow, three elements seem to me to be important.

First, I must already have the book largely in my head before I begin to write – a clear vision and disposition and in addition a good deal of material already worked out.

Secondly, I must work day and night in the semester and the vacations and get by with little sleep. For decades I content myself with around five hours, plus a fifteen-minute siesta after lunch.

Thirdly, there must be as little effort as possible with technical matters. First of all I write everything by hand, line by line, in two or three versions. I have the literature in my library at home, which has a systematic structure and has been built up increasingly over the years, or I can get it from the university library or other libraries. I dictate what has been written out by hand into a machine, check it first by listening to it, and only then have it typed by my secretary. First I correct the typescript, and then it goes for correction and criticism to my assistants – in the case of *The Church* to Dr Gotthold Hasenhüttl and Dr Alexandre Ganoczy. With later books the drafts also go to professional colleagues and friends for critical checking. Then I myself correct, expand, change it all time and again – until immediately before printing. Normal manuscript pages are typed perhaps six times, difficult ones sometimes twelve times. Later the computer will make everything much simpler.

Given this somewhat unusual amount of work and pace of work I am sometimes asked: 'And what else do you get out of life?' Here I can first reply quite simply: 'Don't worry, I get much out of life in every respect. I never get bored. Theology is my life and I've always seen it as an interesting task to be able to reflect on God and the world. In this way my work becomes a hobby, working time becomes leisure time and leisure time working time.'

But I am not a workaholic who cannot relax. As well as a few daily keep-fit exercises, swimming, whenever I have the opportunity, is part of the day, and skiing on my winter holidays. I concede that the correspondence which increases year by year is a chore, the purely administrative work a duty, and physical work a burden – to be avoided as far as possible. But my real intellectual creative work is a pleasure, and I can keep at it from morning till after midnight. However, I use my room at the university mainly for discussions and colloquia and always like putting it at the disposal of colleagues and visitors. I work at home and therefore have always had my secretariat in my house. But I can't be creative at a machine. I need to look out on nature, into the garden and the landscape, and like working outside whenever possible. A block of paper is enough for the first sketches. However, in my lake house I limit myself as far as possible to reading, preferably those big works which demand time.

And what would all work be without music, which makes the spiritual sensual and the sensual spiritual? I lack something if I have to do without it – for example at the Council (RAI has terrible music programmes) or when travelling. I don't like indefinable constant background music but something appropriate to the season. The classical programme in the morning – interrupted by the news and reports on the papers – immediately cheers me up. Of course if I have to read serious literature I can't take in music at the same time. But I breathe again when I get home tired or the time for listening to music has come in another way. Music warms my heart and keeps my head clear. I have invested a good deal of time and money in my record collection, which I have built up historically – from Gregorian chant to modern classical music – as I have my effective library. And whether the music is Renaissance, baroque, classical or romantic, depending on my mood, sometimes I listen more to music that is peaceful and inward, cheerful and lively, or dramatic and solemn. Here over time Mozart has super-seded Beethoven as the master of all masters.

I can relax above all in conversation. I don't live a solitary life: a hermit's existence has never attracted me. Whether in the family, the Germanicum or now at the university, I was never alone. Unlike other professors, who prefer to keep clear of assistance, I initiate my colleagues in as much as possible. I'm interested in their questions, opinions, advice, and I like discussing with them, often until late into the night, not just theology but the state of the church and the world and every possible subject. We work intensively, but we also laugh a great deal. With Immanuel Kant I believe: 'Heaven has given human beings three things as a counterbalance to the many troubles of life: hope, sleep and laughter.'

I like talking with colleagues and friends of all faculties, and I receive and issue a great many invitations. I can live, eat and drink modestly, but I can also enjoy myself. I follow my father's example in keeping good wine in the cellar and show the hospitality to which I have been accustomed since my youth. Countless visitors from all over the world will be my guests over the years. Even if I have guests from other religions or no religion, I never fail to say grace. For me the vertical reaching out to the infinite is naturally part of my horizon on earth. I am too convinced that everything, including my ideas and achievements, is given not to express my gratitude even before breakfast: thanksgiving for a quiet night and a prayer for what I plan, often also thinking of others who I am concerned about. Also a prayer at midday and in the evening: thanksgiving for the day and a prayer for the night. Mahatma Gandhi says that prayer is the key for the morning and the bolt on the door for the evening. I seldom need fixed formulae for this prayer: don't babble like the Gentiles, who think that they will be heard only if they use many words (cf. Matt. 6.7). In everyday life a trusting thought sent 'above' is all that is necessary to ensure transcendence.

And so I do theology every day with joy. A few conflicts apart, I have very good relations with the women and men who surround me. I lead a contented and – despite all cares and fights – a happy life.

IX

⚜

A Relapse into the Old Lack of Freedom?

'Above the pope as an expression
of the binding claim of church authority
stands one's own conscience,
which has to be obeyed first of all,
if need be against the demands of church authority.'

Joseph Ratzinger, 1968

Nervous tension before the third session of the Council

Now that in the second half of the second session of the Council, by contrast
with his predecessor, Paul VI has proved more of a brake on the Council than an
inspiration for it, the hopeful mood of a new beginning has given way to a
nervous uncertainty. Talk is increasingly going the rounds that the atmosphere in
the Vatican has changed. On 24 July 1964 Monsignor Montini's former confidant
in the Engelberg monastery, Fr Dr Anselm Fellmann from Sursee, writes to me
that he has visited the pope in Rome and that the pope has also got round to
talking about me: 'May I tell you – he asked me to – that he is not very happy
with you or your last written works, indeed he is troubled by them. He asks you
to moderate yourself somewhat. He also reads your books. I was able to give the
first of them to him on your behalf. I would have preferred to say this to you
rather than write it; but at that time I had no opportunity. Please be discreet.
With friendly greetings.'

But at the grass roots, as I know all too well, many people are disturbed about
the pope. For example, my friend from my time in Oxford, Peter Nelson, now in
a little parish in Scotland, writes to me on 4 April 1964: 'I personally am very
depressed at the moment. So far I haven't been able to discover a glimmer of
hope in this pontificate. It looks as if everything is once again to be as it was under
Pius XII. Am I wrong? I hope so, but I fear the worst.'

A certain narrow-mindedness is becoming evident even in the Secretariat for
Christian Unity. 'I am again in Rome, to take part in the session of the Secretariat,' Gregory Baum writes to me from Rome on 23 February 1964, 'and want
to take the opportunity to send you my best greetings. It's a pity that you aren't
one of us. I wrote to the Secretariat from Canada, suggesting that you might be

invited, but apparently people think that there are already enough of us.' Professor Johannes Feiner, the extremely sound Swiss member of the Secretariat, has confided in me that this probably isn't the reason: 'You're capable of blowing up any commission.' That's probably true – if this commission veils the truth and gives priority to ecclesiastical self-righteousness.

Of course nobody in the Secretariat for Christian Unity basically wants that – I know most of them personally. But here too the result of the discussion is a compromise, as Gregory Baum immediately goes on to write: 'The schema (on ecumenism) has improved somewhat, but the theology has remained the same: at the centre the church of Rome with the fullness of all wisdom and means of grace, surrounded by other churches and communities which have taken on in different degrees something of the wisdom and the means of grace of the Catholic Church.' That would indeed have been a conception which I would have 'blown up'. And this not out of arrogance but for the reason to which my friend Gregory refers: 'Although the beginnings are there, we haven't succeeded in saying that the goal and norm of all churches is *not* the Catholic Church; the goal and norm of *all* churches is Christ and his act of salvation. Perhaps that will come in the Third Vatican Council. There are already a couple of open doors in our improved schema.'

Baum also complains about the letter from Cardinal Secretary of State Amleto Cicognani to the Council *periti*, which significantly I haven't received: 'In it we are forbidden to open our mouths. The reaction of Rome is that we should take no notice of the letter. Remarkably the letter hasn't got into the press.' But at any rate my American friends have also received it. Mark Hurley, Chancellor of the diocese of Stockton, California and later Bishop of Santa Rosa, writes to me: 'As we say over here, they sent out a muzzle.' During the next session of the Council, along with General Secretary Felici, *le barbu* ('the bearded one', his curial nickname), namely the French Dean of the College of Cardinals, Eugene Tisserant, will be especially prominent in sending public admonitions to the theological experts not to distribute any 'unauthorized' papers in the aula and to restrain themselves generally. It is amazing – no, it isn't amazing – how the various organs of the Curia time and again play into each others' hands. General Secretary Felici will even take action against bishops: he brutally tears a bundle of papers on birth control and the pill out of the hands of Josef Maria Reuss, the suffragan bishop of Mainz. The prophylactic action of a celibate member of the Curia. But much is at stake for him.

The struggle for public opinion

It's clear that in this ambivalent situation our publication of speeches made by bishops at the Council is quite an important political event. As I have reported, the co-editors are Daniel O'Hanlon and Yves Congar. Beyond doubt the Curia is afraid of the truth: the people of the church aren't to hear what has been said in the Council. Therefore there is an insistence on secrecy. The 'Council secret' is a sacred cow in the possession of the Curia. Certainly this secrecy had been relaxed in the second period of the Council. A separate press committee is responsible for giving more comprehensive information to the media. But the official press spokesmen still have a monopoly of information. The bishops continue to be bound to the rule of secrecy and the printed documents all remain *sub secreto* – though often in vain.

Remarkably enough, although in the Vatican I am probably regarded as the 'chief culprit' over the publication of the Council speeches, I don't receive a reprimand: do they fear negative publicity, or do they think that an intervention is no longer useful since the German edition has been published so quickly? However, the American Jesuit Daniel O'Hanlon receives an admonition from Felici, the General Secretary of the Council – as always in such cases it is delivered secretly through the Jesuit General and the provincial (of the province of California) – that publication of these speeches would violate the 'Council secrecy'. But fortunately the American edition had appeared at almost the same time as the German, so here too the Roman intervention comes too late. O'Hanlon sends an explanation to his provincial and thus the matter is initially settled.

But the French edition hasn't yet appeared, and Yves Congar reports to me that he has had a letter from Cardinal Secretary of State Cicognani, i.e. Cardinal Ottaviani, which censures publication of the bishops' speeches. He is considering whether he can still be responsible for the French edition that has been prepared. I reply to him after my return from Sursee, where to my great joy I was able to furnish my little house by the lake, on 22 April 1964: from a legal point of view only the drafts of the Council documents and the Commission meetings are *'sub secreto'*; we had explicit permission from each individual bishop, and some extracts from Council speeches have in any case already appeared in the press. What applies to us is not what the Curia people *declare* to be permissible or not, but what *is* permissible or not. That also applies to Cardinal Cicognani's letter. There is no obligation to ask any curial authority in advance for permission. Of course the Curia likes uniformity of church public opinion. Had we theologians observed the wishes of the Curia before and during the previous sessions of the Council, and had we not created clear currents of opinion, the Council would have made even less progress.

Now Congar too writes to me that the climate in Rome has changed. But this seems to me to be more of a reason *for* publication. 'The main problem evidently is that we have a pope who – for whatever reasons – has not so far followed up his great and bold words with equally great and bold actions. The *ceterum censeo* is: *Romanam curiam esse reformandam*. Unless the Council succeeds in this we can soon begin all over again from the beginning. And here the publication of the Council speeches will be particularly helpful. I think that here we may last of all let ourselves be influenced by the Roman climate. Rather, there is need for an active mobilization of public opinion in the church, in order to support the pope in taking action.'

That, then, is how I express my hope that the French edition may also appear before it is too late. I point out that Congar's name is now known as co-editor of the German and American editions, and it would only lead to misunderstandings if he didn't appear as editor of the French edition or this wasn't published at all. Certainly I want to leave him the freedom to decide the fate of the French edition: he shouldn't have conflicts of conscience on my account. But my view is clear: 'We made our joint decision as *periti conciliares*. Here in principle I don't think that I am in a different position from you, though – after mature consideration and by my own free choice – I have shown no interest as *peritus conciliaris* in collaborating with *this* Theological Commission under *this* leadership. That in our enterprise we should appear as "partisans" of a particular theology was unavoidable from the start and is nothing new. Parente, etc. (of the Sanctum Officium) have many times publicly declared themselves to be partisans of another particular theology. I have to endure with equanimity being regarded by such people as *persona non grata*, something that you yourself have endured for so long in an exemplary fashion. The issue is no more and no less than the unpretentious service of the gospel, without any anxiety, in season and out of season.' I end with the words: 'Our different views on this matter surely don't rule out our continuing to be good friends. All my life I shall never forget what I owe to you and your theology. *Avançons*. Cordially.' And the result? Yves Congar agrees, and the French edition also appears.

Robert F. Quinn writes to me from the Catholic Information Center of the Paulist Fathers in Boston: 'Your Book *Council Speeches of Vatican II* is going very well in the United States. It is being widely accepted and hailed as a great step forward in understanding the true problems of the Council. We are distributing hundreds of them here at the Center' (24 April 1964). In the struggle over public opinion the progressive majority has managed to assert itself: never again in this century will the Catholic Church achieve such a high degree of public approval, extending far beyond its members.

A Roman or an ecumenical point of view?

The third session of the Council begins very early, on 14 September 1964. The previous day, spending the night once again in Sursee, I set off at 4 a.m. and am already in Rome by 3 p.m. In this session I live in the Istituto San Tommaso di Villanova (Viale Romania 7), well looked after by sisters. In American circles this is called 'the rebels' roost'. There is a very pleasant and interesting group of like-minded people and friends: I lunch with the French bishops (Léon-Arthur Elchinger of Strasbourg, Paul Joseph Schmitt of Metz and Pierre Boillon of

Verdun) and theologians (the Dominican Henri Féret and the Louvain church historian Willy Onclin). I spend the evenings, often until midnight, with American bishops (Ernest Primeau of Manchester, Paul Schulte of Indianapolis) and *periti*: John Courtney Murray SJ, Monsignor George Higgins of the National Catholic Welfare Conference in Washington, John Quinn of the Archdiocese of Chicago, and several others. The atmosphere is always lively and friendly, uncomplicated in a way which is unusual among German professors. It is more than a formality when several people write to me later that they very much hope to see me again in this residence in the fourth session. I feel encouraged by such varied friends who are still unanimous about the basic line and are also very well informed. Sometimes interesting visitors appear, like Monsignor Marcinkus from the Secretariat of State (he was deacon and I was subdeacon at the first mass of my friend Robert Trisco); responsible for the Vatican finances, he is later to play the most ominous main role in the Banco Ambrosiano scandal.

At the beginning of the third session of the Council a group of conservative cardinals and religious superiors had drawn the pope's attention in a letter to the dangers which threaten 'the church' (for them identical with the Curia) as a result of the Council (which they reject in principle). In an audience with the pope (according to the note in his diary on 9 October 1964), Cardinal Siri, who belongs to this group, replies to the question when the pope should end the Council: '*Se possibile subito, perché l'aria del concilio fa male* – if possible immediately, the atmosphere of the Council makes one feel ill.' What is worse is that the pope, who wants to be arbiter, increasingly puts himself behind the curial power cartel, as is already evident in the second half of the second session of the Council. Certainly he would 'feel things in a very deep and dramatic way', Yves Congar writes in his journal at the same time. However, Paul VI doesn't have 'the theological vision which his openness would require' but is 'very tied to a Roman point of view' (14 September 1964). That is the decisive reason why this third session of the Council will end with a '*settimana nera*', a 'black week'.

Important topics for discussion in the third session of the Council have been already raised by the second: the schema on the church and the chapter on Mary, the schema on the bishops and the improved schema on ecumenism. Now finally the debate on freedom of religion also begins (introduced by Bishop de Smedt) and then the debate on the Jews and non-Christians (introduced by Cardinal Bea) – I shall report on these separately. It is hardly worth reporting the discussions of the schemata 'Christian Education' and 'The Renewal of Religious Life', for which Bishop Leiprecht is also responsible.

Some curiosities: some women have now also been admitted to the Council as *auditores* (listeners): at any rate a schema on the 'lay apostolate' and another on 'the church in the modern world' are also to be discussed, and this would look comical without women. The pope even grants a special audience to the wives of non-Catholic observers. Wonder of wonders, finally even some parish priests are admitted to the Council. And on one occasion – what a privilege for the *'poveri sacerdoti'* – they are even allowed to 'concelebrate' in St Peter's with His Excellency Felici, who is increasingly giving himself airs. I am not one of those Catholics who can derive maximum enjoyment from minimal progress in an encrusted church system.

In the middle of November 1964 verdicts differ widely on what has been achieved inside and outside the Council, depending on whether the criteria for evaluation are theoretical or practical, within Catholicism or ecumenical, a matter of principle or pragmatic. I have my doubts.

When I think about what has been decided theoretically, I am optimistic, but when I look at the practical achievements I have reasons for pessimism. As an optimist I can welcome, for example, the establishment of a shared leadership of the church by pope *and* bishops as a decisive counterpoint to the one-sided definition of papal primacy at the First Vatican Council. But as a pessimist I must reflect that this resolution on collegiality so far hasn't in fact changed anything in Rome.

If I assess what has been achieved from a standpoint within Catholicism there is much that looks positive, but from an ecumenical perspective much is unsatisfactory. For example, within Catholicism the full affirmation of the historical-critical method in exegesis (in respect of literary genres, literal meaning, etc.) in the new schema on revelation, which takes the human character and the fragility of the words of scripture seriously, represents a great victory of modern exegesis over the reactionary tendencies which still emerged in the first schema under John XXIII. But from an ecumenical perspective the description of the inspiration of the Bible does not take the slightest heed of modern exegesis and history, and despite the profane, scientific and historical errors which can easily be noted today, the Bible is claimed to be dogmatically 'without error'.

If I am concerned with theological solutions in principle, my judgement will be different from what it would be if I contented myself from the start with what is politically possible. As one who thinks tactically and pragmatically I will praise the collegiality of the pope and the bishops which is affirmed both theologically and in practice as the main ecclesiological achievement of Vatican II. But as one who thinks about matters of principle I have to say that collegiality is a characteristic of the church as such (as the fellowship of believers and people of God) and that therefore not only the collegiality of the pope with the bishops but also that of the bishop with the pastors and that of the pastors with the members of the community has to be realized both theologically and practically.

As for the mood in the Council, what I drew attention to from the beginning has now become clear even to the most naïve: the Council is most hampered and hindered by the antagonism which is now having an effect everywhere – not between the 'Council majority' and the 'Council minority', as people like to say, but between the Council and the curial power cartel. Small in number and without the people of the church behind it, under the aegis of Ottaviani, Cicognani and Felici this is extraordinarily powerful: it dominates the most important control centres of the Curia (the Roman congregations) and the Council (the commissions). The presidents are members of the Curia, the vice-presidents are members of the Curia, the secretaries of most of the Council commissions are members of the Curia, and the General Secretariat of the Council under the 'maestro machiavellista' Felici, which interferes everywhere, is also manned by the Curia; it doesn't hesitate to change the Council texts illegally at the Vatican printers. How differently everything would have gone from the beginning of the Council if the commissions had not been led by members of the Curia! It is because of the Curia, not the Council, that many words and actions of the Council are not clear decisions but ambiguous compromises, and some words are not followed by actions. Because the Curia keeps throwing sand into the workings of the Council, the majority and its spokesmen seem to have lost their dynamic. The incessant squabbling and skirmishes in the commissions and the aula cause weariness. And yet – we must look at the whole picture:

A prophecy fulfilled

So is the whole Council after all an empty hope? No, despite all the great difficulties and severe obstacles I still cherish a very well-founded hope because:

No doors have been shut: there have been no definitions and dogmatizations, negative or positive.

Countless doors have been opened: there is now discussion on all questions in the Catholic Church – but on birth control and celibacy only outside the Council.

Principles like *ecclesia semper reformanda*, which in 1960 even Catholic ecumenists thought to be primarily Protestant, now appear in Council decrees.

A new spirit has come to life, a spirit of renewal and reform, of ecumenical understanding and dialogue with the modern world, among bishops, theologians and in the Catholic Church generally. The Catholic Church will never again be as it was before the Council.

After the reform of the liturgy, resolved on at the end of the second session of the Council, in the third session three further important constitutions will now be passed: on the church, on ecumenism and on the Eastern churches. Whereas with its Chapter III on the hierarchy the Constitution on the Church confirms the Roman system at the decisive point, the Constitution 'On Ecumenism' opens up new ways and a new future. A simple count of some key words now makes my book *The Council and Reunion* seem to be a prophecy fulfilled.

Both sides are to blame for the schism. There is a request to other Christians for forgiveness. As a church of sinners the Catholic Church is in need of constant reform, in practical church life, but also in doctrine. The gospel is the norm for renewal. Non-Catholic Christian communities are also called churches or church communities. An ecumenical attitude is necessary; the churches must get to know each other, there must be dialogue, recognition of the good in others, learning from others, collaboration in all spheres, shared prayer with separated Christians, growing fellowship also in the celebration of the liturgy. There must be conversations between theologians at the same level; doing one's own theology, especially also in the historical disciplines, in an ecumenical spirit, and much more. When everything that has been achieved is seen together, what church has done more for its own renewal and ecumenical openness in barely three years than the Catholic Church since the beginning of the Council?

That is what the situation looks like in the middle of November, and this is my stocktaking of the third session of the Council which is published in the *Frankfurter Allgemeine Zeitung* on 18/19 November 1964. That same day Paul VI surprisingly announces his visit to India. I have already flown to India on 14 November. I believed that I might leave the Council early with a good conscience in order to achieve more at another place during its last two weeks. No one suspected that the week of 14 to 21 November 1964 would go down in history as the *'settimana nera'* of Vatican II. The expression 'black week' was coined by the bravest and most beloved bishop of the Netherlands, Monsignor Willem M. Bekkers ('s-Hertogenbosch), another friend who died all too early.

India – Christianity as a minority

During the second session of the Council the theologian Fr Josef Neuner SJ, long active in India, who had earlier translated the 'Denziger' of conciliar and papal doctrinal definitions into German but then had remarkably worked himself into the world of Hinduism, had asked me whether I could come to India in the second half of November 1964. In the third session of the Council I give a lecture in Rome for Cardinal Valerian Gracias of Bombay and the Indian bishops. I have more than one conversation with this head of the Indian episcopate, and it is also Gracias who definitively invites me to India. Immediately before the great eucharistic congress, for which moreover the pope will also come to India for the first time, from 2-5 December there is to be a great symposium of Catholic theologians from all over India.

As the first of four speakers at this symposium, under the title 'Christian Revelation and Non-Christian Religions' I can speak on a topic which has long been of central importance to me: 'The World Religions in God's Plan of Salvation'. I can now present in a synthesis what I thought through during my student years in Rome and later have continually developed, not least inspired by more recent publications of Karl Rahner and Joseph Ratzinger.

I begin from the tolerant view of the Indian philosopher of religion Sarvapalli Radhakrishnan, India's first state president, who allows all religions to be valid in their own way and is therefore accused by Christians of relativism and indifferentism. I compare this view with the rigorous Catholic formulation of the dogma 'Outside the church there is no salvation' by Pope Boniface VIII, who will allow only the 'creature' submissive to the pope to attain eternal salvation. This is an inhuman statement if we look from today's perspective at the past, present and future of all humankind, against which Roman Catholic Christianity appears as a tiny minority.

So I put the Catholic Church's claim to monopoly to the test. In a survey of the different biblical testimonies which show the 'pagans' in a friendly light I demonstrate unequivocally that already in both the Old and New Testaments a quite different universal perspective can be established. There God appears as the creator of all human beings and 'Adam' not as the first Jew, first Christian or first Muslim, but as the first human being. And I draw conclusions from this which need not be described in detail here.

One thing at any rate is certain: the ecclesiocentric view of 'outside the church no salvation' can no longer be maintained; a theocentric perspective must also assign the world religions as such (and not just individual non-Christians) a function in God's saving plan. Here, as I put it in a challenging way in contrast to the usual terminology, the world religions appear as the normal, 'ordinary way' to salvation, and the Christian faith as the great, very special, 'extraordinary way'.

Later I will tend to avoid this terminology, but I shall always be concerned to find the way between the extremes of indifferentism and exclusivism, and here not to advocate any naïve idealizing view of the world religions but a realistic view: the religions in their ambivalence, their truth and their error. However, I shall also make self-critical assessment of Christianity, which may by no means be contrasted, as a complete, 'perfect' entity with an absolute claim to truth and a monopoly of salvation, with the incomplete, 'deficient' world religions, something that Joseph Ratzinger still attempts to do in the year 2000 as supreme guardian of the faith in his declaration *Dominus Iesus*. At the same time, Inquisition proceedings against theologians of religious pluralism, like those against Jacques Dupuis and Tissa Balasuriya, who have already been mentioned, and also against Paul Knitter in Cincinnati, show how little even now people take seriously the Vatican II declaration *Nostra aetate* on the relationship between the church and the non-Christian religions, which has been passed in principle just two weeks before my departure from India.

As might be expected, already in 1964 there is an intensive discussion of this view in Bombay. The press has been excluded for fear of tendentious reports; this was a mistake. But it is impossible to prevent a now really tendentious full-page report appearing in *Le Monde*; this is taken up by the London *Tablet* and causes many misunderstandings, long before an objective summary of the results of the congress produced by the organizers themselves appears in *Informations Catholiques Internationales*. The organizers make it clear that it is not theology that has invented all these problems. They have been posed by the reality of the world, which has entered a new era. And already in view of the hundreds of millions of Hindus whom one encounters in India, one must grasp a more comprehensive view of salvation with heart and mind.

I also give a public lecture in Bombay on 26 November 1964 and get much applause from the public here. But four days later, immediately before the arrival of the pope, for reasons of time I cannot speak at the international eucharistic congress itself. Nor can I accept an urgent invitation by Monsignor Clarizio to speak at the International Mariological Conference in Santo Domingo, which reaches me in New Delhi. I have already long been on a journey further east. Why east?

A journey round the world

A brief flashback: at one point in the semester in Tübingen Herbert Haag and I are at a dinner with the head of the surgical clinic, Professor Naegeli of Zurich. This modest surgeon is now retired, free of all the duties which often claimed him day or night. 'What are you doing with your retirement?' I ask him. 'A journey round the world,' he say, 'three or four months with my brother.'

Who hasn't had such a wish: a journey round the world! Perhaps I too will make one once I'm retired? But that won't be for 33 years. And now hardly a year has passed and I'm already on my first journey round the world, not in three months, nor even like Jules Verne in his futuristic novel *Around the World in Eighty Days*, but in 25 days – science has overtaken fiction. I don't want to contemplate the world just from the ivory tower of academia; I want to get to know the various cultures of the world *in situ*. It's wonderful to fly on PanAm Line One: no mass tourism anywhere, hardly any delays. Later I will no longer dare to make such a journey with every hour calculated; flight times have meanwhile become so uncertain. Of course I and my assistant Dr Gotthold Hasenhüttl have only days at our disposal everywhere, but usually with expert guides. In particular, these intensive, concentrated first impressions of the different 'places of world culture' later make me see the world, and above all Asia, in quite a different way and read books differently. Indeed, seeing a city once means more than reading twelve books about it. I shall see much again later. And I can never read enough, even on journeys.

From Bombay I go first to Teheran, where I arrive on 15 November 1964. The Shah's regime is a model for Western development strategies and policies, based on the presupposition that Islam has become a negligible factor. In these short two days I am also interested not only in the newer mosques and the bazaar, but above all in the national museum with its treasures of Persian art from three millennia. The Shah, the son of an upstart from a military coup, hasn't yet had the megalomaniac idea of going back behind the Islamic calculation of time and legitimating his rule from the time of Cyrus the Great and the ancient Persian Achaemenids; nor is he yet pursuing the disastrous plan of having himself crowned great king in Persepolis. In Teheran, with the help of an acquaintance from the Austrian embassy I buy a reddish-brown Afghan carpet, which still adorns my study. When decades later I am allowed to talk to the mullahs in Teheran, I will pick up on this first visit in my introduction.

But at the same time the date of 14 November reminds me of the beginning of the 'black week' of the Council. Only afterwards do I hear more precise details of the scandalous goings-on in Rome over the next few days: the postponement of the vote on the decree on religious freedom; the enforcement of the *'nota praevia'* on the unqualified papal primacy; arbitrary changes by the pope to the decree on ecumenism which has already been approved by the Council; the proclamation of Mary as 'Mother of the Church', against the will of the Council. Are sometimes not only shahs but also popes in danger of autocratic megalomania?

From Teheran I arrive in New Delhi, where I want above all to see the memorial to Mahatma Gandhi and the great monuments of Indian Islam, and talk with Indian theologians. I have to travel on first by train and then laboriously by car in a triangle to Agra (the Taj Mahal), to Fathepur Sikri (in the sixteenth century the residence of the tolerant grand mogul Akbar the Great, who is important for the understanding of the religions), and finally to rose-coloured Jaipur. Back to Delhi, and from there again by plane to India's earliest and holiest pilgrimage city, Benares: I will repeat the journey there on the Ganges more than 30 years later with our film team for the seven-part SWR television series *Spurensuche* ('Tracing the Way'). Without my countless experiences of travel since the 1960s, this project would neither have been conceived nor realized in the 1990s.

Already at that time I fly over Patna and the original land of Buddha in what was once a military plane, to the Hindu kingdom of Nepal. From the cockpit I can observe the land rising from the brown Indian plains, through the various layers of vegetation, until suddenly well-tended terraces of rice emerge and finally behind a cloud cap there is the whole glorious white range of the Himalayas in the sunlight. In the Kathmandu valley, until the end of the Second World War a closed land, and at the beginning of the 1960s still not visited by masses of tourists, one can see the city with the nearby great Buddhist monastery and stupa buildings in all their tranquillity. I couldn't have had by any means so intensive an experience of this without the companionship of the American Jesuit Marshall Moran, highly respected in Nepal, founder of schools and known as the only Nepalese radio ham in the world.

Then again a flight south, into the sweltering heat of Calcutta, the largest urban region of India with many wretched figures on the streets day and night and gigantic slum areas. As in Delhi, I give a public lecture, which becomes the occasion for the first ecumenical meeting in this city: 'You helped us to "break the ice"', they write to me later, and the immediate consequences of this 'breaking of the ice' are prayer services shared by all Christians during the coming Week of Prayer for Christian Unity in which large numbers take part. With Fr Fallon (of Belgian origin), an expert in Bengal and Hinduism and a firm supporter of indigenization, I take part in a celebration of the eucharist in the Indian form.

By being constantly active and in contact with local people, in a short time I get more information than the average tourist gets in weeks.

From Bombay on 28 November I go further east, my destination Washington, DC. No, that isn't a mistake: after the Bombay symposium, Washington, or more precisely Georgetown University, which has invited me as a guest speaker for its 200th anniversary, is the second reason for my trip. And why should I fly back from India to Europe and over the Atlantic to America if I can also reach my destination via Japan and the Pacific? I will later revisit more than once all the cities to which I fly. But the first tremendous impression will hardly ever be surpassed subsequently. First Bangkok, where there are as yet no traffic problems in visiting the old heart of the city, where there are great temple and monastery buildings (wats) by the river Menam and one can travel along the canals (khongs). Then Hong Kong, behind whose modern façade bustling life teems, all against a background of marvellous countryside. And finally Tokyo, Japan's pulsating capital, with its tremendous crowds of people. In this way I experience Asia for the first time, utterly fascinated above all by the great diversity of people: Indian, Thai, Chinese, Japanese faces; women, men, children. I experience national, ethnic and religious diversity not as a threat but as an enrichment. I am almost bored when – having gained a day over the international date line – in San Francisco, which I know, I finally see predominantly white faces.

I arrive in Washington punctually on 2 December. Georgetown University has made 'Freedom' – my great theme of the past year – the general theme of this symposium. I give my jubilee lecture on 'The Theologian and the Church'. Afterwards I am again briefly in New York; I give the same lecture in Chicago and then finally fly back via New York to Stuttgart, where I arrive on 8 December. Truly, I have taken in what I could in these 25 days: I haven't travelled as a globetrotter but as a theologian who wants to get to know the religions and cultures from direct encounter rather than just from books. At that time I could have had no inkling how much this would help me in later interfaith dialogue.

However, back in Tübingen the reality of the church and the Council again catch up with me. Immediately before my journey round the world, on 9 November 1964, Bishop Léon-Arthur Elchinger of Strasbourg wrote to me from Rome – on 31 October he had made a brave speech in the Council on the rehabilitation of Galileo, which was only later to bear fruit: 'Le combat continue (the fight goes on). Le grand chef est redevenu très "hesitant" sur le chap. 3 de Ecclesia.' In English: the big boss has again become very 'hesitant' about Chapter III of the Constitution on the Church (on the hierarchy). But Elchinger is hoping for the Holy Spirit: one can no longer shut the 'windows' and the 'doors'. Unfortunately, however, that is only partially true.

411

Setback: the Council's 'black week'

In retrospect I very much regret not having been in Rome for the *'settimana nera'* of the third Council session. Certainly I couldn't have prevented everything that took place, but perhaps I could have done something in the case of the declaration on the Jews, the dropping of which could have been prevented by a collaboration of *periti* and bishops. I shall be talking about that later. At least a vigorous public protest could have been organized against everything that took place there, to the indignation of the Council assembly, which would have sounded the alarm at least to the church public, if not the world public.

The tension between the progressive Council itself and the reactionary Curia, which could be detected from the first session onwards, had been charged in the second session and was now discharged in the third – unfortunately in favour of the Curia. If seats in the Council had been assigned only to those bishops who as residential bishops or as suffragan bishops had a church people (diocese) behind them, then all the curial 'honorary bishops', who represented only a church bureaucracy, albeit a very powerful one, would have been excluded from the Council, its leadership and its commissions: going by previous experience and the results of votes, the reactionary 'minority' would have fused into a few outsiders with no influence. But because in fact the opposite is the case, because the Curia largely dominates the conciliar apparatus and the mode of negotiations, there are the painful incidents which deeply infuriate bishops and theologians in the last dramatic week of the third session, and are felt in the world generally to be a setback for the Council and its constructive aims.

However, the obstruction of the Curia, which has already been known for a long time, is not in the first place thought to be serious. What is serious is that the majority of the bishops, theologians and observers of the other Christian churches are getting the fatal impression that Paul VI himself – out of anxiety, weakness or resignation, out of theological uncertainty, concern for his surroundings and Italian domestic politics, or for whatever reason – is now largely putting himself behind the obstructive manoeuvres of the Curia, thus proving Michael Serafian/Malachy Martin right. Now it is no longer possible to overlook the fact that Paul VI wants a modernization of the Catholic Church – but without giving up the way that it is imprisoned in the Roman Middle Ages. He wants collegiality – but without going back on the papalism of the eleventh century. He wants reform of the Curia – but without abolishing the Sanctum Officium and dropping Ottaviani.

He is a pope of contradictions, who wants to beatify John XXIII and Pius XII at the same time; although he has an ecumenical disposition and is open to the world, in this third session of the Council, too, he has allowed the machinations against the declaration on the Jews and constant further delay. He is personally committed to a schema on mission which, worked out completely from the perspective of the Roman Congregation on Mission, is rejected by the Council with a big majority as completely inadequate. He refers the controversial questions of sexual morality, especially those of birth control, from the Council to a commission dominated by the Curia. He drops the support that he had offered to the Council until around the middle of its second session, and now gives speeches with a completely different tone from that of his promising speeches on reform of the Curia and at the opening of the second session.

I needn't describe the development of the crisis at the end of the third session in detail. It is enough to list in summary form what Paul VI was responsible for in the 'black week' in a highly personal way:

At the last minute before the final vote he orders a whole series of petty changes to the schema on ecumenism, which has already been approved many times by the Council; these aren't very kind to non-Catholic Christians and are simply forced on the Council (for example it is no longer said that Protestant Christians 'find' God in Holy Scripture but only that they 'seek' him).

He endorses a further postponement of the Declaration on Religious Freedom, imposed with formal pretexts; this has now already been hindered by the Curia over three Council sessions and is expected impatiently by the Council and by the whole world. The postponement leads to a massive protest by well over 1000 bishops.

Without any need, and contrary to the explicit will of the Council majority, he promulgates the title 'Mary, Mother of the Church' (*mater ecclesiae*), which is open to misunderstanding and provokes in non-Catholic Christianity resistance and doubt as to whether the pope really wants ecumenical understanding.

And he forces on the Council through General Secretary Felici 'by higher authority' a *'nota praevia explicativa'* of four paragraphs in favour of his primacy. This has never been circulated for a vote, totally waters down collegiality, and represents a lapse back to the unqualified definition of primacy made at Vatican I. Many bishops feel that this is sheer blackmail: either they accept this papal 'interpretation' of collegiality or there is no Constitution on the Church. Thus the one-sided curial interpretation of the papacy is inserted between Chapters I-II (the Church as the People of God) and Chapter III (the Church as hierarchy) into the fatally ambiguous compromise by the Council. Again the mediaeval structures of the church!

Anyone who is interested in the curial cabals and intrigues, machinations and ploys to which the Council had been exposed from beginning to end should read the 66 pages in Alberigo's *History of Vatican II* (Volume IV) which L. A. G. Tagle from Tagaytay (Philippines) has written with much effort about the 'November Storm: The "Black week"'. I can only endorse his verdict on the curial party:

Throughout the whole of the third session the minority indefatigably follows a plan, and the 'black week' is the conclusion of their constant and daily zealous concern. It has sought every procedural means to block the work of the Council; it has speculated on the temperament of Paul VI to win little battles. The strategy and the dispute during the 'black week' brings out the ambiguity of the conciliar documents: but to take account of their objections further increases the theological compromises in the texts.

The only remarkable thing is that the same Roman Catholic historian cannot find enough explanations and excuses for the pope to 'interpret' and justify Paul VI's anti-conciliar policy; in the closing section his writing degenerates into sanctimoniousness.

I have to confess that today, when I have very much more precise knowledge of some of the background, I am even more repelled than I was at the time by this ploy, which has little to do with what is really Christian and (despite the differences) much to do with the court and mentality of the Caesars. The majority of the bishops prove shocked, but incapable of any effective reaction. Just how incapable is shown by the moderator on 20 November, Cardinal Julius Döpfner, in an involuntary comedy. At the end of the session he offers our 'beloved Father Paul VI, who has followed . . . the course of this Council with such attention and care, feelings of childlike gratitude . . .' I ask myself whether Felici foisted this Latin text on him. The only thing that is certain is that these 'black days' send out shock waves all over the church and cause a frustration which has abiding consequences. After the black week, many people cannot get rid of their mistrust of this pope.

This is a bad prelude to the coming fourth and last session of the Council. It is a bad prelude above all to the post-conciliar period: will people in the Vatican in all earnestness continue to rule the church in this hitherto absolutist way? The Protestant Council observer Dr Hermann Dietzfelbinger rightly speaks of an 'attack on the very foundations of the Council, from which this emerged the loser': 'Quite apart from its basic intentions, the attack was on three points at the same time: collegiality, ecumenism and freedom of religion.' What use is it when Paul VI, friend of great gestures without great consequences, on 13 November 1964, after a Byzantine liturgy, once for all takes off the expensive 'tiara' which has been customary since the Middle Ages, adorned with three crowns and newly made a year previously in accordance with his own ideas, and gives it to 'the poor'? Which poor? The contradictory nature of this gesture, too, immediately becomes evident: it is Cardinal Francis Spellmann who receives the tiara and presents it in New York, one of the richest dioceses in the world, at a banquet, after which it is put on display in his St Patrick's Cathedral. Alms welcome.

From a pope of the Council to the pope of the Curia

In view of this situation at the end of the third session of the Council, which gets a very critical response throughout the world press, once I have returned to Tübingen from the USA I think it a matter of urgency to correct my relatively hopeful interim stocktaking of the Council published in the middle of November. After all, I have to take note of what all the papers are full of: the prestige, indeed the credibility, of the papacy has suffered a tremendous blow for which no reception in India, however triumphal, can compensate. Indeed I now have to state explicitly that confidence in the pope, which in the days of John XXIII reached an almost unprecedented high point, has sunk to a nadir for many people inside and outside the Catholic Church. Cardinal Ottaviani in the Sanctum Officium will take me personally to task for this public statement.

But should I, to back it up, report the bitter words and reactions which I heard from so many well-intentioned people during and after my lecture trip round the world? The Benedictine Dr Ansgar Ahlbrecht, editor of the ecumenical journal *Una Sancta*, who was present in the aula during the last week of the Council, writes to me that for him my criticism is 'spoken from the soul': 'I still have ringing in my ears what well-known Council fathers and *periti* were boldly saying at that time. That makes the general trivialization on returning home all the more disappointing . . . The relatively independent post of professor at a German university seems to be the last place in which the office of the prophet can still be asserted. But not even all our professors (= confessors) have the courage to honour your name.' The criticism of a theologian from the USA who shows his dismay at 'the pope's weakness and capitulation and his lack of obedience to the voice of the Spirit which is speaking throughout the church' is even sharper: the pope's visit to India is 'nothing but a big show'. The 'papal syndrome' shows 'what is wrong with the Catholic Church'. So 'only a superficial reform can be expected'. These are just two witnesses out of many.

I am convinced that all the critical newspaper commentaries and Michael Serafian/Malachy Martin's book cannot be refuted by an apologetic which neglects the main point, but only by actions on the part of Paul VI himself. Despite all the disappointments I still hope with countless Catholics and non-Catholics for the rapid implementation of what the pope has solemnly promised his church and the world: a serious, far-reaching reform of the Roman Curia which embraces structures and personnel. And in the view of the Council that means:

- An *internationalization* of the Roman Curia;
- A *collegialization* through a council of bishops which assembles periodically in Rome and, set over the Curia, works out collegially with the pope the decisive directives for governing the church;
- A *decentralization* of the power of the Curia to the national conferences of bishops or local churches.

The Council is completely behind this programme. It has laid down the foundations for it especially in the schema on 'The Pastoral Tasks of the Bishops', which, contrary to expectations, likewise cannot be promulgated. However, there is a widespread fear in the episcopate that the Council resolutions could remain a dead letter. The saying is going the rounds in the Vatican: 'Councils pass away, popes pass away, but the *Curia romana* abides.' Will it ever be possible to limit this bureaucratic apparatus, so rich in tradition and wiles, which basically is unfriendly not only to the Council but also the Montini pope, to its due functions in the service of the pope? Will one day the Catholic Church change from being a Roman empire into a Catholic commonwealth?

At any rate Opus Dei, this well-financed, fascistoid Roman Catholic secret organization, has not yet been a decisive influence under this pope. But its growing significance in the Vatican cannot be overlooked. Hans Urs von Balthasar is also disturbed about this: 'Please think about the business with Opus Dei: it is *of decisive importance to me* to know why it is no longer an *institutum seculare* – and whether it is true that there are so many complaints about it in Rome, especially from Spain. Larraona (the cardinal prefect of the Congregation of Rites) will know all about it, but perhaps one will learn more from Philippe.' Balthasar will publish an extremely acute analysis of the Opus Dei ideology, which certainly isn't just prompted by competition – Balthasar has his own ideas about lay orders. I too will be approached in St Peter's by Monsignor Alvaro del Portillo, representative (and later successor) of Escriva de Balanguer, 'founder of the sect', to see whether I would have any interest in a conversation about Opus Dei. I certainly made no friends when I said no. But '*principiis obsta* – beware the beginnings!'

Ominous shifts of direction before the fourth session of the Council

The fourth session will show whether the Council, which has won so many battles, will finally lose the war. Many important themes remain on the agenda: renewed discussion on the draft degrees on 'The Church in the Modern World', freedom of religions, missions, priests. Further votes on the schemata on 'revelation' and the 'lay apostolate'. And finally votes on the improved schemata on the pastoral office of bishops, the religious orders, the training of priests, Christian education, the relationship of the church to the Jews and the non-Christian religions. A mammoth programme.

As early as 23 July 1965 I had received an alarming letter from the bishop of Strasbourg, whom I have already mentioned on a number of occasions. Léon-Arthur Elchinger asks me to write an article on the Council of Bishops, which has unfortunately become very necessary. He has heard 'that the Holy Father is no longer for the project, of which he was formerly the promoter'. Through the commission president Cardinal Paolo Marella the pope has required the text on this to be modified; however, Marella has rejected this with the argument that the pope himself could require this only '*à titre personnel et "auctoritative"*'. I visit Elchinger and Congar a few days later, in connection with an excursion of our

Institute for Ecumenical Research to Strasbourg, and we exchange our information and worries. On 28 August 1965 my extensive plea for a council of bishops is published in the *Frankfurter Allgemeine Zeitung* under the title 'And after the Council?' This is taken up by other organs. It ends with the statement: 'If there is no council of bishops or real council of bishops (which has a share in decisions), then serious fears for the time after the Council are justified.'

The meeting between Paul VI and the patriarch Athenagoras I of Constantinople in Jerusalem at the conclusion of the Council on 7 December 1965 will bring the reciprocal abolition of the excommunication, but paradoxically no restoration of the *communio*, the eucharistic fellowship. Here the bishop of the First Rome should have corrected the primacy of jurisdiction over all the churches and the faithful claimed since the eleventh century and the infallibility defined in the nineteenth century in the spirit of the shared first millennium – which of course is expected by the patriarch of the Second Rome (Constantinople) and above all the Eastern churches.

But Paul VI has yet again acted only symbolically, politically and tactically, as I learn indirectly through Yves Congar. Congar had been at the Jerusalem event with the pope and had asked him, 'Surely there's a theology behind your encounter?' 'No,' Paul VI had replied, 'no theology behind it.' For him the encounter with the ecumenical patriarch was primarily a church-political action designed to attract publicity, which need have no decisive consequences for the Catholic Church. At any rate there is no critical self-reflection on the mediaeval claims to power made by Rome against the East, no recognition of the autonomy of these apostolic churches in the early church. For both Congar and me this confirms once again that Paul VI has only a Roman and not an ecumenical vision of the future of Christianity. This becomes blatantly clear through three isolated preliminary decisions made by the pope, which in a dangerous way prejudice the last session of the Council, indeed the whole period after the Council. The wretchedness of the American church (and unfortunately not only of that church) in 2002 can largely be explained in terms of these three ominous changes of direction.

A first ill omen – after Paul VI's inaugural encyclical *Ecclesia suam* (1964), the unecumenical Romanism and lack of a biblical basis of which now comes more into the foreground – is his encyclical *Mysterium fidei* on the eucharist, which to the annoyance of many bishops he publishes with an eye on the Dutch theologians (Schillebeeckx and Schoonenberg) on 12 September 1965, immediately before the Council meets for the fourth session. In it the pope shows himself indebted to a Roman scholastic theology on which neither the exegesis nor the historical research nor the theological reflections of recent decades have made any impression. John XXIII's statement that the formulations of faith change while the substance remains the same is not only passed over, but in fact denied. One asks oneself, will this mediaeval theology go on as it always has done – as if Roman neoscholasticism didn't suffer shipwreck at the Council?

There is a second ill omen right at the beginning of the fourth session of the Council, on 15 September 1965: in his own perfection of power – the *motu proprio 'Apostolica sollicitudo'* (out of 'apostolic concern') – the pope proposes a council of bishops to his own taste and thus once more overtrumps both the Council and the episcopate. For the assembly of representatives of the episcopal conferences of individual countries and religious communities is to be called 'synod of bishops' – its very name emphasizes that it is not permanent – and, contrary to the will of the Council, will not have the slightest capacity to make decisions. So it is not an authentic council of bishops. The pope alone calls and leads it, defines the subject of the deliberations and confirms the members of the synod to be elected. These may indeed inform and advise the pope. But the pope himself has what are allegedly the wishes of the bishops subsequently summed up by his bureaucrats. Moreover these determine which, if any, will be implemented. One asks oneself, will this mediaeval church government go on as it always has done: the synod of bishops as a collegial fig-leaf for naked papal absolutism?

It should be noted here that the pope and the Curia are not satisfied with just the proclamation of these two documents, which are forced on the Council. As is usual in authoritarian systems, they expect a gesture of submission from the Council and indeed receive it: the assembly assents on 20 September 'with applause' (in other words, without discussion) to a letter which is simply read out. In it the pope is profusely thanked by the Council for the establishment of the synod of bishops and for the encyclical on the eucharist – for which again most courteous thanks are given by the Secretary of State in a letter of 29 September. What shameful Byzantinism!

A third ill omen is that in the middle of the debate on the renewal of the religious life, on 11 October 1965, a letter from the pope is read out in the Council stating that it is not in accordance with his will to discuss the problem of priestly celibacy in the Council aula: possible proposals on this can be addressed directly to him – of course with zero effect. In this case, too, a letter from Cardinal Tisserant the very next day expresses the alleged assent of the Council fathers to the pope's letters. It is as if one were at a totalitarian party congress. One asks oneself: will this mediaeval disciplining of the clergy go on as it always has done – as if the eleventh-century law about celibacy did not contradict the gospel and human rights relating to marriage and increasingly rob the Catholic communities of new priests and pastoral care? What is left of the freedom of the Council in the face of such manipulations? I think back to these events with bitterness as I write in 2002, when all the media are full of reports of scandals involving sexual abuse by priests and the failure of the bishops in this my church, from California to Poland, so that now even the official organ of the archdiocese of Boston, which is particularly hard hit, and a few brave bishops, are opening up discussion of a revision of compulsory celibacy.

A blockade on religious freedom

I remember all too well Cardinal Alfredo Ottaviani giving his lecture on state and church at the Lateran University in 1953. It had also worried us in the Germanicum. The former professor of church law defended the Catholic state at his university with vehemence and insistence in accordance with his textbook on the law of the state and the church (*Ius publicum externum*) – in the same year prescribed by a concordat with Fascist Spain. Error has no rights at all. Compromise with the erring leads to error. Tolerance is merely a matter of putting up with an unjust situation which one must prevent wherever possible and can tolerate only to avoid greater ills. The lecture by the then pro-secretary of the Holy Office was seen as a theoretical justification of the suppression of the Protestants in Spain and South America (no distribution of the Bible, training of ministers, etc.) and provoked a vigorous international reaction. Pius XII saw himself compelled to engage in diplomatic activity and to give his own address on tolerance, which he did at the Gregorian. However, he did not justify tolerance in principle, but purely pragmatically and tactically: otherwise Catholics could also be suppressed in Protestant countries.

At the Council, freedom of religion is the great concern especially of the American bishops (the Europeans are somewhat passive on this question), and the inspiration behind their speeches is my friend John Courtney Murray, attacked by Ottaviani and Fenton. In a number of publications the New York Jesuit had based freedom of religion on modern constitutional law, focusing on inalienable human rights. So he was finally brought to Rome as *peritus* for the second session by the otherwise highly conservative Cardinal Spellman: he is to help with the new version of the Council schema.

But Murray is bitterly disappointed, because through Machiavellian manipulations of the Curia obstacles are time and again put in the way of the present schema throughout the second session of the Council, and also because the American bishops will not make a public protest. On 30 November 1963 I had invited Murray to dinner, together with our friends Bishop Primeau (Manchester, USA) and the American *periti* George Higgins and John Quinn. John is in a bad mood. The next day he writes me a note that he has been 'extremely tired, depressed and dispirited'. The final blow has been the news from Bishop Primeau 'that the American bishops will do nothing (the proposal was that they sent the pope a letter, simply expressing their disapproval and regret over this action of the Curia, which they regarded as a breach of faith with them and a violation of the freedom of the Council; it was also proposed that they issue a statement to the American people, saying that they still held to their position, etc.). In any case, I then got a bit angry and behaved badly. And I am sorry.' I am very moved that this man, who is so much older, adds: 'I have admired you since I read the book on justification. And I am happy now to be your friend. And I am sure that the friendship will abide . . .'

But subsequently Murray did after all play a decisive role in the commission. Whereas French theologians see freedom of religion more as a theological and moral question, from which they draw legal and political conclusions, for Murray (supported by the eminent Monsignor Pietro Pavan, who inspired the encyclical *Pacem in terris*) it is primarily a legal and political question which can be supported by theological and moral arguments; here at the same time the state is seen as absolutely incompetent to judge on the truth of a religion.

Now on 15 September the new version of the Declaration on Religious Freedom was presented, by the eloquent Bishop de Smedt of Bruges: 64 speakers had announced their intention to speak in the debate. One asks oneself: why then does the Curia work so hard to obstruct religious freedom? Because – quite apart from the complicated questions of power – otherwise it would have to concede that the Roman magisterium had seriously erred on this point. Not a trace of 'infallibility'. The popes of the nineteenth century had repeatedly not only sharply repudiated religious freedom but even described it as a 'plague', *delirium* (Gregory XVI) and a pernicious product of the modern spirit of the age.

And how – since it cannot and will not be conceded that the 'church' has made any errors – can there now be a move from the ('infallible') repudiation to the ('infallible') assertion of religious freedom? Vain attempts have been made to apply the scholastic terminology customary in the proofs for the existence of God: the move from negation to affirmation through the *via affirmativa*, *via negativa* and *via eminentiae*. The bishops rightly find such tortuous argument, not supported by history, 'too complicated'. It is finally omitted, and thus there is no foundation whatsoever for the amazing U-turn and with it an acknowledgement of a doctrinal error of the first order. So now the whole declaration stands as it were naked, without any fig-leaf of a neoscholastic 'proof' to cover its historical shame. Now one can say only yes or no to the new decree. And it is already known that the majority of the Council want to say yes. But against their will, they aren't yet allowed to vote. The Council is oceans away from a fair democratic procedure, and is constantly annoyed about the Curia and pope. Now another highly explosive question is linked with the theme of religious freedom: the question of the relationship between the church and the Jews.

The struggle over the declaration on the Jews

It seems too much to many traditional Catholics – especially in the Roman Curia – to ask for a new attitude to Judaism. As early as 23 February 1964 my friend Gregory Baum (Toronto), who with the distinguished Monsignor John Oesterreicher (Seton Hall University) is the decisive champion of a declaration of the Jews in the Secretariat for Unity (he likewise has a Jewish background), had written to me: 'The opposition to Chapter IV on the Jews is quite great: the bishops of Arab countries fear unpleasantnesses and those from the mission countries are militating against preferential treatment for the Jews. But many bishops have also reacted positively. Remarkably, not a single German bishop has written to the Secretariat about Chapter IV. I personally think that a scandal.' Gregory Baum had had to emigrate as a child with his parents from Berlin in the 1930s.

After the painful curial delaying actions of the second session, the Declaration on the Jews had again been on the agenda for the third session in 1964. On 23 September Cardinal Augustin Bea presents the report on the 'Declaration on the Jews and the Non-Christians' in a calm and measured way – there is demonstrative applause at the beginning of his speech and even more at the end. Happily, the German bishops had previously made a statement supporting the planned Council document and at the same time recalling the crimes perpetrated on the Jews in the name of the German people. Indeed this is the first ecumenical council after Auschwitz. And the world pricks up its ears when it perceives that after long centuries of an open or concealed anti-Judaism within the church, the Catholic Church wants to correct deeply-rooted religious prejudices against Israel, God's old people: the Jews are not God's murderers nor are they accursed by God. However, there is no will to adopt a standpoint on political questions, in other words on the state of Israel.

But the curial obstruction had continued even after the conclusion of the Council discussion, which is very positive – only a few negative voices can be heard alongside that of Cardinal Ruffini. On Friday 9 October 1964, towards the evening, our group of French and American bishops and theologians in the Villanova receive news from Cardinal Bea's Secretariat for Unity that Papa Montini has yielded to political pressure outside and inside the church and decided to block the declarations on the Jews and on religious freedom in the Council and submit them to bodies dominated by the Curia for further checking. Speed is of the essence.

Immediately we organize the resistance. On Saturday morning Bishop Elchinger mobilizes the French Cardinals Liénart and Joseph Lefèbvre (Bourges) and the Americans cardinals Meyer and Ritter. I myself telephone Joseph Ratzinger in the Anima so that he can immediately put Cardinal Frings in the picture, and Karl Rahner, so that he can make contact with Cardinals König and Döpfner. The cardinals mentioned meet in the Anima as early as Sunday, at the invitation of Cardinal Frings; Alfrink, Silva Henriquez and Léger are also there (Suenens is in Belgium for the elections). They compose a protest letter to the pope with the opening words '*magno cum dolore* – with great pain'; it finally goes to the pope with the signatures of thirteen important cardinals.

At the same time I take personal responsibility for breaching the secrecy imposed on us and putting the public in the picture. On Saturday I telephone the correspondents of the Roman *Messagero*, the *Frankfurter Allgemeine Zeitung* (Schmitz van Vorst) and *Le Monde* (Henri Fesquet), all known to me, who are quite unsuspecting, and brief them on the scandalous machinations against the two declarations, the main figure behind which is General Secretary Felici (as can be ascertained afterwards). The result early on Monday morning is major reports on the front pages of these newspapers and an indescribable storm in the international press. Unfortunately, however, the director of the Latin American information centre, Antonio Cruzat, loses his job because he is responsible for handing on the letter by the thirteen cardinals to the press. Personal interventions by Cardinal Bea and Frings with the pope follow. The result is that both schemata remain on the Council agenda. And in the basic vote that is at long last allowed on 20 November 1964, 1770 bishops will vote for the draft of the decree on the Jews and only 185 against. So resistance resolutely organized can achieve something with this pope.

At last two epoch-making new orientations

Now *two* completely independent declarations on the Freedom of Religion and on Judaism have been worked out for the fourth and last session of the Council in 1965. The latter is also extended to the Muslims – as Eastern bishops require; indeed on the basis of Asian interventions it finally becomes a declaration on the world religions generally. So some good has finally come out of evil.

But the opponents in the Curia cannot stop weakening the declaration in a petty way right up to the end: instead of 'condemning' (*condemnare*) hatred of the Jews, persecution of the Jews and antisemitism (which is explicitly mentioned for the first time), they want to content themselves with 'deploring' (*deplorare*). Why? Otherwise one would be condemning former (infallible!) popes. But this doesn't alter in any way the extremely welcome fact that with this declaration, prompted by John XXIII, the Catholic Church has accomplished an epoch-making shift towards Judaism. In the final solemn vote on 28 October 1965, the day of the promulgation, 2312 bishops vote for and only 88 against the declaration *Nostra aetate* on the relationship of the church to the non-Christian religions.

Here for the first time it is solemnly stated that the church is uniquely bound up with the Jewish religion; it too appeals to Israel's patriarchs and holy scriptures. Jesus and the young church emerged from Judaism. Even if the majority of Jews at that time rejected Jesus as Messiah, they are not cursed by God. They remain his chosen people. Jesus's death cannot be attributed to all the Jews of that time, far less to all the Jews of today. Preaching, catechesis, studies and conversations are to help towards reciprocal knowledge and esteem. The church deplores all manifestations of antisemitism. It rejects any discrimination on grounds of race, skin colour, class or religion. It confesses the brotherhood of all men and women under the one Father.

However, for me personally all this will once again have an unpleasant sequel. In my commentaries on this declaration I repeatedly make the statement: 'National Socialist antisemitism would not have been possible without the centuries of anti-Judaism in the Christian churches.' This wins me a first official reprimand from the chairman of the German conference of bishops. In a long and furious letter Cardinal Julius Döpfner – now no longer using the familiar *'Du'* of the Germanicum alumni but the official *'Sie'* – asks how the 'Herr Professor' could make such an irresponsible statement. The professor replies to the cardinal with a calm but firm letter and as justification for this sentence refers him to the attached Chapter I, 3 of *The Church*, which has already been written, as planned on the first visit to the USA. In it the author depicts at length the 'indescribably desperate history of suffering and death, which monstrously culminates in the Nazi mass murder of millions of Jews'.

There is no reply to this letter from Cardinal Döpfner. Presumably the vigorous discussion of Rolf Hochhuth's 'Christian tragedy' entitled *The Representative*, first performed in Berlin on 20 January 1963, had contributed to his rebuke. Like the Curia, German bishops, too, react with apologetics instead of reflection in the spirit of the decree on the Jews. It would have been better for them to follow John XXIII who, according to Hannah Arendt, when asked what could be done against Hochhuth's drama, is said to have remarked: 'Do? What can one do against the truth?'

In this fourth and last session on 19 November 1965 there is finally also a vote on the Declaration on Religious Freedom. The result is equally welcome: 1954 yes and 249 no. When I think back – only ten years have passed since my farewell to Rome – how much there has changed! The declaration begins with the fine words *Dignitatis humanae*. But what is to be different in future? It makes the following core statements: 1. Every human being has the right to freedom of religion and conscience. 2. Every faith community has the right to unhindered public practice of its religion in accordance with its own laws. 3. Religious freedom must be protected and furthered by society, state and church.

All this is promulgated in the ninth public session immediately before the end of the Council on 7 December, now with 2308 votes in favour and only 70 against. With the Declaration on Religious Freedom the Catholic Church brings about a further reorientation: an epoch-making shift towards modernity, for which freedom of religion and conscience is one of the fundamental human rights.

At the same time it is becoming increasingly clear that the Second Vatican Council is a fiasco for traditionalist Roman theology. Everywhere in the Council that theology had come up against opposition to the schemata which it had essentially prepared. It could oppose and block in the debates, but it could hardly make a constructive contribution. It was now not even at home in the modern world, but in the Middle Ages; even Thomas Aquinas has hardly ever been cited in this Council as an authority, except that again he was once praised by the pope himself at a Roman Thomistic congress immediately before the first session of the Council as a normative teacher of the church – not to mention the minor figures of neoscholasticism who populated our textbooks at the Gregorian. But people aren't deceived, and the few dozen 'no' votes of the hardliners make one think that the Sanctum Officium and the reactionary core of the Curia have in no way resigned. And all over the world they have like-minded colleagues and helpers whom they encourage. One of them is the primate of Poland.

The church and freedom in Poland

One might expect that interest in the topic of freedom and the church would hardly be greater anywhere than in this brave nation, which had to suffer decades of oppression under two totalitarian regimes, the Nazi regime of 1939–45 and the Communist regime from 1945 to the present. The Catholic Church of Poland, identifying itself with the nation, presents itself over all these years as a bulwark of freedom. But was it really?

The Polish episcopate stood out in the first and second sessions of the Council because it made virtually no constructive contribution to the reform of the church. Rather, it was above all for Marian piety and preserving mediaeval Latin. There was no trace of biblical, liturgical and ecumenical renewal. Evidently it had no desire for a church of *aggiornamento* and preferred to evoke the 'spirit of martyrdom and the fight to the death'. In this way people cherish and cultivate the myth of a church of the resistance and keep silent about how much con-formism and collaboration in the time of National Socialism and above all of Communism made the survival of the church possible. There is no mention of the fact that antisemitism was deeply rooted and widespread even in pre-war Poland (the horrific pastoral letter of Cardinal Hlond in 1936!), and that there is no official statement by the Polish episcopate on the extermination of millions of Polish Jews by the Nazis; in the statistics of those who are murdered they are then simply counted as 'Poles'. The liberated Greek Catholic metropolitan Josyf Slipyi bitterly complains in Rome that the Polish hierarchy didn't even prevent the destruction of the Greek Catholic Church in Poland, which was united with Rome; rather, it promoted compulsory latinization.

Yet among many Catholic intellectuals of Poland the notion of conciliar renewal is very much alive. By that I don't mean the pro-Communist Catholic Pax group, also present among the journalists in Rome, whose representative visits me, more than once asks me for an option on one of my books, but in fact never publishes one – anxiety about the 'left'. Rather, I mean the Catholic Znak group, critical of the regime, which is represented in the Sejm, the Polish parlia-ment, with only five delegates, though in fact it represents the majority of the Polish people. For it, Jerzy Turowicz, the chief editor of the influential weekly *Tygodnik Powszechny* from Krakow, is at the Council; he has made contact with me at an early stage. We get on excellently and agree on a Polish edition of *The Council and Reunion,* which appears in Krakow in 1964 after the English–American, Dutch, French and Spanish editions and even before the Italian (and

Japanese). The next year the Polish theologian Halina Bortnowska has a long article on my theology published in *Tygodnik Powszechny* ('*Ludzie soboru* – Men of the Council: Hans Küng').

Tygodnik Powszechny also prints my American lecture on the church and freedom on 22 September 1963. And who gets very agitated about this publication? Not the Communist party or the Polish state, but the primate of the Polish church, Cardinal Stefan Wyszynski, who has great reservations about the intellectual circles of Krakow. I have often been able to observe him at the Presidium table: beyond question he is an imposing and strong personality, the undisputed symbol of the strength of Polish Catholicism in the face of the Communist regime and of the close connection between Catholicism and the Polish nation. But at the same time he is authoritarian both towards the state and in the church: he is a hierarch who would have fitted better into Vatican I than Vatican II. In Rome he is able to prevent the creation of a second Polish cardinal – presumably Karol Wojtyla, recently made Archbishop of Krakow! – and complains to the government about his scant financial means, although he returns from Rome to Poland with 10,000 officially declared dollars. This gentleman issues a sharp rebuke to the editors of the journal which has published my article and calls for the publication of a response. For while he defends the freedom *of* the church (over against the state) he will not tolerate any freedom *in* the church (for people and clergy). But the editors boldly reject the cardinal's demand. Later, however, the same Wyszynski succeeds in throttling the Polish edition of the journal *Concilium* after only two years. The Polish edition of my Council articles *The Council in Action* is also blocked, despite the efforts of the brave Sr Joanna Lossow of the very active Centre for the Unity of Christians of the archdiocese of Warsaw. Is this by the state, or by the church, or by both?

In the *Concilium* foundation after the Council we will consider whether a delegation should not go to the new Archbishop of Krakow, Karol Wojtyla, who is regarded as more open than the primate: the latter is said at the time to have put the suffragan bishop Wojtyla in sixth and last place on his proposed list. For technical reasons we didn't make the journey, but, as it is said afterwards, it would hardly have been much use. For so far nothing bold has been heard from Wojtyla in the Council either: only a very conventional speech on the call to holiness as the church's goal and on the 'evangelical counsels', of course without even mentioning the problem of renouncing marriage and the law of celibacy. I personally never consciously noticed the suffragan bishop, then archbishop, Wojtyla at the Council, whereas I have good reason to assume that he was very well aware of me, generally known as the youngest Council theologian, with blond hair, in a black suit instead of the usual gown, though he never addressed me. Wojtyla, who, as I reported, was rejected as a doctoral student at the Gregorian, very soon has relations with the wealthy Opus Dei. He is nominated a member of the papal 'pill commission', but doesn't take part in a single session. Instead, engaging in intrigue behind the backs of the progressive majority on the

425

commission, he sends texts to the Vatican which were presumably used for the preparation of the encyclical *Humanae vitae*. Freedom in the church of Poland? And freedom in the church of Rome? For me personally things are coming to a head.

Confronted with the Grand Inquisitor

On Thursday 14 October 1965 at noon he has ordered me to come – to the palazzo of the Sanctum Officium on the first floor. His entry couldn't have been more theatrical: on the first tremendous stroke of the bell of St Peter's the double doors of the room are simultaneously opened with a bang by a monsignore and he stands there in the doorway in all his purple splendour: the much-feared Grand Inquisitor, the head of the Sanctum Officium, Cardinal Alfredo Ottaviani. He strikes his cross and prays aloud: '*Angelus Domini nuntiavit Mariae* – the angel of the Lord brought the message to Mary.' I respond with a firm voice and in Latin: '*Et concepit de Spiritu Sancto* – And conceived by the Holy Spirit.' And so we say alternately the whole of the Angelus Domini with its three Ave Marias. I can't chase away the thought that others, not accustomed to such pious Roman customs, would have stood there flabbergasted.

Only then does the cardinal greet me, and we sit on the baroque red-gold chairs. One eye half closed because of a weakness of old age, he stares all the more at me with the other – but how much does he see? He begins by saying that I mustn't go out into the Piazza di San Pietro afterwards and give a press conference. In fact there is nothing that the Inquisition fears more than publicity. Then the cardinal talks to me with a clearly local Roman pronunciation of Italian ('*romanaccio*') about my critical article after the third session of the Council. He is particularly annoyed that I claim that the credibility of the pope has sunk to a nadir as a result of the events of the 'black week'. He lectures me on the importance of the papacy in a difficult time. After all, I grew up in Rome, have lived here seven years, and have studied and received a great deal. So one may expect me to be loyal to the pope, utterly loyal in unqualified solidarity. I listen to the cardinal without interrupting. He is regarded as a walking lexicon of all the Roman precepts, dogmas and principles, but without any sense of what is stirring up so many Catholics today so deeply.

Of course I could have now told him in detail that I don't repudiate the pope, but papalism; I don't repudiate the Roman centre but its centralism, legalism and triumphalism – which is also being criticized in the Council. But am I to get into a theological discussion with a church lawyer and dogmatic theologian who understands nothing about either exegesis or the history of dogma and who had declared before the Council to the ecclesiastical book censors that modern Catholic theology seems to him to be 'like a crossword puzzle'? Nevertheless he is convinced that he, the supreme guardian of the faith, is in any case right – even over against the Council – because he stands for the pope himself. Ottaviani lives and thinks – though this is something that I will only be able to analyse later – in another 'paradigm'; he still lives wholly in the mediaeval-Counter-Reformation-antimodern constellation of the church and society. And for that reason it is as difficult for me from my modern-postmodern paradigm to discuss with him as it would be for an advocate of the modern Copernican picture of the world to discuss with a representative of the old Ptolemaean picture. Granted, the sun, moon and stars, God, Christ and the church are the same for both of us, but the way in which we see these is utterly different, depending on the 'constellation', the paradigm, in which each of us stands. We live in the same church and yet in different worlds.

I observe the cardinal with his imperial head attentively while he is giving his monologue and feel almost something like sympathy for him. This man, who bears the dangerous saying 'semper idem – always the same' on his coat of arms, has grown old in the service of the Curia, almost blind, and hopelessly left behind by the development of theology and the church. Yet not even an oak can be 'always the same' unless it 'constantly changes', sheds leaves, puts out new shoots and grows.

Sitting opposite him, I remind myself of the almost tragic scene when at the end of the first session Ottaviani had presented the last of his four schemata with the significant title De ecclesiae militantis natura – on the nature of the church militant – with a sharp chapter on authority and the absolute need of the Roman church for salvation. But whereas in his first speech to the Council on 14 October he had spoken with great self-awareness and self-confidence, now he is more muted and sad, probably knowing that he is the target of most of the Council jokes, which are even cruel ('O God, in your omnipotence close his eyes for ever'). Yet with his completely hopeless schema he at least wanted to go down with dignity and said: 'I expect to hear the usual litanies from all of you: it is not ecumenical and is too scholastic; it is not pastoral and is too negative, and similar complaints. This time I will make a confession to you: those who are already accustomed to say "tolle, tolle substitue illud – take it away and replace it" are already prepared for battle. And I also want to reveal something else: even before this schema was distributed an alternative schema had been prepared. So all that is left is for me to be silent. For as scripture says, "where no one listens it is senseless to speak" (Acta I, 4, p. 9).' The cardinal had calmly switched off the microphone and left the aula in a generally cheerful atmosphere. He knew that he had lost in the Council. But not in the Curia.

What am I now to say to the head of the Officium? After listening to him for a very long time I interrupt him in a friendly way: 'Eminenza, may I now also say something?' 'Si, si, si capisce,' he replies. I say, 'Eminenza, Lei sa: sono ancora giovane. – You know, I'm still young.' Then suddenly the feared face of the half-blind 75-year-old baker's son from Trastevere, who all down the years has looked after an orphanage there, lights up: 'Sì, sì, questo è vero. You're still young, and when I was still young I did many things I didn't do later.' And he goes on like this – evidently after all he wasn't so much 'always the same'. I had spoken to his heart and he has opened it up to me a little. Then I attempt to explain a bit to him how I stand over Rome and the pope.

Finally he says: after all, I studied at the Gregorian, I should talk there with two of my professors, with Fr Bertrams, the church lawyer, and with Fr Hentrich, formerly the second private secretary to Pius XII. Then I am graciously released, unpunished. Eight days later I go to the Gregorian and talk with the two Jesuits. They appeal to my conscience but don't threaten me in any way – except for a little outburst of anger on the part of Fr Bertram, who is otherwise so calm. Here I have come to realize one thing: in my sharp criticism of the pope I have failed to mention that from his standpoint he has acted with good intentions. It had been pointed out to me that at least I could have granted the pope what I always explicitly grant the Protestants. I realize that. But I hadn't done so, not because I doubted the pope's good intentions, but because I presupposed them as a matter of course. For me Giovanni Battista Montini is the prisoner of the Roman system!

Already after the publication of my critical analysis of the *'settimana nera'* in the third session of the Council on 17 February 1965 I had written to the pope's personal theologian, now, as Bishop, Sua Eccellenza Carlo Colombo: 'What I wrote about the pope and his attitude I did to support the pope in his original intentions. No one doubts his good intentions and his honest concern for the salvation of the church, Christianity and humankind. But many fear, and fear increasingly, that some people around him are opposed to the decisive actions which the whole world expects in accordance with these intentions. The mistrust which the pope encounters today in very wide and very important circles of the church and the world must be countered with every means. So I hope that my contribution, while critical, is recognized in its whole aim of offering constructive help. Nothing would delight me more than if I could do yet more for the pope in the service of the church. I will leave it to you to pass this article on to His Holiness – if this seems right to you. I would think it extremely important not only to be allowed my bona fides but also for the concerns of so many people expressed in this article to be understood in a positive direction. I cannot say how much the church, Christianity and the world expect of Pope Paul VI.'

But I can't deny that in my – in any case overlong – published article I have neglected to emphasize the good intentions of Paul VI. And so I plan always to mention these in the future. At any rate this is one of the reasons why now at the end of November 1965 I write an explanatory letter to the pope himself. If possible, I want to have personal contact with him once again and to speak to him about the question of birth control, which hasn't yet been decided, before the Council comes to an end on 8 December and I return to Tübingen. However, it must inevitably be extraordinarily difficult to secure an audience. For in these last days of the Council he is overoccupied, since among other things he is saying farewell to all the episcopal conferences individually. I send my letter to the pope via his private secretary Don Pasquale Macchi, and to my amazement get an answer within three days. It's positive. Pope Paul VI – in complete contrast to his Polish successor later – is immediately ready to receive me: not, as so often, in a small group (special audience), but just the two of us (private audience).

Audience with Paul VI: 'entering the service of the church'?

Yves Congar also reports on a private audience with Paul VI in his memoirs. The pope told him that the Roman Curia urgently needed capable younger forces, and he had thought here particularly of Küng and Ratzinger – but Küng didn't seem to have enough 'love of the church'. How Joseph Ratzinger indicated his 'love of the church' to the pope I don't know. But I remember precisely what I said to the pope.

Thus immediately before the end of the Council, on Thursday 2 December 1965, around 12.15 I am on the way to the private audience with Paul VI. With my *peritus* pass I drive up to the Damasus Court and from there go up in the little lift to the fourth floor. Recognizing one of their countrymen, the Swiss guards salute in a friendly way. There is a reception by the monsignori of protocol (*anticamera*). I go through around a dozen big rooms, tastefully modernized under Paul VI, no longer in red and gold but in beige and grey and decorated with precious works of art; these are used for special audiences. There is a mysterious tinkling. I finally discover that this comes from the medals of the *cameriere della spada* in Spanish court dress who is accompanying me. After a brief wait in the last room, the door to the grand papal private library, which has been similarly renovated, is opened to me by the monsignore serving in the antechamber. But instead of being at the other end of the long room, like Pius XII, Paul VI awaits me on the right by the door, sitting at his desk. Is this to remove the visitor's inhibitions and to save the three genuflections which used to be customary? Be this as it may, whether intentional or not, it's a successful little surprise.

As I know from previous encounters, Papa Montini seems far more congenial and human when there are just two persons than he does in his often stiff public appearances. He has receding hair, a sharply etched nose, and the eyes under his bushy eyebrows are directed towards me in a way which is both friendly and searching. When I sit down he gives a little address. His voice is rougher than his delicate figure leads one to expect. Evidently he has thought hard about how to conduct the conversation. First of all he praises me unduly with a correct but ultimately impenetrable smile for my 'doni', 'gifts'. He is reminded of my Tübingen predecessor Karl Adam, whose *Essence of Catholicism* was translated for him into Italian by a friend in the 1920s and which he had still kept working on after the intervention of the Sanctum Officium (he doesn't reveal this last to me). Like Adam I want to present the Christian truth in public beyond the 'mura della Chiesa', 'the walls of the church'; today that is more important than ever.

Of course I'm delighted at this recognition; after all, the Summus Pontifex is sitting in front of me. However, suddenly Paul VI makes a surprisingly abrupt change and stops smiling: but when he looks over everything that I have written, he would really prefer that I had 'written nothing'. *'Niente'* – that isn't exactly an encouraging compliment for a young Catholic theologian to hear personally from the mouth of the supreme boss. Having learned in his career to calculate the effect of his words precisely, he certainly hopes that this is the stick after the carrot.

I would now write a good deal about *libertà*, freedom in the church, Pope Paul continues, now with a slightly ironic smile (this is how the Caesars must have smiled at poor poets), and then gets round to his real concern. 'How much good you could do,' Paul now says emphatically, ' if you were to put your great gifts at the service of the church': *'nel servizio della Chiesa'*! 'At the service of the church?' I answer gently, now smiling myself: *'Santità, io sono già nel servizio della Chiesa.'* 'But I'm already at the service of the church.'

However, in good Roman fashion Paulus Papa Sextus has meant by 'church' the specifically Roman church. He continues: *'Deve avere fiducia in me.'* 'You must trust me.' I reply: 'I trust you, *Santità, ma non in tutti quelli che sono intorno a Lei*, but not all those around you.' Such directness, which is unusual in the curial milieu, makes the otherwise always moderate church diplomat burst out with an emotional *'Ma* – but', arms held high. But – if he came to 'Tubinga' and went through the streets there, first of all he would also encounter many unknown, closed, dark faces, but these would light up when he got to know them more closely. So too it is in the Curia Romana.

Once again completely in control, Papa Montini continues: I need by no means be a priori in agreement with everything that happens here. But I must conform a little – and here the pope's slim hands make the gesture of bringing into line. So that is the condition: conform, adapt – that's the issue. What this means is quite clear to me, since I've been educated in Rome. It's possibly clearer to me than to the non-Roman Ratzinger, who evidently has subsequently taken the way offered to him directly or indirectly in some form by the pope – and with no little success.

Should I perhaps have decided to follow the pope's line? The great opportunity of my life – have I missed it? The answer is: I won't dispute that I could have done some good in the Roman system; that's the first thing. And that at any time I could have fallen in with the Roman way; that's a second thing: soon a further exchange will take place. And that there are good reasons why I can't do this, cannot, will not become a conformist, that is a third thing.

I go on to bring the conversation round to the disputed question of contraception, offer him a small memorandum consisting of a dozen points for him to hand on to the commission, and finally on the basis of the papal reservations about the pill unexpectedly end up with the question of infallibility, which will be discussed in detail in the second volume of my memoirs. At all events I am later informed of the annoyance of the conservative American moral theologian

John Ford SJ that the pope, whom he had previously won round to his conservative attitude, had again vacillated after his conversation with me.

Between ten and fifteen minutes had been allotted for the conversation. The monsignore in waiting had already opened the door gently twice, to indicate the time. But he is sent away with a gentle movement of the left hand (here the pope says when time is up). In the end the conversation has been extended to almost three-quarters of an hour. Paul VI bids me farewell with great friendliness. He gives me a rosary of white pearls for my mother. And he gives me a New Testament in Greek and Latin (the Merk-Lyonnet edition from the Pontifical Biblical Institute). He slowly signs it: 'Paulo P. P. VI – 2.XII.1965'. And gives me his blessing.

Of course I wonder who has had to wait out there so long in the reception room. When I leave the private library in an ordinary black suit, I see sitting there in all his hierarchical splendour with his violet cloak the General Secretary of the Council, Archbishop Pericle Felici, who is important in every respect. For certain he was doubly annoyed at the delay when he heard about the highly dangerous theologian to whom the pope was giving so much time. But of course I know what is seemly: '*Eccellenza!*' – I bow to him smiling with great *gentilezza* as I go past, and his excellency, in good Roman style, greets me with a smile (this must be what it is like if a lemon tries to smile).

But that 1965 papal audience suddenly confronts me vividly with the question: for whom are you doing theology, if you really want to go on doing theology? My theology obviously isn't for the pope (and his followers), who clearly doesn't want my theology as it is. In that case it's for those people who may need my theology. And here I comfort myself by remembering the one who didn't say 'I have compassion on the high priest' (although the high priest would perhaps also have deserved compassion), but 'I have compassion on the people.' Therefore from now on even more resolutely, my theology is for my fellow human beings. Yes, in all freedom, that is my way. With the young and also not completely conformist assistant priest, played by Bing Crosby, I am 'going my way'. And soon I receive confirmation that I'm on the right way. It now becomes clearer how Papa Montini understands '*servizio della Chiesa = della Curia*'.

A two-faced reform of the Curia

Janus isn't a Catholic saint. Janus is a Roman god, the god of the *janua*, the gate: the god of going in and going out, who looks both backwards and forwards, into the past and into the future. So he is depicted as a god with two faces and from of old symbolizes being two-faced, ambiguous, even contradictory.

Only at the solemn conclusion of the Second Vatican Council, on 6 December 1965, does Paul VI publish the *Motu proprio* ('on his own initiative') *Integrae servandae*: here the first important step is taken towards a reform of the Curia with a reform of the Sanctum Officium; the overall conception of the reform will then become visible in 1967 with the Apostolic Constitution *Regimini Ecclesiae*. It is a reform with two faces, and needs to be analysed precisely here. For here is the root of the ambivalence of the development after the Council and the crises caused by the Vatican apparatus of government; the many problems which I too will subsequently have quite personally with the Roman church also have their foundation here.

Beyond doubt, from the beginning Papa Montini wanted a serious reform of the Curia and worked on it from 1963 onwards. There was also talk about it in the circles around the Sanctum Officium which caused concern. Now that this document is published, people in these circles are dismayed, but of course may not oppose it in public. 'Remember, this is a *giorno nero,* a black day in church history,' declares Cardinal Alfredo Ottaviani to a group of colleagues. Why? Because the Sanctum Officium is forfeiting the proud title *'suprema'* = 'supreme' congregation.

This in fact does not just deny it a title which it had not given itself until the twentieth century on the model of the Spanish Inquisition. It also denies it the *de facto* primacy it had arrogated on all matters of faith and morals. Even the popes – though formally prefects of the congregation – hardly dared to contradict when the secretary of the congregation presented the most important decisions of the week for signature each Friday; they had been prepared by the *consultores* on the Monday, and on the Wednesday (each time a week later) had been approved by the members of the congregation, including the members of the Vatican Pentagon. The *suprema congregatio* assumed that the pope, its prefect, would sign all its decisions as a matter of course.

And what now happens to this Sanctum Officium? The Germanicum alumnus Hermann Schwedt, himself formerly a member, analyses it precisely in the report *Studientag Bistum Aachen* (29 November 1997): Paul VI degrades the 'security headquarters' of the Catholic faith to a normal congregation of the Roman Curia, with a cardinal as prefect and a new name, 'Congregation for the Doctrine of Faith'. And this is no longer to be responsible only for 'safeguarding' the faith but above all for 'promoting' it. Here the congregation is no longer to prohibit (*prohibere*) books as laid down in *CIC* Canon 247, but only to 'disapprove' (*reprobare*) of them. In the process, quite incidentally and hardly noticed to begin with, the Index of Prohibited Books is in fact abolished, though the pope doesn't make a clear statement about this.

Cardinal Ottaviani is so furious at this redefinition of the Sanctum Officium that not until four months later, on 13 April 1966 – and then only in reply to a question in an interview for an illustrated magazine – does he confirm that the Index will no longer be imposed; it remains a 'historical document'. And only on 14 July 1966, because there are many enquiries, does an official notification come from the ex-Sanctum Officium itself that the Index is no longer a legal norm and has only 'moral value'. Meanwhile the Congregation has received as a new sub-secretary the Louvain professor Charles Moeller, though in this power structure under the old boss his influence is to remain limited. Because things still aren't clear, on 15 November 1966 the ex-Sanctum Officium finally publishes an official 'decree' which formally abolishes all the relevant canons and repeals the church penalties imposed on the reading of forbidden books. Only now are the canon lawyers content with the information from the Congregation. So the 'digestive process' of the Congregation over the Index has taken almost a year. But one is very deceived if one thinks that the old guard round the *'vecchio carabiniere'* Ottaviani has already resigned.

The repression of the undue influence of the Sanctum Officium (of which Montini too was an ex officio member for many years) is only part of the reform of the Curia. The central measure will be published in 1967: the elevation of the 'papal Secretariat of State' in which Montini had literally had his home for decades, to become the Vatican 'super ministry'. And it is this that redoubles the wrath of Ottaviani and his men: is the ideological leadership of the church – which is how he understands his office – now to change from theology to diplomacy? Is what Catholic faith is in disputed cases no longer to be decided, as it has been for centuries, by this venerable inquisitorial authority, but by the political organ of the Curia? This endangers the strict coherence and consistency of the Roman Catholic doctrine of faith. It endangers the foundations of the *'baluardo'*, the Roman 'bastion'.

But Ottaviani is worrying too much about this. Pope Paul doesn't want to raze the bastions of the fortress but to consolidate them. As an absolute ruler and his own Secretary of State, Pius XII had largely ruled with the help of a German 'kitchen cabinet'. John XXIII had allowed the various offices of the Curia to go on in the old style, but had reserved for himself the freedom to make individual decisions on actions which were important to him, like the calling of the Council. Now Paul VI wants to reorganize the Curia: to end the way in which the Sanctum Officium and other offices 'go it alone' and put them all under a co-ordinating head office over which he himself has daily control. And this is the Secretariat of State, located immediately below him on the third floor of his own palace and always available.

I recall my conversation with Cardinal Montini before the Council, in which in view of my desire for decentralization he said that the services of the Curia were now *'molto svelte*, very quick'; one could easily telephone and do other similar things. In fact his reform of the Curia is a centralization and restructuring of the Curia; its efficiency is to be heightened and the pope's own freedom of action is to be regained. In short, this is basically not a fundamental reform but a modernization of the Curia – in the spirit of the old absolutism. It is no coincidence that already in his speech on reform of the Curia in 1963 the pope had required 'absolute obedience' from the Curia.

But is one to kneel like this in obedience before the pope, arms crossed, as the new Jesuit General Pedro Arrupe does in a photograph circulated by the Vatican during these days, with Paul VI raising his right hand high in blessing (or in threat)? No, that contradicts my understanding of the freedom of a Christian. And my lectures in the last weeks of the Council, on 'Church and Freedom' and 'Church and Truthfulness', say precisely the opposite. They find a widespread response both among the Council fathers and in the media. I write a programmatic article on the 'charismatic structure of the church', completely following the line of Suenens' speech, for the first ecumenism issue of our new international journal of theology *Concilium*, which I edit: charism understood as service; not, however, of the pope but of the community of Christians who all (including the Bishop of Rome) stand as brothers and sisters in obedience under the one Lord and God. That is Christian, the other is 'Roman'.

Contrary to the intentions of the Council

Is such a 'reform' of the Curia what the Council wants? No, such modernization of the Curia has little to do with the great aims of the Council. Hadn't this Council been characterized from the first session on by its activation of the college of bishops and the local church? And to match this, by a retreat of the central administration, supported by John XXIII through a restrained use of primatial authority? And precisely by doing this didn't pope, Council and church gain a completely new credibility? But Paul VI, above all a pope of the Curia, has with good reason forced on the Council his notorious *'Nota previa'* on his primacy of rule: in intrinsic contradiction to the clear statements of Vatican II about the collegiality of the college of bishops and the will of the episcopate, an unhindered, unqualified exercise of primacy along the lines of Vatican I is to be made possible and legitimated again. Surrender power in the spirit of the Sermon on the Mount? The pope didn't think of this for a moment. Share his power with bishops and local churches along the lines of the ancient Catholic tradition? This isn't what the pope wants.

The two-facedness of this reform of the Curia oppresses me. At any rate there is hardly any trace of a new, conciliar spirit. Measured by the great intentions of the Council, this is a tremendous disappointment. For what in particular will the post-conciliar church suffer from into the third millennium? Not being led in the spirit of the Council. Indisputably the Council had called for an internationalization, collegialization and decentralization of the central Roman administration. But what has it received from this pope? That can be said in three sentences:

An *internationalization* which is only external: greater representation of the various nationalities in the Vatican but not of the various mentalities.

A *collegialization* which is only apparent: the council of bishops, castrated so that it is only an occasional synod of bishops, will debate and 'consult' endlessly, but may decide absolutely nothing.

A *decentralization* which is only cosmetic: insignificant powers are now given back to the bishops at the end of the Council, as a privilege graciously granted by the Roman pontifex, but not to restore the original Catholic order.

Peter Hebblethwaite called Paul VI 'the first modern pope'. But on this point unfortunately he was only half right. And precisely because of this, Montini – the number VI is neither here nor there – will become a *'papa infelix'*, tormented and inwardly split. Certainly he looks forward: he wants to 'modernize' the Curia and the church, win people like Ratzinger and me over to it, and in 'foreign policy' work honestly for peace and social reforms in the world. His visit to New York and speech to the United Nations on 4 October 1964 also serve this end. So does his social encyclical *Populorum progressio* of 21 March 1967, which isn't forgotten. At the same time, however, despite valuable advances on behalf of the Third World and development policy this pope orientates himself backwards: on the past, but not, say, on the New Testament and the church of the first millennium. Or rather, on the principles of the eleventh-century Gregorian reform, which he doesn't see through, because he has no training in exegesis and historical criticism. Only on this presupposition, if at all, can his fixation on the papacy and on Rome be excused. The mediaeval Roman system is to remain intact; there is no question of serious internal political reforms of the structure of the power. Therefore immediately after his return from New York he gives a traditional Latin(!) speech in the Council aula and rather later announces the beatification not only of John XXIII but also of Pius XII. Only to the outside world does he show himself as modern, social and liberal. No, Pope Montini is not a liberal or even a collegial pope; unfortunately it has to be said that he is through and through a curial pope.

And am I to hand myself over to such a pope 'in absolute obedience in the service of the church'? After all I have related, the reader will understand that it really is no spiritual arrogance and moral superiority if I, born a republican and baptized a Christian, do not want to engage in this service, no matter how fine the posts, or the violet or scarlet cloaks and prelates' caps that may come my way. It should be remembered that the pope hasn't even conceded to the Council a transition from the absolutist to the constitutional monarchy. His Secretary of State with the members of the Curia will supervise the new *Codex Iuris Canonici* which is planned, and he himself will issue decrees on the basis of his own perfection of power. In other words, this completely obsolete princely absolutism and its fawning courtiers (seeming in many respects absurd in their robes) have nothing in common with the free commonwealth in which I grew up. Nor do they have anything in common with my republic of scholars, in which the constitution guarantees me freedom of research and teaching. Even more, they have nothing in common with the free nature of the church which is shown us in the New Testament and lived out in the history of the early church. Nor do they have anything in common even with the best Tübingen tradition as it was formulated almost 200 years ago by the young J. A. Möhler, who at a very early stage also enthused Congar and the great Frenchmen, 'in the spirit of the church fathers of the first three centuries': 'But neither one nor any must want to be all; only all can be all, and the unity of all only a whole. That is the idea of the Catholic Church' (*Die Einheit in der Kirche*, §70, 1825).

There is something that I have to concede: at the end of the Council I too didn't reckon that the defeated old guard around the Sanctum Officium would succeed so easily and so quickly after the departure of the Council fathers in putting the pope, concerned for his own freedom of action, under pressure so that it could win back the positions it had lost and establish its own doctrinaire line in dogma, morality and church discipline. And this despite all the fine statements in the Pastoral Constitution on 'The Church in the Modern World', passed in this last session of the Council, in which the Council attempts honestly all along the line to make the second epoch-making paradigm shift – after the Protestant Reformation: the turn towards modernity.

From the general condemnation of modernity to its acceptance

The church and the modern world: there is a tremendous amount to say about it. And I joined in the applause when Cardinal Suenens, as clear and powerful as ever, criticized the lack of structure in the work of the Council as early as the end of its second session, on 4 December 1962. He proposed that the Council should take two directions in its future work. On the one hand *ad intra* = inwards. What does the church say about itself? And on the other hand *ad extra* = towards the outside world. How does the church understand itself in dialogue with the world?

However, I concede that together with the other German-language *periti* from the beginning I had some reservations about an all-embracing pastoral constitution on the church and the modern world which was long-windedly to deal with everything conceivable, from the church's attitude to human life through the questions of social justice and the evangelization of the poor to the safeguarding of international peace – so to speak from the pill to the bomb. These questions seem to me to be too complex, and to vary too much from region to region.

I personally would have preferred a concentration on a few less controversial questions. For example questions like contraception, divorce or mixed marriage, where the church government could and should not only preach to others (which it loves) but also contribute to a constructive solution (which it doesn't). Above all, it seemed important to me to reflect on some of the basic values and attitudes which have been regarded as the fundamental virtues since the eighteenth-century Enlightenment and are of decisive importance for modern society – modern basic virtues which have, however, been neglected, ignored and even suppressed by the Catholic Church at decisive points.

I am thinking above all of the basic value and basic virtue of freedom, which during these years I illuminated time and again from different sides, also in my journalism. Papa Montini evidently doesn't value this. For the series I edit I write a sequence of 'Theological Meditations': on the freedom of the individual, *Freedom in the World* (Thomas More); on the freedom of theology, *The Theologian and the Church*; on freedom in the church, *The Church and Freedom*; on freedom of religion, *Christian Revelation and World Religions*. They appear as early as 1964/5, and then in 1966 collected in one volume, first in English under the title *Freedom Today*, later also in German and in other languages: 'the freedom of the Christian' is the general theme.

But the basic value and basic virtue of truthfulness, about which so far I have said little, has also become increasingly important to me. In fact on 7 October 1964 I already feel called, during the third period of the Council, for the first time to give a lecture on 'The Church and Truthfulness' at the Centro Unitas in Piazza Navona; it meets with a great response, and through newspapers like *Le Monde* is also circulated among a great many Council fathers. I shall have to discuss this later in another context. It is enough here to bring out some central points.

The introductory part discusses the importance of truthfulness in the twentieth century, from modern art and literature through psychology, sociology and philosophy to everyday life, and from there, truthfulness as a basic demand to the church in the modern world. The second part is about the historical background to the neglect of truthfulness (in favour of 'chastity') in moral theology and theology generally. The third part is about truthfulness as a demand of the message of Jesus, his sharp speeches against hypocrisy and their application to the church. Finally, in the fourth part I draw conclusions for the future: no fanaticism about truthfulness but truthfulness of action – in the preaching of the church, dogmatics, exegesis and above all moral teaching. I say that instead of proclaiming many fine and profound generalities about love and marriage, the Council should give a concrete, honest and understanding positive answer in questions, say, of contraception – untroubled by former time-conditioned answers. That means that responsibility for birth control is to be left to the conscience of the couple: questions of method are a matter for competent professionals.

Does the new Pastoral Constitution fulfil this demand for truthfulness? One cannot dispute the fact that as a whole, like the Declaration on Religious Freedom before it, it expresses a decisive move of the Catholic Church towards the modern world and attempts to take seriously the epoch-making paradigm shift since the Enlightenment. One has only to compare the new 1964/5 document with the general condemnation of modernity in 1864, just 100 years previously, in which the infallibility pope Pius IX had condemned a 'collection (*syllabus*) of modern errors' and uncompromisingly defended the mediaeval Counter-Reformation structure of teaching and power. This Syllabus culminates in the 'error' that the Roman Pontiff can and must 'be reconciled and united with progress, with liberalism and with the new culture' (Denzinger 1780). And now?

The 1964 Pastoral Constitution *Gaudium et spes* on 'The Church in the

Modern World' is quite different: in future the attitude of the church to the progress of humanity is to be in principle positive, though not uncritical. The church is to declare itself to be profoundly in solidarity with the rest of humankind and to collaborate with it. Everywhere it must recognize the signs of the time and interpret them in the light of the gospel; answer the questions and not reject them. So there must be dialogue instead of polemic, convincing witness instead of conquest. Precisely in the light of its own message there must be a resolute advocacy of human dignity, freedom and rights, of the development and improvement of human society and its institutions, of a healthy dynamic in all human activity. What would the Pius popes have said to all this? Truly, there is undoubtedly a shift.

And where specifically does this positive attitude show itself? In an understanding and self-critical attitude to the various forms of atheism (despite a request from a large number of Council fathers, Communism is not mentioned, to avoid misunderstandings). And also in the affirmation of responsible freedom in spiritual and cultural activity, the justified autonomy of the sciences and the living research of theology. Then in special advocacy of the weak (peoples and individuals) in economic, social and political life. Likewise in a sharp rejection of war and in an agreement to collaborate towards an international community of nations. All these are clear signs of a shift towards modernity. But precisely on this last point the Achilles' heel of this Constitution becomes evident – once more a consequence of the well-known compromise between Council and Curia.

Birth control as a test case

Subsequently the conservative side has criticized the pastoral constitution for being too positive about progress. But that is easier to say in retrospect than it was in the early 1960s, when people didn't yet perceive quite so clearly the negative aspects of progress in society, and the church had to catch up on a great deal. We rightly wanted to set a counterpoint to the church's cultural pessimism and the self-righteous moralism of past centuries. No, the weakness of the Constitution is that on topics like marriage and family – beyond doubt the focal point of interest also among a wide public – it speaks very sweepingly on general aspects like holiness, love and fertility, but at the decisive point, namely responsible parenthood, and specifically birth control and contraception, it remains deeply ambiguous.

There were already vigorous arguments in the commission between the Council and members of the Curia, above all between Archbishop Mark McGrath, who was in favour of reform and at whose invitation I had once addressed a group of Council fathers from the Holy Cross Order, and Ottaviani's man, the Franciscan Fr Ermengildo Lio, who will later write a fat work supporting the infallibility of the teaching put forward in the encyclical *Humanae vitae* against contraception. The morning with three speeches by Patriarch Maximos, Cardinal Léger and Cardinal Suenens is a high point of the debate in the aula during the third session – after the vigorous attacks by Cardinal Ruffini (Palermo) and Archbishop Heenan (London). All three speak out clearly in favour of the revision of church teaching on 'artificial' birth control (the pill or other methods) and are greeted with great applause in the plenary. At the end of the session I leave St Peter's with Cardinal Suenens. I congratulate him on his bold intervention. He thinks that the demand for a theological reorientation must now be made publicly in the Council for the first time. The pope now wants to leave things to a papal commission, he thinks, but one can be optimistic about that. We are both to be mistaken.

Of course the curial party had by no means given up. There are the usual tricks: manipulation of the commission, the exclusion of theologians and lay experts, direct interventions from the pope. The curials certainly cannot establish the short-cut solution ('continence as a means of birth control'), but they hope to be able to prevent a consistent solution along the lines of responsible parenthood. The equally urgent question of mixed marriages, mentioned by Cardinal Frings and originally addressed in the same Council document, is likewise dropped; the pope also wants to reply to this personally – unfortunately in the negative. The proposal for toleration of the remarriage of the deserted spouse, which is proposed after the practice of the Eastern churches and applauded at the Council, also doesn't get a hearing in the commission. There are no discussions of such pressing questions in the Council plenary, but rather many superfluous interventions over particular formulations and arguments.

On 16 November 1965 the chapter on marriage and family which has been revised and discussed time and again is presented for a first vote. Again there are stern warnings from Cardinal Ottaviani that the principle of responsible parenthood is incompatible with Catholic faith. Two votes produce more than 2000 *placet* and only 91 or 144 *non placet*. But thousands of proposals for emendation are sent in and are worked on day and night by the sub-commission concerned.

However, at the end of November there is again a dramatic intervention by Paul VI. A whole series of *'modi'* are urged by the Secretariat of State. These would change the text, already accepted by the necessary two-thirds majority, in the direction of the curial minority. The most elementary rules of any parliamentary assembly are time and again arbitrarily passed over by the absolute ruler in this assembly of the church. The commission is perplexed, annoyed, confused: is this an order from the pope or only a suggestion? Only a suggestion, it is said soothingly, but nevertheless notice must be taken of it. So what is to be done? My fellow *peritus*, the famous moral theologian Bernhard Häring, who did the main work on this text and showed brave resistance to the pressures from the Curia, will say in a post-conciliar Herder Commentary that the 'commission majority acted with such wisdom and dignity that it deserves the admiration of posterity'. But I can't go along with his mitigating verdict. Realistically considered, the text modified in accordance with the papal 'suggestion' and definitively accepted in the final vote is one of the laziest compromises between the Council and the Curia in the history of Vatican II. Why? The reader has only to compare two decisive texts briefly.

On the one hand, in Article 50 responsible parenthood is affirmed in a welcome way: 'The married couple must in the end themselves decide.' The way in which previously the hierarchy has put one aim of marriage (procreation) above the other (loving union) has been abandoned in favour of a fusion of both (as had been proposed many years earlier by Doms of Münster, who was condemned at the time) and thus the purely physiological and biological approach to sexuality is abandoned in favour of a holistic personal one.

On the other hand, Article 51 challenges the personal 'responsibility of the children of the church': 'All this is possible only if the virtue of married chastity is seriously practised. In questions of birth control the sons of the church, faithful to these principles, are forbidden to use methods disapproved of by the magisterium of the church in its interpretation of the divine law.' The 'magisterium'? Is that suddenly no longer the ecumenical council but the *Diktat* of the pope? This is unmistakably insinuated by the reference to Pius XI's encyclical *Casti connubii*, which in 1930 disastrously committed the Catholic Church, as opposed to the Anglican Church, to the rejection of any form of contraception. And to cap it all, there is yet one more reference to the scandalous address of Pius XII to the midwives, composed by my teacher Hürth, which I mentioned in connection with my student years.

And as always, to make it abundantly clear that the episcopate, Council and church ultimately have to decide nothing and the pope everything, under the pressure of the Curia the following addition has to be made: 'By the order of the Holy Father, specific questions requiring further and more careful investigation have been given to a commission for the study of population, the family and births, in order that the Holy Father may pass judgement when the task is completed. With the teaching of the magisterium standing as it is, the Council has no intention of proposing concrete solutions at this moment.'

Thus it is clear that the Council hasn't succeeded in asserting itself against the Curia on such a decisive question because the Curia has the pope behind it. Cardinal Ottaviani and his men, who in the Council aula appear outwardly as losers, will prove victors as early as 1968, the year in which Bernhard's commentary mentioned above appears: in the encyclical *Humanae vitae* Paul VI, wrongly appealing to the Council, indeed even scorning the papal commission which he has set up, will speak out clearly against any contraception and thus hurl the Catholic Church into a crisis of trust which has yet to be overcome. It is the occasion for my book *Infallible? An Enquiry* (1970).

This is a sorry story. It must be discussed later, but I shall conclude it provisionally here with a quotation from Josef Ratzinger shortly before *Humanae vitae* (1968):

Above the pope as an expression of the binding claim of church authority stands one's own conscience, which has to be obeyed first of all, if need be against the demands of church authority. With this emphasis on the individual, who in the conscience faces the highest and last authority which is ultimately withdrawn from the claim of external communities, including the official church, at the same time the counter-principle to rising totalitarianism is given, and true obedience in the church is acquitted of the totalitarian claim that cannot accept such an ultimate compulsion that opposes its will to power.

Did Ratzinger also have in view the rising totalitarianism of the 'official church', the main defender of which he himself would one day be? It would certainly be wrong to limit oneself to the problem of contraception in answering this question.

Demands which are met

What has the Council achieved? At the end of the fourth session we theologians take pains to survey the results. On Monday 29 November 1965, Daniel O'Hanlon SJ, Godfrey Diekmann OSB, Edward Schillebeeckx OP and I meet with English-speaking Council observers and journalists. However, for the next day I have personally invited a dozen Council theologians to our residence, the Istituto San Tomaso di Villanova, to discuss four questions for mutual information and in order to form a balanced judgement. What are the epoch-making results in the Council decrees? And what are they outside the Council decrees? What are the main difficulties in the period after the Council? And what are the main tasks? Those who have accepted include Gregory Baum (Toronto), Yves Congar (Strasbourg), Henri Féret (Paris), Jorge Medina (Buenos Aires), Daniel O'Hanlon (Los Gatos, California), Joseph Ratzinger (Münster) and Edward Schillebeeckx (Nijmegen). I have the opportunity to give my impressions later in the Dutch documentation centre I-Doc, and also on German and Italian television, and work the results into articles for the *Frankfurter Allgemeine Zeitung*, the Swiss *Civitas* and the Italian *Epoca*.

On 8 December the Second Vatican Council is ended at a solemn closing ceremony in St Peter's Square at precisely 1.20 p.m. with Paul VI's *'Ite in pace'*. So what has the Council achieved? I can only give my own assessment. Unfortunately I know only too well what it hasn't achieved. There are certain decrees – for example that on the mass media or the Declaration on Christian Education – which contain hardly any pointers to the future, though they are also harmless and therefore will soon be forgotten. There are others which are very unbalanced, indeed ambiguous at some points or backward-looking. There isn't a single decree that completely satisfies me and probably most of the bishops. Much that the Council fathers wanted hasn't been incorporated into the decrees. And the Council fathers didn't want much that has been.

Almost everywhere, particularly in the doctrinal decrees, I miss a solid exegetical and historical foundation – I have often complained about the almost total absence of historical-critical exegesis at the Council as a fundamental defect. Often the most difficult points like scripture/tradition or primacy/collegiality have been plastered over: as I have said time and again, there are compromises between an overwhelming majority at the Council which generally has serious and living theology on its side, and the tiny curial party which has control of the power of the apparatus in the commissions dominated by the members of the Curia and uninhibitedly exploits it to the end. I had seen these defects from the beginning and constantly expressed my fears for the future. I keep warning: 'The episcopate and the church will have to be careful not to lose some things that have been achieved as a result of the cold course of bureaucracy.'

But despite everything, we now seem to have reached a point when the indisputable obscurities, compromises, omissions, one-sidednesses, lapses and mistakes aren't complained about as a defect of the past, in a retrospective critique of manoeuvres. Rather, they are now seen in a forward-looking hope as tasks for the future, and attempts are made, in keeping with the Council, not to shut any doors. In some respects, in fact, the Council, the authentic realization of what happened at the Council, only began on 8 December 1965.

Be this as it may: since Vatican II the age of the Counter-Reformation which restored the Middle Ages, of a defensive attitude, polemic and conquest for the Catholic Church, is over – despite all the abiding resistance, in particular at the Roman centre. A new, more hopeful, age has begun for it: an age of constructive renewal in all spheres of church life, of an understanding encounter and collaboration with the rest of Christianity, the Jews and the other religions, with the modern world generally.

Precisely what this means is shown by an analysis of the sixteen decrees which the Council has approved in the four years of its work. They are going to be the pillars of the church after the Council. Along these lines, the journal *Epoca* publishes a richly illustrated leading story of mine which gives a documentary closing report on the Council under the title: 'The Sixteen New Pillars of St Peter'. I say clearly that these pillars have differing load-bearing capacities. In any case it is a risk briefly to report the results of these sixteen decrees without being specific. Some aspects of them are incomplete and will prove provisional; some elements are fake decoration from the long history of the Catholic Church. Be this as it may, they all represent documents of a transition in the history of the church in which, despite everything, the new and better clearly comes to light. No one can dispute that the post-conciliar church will be different from the preconciliar church!

I have already reported on most of the results of the decrees in these memoirs and made it clear how, for example, through the Decree on Ecumenism an ecumenical age has irrevocably begun for the Catholic Church too. It has also become clear that the Council has adopted a whole series of central concerns of the Reformation. Be this as it may, the main concerns of my book *The Council and Reunion* have largely been fulfilled:

- The Reformation is being taken seriously as a religious event;
- The Bible is being valued highly in the liturgy, in theology and in the whole life of the church;
- An authentic liturgy of the people of God has been achieved in preaching and the eucharist;
- The laity has been revalued in worship and community life;
- The church has adapted to the various cultures and there is dialogue with them;
- There is a reform of popular piety;
- There is a 'reform' of the Roman Curia.

Peter Hebblethwaite confirms this assessment in his biography of John XXIII (1984): the author of *The Council and Reunion* has proved to be 'an accurate and far-sighted prophet'. 'All of his seven demands were embodied, even if in modified form, in the final documents of the Council.'

Demands which are not met

Does this stocktaking mean that all this will be implemented? Truly, I was never naïve in matters relating to the Council. I wasn't seized by euphoria over the Council either before, during or after it. And time and again I drew attention to the basic tension between a church pressing for reform and a Curia hindering reform, making myself unpopular with some people in the process.

That is why I also write quite unmistakably in my stocktaking of the Council on 17/18 December 1965: 'The tension between a church intent on reform and a Curia unwilling for reform could only bring about a serious crisis – as it already did at the Council. If at least with the passing of time the forces of renewal, though less numerous, did not get the upper hand in Rome (not least by new appointments to senior posts in the Curia), and should attempts be made there, as has in part been indicated, to restore the situation as it was before the Council, then this would inevitably lead to a great crisis of trust. Only the reform of the Curia in personnel and structure can help to avoid such a crisis. Here, too, the renewal of the Spirit and the conversion of the heart is the decisive thing.'

And then I formulate quite clearly the questions which were not discussed at the Council or were not allowed to be discussed at all. So what are 'the questions not resolved by the Council'?

- Birth control as a matter of personal responsibility;
- Regulation of the question of mixed marriages (validity of the marriage, upbringing of the children);
- Priestly celibacy in the Latin church;
- The reform of the Roman Curia in structure and personnel;
- Reform of penitential practice: confession, indulgences, fasting (on Friday);
- Reform of the dress and titles of prelates;
- The involvement of the church regions concerned in the appointment of bishops;
- Election of the pope by the Synod of Bishops, which is more representative of the church.

In listing these desiderata I am thinking not least of Pope Paul VI himself, to whom moreover I will send my stocktaking in *Epoca*. But when now, after the end of the Council, I think back once again to the proposals in *The Council and Reunion* (1960), which at that time five years ago could very well have been regarded as extreme demands, I may say that the Council has been worthwhile despite all the disappointment.

Indeed, where would we be without this Council: in the liturgy, in theology, pastoral care, ecumenical relations, relations with Judaism and the other world religions, and with the secular world generally? Vatican II may not have been allowed to do much of what it could have done. But it has achieved far more than most people expected. At that time I wrote the sentence: 'The Council will be the fulfilment of a great hope or a great disappointment. Given the seriousness of the world situation and the needs of Christianity, the fulfilment of a little hope would be a great disappointment.' And even today, looking back after almost 40 years, I may say that for all the disappointments, which were by no means small, the Council brought a great hope.

So what I wrote in 1965 is still my view as I write in 2002. However, unfortunately my fears of the time have also been confirmed. Still, first of all, having returned to Tübingen from Rome, instead of dealing with great church politics I must necessarily occupy myself with small faculty politics.

A faculty drama in three acts

Hardly am I back from the Council when on 10 December 1965 – with amazing unanimity – I am appointed dean of the Catholic theological faculty for the second time: during my months at the Council, pro-dean Haag has represented me admirably. Whereas my first year as dean was highly successful, my second was to prove extremely depressing. Had it not had so many effects on the further history of the Catholic theological faculty of the University of Tübingen, I would prefer not to report on it at all, just as I have also reported on virtually nothing of normal everyday university life: all the lectures and seminars and their preparation (spending most of my life at my desk), the sessions of the faculty, commission and senate (not always very exciting). Nor stories like that of the new appointment to the chair for comparative philology in January 1966, in which as senate reporter in a long plea I overturn the list presented by the philosophical faculty – finally with 44 votes for, 8 against and 10 abstentions – and help the polymath and multilingual anti-Fascist Spaniard Antonio Tovar, ex-Rector of the University of Salamanca, to get the Tübingen chair.

The reader will understand that the great church-political controversies with Rome are much less of an emotional burden for me (they are simply rooted in the nature of the case) than those in my own faculty, which are closer to me and in which from the beginning good personal relations have been so important to me. So, while sparing those still alive as far as possible, I will give a brief summary of this little *historia calamitatum,* unfortunate history, which now follows.

Act I: After the 'air of the great wide world', here I am suddenly back again, though not quite as in the Germanicum, in a *'piccolo mondo chiuso',* a 'little enclosed world' of a faculty, at that time still protected from outside view by the most sacred 'faculty secrecy'. The conflict breaks out where underground tensions in faculties so often explode: in new appointments. The situation is as follows. After the chair for dogmatics, the chair for moral theology is also to be duplicated. And here I cannot avoid naming names. The ordinarius for moral theology, Johannes Stelzenberger, insists on seeing one of his pupils, the lecturer Josef Rief, who has only recently gained his habilitation, as his colleague for the newly created chair of moral theology and social ethics. This is inbreeding not appreciated by the university and barely tolerated by the Kultusministerium (a 'house call'): someone who has studied, taken his examinations, gained a doctorate and a habilitation in Tübingen should be the last person to be given a chair there for the rest of his life. However, in the case of a favourite pupil the Herr Ordinarius will not see this.

As dean I see no reason for opposing the majority in the faculty. Certainly one can think that a man from the school of the Münster social scientist Joseph Höffner has better qualifications in empirical social research; in this respect Höffner's prize pupil and later successor, Willy Weber, closely associated with me by seven years at the Germanicum and the social circle, would be the better candidate. And in fact in the Great Senate especially, the economists indicate their preference for Weber over Rief. But as dean I ward off all criticism without scorning the merits of Weber, whom I value highly: after all, I argue, the faculty rightly wants a colleague who deliberately starts from theology, in order to engage in dialogue with the social sciences from there. The vote produces a big majority in the senate for our local candidate with only isolated votes against.

The faculty has every reason to be content with its young dean. And everything would have gone well had not Stelzenberger had the unfortunate idea a year later of wanting to see this same Rief as the successor in his own chair.

Act II: There are eminent university teachers who are tacitly of the view that in any case no one better could succeed them and so they are not particularly concerned about their successor. And there are others, not always eminent, who fight for a successor from their own circle of pupils as if they were fighting for their ancestral estate. Now Stelzenberger, too, fights for his pupil as for his own son. And unfortunately this friendly man proves to be very malleable.

While I have decisively backed Rief in the first call, from the beginning I equally decisively object to a second call. After all, it is impossible for me a year later again to go before the senate and once again defend this man as the right and only candidate for moral theology I, although there were already problems over his call to moral theology II. Moreover he has no new academic achievements to show. As later in my own discipline too (the call of Ratzinger to Tübingen), I am simply concerned to get the best person in Germany for this chair, which is so important. I am thinking primarily of Professor Franz Böckle of Bonn (that he is Swiss is no more relevant to me than the fact that Weber is a Gemanicum alumnus). Now, when the discussion on contraception and similar questions is coming to a climax, Böckle has already worked intensively in medical ethics and has argued in an expert way for a new basis for ethics, an 'autonomous' ethic. Without doubt he would be a brilliant first choice for Tübingen.

Secondly I think of Professor Alfons Auer from Würzburg, an equally well-tried moral theologian, whom I have also come to know as a most congenial person through giving a lecture there. However, Auer still teaches moral theology in a very traditional way, within the framework of the seven sacraments, and is cautiously holding back from the dangerous questions of sexual morality. But if there is to be no agreement on Böckle, then I would accept Auer as a compromise candidate – Herbert Haag is of the same view: thus Böckle in first place and Auer in second (or vice versa), and in third place the largely unknown Rief, wanted by his predecessor, who so far has publications only on the church father Augustine and the Tübingen school.

However, in the faculty meeting (11 January 1966) I note very quickly that neither Auer nor Böckle are acceptable to the majority, Böckle presumably because he is too exposed in matters of sexual morality and is moreover Swiss (a third Swiss), Auer presumably because he is too much associated with the church establishment in Rottenburg. No, only Rief is said to be worthy of this chair. I state once again that I cannot present this to the senate. Days after the meeting a delegate from the majority comes to me at home in the hope of being able to make me change my mind. When he doesn't succeed, he threatens me with a friendly smile: 'Then there will probably be a row . . .'

Still innocent in the field of academic intrigues, I have no inkling what a row awaits me. In the decisive meeting it immediately becomes clear that the Stelzenberger party has a slight majority and intends to exploit its power. I cannot gain the slightest thing for myself personally out of this controversy (for me this is always an important criterion of judgement), and it has even less to do with the

'Swiss team' (as can later be read in the local press). Quite apart from the fact that we two Swiss and with us two Swabians use our freedom to vote in accordance with our best knowledge and conscience in a decision which is important for the whole faculty.

In the decisive meeting (1 February 1966) I make the compromise proposal: 1. Auer, 2. Böckle, 3. Rief. The proposal is rejected; indeed Böckle, who in my view has the best qualifications, is struck off the list. Then comes the surprising proposal by the Stelzenberger party: 1. Auer, 2. Rief, 3. others. Böckle is eliminated with no reasons given. But why suddenly make the unpopular Auer favourite? I learn afterwards that this is because the gentlemen concerned are sure that he will not accept the call; they have heard very recently that Auer has just built a new house in Würzburg and certainly wouldn't want to give it up. And if Auer refuses the call, because Böckle has simply been deleted, the call automatically goes to the second candidate, who is wanted, namely Rief. As soon as the result is fixed for Rief, I formally state that as dean I cannot present this list to the senate. But I am told that I must. No, I must not. Then the pro-dean is approached. That is Herbert Haag, and he too refuses. They insist. In vain. Consternation. A shameless intrigue! They necessitate a further meeting of the faculty (9 February 1966).

They are afraid of a special statement by the dean and pro-dean in the Great Senate. I offer my colleagues three possible ways of settling the conflict. That perplexes the 'majority'. There is a request to adjourn the meeting. I adjourn the meeting. Those committed to Rief leave the room. There is a long conference in the corridor. Then they return and say that they would 'welcome it if colleagues Haag and Küng would refrain from making special statements . . . and . . . want the dean to stay away from the meeting of the Great Senate'. Very well. Finally the member of the majority who threatened me with the 'row' thunders that he will present the list in the senate himself. After a few questions the unsuspecting body passes this. The majority on the faculty triumphs. But too early. For wonder of wonders, Auer accepts the call to Tübingen. To my delight. It really could have been achieved much more cheaply. And Rief, in embarrassment, remains sitting on his unpopular chair.

Act III: This whole affair, which occupied us for weeks on end, for a long time poisons the atmosphere, which in my first year as dean had been excellent, and brings me very bitter days and sometimes also nights. For those who have been deprived of victory want no peace. They now act as a power cartel and plan vengeance, in three directions:

The Institute for Biblical Kerygmatics promised to Herbert Haag, founded especially for critical investigation of the biblical basis of the books of religion, is simply written off. Resolved on unanimously by the faculty, approved unanimously by the senate and already authorized by the ministry, it is now to stop business. The assistant has already been appointed. But on the proposal of the church historian Fink, 'the faculty', the power cartel, makes the decision after

447

vigorous debates, with five votes for (three against and three abstentions). The institute is abolished, the money for it can go back to Stuttgart. Whoever heard of such a thing?

The second chair for New Testament exegesis, long decided on (the Protestant faculty has three!), is likewise torpedoed. Having advanced to sixth place on the university list in my first year as dean, in my second year, on the basis of my plea – Catholic exegesis has a great need to catch up – it is safely placed first. But a new decision is made by the 'faculty': this chair too is unnecessary. It is to be changed into a post for an academic councillor (with no voting rights in the faculty). In this way the power cartel retains the voting majority. For how long?

The habilitation of my assistant Dr Alexander Ganoczy is squashed by four votes to four and the casting vote of the new dean, Max Seckler, who the evening before had invited the candidate to a very friendly 'condemned man's last meal'. Ganoczy lodges an objection. But after further indescribable faculty meetings I sadly have to realize that this best-qualified Catholic specialist on Calvin has no future in Tübingen. So I make contact with the Reformation historian Erwin Iserloh, whom I know from Rome, and who knows and values Ganoczy's work. All credit to him and his Münster faculty that a year later they grant Ganoczy his habilitation in Münster without any difficulties. Ganoczy is soon called as Professor of Dogmatics to the University of Würzburg.

The whole activity of this power cartel – hidden from the public and also from the students and assistants by 'faculty secrecy' (after 1968 I will argue resolutely for the abolition of this) and well prepared by relevant conversations ('pastoral care by telephone') – repels me so much that for months I do not attend any faculty meetings. With Seckler as my successor as dean in any case I cannot prevent further unhelpful decisions at them. Happily, in the summer vacation of 1966 I am back in Sursee, now in my lake house. There I often think that it would be best for me not to return to this Tübingen faculty again.

But nothing under the sun remains as it is. Some time later I receive in Sursee by telephone the sensational news that Rief and the spokesman of the cartel will leave Tübingen: they have both accepted calls to Bavarian faculties. Thank God: the power cartel has blown up! There is an end to the provincial farce. Now the faculty can steer back into smoother waters. Above all Haag, Auer, Johannes Neumann, the new church lawyer who is happily open (Heinrich Fries had recommended him to me as dean), and I work hard with success in the meetings, without any conspiratorial agreements, to bring about a matter-of-fact and collegial atmosphere.

A surprise at Easter

In Easter week 1966 a small packet arrives for me from the Vatican. It is in fact an Easter gift from Pope Paul VI. Beautifully packed in a box with yellow and white ribbons and a little palm branch, I find bound in leather and set on velvet for display a gilded plaque of the risen Christ. Attached is a confidential letter from the substitute of the Secretariat of State Monsignor Dell'Acqua dated 16 April 1966 with the protocol number 68844 (happily different from the one I have at the Sanctum Officium). This is what the letter says:

> The Holy Father has commissioned me to send you his Easter greetings. For some time now he has wanted to let you know what good memories he has of the visit that you made to him at the end of the Council and that he has noted your newspaper articles in *Vaterland* and *Epoca*, though not without certain reservations. Of course the Holy Father does not want to go into your reports in detail. But is it not legitimate to ask whether one really does the church true service by unrestrained discussion of questions which relate to the external and internal state of the church and its future in a way which here and there shows a lack of the conscientious consideration that is needed? Could not a theologian who wants to serve the truth and the church have made a contribution to the Council in a more positive form and brought it to an ever deeper knowledge of the Catholic truths of faith?
>
> That, revered Herr Professor, is what the Holy Father expects of you, in the high esteem in which he holds your gifts and your cultural education. Confident of this, the Holy Father asks for the support of the Holy Spirit for your scholarly and pastoral activity. At the same time he addresses to you the urgent and paternal request to love the holy church and to give it your powerful help by building it up.
>
> In reporting this to you, may I send you the enclosed gift from the Holy Father and personal good wishes, Yours most sincerely, A. Dell'Acqua.

So once again there is praise and blame, love of the church and a request for collaboration in building it up. In my reply to Archbishop Dell'Acqua of 6 June 1966 I express my delight at the 'valuable, fine Easter gift of the Holy Father': 'I am very surprised by this wholly undeserved kindness, and I allow myself to ask you to pass on to the Holy Father my deeply felt thanks.' Then comes my real answer:

> I am delighted to hear that in the midst of the far more important claims on him the Holy Father has taken the trouble to read my two articles and that he has accepted them in a benevolent way. I have tried to give a credible account of the positive results of the Council for people today.
>
> I am glad to follow the suggestion of the Holy Father in making a positive contribution to the deeper knowledge of the truth of faith and the church. I will continue to make an effort to give honest expression to my love of the church in my theological works. I am particularly grateful for this benevolent concern of the Holy Father for my theological work.

Even to the non-insider, the tone and content of this letter are very clearly different from what anyone who wanted to rise in the service of the Curia and the hierarchy would say. This is still in no way on my mind. Once again, not out of arrogance, but out of the thought that I wouldn't be able to avoid fitting in with the unreformed Roman system. Had the pope invited me to collaborate in some serious plan for reform, I would have collaborated just as naturally as I did in the international theological journal *Concilium*, in memoranda on reform, or later in the framework of the World Economic Forum, in UNESCO or UNO projects. But I cannot and will not promise to tie myself down in so to speak 'absolute obedience' to a line which aims at the stabilization of the modernized mediaeval system. Think of all the things that I would have to agree to!

In short, I am and remain a professor of theology – that fulfils me completely, it gives me many possibilities and I enjoy it. And I am grateful that soon the book which makes clear in a comprehensive way my view of the church and service in the church and which has cost me infinite hours by day and night during the Council and the subsequent period will soon see the light of day: *The Church*.

So contrary to my usual habits I have to remain in Tübingen during August 1966. Finally, on the morning of 27 August, around 5 a.m., I can complete the manuscript – totally exhausted and ready for a holiday. I have around half an hour's sleep and then drive to Sursee, where at 9.30 I have to take part in a colloquium with important Swiss figures, planned months ago, at the other end of the lake. Then finally a holiday in my lake house – some relaxed days with my friends Peter Lengsfeld and Josef Fischer from the Germanicum. I visit Karl Barth twice during this time. The big book, around 600 pages long, immediately goes to press with the Catholic publishing house Herder Verlag in Freiburg. I write the preface, with the date New Year 1967, and on 30 January receive the imprimatur from the episcopal ordinariate of Rottenburg. Now, in April 1967, the book appears in German and a little later in Dutch with Paul Brand's publishing house. *'Iacta alea est'*, say the Romans, 'the die is cast!'

My service of the church

Before the Council in 1960 my book *The Council and Reunion* was the constructive offer of a theologian to the church and its leaders, showing the way into a new future. The offer was accepted: 'Like it or not, in historical perspective this book has done more than any other to get the Council going', writes the English Dominican Fergus Kerr 25 years later. Likewise, after the Council, in 1967, my book *The Church* is such an offer, showing how to realize the great concern of the Council. With a consistent foundation in the New Testament, in a truly Catholic manner (and precisely for that reason sometimes deviating from what is customarily Roman Catholic), I have attempted to show a way: what the church can and should be in the light of its origins in a difficult present with a view to a better future. Will this offer also be accepted by the church and its leaders – the 'service in the church' that I desire? In 1960 I knew that I had the Council and the pope behind me – whom do I have behind me now, in 1967?

Soon rumours are going around in Rome that the Sanctum Officium, now called the Congregation for the Doctrine of Faith, has its eyes on the book. Later I learn that an action is being prepared which can be dangerous for me. Will people in Rome really not note that despite some objections in detail, the reaction of key Catholic and Protestant theologians is amazingly positive? Karl Barth says to me after reading it: 'That is a deeply evangelical book.' And in his lecture in the Festsaal of the University of Tübingen, after reporting the main thesis of *The Church*, Ernst Käsemann declares: 'With this book the schism between me and Küng is ended.' What a blessing, I think, it would be for the Catholic Church and the whole ecumenical world if there could be some agreement on the line taken in this book, despite all the corrections? Very soon it will be introduced as a textbook in some seminaries, both Catholic and Protestant.

But people in the 'Holy Office' see things differently, and will soon initiate an Inquisition procedure which will lead to an ongoing conflict with the Vatican and in the 1970s will reach its climax in the dispute over infallibility. I mention this only to explain why here – in order to offer a counterweight to the denouncers and inquisitors – I allow myself to quote some significant witnesses to the catholicity and ecumenicity of this book. The Council theologian Yves Congar OP:

Küng's constructive contribution on ecclesiology is extraordinarily rich. No one so far has thought through the reality of the 'church' in such a comprehensive and consistent way in the light of the gospel, so thoroughly in its conceptuality. The biblical exegetical, historical-critical method followed here leads less to a 'theology' of the church, especially the 'church which is believed' than to a very varied description of the primitive church, above all the Pauline church, in which the characteristics of the 'essence' of the church are critically examined for their 'perversion' (*Revue des Sciences Philosophiques et Théologiques*).

The Council father Otto Semmelroth SJ:

Here Küng offers a unique book on the church. The marked personal commitment and the lively language make reading the book more than sober study . . . Although some statements are unusual and do not shrink from shocking, the book offers a completely Catholic ecclesiology (*Theologie und Philosophie*).

Hans Urs von Balthasar:

A book of passion, but well considered and powerful in s_____re, clear in the lines that it takes, written in a hard, clear, sometimes high-speed rhetorical style. It deliberately offers an ecumenical doctrine of the church, at the end of which basically any offence caused by Catholics to Protestants is removed (*Civitas*).

The Lutheran theologian Herman Dietzfelbinger:

Anyone who knows Küng's theological intentions will not be surprised that in him the Bible speaks. But the way and the extent to which this happens is breathtaking. Küng knows how to give a hearing to the *whole* of the New Testament, and with a remarkable sense of the importance of the individual authors, depending on how close they are in time and substance to the origin of the gospel. For Catholic exegesis to have taken over the results of his-torical-critical research is nothing new; but a systematic theological eva-luation which is concerned only for the Bible to have its say to the end, without at any time or in any way wanting to protect any of the traditional and familiar dogmatic premises and without on the other hand regarding the craft of exegesis as art for art's sake – something like this is unique in the theological literature of both confessions (*Nachrichten der evangelisch-lutherische Kirche in Bayern*).

The Anglican Cambridge professor Hugh Montefiore:

I had only to glance at the book to see that it was good. By page 100 I realized it was very good. On page 250 I knew that it was a classic. By page 500, though panting somewhat, I stood firm in my conviction. When you do get to the end, you feel as though you have successfully completed an Oxfam walk. You certainly need your second wind before page 388, where you are somewhat daunted to read in small type, with reference to Küng's earlier work *Structures of the Church*, that Chapters VI-VII (pp. 95–352) of that book must be presupposed here (*New Christian*).

But enough of the kind of boasting which seemed necessary even to the apostle Paul in his defence against the 'super-apostles' (cf. 2 Corinthians 11–12). Of course substantive objections on matters of detail will be made from various sides, and some will even formulate a rejection of the book. My pupils Hermann Häring and Josef Nolte will document the discussion comprehensively in a book *Diskussion um Hans Küng, Die Kirche* (1971). But on the whole the discussion went well and could lead to a positive result. Not least the reactions from the Anglican Communion show me how on this basis a reconciliation between Rome and Canterbury would one day be possible – a model for further progress in the Christian ecumene. Here I set special hopes on a colleague who is the same age, is like-minded and equally competent: Joseph Ratzinger.

Joseph Ratzinger in Tübingen

When my colleague in dogmatics, Professor Leo Scheffczyk, receives a call to the University of Munich from which he comes, I do all I can as dean to persuade him to remain in Tübingen. But I can't close my ears to his arguments. He thinks that the critical intellectual atmosphere here is right for me to work in, but he would feel much more at home in the conservative atmosphere of Munich. Apart from lesser frictions (in connection with the foundation of the institute and a habilitation), which can hardly be avoided completely in everyday faculty life, we had got on well with each other. And Scheffczyk's predecessor and promoter Michael Schmaus is kind enough to send me the sixth edition of his 'Doctrine of Grace', which brings out the concerns of my book *Justification*. Scheffczyk could certainly be a good successor there. So at a dinner given for him in Bebenhausen near Tübingen on 5 November 1965 we bid farewell in a friendly way. However, as a neoscholastic who is perfectly loyal to Rome, he will later write a malicious pamphlet against my theology, will receive an honorary doctorate from the Opus Dei university in Pamplona, Spain, and at the age of almost 81 (because those over 80 do not vote in a papal election) will be made a cardinal.

But who will be his successor? I would like none other than Joseph Ratzinger, at the time Professor of Dogmatics in Münster. Although he is only 37, he enjoys great respect, as his career so far shows. He has his own direction of research and at the same time is very open to contemporary questions – the basis for a good collaboration. I had also found him personally congenial at the time of the Council. So he seems to me an almost ideal appointment. And this is the argument which, contrary to all custom, I present right at the beginning of the meeting of my faculty. As dean and at the same time occupant of the parallel chair I feel justified in doing so. With resounding success. My proposal is accepted unanimously: Joseph Ratzinger – and this is very unusual – is to be put on the list for the call *unico loco* (in other words, without mentioning a second or third candidate).

Previously, of course, I have checked things out with Ratzinger. Already after my election as dean I had proposed him to the faculty for a university lecture on 8 July 1964. Ratzinger writes back that he would like to tackle one of the 'hottest potatoes' in the doctrine of the eucharist: 'Transubstantiation, the doctrine of the change of substance and the meaning of the eucharist'. The lecture, which at first alienates the audience because of the high pitch of the speaker's voice, meets with much approval among both colleagues and students. On 2 May 1965 I then visited Ratzinger once again in Münster – after a meeting of Catholic and Protestant journalists in Hardehausen – and talked with him about the possibility of a call to Tübingen. In a letter of 11 May I again pointed out to him 'everything that makes Tübingen attractive for you: the scholarly collaboration with Catholic and Protestant colleagues at a place with a great free tradition, the excellent conditions for work, the nearness to your home . . . So I think that everything that didn't draw me from Tübingen to Münster at that time can persuade you to go from Münster to Tübingen.' Immediately before the decisive faculty meeting Ratzinger assures me by telephone that he would accept a call proposed by me *unico loco*.

The unanimous resolution of the faculty is followed a couple of weeks later by the unanimous resolution of the Great Senate. However, Ratzinger will come to Tübingen only in the summer semester of 1966, when he has completed his three years in Münster. By then I will have found what I had promised him and his sister, whom he cannot ask 'to spend endless time sitting here alone in the north': an attractive new house to rent in a good area of Tübingen, in Dannemannstrasse.

Our fundamental theologian Max Seckler, who possibly had also had hopes for the chair in dogmatics, but either could not or would not compete with Ratzinger, tells me later that it made a great impression on colleagues in the faculty that I had got my strongest rival. I say that I think it natural that the best should be called. No, he says reflectively, that is by no means a matter of course. Evidently I must gain further experience to understand certain mechanisms in calling: only the strong call strong colleagues, and the average call the average. And this is the secret of why certain faculties – and truly not just theological faculties – remain average.

'I am tremendously delighted about your yes,' I write to Ratzinger on 8 July 1965. But won't I be running some risks with this call? I am aware that he remains more rooted in the neoscholastic tradition than I am and attaches more importance to the authority of the church fathers (and that of Augustine in particular), to which he will also devote his inaugural lecture. But different emphases and directions of research can only be an advantage. And in fact his chair is 'of dogmatic theology and the history of dogma', whereas mine is 'of dogmatic and ecumenical theology'.

What is more important to me is that we are both like-minded over the significance of the Second Vatican Council: in the direction of the renewal of theology and the church and ecumenical understanding. Freedom in the church is fundamental to this. At an early stage I have sent Rahner my lecture, which is now available as a Theological Meditation. His answer: 'First of all warmest thanks for sending me your *The Church and Freedom*. I need not tell you how much I agree with you on this particular matter.'

Our like-mindedness becomes evident in the introduction to the series 'Ökumenische Forschungen', edited by him and me, which will begin with my book *The Church*. This says in 'January 1967':

The time is ripe for a systematic purging of the theological differences between the Christian churches. The ecumenical encounter of the various Christian theologies has not kept pace with the surprising ecumenical encounter of the various Christian churches in recent years. Yet the Christian churches will at best do no more than come within calling distance of one another unless the theological blocks and sometimes even sandbanks which lie between them are removed or new ways of encounter are found which make possible an exchange of their gifts – often after throwing out unnecessary theological ballast . . . Not all the questions between the Christian churches can be resolved. But those questions which divide the churches must be solved.

Beyond doubt we now have an extraordinarily favourable constellation of theologians in Tübingen, documented in the university journal *Attempto* of December 1968: from the Protestant side Jürgen Moltmann writes on 'God and resurrection' and Herman Diem on 'The church's task and address to the public'; from the Catholic side Joseph Ratzinger writes on 'Present tendencies in Catholic theology' and I write on 'Infallible magisterium?'. In the introduction the editor, Walter Jens, remarks: 'And then this stroke of luck! A basic article from Ratzinger's pen, the foundation for ongoing reflections, and alongside it, boldly rising into the air, a rocket with Swiss markings, fired from Tübingen and now circling overhead . . . and in the editorial board prompting the question: shouldn't the pope be a reader of *Attempto* . . . how can we get our journal to him? Thanks to the theologians . . . editors do not experience such a favour every decade!'

So I have the well-founded hope that we in Tübingen, supported by capable exegetes and historians, and in collaboration with interesting Protestant colleagues, can form a strong theological group. At the same time I set my hope on Karl Rahner, together with whom after the Council, in Munich on 8 December 1965, I share a television broadcast directed by Hans Heigert, chief editor of the *Süddeutsche Zeitung* – I have him invited for lunch in Tübingen in connection with a lecture. He is accompanied by his competent and hopeful assistant Dr Karl Lehmann, who comes from nearby Veringenstadt by Sigmaringen. Lehmann is already known to me from the Germanicum and now carries on the correspondence for Rahner in a brotherly tone – above all about Rahner's fine 'theological meditation' *Belief Today*. Remarkably, the episcopal ordinariate of Chur now asks for an opinion (from me!) on Rahner's 'theological meditation'. 'It's a long time,' Lehmann writes, 'since anyone interfered in an imprimatur for Rahner . . . I envy you your quiet days (at least outwardly) in Sursee. Things are busy here (in Munich) because the *Lexikon für Theologie und Kirche* X and the *Handbuch für Pastoraltheologie* II are nearing completion.'

Yes, that's my dream: Rahner, Ratzinger and I, supported by the rising Hermann Häring, Walter Kasper, Karl Lehmann, Johann Baptist Metz, Otto Herman Pesch and as many others as possible – the *avant-garde* of a renewed Catholic theology in Germany, also in connection with *Concilium*. But I am all too well aware that I depend on allies. I was never a 'lone wolf'.

I am certain that in Rome people aren't sleeping. It's already evident that the Curia, and the Sanctum Officium in particular, will do everything possible to recapture the position lost through the Council as quickly and completely as possible. And in fact I am now confronted with the Roman counter-offensive in a quite personal way.

Rome's reaction

As early as 29 November 1967, as I learn subsequently, a session of the cardinals' congregation of the Congregation for the Doctrine of Faith – as the euphemistic name of the Inquisition now runs – takes place, in secret as ever, in the palazzo of the Holy Office. There is concern about the publication of my book *The Church*. The Congregation resolves the following decree: the episcopal ordinariate of Rottenburg is to be censured for giving the imprimatur. The author of the book is authoritatively to be invited by the Bishop of Rottenburg not to distribute the book further and not to have it translated into another language 'before he has had a colloquium with men to be selected by this Holy Congregation to which he will soon be invited'.

On 19 December 1967 this hardly Christmaslike decree is communicated by Cardinal Alfredo Ottaviani to Bishop Carl-Joseph Leiprecht without any substantive reasons given. There is a great stir in Rottenburg. I have travelled to Switzerland to celebrate Christmas with my family and there in my lake house on 27 December 1967 receive this Roman decree by express letter to my Swiss address from the episcopal ordinariate of Rottenburg (another goes to my Tübingen address). The Inquisition in action. I am celebrating with my parents and sisters in our old house in the Town Hall Square. But I don't want to disrupt the Christmas mood, and show nothing of my anxiety and agitation. However, speed is of the essence. What is to be done?

I consider: Rome has suppressed an infinite number of books in this infamous way – I think particularly of the works of Teilhard de Chardin and Congar's book on reform in the church. Am I to allow freedom of distribution in German and other languages to be taken from me? No, for me there is no question of that – less than ever now, after the Council declaration on religious freedom and human rights, which in fact also includes freedom of the press. On the contrary, resolute action is now called for if I am not to be beaten from the start. And specifically that means that I immediately get in touch by telephone with my publishers in Paris, London and New York and tell them that the publication of the French, English and American editions must be speeded up. I inform the Spanish publisher Herder in Barcelona via the German mother house Herder Freiburg: I insist on the conditions of the contract being kept, even in the face of possible attempts at intimidation over the further publication of the book.

The publishers go along with this: both the English and the American editions appear soon, and the Spanish and Italian editions follow later. In Chicago the book is honoured with the Thomas More medal as the 'most outstanding contribution to

Catholic literature in 1968'. It is clear to me that the Vatican will not simply accept all this. We are moving towards a great controversy. But what is the alternative?

A march through the institutions?

A brief personal letter to Pope Paul would have been enough to stop the action of the 'Sanctum Officium'. But of course in such a letter – wholly in keeping with the pope's wish in the private audience and the Easter letter – I would have to give 'a sign' that I was intending to fall in with the Roman line. *'Deve dar un segno'*, the pope will later write on my Inquisition documents: 'He must give a sign.' But with an addition of which his Polish successor will take no notice: *'Ma procedere con carità* – but proceed with love.' Which for the Sanctum Officium means, not with disciplinary measures.

Indeed, what would I have had to promise then in 1967/8? A sign of submission: and adapt, correct, retract. If not a total capitulation, at least an ongoing obedient silence (*silentium obsequiosum*) on controversial or taboo questions, which one can time and again observe almost painfully in the case of episcopal candidates and bishops who blossom from being progressive Catholic professors or pastors into reactionary Roman dignitaries. In other words, I would have to 'put myself at the service of the church' – if not voluntarily, now under Roman pressure. This is what is now expected of me in the well-meaning but narrowly Roman perspective of this pope: not 'just' at the service of the church of Jesus Christ, in whose service I in any case stand and which I attempted to describe comprehensively and in detail in my book. But at the service of the Roman church, or more precisely at the service of the Roman system, as it has been dominated and directed by the Curia since the eleventh century. Had I done so, I would then not only have had no further difficulties with the Sanctum Officium but could have made my way as a 'Roman' just as fast as others to some important, privileged church post in the north or in Rome, perhaps even into the Sanctum Officium – like another Tübingen theologian who, having hardly settled properly in Tübingen, leaves again: for Regensburg at the end of the summer semester of 1969. Why?

Time and again people puzzle over how so gifted, friendly, open a theologian as Joseph Ratzinger can undergo such a change: from progressive Tübingen theologian to Roman Grand Inquisitor. Ratzinger himself has always described this as a straight line which he has followed since Tübingen. The truth about that will be investigated in detail later. Certainly, even in Tübingen my colleague, who for all his friendliness always seems somewhat distanced and cool, had kept something like an unenlightened 'devotional corner' in his Bavarian heart and shown himself to be all too stamped by Augustine's pessimistic view of the world and Bonaventura's Platonizing neglect of the visible and empirical (in contrast to Thomas Aquinas).

In an acute analysis of more than 200 pages, Professor Hermann Häring, my assistant in Tübingen at that time, shows how from the beginning 'Theology and Ideology in Joseph Ratzinger' (2002) have been interwoven. He simply didn't put certain questions to himself; he always had a sceptical attitude towards modern exegesis, and was open to historical arguments only to a limited degree. In his Tübingen 'Introduction to Christianity' (1967) he contented himself with a caricature of contemporary research into Jesus and here already showed the beginnings of the misinterpretations, insinuations, caricatures and condemnations of which he is capable. I had to experience this personally, in a way which was very painful to me, seven years later in his invective on my book *On Being a Christian*. Hermann Häring may be right that I overestimated Ratzinger's readiness for co-operation; that in the end he liked to keep under cover and avoided direct argument. It was just the same in that 1968 faculty meeting in which as dean he alone opposed all his professional colleagues when they were in solidarity in wanting to make a plea to the ordinariate of Rottenburg for the religious educationalist Professor Hubertus Halbfas of Reutlingen, who had incurred his enmity. The perverse technique of arguing with which the skilled orator Ratzinger rejected that plea for Halbfas, without bothering in the least about the coherence of his sometimes contradictory arguments, was perplexing to me.

However, it wasn't this discussion, which eventually proved pointless since the priest Halbfas soon got married, that was responsible for Ratzinger's departure from Tübingen, but the 1968 student revolts. We were both more than once vociferously prevented from teaching by sit-ins of protesters from other faculties in the lecture room. What for me remained merely a temporary annoyance evidently had a permanent shock effect on Ratzinger. He didn't want to remain in Tübingen a semester longer. Above all the agitation of a revolutionary group within the Catholic students' chaplaincy which wanted the appointment of a new chaplain to be completely in the hands of the chaplaincy (which came up against our joint resistance) had affected him deeply. To the present day Ratzinger has shown phobias about all movements 'from below', whether these are student chaplaincies, groups of priests, movements of church people, the *Iglesia popular* or liberation theology.

Ratzinger's march through the institutions doubtless began with his departure from Tübingen after three years in which we were both in harmony, and his move to Regensburg under the wing of Bishop Graber, the extreme right-winger of the conference of bishops: Archbishop of Munich and Cardinal (1977), then Prefect of the Congregation for the Doctrine of Faith (1981). But there can certainly also be spiritual power without much worldly satisfaction. He complains that he had to give up 'an *oeuvre*', an overall theological work, for the sake of his career. '*Tu l'as voulu, Georges Dandin, tu l'as voulu,*' I would reply to him in Molière's words. It is to be hoped that despite the lack of an *oeuvre* he will not be so quickly forgotten as the likewise near-almighty Cardinal Merry del Val,

Secretary of State to the anti-modernist pope Pius X, or even Cardinal Ottaviani, whose name even young theologians hardly remember today, despite his many speeches and declarations.

Could I have achieved more on the 'march through the institutions'? Time and again, when there is talk of my good personal relations with Paul VI, the private audience and the subsequent correspondence, friends put to me the question which some readers of this memoir may have on their lips: didn't you miss a big opportunity? So for a last time: I don't dispute for a moment that I could have made some contribution in the church apparatus, as was shown after Ratzinger in one way or another by the theologians and later cardinals Dulles, Lehmann, Mejía, Kasper, Tucci and other friends from the time of the Council. Nevertheless it was and is true for me that in the circumstances I could in no way have gone on this march through the institutions. Happily I have no regrets that I followed my conscience. For meanwhile the price that my friends have 'paid' has become clear: one has only to think of what they all said, have had to say, Yes and Amen to.

Should one say Yes and Amen to everything?

Meanwhile, since the Council, the sober question has arisen for me: should I, can I, may I be content with all the papal doctrinal documents which Paul VI 'decrees' in the old Roman self-glorification – quite unconcerned about the collegiality of the pope with the episcopate solemnly resolved on by the Council – and which now also annoy, infuriate, oppress countless bishops and theologians? Am I, like many of them, to content myself with private indications of annoyance and in public declare that I am in agreement with them? Am I perhaps to say Yes and Amen (Hebrew 'So be it') to all of them with grumbling and muttering and in the end by the skin of my teeth?

- Yes and Amen to the encyclical *Sacerdotalis coelibatus* (1967)? This outrageously appeals to the highest truths of the gospel and still cannot produce a QED: that the government of the church may turn what according to the gospel is a meaningful free call to celibacy into an obligatory law which does away with freedom.
- Yes and Amen to the pope's 'Credo' (1968)? With typically Roman gestures of identification, Paul VI declares this to be the 'Credo of the people of God' without asking the church or even the episcopate; here the 'hierarchy of truths' established by Vatican II is completely neglected, and problematical theological constructs of Roman tradition are put on the same level as central statements of the biblical message.
- Yes and Amen to the encyclical *Humanae vitae* (1968) on birth control? It too shows the astonished public of the world just how weak and backward Roman

459

moral theology is and demonstrates the danger of an ideology of infallibility; within the Catholic Church it sparks off an unprecedented revolt and exodus of church members and statements of dissent from theologians, bishops and whole conferences of bishops.

- Yes and Amen also to the decree on mixed marriages (*Matrimonia Mixta*) which will soon follow (1970)? This reveals behind all the ecumenical assertions the still deeply unecumenical attitude of the Roman central administration, the mentality and style of which time and again bear witness to short-sightedness, stubbornness and arrogance, and sometimes even megalomania. And so on?

These wrong decisions of Rome after the Council (and similar personal decisions) have caused infinite sorrow to Catholic believers. Any pastor can tell countless stories about them. But with the Roman system the pope also personally shares the responsibility for the wretchedness of the church which has lasted to the present: a rigoristic sexual morality; the collapse of pastoral care because of a lack of priests; hindrances to ecumenical understanding and ecumenical fellowship; a failure in the face of the catastrophic population explosion and the AIDS epidemic. Am I to say Yes and Amen to all this? I just can't, with the best will in the world! Not only can't I identify as a Catholic theologian with this Roman theology and politics; I must oppose it in all loyalty to the church and also to the pope. Spiritual dictatorship in particular – which has devastating consequences for countless people – must be resisted. Church totalitarianism in particular must be opposed with the freedom of the conscience, the freedom of a Christian.

1968: for many people this is the year of the birth of the 'Loyal Opposition of His Holiness'. But not for Joseph Ratzinger. As will be written on the occasion of his seventy-fifth birthday in 2002:

A rapid career. And a spectacular change of sides: as a theologian and adviser to Frings he is one of the 'young savages' who fought against the status quo of the church, did not conceal their aversion to the absolute power of the papal office, fought for the freedom of theology, complained about exaggerated Marian piety as an obstacle to the ecumene and interpreted tradition as something which is not given once and for all but must be understood in connection with growth, progress and knowledge of the faith . . . 'Collegiality' would become a key word of the theological *avant garde*, which concentrated its criticism on Cardinal Alfredo Ottaviani, the strictly conservative head of the then Holy Office. Today Joseph Ratzinger stands in his place, and like Ottaviani 40 years ago is concerned for Catholic identity. Has the Bavarian in the Vatican betrayed his former convictions? (G. Facius in *Die Welt,* 16 April 2002).

1968: I am now 40 years old and statistically have half my life – or perhaps very much more – behind me. 1968: not only the encyclical *Humanae vitae* and the epoch-making breach of trust for the pope and the church, but in addition a turning-point in human history generally, with student revolts from California through Paris and Berlin to Prague, a cultural revolution which can also be felt at the university of Tübingen. 1968: a turning-point which makes me break off my memoirs here. Later, in a second volume, I also want to describe the new period of my life which now begins, the new struggles, and finally a dramatic culmination of the controversy with Rome. In my farewell lecture in Tübingen on my retirement in 1996 I will state: 'I could not have gone another way, not just for the sake of freedom, which has always been dear to me, but for the sake of the truth. I saw then, as I see now, that had I gone another way, I would have sold my soul for power in the church. And I can only hope that my contemporary and colleague Ratzinger, who took the other way, is also as content and happy as I am as I look back on my life, despite all the suffering (and I say this without the slightest touch of irony).'

On 16 April 2002 Joseph Ratzinger celebrates his seventy-fifth birthday in the Vatican to a salute (only blanks) by 400 Bavarian mountain guards from the Tegernsee. He has reached the age limit laid down by the Council. But untroubled by the spirit and letter of the Council regulation, people in the Curia over-ride this. Recourse is had to the papal dispensation that one can continue in office if one is indispensable.

On 19 March 2003, having vacated my chair in 1996 at the age of 68 in accordance with the rule in order to make room for a successor, I hope to celebrate my seventy-fifth birthday in Tübingen. And I can guarantee now that there will be no such shooting at my celebrations. There will be plenty of people. The UN General Secretary Kofi Annan, with whom most recently I have collaborated over the manifesto *Bridges into the Future* (2001), intended for him and the UN General Assembly (quoted at the beginning of these memoirs), has accepted my invitation, and will give the Third Global Ethic Lecture at the University of Tübingen. All, of course, *Deo bene volente*.

Prospects

On 23 March 2002, on the eve of Palm Sunday, after a long time I am again in Rome up on the terrace on the ninth floor of my old Collegium Germanicum. I have been invited by the Rector, Fr Gerwin Komma SJ. The occasion: tomorrow my pupil, colleague and friend Professor Karl-Josef Kuschel will give an impressive illustrated meditation on '*Ecce homo*', and the day after, in a 'college academy', I will give a lecture, not on church politics but on 'Global Politics and Global Ethic. The New Paradigm of International Relations'.

Night is already falling on the city, and the spectacular panorama with all the domes and palaces which is so familiar to me is bathed in the intense Roman twilight. The renovated St Peter's stands above it in festal illumination like a jewel. Early in the morning, before the stream of visitors, an old Germanicum alumnus will show us with the expertise of an art historian the Sistine Chapel, which is again gleaming as if brand new. A miracle of colours, forms, shapes, gestures – there is so much that moves me in it.

Here Michelangelo, originally a sculptor, has proved to be not only a brilliant painter but also a Christian who did not want to present primarily popes but the whole of salvation history, from the grandiose beginning of the creation of the world and human beings to the gracious Last Judgement (hell as a threatening possibility which no one enters). This is a universal vision which includes the women seers of the pagans as well as the prophets of Israel.

The friend of the poetess Vittoria Colonna, to whom he dedicated his most important sonnet and with whose Viterbo circle he wanted to remain Catholic when the Reformation then broke out and yet to have an evangelical disposition, thought deeply about its form. My ideal.

Together with numerous humanists, theologians and politicians, here is that 'third force' which was lost in the sixteenth century but revived again at Vatican II and proves effective. My direction.

To the present day the dispute of the century over the true form of the Catholic Church, the ecumenical world, indeed Christianity generally in these revolutionary times which began at the Council, has not yet been decided. My suffering.

And no one knows whether in a couple of years the church and the world will not perhaps look better. My hope.

Do I feel uneasy?, Karl-Josef Kuschel asks me on returning to the house in which I lived and worked, suffered and fought for seven years. On the contrary, I say, quite naturally I feel 'at home' again; I look around with curiosity at what has remained the same in the house and its customs and what has changed. And I am simply glad to be here again: different, and yet the person who said goodbye almost five decades ago. And after all that has happened in the meantime, I am given a friendly welcome by a young generation of Germanicum students who evidently share my great concerns with enthusiasm. This is an experience which I have been granted time and again all over the world, of having kept my spiritual home in the great Christian community of faith, whatever the verdict on its apparatus and its administrators. I feel that I belong to it as much as I belong to democracy in the political sphere (likewise much misused and damaged). Precisely in this way – in critical solidarity – I can affirm a great story and, with so many others, live by it.

Indeed, looking back on the now almost 75 years of my life, can't I feel infinite gratitude? I am grateful that I have kept the freedom which because of fortunate circumstances was as it were laid in my cradle. This civic freedom has purged itself and become freedom of conscience. I have been allowed to experience it as the freedom of a Christian. It has proved itself as freedom in the church and theology. In all modesty, which I have learned in my childhood, in the tumult of the times I have been able to assert myself as a free man, a Christian and a theologian. This is a freedom which has been fought for and at the same time given. I can never sing the hymn 'Praise to the Lord' without emotion when it comes to the words: 'who guides me safely on eagle's wings, preserves me as it pleases him. Have you not sensed this?' Those who sing the English version of the hymn miss something of its evocative power!

Indeed, contrary to all appearances I have time and again confidently 'detected' the reality of God – the great theme of my life. With all the experiences and encounters, suffering and joys, up to 1968 I have been able to lead a fulfilled and rich life for four decades. And through the struggles and conflicts, the good days and bad days of the second half of my life, it will be an even more fulfilled, an infinitely rich life.

Had I turned to the Roman system at that time in the 1960s and put myself at the service of a world church, I would have been limited to the church world and would by no means have been involved so intensively with the themes of world literature, world religions, world peace and a global ethic as I would be forced to do *Dei providentia hominum confusione* – through God's providence and human confusion.

I shall be talking about all this in my second volume, which, God willing, will describe the decades in which the main emphasis increasingly shifts from freedom to the truth: the truth, which, I am firmly convinced, can and may be proclaimed, defended and lived out only in truthfulness. And in the years to come I shall be tested as much over truthfulness as I was tested in the previous years over freedom.

At New Year 2002 a Catholic Swiss pastor writes to me of the prophet Elijah, who wants death in the wilderness: 'What was said to the prophet Elijah will probably also apply to you too: arise, eat and drink, you have still a long way before you. May God accompany you on it, strengthen you and confirm you when the rough wind of opposition, indeed hostility, blows against you. The fate of a prophet!' Oh no, the fate of a professor is enough for me.

꧁꧂

Select Bibliography
of Hans Küng's Books in English

(The date of the German publication is given in brackets)

Justification. The Doctrine of Karl Barth and a Catholic Reflection (1957), New York: Thomas Nelson and Sons 1964 and London: Burns and Oates 1965

The Council and Reunion (1960), London: Sheed and Ward 1961; American edition *The Council, Reform and Reunion*, New York: Sheed and Ward 1961

That the World May Believe. Letters to Young People (1962), London and New York: Sheed and Ward 1963

Structures of the Church (1962), New York: Thomas Nelson and Sons 1964 and London: Burns and Oates 1965

The Living Church: Reflections on the Second Vatican Council (1963), London: Sheed and Ward 1963; second edition (1964) *The Changing Church. Reflections on the Progress of the Second Vatican Council*, London: Sheed and Ward 1965. American edition *The Council in Action*, New York: Sheed and Ward 1963

The Church and Freedom (1964), London and New York: Sheed and Ward 1965.

Freedom Today (1971), New York: Sheed and Ward 1966

The Church (1967), London: Burns and Oates and New York: Sheed and Ward 1967

The Incarnation of God. An Introduction to Hegel's Theological Thought as Prolegomena to a Future Christology (1970), Edinburgh: T & T Clark 1987

Infallible? An Enquiry (1970), London: Collins and New York: Doubleday 1971

On Being a Christian (1974), London: Collins and New York: Doubleday 1977

Does God Exist? An Answer for Today (1978), London: Collins and New York: Doubleday 1980

Eternal Life? (1982), London: Collins and New York: Doubleday 1984

Global Responsibility (1990), London: SCM Press and New York: Crossroad 1991

Judaism (1991), London: SCM Press and New York: Crossroad 1992

Christianity: Its Essence and History (1994), London: SCM Press and New York: Crossroad 1995

The Catholic Church: A Short History, London: Weidenfeld and Nicolson and New York: Random House 2001

Tracing the Way: Spiritual Dimensions of the World Religions (1999), London and New York: Continuum 2002

Women in Christianity, London and New York: Continuum 2002

Index of Names